Iberia and the Americas

Other Titles in ABC-CLIO's

Transatlantic Relations Series

Africa and the Americas, by Richard M. Juang, Kim Searcy, and Noelle Searcy
Britain and the Americas, by Will Kaufman and Heidi Slettedahl Macpherson
France and the Americas, by Bill Marshall, assisted by Cristina Johnston
Germany and the Americas, by Thomas Adam
Ireland and the Americas, by Philip Coleman, Jason King, and Jim Byrne

Iberia and the Americas

Culture, Politics, and History

A Multidisciplinary Encyclopedia

VOLUME II

EDITED BY

J. Michael Francis

Transatlantic Relations Series

Will Kaufman, Series Editor

Santa Barbara, California Denver, Colorado Oxford, England

Library of Congress Cataloging-in-Publication Data
Iberia and the Americas : culture, politics, and history : a multidisciplinary encyclopedia / edited by J. Michael Francis.
p. cm. — (Transatlantic relations series)
Includes bibliographical references and index.
ISBN 1-85109-421-0 (hardcover : alk. paper) — ISBN 1-85109-426-1 (ebook) 1. America—Relations—Spain—Encyclopedias.
2. Spain—Relations—America—Encyclopedias.
3. America—History—Encyclopedias. 4. Spain—History—Encyclopedias.
5. North America—History—Encyclopedias. 6. Latin America—History—Encyclopedias. 7. South America—History—Encyclopedias. 8. America—Politics and government—Encyclopedias. 9. Spain—Politics and government—Encyclopedias. I. Francis, J. Michael (John Michael) II. Series.

E18.75.I24 2006
303.48'2181204603--dc22

2005025407

09 08 07 06 10 9 8 7 6 5 4 3 2 1

This book is also available on the World Wide Web as an e-Book. Visit abc-clio.com for details.

ABC-CLIO, Inc.
130 Cremona Drive, P.O. Box 1911
Santa Barbara, California 93116-1911

This book is printed on acid-free paper ♾.
Manufactured in the United States of America

CONTENTS

Defense—Colonial Brazil

Colonial Brazil's defense system was formed by a combination of professional troops and militia, whose main function was to fight Native Americans, rebel slaves, and invading European powers. The organization of the armed forces was extremely complex, uniting elements of Portuguese military and administrative structures with original adaptations to unique local circumstances.

Paid troops, called *tropas de primeira linha* (first-line troops), or simply *tropas de linha,* arrived in Brazil with the first governor-general in 1548. They were positioned in forts (called *presídios*) that represented an important mechanism to populate the territory. Several Brazilian cities, such as Rio de Janeiro, Natal, and Belém, developed in the surroundings of these forts. In tactical terms, the tropas de linha were organized (from 1618 onward in Portugal and from 1626 in Brazil) under the system of *terços,* based on the Spanish system of *tercios.* In theory, the terços were made up of ten companies of 250 men, with each company commanded by a captain subordinated to a *capitão-mor* or *mestre-de-campo.* Ideally, terços would form a compact structure of pikemen supported by squares of infantrymen with firearms; however, conditions in Brazil never allowed these terços to have the appropriate number of components or tactical formation.

A good portion of the forces came from Portugal, with the main command positions reserved exclusively for native Portuguese; lower positions were usually occupied by the incipient colonial middle class in search of the influence that often came with wearing a military uniform. To complete their permanently insufficient soldiery, the colonial population was recruited, including mixed-blood individuals, which was forbidden by Portuguese law. The civilian population feared these drafts because the soldiers lived in deplorable conditions, and, although they were called *soldados pagos* (paid soldiers), in reality they were very rarely paid. Several urban rebellions and riots, such as the ones in 1660 (Rio de Janeiro), 1688 (Bahia), and 1723 (Pernambuco), were fueled by the lack of payment to the "paid" soldiers. Often soldiers were forced to beg on the streets, to extort civilians (charging "rights" to the use of water fountains, for example), or simply to steal. To the free population, to become a soldier through compulsory drafting was considered a fate worse than death, and this made soldiers the least valued of free men.

Not surprisingly, professional troops were of little military use in colonial times, and they were used much more as repressive tools to urban populations. Theoretically, the Portuguese Crown was responsible for supporting the tropas de linha; however, the Crown frequently alleged not to have the resources because of the costly seventeenth-century war against Spain and the Netherlands. Therefore, the expenses were sent to *Câmaras* (municipal councils), which charged heavy taxes on products such as wine and liquors to cover the military expenses; this encouraged smuggling and also incited uprisings from the population against excessive taxing.

In all circumstances, the real armed forces of colonial Brazil were the *tropas auxiliares* (auxiliary troops), which were divided into *milícias* (irregulars and unpaid troops) and *corpos de ordenanças* (second-line militia troops composed of men aged fifteen to sixty who were considered militarily or physically unfit to be enrolled in milícias). The milícias, regulated in 1641, had existed informally since the beginning of Brazil's colonization, when municipal councils, governors, and rural landowners used troops formed by allied or enslaved Native Americans, supported by a small number of soldiers with firearms, to fight against unfriendly natives and European invaders.

These troops were not paid, and were also organized in terços; but command positions could be occupied by Brazilians, usually rich landowners and other *homens bons* (good men) who formed the colonial elite. Each village gathered as many militia corps as possible. This often happened because of the inclination of the landowners to reach for militia command positions as a way of gathering political and military power as well as social prestige, which led the Portuguese Crown in the eighteenth century to try to limit the formation of new troops.

Besides being recruited locally, troops were gathered among some professions (such as tradesmen and artisans) and different ethnic groups, as seen in the militia of Native Americans, *pardos* (mixed-blood men), and freed Afro-Brazilians. For the last-named, to be part of a militia was an important way of showing their status as free men (slaves could not be part of a militia), which was fundamental in a society marked by racial discrimination. Europeans who visited Brazil at the end of the colonial period remarked that Afro-Brazilian troops were the best dressed and trained among Brazil's soldiers.

Different from the militia, which could be deployed to fight anywhere in Brazil, the corpos de ordenança, regulated in 1570 and 1574, consisted of all local able-bodied men who were not part of the paid militia; these forces could not be moved from their localities. Command positions were appointed by municipal councils and governors, and commanders were always homens bons. These troops had little military value, since the best soldiers were already enlisted in the militia; however, they were paramount to the administration because of the poor bureaucratic organization in Portuguese America. Through these troops the free population was disciplined and forced to work. For example, the corpos de ordenança were often employed in public services without payment, since they were theoretically conducting "military" functions. The ordenanças were the most perfect evidence of the power exercised by the colonial elite, uniting all associate and subordinate men under a legal and juridical structure that ensured the elite's political and economic power.

This double structure (paid troops and auxiliares) was the foundation of the military organization in independent Brazil: a paid army, poorly armed and poorly trained, that continued to make use of the draft, and a *Guarda Nacional* (National Guard), which replaced the militia and ordenanças, and was supported by the power of Brazil's wealthy landowners.

João Azevedo Fernandes

References

Alden, Dauril. *Royal Government in Colonial Brazil with Special Reference to the Administration of Marquis de Lavradio, Viceroy, 1769–1779.* Berkeley and Los Angeles: University of California Press, 1968.

Boxer, Charles R. *The Portuguese Seaborne Empire, 1415–1825.* New York: Knopf, 1969.

Kraay, Hendrik. *Race, State, and Armed Forces in Independence-Era Brazil: Bahia, 1790s–1840s.* Stanford, CA: Stanford University Press, 2001.

Salgado, Graça, ed. *Fiscais e meirinhos: A administração no Brasil colonial.* Rio de Janeiro: Nova Fronteira, 1985.

Schwartz, Stuart. "A Note on Portuguese and Brazilian Military Organization." In *A Governor and His Image in Baroque Brazil—The Funeral Eulogy of Afonso Furtado de Castro do Rio de Mendonça,* edited by Juan Lopes Sierra. Minneapolis: University of Minnesota Press, 1979.

See also: Alcohol; Amazon; Armies—Colonial Brazil; Colonists and Settlers II—Brazil; Conquest II—Brazil; Contraband; Defense—Colonial Spanish America; Donatary Captaincies; Enlightenment—Brazil; Monopolies; Native Americans I–II; Race; Slavery I—Brazil; Travel Literature—Brazil; Wine.

DEFENSE—COLONIAL SPANISH AMERICA

The defense of colonial Spanish America required a constant balance between indigenous and imperial threats. Within decades of the conquest, colonial authorities faced rebellions by both recently subjugated Indians and the conquistadors and their descendants in the interior as well as resistance from unconquered Indians on the frontiers, all while contending with the threat of piracy on the sea lanes between the New World and Spain. By the seventeenth century imperial threats emanated from European competitors, especially France in North America and, eventually, Great Britain in the Caribbean. Thus, when a general revolt broke out during the late seventeenth century among the Indian peoples of northern Mexico, imperial and indigenous defense became nearly one and the same. Attempts to fuse the two concerns from the early eighteenth century by the new Bourbon dynasty in Spain resulted in the establishment of a regular colonial military, backed by a large local militia. Many of the reforms needed to pay for colonial defense resulted in internal distress and resistance during the latter half of the eighteenth century, especially in the Andean regions of South America. Although these revolts were contained, the increasing domination of the colonial defense establishment by Spanish Americans eventually led to general revolts and ultimately to rebellion for independence.

The first threats to Spanish colonial control were local rebellions, both from indigenous forces and from disgruntled Spanish conquistadors and early settlers. When Francisco Vázquez de Coronado led an *entrada* (expedition) from Mexico to present-day Arizona, New Mexico, Texas, and Oklahoma in 1541, he took a large number of the colonies' men with him. The Mixtón Indians took advantage of their absence to revolt, leading to the Mixtón War (1541–1542). The Indians attacked Spanish settlements from fortified hilltops, and all attempts to dislodge them failed. Not until Viceroy Don Antonio de Mendoza led an army of 500 Spaniards and 50,000 Indian allies were the Mixtón defeated. In Peru, the southern center of Spanish America, colonial control of the conquest was threatened by a civil war among the conquistadors. In 1538 Francisco Pizarro defeated Diego de Almagro, but Almagro's son led an unsuccessful civil war in 1542. In 1544, Francisco's brother, Gonzalo Pizarro, led a revolt against the Viceroy of Peru, but he was defeated in 1549. In all of this fighting, as in the Mixtón War, a number of Spaniards were supported by larger numbers of Indian allies and auxiliaries.

Within a few decades of dealing with these challenges, a new threat arose, this time on the frontiers of colonial expansion. In South America a 1540 expedition from Peru led by Pedro de Valdivia into what is now Chile incurred resistance from the Araucanian Indians. The Araucanians quickly adopted the horse, and by the early seventeenth century they had created a stalemate along the Bío-Bío River. The Araucanians utilized hit-and-run tactics against the Spanish frontier forces, which rarely numbered more than 1,500 men. Meanwhile, in Mexico, discovery of silver mines at Zacatecas in 1546 caused a rush of men into the region inhabited by peoples known collectively as Chichimecas. Resistance by these Indians, including attacks on ranches and wagon trains, continued from the 1550s until the end of the century and resulted in the creation of a frontier defensive system based on *presidios* (fortified garrison communities). The search for and exploitation of silver mines pressed Spanish expansion northward and caused revolts among the Xiximes (1601), Tepehuanes (1616–1620), Tarahumaras (1648, 1650, 1652), and Pueblos (1680–1692). Again a large force of settler militia, supported by a small number of royally paid soldiers, and with help from Indian auxiliaries, was ultimately able to deal with these threats.

Although indigenous rebellions and resistance required a land-based defense on the frontiers, threats from corsairs preying on the treasure fleets and supply convoys demanded a more involved defensive system. From the mid-1500s, the Spanish strategy in the Caribbean defended the coasts with forts (also called presidios), artillery, and militias, while fleets patrolled those parts of the sea where the threat from corsairs was the greatest. By the end of the century, the strategy included escorting convoys to and from Spain, with one convoy departing the Americas in midsummer and the other leaving Spain in late spring. Pirates also threatened the Pacific coast, launching at least twenty-five incursions from 1575 to 1742, attacks that local militias, led by colonial authorities, mobilized to resist. Given the widespread threat, Spanish militias were no longer composed exclusively of Spaniards. Indians and, especially, free blacks served in coastal militias in ever-increasing numbers.

By the seventeenth century, however, threats from the sea would not be limited to corsairs. European imperial competitors also threatened Spain's empire. In 1624 the Dutch took Bahia on the coast of Portuguese Brazil, then part of Spain's empire, before a Spanish fleet ejected them in 1625. Emboldened by the seizure of an entire treasure fleet in 1628, the Dutch seized much of Brazil in 1630 and held it until 1654. In the 1620s, the British too began to seize parts of the Spanish Empire in the Caribbean, culminating in the occupation of Jamaica in 1655, which soon became the base for a new generation of pirates, the buccaneers. Buccaneers attacked Spanish possessions in the Caribbean and Central America, most notably in Panama, throughout the 1660s. Since Spain was embroiled in the Thirty Years' War (1618–1648) in Europe, much of the defensive burden was borne, again, by local forces and funded with local money. As most of the money came from the silver mines of northern Mexico, French expansion down the Mississippi Valley from Canada toward the Mexican north greatly concerned Spanish authorities. When royal officials learned in 1685 that the Sieur de La Salle was attempting to establish a French colony at the mouth of the Mississippi River, they were certain its purpose was to threaten the northern mines of Mexico. La Salle's attempts failed miserably since he missed the Mississippi altogether and ended up in what is now Texas, but it took six land expeditions and five maritime explorations in four years to discover La Salle's fate.

La Salle's attempt was even more worrisome to the Spanish Crown because it took place at the same time as a general uprising in northern Mexico, instigated by the Pueblo Revolt in New Mexico in 1680. Indian revolts and imperial defense thus merged by the eighteenth century. An example of this occurred in northern Mexico in the 1720s. Given the ongoing Indian resistance and fears of French interference, the Spanish viceroy, the Marquis de Casafuerte, ordered an inspection of the region's presidios. The result of the inspection was a regulation in 1729, whose example was an earlier regulation for the presidio that protected the critical Caribbean port of Havana. Thus, the presidios of northern Mexico were to defend against both imperial and indigenous threats, indeed as was the entire colonial defense establishment. And such threats continued to mount throughout the first half of the eighteenth century. On the northern frontier the war with the Apaches escalated by midcentury, and a new foe, the Comanches, entered the scene as well. In the Caribbean, during the War of Jenkins' Ear (1739–1742), the British again launched attacks on shipping and ports and, together with their Indian allies, on Spanish forts in Florida. In South America from the mid-eighteenth century, rivalry broke out on the frontiers between the Portuguese and Spanish Empires. Yet the tried-and-true means of colonial defense, relying upon fortifications and local militia forces backed by a few regulars, proved to be inadequate by midcentury, when British forces seized Havana in 1762.

The ongoing struggle with Indians on the frontiers and the persistent threats from the British led to the establishment of a regular army and provincial militia force in the colonies from the mid-eighteenth century. The shift was part of the general administrative and fiscal reorganization of Spanish America known as the Bourbon reforms. This reorganization reversed earlier practices for provincial militias; rather than being the mainstay for any defense, it now supported a regular army of troops rotated from Spain. In Mexico and Peru, the two largest colonies, the number of regular troops tripled from the 1760s to 1800. By 1800, Mexico fielded a regular force of 6,000 men, while Peru had nearly 2,000. Militia forces composed of and commanded by Spanish Americans also grew in the last decades of the eighteenth century to 24,000 in Mexico and 18,000 in Peru. However, in spite of the increase, militia forces often were inadequately trained and equipped.

Similar military establishments existed in Cuba, New Granada (present-day Colombia and Venezuela), and Argentina. The Spanish navy also reformed and reorganized in the eighteenth century. Cuba and the shipyards of Havana were central to this effort. Between 1700 and 1788 the Havana yards built seventy-one warships, while many colonial-born officers also served with the revitalized navy. The plan to rotate regular Spanish army troops from Europe to serve in the American colonies soon broke down, however, as a result of distance, expense, and the outbreak of the French revolutionary wars in the 1790s. Colonial Spanish Americans thus came to dominate not just the militia forces, but also the regular units.

Besides serving in the forces, Spanish Americans had to pay for their own defense. By 1800 roughly 60 percent of Mexico's budget was spent on defense. Thus the Bourbon reforms upset traditional arrangements and practices, resulting in a new round of internal resistance while preparing for external defense. In the Andes an Indian leader took the name Túpac Amaru, the last Incan emperor, and led an armed rebellion in 1780 protesting long-standing abuses and the new reforms. By May 1781, colonial forces, mainly provincial militia, captured and executed Túpac Amaru, but the rebellion in his name lived on for another two years and cost 100,000 lives. Soon after the start of the Túpac Amaru rebellion, though separate from it, colonial authorities faced a protest from the middle-class inhabitants of what is now Colombia and Venezuela over increases in the sales tax to pay for defense (the Comuneros Revolt). The protest turned into a rebellion in 1781, and while colonial officials initially surrendered to the rebels' demand, the arrival of loyal militia troops allowed them to reestablish control.

By the early nineteenth century colonial defense was in the hands of primarily Spanish American forces, a fact that is evidenced by the attempted British invasion of Argentina and the outbreak of rebellion in Mexico. In 1806 a British expeditionary force took Buenos Aires in Argentina, the Spanish viceroy tasked with its defense having fled. The citizens organized resistance to the British and formed a military force that drove the British out within a few months. A year later the British tried again, and again militia and irregular forces—not the regular army—defended the city. Spanish American colonists now dominated the defense of the Spanish colonies, and when the Spanish king abandoned his throne in 1808, under pressure from Napoleon, the question of who should rule, Spaniards or Spanish Americans, came to dominate the empire. In 1810 royal officials discovered a Mexican conspiracy to throw out the Spaniards, with three Spanish American militia officers at its core, although its leader, Miguel Hidalgo, was a parish priest. The authorities proved unable, however, to stop the rebellion in September 1810, and it quickly spread across north-central Mexico. A force of Mexican Royalists initially defeated the rebellion, but an insurgency continued for another decade until independence. The situation was repeated in South America, where Spanish Americans decided to take matters into their own hands and, ultimately, they declared independence from Spain. After facing imperial and indigenous threats for nearly three centuries, the Spanish colonial empire fell to those who, in the main, had long been the bulwark of colonial defense.

Lance Blyth

References

Archer, Christon I. *The Army in Bourbon Mexico, 1760–1810.* Albuquerque: University of New Mexico Press, 1977.

Campbell, Leon G. *The Military and Society in Colonial Peru, 1750–1810.* Philadelphia: American Philosophical Society, 1978.

Harbron, John D. *Trafalgar and the Spanish Navy.* Annapolis, MD: Naval Institute Press, 1988.

Hemming, John. *The Conquest of the Incas.* New York: Harcourt Brace Jovanovich, 1970.

Hoffman, Paul E. *The Spanish Crown and the Defense of the Caribbean, 1535–1585.* Baton Rouge: Louisiana State University Press, 1980.

Lynch, John. *The Spanish American Revolutions, 1808–1826.* 2nd ed. New York: W. W. Norton, 1973.

Weber, David J. *The Spanish Frontier in North America.* New Haven, CT: Yale University Press, 1992.

See also: Atlantic Economy; Bourbon Reforms; Armies—Colonial Brazil; Armies—Colonial Spanish America; Colombia; Comuneros—New Granada; Fleet System; Independence I–VI; Peru; Pirates and Piracy; Rebellions—Colonial Latin America; Túpac Amaru Revolt.

Defensor de Indios

The defender or *protector de Indios,* an institution created to safeguard the legal rights of American natives, drew upon peninsular antecedents and underwent substantial shifts during the colonial period. The Spanish Crown initially understood the defense of indigenous peoples as a collective responsibility that it shared with civil and ecclesiastical authorities as well as colonists. However, it soon became clear that the *encomienda* system officially envisioned to protect the natives actually had the opposite effect. The position of the defender or protector de Indios, assigned first to bishops and subsequently to lay authorities, attempted to prevent abuses against natives while upholding the norms established for their acculturation and evangelization.

The institution of the defender of the Indians juridically situated Native Americans in the position of permanent minors requiring legal tutors or guardians. Peninsular antecedents for this situation can be found in the Roman figure of *defensor plebes* or *defensor civitatis,* which became the highest municipal official under the Visigoths. The spread of poverty in the later Middle Ages led to growing demands for the monarch to protect the weak and the creation of a new charge, the defender of the poor. The Catholic Monarchs, Ferdinand and Isabel, sent the court's defender of the poor to protect the natives of the Canary Islands, a more immediate precedent for the American institution.

In Spanish America the Crown initially entrusted ecclesiastics, and particularly bishops, with protecting the natives. In 1516 the first and foremost *defensor de Indios,* Bartolomé de las Casas, received the

Cardinal Francisco Jimenez de Cisneros (1436–1517), Archbishop of Toledo, Primate of Spain, and Grand-Inquisitor. Private collection. (Snark/Art Resource)

title "universal defender and protector of the Indians" from the archbishop of Toledo, Francisco Jiménez de Cisneros, acting as regent, with orders to travel throughout the colonies, informing royal governors, their deputies, and the Crown of the plight of Native Americans. Early bishops named protectors of the natives included Diego Álvarez Osorio in Nicaragua and Hernando de Luque, who never actually exercised the office, for Peru. These first defenders received broad powers to dictate laws, impose penalties, name deputies, and judge and imprison offenders, leading to numerous clashes with civil authorities. Subsequent instructions tended to limit the defenders' functions to informing the appropriate *audiencia,* governor, or viceroy, as well as the Crown, of abuses against natives.

In response to frequent conflicts and complaints, the position of defensor de Indios passed to lay officials beginning in the 1560s. The Crown suppressed it altogether in 1567 and, more resolutely, in 1582, only to restore the protector de Indios in 1589. Among other duties the defenders upheld natives' rights to possess land, often through long and complex legal proceedings, and limited the tributes required of them. Mestizos, suspected of greater cruelty than peninsulars toward natives, were barred from the position after 1578. In the early 1640s the charge became termed "fiscal [public prosecutor] protector" and could be purchased until still more complaints led to a royal decree of 1646 renewing the provision of secular protectors by viceroys, presidents of the audiencias, and governors. In the eighteenth century, the appointment of protectors passed to the public prosecutors of crime.

Bethany Aram

References

Bayle, Constantino. *El protector de indios.* Seville: Escuela de Estudios Hispano-Americanos, 1945.

Olmedo Jiménez, Manuel. *Jerónimo de Loaysa, O.P. Pacificador de españoles y protector de indios.* Granada: University of Granada, 1990.

Recopilación de leyes de los reynos de las Indias. Vol. 2, book 6, title 6. Madrid: Viuda de D. Joaquín Ibarra, 1791.

Ruigómez Gómez, Carmen. *Una política indigenista de los Habsburgs: El protector de indios en el Perú.* Madrid: Ediciones de Cultura Hispánica, 1988.

See also: Administration—Colonial Spanish America; Audiencias; Catholic Church in Spanish America; Encomienda; Laws—Colonial Latin America; Laws of Burgos; Mestizaje; Native Americans I–VIII; New Laws of 1542; Race; Viceroyalties.

DEMOCRACY

The rise of democratic ideas and institutions in the Iberian world took place in the context of the Napoleonic invasion of the Iberian Peninsula (1808–1814). The French occupation sparked monarchical crises in Spain, Portugal, and their empires. The consequent destabilization of social and political colonial hierarchies led to the spread of formal aspects of democracy, namely constitutions, elections, and citizenship. This process occurred on both sides of the Atlantic. Democratic rule and its discourses have since then been fundamental elements of the modern Ibero-American political culture. In spite of this, democracy was not always the regime of either Iberian or many Latin American nations throughout the nineteenth and twentieth centuries. As ongoing political struggles demonstrate, democracy continues to be a contested term and is the site of the dynamic construction of citizenship in terms of racial, ethnic, gendered, and class identities.

Between 1808 and 1814, while the Spanish king Ferdinand VII was in Bayonne (after being abducted by Napoleon Bonaparte), a fundamental transformation in political language accompanied the emergence of constitutionalism in Spain and Spanish America as the modern institutional expression of political communities. In this process, the language of popular sovereignty and representation assumed greater importance, replacing absolutist language, monarchic symbolism, and institutions, all of which had been central to Bourbon reformism throughout the eighteenth century. The transformation in the uses of these political concepts had different consequences on each side of the Atlantic. The installation in Spain of a new legitimacy based on the nation signaled the transition to a modern and increasingly liberal political culture. Overseas, this was the principal cause of the dissolution of the empire. Spain's refusal to accept real equality of representation intensified colonial conflicts and gave rise to American independence movements.

Countering the long-held explanation of the Hispanic revolutions as being "externally motivated" by the expansion of the French Revolution, recent reassessments of the period highlight the profound influence of democratic institutions and liberal constitutionalism as part of a Hispanic model of political legitimacy. These revisionist views show that a Hispanic brand of liberalism was at the base of these institutional changes and that juntas, or local councils, were established in major cities to govern in the absence of the Spanish monarchs. Spanish political culture influenced this process because the institutional concept of the juntas and the re-creation of the Cortes ultimately transformed the monarchical government into a national model in which the Hispanic legal principle declared that, in the absence of the king, sovereignty would revert to the people. This explains why the early constitutional documents were formulated in the name of the people as the sovereign ground. The main symbol of this transition was the Cádiz constitution, drafted by the Spanish Cortes in 1812 with the participation of American deputies.

In Spanish America by 1810, a series of revolts led by Creole leaders with popular support successfully negotiated local independence from Spain, and governments were then elected to exercise sovereign rule. The first act of these governments was always to write a constitution. Although the local juntas initially expressed their loyalty to the king in their constitutions, they shortly called for independence.

Brazilian independence was also triggered by the Napoleonic invasion of the peninsula and tied to the shift to liberalism in the Iberian world. In 1822, Emperor Pedro I, the son of the Portuguese king, became head of the Brazilian constitutional monarchy. While Spanish America fragmented into multiple nations, Brazil remained a single polity even after it became a republic in 1889. As the writing of an imperial constitution in 1824 shows, Brazilian liberal elites had advocated modern forms of representation since the first decades of the nineteenth century, and when institutionalized, they changed the nature of the regime and political power in Brazil. However, the pro-independence patriots' commitment to slavery and their exclusion of the masses from the electoral process show their paradoxical use and their limited practice of the language of popular sovereignty and equality.

Eventually, the early liberal ideological hegemony in the Spanish American republics was challenged by conservatives in response to increasing political instability and social unrest. However, because popular sovereignty and modern representation were at the base of the independence process, constitutions as the main institutional expression of the modern principles of sovereignty and representation remained the norm throughout the nineteenth century across Latin America.

Citizenship and the constitution of a citizenry also were central aspects of nation building in the nineteenth century. Citizenship was founded on the basis of local forms of communitarian recognition. Elections also became a key aspect of the new system of government. In this process, traditional forms of representation were challenged and eventually displaced by the new forms advocated by the French Revolution, American democracy, and Spanish liberalism. The election of representatives was the people's main and ideal form of political action. Modern representatives were different from those of the ancien régime societies in that they were not supposed to act as delegates of any group or sector in particular. They represented and produced the will of the nation, the abstract community formed by individual citizens.

Elections were practiced in the Spanish colonies, but in 1812 with the changes introduced by the Cádiz constitution, old forms of representation started to change. After independence, the right to vote was fully extended to the male population. All free, nondependent, adult males were enfranchised, including Indians. This marked a notable step toward erasing, albeit partially, colonial hierarchies in favor of new political categories. In many areas of Latin America where Indians and mestizos were a significant percentage of the population, this opened a process of contestation of the definition of citizenship rights according to ethnic values. And it was precisely on racial criteria that the initial boundaries of citizenship were once again modified in the 1830s. Aided by the introduction of the French doctrinaire's differentiation between passive and active citizens, changes in the definition of the ideal citizen were proposed. The propositions were to introduce property, income, or literary qualifications to the franchise, limiting the democratic potential of republican institutions.

The complex and uneven history of suffrage is an expression of the dynamic between ideal and practical limits of popular sovereignty. Furthermore, competing ideas of the nation nurtured diverse national projects, endorsed by different social and political groups. This sometimes resulted in struggles between corporate and plural notions of the nation, and liberal projects. Primary examples of these different definitions are indigenous communal notions of rights, which remain to this day as a counterpoint to the liberal abstract citizenship model. Another important oppositional project, waged by workers in the late nineteenth century and the first three decades of the twentieth century, embraced social rights, adding a social dimension to liberal individual citizenship.

In the twentieth century, democracy became a central precept of the United States' endeavor to use aid and diplomacy to promote democratization overseas. Already in 1913 President Wilson had declared that his administration was the champion of constitutional governments in the Americas. In 1948 the Organization of American States (OAS) was established, and its member states endorsed the "Final Act of Bogotá," which, exemplified by the United States' democratic model, proclaimed the existence of a common democracy throughout the Americas. Pan American states debated the degree to which inter-American institutions could intervene to further guarantee the existence of democracy in the whole continent.

This American commitment to democracy was tied to a process in the whole Atlantic, in tune with Europe's post–World War II struggle to overcome Fascism and stabilize internally through constitutional democracies. In the second half of the century, democracy was filled with new meanings. Apart from the original republican representational and constitutional frameworks, an emphasis on the existence of stable party systems and recurrent elections characterized the new prevalent procedural definition. Democratization was promoted internationally by leading capitalist countries through a discourse that emphasized private ownership and anti-Communism. In the midst of the cold war, a second variant, one that espoused social rights and economic equality, lost much of its international support. Both Iberian and Latin American countries entered the American-led alliance, promising to introduce a system of commitments that could guarantee stability in these regions. From the 1950s to the 1980s, democracy was also a fundamental value used by the United States and its allies to counter Communism, portrayed as implicitly authoritarian and a threat to democratic values. For this reason, and paradoxically, the struggle for democracy and development was recurrently aided by violence and interventionist force. In cases where democratic experiences were tied to socialist values as in Chile (1970–1973), the interventionist pressures of the United States overcame the principles of national sovereignty.

The Allied victory in 1945 promised an extension of the practices of "democracy" understood in the Anglo-American sense as competitive electoral systems and separation of powers under the rule of law. A democratic opening was visible throughout Latin America, and a number of undemocratic regimes in the Caribbean were liberalized. The political climate of democratization, in social settings where the working class had expanded considerably, also led to the widespread expansion of union membership. The working class was incorporated into democratic politics and institutionalized in parties as well. Nevertheless, by 1947 popular mobilization often was repressed, and participation was restricted, signaling the closure of the democratic opening of previous years. Notably the authoritarian governments of the Southern Cone, Brazil, Argentina, Uruguay, and Chile, were regimes in which state power aimed to control popular forces and powers, such as unions. In tune with global forces that sought to counter socialist movements, in these countries the goal of economic modernization was pursued by recourse to authoritarian rule.

The twentieth century also saw the demise of authoritarian regimes in the Iberian Peninsula. Following a series of authoritarian cycles in the nineteenth century, Spain struggled to consolidate a democratic government and institute a solid republic. Portugal and Spain were ruled by authoritarian regimes aligned with Fascist European currents, namely, General Francisco Franco's dictatorship in Spain and António de Oliveira Salazar's thirty-year military regime in Portugal. Spain's democratic transition from 1976 to 1978 came as a crucial example of a successful dismantling of a long-lasting and deeply institutionalized authoritarian regime. In this way it became the model of democratization for southern European nations and for Latin America as well. The Spanish transition resulted in the writing of a new constitution, signaled the conciliation between the monarchy and the Spanish Cortes, and instituted a parliamentary monarchy headed by King Juan Carlos I of Spain. The election of Felipe González as prime minister in 1982 completed the transition to democratic government. Portugal's transition in 1976 ended Europe's oldest authoritarian government and led to the creation of a new democratic constitution. Both Portugal and Spain turned to democratic consolidations with the aim of enhancing their integration into the European Community.

Transitions to democracy in the Southern Cone during the 1970s and 1980s engendered social movements that constituted important sources of democratic power, as in the case of women's movements in Argentina and Brazil. This has become another example of the possible redefinition of contemporary politics outside of state-centered notions and reflects the crucial role of civil society in promoting democratic transitions and consolidations.

Where ethnic movements have been resilient, these have proven to be bearers of communal and popular notions of democracy. In the late twentieth century, indigenous movements for Indian rights, territorial justice, and participatory democracy in the Andes had constitutional effects that tinted the definition of national politics with issues of cultural pluralism and collective rights.

Marcela Echeverri

References

Bethell, Leslie, and Ian Roxborough. "The Impact of the Cold War on Latin America." Pp. 293–316 in *Origins of the Cold War: An International History*, edited by Melvin Leffler and David Painter. New York: Routledge, 1994.

Da Costa, Emilia Viotti. *The Brazilian Empire: Myths and Histories.* Chapel Hill: University of North Carolina Press, 1999.

Guerra, Francois-Xavier. *Modernidad e independencias: Ensayos sobre las revoluciones hispánicas.* Mexico City: Fondo de Cultura Económica, 1992.

Posada-Carbó, Eduardo. *Elections before Democracy: The History of Elections in Europe and Latin America.* New York: St. Martin's, 1996.

Rodriguez, Jaime. *The Independence of Spanish America.* New York: Cambridge University Press, 1998.

Sábato, Hilda, ed. *Ciudadanía política y formación de las naciones. Perspectivas históricas de América Latina.* Mexico City: Fondo de Cultura Económica, 1999.

Whitehead, Laurence. "International Aspects of Democratization." Pp. 3–46 in *Transitions from Authoritarian Rule: Comparative Perspectives,* edited by Guillermo O'Donnell, Philippe C. Schmitter, and Laurence Whitehead. Baltimore, MD: Johns Hopkins University Press, 1986.

See also: American Revolution; Bourbon Reforms; Cold War—Portugal and the United States; Cold War—Spain and the Americas; Constitution of Cádiz; Cortes of Cádiz; Creoles; Fin de Siècle; Independence I–VI; Liberalism; Napoleonic Invasion and Luso-America; Napoleonic Invasion and Spanish America; Nationalism; Organization of American States; Positivism; Slavery I–IV; Spanish Civil War and Latin America; Women—Modern Spanish America; World War I; World War II.

DEPENDENCY THEORY

Dependency theory is a theoretical critique that attributes Latin American underdevelopment to capitalism. The theory, widely influential in much writing about Latin America from the 1960s to the 1980s, holds that capitalism generates not only development in the core or metropolitan sectors, but also underdevelopment in the periphery. This occurs because the capitalist metropolis dominates the conditions of exchange between the center and periphery. Its control makes the exchange unequal, with most of the profits from economic activity in the periphery flowing to the metropolis for its progress and development.

Dependency theory grew, in part, from the work of the United Nations Economic Commission for Latin America (ECLA), founded in 1948. Headquartered in Santiago, Chile, ECLA was directed by Raúl Prebisch, who was a central figure in elaborating the idea of unequal exchange in works such as *The Economic Development of Latin America and Its Principal Problems* (1950). The theory of unequal exchange held that in Latin America, low wages meant low prices for the region's export products. Prebisch concluded that over the long term, the technological and industrial advantages of the capitalist center allowed it to dominate terms of trade with the periphery. This led to high wages for workers in the center and high prices for its trade goods, whereas in the periphery trade competition resulted in lower prices for export products and lower wages. International trade created structures in the periphery, which perpetuated the imbalance and accentuated Latin America's poor development. Hans W. Singer independently advanced similar ideas, and their position became known as the Prebisch-Singer thesis.

Prebisch and his associates, such as Brazilian Celso Furtado and Chilean Osvaldo Sunkel, concluded that Latin America's liberal capitalist policies made the region backward, poor, and miserable. They critiqued developmentalist thought, which posited that underdeveloped nations were on the path to progress and development and that their traditional, backward sectors would eventually give way to the modernizing power of international capitalism. The early structuralists such as Prebisch saw unfettered capitalism as the cause of backwardness in Latin America rather than its cure. They were not anticapitalist, however, but advocated protectionism, in which Latin American governments adopted nationalist policies that promoted import substitution and industrialization.

This required the governments to break out of the political and social controls exerted by international capitalism. It also provided much of the intellectual support for nationalist and statist economic policies in much of Latin America from the 1960s to the 1980s.

Some proponents of dependency theory opted for Marxist solutions to the problem of unequal exchange. These included political economists such as Paul Baran, Paul Sweezy, and Samir Amin. They combined Marxian analysis with the Prebisch-Singer thesis and concluded that underdevelopment would worsen unless Latin American nations freed themselves from both international and domestic capitalist structures. They did not see capitalism as a progressive force preparing the way for the struggle in which the proletariat would triumph over the bourgeoisie and create a classless society.

No figure in this neo-Marxist theoretical strain was more influential than André Gunder Frank, a German-born, University of Chicago–trained economist. Frank wrote in a nontechnical, popular style that resonated with a broad audience troubled by the problems of Latin America. His *Capitalism and Underdevelopment in Latin America* (1967) became the most widely read and most influential of the dependency theory treatises. In this work and in hundreds of other publications, Frank argued that development and underdevelopment were the two faces of the capitalist coin. Before international capitalism began to transform the New World, the Americas might not have been developed, but they were not underdeveloped. Liberal modernization theorists held that Latin American nations consisted of traditional "feudal" and progressive capitalist sectors and that growth of the capitalist sectors would eventually eliminate the feudal. Frank contended that both the traditional and the modernizing sectors existed as a result of capitalist imperialism, that the modern sector lived by impoverishing what was neither traditional nor feudal but what was in reality the capitalist periphery. He further argued that only during times of capitalist crisis, such as the Great Depression of the 1930s, could authentic development occur in the periphery.

In terms of economic and social analysis, dependency theory was particularly important for its emphasis on global analysis. The monumental synthesis of sociologist Immanuel Wallerstein reflected this concern. In three volumes published between 1974 and 1989, Wallerstein analyzed the growth of what he termed the capitalist world system. He divided the world system into capitalist core, semiperiphery, periphery, and external areas. The core exploited the semiperiphery and periphery, and the semiperiphery also appropriated surplus from the periphery. Wallerstein sought to unearth the social manifestations of global capitalism. Coercive labor systems such as slavery and the *mita* (system of rotating forced labor in the Andes) flourished in the periphery, for example, whereas proletarianization typified the capitalist core. Social relations also reflected the shift from agricultural to industrial capitalism. A synthesis rather than a work of primary research, Wallerstein's study attracted readers with its interpretative boldness and its survey of a vast, global literature. Many pages devoted more space to explanatory footnotes than to the main text.

By the 1990s, dependency theory had lost some of its dynamism. In Latin America the military regimes that had ruled almost every country gave way to civilian governments. Statist policies failed to resolve the economic crises that afflicted the region, and governments began to sell off state-owned enterprises and remove protectionist barriers in an attempt to improve efficiency and stimulate growth. They often sought guidance from technocrats and economists inspired by the classical liberalism of the University of Chicago. The theory also seemed to lack sufficient predictive value. New World colonies exploited by European capitalism had decidedly different outcomes. Despite its colonial status, for example, the United States developed, and even Brazil, with its huge disparities in income distribution and widespread poverty, has developed one of the world's largest gross national products. Nor did the theory provide practical solutions to the problem of dependence.

Kendall W. Brown

References

Cardoso, Fernando Henrique, and Enzo Faletto. *Dependency and Development in Latin America.* Translated by Marjory Mattingly Urquidi. Berkeley and Los Angeles: University of California Press, 1979.

Cockcroft, James D., André Gunder Frank, and Dale L. Johnson. *Dependence and Underdevelopment: Latin America's Political Economy.* Garden City, NY: Anchor, 1972.

Frank, André Gunder. *Capitalism and Underdevelopment in Latin America: Historical Studies of Chile and Brazil.* New York: Monthly Review, 1967.

Lehmann, David. *Democracy and Development in Latin America: Economics, Politics, and Religion in the Postwar Period.* London: Polity, 1990.

Oxaal, Ivar, Tony Barnett, and David Booth, eds. *Beyond the Sociology of Development: Economy and Society in Latin America and Africa.* Boston: Routledge and Kegan Paul, 1975.

Wallerstein, Immanuel. *The Modern World System.* 3 vols. 1: *Capitalist Agriculture and the Origins of the European World-Economy in the 16th Century;* 2: *Mercantilism and the Consolidation of the European World-Economy, 1600–1750;* 3: *The Second Era of Great Expansion of the Capitalist World-Economy, 1730–1840s.* New York and San Diego: Academic, 1974–1989.

See also: Atlantic Economy; Communism; Democracy; Liberalism; Mita; Nationalism; Positivism; Trade—Spain/Spanish America.

DIABOLISM IN THE NEW WORLD

Diabolism can be defined as belief in the devil. In some exceptional instances, the definition can be extended to worship of the devil, or Satanism. In the Americas, belief in the devil began with attempts by Europeans to categorize the newly discovered civilizations and their religious practices. By the mid-eighteenth century, Satan had become a real presence in the new continent, but he had undergone considerable transformation. The varying degrees of communication and interaction between European and indigenous cultures, and the diverse theological trends within Hispano-American Christianity itself, markedly affected the devil's perceived nature and purpose.

Throughout the early modern period the devil was a paradoxical figure. The same missionaries responsible for his arrival and dissemination believed that they were in the process of dislodging him from his last worldly bastion. Meanwhile, theological trends in the late seventeenth century juxtaposed the more usual image of Satan as the eternal enemy of humankind with more surprising appearances of him as a servant of the divine will, sent by God to purge individuals of their sins by attacking their bodies and minds. In this respect Satan was sometimes believed to assist rather than obstruct individuals on the road to salvation.

Upon the discovery of the Americas, there sprang an immediate need to classify and understand the New World and its inhabitants. The arrival of missionaries and the potential for the conversion of untold numbers of indigenous people appeared to herald a new phase in the progression toward Satan's final defeat. This millenarianism, championed by the early Franciscan friars in New Spain, was seemingly confirmed by the baptism of thousands of Indians in the first few years after their arrival in 1524.

The vast majority of missionaries believed that the sacrificial rites of the Mexican Indians were diabolical. Initially, however, some missionaries came to believe that such rites had developed for want of Christianity's presence. As they perceived it, even such practices as human sacrifice might have grown from the human's innate desire and need to worship God. Without proper guidance, it was quite understandable that these religions would not reach the ritual perfection of Christ's Church. The influential Dominican Bartolomé de las Casas championed this view, even arguing that, far from being diabolical, human sacrifice, as the most precious sacrifice a society could make, was the natural culmination of human religious expression. Once the truth was presented to the indigenous peoples, human reason would be enough for them to realize the errors of their ways.

Such optimism was not to last, however, and this is nowhere so clearly in evidence than in the later evangelization project in Peru. As the sixteenth century progressed, it became harder for Europeans to believe that the continuation of indigenous rites was merely the result of ignorance. Similarities between Christian and indigenous rites began to be more frequently explained as diabolical imitations. However, for the indigenous peoples, the concept of a totally evil supernatural being was fundamentally alien. Both the Mesoamerican and Andean cosmologies attributed both destructive and creative powers to their deities in cycles of destruction and renewal. Without the essential power to destroy, a god would be unable to create, and one who could not destroy could never renew. *Ucupacha,* for example (the word designated by missionaries in the Andes to mean "hell"), in fact referred to a dark place beneath the earth in which new life was germinated. Therefore, Satan could not be introduced to the indigenous peoples without undergoing considerable transformation. In turn, there was no contradiction in the devil being accepted into the American pantheons alongside God and the saints, all of whom had the power to protect individuals and communities and could vent their wrath in the natural world. In Mesoamerica, the evidence suggests that the more the missionaries insisted that indigenous sacrifices were diabolical, the more indigenous peoples internalized the notion that the devil was actually on their side. Illicit sacrifices thus continued within indigenous society, but they were now increasingly offered to the devil in the same way as they had been offered to autochthonous deities in the past.

The extent of the devil's naturalization depended largely on the degree of contact between indigenous peoples and the Hispanic world. In central Mexico, where indigenous peoples were generally concentrated in large metropolitan centers, as opposed to the peripheries where missionary activity struggled against geographical extremes and dispersed and resistant populations, Christianization had been largely successful by the late sixteenth century. Despite varying degrees of religious syncretism, Christianity in central Mexico largely replaced indigenous religion at the heart of communal ritual practice. In Peru, by contrast, where communities were much more isolated owing to the extreme geography of the Andes, worship of *huacas* (local gods) continued throughout the Spanish colonial period, notwithstanding various extirpation campaigns. Nevertheless, a gradual process of the diabolization of indigenous huacas did occur for Andeans who maintained regular contact with Christian society. Huaca worship was forced from its central position within community life to a private and surreptitious role in isolated places. Like devils, huacas in exile became linked to considerable dissension within communities as Christian and nativist factions vied for political and religious control.

In the minds of many Hispanic writers, Satan was to find a useful ally in the various non-Hispanic communities that encircled and penetrated the main colonial cities. This perceived threat was to combine during the Baroque period, with a shift in Christian spirituality giving rise to altogether new diabolical phenomena. Toward the second half of the seventeenth century, an exaggerated form of Augustinianism that condemned the human body and the senses as essentially corrupt began to gain ground. Individuals could contribute to their own salvation only by rejecting nature and mortifying their flesh. The physical torment of possession became a vehicle for such mortification, a way of purging the body of the stain of sin. In extreme cases, such as the possessions of the Franciscan nuns of Trujillo (Peru) in the 1670s and of Querétaro (Mexico) in the 1690s, possessed individuals claimed to be suffering for the sins of the entire community. Meanwhile, others looked for the causes of these diabolical infestations in the autochthonous ritual practices of the surrounding rural communities, or otherwise passed them off as delusions. What was clear to the majority was that the possessions caused chaos, fear, and even skepticism in the communities, disrupting normal liturgical and secular life. Satan thus remained a paradoxical figure to the end: on one hand, he threatened individuals and their communities; on the other, he was increasingly perceived as an instrument of salvation.

Andrew Redden

References

Cervantes, Fernando. *The Devil in the New World: The Impact of Diabolism in New Spain.* New Haven, CT: Yale University Press, 1994.

Farriss, Nancy. *Maya Society under Colonial Rule: The Collective Enterprise of Survival.* Princeton, NJ: Princeton University Press, 1984.

Griffiths, Nicholas. *The Cross and the Serpent: Religious Repression and Resurgence in Colonial Peru.* Norman: University of Oklahoma Press, 1995.

MacCormack, Sabine. *Religion in the Andes: Vision and Imagination in Early Colonial Peru.* Princeton, NJ: Princeton University Press, 1991.

Mills, Kenneth. *Idolatry and Its Enemies: Colonial Andean Religion and Extirpation, 1640–1750.* Princeton, NJ: Princeton University Press, 1997.

See also: Cannibalism; Catholic Church in Brazil; Catholic Church in Spanish America; Clergy—Secular, in Colonial Spanish America; Human Sacrifice; Idolatry, Extirpation of; Native Americans I–VIII; Religious Orders; Syncretism; Witchcraft.

DONATARY CAPTAINCIES

Donatary captaincies were the political, territorial, and administrative units of colonial Brazil. *Capitanias* (or donatary captaincies) first appeared in Brazil in the sixteenth century. In order to promote the settlement of Brazil, Dom João (King John III) of Portugal divided Brazil into fifteen hereditary captaincies in the 1530s. Using late medieval and early modern Portuguese grants as the model, the king transferred specific rights and privileges normally held by the Crown to individuals. The recipient, known as a *donatário,* received extensive powers, including the right to grant land, administer justice, and collect rents. The original captaincies extended, on average, 50 leagues (approximately 300 kilometers) along the coast and inland due west to the line (between 48° and 49° W) set by the Treaty of Tordesillas. Although such a line could be drawn on maps such as the one below, in reality the interior of Brazil was a vast wilderness unknown to Europeans and effectively under the domain of hundreds of independent Indian tribes. Nevertheless, the Crown gave these lands in donations as rewards for service to wealthy men in Portugal, primarily to merchants and prominent officials of the Crown who had the financial means and expertise to promote colonization. Through this policy, the Crown hoped to pass the cost of claiming the huge territory of Brazil, then contested with France, to private individuals.

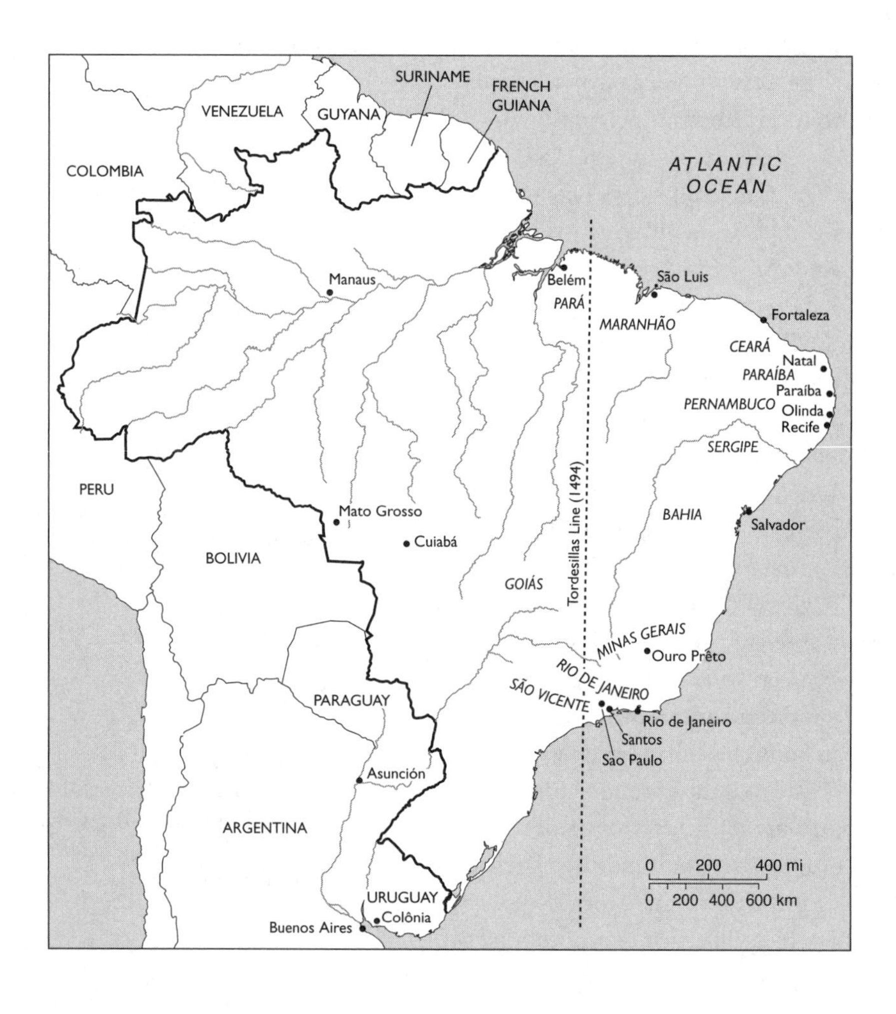

Of the fifteen original captaincies, ten were settled in the sixteenth century; among them from north to south were Maranhão, Pernambuco, Bahia, Ilhéus, Porto Seguro, Espírito Santo, São Tomé, and São Vicente. Only two of the capitanias met with modest initial success: Pernambuco and São Vicente. The Crown reclaimed the captaincy of Bahia from its heirs in 1549 in order to establish an effective royal presence in Brazil. Bahia became a royal captaincy and the site of Brazil's first capital, Salvador. There resided the king's governor-general for Brazil, as well as the most important Crown officials. The power of the donatários began to decline thereafter. During the seventeenth and eighteenth centuries, administrative reforms continually reorganized Brazil. Captaincies, administered by Crown-appointed governors, were the core territorial units of the colony.

By the second half of the eighteenth century, the Crown resolved to terminate the rights of the remaining hereditary captaincies during the reforms initiated by the powerful Marquis de Pombal, first minister to King José I (1750–1777). Other reforms created the *capitanias gerais* (captaincies-general), the most important of the territorial divisions of Brazil. By the late eighteenth century, the capitanias gerais included, from north to south, Grão Para, Maranhão, Pernambuco, Bahia, Goiás, Minas Gerais, Mato Grosso, Rio de Janeiro, and São Paulo. The administrators of these vast territories (*capitais gerais* or captains-general) had extensive powers that rivaled those of the governor-general for all of Brazil and later those of the viceroy. Smaller captaincies, administered by governors, included, from north to south, São José do Rio Negro, Piauí, Ceará, Rio Grande do Norte, Paraíba, Sergipe, Espírito Santo, Santa Catarina, and Rio Grande do São Pedro. After independence in 1822, the captaincies-general and captaincies became provinces.

Alida C. Metcalf

References

Alden, Dauril. *Royal Government in Colonial Brazil.* Berkeley and Los Angeles: University of California Press, 1968.

Johnson, H.-B. "The Donatary Captaincy in Perspective: Portuguese Backgrounds to the Settlement of Brazil." *Hispanic American Historical Review* 52 (1972): 203–214.

———. "Portuguese Settlement, 1500–1580." Pp. 1–38 in *Colonial Brazil,* edited by Leslie Bethell. Cambridge: Cambridge University Press, 1987.

See also: Administration—Colonial Spanish America; Colonists and Settlers II—Brazil; Conquest II—Brazil; Engenho; Enlightenment—Brazil; Gold; Mining—Gold; Monarchs of Portugal; Slavery I—Brazil; Sugar; Tordesillas, Treaty of.

DRUGS

Drugs pose serious challenges to societies and governments throughout the world, but especially in the Americas, where the United States is the world's leading consumer, and Latin American countries are some of the leading producers of illicit drugs. As the world's only superpower, the United States and its drug policy tend to overwhelm all other issues in those countries caught up in international drug trafficking, such as Colombia, Peru, Bolivia, and Mexico. There are many inconsistencies, if not downright contradictions, in this policy, whether pursued domestically or abroad. The unsatisfactory results to date have led to a heated debate in the United States and abroad over how drugs, their consumers, suppliers, and producers should be treated. In many countries drugs became one of the defining political issues in the late twentieth century.

U.S. drug policy has been directed toward reducing both the demand and supply of illegal drugs. In monetary terms, the demand side of the equation is in the United States, and the supply side is in Latin America, where cocaine and increasing amounts of heroin are produced. In the year 2000, Colombia produced 266,000 tons or 80 percent of the coca leaf. Peru produced 54,000 tons or 16 percent, and Bolivia produced 13,000 tons or 4 percent, most of which was organized, processed into cocaine, and then transported by Colombians. Mexico, with its long border with the United States, is often an essential pass-through country. As a result, Colombians have found it useful to form joint partnerships with Mexicans in transporting cocaine and then, in some instances, in its distribution. While Afghanistan and Myanmar produce most of the world's opium, increasing amounts of heroin come from Colombia and Mexico, using the same distribution networks as for cocaine. Again, Colombia leads the way in the Western Hemisphere's opium production. In the year 2000, Colombia produced 88 tons or 81 percent and Mexico 27 tons or 19 percent of the opium made in the Western Hemisphere.

Why Colombians assumed the leadership role of the international drug trade and not Peruvians, Mexicans, or Bolivians has much to do with Colombia's unique history. Colombia's strategic location, complex geography, weak national institutions, and traditional entrepreneurial skills brought it to the forefront of the drug trade by the late 1960s, where it has remained since. For many of the same reasons, Colombia is also the site of the longest-running guerrilla movement in Latin America, and when the power of the Medellín and Cali drug cartels was broken in the 1990s, the guerrillas and the paramilitaries moved into the vacuum and became significant factors in the drug trade.

Colombia's strategic location helped it to monopolize many of the key trade routes. Colombia is positioned close enough to the United States to control much of the flow of cocaine, yet far enough away and complex enough geographically to resist the United States' war on drugs. Its overlay of three mountain ranges is unique even in Andean America, where mountains and rough terrain are dominant geographical features. The country remains a sieve of ingress and egress points. Colombia's border with five countries and its long coastlines on both the Pacific and the Caribbean, with hundreds of seaports and airstrips, delight tourists, adventurers, romantics, smugglers, drug traffickers, and money launderers. Of course, they also bring despair to statisticians, customs agents, the police, military, and other "honest" officials of both the United States and Colombia.

Geography blessed Colombia with great diversity but burdened it with a shattered mosaic that to date has never been molded into an orderly functioning whole at the national level. Instead, it left Colombia with ineffective state institutions and a culture of clientalism where the powers of the president and the military have historically been weak. Out of this power vacuum emerged classic wheeler-dealer, adventurer types, most often personified by the stereotypical Antioqueños from Medellín, the capital city of the Department of Antioquia, who were long known for their dynamic colonization and entrepreneurial

A Colombian antidrug policeman gives instructions to a Black Hawk helicopter pilot after destroying a cocaine lab during an operation in northeastern Colombia, May 2000. (Reuters/Corbis)

success and who, by the 1970s, had successfully organized the international drug trade. Every Colombian city of any size has a place where black-market goods and contraband are sold illegally. Today these contraband operations are so pervasive that they are nationally organized into the Colombian Sanandresito Federation, which represents the interests of 20,000 store and 180 shopping-mall owners. Colombians have a long tradition of moving contraband goods in and out of the country. These networks and contraband skills have four centuries of tradition behind them. Thus, Colombia was primed to organize the international drug trade between the United States and Bolivia and Peru.

When the consumption of illicit drugs grew in the United States to alarming proportions in the 1980s, moralizing politicians played on the fears of the general public and produced legislation that attacked both the supply and demand sides of the drug equation. There were significant problems with this legislation both at home and abroad. Most legislation to stop consumption emphasized punishment rather than treatment, and the results did not reduce demand. In 1997, more than 220,000 teenagers were arrested for drug transgressions in the United States, an 82 percent increase since 1993. Mandatory sentences of five to ten years for the possession of a few grams of a drug have incarcerated thousands, so that half of those in federal prisons are there for drug offenses. Only 12 percent of these offenses involved a violent crime in which a weapon was used. The rate of incarceration in the United States for drug offenses now exceeds the rate of imprisonment for all crimes in most European countries. Even though drug use is more or less the same across racial lines, nonwhites suffer a disproportionate amount of the punishment and account for three-fourths of those arrested. There are more black males in prison for drug offenses than are in college. Clearly, the punitive approach has been less than successful in reducing the demand for drugs and has tended to divide the United States along racial and class lines.

The punitive approach has had other negative repercussions. It has spawned new bureaucracies dedicated to enforcing drug laws and generated a whole industry of prison building. Most drug offenses involve willing consumers who do not see themselves as victims, so that law enforcement must use informants, wiretapping, and undercover operations that are not used in most other crimes and that can easily endanger civil liberties. The inability "to win the war on drugs" to date has led voters to accept the arguments of self-serving bureaucrats, politicians, and prison builders that more law enforcement and punitive measures are needed. But eventually taxpayers may resent the escalating bureaucracies and expenditures. In fact, an increasing number of people see the drug laws as having missed their mark and as having been ill-conceived from the beginning. They argue that the social damage has been incalculable. People in prison for nonviolent crimes, the case with most drug offenses, often emerge embittered and a much greater threat to society as a result of harsh prison conditions. Human Rights Watch estimates that 20 percent of imprisoned males are subjected to forced sex. Increased drug use often results from being in prison. When finally released to the general population, they face the world with the training they received in the violence of prison life. The outmoded model employed in the United States and many of its underlying arguments are replicated in other countries with even sadder results. There police run amok, civil liberties are more frequently violated, and prison conditions are inhumane.

It is important to note that tobacco and alcohol, both legal in the United States, are far more injurious to U.S. society than all illegal drugs combined. The number of deaths caused by tobacco and alcohol are hundreds, if not thousands, of times more than those caused by all illegal drugs. Why tobacco and alcohol should be exempt and not other drugs is not clear, other than the fact that tobacco and alcohol have long been socially acceptable while the others have only gained some social tolerance since the 1960s. Half of the people under forty years of age in the United States have tried marijuana. One argument justifying the double standard is the gateway theory, which states that soft drugs like marijuana are the first step toward using more powerful and dangerous drugs like cocaine or heroin. But the same argument does not lead to a ban on tobacco and alcohol. And undermining the gateway theory are the statistics showing that few marijuana users replace this with other illegal drugs.

Another argument advanced for banning drugs rests on the belief that using drugs makes you forever addictive, ruined, and lost to society. In fact, most drugs are probably not physically addictive. Among users the most addictive is nicotine. The rate of addiction among cigarette smokers is 80 percent, among heroin users 50 percent, and among cocaine consumers 20 percent. Many have tried these drugs but are no longer consumers and are not included in these percentages.

It is a mistake to think that the demand side of the drug equation in the future will only be in the United States. The same willingness of the young to try something new has spread the drug culture throughout Western Europe and Latin America. Many acquired their popular culture in the United States before returning to their home countries. Many more will follow. The demand side of the drug equation will have increasing relevance in Latin America. If governments there follow the United States' unsuccessful domestic drug policy, they will probably experience the same failures. But to do otherwise will put them at variance with U.S. policy and will be another sore point in U.S.–Latin American relations.

The United States has attempted to deal with the supply side of illicit drugs by reducing availability. It has pressured Latin American countries to prosecute producers as criminals and to destroy coca cultivation. As the principal market for many of their legal exports, as the chief architect of economic globalization, and often as the chief supplier of vital foreign aid, the United States has enormous leverage over the economies and governments of Latin America. To follow or not to follow U.S. drug policy has invariably created major political problems. Much of the negative feeling in Latin America toward the United States has resulted from the unilateral way in which it has attempted to impose its drug policy on individual Latin American countries.

The United States has faced unique problems in different Latin American countries. It did not see or did not care what the long-term impact of its drug policy would be individually or collectively, and the results have almost never satisfied any of the parties. In Peru and Bolivia the coca leaf has been legal since time immemorial. There poverty-ridden peasants experienced in its cultivation easily increased output to satisfy the new international demand. Production in Peru concentrated in the Upper Huallaga Valley in the late 1980s with estimates of between 60,000 and 100,000 hectares (132,000–220,000 acres) planted in coca leaf, employing 40,000 to 50,000 peasants. Another 100,000 hectares elsewhere in Peru could also have been dedicated to coca production. Estimates for Bolivia at the same time were 60,000 hectares in coca leaf production, employing upwards of 120,000 peasants, mainly in the Chapare region.

Throughout the 1980s, the United States increased its overt and covert military operations and intelligence gathering in the Caribbean, Central America, and South America to stem the flow of cocaine from Andean countries. In 1986, President Ronald Reagan promulgated a National Security Directive, making drug trafficking a "lethal" threat to U.S. national security. A more concerted effort to stem the flow of drugs northward followed.

In response to U.S. moves to cut off vital aid, Bolivian president Victor Paz Estensorro allowed Operation Blast Furnace to take place in 1986. U.S. Army personnel and their Blackhawk helicopters transported U.S. agents and Bolivian police forces to Chapare to destroy cocaine laboratories and arrest traffickers. The resulting outcry almost brought about Estensorro's impeachment. Coercive efforts to curtail coca production have continued to produce a strong backlash among peasants who have everything to lose from the disruption. Bolivian peasants have been well organized since the Revolution of 1952 and have endangered the survival of every government that has put their interests in jeopardy.

In 1989, the United States launched a military invasion of Panama to arrest its dictator, General Manuel Noriega, for drug trafficking and money laundering. The invasion of Panama brought widespread condemnation from throughout Latin America. As a result, U.S. militarization of the drug war was concealed in the civilian employees of its Drug Enforcement Administration (DEA), State Department, Central Intelligence Agency (CIA), and private contractors supported by the U.S. military.

In Peru, U.S. manned and bunkered bases were established in the Upper Huallaga Valley in 1989 to control drug trafficking. Eradication efforts led to alliances between peasants and Sendero Luminoso (Shining Path) guerrillas, an alliance that was maintained until the capture of the guerrilla leader Abimael Guzmán in 1992. Overall U.S. drug policy emphasized military strategies and tactics at the expense of socioeconomic development, and in Peru it may have upset the balance between civilian and military forces that eventually led to some of the worst abuses and corruption during the presidency of Alberto Fujimori (1990–2000).

In Colombia, the United States wanted drug traffickers captured and extradited, and consequently supplied police officials with military and intelligence support. Efforts at curtailing drug production by extraditing drug lords led to the murder of justice minister Rodrigo Lara Bonilla in 1984, *El Espectador* newspaper editor Guillermo Cano in 1986, Attorney General Carlos Mauro Hoyos in 1988, and Liberal presidential candidate Luis Carlos Galán on August 18, 1989. In the last-named case, the Colombian government found itself in a total war with the "Extraditable Ones," the *nom de guerre* of the Medellín cartel leaders made up of Pablo Escobar, Gonzalo Rodríguez Gacha, and Jorge Luis Ochoa. The Colombian political elite and the drug lords had dueled on and off and in different negotiations since 1980 as to what their power would be. With the killing of Rodríguez Gacha in 1989 and of Escobar in 1993, the Medellín cartel came to an end; however, it was replaced with that of the much less confrontational Cali cartel, led by Gilberto and Miguel Rodríguez Orejuela, José Santacruz Londoño, and "Pacho" Herrera. The Cali cartel put the police and army officials, congressmen, and judges on their payroll, and corrupted the Colombian system in a way from which it still has not recovered.

When it became public knowledge in early 1995 that Liberal president Ernesto Samper (1994–1998) had been elected with the help of Cali cartel money, the United States made President Samper *persona non grata* by denying him a visa. Even though there was much greater cooperation under Samper—the Rodríguez Orejuela brothers were arrested, the Cali cartel was dismantled, and the power of the drug kingpins was broken—the United States decertified

Colombia in 1996 and again in 1997 for not cooperating sufficiently on counternarcotic efforts. Colombia was denied foreign aid and U.S. support within international lending agencies. U.S. Embassy officials dealt directly with Colombian police and military authorities like General Rosso José Serrano rather than with President Samper, who had become a virtual nonentity. This led Colombians to elect U.S.-backed Conservative Andrés Pastrana as president (1998–2002) over the more politically talented Liberal candidate Horacio Serpa.

Another major irritant of U.S. drug policy has been the emphasis on eradication through the aerial spraying of herbicides. Coca leaf cultivation declined significantly in Bolivia and Peru as a result of spraying, but Colombia more than made up the difference, increasing production from 44,700 hectares in 1994 to 86,300 in 2003. Nevertheless, Colombian production in 2003 declined 50 percent from its high in 2000 of 163,300 hectares. Despite the drop, there was no measurable impact on the supply or cost of cocaine in the United States. Unfortunately, herbicides destroy subsistent food crops and are probably an environmental and health hazard as well. It certainly has been a propaganda disaster for the United States and politicized significant numbers of *campesinos* (farmers), driving many into the ranks of Colombian guerrillas and paramilitaries. Crop substitution programs have invariably failed, since only monetary returns from illegal coca and opium production are sufficient to overcome the transportation barriers to a market economy.

An unintended result of U.S. drug policy has been to significantly weaken the Colombian state. The years since 1994 have seen drug operations in the field taken over by Colombian guerrilla and paramilitary groups. Their forces and power have increased by leaps and bounds, fueled in large part by money earned through the international drug trade. This further weakened the Colombian state. Its inability to protect Colombian citizens from the kidnappings and blackmail of the guerrillas led to the explosive growth of paramilitary forces, which in turn committed major human rights violations against social activists and those in areas with a significant guerrilla presence. Colombia now faces a major guerrilla or civil war that is inextricably linked to the traffic in illicit drugs.

Maurice P. Brungardt

References

Clawson, Patrick L., and Rensselaer Lee. *The Andean Cocaine Industry.* New York: St. Martin's, 1996.

Crandal, Russell. *Driven by Drugs: U.S. Policy toward Colombia.* Boulder/London: Lynne Rienner, 2002.

MacCoun, Robert, and Peter Reuter. *Drug War Heresies: Learning from Other Vices, Times, and Places.* Cambridge: Cambridge University Press, 2001.

MacDonald, Scott B. *Dancing on a Volcano: The Latin American Drug Trade.* New York: Praeger, 1988.

Perl, Raphael, ed. *Drugs and Foreign Policy: A Critical Review.* Boulder, CO: Westview, 1994.

Sierra, Alvaro. "Día mundial de lucha contra las drogas [Analysis of 2004 *World Drug Report*]." *El Tiempo,* June 26, 2004.

Smith, Peter H., ed. *Drug Policy in the Americas.* Boulder, CO: Westview, 1992.

"A Survey of Colombia: Drugs, War, and Democracy." *The Economist,* April 21, 2001, pp. 1–16.

"A Survey of Illegal Drugs." *The Economist,* July 28, 2001, pp. 1–16.

See also: Alcohol; Bolivia; Coca; Colombia; Communism; Contraband; Guerrillas; Human Rights; Mexico; Monopolies; North American Free Trade Agreement; Organization of American States; Peru; Tobacco; World War II.

DYES AND DYEWOOD

Unlike pigments, natural dyes, which chemically bond to a substrate, are rare. Historically, dyes of red and blue were particularly scarce, and successful American dyestuffs—cochineal (bright red), indigo (deep blue), brazilwood (red to purple), and logwood (brown to charcoal)—met the needs of an existing European market that would grow over the next few centuries.

Cochineal (*cochinilla*), a superior red dye derived from an insect of the same name, was Mexico's second most valuable export. The Aztecs gathered the red insects from the wild *nopal* cactus and sold them in public markets. Only under Spanish rule did the Indians of Oaxaca domesticate the insect. In fact, Oaxaca's Indians enjoyed almost exclusive control of cochineal, which explains, in part, why their communities survived colonization better than many native groups in Mexico. Indians planted fields of nopal that, once established, were seeded with cochineal nests. The insects parasitized the cactus and quickly matured if protected from bird and insect predators. Once they were mature, skilled workers brushed the insects off the plants with a tuft of animal hair, suffocated them, and set them to dry. Desiccated, the insects looked like red grain, hence cochineal's popular name, *grana.* A single pound consisted of 70,000 insects. By the 1770s, Oaxaca produced 1.5 million pounds annually, but after independence from Spain, production moved to Guatemala.

Indigo *(añil* in Spanish) was a plant native to Mesoamerica that Spaniards recognized as a close relative of the East Indian variety. The Maya had employed it to dye both textiles and ceramics, and indigo's blue was the traditional color for sacrifice. Only after a century of colonial rule did Spaniards plant indigo, and thereafter its cultivation spread from its source in Guatemala to Venezuela, the Caribbean, and eventually South Carolina. French Saint Domingue and Guatemala were the major producers in the late eighteenth century. Slaves and Indian tributary labor (*repartimiento*) provided the labor, which was seasonal, as the plants required little care. At harvest, workers placed the plant in a large vat of water to macerate. Within a day, the leaves began to effervesce violently, releasing blue matter to the solution that was soon channeled to a second vat. Here, workers beat the surface with wooden poles (an operation soon mechanized) until a skilled foreman ordered the water drained and the blue sediment collected, dried, and sawn into 214-pound chunks. The stench from the vats attracted biting insects and, with them, disease; the odor was so unpleasant that indigo manufactories were legislated away from human habitations. While in most areas indigo remained in the exclusive hands of Europeans, in Saint Domingue the free colored employed indigo and slave ownership as vehicles of upward mobility. Their rise resulted in elite racial conflict upon which slaves later capitalized in the Haitian Revolution.

Brazilwood *(pau brasil)* was Portuguese America's first export. Similar to a well-known dyewood from East Asia, its value was immediately recognized. The Crown made it a strict royal monopoly, but contraband was common, and excluded colonists burned it as an obstacle to agriculture. The tree was harvested initially by free Indian workers who labored in exchange for European trade goods, especially iron tools and textiles. To expose

Indigenous Brazilians harvest brazilwood for export in this scene from a sixteenth-century book. Exploitation of the wood and other natural resources drove the early colonial economy. (Library of Congress)

the dark heartwood, the source of the red dye, workers removed the bark and sapwood; then they shouldered the heavy timbers to coastal warehouses to await the arrival of transport to Dutch and British markets. Today, Brazil's namesake has all but disappeared.

Logwood (*campeche*) exploration in Belize and the Yucatán was a Spanish monopoly until the mid-seventeenth century when British incursions caused the price to fall considerably. The tree grew in swampy land and was processed much like Brazilwood. Its primary use was as a darkener in conjunction with other colored dyes.

Although the fortunes of the dye trade rose and fell with various conditions, the Industrial Revolution spurred general growth. However, the trade in natural dyes virtually disappeared in the late nineteenth century with the development of synthetic dyes by German industry.

Shawn William Miller

References

Baskes, Jeremy. *Indians, Merchants, and Markets: A Reinterpretation of the Repartimiento and Spanish-Indian Economic Relations in Colonial Oaxaca, 1750–1821.* Stanford, CA: Stanford University Press, 2000.

Garrigus, John D. "Blue and Brown: Contraband Indigo and the Rise of a Free Colored Planter Class in French Saint-Domingue." *Americas* 50, no. 2 (October 1993): 233–263.

Souza, Bernardino José de. *O pau-brasil na história nacional.* 2nd ed. São Paulo: Companhia Editora Nacional, 1978.

See also: Atlantic Economy; Brazil; Colonists and Settlers II—Brazil; Columbian Exchange—Agriculture; Conquest II—Brazil; Guatemala; Mexico; Native Americans I—VIII; Trade—Spain/Spanish America.

ECUADOR

Ecuador is a republic located on the west coast of South America, bordered by Colombia on the north and Peru on the south and east, encompassing an area of 109,000 square miles with a population of approximately 13 million in 2004. Though small in area, Ecuador has diverse geographical features, including lush tropical coastal lowlands, temperate highland valleys, rainforests, arid deserts, and numerous active volcanoes. The Galapagos Islands are also part of Ecuador.

Present-day Ecuador comprises the northern quarter of the Inca Empire with the administrative center at the city of Quitu (Quito). The area was conquered and colonized by the Incas ca. 1515 and retained a distinct identity within the realm. Ecuador's connection to the Iberian world began in 1526 when Francisco Pizarro probed the Ecuadorian coast in search of the riches of the Inca Empire. In 1532, Pizarro led an expedition with 167 Spaniards and a dozen horses. On November 18 of that year, Pizarro captured Inca emperor Atahualpa during a daring surprise attack at Cajamarca and thus began the Spanish conquest of Peru.

The task of conquering Ecuador was assigned to one of Pizarro's lieutenants, Sebastián del Benalcázar. Benalcázar's force of 140 Spaniards, assisted by Indian allies, the fierce Cañari, defeated an Inca army led by the legendary Inca general Rumiñahui, at the base of Mount Chimborazo near the city of Riobamba. Rumiñahui burned Quito rather than surrender the city to Benalcázar's forces. Thus, when Benalcázar founded the city of San Francisco de Quito on December 6, 1534, he did so amidst its smoldering ruins. Colonial Quito, unlike Cuzco, had no architectural evidence of its pre-Columbian past. Rumiñahui was eventually captured and, on January 10, 1535, he was executed. On July 25, 1535, Benalcázar established the port city of Guayaquil, which later became the commercial center of Ecuador as well as the political rival of the colonial capital, Quito.

In February 1541, an exploratory expedition, led by Gonzalo Pizarro, with Francisco de Orellana as second in command, set out from Quito to the east in search of cinnamon and gold. The party, which consisted of 210 Spaniards and 4,000 Indians, traversed the eastern cordillera and suffered great hardships in the rainforest. Over half the force was lost to disease, desertion, and encounters with fierce warrior tribes. Upon reaching the Coca River, the expedition was near collapse from a shortage of food. Pizarro then ordered Orellana to build a small ship and sail down the Coca in search of food. Orellana never returned; instead, he navigated the Coca until he discovered that it was a tributary of the mighty Amazon River. Orellana then sailed the length of the Amazon to its mouth at the Atlantic Ocean. He eventually sailed to Venezuela and then to Spain. Meanwhile, assuming that Orellana and his men had been killed by hostile natives, Pizarro limped back to Quito with a handful of survivors. The discovery of the Amazon has great significance for Ecuador's national identity as it was later used as a basis to claim jurisdiction over a vast area named the Oriente, which would be in dispute with Peru until 1999.

Sebastían de Benalcázar, Gonzalo Pizarro, and many other Spanish conquistadors attempted to establish themselves as the self-proclaimed grandees of Ecuador by introducing the *encomienda* labor system. To curb the power and abuses of the conquistadors, the Spanish Crown proclaimed the New Laws in 1542. The Viceroyalty of Peru, of which Ecuador was a part, was established in 1544 in an attempt to enforce royal administrative control. Ecuador became an *audiencia* in 1563. The Audiencia of Quito was both a court and a political unit, headed by a president with several judges (*oidores*). Although an audiencia was a subunit of the viceroyalty, it could deal directly with Madrid on certain matters. Moreover, the boundaries of the audiencia were an early definition of Ecuador's territory and would later lead to disputes in the postindependence period.

Ecuador had little gold and silver, and thus the colonial economy developed around textiles and foodstuffs needed to supply the mines of Peru. In the highlands, from Otavalo in the north to Riobamba south of Quito, numerous textile mills, known as *obrajes de comunidad,* were established, employing as many as 200 Indian weavers in the larger mills. In some instances, these obrajes were operated directly by the Crown, while others, in theory, were the communal property of Indian towns. However, by the eighteenth century, most obrajes were privately owned under licensing arrangements with the Crown. Working conditions in most of the obrajes were oppressive and included low wages, long hours, and debt peonage, which bound workers, and often their families, to the enterprise as well as to the whims of the owners. To support the workforce in the obrajes, the hacienda system became prevalent throughout the Ecuadorian highlands. The haciendas provided the obrajes with foodstuffs and wool.

Ecuadorian textiles were of superior quality and thus were exported to Lima. Since the import of European textiles was forbidden, the economy thrived until 1740, when the monopoly on woolens was broken by a change in royal policy that allowed the importation of cheaper and superior-quality European goods. Then the northern and central highlands suffered a sharp economic decline, although the southern highlands, centered at the colonial town of Cuenca, experienced increased prosperity as cotton and woolen textiles were exported on a more competitive basis. In addition, some landowners found an alternative product in the bark of the cascarilla tree, which contains quinine.

In the littoral, economic development was much slower. In 1778, Spain's Bourbon monarchs began to allow open trade within the empire. The Ecuadorian coast benefited from this change with the exportation of cacao, which became the mainstay of the regional economy. In addition to cacao, Ecuadorian coastal plantations produced tobacco, sugar, and other products for export. In the colonial period, the different economic patterns of the coast and the sierra served as a further bifurcation of the identity and interests of the two regions.

Spain also brought Roman Catholicism to Ecuador. The Belén church (1541) was among the first permanent structures erected in Quito. The major religious orders—Dominicans, Franciscans, Augustinians, and Jesuits—were well represented in Ecuador and built magnificent churches and convents in Quito. The Church established schools, almshouses, hospitals, monasteries, and nunneries to provide for the educational and social needs of the colony. In addition, the Church acquired vast wealth through the accumulation of property that included the operation of haciendas, obrajes, and other commercial enterprises. The cultural life of colonial Ecuador was dominated by the Church, which sponsored the arts in the form of religious sculptures and paintings to decorate the churches and chapels of the convents. The Quito School became renowned for training some of the most skilled artisans of the day.

During the colonial period, Spain's imprint on Ecuador was indelible. However, two distinct Ecuadors emerged, as the Crown, in a futile attempt to protect its Indian subjects, segregated the population into Spanish and Indian towns (*Repúblicas de los Indios*). The pattern of trade and commerce emerged with obrajes and haciendas in the highlands and the plantation system on the coast. The two political and commercial centers of the country, Quito and Guayaquil, became rivals rather than partners. Finally, the ecclesiastical aspect of Ecuador had been determined when both the secular and regular clergy of the Roman Catholic Church had arrived, proselytized tens of thousands of Indians, built the religious infrastructure, and guided the moral and cultural life of the colony.

By 1790, Spain's grip on its New World possessions was weakening, and intellectuals were gathering in committees known as Friends of the Country *(Amigos del País)*. In Quito, the leading figure of the local committee was Eugenio de Santa Cruz y Espejo. Espejo was of mixed blood but had obtained a university education and was a physician, political satirist, and library director. Espejo was deeply affected by the ideas of the Enlightenment and the American Revolution; he advocated independence from Spain, local control of the clergy, the expulsion of Iberian priests, and the creation of a republic. Espejo's writings and activities were soon considered subversive by the Crown, and he was imprisoned until he died in 1795. He is regarded as the precursor of Ecuador's independence.

Disputes and antagonisms within the elite widened after Espejo's death. Important government and church positions tended to be assigned to the peninsular elite, and Ecuador's Creoles continually felt left out. Moreover, commercial regulations tended to inhibit the ambitions of local Creoles, many of whom were large landowners and wealthy merchants. However, it was Napoleon's invasion of Spain in 1808 that fanned the flames of independence. In December of 1808, a revolutionary committee, or junta, was formed in Quito and led by Juan Pio de Montufar, the Second Marquis of Selva Alegre. The junta declared its support for Ferdinand VII but remained under the authority of the president of the audiencia and was eventually suppressed by viceregal authorities. A second attempt was made on August 10, 1809, when a new junta was formed, which, with the support of the Spanish garrison, deposed the president of the audiencia and decreed an open council (*cabildo abierto*). August 10 is Ecuador's official independence day. The junta maintained power until October, when internal dissension led to its collapse. Many of the rebels were eventually jailed in the Conde Ruíz de Castilla prison. On August 2, 1810, an angry mob attempted to storm the prison and liberate the patriots. Panic spread among the Spanish guards, who shot and killed forty-six prisoners in their cells. The slaughter at the prison touched off another rebellion, which resulted in a new junta that retained the president of audiencia as a figurehead. In December 1811 another junta proclaimed the Free State of Quito, declared independence from Spain, and named Selva Alegre as its president. This break from Spain lasted until December 1812 when a Spanish army crushed the revolt at a battle near Ibarra, 80 miles north of Quito.

Ecuador remained quietly under Spanish control until 1820, when a new revolt broke out, this time centered in Guayaquil. Led by José Joaquín Olmedo (and soon joined by Captain León Febres Cordero and other members of the Numanica Battalion), the insurgents formed a junta and liberating army, the *Protectora de Quito,* and began a campaign to liberate the entire audiencia. The junta sought assistance from the great liberators, Simón Bolívar and José de San Martín. Bolívar dispatched a force commanded by Antonio José de Sucre, while San Martín augmented the army with additional troops. The culminating battle for the liberation of Ecuador came on May 23, 1821, when Sucre defeated the Spanish army on the slopes of the Pichincha Volcano high above Quito.

In the aftermath of the war of independence, Ecuador was incorporated into the Republic of Gran Colombia, which also included present-day Colombia, Venezuela, and Panama. This union lasted for eight trying years; however, in 1830 both Venezuela and Ecuador seceded and formed independent republics.

Ecuador's first president was Juan José Flores, a Venezuelan general who had married an Ecuadorian. Flores favored mending relations with the mother country, but Spain's refusal to recognize Ecuador kept the two countries officially at war. Vicente Rocafuerte, Ecuador's second president (1835–1839), vehemently opposed any concessions to Spain. Flores returned to the presidency in 1839, and on February 16, 1840, Ecuador and Spain signed a Treaty of Peace and Friendship in Madrid. The treaty officially recognized Ecuador's independence and paved the way for improved commercial relations. In addition, the treaty fostered a Pan Hispanic attitude by the Ecuadorian government as Flores promulgated racial and cultural links to Spain. Flores was deposed in 1845 but used careful wooing of Spain during his second presidency in a later attempt to resume power. In 1847, Flores began to recruit mercenaries in Spain for a private military expedition to Ecuador. Initially, the formation of the expedition had the support of the Spanish government. However, Flores's diminishing credibility as a military leader, the British government's detention of the expedition's ships, and an active diplomatic campaign by Ecuador caused Spain to withdraw support.

The legacy of Ecuador's colonial past continues to the present. Ecuador's recent territorial dispute with Peru over a vast area of the remote upper Amazon Basin has deep roots in the Spanish colonial period. Both Peru and Ecuador submitted the issue to the king of Spain for resolution in 1904. The Spanish foreign ministry established a special commission to review the competing claims. The arbitration took over four years and ended in 1910 when Ecuador rejected the king's proposal for a final settlement. The dispute led to war in 1941, the Rio Protocol of January 1942, and armed clashes over the next five decades, with the most serious occurring in 1995. Final resolution of the dispute was not reached until 1998.

World War I represented a turning point in Ecuadorian foreign relations, as the United States increasingly became the most influential military and economic power in the Western Hemisphere. Nevertheless, Ecuador continues on cordial terms with Spain, and cultural ties with the "mother country" remain especially strong.

George Lauderbaugh

References

Linke, Lilo. *Ecuador, Country of Contrasts.* London: Oxford University Press, 1960.

Phelan, John Leddy. *The Kingdom of Quito in the Seventeenth Century.* Madison: University of Wisconsin Press, 1967.

Spindler, Frank MacDonald. *Nineteenth Century Ecuador: A Historical Introduction.* Fairfax, VA: George Mason University Press, 1987.

Van Aken, Mark J. *King of the Night: Juan José Flores and Ecuador 1824–1864.* Berkeley and Los Angeles: University of California Press, 1989.

Zook, David H., Jr. *Zarumilla-Marañón: The Ecuador-Peru Dispute.* New York: Bookman Associates, 1964.

See also: American Revolution; Audiencias; Bourbon Reforms; Cabildo; Cacao; Catholic Church in Spanish America; Colonists and Settlers I—Andes; Conquest I—Andes; Conquistadors; Cotton; Encomienda; Enlightenment—Spanish America; Gran Colombia; Hacienda; Independence IV—Colombia, Ecuador, and Venezuela; Monopolies; Napoleonic Invasion and Spanish America; Native Americans VI—Northern Andes; New Laws of 1542; Obraje; Religious Orders; República de Indios; Sugar; Tobacco; World War I; World War II.

EDUCATION—BRAZIL

Throughout the colonial period, formal education in Portuguese America (Brazil) was a task performed by the religious orders, in particular the Jesuits. The educational standard for the Jesuits, both in Portugal and in the discovered lands of America, Asia, and Africa, was set by the Royal College of Arts of Coimbra (Real Colégio das Artes de Coimbra). The masters of ultramarine colleges were subsidized by the Portuguese Crown, and their primary goal was to train priests for the evangelization process. However, these colleges were not strictly devoted to the formation of missionaries, since they were also responsible for education in colonial areas.

The first colleges founded by the Jesuits were located in São Vicente (São Paulo's littoral) and in Salvador (Bahia). With the expansion of the indoctrination work, new colleges were founded in São

Paulo (1554); Rio de Janeiro (1568); Olinda (1576); Ilhéus (1604); Recife (1655); São Luís, Paraíba, Santos, Belém, and Alcântara (1716); Vigia (1731); Paranaguá (1738); and Desterro (1750). In the settlements, villages, and cities, the Jesuit schools were known for reading, writing, and basic mathematics.

The organization of Jesuit teaching was based in the *Ratio Studiorum,* in which the curriculum was divided into two distinct sections. The first, which lasted six years, designed for inferior classes, focused on rhetoric, the humanities, and grammar. The advanced section, which lasted another three years, focused on the study of philosophy, including logic, physics, metaphysics, and mathematics.

Jesuit education, both in Portugal and in Brazil, was public and free. Natives were given only minimal formal education, however, which emphasized the transmission of Portuguese culture and the Catholic religion. Slaves and women of all classes had no access to formal education.

Unlike the situation in Spanish America, Portugal did not establish universities in Brazil. In Portuguese America, a university education, besides being restricted to the sons of the elite, could be obtained only in Portugal, at the University of Coimbra (Universidad de Coimbra). In 1768, the province of Minas Gerais attempted to establish a school of medicine; however, it was unable to procure the necessary authorization from the metropolis. The Crown insisted that university studies had to be conducted only in Portugal, which proved to be an effective tool of control over the colonies. The absence of universities made intellectual debate highly difficult, an issue exacerbated by the fact that it was also prohibited to print books in the colony. Even the importation of books was subject to rigid control from Portugal.

During the administration of the Marquis of Pombal (1750–1777), the University of Coimbra went through a series of reforms destined to introduce Enlightenment ideas. The priest Luís Antônio Verney (1713–1792) was largely responsible for implementing these changes. A graduate in theology at the University of Évora (Universidad de Évora), Verney obtained a doctorate in jurisprudence and theology in Italy. A close friend to the Marquis of Pombal, Verney returned to Portugal to head the reform of the University of Coimbra. From then on, the Jesuit monopoly over teaching was abolished. In 1772, the university's reform program began under the direction of rector Francisco de Lemos, who had been born in colonial Brazil. From that point, the emphasis turned toward the natural sciences, such as chemistry, zoology, mineralogy, and botany. It was hoped that the new emphasis would help to improve Portugal's lagging economy and would serve to enhance the exploitation of the available natural resources of the colonies, especially in Brazil. In spite of the emphasis on scientific knowledge, other Enlightenment ideas were still prohibited; for example, the *Mesa Censória* (the institution responsible for censorship) forbade the publication of John Locke's *Essay on Human Understanding.*

Educational reforms were not limited to Portugal. Following the Marquis of Pombal's lead, Bishop Dom José de Azeredo Coutinho proposed a new school in Pernambuco that would offer dramatically different education from that offered by the Jesuits. The purpose of the new school was to train individuals who would be qualified to inventory the colony's wealth, in order to help generate new revenue for the Portuguese Crown.

After the Jesuits were expelled from Brazil (1759–1760), the basic education system in Brazil was reformulated. "Royal Classes" were established, designed to teach fundamentals (Latin, Greek, geography, grammar, rhetoric, and mathematics); such classes were financed through the collection of a new tax, named the literary tax. From its outset, the system was very precarious; the new tax was never systematically collected, and on many occasions revenues were sent directly to Portugal. Thus, formal education remained the province of religious schools, seminars, and private teachers.

With the arrival in 1808 of the Portuguese royal family following Napoleon Bonaparte's invasion of Portugal, Brazil became the seat of the Portuguese kingdom. The arrival initiated a period of significant changes in education and culture. The Royal Press, the Public Library, and the Botanical Garden were all founded in this period. The prince regent, the future Dom João (King John VI), stimulated primary education and carried on the policy of secularization in public teaching started by the Marquis of Pombal. Medical schools were established in Bahia and Rio de Janeiro (1813 and 1815). At the same time, the Royal Academy of the Marine Guards and the Royal Military Academy (1808 and 1810) were established, followed in 1820 by the foundation of the Academy of Beaux-Arts. However, little was done in relation to elementary education, which remained the responsibility of local families, who generally relied on private teachers. Nevertheless, ideas of universal education began to spread in the large rural estates. The education of settlers' sons was performed by priests, and those who knew the rudiments of reading and writing were generally put in charge of teaching illiterate people.

With Brazil's independence in 1822, several law schools were established, mainly because the new state needed legal expertise in order to build its institutional and political basis. In 1828, the first law schools began to function, one in the city of São Paulo and another in Olinda. However, there were still many obstacles to overcome. The first challenge was to find buildings where the courses could be taught. In São Paulo, courses were offered in the Saint Francis Convent; in Olinda, they were taught at the São Bento Monastery. These locations were hardly ideal, and gradually the courses were moved to new locations. After two or three years, entirely new buildings were constructed to serve as the law schools.

In addition to the challenge of finding appropriate buildings to offer courses, the new law schools had trouble obtaining qualified lecturers; most of the first professors were ex-students of the University of Coimbra. As far as course content was concerned, there was a significant change because Roman law was abandoned, replaced by subjects more directly related to local needs. Emphasis was placed on maritime and mercantile laws, as well as political economy. It was hoped that the new law schools would train judges, lawyers, political representatives, diplomats, and qualified members of the state bureaucracy. However, the difficulties in finding qualified teachers emerged almost immediately; on August 5, 1831, the minister of the empire issued a statement about the carelessness and neglect of some professors who did not care if students even attended class.

In 1854, Brazil's legal studies were reformed, and specific regulations were applied to all courses taught.

Law schools were not the only professional schools established. In 1839, a school of pharmacy was founded in the city of Ouro Prêto, Minas Gerais; and in 1876 a Mining Academy was established in this same city. In 1858, the study of civil engineering was removed from the Military Academy and transferred to the Central School, which was renamed the Polytechnic Institute in 1874.

Important changes also occurred in primary and secondary studies. Although the 1824 constitution stipulated that education should be free and universal, this did not occur. Up to a certain point, this was understandable because the new state had upheld the institution of slavery, and men from the elite classes remained its priority, at least as far as education was concerned. In 1827, the General Teaching Law (*Lei Geral do Ensino*) was approved, which aimed to achieve the training of primary and secondary schoolteachers. Soon thereafter, this responsibility was transferred to the provinces. By then, schools dedicated to the training of teachers, the *escolas normals,* began to appear. The first such school to go into operation, founded in 1830, was located in the city of Niterói, Rio de Janeiro. The first *escola normal* of the court was not established until 1881.

In 1837, minister of the empire Bernardo Pereira de Vasconcelos presented ruler Pedro de Araújo Lima a proposal for establishing the first official secondary school in Brazil. Pereira de Vasconcelos believed that public teaching should be better than private, which he argued was inadequate because it was offered in unsuitable locations and often by ill-prepared teachers. Therefore, in 1837 the Colégio Pedro II was founded in Rio de Janeiro; the new school was devoted mainly to the sons of wealthy families. There were also a music school, a school of commerce, as well as some other professional schools.

The wealthy families' sons began their education with private tutors and afterwards went to Colegio Pedro II. Those who lived too far from the court attended a lycée or a seminar. After that, they transferred to an Imperial Law University, the Navy School, or a European university. Those who were not wealthy obtained their education in public schools or seminars. Some followed either an ecclesiastic career or entered a military academy; those who aspired to a technical career attended a mining academy. Throughout the empire, the military academies became the center for the diffusion of the Marquis of Pombal's reformist ideas, since they emphasized the study of both technical and professional subjects.

Education was one of the factors that distinguished the political elite in Brazil. The gap that separated them from the rest of the population was enormous. The number of students enlisted in primary and secondary schools was extremely low. For a free population of 8,490,910, the 1872 Census revealed a total of just 12,000 students enlisted in secondary schools. The illiteracy rate was extremely high, surpassing 90 percent of the population.

In 1889, with the establishment of the Brazilian republic, a greater concern for universal education began to emerge. Soon, the development of a school system based on the ideals of the French Revolution came under increasing consideration. In 1924, the Brazilian Association for Education was created, which from 1927 on promoted National Conferences on Education; these conferences served as forums for national debate, during which authorities and specialists discussed national education policies. In 1935, Fernando de Azevedo, Anisio Teixeira, and Lourenço Filho (among others) published the *Manifesto dos Pioneiros* (Pioneers' Manifesto), an influential manifesto that defended the democratization and the universal access to primary education throughout Brazil.

Maria Emilia Prado

References

Alden, Dauril. *The Making of an Enterprise: The Society of Jesus in Portugal, Its Empire, and beyond, 1540–1750.* Stanford, CA: Stanford University Press, 1996.

Burns, E. Bradford. *A History of Brazil.* 2nd ed. New York: Columbia University Press, 1980.

Kiemen, Mathias C., O.F.M. *The Indian Policy of Portugal in the Amazon Region, 1614–1693.* Washington, DC: Catholic University Press, 1954.

See also: Art and Artists—Brazil; Brazil; Censorship—Brazil; Education—Colonial Spanish America; Enlightenment—Brazil; Independence II—Brazil; Jesuits—Brazil; Jesuits—Expulsion; Laws—Colonial Latin America; Monarchs of Portugal; Napoleonic Invasion and Luso-America; Science and Scientists—Brazil/Portugal; Universities; Women—Brazil.

EDUCATION—COLONIAL SPANISH AMERICA

In a broad sense, education in colonial Spanish America can be defined as the process by which knowledge, skills, and beliefs were transmitted to millions of Indian inhabitants of two continents and to the immigrants who arrived during the 300-year period. New educational methods and transferral of European instructional practices characterized the period. This educational effort can be divided into four areas: Indian education during the sixteenth century, the creation of institutions of higher learning, elementary schools for urban centers, and educational reforms during the eighteenth century.

When the first twelve Franciscan friars arrived in the Aztec capital of Mexico—Tenochtitlan—in 1524, they were astounded by the highly developed urban culture of the Indians and, at the same time, perplexed as to how to evangelize the natives. They immediately decided that it would be necessary for them to learn Nahuatl (the Aztec language) instead of trying to teach Spanish to the natives. Moreover, influenced by the linguistic and biblical studies being carried out at the University of Alcalá in Spain, they decided that it would be necessary not only to learn the native tongues, but also to compose dictionaries, grammars, and catechisms in those languages. During the sixteenth century, sixty-one books were published in Nahuatl, thirteen in Tarasco, six in Otomi, five in Matlalzinca, five in Mixteco, five in Zapoteco, four in Huaxteco, two in Totonaco, and one in Zoque. In Peru, texts were printed in Quechua, and in Guatemala in Quiche, Cakchiquel, and Mame.

With an attitude uncharacteristic of other colonizing nations, the friars not only dedicated themselves to learning languages, but also decided that in order to educate, they had to understand the culture of the conquered people. One of the Franciscans, Bernardino de Sahagún, spent forty years gathering information about the pre-Hispanic culture by asking the elders to describe orally and in pictographic form their religious beliefs and ceremonies, legal system, history, educational practices, and social traditions. He recorded their conversations in Nahuatl and later transcribed them in Spanish, forming twelve great volumes of text with over 1,500 paintings. His method and writings have earned him the title of the founder of modern anthropology. In Peru the Jesuit José de Acosta gathered information about the society and the flora and fauna of the Andes, thereby contributing to an understanding of Inca culture.

Aware that Aztec society had two types of formal educational institutions for their youth, the *calmecac,* or boarding schools for nobles, and the *tepolchcalli,* or daily sessions for learning crafts, the priests decided to educate the sons of the nobility within their monasteries and to impart daily religious and craft instruction in the church courtyards to the children of the commoners. Members of the clergy employed a variety of methods based on pre-Hispanic practices, such as catechisms containing only drawings instead of words, which conveyed the mysteries of faith; they utilized large paintings with scenes from the life of Christ or the Last Judgment, which were explained to children and adults, and they produced theatrical pieces in Nahuatl, dramatizing biblical stories. Words of prayers were put to music and accompanied by ritual dance.

In 1536, the Franciscans opened a college for Indian students in Mexico City, called Santa Cruz of Tlatelolco; there, young Indian nobles studied Spanish, Latin, rhetoric, logic, theology, philosophy, music, and medicine. The objective of the college was to prepare the eighty students for the priesthood and for leadership positions in their society. Two of the graduates were the authors of a medical and botanical compendium about the plants of Mexico. Written in Nahuatl and Latin, it conveyed to Europe the remedies discovered by the Indians; these remedies were then incorporated by Nicolás Monardes, a doctor in Seville, into a best-selling book, translated into Italian, Latin, English, and French and used for two centuries. However, after thirty years, opposition by Spaniards and financial difficulties forced the college to discontinue its advanced studies and only offer elementary education. In 1585, the Church hierarchy declared that Indians could not be ordained priests since they were judged to be unsuitable for the religious life.

Even though the monarch declared in 1550 that the religious orders should teach Spanish to the Indians, the missionaries and the Church Councils of Mexico and Lima insisted that the education of the native population could best be carried out by communicating with them in their own language. King Philip II accepted their arguments and, despite the protests of various Spanish authorities, decreed in 1596 that the Indians should not be forced to learn Spanish and that no parish priests could be appointed unless they spoke the language of their parishioners.

By the mid-sixteenth century, the increase in the Spanish population caused the municipal councils of Mexico City and Lima to petition the king for permission and funds to found a university. Lima received its decree on May 12 and Mexico on September 21, both in 1551. The latter was the first to begin classes (in 1553). Santo Domingo opened a university in 1558 (Harvard University would not be founded until 1636). Similarly, to support linguistic, religious, and university studies, the first printing press in the Americas began operating in Mexico City in 1539 and another in Lima in 1580, a century before the first press appeared in the English colonies.

Smaller cities, rather than open universities, supported Jesuit colleges, which offered pre-university courses in Latin, philosophy, and science. Many of these colleges later were given university status. Mexico and Lima had five faculties: theology, canon law, civil law, medicine, and humanities, which qualified them to be considered major universities. In addition, they soon received the title of pontifical universities, which meant that the Vatican judged the level of their studies to be on a par with those enjoyed by the four best centers in Europe (Oxford, Salamanca, Bologna, and Paris), and their degrees had universal validity. Mexico, Lima, and Guatemala also offered courses in Nahuatl, Otomi, Quechua, and Cakchiquel.

Classes were held in the early morning and late afternoon, with the professors dedicating themselves to their own secular or ecclesiastical professions during the day. The rector was elected annually by faculty members and students. He served for one year, and the post alternated between a cleric and a layman. Tenured chairs were won in public oral examinations, some having as many as fifty candidates and lending themselves to heated Latin debates and even physical altercations between members of the religious orders or among the students who favored one or another of the participating professors. In Santiago de Chile, Quito, Caracas, Bogotá, and Guatemala, considerable rivalries existed between the Jesuit and Dominican colleges.

Since the universities and colleges were endowed, higher education was virtually free. However, in order to receive a graduate degree, the cost was extremely high due to the extravagant procession, very high fees given to the examiners, and gifts that accompanied the ceremony. Thus, many talented but poor students remained with only the first university degree. In total, there were ten major universities and thirteen minor ones in colonial Spanish America. By 1821, the University of Mexico had granted 29,882 bachelor's degrees and 8,323 doctorates. During the colonial period, the universities in all of Spanish America awarded about 150,000 degrees.

During the seventeenth century, rote memory and the principle of authority characterized university studies and caused the institutions to lag behind developments in Europe. As in many countries, individual scholars led the way in original research. One such savant was Carlos de Sigüenza y Góngora in Mexico, who published studies in 1681 based on mathematics and astronomy, which showed that comets were not the cause of calamities on Earth and combated the astrological ideas of the German Jesuit Eusebio Kino. Sigüenza based his conclusions on Copernicus, Kepler, Galileo, Descartes, and Tycho Brahe. John Tate Lanning, upon examining university theses in Guatemala, has concluded that advances in European research generally reached Spanish America one generation after being published.

In Spanish America's urban centers, elementary education developed haphazardly. In general, private individuals taught groups of children whose parents paid an agreed fee. Some of the religious orders established free schools in the cities and villas, but their number declined during the seventeenth century. The schoolmasters formed a guild in Mexico City and set minimum standards for aspirants, as well as limiting the number of schools to thirty-four. The city council issued licenses to teachers approved by the guild.

Hundreds of women taught Christian doctrine, reading, and sewing to girls in private schools, called *amigas*. Some of these were little more than day-care centers, and many of the amiga teachers did not know how to write. In some cities, nuns taught small numbers of girls basic literacy, crafts, and music, while groups of laywomen, known as *beatas*, offered formal instruction to larger numbers of middle- and lower-class students. In Mexico City in 1755, the first order of teaching nuns opened a school for 300 girls.

During the colonial period, three texts served as the basis for literacy. The *cartilla*, an eight-page summary of the alphabet, syllables, prayers, and the multiplication tables, was printed by the thousands every year. The privilege to publish such elementary books was awarded by the king to charitable hospitals in Mexico, Lima, and Buenos Aires as a means of providing them with some income. Then the student read, recited, and memorized the sixteenth-century catechism written by Gerónimo Ripalda. A third small book had the generic title of the *Caton*, named after the statesman of ancient Rome, which contained in verse or prose moral advice for children. As in Europe and the English colonies, children learned to read first and, only after two or three years, were taught to write. Teachers charged more for instruction in calligraphy because of the high cost of ink and paper. Thus, in the occidental world, until the end of the nineteenth century, many more people knew how to read than to write because many dropped out of school once they mastered the skill of reading. Schools were in session Monday through Saturday, with Thursday as a day off and Saturday as the time when the boys paraded through the streets answering in chorus the questions of the catechism. In most parts of Spanish America, children of all classes and racial groups attended classes together, except in Caracas and the Caribbean where blacks were excluded. Lima in 1725 had twelve free schools with 1,000 students; in 1802, Mexico City had forty-three schools for 2,711 boys, of which twenty-three offered free instruction, and seventy schools for 3,103 girls, of which eight large institutions taught 1,367 without cost; in 1803 there were nine schools in Quito for 644 children.

In the eighteenth century, important changes occurred in Indian education. In 1697 and again in 1727, the king revoked the previous Church legislation that had prohibited the ordination of Indians, ordering that scholarships be provided for the natives in the diocesan seminaries. In mid-century the archbishop of Mexico City promoted the opening of elementary schools in the Indian towns of his diocese, with funds from the parish priest or from the Indian municipal councils. King Charles III extended this policy to all Indian towns in the territory, from Durango to Yucatán, putting them under governmental, rather than Church, supervision. By 1808, lay teachers paid by municipal funds existed in 24 percent of the 4,468 Indian towns of New Spain. Similarly, in the major Spanish cities and villas, the municipal councils began to finance schools and to order the religious orders to reestablish free education.

In 1767, Charles III expelled the Jesuits from Spanish America. In New Spain, 678 Jesuits were expelled, 479 of them being Mexican-born. A third had been professors in the colleges; others were preachers and confessors in the cities, and many served as missionaries among nomadic Indians in the northern frontier and the Californias. The expulsion of the Jesuits caused the closure of their colleges and primary schools and the expropriation of their properties. However, the largest institutions were reopened a few years later; they were called Caroline Colleges in honor of the monarch and funded by the government. Many other colleges were never reestablished. In smaller cities, other religious orders opened institutions and, together with the diocesan seminaries, began to educate lay students not destined for the priesthood; this practice continued for the next two centuries.

The absence of the Jesuits also affected educational reforms, which had begun in some of their colleges, such as the teaching of experimental physics instead of Aristotelian doctrines, as well as the simplification in the rhetorical forms of sermons, criticism of the excessive dialectical arguments and subtleties, and the study of archaeology, history, and Greek. The Spanish government promoted new institutions in science, technology, and art, since it was difficult to change the curricula of the universities. Botanical expeditions were sent to all parts of Spanish America, and the Linnaean system of plant classification was introduced. A Mexican scientist, José Antonio de Alzate, proclaimed that the Aztec method, already developed in New Spain, of naming and classifying specimens according to their usage was superior to that being used in Europe. At times the practices and discoveries of Mexican intellectuals in the areas of mining, architecture, botany, and medicine clashed with the doctrines of the highly paid Spanish professors who staffed the new School of Surgery, the Mining College, and the Academy of Fine Arts. When the German scientist and explorer Alexander von Humboldt visited these institutions in 1803, he wrote that no city in the new continent, without excluding the United States, presented scientific establishments as large and solid as the capital of Mexico.

Although the Inquisition restricted the reading of theological and political texts judged dangerous to the faith or the monarchy, in other fields of knowledge the prohibitions did not apply. Large libraries such as that of the cathedral, with 6,922 volumes, were open to the public, and many of the Jesuits' books were given to other colleges. However, new publications were difficult to obtain because of their high price, the low salaries of the professors, and the lack of university funds. In Quito, Guatemala, Lima, and Havana, clerics and scholars formed Patriotic Societies, similar to those in Spain, to promote knowledge useful in agriculture and industry. Newspapers, such as the *Mercurio Peruano,* published their findings. In Peru, Toribio Rodríguez de Mendoza promoted university reform, and Hipolito Unanue introduced advances in medicine.

Dorothy Tanck Jewel

References

Klor de Alba, J. Jorge, ed. *The Work of Bernardino de Sahagún: Pioneer Ethnographer of Sixteenth Century Aztec Mexico.* Austin: University of Texas Press, 1988.

Lanning, John Tate. *Academic Culture in the Spanish Colonies.* New York: Oxford University Press, 1940.

Mörner, Magnus. *The Expulsion of the Jesuits from Latin America.* New York: Knopf, 1965.

Ronan, Charles E., *Francisco Javier Clavigero, S.J. (1731–1787), Figure of the Mexican Enlightenment: His Life and Works.* Chicago: Loyola University Press, 1977.

Tanck de Estrada, Dorothy. *Pueblos de indios y educación en el México colonial, 1750–1821.* Mexico City: El Colegio de México, 2000.

See also: Beatas; Borderlands; Bourbon Reforms; Catholic Church in Spanish America; Cities; Clergy—Secular, in Colonial Spanish America; Creoles; Education—Brazil; Hospitals; Inquisition—Spanish America; Jesuits—Expulsion; Jesuits—Iberia and America; Languages; Medicine; Mexico; Migration—From Iberia to the New World; Missions; Monarchs of Spain; Native Americans I–VIII; Religious Orders; Science and Scientists—Colonial Spanish America; Syncretism; Universities; Women—Colonial Spanish America.

EL DORADO

El Dorado literally translates as "the Golden One" and refers to the legendary king of a fabulously wealthy land. As part of a ritual offering to the gods, his body was said to have been coated with fine gold dust after which the gilded king carried offerings of gold and emeralds on a raft into the middle of Lake Guatavita (in modern-day Colombia) and cast them into the water. Then, to bring the ceremony to a close, he dived into the lake and washed the gold from his skin. The title El Dorado has been understood in different ways, some taking it to mean the golden land; others, the golden lake; and still others, the golden king. Yet the veracity of the El Dorado legend has long been debated, and the persistence of such rumors was the cause of numerous ill-fated expeditions.

The subjugation of Mexico in 1519 and the Inca Empire in 1532 spurred on European exploration and conquest. In the years 1536–1539, three separate expeditions converged on the prosperous Muisca Kingdom of Bogotá. The first expedition, under the captaincy of Don Gonzalo Jiménez de Quesada, left from the coastal city of Santa Marta (in modern-day Colombia); the second left from Quito under the leadership of the veteran conquistador Sebastián de Benalcázar; and the third from Coro (Venezuela) left under the command of an Austrian named Nicolaus Federmann. The search for gold was certainly a driving force behind these penetrations into Colombia's interior. However, contemporary accounts make little mention of El Dorado, and the legend only began to take shape in the 1540s, once the Muisca had been conquered.

Despite this background, the conquest of the Muisca was later credited to the incentive provided by the El Dorado legend. In 1615, the chronicler Antonio de Herrera wrote an account that attributed the source of the legend to an Indian ambassador who had traveled to Quito to request military assistance. According to Herrera, the ambassador was captured by the Spanish and subsequently interrogated by Benalcázar, whom he told of a land of great wealth that was only twelve days' march from Quito.

These chronicles inspired numerous expeditions that were at once disastrous and epic, such as the 1542 expedition led by Gonzalo Jiménez de Quesada's brother, Hernando Pérez de Quesada, in which thousands died. However, perhaps the most famous of the ill-fated expeditions was the one led by Gonzalo Pizarro and Francisco de Orellana. Lost and starving in the jungles east of Quito, Orellana offered to take the boats to search for food. Once downstream, they were unable to fight the current to rejoin Pizarro's group, so instead they decided to navigate the entire length of the Amazon until they reached the Atlantic. Another infamous expedition was that led by Pedro de Ursúa in 1560. Ursúa was killed in a mutiny led by Lope de Aguirre, who then led a crazed and bloody attempt to seize the Kingdom of Peru for himself. El Dorado even inspired English attempts under Sir Walter Raleigh to explore Guiana in search of the mythic golden land. As with the other expeditions, El Dorado remained undiscovered, and Raleigh's failure resulted in his execution on his return to England in 1618.

Andrew Redden

References

Bray, Warwick, and Julie Jones. *El Dorado: The Gold of Ancient Colombia.* New York: New York Graphic Society, 1974.

Freile, Juan Rodríguez. *The Conquest of New Granada.* London: Folio Society, 1961.

Hemming, John. *The Search for El Dorado.* London: Book Club Associates, 1978.

See also: Amazon; Colombia; Colonists and Settlers I—Andes; Conquest I—Andes; Conquest V—Mexico; Conquistadors; Ecuador; Emeralds; Explorers; Gold; Mexico; Peru; Silver.

El Niño

El Niño, meaning "the [Christ] Child," is a recurring oceanographic and meteorological phenomenon that affects climate on a global scale and often causes widespread devastation throughout coastal Peru and Ecuador. The name, first recorded by scientists in the nineteenth century, had long been used by fishermen from the north coast of Peru to refer to a phenomenon that arrives around Christmas and lasts until well into the following year.

In normal circumstances, a cold current of water travels up the Peruvian coast until it reaches the equator, where it is turned eastward by the lay of the land and the rotation of the Earth. The cool arctic waters cause relatively little evaporation and very low rainfall along the desert coast. This cold current is assisted by prevailing easterly winds that blow the sun-heated surface water of the Pacific along the equator, thus causing the heated water to "pile up" on the far side of the ocean in what is known as a thermocline. In some years, however (and for reasons still not fully understood), the prevailing winds and the easterly current slacken, causing the heated water to flow back westward until it strikes the coastline of Peru and Ecuador.

The arrival of El Niño dramatically affects the regional environment. Fishing stocks that thrive in the normally cold and plankton-rich Pacific waters collapse, affecting the seabird and seal populations that feed on them. El Niño years are characterized by the disappearance of much marine life, with bird and seal carcasses littering the beaches. The fishing industry of Peru is also seriously affected, for the industry's capital is largely derived from exploitation of the cold-water anchovy stocks.

The warm waters increase evaporation and humidity in the air, causing extraordinary rainfall in a short space of time. This in turn causes normally placid rivers to be transformed into raging torrents that burst their banks, destroying houses, cultivations, roads, and bridges. Such was the rainfall of the 1997–1998 El Niño that a lake second only in size to Lake Titicaca was formed in the Sechura Desert. As well as destroying state infrastructure, El Niño years are times of increased epidemics, especially typhoid, malaria, dengue, and yellow fever. Before it was possible to predict its return, El Niño was often followed by years of famine resulting from the loss of crops and stores, and the drought-inducing reverse phenomenon now known as La Niña.

El Niño has even been credited with causing the downfall of civilizations. The collapse of the Classic Maya in tenth-century Mesoamerica might have been caused by years of prolonged drought normally associated with the El Niño effect. Similarly, severe flooding followed by famine in AD 700 largely destroyed the Moche civilization of the northern Peruvian coast. The ease of Pizarro's penetration into the Inca Empire in 1527 has also been attributed in part to the effects of El Niño. Chroniclers write of the rain-sodden country (coastal Ecuador) that exhausted their men and horses, and the fast-flowing rivers (normally shallow and slow) in northern Peru that drowned some of the conquistadors as they tried to cross.

Andrew Redden

References

Caviedes, César N. *El Niño in History: Storming through the Ages.* Gainesville: University Press of Florida, 2001.

Fagan, Brian. *Floods, Famines and Emperors: El Niño and the Fate of Civilizations.* New York: Basic, 1999.

Glantz, Michael H. *Currents of Change: Impacts of El Niño and La Niña on Climate and Society.* Cambridge: Cambridge University Press, 2001.

See also: Atlantic Economy; Ecuador; Environment; Explorers; Native Americans IV, V, VII; Navigation; Peru; Ships and Shipbuilding; Trade—Spain/Spanish America.

EL SALVADOR

El Salvador is the smallest country and the most densely populated in the Western Hemisphere. In 2004, its population was 6.57 million, with an average population of 292.5 per square kilometer and annual population growth of 2.1 percent in the 1990s, which includes an emigration rate of 0.6 percent. The population is 94 percent mestizo, 5 percent indigenous, and 1 percent white, with few ethnic and racial tensions; however, class conflict is intense. Catholics comprise about three-quarters of the population, with Protestant evangelicals expanding.

El Salvador was a center of Native American civilization, which included several Amerindian groups. When the Spanish invaded in 1519, El Salvador was controlled by the Pipils, who were related to the Aztecs through their Nahuatl language. The country was then called Cuzcatlán, the Land of Jewels. The Pipil Indians, descendants of the Aztecs, likely migrated to Central America in the eleventh century. In 1525, Pedro de Alvarado, a lieutenant of Hernando Cortés, conquered El Salvador. All the countries of Central America declared independence from Spain on September 15, 1821. El Salvador was part of a federation of Central American states until that union dissolved in 1838. For decades after independence, El Salvador experienced numerous revolutions and wars against other Central American republics.

With a large population density and an organized state with laws, taxes, and temples, the indigenous peoples that resided in the territory of contemporary El Salvador traded across two continents and understood advanced astronomy and mathematics. As in other Central American countries, Spanish colonialism destroyed much of the indigenous culture. The Spanish created large plantations for cotton, balsam, and indigo (a plant used for making blue dye), using indigenous labor.

On September 15, 1821, El Salvador gained freedom from Spanish domination, but the land was still controlled by a wealthy elite. El Salvador's economy is one of the poorest in the Western Hemisphere, affected by years of war, the aftermath of colonialism, and vulnerability to international price swings, particularly those of coffee. With an economy based predominantly on agriculture and a history of inappropriate land tenure and ownership practices that date back to colonialism, El Salvador's major environmental challenges tend to be derived from these conditions. Spanish colonialism may also have led to the large amount of corruption present in El Salvador.

With few natural resources and unused agricultural land, about 60 percent of the population lives in rural areas, and over 80 percent of El Salvador's farmers work farms of less than 3 hectares. Beginning in the 1880s, coffee cultivation led El Salvador to become the most prosperous economy in Central America. Political and economic power was concentrated in a few hands, however, epitomized by the metaphor of the "fourteen families," which, with the mutual support of the military, supposedly governed the country and controlled the economy. However, falling coffee prices in the early 1930s induced peasant revolts, which were violently suppressed by the minister of war, General Maximiliano Hernández Martínez. Repressive, military-dominated rule continued through the 1970s.

Although El Salvador poses no conventional military threat to its neighbors, demographic pressures resulting from its high population density have provoked occasional tensions, especially with Honduras. In July 1969, 300,000 Salvadorans moved into sparsely populated areas of Honduras, an action that was initiated after Honduran landowners deported several thousand Salvadorans. The four-day conflict became known as the "football war" because it broke out during a soccer game between the two countries. Later, in a 1992 ruling, the International Court of Justice granted most of the land to Honduras, a ruling that was not recognized in treaty until 1999.

The 1979 Sandinista revolution in Nicaragua exacerbated tensions between the two countries, particularly when the Sandinistas provided headquarters in Managua to the FMLN (Farabundo Martí Liberation Front) command during the early 1980s, as well as probably providing arms transfers. From their Managua base, the guerrillas waged a successful rural and urban guerrilla campaign throughout the 1980s. By mid-decade, the FMLN began targeting elected mayors and lost significant support among European and U.S. moderates. However, its large offensive against the capital, San Salvador, in November 1989, the second in a decade, was a significant inducement to both sides to begin negotiating a solution.

Under U.S. pressure, a coalition of Salvadoran military officers and civilians ousted the government in 1979 and formed a military junta, a governing council or dictatorship, which attempted to return the country to civilian rule. José Napoleón Duarte returned from exile abroad to El Salvador to join the junta. Also under U.S. pressure, political parties competed in a constituent assembly election in 1982. The newly elected body wrote and ratified the constitution. Duarte won the presidential elections, and his Christian Democratic Party won the majority in the legislative assembly elections, both in 1984.

The elected government never established full control over the military and paramilitary forces that conducted repressive campaigns against the guerrillas, their suspected civilian supporters, and innocent civilians. The level of death squad killing, which apparently reached about 800 monthly in the early 1980s, decreased dramatically after a visit in December 1982 to the country by then U.S. President George H. W. Bush. In addition, the United States sent dozens of military advisers, which created an air force that was accused of bombing villages.

After his election in March 1989, Alfredo Cristiani succeeded Duarte as president, while his right-wing Republican National Alliance (ARENA in Spanish) Party took control of the legislative assembly the year before in parliamentary elections. The Christian Democrats were punished by voters who were tired of the war as well as the party's corruption. In 1991, the United Nations established the first multilateral human rights monitors inside the country, based on the peace talks that had begun in the spring of 1990. The talks continued over a two-year period, with important agreements reached in New York in September 1991 and the final Chapúltepec Accords signed in Mexico City in January 1992.

The pact called for demilitarization and integration of the guerrillas into political and agricultural life, as well as demobilization and demission of the most repressive units and individuals in the military. A new national police force was established, which included both FMLN and Salvadoran military elements that had passed tests for their human rights records. The Treasury Police and National Guard were abolished, and the size of the military was reduced from 63,000 to 24,600. As a result of El Salvador's twelve-year civil war, 75,000 people died, 8,000 disappeared, and 12,000 were left disabled.

A UN-sponsored Truth Commission issued a report on violations by both sides and blamed the government for the majority of summary executions during the civil war. The guerrillas were also involved in killings, kidnappings, and the abuse of noncombatants. Paramilitary death squads linked to ARENA Party founder Roberto D'Aubuisson were also involved in the deaths of thousands of civilians. A Human Rights Ombudsman's Office was also established as a result of the peace accords.

Both the 1992 peace accords between the Salvadoran government and the FMLN and the 1990 electoral defeat of the Sandinistas in Nicaragua greatly reduced tensions in the region. In 1993, the United Nations declared that the government had successfully removed all identified human rights offenders after the dismissal of a final group of 103 officers from the military. In 1994, a joint UN-government commission declared that death squads were no longer as active but that violence was still being used to achieve political ends. Still, El Salvador's crime rate has been very high, and the country is among the most violent in the hemisphere.

There is also a growing problem with common crime, most notably kidnapping. Organized crime syndicates are involved in narcotics trafficking. In an attempt to demilitarize the country, El Salvador's government has initiated a program to buy back arms. This project has exchanged cash and goods for rocket launchers, grenades, and assault rifles. However, there is skepticism as to whether this process will make any concrete contribution to internal security in the long term.

El Salvador, like all Central American states, has been significantly affected by the departure of the U.S. Southern Command from Panama. The U.S. military presence in guaranteeing regional security has effectively been replaced by a network of economic agreements and international aid agencies.

Henry F. Carey

References

Boyland, Roy C. *Culture and Customs of El Salvador.* Westport, CT: Greenwood, 2000.

Human Rights Watch, *El Salvador's Decade of Terror: Human Rights since the Assassination of Archbishop Romero.* New Haven, CT: Yale University Press, 1991.

Menzel, Sewall H. *Bullets vs. Ballots: Political Violence and Revolutionary War in El Salvador, 1979–1991.* Miami, FL: North-South Center, 1994.

Pearce, Jenny. *Promised Land: Peasant Rebellion in Chalatenango, El Salvador.* London: Latin American Bureau, 1986.

Schwarz, Benjamin C. *American Counterinsurgency Doctrine and El Salvador: The Frustrations of Reform and the Illusions of Nation Building.* Santa Monica: RAND, 1991.

Wood, Elisabeth Jean. *Collective Action and Civil War in El Salvador.* Cambridge: Cambridge University Press, 2003.

See also: Catholic Church in Spanish America; Coffee; Cold War—Spain and the Americas; Colonists and Settlers IV—Mexico and Central America; Conquest IV—Central America; Conquistadors; Democracy; Drugs; Guerrillas; Honduras; Human Rights; Native Americans IV—Mesoamerica; Nicaragua; Panama; Terrorism.

EMERALDS

Since the time of the Spanish conquest, beauty and violence seem to go inextricably together in the case of Colombian emeralds. In 1560, following intense battles between the Spaniards and the local Muzo Indians for control of the emerald territory, New Granada's (modern-day Colombia) *real audiencia* (High Court) authorized Captain Luis Lancheros to establish a town, which he named Villa de la Santísima Trinidad de Muzo. Unfortunately, emeralds have been more a problem than a valuable resource to be enjoyed by the inhabitants of northwestern Boyacá, the department where the mines are located, in the eastern part of the Andes. Though important mines can be found throughout the region, locals consider the Muzo mine to be the "princess" of them all. The town of Muzo is located 235 kilometers from Bogotá; it borders Otanche and Borbur (where the mine of Coscuez is located) to the north, and Coper and Maripí (where the mine of La Pita is located) to the east.

The region's inhabitants still recall the creation legend of the Muzos as an explanation for the apparently endless violence associated with the mines. The myth tells of the first man, Tena, and the first woman, Fura. The two lived together happily for many centuries, and their descendants formed the Muzo world. One day a foreigner named Zarbi arrived. Fura fell in love with him and was unfaithful to Tena. The desperate husband killed Zarbi and then stabbed himself and died in Fura's lap. Fura was inconsolable, and the passage of time did little to ameliorate her anguish. For centuries she cried. Her tears turned to emeralds and beautiful butterflies, while her lover Zarbi's blood became a furious torrent of water, later named the Minero River, which separated the couple. Local people proudly tell this legend while showing the mountain of Furatena, composed of two long ridges divided by the river.

The best-known emeralds of Muzo are the "oil drops" *(gotas de aceite).* It is said that before the Spaniards arrived, the mines were already being exploited by the Muzos, who considered the emeralds to have medicinal properties. Apparently, and notwithstanding the stories of the conquest, emeralds are rare in pre-Columbian jewelry. Emeralds were used by the Muzos as coins for economic transactions with the Incas and the Mayas; however, the nature of this exchange is still poorly understood. In 1519, Hernando Cortés received jewels from emissaries of Moctezuma (Montezuma), some of which contained emeralds. Cortés believed the gems came from Mexico or Peru, a belief that was held for some time, until it was found that the only emerald mines were in Colombia. In 1522, Cortés reported a huge emerald in the form of a pyramid, but in reality it was a conglomerate of emeralds. It was sent to King Carlos V by Cortés and was given by the king to the Habsburgs. The gem that is believed to be "La Gran Esmeralda de Montezuma" currently is on display in the Secular Treasury in Vienna.

Notwithstanding the strong symbolism that emeralds possess in Colombian popular history, the effort to exploit them only began in earnest in the mid-1940s. According to reports from the Central Bank, for a brief period during colonial rule, a rather productive exploitation existed, but the emerald enterprise was never a major business. Usually leased to small companies, some of them foreign, or to private individuals, the economic benefits did not compensate for the resulting social problems. Mining was risky and state control extremely difficult, causing closures of the mines for long periods of time. The particular geographical characteristics of the area, surrounded by mountains from the *cordillera oriental,* made it a safe haven for poor peasants forced to leave their lands during periods of political violence. The possibilities of surviving and finding emeralds were good reasons to migrate to the region. But the area also became a haven for *bandoleros* (bandits) and outlaws looking for a "frontier" far from the political centers.

In 1946, the government signed a contract with the Central Bank, making it responsible for the exploitation of the mines of Muzo and Coscuez. In October of 1947 the exploitation of the mines officially began. It was also the beginning of frequent complaints because of the government's inability to control corruption and smuggling. In 1973, the mines were closed and militarized, and the government announced that they were to be leased to private contractors, who, already in the business, became the emerald lords, with almost absolute power in the region. A fierce competition between them for control of the mines and the territory resulted in what is commonly known as the "Emerald War" *(la Guerra de las Esmeraldas)* a name describing three periods of acute violence in the region that started in the 1960s and ended in 1991, when a peace treaty was signed among the different patrons of the mines.

Currently, it is believed that the emerald business is in a deep crisis: in 1995, export revenues were around US $456 million; by contrast, in 2003 revenues did not reach US $80 million. But official records are difficult to accept because of the volume of illegal commerce. Notwithstanding some efforts to create a stock market exchange for emeralds, their commerce is notably disorganized. With an uncontrolled street market in Bogotá, a considerable amount of illegal exports, and a proliferation of transaction agents, the business lacks the consistency of other economic enterprises. According to a specialized report by the magazine *Semana,* in 1993 Colombia controlled 55 percent of the world production of emeralds. The most important commercial agencies were in the hands of Japanese who had the most efficient export system.

Poverty in northwestern Boyacá, in some cases, surpasses that of other regions of Colombia. The past, with the tragic legend of Fura and Tena, who lost their happiness when a foreigner arrived, has served more than once to legitimate an ambiguous relation to the state and a fatalistic conviction about the persistence of violence in the region.

Claudia Steiner

References

Acevedo, Leticia, Margoth Pachón de Upegui, and Elvia Rubiela Pardo Moreno. *Cuentos, mitos y leyendas del municipio de Muzo.* Bogotá: Universidad de La Sabana. Lingüística y Literatura, 1995.

"Crece la fiebre verde: Las esmeraldas duplican sus ventas al exterior y la bolsa mundial de piedras preciosas marcha a todo vapor." *Dinero* (Bogotá),no. 7 (October 1993): 24–30.

El gran libro de la esmeralda. Bilbao: Editorial La Gran Enciclopedia Vasca, 1990.

"La reinserción de los esmeralderos." *Semana* (Bogotá), April 14, 1992, pp. 29–31.

Muñoz G., Otero. *Esmeraldas de Colombia.* Bogotá: Banco de la República, 1948.

See also: Audiencia; Bandits and Banditry; Colombia; Conquest I—Andes; Conquest V—Mexico; Conquistadors; El Dorado; Gold; Gran Colombia; Mining—Gold; Mining—Mercury; Mining—Silver; Silver.

ENCOMIENDA

The *encomienda* was a grant of Indians to Spanish conquistadors for their individual effort in the Spanish conquest of the New World. Because the Crown did not itself have the resources to finance the conquest, it therefore depended on the contributions of private individuals. Legally, only the Crown could grant encomiendas, but leaders of successful expeditions, such as Hernando Cortés in Mexico, Francisco Pizarro in Peru, Gonzalo Jiménez de Quesada in Colombia, and Pedro de Valdivia in Chile, parceled them out to their followers, and the Crown was left with a *fait accompli.*

Royal authorities reacted against the worst abuses and potential threats to Crown authority. They set limits and worked to circumscribe the power of the grantees, the *encomenderos.* In 1542, the New Laws banned Indian slavery, prohibited the granting of new encomiendas, and programmed the return of existing ones to the Crown upon the death of the current holders. However, the promulgation of the New Laws sparked significant unrest in the New World. A revolt in Peru and dissatisfaction elsewhere led to a suspension of the provisions. Piecemeal implementation became the order of the day and depended on the individual circumstances of each region and on the presence of royal authorities. Sometimes the only royal authority was the encomendero, and in some frontier areas Indian slavery and unregulated encomiendas continued to the end of the colonial period. In more settled areas, like Central Mexico and the Andean Highlands, the inheritance of encomiendas was limited to two or three successive heirs, so that by 1600 most encomiendas had reverted to the Crown. And whatever the encomenderos were to receive from the Indians was to be overseen and regulated by royal authorities who fixed and collected the annual tribute payments. These limits and the demographic disaster visited upon the Indians made encomiendas far less important by the seventeenth century.

Where Amerindian civilizations were highly developed, encomenderos had at their disposal native institutions that could deliver tribute and labor of another order and magnitude when compared to frontier regions. An encomienda of nomadic Indians was practically worthless, whereas encomiendas with large numbers of sedentary Indians could provide an encomendero with an annual income worthy of a prince. It also made it worthwhile for the Crown to bring in royal officials who would move the flow of labor and tribute away from the encomendero. Encomiendas in Peru before 1560 regularly brought in 5,000 to 10,000 pesos a year in income, with some totaling as much as 50,000 pesos.

In return for their encomienda grants, encomenderos had certain responsibilites. They were viewed as guardians of the kingdom with military obligations that required them to be available and properly equipped with horses, weapons, men, and Indians whenever called into the service of the Crown. Over time the Crown replaced this personal military service with a monetary payment. Encomenderos were required to provide for the Christianization of their Indians and pay the necessary costs of building a church as well as a stipend for a priest. Of course, not all encomenderos fulfilled their obligations.

Maurice P. Brungardt

References

Bakewell, Peter. *A History of Latin American Empires and Sequels, 1450–1930.* Oxford: Blackwell, 1997.

Lockhart, James. *Spanish Peru, 1532–1560: A Colonial Society.* Madison: University of Wisconsin Press, 1968.

Lockhart, James, and Stuart B. Schwartz. *Early Latin America: A History of Colonial Spanish America and Brazil.* Cambridge: Cambridge University Press, 1983.

Villamarin, Juan A., and Judith E. *Indian Labor in Mainland Colonial Spanish America.* Newark: University of Delaware Press, 1975.

See also: Armies—Colonial Spanish America; Borderlands; Catholic Church in Spanish America; Civil Wars; Colonists and Settlers I–VI; Columbian Exchange—Disease; Conquistadors; Corregidor/Corregimiento; Laws—Colonial Latin America; Native Americans I–VIII; New Laws of 1542; Repartimiento; Slavery I–IV.

ENGENHO

For Iberians, the *engenho* (Spanish *ingenio*), adequately translated as "mill," referred to the entire complex of the sugar plantation. The technology of the sugar mill was transferred with little modification from Iberia's Atlantic islands to Hispaniola by 1515 and to Pernambuco by 1516. Brazil's mills dominated sugar production until the 1650s when the Dutch, who had occupied northeast Brazil, retransmitted milling technology to the Caribbean, where it was successfully adopted in the British and French islands. Sugar mills were also established in scattered locations across Spanish America but only took a central economic position in the Spanish Caribbean in the nineteenth century.

The workings of the mill, which were remarkably similar across the Americas, consisted of three substantial outbuildings, sometimes connected: the mill itself, the boiling house, and the purging house. The mill, a simple, yet substantial, mechanism that required considerable horsepower, expressed the juice from the harvested cane. Although there were variants, until the nineteenth century the standard mill consisted of three vertical rollers driven by water or oxen. A slave fed cane between the first and second rollers, while another slave, on the other side, returned the cane for a second ringing. The cane juice ran in gutters to the boiling house, where it moved progressively through five to seven kettles of diminishing size, over as many furnaces. Workers added lye or lime to clarify the juice, skimmed the surface for impurities, and ladled the increasingly viscous syrup to the next smaller kettle. In the final kettle, the foreman, by experienced eye or empirical test, announced the striking point, and the syrup was poured into forms in the shape of an inverted cone, which were carried to the purging house. There the remaining impurities and molasses were drained from the crystallizing sugar. In a final process to whiten the sugar, known as claying, a layer of wet clay was placed on the top of the sugar through which water was slowly passed, dissolving the remaining molasses. Once removed from the form, the sugar was divided into grades, dried, and packed in chests for export.

The mill's multiple furnaces, which were sometimes compared to the fires of hell, consumed firewood at tremendous rates. Even modest mills could consume between 3,000 and 5,000 tons of firewood each year, and fuel might account for a fifth of a mill's production costs, often greater than the cost of slaves. Regions like Brazil, with extensive forest reserves and coastal mangroves, held a distinct advantage over producers on the smaller Caribbean islands. British planters compensated by developing the Jamaica train, which employed an efficient flue and chimney to direct the heat of a single furnace under all of the kettles, saving more than half the fuel of the old multiple-furnace Spanish train. The British also resorted to burning bagasse, the dried stems of the crushed cane, converting it to Tahitian cane, with its woody stem, for that purpose. As each sugar region faced increasing fuel costs, millers turned to the new technology.

Sugar mills were highly specialized, relying on external sources not only for firewood but also for food, hardware, slaves (who never reproduced themselves), and even sugar, which was sometimes provided by local planters. Mills operated nine months of the year, seven days a week, and twenty hours a day, which, combined with their furnaces, smokestacks, assembly lines, and shift work, gave the mill a protoindustrial aspect, even though feudal sympathies dominated social relations.

Shawn William Miller

References

Barrett, Ward. *The Sugar Hacienda of the Marqueses del Valle.* Minneapolis: University of Minnesota Press, 1970.

Miller, Shawn W. "Fuelwood in Colonial Brazil: The Economic and Social Consequences of Fuel Depletion for the Bahian Recôncavo, 1549–1820." *Forest and Conservation History* 38 (October 1994): 181–192.

Moreno Fraginals, Manuel. *The Sugarmill: The Socioeconomic Complex of Sugar in Cuba, 1760–1860.* Translated by Cedric Belfrage. New York: Monthly Review, 1976.

See also: Atlantic Economy; Cimarrones; Colonists and Settlers II—Brazil; Columbian Exchange—Agriculture; Conquest II—Brazil; Donatary Captaincies; Obraje; Palenque; Rebellions—Colonial Latin America; Slave Rebellions—Brazil; Slavery I—Brazil; Slave Trade; Sugar; Trade—Spain/Spanish America.

ENLIGHTENMENT—BRAZIL

On the surface it might seem surprising that the Enlightenment exerted a significant influence in Brazil, the distant colony of a reactionary, staunchly Catholic nation with not a single university or even a printing press before the nineteenth century. Nevertheless, the ideas that emerged from the revolution in European thought in the eighteenth century played an important role in shaping Brazil's economic, political, and social development. The Enlightenment's emphasis on reason and the empirical method helped to transform the way Brazilians saw themselves and the world around them. Ideas rooted in the Enlightenment provided the intellectual rationale and inspiration behind the stirrings for independence that began in the late eighteenth century and, a century later, for the creation of a republic.

Paradoxically, it was colonial officials who first brought Enlightenment ideas to Brazil. Sebastião José de Carvalho e Melo, the Marquis of Pombal, Portugal's de facto prime minister from 1750 to 1777, implemented empirewide reforms that sought to increase administrative efficiency by applying rational forms of organization. The discovery of gold in Minas Gerais at the turn of the eighteenth century had increased the colony's economic importance, and Portugal sought to maximize its economic benefit. In the Pombaline context, the strain of Enlightenment thought that stressed progress through the application of scientific methods to political organization, not ideas about liberty, shaped Portuguese policies in the eighteenth century. Under Pombal, the state sought to increase the power and wealth of an enlightened but no less despotic monarchy. The Crown sought to suppress individual liberties by strengthening royal institutions.

An unexpected source of Enlightenment thought in eighteenth-century Brazil was José Joaquim da Cunha de Azeredo Coutinho, a royal official and General Inquisitor. Born in Rio de Janeiro in 1742, Azeredo Coutinho studied at Coimbra soon after Pombal had implemented curricular reforms that incorporated, in a modest way, Enlightenment thinking into the venerable Portuguese university. At Coimbra, Azeredo Coutinho became familiar with the Cartesian methods advocated by the French physiocrats. Upon his return to Brazil, Azeredo Coutinho quickly ascended the ranks of the colonial administration. He founded a school in Pernambuco, which incorporated the new thinking he had acquired during his European studies. While religious in orientation, the school taught natural sciences and Cartesian methodology alongside more traditional subject matter rooted in the scholastic tradition. In a modest way, the seminary at Olinda helped spark interest in the European Enlightenment, which subsequently grew as groups of educated Brazilians began circulating banned texts and organizing secret societies based upon Enlightenment thinking. Azeredo Coutinho also became one of the first writers to enunciate the interests of Brazilian Creoles by applying the ideas of the Enlightenment to the Brazilian economy. Thus a colonial administrator, an official of the ultraconservative Inquisition at that, became one of the first to articulate the kind of thinking that the independence leaders would put into practice decades later.

By the end of the eighteenth century, Portugal had lost its place as Brazil's principal intellectual influence. Crown attempts to censor the colonials' consumption of revolutionary ideas never succeeded in preventing the small number of educated Brazilians who sought out the writings of the Enlightenment from doing so. Smuggled texts, along with the precedents set by the American, French, and Haitian Revolutions, helped fuel the political unrest that characterized the late colonial period in Brazil. Elites in various Brazilian cities began holding salons and forming secret societies that helped spread Enlightenment thinking and applied its tenets to formulate a critique of the colonial system. Scientific investigation helped foster a nativist sensibility among Brazilian Creoles. Intellectuals began to become conscious of heady ideas about political and economic liberty and to see the Portuguese colonial system as impinging on the rights of its American subjects.

In spite of Crown attempts to stem the flow of revolutionary ideas to Brazil, colonial intellectuals managed to read and circulate fundamental works of the Enlightenment. French theorists exerted the greatest influence, but the example of the English Americans in securing their independence offered both precedent and inspiration. Elite Brazilians who studied at Coimbra and elsewhere in Europe in the eighteenth century helped spark an interest in the natural sciences and empiricism in Brazil. Increased interest in and knowledge of Brazil's rich flora and fauna fed nascent nativism and resentment over its subordinate place in the imperial system.

The Enlightenment furnished the intellectual basis for numerous challenges to Portuguese authority in Brazil. Liberal ideology spread through the salons or *tertúlias* and secret societies that flourished in the late eighteenth century. As the eighteenth century drew to a close, Enlightenment ideas helped inspire and justify a number of revolts against colonial authorities in Brazil. The earliest and most famous case was the *Inconfidência Mineira,* an aborted independence plot uncovered in the captaincy of Minas Gerais in 1789. In its inquiry into the foiled rebellion, the Crown turned up banned works by Montesquieu, Diderot, and others. Among the charges the colonial authorities launched against executed coconspirator Joaquim José da Silva Xavier, or "Tiradentes," was an illegal translation of the recent constitution of the United States.

While the participants of the Inconfidência Mineira were predominately members of the elite, in a handful of other rebellions nonelites played central roles. For example, the Conspiracy of the Tailors in Bahia in 1798 took its name from the large number of artisans, tailors in particular, who participated in the rebellion. They were joined by slaves and free blacks, and the group demonstrated a familiarity with the concept of political liberty. Unlike the Inconfidência Mineira, the Bahian rebellion was a truly popular uprising, representing a cross-class coalition of slaves, artisans, and intellectuals. What is most significant about the Tailors Conspiracy is that it provides clear evidence that the ideas of the Enlightenment had permeated Brazilian society beyond the intelligentsia. In Bahia in 1798 and Pernambuco in 1817, cross-class coalitions challenged colonial authority. Clearly, a number of nonelites were familiar with Enlightenment ideas and applied them to formulate a critique of the colonial system.

The transfer of the Portuguese court to Rio de Janeiro in 1808 brought important changes to Brazil. Elevation to the status of co-kingdom changed Brazilians' perceptions of themselves as well as their legal status vis-à-vis the metropolis. During the

Crown's thirteen-year residence in America, the former colony underwent a period of cultural and intellectual fluorescence. Brazil's ports opened to direct foreign trade in 1808, after which its economy became increasingly tied to the emerging international capitalist system dominated by Great Britain. Along with ideas about economic liberalism, the Brazilian elite became increasingly acquainted with political liberalism. The thousands of foreign nationals who arrived in Brazil during the Portuguese court's residence in Rio de Janeiro contributed to the spread of liberal ideology. For example, the French cultural mission of 1816 brought new methods of inquiry and investigation to Brazil. In the early eighteenth century, new institutions of higher learning contributed to the growth of a Creole elite trained in the latest scientific methods. In numerous tertúlias and secret associations, the elite circulated contraband texts and educated themselves in the political and economic doctrines of the Enlightenment.

It did not take long before Brazilians followed the example of their neighbors and put into practice the ideas of the Enlightenment to secure independence. However, in the Brazilian case the independent nation would be ruled by a constitutional monarchy rather than a republic for most of the nineteenth century. It was the heir to the Portuguese throne who declared Brazil's independence on September 7, 1822. The framers of Brazil's constitutional monarchy were profoundly influenced by French theorists above all, although England and North America also provided inspiration. Notably, most of those who led the call for Brazilian independence had studied in Europe. The "patriarch" of Brazilian independence, José Bonifácio de Andrada e Silva, who presided over the constituent assembly that drafted the Constitution of 1824, was well acquainted with the ideas of the Enlightenment and helped apply them to the administration of the new Empire of Brazil. Like most elite Brazilians of his generation, José Bonifácio traveled to Coimbra to receive his education. When José Bonifácio attended the august institution in the 1780s, a counter-Enlightenment wave had recently swept the university and numerous professors were tried for assigning radical texts, particularly those penned by French *philosophes.* Despite the climate of repression, the young José Bonifácio nevertheless became immersed in the ideas emanating from the Enlightenment. Though these ideas officially banned throughout the Portuguese Empire, the framers of the new system were familiar with the writings of Enlightenment thinkers such as Locke, Rousseau, and Montesquieu.

Britain provided the primary model for the Brazilian constitutional monarchy. The Brazilian imperial government reflected Enlightenment principles by providing a division of powers and suffrage, albeit highly restricted. Moreover, the constitution provided for an extremely strong executive by bestowing on the emperor the additional "moderating" power that made him the ultimate arbiter in all political disputes. The constitution demonstrated that the state was preoccupied with maintaining order above all, a tendency that would long prevail among Brazil's ruling class.

Throughout the nineteenth century, regional revolts presented challenges to imperial authority. The existence of slavery until 1888 provided another omnipresent threat of rebellion. That the Enlightenment had provided the intellectual rationale behind the slaves who secured Haiti's independence was never far from the minds of Brazilian elites, most of whom were slave owners. Large numbers of slaves in Brazil resided in the coastal urban centers where they enjoyed a degree of autonomy and opportunity to come into contact with revolutionary ideologies. Slave participation in various rebellions offers evidence of their familiarity with ideas that originated in the European Enlightenment. Although the abolitionist movement in Brazil remained quite weak for most of the imperial period (1822–1889), ideas about liberty and equality helped underscore the case for the abolition of slavery. It must be stressed that, although the Enlightenment helped shape Brazilian history in the nineteenth century, its permeation was only partial. Iberian and Catholic traditions remained a significant presence. While elites paid lip service to ideas of liberty and equality, they perpetuated a profoundly antidemocratic society, with power disproportionately resting in the hands of a small planter class whose wealth derived from the practice of slavery.

Toward the end of the nineteenth century, the Enlightenment helped bring about fundamental change in Brazil. The monarchy and slavery were key institutions in the evolution of Brazilian history from the sixteenth through the nineteenth centuries. Advocates of abolishing both institutions, often the same individuals, rooted their critiques in liberal thought, which had steadily gained adherents in the nineteenth century. The Paraguayan War (1864–1870) helped accelerate discontent among members of the small, yet growing, middle classes, among them junior military officers. The positivist goals of order and progress provided the cornerstone of the republic that emerged in 1889.

Enlightenment ideas made their first modest mark on Brazil in the latter half of the eighteenth century. Throughout the nineteenth century and well into the twentieth, ideas about liberty and progress played a powerful role in shaping the nation's political and social evolution. Brazilian elites found themselves preoccupied with the latest European ideas as they pursued the elusive goals of order and progress. Both the destination and the path chosen emerged directly from the ideas unleashed by the Enlightenment.

Emily Story

References

Burns, E. Bradford. "The Role of Azevedo Coutinho in the Enlightenment of Brazil." *Hispanic American Historical Review* 44, no. 2 (May 1964): 143–160.

———. "The Intellectuals as Agents of Change and the Independence of Brazil, 1724–1822." In *From Colony to Nation: Essays on the Independence of Brazil,* edited by A. J. R. Russell-Wood. Baltimore, MD: Johns Hopkins University Press, 1975.

Marchant, Alexander. "Aspects of the Enlightenment in Brazil." Pp. 95–118 in *Latin America in the Enlightenment,* 2nd ed., edited by Arthur P. Whitaker. Ithaca, NY: Cornell University Press, 1961.

Maxwell, Kenneth R. *Conflicts and Conspiracies: Brazil and Portugal, 1750–1808.* Cambridge: Cambridge University Press, 1973.

———. *Pombal: Paradox of the Enlightenment.* Cambridge: Cambridge University Press, 1995.

See also: Abolition and Emancipation; Amazon; American Revolution; Brazil; Catholic Church in Brazil; Censorship—Brazil; Contraband; Creoles; Education—Brazil; Enlightenment—Spanish America; Independence II—Brazil; Inquisition—Luso-America; Monarchs of Portugal; Napoleonic Invasion and Luso-America; Paraguayan War; Positivism; Science and Scientists—Brazil/Portugal; Slave Rebellions—Brazil; Universities.

ENLIGHTENMENT—SPANISH AMERICA

The subject of the Spanish American Enlightenment is one of great importance for Latin American history—but one that involves both controversy and complexity. In fact, the historiography of this topic has undergone a long and transformative evolution over the course of the last century. Therefore, in order to appreciate how the Enlightenment developed in Spanish America, it is first necessary to understand its treatment by historians whose work has focused on the following issues. First, given Spain's traditional reputation for ideological conservatism in the early modern period, Spanish American historians had to determine whether or not the Americas experienced an Enlightenment at all, and if so, to define its nature. Was the Enlightenment, as some have argued, strictly based on safe, utilitarian topics that did not challenge the political or religious status quo, or did it involve more subversive, revolutionary ideas as well? Similarly, did ideas flow only from Europe to America, or did Spanish Americans develop their own unique version of enlightened ideals? And finally, what role did the Enlightenment play in the nineteenth-century movements for Spanish American independence?

Scholars of the Spanish American Enlightenment first sought to answer these questions in a comprehensive way and to combat powerful "Black Legend" assumptions of American intellectual stagnation. Scholars such as Arthur P. Whitaker and John Tate Lanning argued that educated Spanish Americans were not only well versed in the political, philosophical, and scientific literature of the Enlightenment, but were able to determine which ideas contained in it were useful to their particular context. Whitaker was also able to explain Spanish America's absence from general treatments of the Enlightenment by arguing that Spanish America played a "dual role" in the movement: On one hand, it provided an example for Europeans of a place without reason or enlightenment—a place where European imperialism had gone awry. Hence the publication of Abbe Raynal's highly popular *History of the Two Indies* and of George Louis LeClerc, Comte de Buffon's *Natural History,* both of which held America and Americans to be backward, degenerate examples of a land and a people without reason. On the other hand, according to Whitaker, Spanish Americans played an active role in the Enlightenment in welcoming its ideas, particularly those related to science, and applying them to "useful" pursuits, such as trade and mining.

It has been suggested that the Spanish American Enlightenment was geared more toward political economy and utilitarianism than toward religious or philosophical ideas that may have challenged the status quo. As a result, the intellectual transformations that occurred during the Spanish American Enlightenment have been labeled erroneously as a hispanicized "Catholic" or "Christian" Enlightenment. However, recent scholarship has demonstrated that the Spanish American Enlightenment was based largely on the acceptance of the "sensationalism" of Locke (the idea that true knowledge derives only from the senses), the critical method of Descartes, and the mathematical laws of Newton; all three seventeenth-century philosophers provided the epistemological basis for the later ideas of the *philosophes.*

Recent scholarship also has challenged the idea of a conservative, "Christian" Enlightenment by showing that there was remarkably free circulation of Enlightenment literature, in contrast to assumptions of Spain's religious orthodoxy and rigid conservatism embodied in the Inquisition's prohibition of heretical books. This was especially true in the universities, which conferred over 150,000 degrees during the colonial period. Thus, even if many of Bourbon Spain's Enlightenment reforms were directed toward practical purposes, this did not mean that the only acceptable ideas were those divorced from theological, philosophical, or political radicalism. And finally, recent scholarship has begun to take the bold step toward claiming originality of ideas for the Spanish American Enlightenment. In other words, some scholars reject the assumption that enlightenment ideas flowed only from east to west and that Spanish America was largely the passive recipient of Enlightenment ideas. Rather, in arguing against European detractors, in establishing a mining school in Mexico, and in writing their own versions of New World history from their own documents, Spanish Americans forged their own version of the Enlightenment.

Perhaps the most important contribution to our understanding of the Spanish American Enlightenment lies in Jorge Cañizares-Esguerra's *How to Write the History of the New World* (2001). In a chapter aptly entitled "Whose Enlightenment Was It Anyway?" Cañizares-Esguerra points out that all earlier treatment of the Enlightenment in Spanish America made a fundamental—and fundamentally flawed —assumption: that the only way to judge the Spanish American Enlightenment lay in evaluating the degree of acceptance or rejection of innovative ideas, ideas of an elite minority from the so-called center of the Enlightenment, namely, England and France. Such Eurocentric ideas neglect the key factor of the Enlightenment, which involved a new epistemology based on a new historical methodology that, according to Cañizares-Esguerra, developed first and most radically and creatively in the Americas. By focusing on this new epistemology, Cañizares-Esguerra has been able to show the absolutely crucial role of the Spanish American colonies in creating a new historical method based on what he terms a "patriotic epistemology," or the idea put forth by patriotic Spanish Americans that only they, and not European foreigners, could truly understand and study the documentary and archaeological traces of their history. The results of this patriotic epistemology were a series of truly original histories of the New World, many of which were geared toward refuting the theories of Raynal, Buffon, and others.

Cañizares-Esguerra's attention to the question of American degeneracy brings out one more issue of debate concerning the Enlightenment in Latin America: whether or not Enlightenment ideas led to the independence movements and thus whether they were compatible with patriotism and early nationalist sentiment. Early in the twentieth century, historians assumed a direct causal connection between the Enlightenment and Spanish American independence movements, or posited that the ideals of liberty, equality, and fraternity embodied in the French Revolution and the writings of the French philosophes had similarly influenced elite Spanish Americans. Simón Bolívar is probably the most famous example of Spanish American elites who were exposed to revolutionary ideals through travel to Europe. However, a richer understanding of the independence movements has led subsequent authors to reach different conclusions. While Enlightenment ideas may have provided some of the groundwork for a spirit of revolution or separatist politics, they did not lead directly to independence. Rather, the independence movements are better understood as products of civil unrest and the lack of legitimate leadership brought on by Napoleon's capture of the Bourbon monarchs. Once the independence revolts were underway, Enlightenment ideals then provided direction for subsequent liberal state formation, but that would make their application a consequence, rather than a cause, of independence.

Spanish America did unequivocally experience an Enlightenment, and it was indeed an original one. Still, most scholars agree that enlightened ideas reached the Spanish American colonies through Spain. The accession of Bourbon rulers to the throne meant a close intellectual relationship with France, at least in the early decades of the eighteenth century, and the policies of Charles III (1759–1788) further encouraged this openness to many enlightened ideas, particularly in the areas of science; political economy, both domestic and international; and technological improvement.

Thus, enlightened ideas, most of which were officially condoned, reached Spanish America through Spain, mainly in the form of books. Once circulated in the Americas, these ideas were disseminated through various institutions: economic societies, periodicals, or the *Gazetas,* which sprang up in virtually every colony, and finally in the Spanish American universities, which underwent significant education reform in the eighteenth century. Economic societies, usually called *sociedades de amantes del pais,* were, as their titles indicate, patriotic societies geared toward the promotion of progress and modernization through the useful application of science. Modeled after French institutions, they were founded throughout Spain as well as Spanish America, in the capital cities of the viceroyalties as well as the captaincy of Guatemala. Members of these societies regularly competed for prizes by writing treatises about technological improvement, particularly in the areas of mining, agriculture, and agronomy.

Several of these societies also sponsored the publication of periodicals called Gazetas in the late eighteenth century. Though initially established to report mundane events, the Gazetas that appeared in Lima, Buenos Aires, Guatemala City, and Mexico City soon betrayed their liberal, enlightened roots. The Gazetas routinely had sections devoted to the pursuit of scientific discoveries and new inventions and thus clearly advocated the new, experimental philosophy. They also contained political writings critical of the colonial government and advocated liberal reforms such as free trade and freedom of the press. The most famously controversial series were the *Mercurio Peruano,* published by the economic society of Peru, whose liberal philosophy led the Spanish Crown to shut it down in the 1790s; and the *Gazeta de Literatura de México,* founded by José Alzate y Ramírez, one of the most well-known original thinkers of the period who harshly criticized Bourbon efforts to enforce peninsular authority in the colonies. Finally, the *Gazeta de Buenos Aires* provided a platform for Argentine statesmen such as Mariano Moreno to put forth their views, based on the works of Rousseau and Montesquieu, as to how an independent Argentina ought to be governed.

In addition to these societies and the Gazetas they produced, Spanish American universities welcomed the philosophical as well as the practical ideas of the Enlightenment. University courses in the faculty of arts included the works of the new philosophy from Newton and Descartes to Condillac and Benjamin Franklin, and students wrote theses throughout the eighteenth century that demonstrate clear acceptance of innovative ideas in the areas of science, philosophy, political economy, and law. The University of San Carlos de Guatemala underwent a series of reforms in the eighteenth century that indicate the influence of the Enlightenment and provide a representative example for what was happening in other Spanish American universities as well. The Franciscan José Antonio Goicoechea, hired to teach philosophy at the university after the expulsion of the Jesuits in 1767, advocated a successful and thorough reform of the curriculum in which Castilian would replace the traditional use of Latin, and the study of mathematics, experimental physics, natural history, and political economy would provide alternatives to the traditional scholastic training.

The existence and dissemination of Enlightenment ideas among intellectuals throughout Spanish America are evident through the many achievements of the period. One important outcome of the emphasis on science and its practical applications was the mining school established in Mexico City in 1792. The first of its kind in Latin America, the school helped Mexico produce more silver in the last three decades of its colonial existence than ever before. Spanish America also provided rich opportunities for botanists and natural historians to investigate and classify thousands of plants through no less than twenty-six scientific expeditions organized and funded by the Crown in the eighteenth century, including one that provided smallpox inoculations for the colonial populace. Along similar lines, botanical gardens and natural history museums were established in Mexico City, Lima, Guatemala City, and Havana. Finally, the new historical methodology described by Cañizares-Esguerra is clearly evident in the defenders of America's rich past and promising present, with Francisco Clavijero's *History of Mexico* considered the most well-known example. Given these achievements and given the role of the economic societies, the Gazetas, and the Spanish American universities in disseminating the new philosophy, it is clear that Spanish America not only participated in the Enlightenment but created one of its own.

Paula De Vos

References

Aldridge, A. Owen, ed. *The Ibero-American Enlightenment.* Urbana: University of Illinois Press, 1971.

Cañizares-Esguerra, Jorge. *How to Write the History of the New World: Histories, Epistemologies, and Identities in the Eighteenth-Century Atlantic World.* Stanford, CA: Stanford University Press, 2001.

Lanning, John Tate. *The Eighteenth-Century Enlightenment in the University of San Carlos de Guatemala.* Ithaca, NY: Cornell University Press, 1956.

Shafer, Robert J. *The Economic Societies in the Spanish World, 1763–1821.* Syracuse, NY: University of Syracuse Press, 1958.

Whitaker, Arthur P. *Latin America and the Enlightenment.* New York: D. Appleton-Century, 1942.

See also: Bourbon Reforms; Censorship—Brazil; Censorship—Spanish America; Conquest and the Debate over Justice; Enlightenment—Brazil; Independence I–VI; Inquisition—Spanish America; Jesuits—Expulsion; Medicine; Napoleonic Invasion and Spanish America; Science and Scientists—Colonial Spanish America; Universities; Viceroyalties.

ENVIRONMENT

The Iberian colonies, despite their small populations, had a notable impact on the New World's environment. On the frontier of an expanding world commerce, Iberian colonists did their utmost to turn everything within their reach to profit. Where settlements flourished, plantations replaced tropical forests, mines gouged the land, and ranches decimated native plant species. However, in many areas, the frontier remained open until the nineteenth century, leaving much of Latin America unscathed by European enterprise. And even in settled areas, colonial governments made some small efforts to conserve natural resources.

Upon the Iberians' arrival, the New World was not exactly new. Indians, particularly those of Mexico and Peru, inhabited landscapes that were painstakingly managed and unequivocally prosperous. The Incas terraced mountain valleys in massive works that often extended for many miles, and they watered their terraced crops by extensive irrigation canals. They also engaged in mining. The peoples of central Mexico practiced an intensive agriculture and exploited nature for utilitarian needs, religious compulsions, and worldly obsessions. Jaguar skins, bird feathers, rabbit furs, jade objects, and colorful flowers, among many other such commodities, formed part of Aztec tribute lists or could be purchased in bustling city markets. Some goods were traded over considerable distances. Aztec and Tarascan religion demanded flesh for sacrifice, which disturbed local animal populations, and consumed large quantities of firewood to fuel perennial ceremonial fires. A few communities were aware they were damaging their resource base and attempted to conserve forests and regulate activities such as fishing.

Even tribal peoples scattered in villages across tropical forests had manifestly altered nature, managing the land with simple techniques that favored food-bearing trees and plants. They employed slash-and-burn strategies to clear the land for cassava and corn production, and when the soil's fertility declined after a few years, they abandoned their plots and burned forest anew elsewhere. They also used fire to create pastures to entice deer and other animals for the hunt near their settlements. However, tribal impacts were more limited than in Mexico and Peru by their small populations and their migratory subsistence strategies that were determined by seasonal abundance.

In contrast to the Europeans' enmity for nature, Indian attitudes tended toward harmony. As part of indigenous animism, Indians regarded themselves as part of the natural world rather than distinct from it. The Maya wrote poetry about nature's beauty, and the Aztecs established aviaries, zoological and botanical gardens, and parks, long before Europeans considered such institutions. Many Indian cultures apologized to trees before they felled them and to animals after they had killed them, as they saw living things as their fellow beings. Nevertheless, they felled trees, hunted animals, and greatly disturbed the land upon which they lived. None of America's pre-Columbian inhabitants had achieved ecological sainthood; neither did they inhabit a mythical Eden. The human imprint on the land was quite legible before 1492.

When the Europeans arrived, there was a qualitative change in the way nature was used. Trade was a major factor. The Aztecs and the Inca had engaged in local and limited long-distance trade, but now markets became global, and Iberians began

Inca ruins on a mountainside surrounded by terraces. The Inca used agricultural terraces to increase the amount of arable land in the steep and rugged terrain of the Andes Mountains. (David Owens/iStockPhoto)

to produce commodities not just for local and regional markets, but for Europe, Africa, and Asia. This placed greater demands on the settled land. However, during the first century and a half of colonization, American nature experienced a significant respite. For the environment, the intensification of production by a tiny number of Europeans was less important than the rapid decline in the indigenous populations. As many as 90 percent of the Indian peoples died within the first century of contact due largely to the introduction of Eurasian diseases to which the Indians had no immunity. As a result, the area under intensive agriculture in central Mexico fell by 80 percent. The Iberians, even with African additions, were not up to the task of repopulating the lands they were emptying. In the colonial era, fewer than 800,000 Spaniards immigrated to the New World. In preconquest central Mexico alone, there were an estimated 25 million inhabitants; and despite the fact that the Indian populations began to recover in the mid-seventeenth century, there were still fewer people in the region in 1800 than there had been in 1500. The result, especially during the first half of the colonial era, was that nature experienced fewer human demands. In documented cases in Mexico, the Caribbean, and Brazil, forest habitats recovered and former farmlands went fallow.

Sugar, which was introduced to much of tropical America before 1520, exemplifies the local, but considerable, impact of European commercial agriculture. The first act of sugar planting was to fell the magnificent forests that encumbered the lowland tropics. Settlers generally followed the shifting agricultural practices of their Indian predecessors, but on a grander scale, and sugar monoculture depleted the soil's fertility more rapidly than had the Indians' mixed plantings. Depending on the soil, sugar might do well for five to thirty years on the same plot of ground, but once fertility fell below an acceptable minimum, more forest was felled and burned. In Brazil and on the larger islands of the Caribbean, there were sufficient forests to permit this strategy into the nineteenth century, but on the smaller islands, sugar planters closed the frontier quite rapidly and had to resort to manuring their fields to maintain fertility. Erosion and soil loss were concerns due to the forests' removal, particularly in steep locations. In the Caribbean there were reports of entire cane fields sliding off hillsides, and slave tasks included replacing eroded soil. The plow was rarely used in sugar cultivation, but when used in other locations, it exacerbated soil erosion. In addition, the sugar mill consumed several thousand tons of firewood every year to process the harvested cane, further contributing to regional deforestation. When local firewood sources gave out, sugar producers resorted to burning bagasse, the dried husk of the sugarcane's stalk, in improved furnaces. Although sugar's environmental impact reached well beyond the borders of the plantation, importing food, fuel, and other material, most of the transformation remained within the immediate lowland, coastal zones.

Ranching, however, quickly became and remained the most extensive economic activity in Ibero-America, from Argentina to the American Southwest. Ranching required little labor, which was part of its appeal, and Spain already had a long tradition of pastoralism. Where immigration failed to settle empty lands, Iberian cattle, sheep, pigs, and horses encountered open forests and pastures with few predators and even fewer competitors. Under these conditions, the invaders reproduced rapidly. By the early seventeenth century, New Spain already had an estimated 10 million European domesticates. Animals in many ways were the most effective colonists: many turned feral, wandered beyond the frontier, and were hunted and adopted by indigenous cultures years before the arrival of the Europeans themselves.

Iberia's domesticates had a significant impact on the land, although its nature is disputed. Cattle, and particularly sheep, have been accurately labeled "hooved locusts," as they consume most kinds of vegetation at remarkable rates. Many native plants, ill adapted to being grazed, disappeared and were replaced by other native plants with thorns and spines, or by European grasses that withstood constant grazing. Hooves also trampled plant growth and compacted soils that were now exposed and susceptible to erosion. In one region of central Mexico, eruptions in sheep populations are blamed for transforming a rather fertile valley, where the Otomi grew spring-irrigated crops, into something of a desert. Others, however, have found little evidence of widespread pastoral damage in New Spain and instead argue that ranching was generally sustainable due to the Iberian practice of transhumance, which separated summer and winter pasturing.

Mining was colonial Latin America's economic engine. The silver of Mexico and

Peru, Colombia's gold and emeralds, and Brazil's gold and diamonds provided the primary impetus to Iberian migration, fostered urbanization, and formed substantial domestic markets for all kinds of goods. Ranching played a central role in supplying mining towns with food and also supplied the mines directly with cowhide sacks for ore and tallow candles to illuminate the mine shafts. In addition to the obvious impacts of shafts and tailings created by miners, timber was employed to support mine shafts, which resulted in deforestation. Initially, silver refining relied on firewood (and grass in the Andes when wood was unavailable) to smelt silver ores, which also denuded the local hillsides. The introduction of mercury, which was employed to refine the silver from its ore by amalgamation, reduced the demand for fuel considerably but involved other, more serious, environmental costs. Before the silver could be amalgamated, it had to be pulverized to a powder by stamp mills, which themselves required water power. Numerous reservoirs, dams, canals, and mills were established along narrow stream channels. Mercury, one of the most dangerous and insidious poisons, contaminated local waters and soils and even entered into world air currents, creating what was the first industrial pollution in the Americas. Miners, both at Almaden, Spain, and Huancavelica, Peru, as well as laborers involved in the amalgamation process itself, suffered from mercury poisoning. Death rates, particularly in the mines, were catastrophic, and mercury entered the food chain through various avenues.

In Brazil, gold and diamond mining had a different aspect because both were extracted from placer deposits. Mines were referred to as washings, and miners diverted rivers and tore up riverbeds and other alluvial deposits in order to sort through the auriferous gravels. Washings could be quite substantial, and observers described the gold and diamond regions as pockmarked, denuded, and gullied. But as the gold was in nugget form, there was no need for mercury. Like Spanish America, Brazil's mines, and the cities associated with them, drew on a large hinterland that supplied food, cattle, fuel, and other goods.

Environmental damage and resource depletion did not go unnoticed by the colonial powers, and a few observers lamented the degradation of local resources. However, conservation measures concerning water, erosion, and game were limited in the colonial period and tended to be local. American nature was generally perceived to be exceedingly abundant in contrast to Iberian constraints. Only in one aspect, namely deforestation, did the Iberian experience condition colonial officials to act. Timber was quite scarce in much of Iberia, and some officials feared similar constraints in America's future. Lumber and fuel for mines and cities were the most immediate concerns, but both Spain and Portugal, which had based their empires' initial successes on maritime power, saw the great American forests as military assets and passed various laws to protect ship timbers. In Spanish America, these laws were often local, such as prohibitions against burning the forests in silver regions, or edicts against cutting ship timbers near shipbuilding centers like Guayaquil and Havana. In Brazil, a general law from 1652 prohibited the felling of the *madeiras de lei* (timbers under the law) that were prized for their utility in buildings, furniture, and ships. Colonists were not permitted to harvest trees so designated whether they were found on private or public land. Both Portugal (1799) and Spain (1803) decreed substantial forest regulations at the end of the colonial era, but these faced the same difficulties of enforcement as previous, less ambitious, policies. Colonists chafed under such restrictions, and colonial officials found it difficult to enforce the law in their expansive territories. In Brazil, if colonists found it difficult to engage in timber contraband, setting fire to the king's trees in order to open new fields could be done with impunity. Some conservation measures were intended to protect Crown revenue rather than enhance colonial well-being. Brazil's brazilwood and Mexico's pearl oysters, for example, were protected in the interest of Crown monopoly profits or royal tax revenues. Exceptions to conservation law, however, were sometimes made in the interest of subsistence. In Spanish America, exemptions from forest restrictions were granted to Indians and the poor who relied upon the forests for fuel and game. In Brazil, local mangrove forests were preserved in the interest of subsistence fisheries conservation. Sugar millers, who used the mangrove for fuel, and tanners, who stripped its bark for tannin, were barred from the mangroves in many municipalities so that the free poor could exploit the habitat's abundant fish and shellfish without detriment.

In comparison to subsequent centuries, colonial Latin America had a relatively limited impact on the natural world. Small populations in a vast land and limited technologies restricted their destructive powers. Mexico, the most heavily populated region, is estimated to have destroyed a third of its forests by 1800; Portuguese America deforested 30,000 square kilometers of forest in southeastern Brazil alone in the eighteenth century, which included the now naked mining districts. The colonial powers, despite their failures, and despite their own contributions to the land's degradation through mining and timbering, did make efforts to reduce human impacts and conserve resources for the future. Their independent successors, by contrast, made almost no similar attempts but exploited without restraint for the building of the new nations. Control over land fell entirely into private hands. Free trade and foreign investment, both restricted under the colonial regime, provided additional incentives, technologies, and markets to extract the still considerable abundance that survived the colonial era.

Shawn William Miller

References

Dean, Warren. *With Broadax and Firebrand: The Destruction of the Brazilian Atlantic Forest.* Berkeley and Los Angeles: University of California Press, 1995.

Melville, Elinor G. K. *A Plague of Sheep: Environmental Consequences of the Conquest of Mexico.* Cambridge: Cambridge University Press, 1994.

Miller, Shawn W. *Fruitless Trees: Portuguese Conservation and Brazil's Colonial Timber.* Stanford, CA: Stanford University Press, 2000.

Richards, John F. *The Unending Frontier: An Environmental History of the Early Modern World.* Berkeley and Los Angeles: University of California Press, 2003.

Simonian, Lane. *Defending the Land of the Jaguar: A History of Conservation in Mexico.* Austin: University of Texas Press, 1995.

Watts, David. *The West Indies: Patterns of Development, Culture and Environmental Change since 1492.* New York: Cambridge University Press, 1987.

See also: Amazon; Atlantic Economy; Columbian Exchange—Agriculture; Columbian Exchange—Disease; Columbian Exchange—Livestock; Dyes and Dyewood; Emeralds; Engenho; Henequen; Human Sacrifice; Mining—Gold; Mining—Mercury; Mining—Silver; Monopolies; Potosí; Sugar.

ESTANCIA

Estancia comes from the Spanish word *estar,* a ranch or large farm typically dedicated to cattle-breeding. South American estancias were a key element of social and economic development in the colonial and postindependence periods, and were perceived as a status symbol of landed elites. Estancias were first recorded in 1514 to denote land divisions in Santo Domingo and in 1573 appeared in documents in Paraguay.

Rather than land, colonial estancias began with the ownership of cattle and slaves. Since 1589, the town council of Buenos Aires had adopted a registry of brands for all proprietors of cattle and slaves. These brands represented ownership deeds, granting the *estanciero* (ranch owner) specific rights. To avoid the trespassing of neighbors' cattle into their own grasslands, in the eighteenth century estancieros began to mark their land with boundary humps. The Creole estancia was characterized by an ambiguous landownership status. By 1790, only six landlords owned enormous states in the Río de la Plata, but most estancieros occupied lands owned by the Spanish Crown (*realengas*). Following independence from Spain, the Argentine government encouraged rural settlements through the implementation of land grants. In particular, President Bernardino Rivadavia established the emphyteusis system in 1822, by which the national government retained titles, earned revenue, and tried to promote agriculture. However, as late as 1840, 160 estancias in Buenos Aires occupied 2,100 leagues (3.8 million hectares). In addition, emphyteusis grants displaced prior settlers who generally worked the land.

Modern estancias began with wire fencing in the mid-nineteenth century. In the 1840s, when sheep production increased significantly, landowners marked the limits of their estancias with ditches. In 1845 Alejandro Codwell wire-fenced Richard Blake Newton's vegetable garden in Chascomús to protect it from cows and sheep; the first estancia to be completely wire-fenced was John James Murphy's *La Flor del Uncalito* in Salto. Wire fencing represented both a symbol of landed social status and a limit to those classes perceived as inferior, such as Indians and gauchos, who perceived land and all its contents as communal property.

In the second half of the twentieth century, owing to the inheritance system in force, a typical estancia in the Argentine pampas and Uruguay was reduced in area to an average of less than 1,000 hectares, ranging from a few hundred to over 10,000. However, in northeastern Chaco, Patagonia, and other regions, some estancias are still 50,000 hectares or more. The headquarters or *casco* include the main house, workers' dwelling, storehouses, and machine or repair shops. These buildings are usually surrounded by eucalyptus trees and other species brought from Europe and Australia. Strategic outposts *(puestos)* are located near watering places, and *puesteros* oversee one or several *potreros* (internal divisions of an estancia).

Estancia labor is divided according to the type of production. In the traditional Argentine and Uruguayan estancias, the estanciero (owner or tenant) manages the business and is aided by the foreman or foremen, peons or cattle-hands, shepherds and puesteros, and at times joiners, butchers, bookkeepers, and other employees. From the nineteenth century the estancia was fully integrated in the capitalist network of production units; however, until the 1940s, feudal structures remained, particularly when the workers were contractually bound to a patron and paid with locally issued currency and were obliged to purchase their needs in the estancia's retail store, or *pulpería.* The social structure and spatial settlement of estancieros and workers changed dramatically between 1820 and 1920, when the original production of hides and tallow was replaced by jerked beef, wool, quality meat and mutton, and finally cereals.

Edmundo Murray

References

Capdevila, Pedro V. *La estancia Argentina.* Buenos Aires: Plus Ultra, 1978.

Sbarra, Noel H. *Historia del alambrado en la Argentina.* Buenos Aires: Eudeba, 1964.

Slatta, Richard W. *Gauchos and the Vanishing Frontier.* Lincoln: University of Nebraska Press. 1992.

See also: Argentina; Columbian Exchange—Livestock; Conquest VII—Southern Cone; Encomienda; Gaucho; Independence I—Argentina; Jesuits—Iberia and America; Jesuits—Paraguay; Native Americans V—Central and Southern Andes; Repartimiento; Slavery I–IV.

EXILES—IBERIANS IN THE AMERICAS

The American continent has been a destination for exiles from the Iberian Peninsula ever since the two lands became historically linked at the end of the fifteenth century. The first wave came in the form of Jews and "New Christians" with relatively recent Jewish heritage, who faced increased persecution on the peninsula over the course of the fifteenth century and were expelled altogether in 1492. Within a decade after the expulsion, which coincided with Columbus's initial voyage across the Atlantic, a settlement of New Christians emerged on the Caribbean island of Santo Domingo. Over the next several decades, the West Indies became a kind of promised land for Jews and New Christians from both Spain and Portugal seeking to escape the peninsular jurisdiction of the Inquisition.

As Spain's project of establishing an ideal Catholic society in America took shape during the reign of Charles V (1519–1556), the Spanish Crown imposed a series of measures to restrict this safety valve for persecuted Jews and New Christians. A 1522 law attempted to restrict emigration to America only to Castilian Old Christians. However, as with contraband commercial goods and precious metals, the flow of humans across the Atlantic proved difficult to regulate; forged documents and bribes were common. Consequently, the Jewish and New Christian population in Spanish and Portuguese America continued to grow throughout the sixteenth century. The establishment in 1570 of Inquisitions in Peru and Mexico did not hinder the flow, but there were some periods of intense persecution during the seventeenth century. However, by that time most Jews and New Christians were drawn to America by commercial possibilities rather than as exiles. Still, it may be noted that Buenos Aires, a major American port where no Inquisition was established, became an attractive settlement for Iberian Jews, who made up one-fourth of the city's white population by 1650.

During the latter stages of the colonial period, Latin America became less hospitable to Iberian exiles. Groups expelled from the peninsular domains, notably the Jesuits, were banished from the American colonies as well. Rationalist reformers in

Portugal created penal exile colonies of criminals and heretics as a means to bring manpower to underpopulated regions of the empire, including northern and northeastern Brazil. Clandestine revolutionary movements on both sides of the Atlantic at the end of the eighteenth century did not produce transatlantic exiles per se, as neither America nor Iberia was entirely hospitable to their cause.

The first Iberian exiles of note in Latin America during the modern period were the Portuguese royal family and court, whose members waited out the 1807 Napoleonic invasion of the peninsula in the relative safety of Rio de Janeiro. Some remained in Brazil and participated in the newly independent Brazilian empire, but the Portuguese monarch returned to Lisbon in 1821 in the face of several rebellions demanding Brazilian independence.

Liberal politicians constituted the main exile group from Spain during the first half of the nineteenth century, but America was not an attractive place to settle. Given the frequency of political change and the constant possibility of revolution in Spain, opposition leaders preferred to remain in Europe, principally France, Gibraltar, and Great Britain, rather than banish themselves to the far-flung domains of the former colonies where delays in communication and return passage might weaken their political influence. Later in the century, the activities of anarchist and socialist revolutionaries tended to be labeled criminal by authorities on both sides of the Atlantic; therefore, although such movements maintained transatlantic contacts, emigration did not amount to exile.

The twentieth century constituted the most intense era of transatlantic exile within the Iberian world. This process was a product of the political polarization, civil conflict, and dictatorship prevalent throughout the Iberian world during the period. The first wave of exile originated from the fallen Portuguese republic. A community of exiled Republicans prospered in Rio de Janeiro and São Paulo after the emergence of the Salazar dictatorship in the late 1920s. By the 1960s, this community had become the source of considerable propaganda and funding for the growing left-wing resistance to the Salazar regime. Among the prominent opposition figures to seek exile in Brazil was Humberto Delgado, who had mounted a serious challenge to Salazar in Portugal's presidential election of 1958 despite rules designed to favor the incumbent. Several opposition military figures also took refuge in Brazil, though the Brazilian government, seeking to maintain stable relations with Portugal, denied entry to the most notorious. For example, Henrique Galvão turned to Venezuela, home to a somewhat smaller community of Portuguese Republican exiles. The most dramatic single act of the exiled opposition occurred on January 22, 1961, when dissidents hijacked the *Santa Maria,* a Portuguese cruiseliner, off the coast of Venezuela. The hijacking generated ample international press for their cause before the dissidents surrendered to Brazilian authorities thirteen days later. Leftist opposition activity continued but increasingly originated from Portuguese enclaves in Africa, notably the rebellious colony of Angola, rather than in the Americas.

Spanish Republicans formed by far the largest and best known transatlantic exile group of the twentieth century. Having been defeated in the Spanish Civil War (1936–1939) and subsequently persecuted by the victorious Franco regime, Republicans of various political stripes poured northward into France in 1939; thousands made their way across the Atlantic, primarily to Mexico, during the early stages of World War II. Others, including about 500 children and a handful of Republican intellectuals, had found refuge in Mexico before the war's conclusion. Mexico became the largest recipient of Spanish exiles, mainly because of its government's active commitment to organizing Spanish refugees' transport and care. Although precise figures are unknown, estimates on the number of Spanish exiles who arrived in Mexico during War World II range from 15,000 to 40,000. Mexico quickly became the intellectual and cultural center of the Spanish Republican exile; in fact, the Mexican government had established programs to attract intellectuals before the Iberian conflict even ended. Republican intellectuals were noted for their prominent role in Mexico's cultural and academic circles throughout the 1940s and 1950s. Many exiles unaffiliated with cultural organizations were displaced to sparsely populated regions, where they were often viewed with considerably more skepticism by rural conservative Mexican society. Smaller communities developed in Chile, the Dominican Republic, Cuba, Venezuela, and Argentina. Argentina was a significant case, as numerous luminaries of Spanish culture established themselves there, including the historian Claudio Sánchez Albornoz and the poet Rafael Alberti. However, there was much less Spanish influence on Argentina's national culture than in Mexico, especially after the rise in 1946 of Juan Perón, an antiliberal populist and close ally of Franco.

In terms of political organization, Spanish Republicans encountered much the same problems in exile as they had during the civil war—namely, division and bitter factionalism. With support from the Mexican government, an exiled Republican delegation headquartered in Mexico City prevented Franco's Spain from gaining entry into the United Nations in 1945. Yet this would be its only success, as rivalries and ideological disputes fractured the exile community, which eventually moved its increasingly irrelevant government-in-exile to Paris. By 1950, some segments of the exile community had relinquished the idea of overthrowing the Franco government, instead seeking to gain some kind of reconciliation. This attitude drew sharp criticism from others, who held that no accommodation would be possible until the current regime was replaced. Most Republicans blamed their defeat on the Spanish Communist Party (PCE), which they claimed had hijacked the mission of the left-leaning liberal republic. As a result, PCE members, numbering perhaps 2,000 in all of Latin America, initially were shunned by the greater part of the exile community. Yet the PCE, which maintained offices in Buenos Aires and Mexico City, proved far more effective at subversion inside Franco's Spain than did any other group. This gained the Communists a certain amount of prestige, such that by the 1960s, although they had relocated to France and Romania, they were perceived among Spanish exiles in Latin America as the most effective of the anti-Franco groups.

The thirty-six-year duration of the Franco dictatorship meant that most exiles never returned to Spain to live; nevertheless, de facto reconciliation was achieved by the 1960s, and some exiles began to visit their home country with some frequency. The longevity of the Franco dictatorship also made Spain a home for several deposed Latin American dictators and their entourages, most notably Perón. A handful of Cuban refugees from Fidel Castro's dictatorship settled in Spain during the Franco years as well. At the turn of the twenty-first century, emigration from South America to Spain was brisk, though this was motivated by economic crises rather than political exile. Once the Iberian countries attained political stability in the latter part of the twentieth century, transatlantic exiles began to flow in the opposite direction from the prevailing pattern of the previous four and a half centuries.

Sasha D. Pack

References

Abellán, José Luis. *El exilio español de 1939.* 6 vols. Madrid: Taurus, 1976–1978.

Bernardini, Paolo, and Norman Fiering, eds. *The Jews and the Expansion of Europe to the West, 1450 to 1800.* New York: Berghahn, 2001.

Coates, Timothy J. "Exiles and Orphans: Forced and State-Sponsored Colonizers in the Portuguese Empire, 1550–1720." Ph.D. dissertation, University of Minnesota, 1993.

Fagen, Patricia W. *Exiles and Citizens: Spanish Republicans in Mexico.* Austin: University of Texas Press, 1973.

Raby, David L. *Fascism and Resistance in Portugal: Communists, Liberals, and Military Dissidents in the Opposition to Salazar, 1941–1974.* New York: Manchester University Press, 1988.

See also: Argentina; Bolivia; Colombia; Communism; Cuba; Democracy; Enlightenment—Brazil; Enlightenment—Spanish America; Fin de Siècle; Habsburgs; Independence I–VI; Inquisition—Luso-America; Inquisition—Spanish America; Jesuits—Expulsion; Jews—Colonial Latin America; Liberalism; Migration—From Iberia to the New World; Monarchs of Spain; Moors; Napoleonic Invasion and Luso-America; Populism; Spanish Civil War and Latin America; World War I; World War II.

EXPLORERS

The Spanish Crown claimed lordship of all of the Americas west of the Tordesillas Line and from 1492 onward licensed the exploration, conquest, and settlement of that area. Prior to the eighteenth century, explorations were of two types: scouting expeditions into unknown areas, usually by sea, and explorations that formed part of a conquistador's march inland in search of peoples and resources to subjugate and exploit. Each of these types of exploration was funded either by private individuals or by the Crown, or by some combination of royal and private funding. Unfortunately, we know few specific details of these arrangements. In addition, prior to 1573, private individuals and officials in the Indies, acting on their own without prior royal orders, sometimes sent out their own explorers. The 1573 Ordinances for New Discoveries and Settlements outlawed such private initiatives because they were more often thinly disguised slave-raiding expeditions or attempts at conquest rather than true explorations. The exception to this rule seems to have been the scouting activities of some Jesuits and Franciscans who ventured beyond the frontiers in search of new souls to save. The actual expansion of missions into new areas always required royal approval and usually took the form of an armed expedition that, like the earlier conquests, explored as it went forward. In the eighteenth century a new form of royally authorized exploration arose: the scientific mission to study Latin American flora and sometimes fauna and to answer a variety of scientific questions. Yet even after these more systematic expeditions, some of the area that Spain claimed in the Americas remained unknown in any official sense.

In the early sixteenth century, the Crown's basic license for exploration was like the one it granted Christopher Columbus: a right to explore and then to settle or conquer the new "discovery" and to govern it for the life of the explorer/discoverer and at least one generation thereafter. Francisco Pizarro (who had already scouted the west coast of South America from Panama to Ecuador) and Hernando de Soto are examples of this sort of license. A common variant assigned an area already known (from being seen from the sea, usually) but not explored in detail to an individual who agreed to undertake a conquest or settlement. Pedro de Valdivia's license to subjugate Chile is an example of the first; Lucas Vázquez de Ayllón's contract to build two settlements in what is today the U.S. South is an example of the second.

The Crown also licensed a number of explorations simply to answer particular geographic questions, with trade with native peoples as a possible side benefit to ship crews or the men they represented. Between 1499 and 1502, Alonso de Ojeda, Juan de la Cosa, Cristóbal Guerra, Rodrigo de Bastides, and others (the so-called Andalusian voyages) were authorized to discover (at their own expense) what lay west of Columbus's discoveries around Trinidad. In 1508, the Crown ordered and paid Vicente Yáñez Pinzón and Juan Díaz de Solís to determine if there was open water leading to Asia north of Honduras and west of Cuba; that is, was the Gulf of Mexico really a part of some Asian sea, as Columbus had claimed? Fernão Magalhães (Magellan) and Juan Sebastian Elcano's circumnavigation of 1519–1522, also a royal venture, was sent to determine if it was possible to get around the Americas to Asia. Sebastian Cabot sailed under royal sponsorship in 1526–1530 to follow up on Magellan's discoveries, but Cabot ended up exploring the Río de la Plata drainage instead. The Crown sent Estevão Gómes to Nova Scotia and the northern part of North America in search of a strait to the Pacific Ocean in 1524–1525. All of these voyages began at Seville. Juan Rodriguez Cabrillo sailed from New Spain (Mexico) in 1542–1543 to see if Baja California was an island. Sebastian Vizcaino was sent north from Acapulco in 1602–1603 to gain a better understanding of California's ports that the Manila Galleon might have to use in emergencies when returning to Mexico from the Philippines. In the late seventeenth century (1686–1689), the Crown sent Captain Alonso de León, Juan Enríquez Barroto, and Antonio Romero from New Spain to seek the La Salle colony and thoroughly map the northern shores of the Gulf of Mexico. In doing so, they located and accurately mapped the mouths of the Mississippi River. Later, in 1774 Juan José Pérez Hernández was sent to scout the Pacific coast of North America north of Monterey, California; Pérez was the first of several explorers of what are today the Canadian west coast and the states of Washington and Oregon. He was looking for Russian fur traders reported to be advancing down the coast; he was also checking on the existence of the legendary Strait of Anian. Like Cabrillo and Vizcaino, Pérez sailed from New Spain's west coast.

Explorations sent out by Crown officials with royal approval include those of Fr. Marcos de Niza (1539) and Francisco Vázquez de Coronado (1540–1542) to explore New Mexico and verify Alvar Núñez Cabeza de Vaca's reports of cities there. The royal treasury in New Spain paid part of the expenses of these expeditions. Most of

Spanish explorer Francisco Vásquez de Coronado led a two-year search in North America for the legendary Seven Cities of Cibola in the 1540s. (Library of Congress)

the seventeenth-century explorations of New Spain's northern frontiers were paid for either by private interests prospecting for silver mines or by the Crown sponsoring missionary work; however, all had the permission of the Viceroy of Mexico. The viceroy also ordered and paid for the search for La Salle and Rodriguez Cabrillo's and Vizcaino's explorations along the California coast. In Chile, Pedro Valdivia acted as the royal governor when he sent Francisco de Ulloa and Francisco Cortés Hojea (1553) and Juan Fernández Labrillero and Cortés Hojea (1557) to explore the western entrances of the Straits of Magellan. In the eighteenth century, examples of explorations sent by royal officials pursuant to royal authorizations include Pedro Vial's pioneering trail from San Antonio, Texas, to Santa Fe, New Mexico (1786–1787), and Captain José de Zúñiga's trail from Santa Fe to Tucson. Most of the costs of these latter expeditions were borne by the royal treasury.

Expansion of the mission frontier during the seventeenth century was always under royal license and at royal expense; nevertheless, unauthorized exploration might precede it, and the soldiers who accompanied the friars often took trade goods for their private accounts. More commonly, missionaries ventured into new territories, exploring as they went, at the head of small, armed expeditions. Examples of such ventures include Fr. Eusebio Kino, who in 1663 led a mission into Arizona, and Fr. Juan María de Salvatierra's 1697 foray into Baja California. Gaspar de Portolá's 1769 expedition to establish the missions in California is yet another example, although the coastal geography of the area was well-known by then. And although these examples come from New Spain, similar expeditions moved the mission frontier onto the eastern slopes of the Andes in Ecuador, Peru, and what is now Bolivia.

Privately authorized and funded explorations were less common and confined to the early sixteenth century. Francisco Hernández de Córdoba and Juan de Grijalva, the pioneers of the Mexican coast in 1517–1518, sailed under orders of the governor of Cuba, who was pursuing his own program of exploration and conquest during the period. Alonso Álvarez de Pineda, the first European to circumnavigate and map the Gulf of Mexico (1519), did so under orders from Francisco de Garay, the royal governor of Jamaica. Lucas Vázquez de Ayllón gave Francisco Gordillo orders to go beyond the Bahama islands should he not find (as he did not) slaves there, with a resulting (re)discovery of southeastern North America (1521). Hernando Cortés sent a number of scouting expeditions along the shores of the Gulf of California in the 1520s, and he himself led an overland expedition from central New Spain to Honduras in 1526. His lieutenants pushed the frontiers of New Spain outward during the same period on Cortés's authority, rather than that of the Crown. Similarly, in the late 1530s Francisco Pizarro encouraged a number of his lieutenants to explore the eastern slopes of the Andes.

Finally, mention should be made of the scientific explorations of the eighteenth century. The first was organized by the French Academy of Sciences in 1735 to measure the length of the degree of latitude at the equator. It was led by French scientists Louis Godin, Pierre Bouguer, and Charles de la Condamine, and the Spaniards Antonio de Ulloa and Jorge Juan y Santacilia. Growing interest in classifying plants and discovering their potential economic value led to the botanical expeditions of Hipólito Ruiz, José Antonio Pavón y Jiménez, and Joseph Dombey to Peru in 1777; José Celestino Mutis to New Granada (central Colombia) in 1782; and Martin de Sessé y la Casta and José Mariano Mociño to New Spain in 1787–1803. From 1789 to 1792, Alejandro de Malaspina and Antonio de Pineda y Ramírez examined all kinds of natural phenomena along the west coast of South America and in the Philippines. But perhaps the most famous of the scientific explorers of the eighteenth century was Alexander von Humboldt, who roamed the Spanish Empire from 1799 to 1804 recording human, botanical, faunal, and mineral findings. The costs of these expeditions, with the exception of the first, were borne almost entirely by the Spanish Crown.

In sum, Spanish explorers of the Americas were a highly varied group, with diverse motivations, goals, and sources of funding. Collectively they revealed the coastlines of much of the Americas and provided rich details of many parts of the interiors of those continents. In the eighteenth century, Spanish scientific explorations added greatly to botanical knowledge and helped advance scientific knowledge of the Americas.

Paul E. Hoffman

References

Allan, John L., ed. *North American Exploration.* Vols. 1–2 of 3. Lincoln: University of Nebraska Press, 1997.

Cook, Warren L. *Flood Tide of Empire: Spain and the Pacific Northwest, 1543–1819.* New Haven, CT: Yale University Press, 1973.

Gillispie, Charles C., ed. *Dictionary of Scientific Biography.* 16 vols. New York: Scribner's Sons, 1970–1980.

Parry, John H. *The Discovery of South America.* New York: Taplinger, 1979.

Wagner, Henry R. *Spanish Voyages to the Northwest Coast of America in the Sixteenth Century.* San Francisco: California Historical Society, 1924.

Weber, David J. *The Spanish Frontier in North America.* New Haven, CT: Yale University Press, 1992.

See also: Borderlands; Capitulations of Santa Fe; Catholic Church in Spanish America; Colonists and Settlers I–VI; Conquest I–VII; Conquistadors; Encomienda; Jesuits—Iberia and America; Missions; Native Americans I–VIII; Religious Orders; Science and Scientists—Brazil/Portugal; Science and Scientists—Colonial Spanish America; Tordesillas, Treaty of; Travel and Tourism; Travel Literature—Colonial Spanish America; Travel Literature—Modern Spanish America.

FAMILIARES

Familiares were lay officials of the Spanish and Portuguese Inquisitions who assisted inquisitors in investigating and apprehending suspected heretics and in confiscating their property. They also accompanied condemned heretics in the infamous autos-da-fé. These familiares formed a network of inquisitional officials throughout the Iberian empires that extended to most of the important towns and villages.

Myths abound regarding the familiares, which are mostly erroneous carryovers from their function in the thirteenth century. Originally, they served as bodyguards for the medieval inquisitors general. In Spain, familiares were drawn from the young members of the Third Dominican order; they were called familiares because of their close association with the inquisitors. Historian Henry Charles Lea portrays these medieval familiares as a reckless and evil-minded social scourge who acted at will, protected by the cloak of inquisitional immunity. This dim portrayal may be appropriate for the medieval familiares, but, by the early modern period, things had changed significantly.

Familiares in both Spain and Portugal from the sixteenth to the nineteenth centuries were primarily laymen; few of them ever met the inquisitors general. Nonetheless, the title familiar remained, as did the inaccurate perception of them as ruthless spies and unprincipled bandits. The Inquisitions regulated their activities and even tried them for abusing their authority.

The Portuguese Inquisition did not officially recognize familiares until 1613. The 1640 *Regimento* (bylaws) required that familiares be Old Christians, persons of good behavior, of confidence, of known capacity, and of abundant living. The 1774 Regimento eliminated the purity-of-blood requirement. Spanish requirements were similar and included age (twenty-five years) and marriage requirements. Portugal never had these requirements, and many familiares were minors (under twenty-five) and unmarried; in fact, some were as young as ten years old.

All familiares underwent a costly and rigorous investigation into their ancestry and personal conduct before being appointed. They also enjoyed substantial privileges granted to them by the Iberian monarchs and the pope. These privileges included exemption from certain taxes and forced military service, the right to bear offensive and defensive weapons, and the right to private adjudication in both civil and criminal cases. They also wore habits displaying the crusader's cross and a golden medallion with the coat-of-arms of the Inquisition.

The Spanish tribunals placed limits, or quotas, on the number of familiares permitted in a given town or city. The Portuguese tribunals never limited the number of familiares, but Dom Pedro II limited the number of familiares who could enjoy inquisitional privilege in Portugal in 1693 and in Brazil in 1720. These familiares came to be known as *familiares do número* (familiares of the number).

The familiares and other officials also created corporate bodies, such as a brotherhood to celebrate the cult of Saint Peter Martyr, and in Portugal and Brazil, militia companies called the *Companhias dos Familiares* were formed.

In Spain, nobles formed an important segment of the familiares, but most of the familiares were peasant farmers and merchants. In Spanish America, familiares were often nobles and merchants, although some Indians were also appointed. In Portugal and Brazil, familiares came from a broad social base including merchants, agriculturists, and artisans.

James E. Wadsworth

References

Bethencourt, Francisco. *História das Inquisições: Portugal, Espanha, e Itália.* Lisbon: Temas e Debates, 1996.

Lea, Henry Charles. *A History of the Inquisition of Spain.* 4 vols. New York: Macmillan, 1922.

———. *A History of the Inquisition of the Middle Ages.* 3 vols. New York: Macmillan, 1922.

Veiga Torres, José. "Da repressão religiosa para a promoção social: A Inquisição como instância legitimadora da promoção social da burguesia mercantil." *Revista Crítica de Ciências Sociais* 4 (October 1994): 109–135.

Wadsworth, James E. "Agents of Orthodoxy: Inquisitional Power and Prestige in Colonial Pernambuco, Brazil." Ph.D. dissertation, University of Arizona, 2002.

See also: Brazil; Catholic Church in Brazil; Catholic Church in Spanish America; Clergy—Secular, in Colonial Spanish America; Comissários; Confraternities; Diabolism in the New World; Donatary Captaincies; Idolatry, Extirpation of; Inquisition—Luso-America; Inquisition—Spanish America; Jesuits—Iberia and America; Monarchs of Portugal; Monarchs of Spain; Papacy; Race; Religious Orders.

FAMILY—COLONIAL BRAZIL

The teachings of the Catholic Church and the Portuguese laws of marriage and inheritance, combined with economic development patterns, created the colonial Brazilian family. The ways that families were organized, the values they held, the roles they defined for men and women, and the power that family leaders held over land, capital, and labor profoundly influenced all in the colony. However, there was not one dominant family type in colonial Brazil. Instead, there were several.

The first families in Brazil were those of the indigenous Tupi, Guaraní, Gê, and Arawak peoples. Along the coast, where the Tupi-Guarani-speaking peoples lived, family life was enmeshed in tribal society. Groups of related kin lived in large multifamily longhouses (*malocas*), presided over by a headman. Several such longhouses clustered together around a central space, the whole surrounded by a palisade, forming a village. Prominent men had several wives, and much of their power derived from their extensive group of descendants. Outsiders were often incorporated into the village through marriage; for example, a headman or a chief might arrange a marriage of a daughter to a desirable outsider male, so that the man would become a son-in-law. Children were reared with clearly specified gender roles: Boys were taught to become hunters, fishermen, and warriors. Girls were raised to become agriculturalists, responsible for planting small fields of corn, beans, and manioc roots; preparing food and drink; and bearing and raising children.

When the first Europeans arrived in Brazil in the first years of the sixteenth century, a Portuguese Catholic family did not automatically transfer to Brazil. Instead, European men incorporated themselves into extant indigenous family patterns. One such man was Diogo Álvares Correia, known also by the Indian name Caramuru, who lived in the region of the Bay of All Saints. Caramuru married a daughter of a prominent chief, and through this alliance he became an important intermediary between Tupi Indians and Portuguese merchants seeking brazilwood. As more European men came to Brazil with the advent of colonies, the European Catholic model of family life still remained an ideal but not a reality. When the first Jesuits arrived in Brazil in 1549, they were shocked by the fact that European men preferred multiple women, in the fashion of prominent Indian headmen and chiefs. Because Indian slavery had become pervasive, many European men lived in concubinage with their female slaves. Only when the European population grew, and in particular as more European women arrived in Brazil and the institutions of the Catholic Church became established, did a Portuguese Catholic family pattern begin to emerge in Brazil.

Sugar became the economic focus of Brazil by the last decades of the sixteenth century. An elite of sugar mill owners (*senhores de engenho*) and sugar farmers (*lavradores de cana*) formed, and their families became extremely influential in the sugar-planting regions of northeastern Brazil. Families of slaveholders elsewhere in Brazil later reflected many of these same characteristics. Elite families of slaveholders took on distinct characteristics. Large in size and hierarchical in structure, these elite families included not only the immediate nuclear family, but dependent kin, servants, and slaves. Women in these families are often assumed to have played subordinate roles, but Portuguese inheritance and marriage law gave women specific rights to the family property. Men of these families fathered many illegitimate children by slave and free poor women. Some of these children were recognized by their fathers; others were not. Although the work of Gilberto Freyre led many to accept this elite family model as normative, much research documents the fact that the majority of the population in colonial Brazil did not live in such families.

The families of the free poor population were the most numerous in colonial Brazil. These were families that did not own slaves and therefore depended on family members for labor. Typically, free poor families were formed by simple families (parents and children) but occasionally extended to include dependent kin, a servant, or an occasional slave. These families primarily were subsistence farmers (*roçeiros*) who grew corn, beans, and manioc roots; grazed domestic animals; and harvested small amounts of cash crops such as tobacco, sugar, or cotton for sale in local markets. In these families, the labor of all was crucial: men and women, girls and boys all worked in the fields and in the preparation and storage of food. These families planted on the fringes of established agricultural regions, and they were among the first to settle new frontiers. These families were often multiethnic and multiracial. The ranks of the free poor included poor Portuguese colonists, mixed-race Indian and Portuguese *mamelucos,* mixed-race African and Portuguese mulattoes, and freed slaves. Illegitimacy rates could be very high, in part because these families lived outside of the reach of parish priests. Female-headed households were also common, particularly in town centers and in declining agricultural regions.

The slave family had its own unique character. Slavery became established early in Brazil, with the enslavement of Indians. Subsequently, a slave trade with Africa developed, and by the last decades of the sixteenth century, a sizable population of African slaves lived in the sugar regions. Over the seventeenth and eighteenth centuries, the slave trade increased substantially, bringing hundreds of thousands of African men, women, and children to Brazil. Slavery forever altered African family patterns, but while slavery placed many limitations on family life, it did not prevent slave families from forming. In conjunction with the Catholic Church, slavery shaped the character of the slave family in Brazil. The slave trade created a highly unbalanced ratio of men to women in the slave population. The dominance of male slaves, especially on new plantations or in newly developing regions, meant that it was difficult for slave families to form. However, as sex ratios equalized, slaves married and created families on agricultural estates. Not only did African slaves marry other African slaves, but marriages between Africans and Indians, and between slaves and the free poor, occurred. Slave marriages were celebrated by local priests, many of whom also baptized slave children. Illegitimacy rates were high, and within the baptismal registers many slave children had their father's name listed as "unknown." Slave families were vulnerable to events in the life course of the master, particularly death and inheritance. At the death of the master, slaves often found themselves sold. This broke up slave families. However, inheritance also offered a time when slaves might receive their freedom, either through a bequest in their master's will or the opportunity to purchase their own freedom or that of their kin, for the assessed value recorded in the estate inventory. Over time, rates of manumission in Brazil were such that a population of freed slaves gradually formed; these former slaves found themselves part of the free poor population with greater control over their family lives.

Ideally, the Catholic Church presided over the key moments in family life: birth was followed by the sacrament of baptism, the sacrament of marriage accompanied procreation, and death followed the sacrament of final unction. But there were too few local parish priests to minister to the growing population in Brazil, particularly in frontier regions and in the port cities. In established parishes, priests ensured that baptism and marriage brought important social as well as religious connections. At baptism, a baby had two godparents present, who could be important patrons for the child throughout his or her life. Similarly, at marriage, marriage sponsors supported the bride and groom, creating another significant social bond.

The *Ordenações Filipinas* codified Portuguese law in 1603 and established clear procedures that governed marriage and inheritance in Brazil. These laws gave the aristocracy of Portugal special rights and privileges that diminished the fragmentation of property each generation. Members of the nobility could establish *morgados* (entailed property) that passed undivided to the oldest male heir each generation. However, the laws of inheritance for ordinary people stipulated that the family property be divided equally between all children of each generation. The laws of marriage allowed the nobility to sign marriage contracts, which established how property was to be owned during the marriage. A bride's *dote* (dowry) was reciprocated by the groom's presentation of an *arras* (bride gift). But common people married by a *carta de ametade* (charter of halves) that made husbands and wives the equal co-owners of the property. Whatever property they accumulated within their marriage was considered to be community property, that is, half belonged to the husband and half to the wife.

The dominant marriage and family pattern transferred to Brazil was that of the Portuguese common man, the *lavrador* (farmer), and not that of the Portuguese nobleman *(fidalgo)*. Few morgados were established in Brazil, and the dominant inheritance pattern in Brazil, even among the elite, was the equal division of property among children. Marriage by contract was not common in Brazil, except among the very rich. The typical form of marriage in Brazil followed the rules laid down for community property. This community property was passed in equal shares to the children after the deaths of the parents. After the death of the first parent, one-half of the community property passed to the adult children. The surviving spouse managed the remaining half of the family property, as well as the shares of the minor children. In the event that the surviving spouse was a woman, the law required a *tutor* (trustee) to be appointed to oversee the property of the minor children, which placed limits on what the widow might do. After the death of the surviving spouse, the remaining half of the community property passed to the adult children. When a bride received a dowry at marriage, it was considered to be an advance on her future inheritance from her parents.

The law paid particular attention to the rights of illegitimate children. According to law, the children of an unmarried man or woman were considered *naturais* (natural), and therefore were entitled to inherit an equal share of their parents' property, even if one or both parents had married and had children from their marriages. Any children born out of wedlock to a married man or woman, or to a priest, however, did not have a right to an equal share of the property. These children might only receive simple, charitable bequests from wills.

It is important to recognize that the gap between law and practice was considerable in colonial Brazil, particularly in the sixteenth and seventeenth centuries. The survival of key economic assets, such as sugar plantations and mills, cattle ranches, tobacco farms, and merchant trading companies, depended on crucial moments in the lives of families, such as marriage and death. Then, the laws of marriage and inheritance placed considerable strain on family businesses; as a result, elite families developed strategies to counteract their full effect. Large marriage dowries that far exceeded a daughter's fair share of the family property attracted desirable sons-in-law, particularly from Portugal, for the family business. Not all daughters married; some unmarried daughters continued to live at home, where they cared for parents and elderly kin. Others entered convents, where a few became managers of considerable financial assets. Sons often migrated out of their natal communities and became an important force in the settlement of the Brazilian frontier. Other heirs experienced downward social mobility. Strategies of elite families profoundly affected the lives of the free poor and of slaves. Natural children, who held full rights of inheritance, were often excluded, especially when their fathers subsequently married and had children from their marriages. The auctioning of slaves at inheritance could break apart slave families, depending on how properties were evaluated and divided. Over the course of the colonial period, but with regional variations, many of the deviations from inheritance law began to be corrected by probate judges. The size of dowries began to be limited, and the rights of natural children recognized. As a result, the numbers of free poor families increased. Still, the booming slave trade and expanding agricultural frontiers precluded any demise of the powerful elite family.

Alida C. Metcalf

References

Freyre, Gilberto. *The Masters and the Slaves (Casa-grande and senzala): A Study in the Development of Brazilian Civilization.* Translated by Samuel Putnam. New York: Knopf, 1956.

Gudeman, Stephen, and Stuart B. Schwartz. "Cleansing Original Sin: Godparentage and the Baptism of Slaves in Eighteenth-Century Bahia." Pp. 35–58 in *Kinship Ideology and Practice in Latin America,* edited by Raymond T. Smith. Chapel Hill: University of North Carolina Press, 1984.

Metcalf, Alida C. *Family and Frontier in Colonial Brazil: Santana de Parnaíba, 1580–1822.* Berkeley and Los Angeles: University of California Press, 1992.

Nazzari, Muriel. *Disappearance of the Dowry: Women, Families, and Social Change in São Paulo, Brazil, 1600–1900.* Stanford, CA: Stanford University Press, 1991.

Ramos, Donald. "From Minho to Minas: The Portuguese Roots of the Mineiro Family." *Hispanic American Historical Review* 73 (1993): 639–662.

See also: Brazil; Catholic Church in Brazil; Childhood in Colonial Latin America; Dyes and Dyewood; Engenho; Native Americans II—Brazil; Slave Rebellions—Brazil; Slavery I—Brazil; Sugar; Women—Brazil.

FAMILY—COLONIAL SPANISH AMERICA

Family models of different types existed in colonial Spanish America. The various family types that developed after conquest were the result of the encounter between indigenous, Iberian, and African kinship systems, where the Catholic and Iberian model was the dominant; not surprisingly, it was the one that the Spanish monarchy and the Church sought to instill.

Preconquest societies in the Americas had widely different kinship systems, although our knowledge of them is still scanty. Pre-Columbian societies frequently classified relatives according to systems fundamentally different from Iberian models. Indeed, the very term *family* had no accurate corresponding terms in many native languages, whereas specific kinship terms such as *father* or *sister-in-law* could not always be translated precisely to native tongues. This, in turn, led missionaries, priests, and civil authorities to serious misunderstandings when describing Indian kinship systems and made them believe that most native societies were corrupt, incestuous, and licentious. Their errors of interpretation still make study of precontact and early colonial societies difficult. It is known, however, that matrilineal descent was common among many pre-Columbian societies. In these communities, each individual traced his or her ancestry through the maternal line; children belonged to the lineage of the mother, which also implied that children often belonged to the territory and clan of the mother, even if they resided elsewhere.

Pre-Columbian marriage patterns could be of many types, and could vary within each community. The Mexica (Aztecs), for instance, had a formalized marriage ritual, but the consensual unions that preceded them and the marriages themselves both were dissolvable. Marriages were commonly arranged but not necessarily by parents, who, given the high mortality rate, were often dead by the time children reached puberty. In Mexico, as with many places in the Americas, matchmaking was a community affair, in which relatives, community members, political leaders, and even astrologers took part. During the pre-Hispanic period, men and women alike appear to have married early, between the ages of fifteen and twenty. Polygamy was also common among many societies and particularly among the nobility of the most highly stratified pre-Columbian societies.

Spanish clergy and civil authorities sought to implant Catholic family norms among the neophytes, which meant eradicating polygamy, forcing the native population to register their unions, teaching them that marriages were permanent and that extramarital sex was a sin, preventing arranged marriages that were against the will of the future spouses, and promoting the system of patrilineal descent. One of the great puzzles of the Spanish conquest is the general and swift success of these fundamental modifications in the basic social structures of indigenous society. In the central areas of Spanish America, where Indian communities were reorganized into *pueblos de indios,* the native inhabitants in general conformed to many of these ideals within a generation or two after conquest. Indeed, throughout the colonial period, the village-dwelling Indians displayed the most orderly practices of family formation from the perspective of the Church. Illegitimacy rates among Indians in pueblos were low compared to all other groups; most Indians married legitimately and at an earlier age than most other groups. Admittedly, the polygamy of the nobles proved more difficult to uproot, and matrilineal descent continued to have great importance centuries after the conquest where this principle had been the rule before the arrival of the Spanish. Furthermore, change was slower on the fringes of the Spanish American empire, and many groups in the frontier zones of northern Mexico and in the lowlands of South America were never completely drawn into the Spanish system of family organization.

Regarding the Hispanic population, Iberian family practices were not automatically transferred from Spain to the Americas. Although norms continued to emphasize the importance of the nuclear family and monogamous relationships between Catholic believers, marriage practices in Spanish America deviated in important aspects from those of the peninsula. Owing largely, it seems, to demographic and economic factors particular to the Americas, illegitimacy rates among the elites were far higher in the colonies than they ever had been in Spain. Spanish males were expected to marry their social equals in order to preserve the status of their lineage, but because of the unbalanced sex ratio of immigrants to Spanish America, there was a scarcity of available unmarried Spanish females in the Americas. This implied that males generally married at a later age in the Americas than in Europe; that most Spanish men ended up marrying Indian, African, or mixed-race women; and that many did not contract formal marriages at all. Spanish men who succeeded in marrying peninsular women, or women of Spanish descent, were normally wealthier and of higher social status than those who married non-Spanish women, but they frequently had so-called natural children with partners of an inferior social status. Spanish males, then, often presided over two or more sets of families, sometimes grouped together in the same household. The social status of the women and children in these households depended in part on their legitimacy. Although the Crown discouraged men from emigrating to the Americas without their wives, many Spanish men had a legal family in the peninsula and one or several consensual unions in the colonies.

The extended family could be of utmost importance for the elites in cementing political and commercial alliances. Despite the fact that colonial legislation prohibited men from holding high administrative posts in areas in which they were born or had relatives, in practice these rules were often circumvented. Patronage and clientilism permeated the family, especially the extended family networks of the wealthy. Material concerns evidently played an important role in the formation and working of the colonial family, even though the Church insisted that marriages should be the result of the spontaneous and free will of the couples. Spanish laws stipulated that inheritances should be divided equally between legitimate heirs, and custom dictated that natural children should be provided for, although not as generously as the legitimate family. In order to keep property intact, wealthy Creoles and peninsulars sought to establish *mayorazgos* (entails), but this institution was beyond the means of most provincial elites. Recently arrived peninsular merchants often avoided formal marriages altogether in order to keep their properties undivided. A normal arrangement among them was to invite nephews or other young male relatives from Spain to come as apprentices and serve in the business, and eventually arrange a marriage with socially prominent local elites for them. Elite households were normally considerably larger than Indian or lower-class Hispanic households, as the elite households frequently included servants and domestic slaves in addition to the nuclear family and at times more distant relatives.

Elites often dismissed the family arrangements of the great majority of the population as disorderly and immoral. Mixed-race plebeians, especially in the large cities of Spanish America, seem to have had a casual attitude toward the sacrament of marriage. Illegitimacy rates of over 50 percent were common, but many of the children whose baptisms were registered as illegitimate were born to parents who lived in permanent consensual unions and who themselves may not have felt that their union was contrary to religion. Plebeian households were normally much smaller than those of the elites. In some places female-headed households were the norm, although this was not generally the rule for Spanish America as a whole and was probably less widespread than what contemporary elites as well as some subsequent historians imagined.

The family structure and relations of slaves in colonial Spanish America are still topics that need further study. Even though there are examples of fugitive slave communities in the early colonial period whose kinship organizations seem to have represented a continuation of African patterns, with time the great majority of slaves in Spanish America were born and raised in the New World. They were socialized into a Catholic cultural context that placed great emphasis on marriage and belonging to a family. However, for slaves it was difficult to get married and problematic to keep families together. Female slaves, especially domestic servants, were prized sexual objects for owners. Slave families risked being sold individually rather than together; in fact, several slave revolts occurred precisely as a reaction to this threat. Overall, urban slaves had a greater chance of forming their own families and saving money to buy their own freedom. However, even among the relatively privileged slaves, formal marriage was infrequent and family life intrinsically unstable.

Steinar Sæther

References

Almécija, Juan. *La familia en la provincia de Caracas.* Madrid: Mapfre, 1992.

Hunefeldt, Christine. *Paying the Price of Freedom: Family and Labor among Lima's Slaves, 1800–1854.* Berkeley and Los Angeles: University of California Press, 1994.

Lavrín, Asunción, ed. *Sexuality and Marriage in Colonial Spanish America.* Lincoln: University of Nebraska Press, 1989.

Lockhart, James. *The Nahuas after the Conquest: A Social and Cultural History of the Indians of Central Mexico, Sixteenth through Eighteenth Centuries.* Stanford, CA: Stanford University Press, 1992.

Rodríguez, Pablo. *Sentimientos y vida familiar en el nuevo reino de Granada.* Bogotá: Editorial Ariel, 1997.

See also: Bigamy, Transatlantic; Catholic Church in Brazil; Catholic Church in Spanish America; Children in Colonial Spainish America; Cimarrones; Clergy—Secular; Clothing in Colonial Spanish America; Creoles; Family—Colonial Brazil; Laws—Colonial Latin America; Marriage; Migration—From Iberia to the New World; Native Americans I–VIII; Palenque; Poverty; Race; Religious Orders; Slavery I–IV; Syncretism; Women—Colonial Spanish America.

FICTION—PORTUGAL AND THE UNITED STATES

Although there was some Portuguese presence in North America well before the American Revolution, the Portuguese did not immigrate to the United States in appreciable numbers until the nineteenth century, becoming what some have called the nation's "silent minority." Paralleling the lack of an identifiable Portuguese voice in U.S politics and culture has been the relative Portuguese silence in the literary realm. Only in recent generations have Portuguese voices, if only in modest numbers, been heard.

Conceived broadly, the rubric "Luso-U.S. Fiction" will enable a consideration of the fiction of John Philip Sousa, John Dos Passos, Frank X. Gaspar, Katherine Vaz, Charles Reis Felix, Art Cuelho (Coelho), Alfred Lewis, Joseph M. Faria, José Rodrigues Miguéis, Onésimo Teotónio Almeida, José Francisco Costa, José Brites,

Caetano Valadão Serpa, Manuel Ferreira Duarte, and Urbino de San-Payo. The first six are U.S.-born Luso-descendants. The last nine are immigrants, six of them from the Azores and three from continental Portugal. The fiction of the first eight is written in English, that of the other seven in Portuguese.

Sousa and Dos Passos are included because they are Portuguese descendants—in Sousa's case, his father (possibly an Azorean), and in Dos Passos's case, his grandfather (a Madeiran). Neither Sousa nor Dos Passos writes about the experiences of Portuguese Americans. Sousa, who is almost exclusively known for his music (though he once identified himself as "Composer, Novelist, Conductor of Sousa Band"), was the author of two novels and a novella, *The Fifth String* (1902). His novella tells a version of the Faust myth in an American setting and was his first published work of fiction. *Pipetown Sandy* (1905), his engaging first novel, falls within the tradition of earlier American boyhood fiction, best exemplified by Thomas Bailey Aldrich's *The Story of a Bad Boy,* Mark Twain's *The Adventures of Tom Sawyer* and *Adventures of Huckleberry Finn,* and Stephen Crane's *Whilomville Stories.* His third (and last) novel, *The Transit of Venus* (1920), has for its principal setting an ocean liner. Sousa, who always insisted on his American patriotism, never discussed his Portuguese origins, though he was always happy to talk about his German mother.

Dos Passos, once considered one of the three or four most important post–World War I writers in the United States, is best known for his inventive narratives and structural innovations. But like Sousa, his fiction is largely void of references to the experiences of Portuguese Americans. In his most famous work, the trilogy under the collective title *U.S.A.,* there are just two brief references in the first volume, *The 42nd Parallel* (1930), one to the father of one of the characters, who spoke Portuguese, and another to the presence of some "Portagees," who are listed along with members of other national groups. In his last years, Dos Passos turned to Portuguese history, publishing *The Portugal Story: Three Centuries of Exploration and Discovery* (1969), a celebratory account that falls somewhat short of dealing with Portuguese emigration to the United States.

Born in the Azores (on the island of Flores), Alfred Lewis immigrated to the United States when he was a child; he ultimately became a successful businessman in California. As a poet, Lewis wrote in both both Portuguese and English, but as a writer of fiction, he limited himself to English. The author of several short stories, in which he appears to disguise his characters as Latinos, his sole published novel, *Home Is an Island* (1951), is a lightly fictionalized account of his life on the island of Flores until the moment of his departure, full of hopes, dreams, and fears, for the United States. Lewis's novel was praised for its tender evocation of the author's exotic home and generally effective emotive style. "Lewis' style is most refreshing," wrote a reviewer for the *New York Times.* "Some of his descriptive passages, in the pellucid simplicity and rich imagery, ring with the lyricism of poetry." At his death in 1977 he left several novels in manuscript. *The Land Is Here* is a continuation of the life of the hero of his published novel. A second unpublished novel, *Sixty Acres and a Barn,* which deals with the vicissitudes and triumphs of a Portuguese immigrant in the

John Dos Passos wrote fiction and history that lionized the rights of the individual against the corruptions of capitalism and war. The radical structure of his three-part U.S.A. *earned it praise as one of the most ambitious American novels of the twentieth century. (National Archives)*

dairy country of the San Joaquin Valley, is scheduled for publication. Other manuscripts, *Rockville,* a work of science fiction; *The Mark of the Trespasser,* which deals with illegal immigration from Mexico; and *A Ship Full of Corn,* which returns to the island setting of his first novel, remain unpublished.

Born in New Bedford, Massachusetts, Charles Reis Felix has lived in California for the past sixty years. He is the author of two autobiographical volumes, *Crossing the Sauer,* which follows his military service in Europe during World War II, and *Through a Portagee Gate* (2004), an account of his own life and his father's during the 1920s and 1930s in New Bedford. Reis is also the author of an as-yet-unpublished novel about growing up as a Portuguese American in New Bedford, Massachusetts. This novel of comic realism is titled *Da Gama, Cary Grant, and the Election of 1934.* Like Gaspar's *Leaving Pico,* Reis's novel is also a novel about a boy's initiation, with an emphasis on local politics.

Frank X. Gaspar's one novel, *Leaving Pico* (1999), tells the adventures of a young Portuguese American boy growing up in Provincetown, Massachusetts—very much a Portuguese town. Best known for his poetry (much of it dealing with Portuguese American themes and characters), Gaspar wrote a fine novel of initiation that, like Sousa's *Pipetown Sandy,* is in the best tradition of the American boy novel. The book is replete with Portuguese Americans (both from the Azores and from the Continent) living and working among Anglos, especially summer people. In a narrative within the narrative, the boy's grandfather tells a story (missing in the historical accounts) of the primacy of the Portuguese in the discovery of America, a story that is finally finished by the boy himself.

Katherine Vaz, a native of California of Azorean descent on her father's side, is the author of two novels and a collection of short stories. *Saudade* (1994), her well-received first novel, takes its title from that quality of almost free-standing longing that the Portuguese insist is indefinable or, at least, untranslatable. The novel deals with a young blind woman's experiences on her father's native island in the Azores. In what has become a strong characteristic of her fiction, Vaz incorporates lore and legend about life in the Azores, some of which reads like a lightly fictionalized travel account. Her second work of fiction, the collection of a dozen Portuguese American stories under the title *Fado and Other Stories* (1997), won the Drue Heinz Literature

Prize. Some of Vaz's strongest writing appears here, in stories such as "My Hunt for King Sebastian" and "Original Sin." Her second novel, *Mariana* (1997), was first published in London; then, in Portuguese translation, in Lisbon; and finally (and only recently—2003) in the United States. It dramatizes in wonderfully imagined detail the quotidian life of Mariana Alcoforado, the seventeenth-century nun from Beja, Portugal, who is, putatively, the author of the famous (and notorious) *Lettres portugaises.*

Art Cuelho, descended from Azoreans transplanted to California, now lives in Montana. A prolific poet, editor, and publisher of Seven Buffalo Press, he has published chapbooks of his own poetry and fiction as well as contributions to journals. The author of *Fresno County Tales* (1979), he has in recent years written a good deal about his Azorean heritage.

In the Portuguese-speaking world, José Rodrigues Miguéis is widely considered to be one of the most influential writers of Portuguese fiction in the twentieth century. Emigrating to the United States from Lisbon in 1935, when he was thirty-three years old, he spent most of his life in New York City, where he died, at the age of eighty, in 1982.

Miguéis's experience as a Portuguese exile living among Portuguese Americans is reflected in some of his best short stories—all of them written in Portuguese. Among them one might call attention to "O viajante clandestino" (translated as "The Stowaway's Christmas"), "Beleza orgulhosa" ("Proud Beauty"), "A inauguração" ("The Inauguration"), "O natal do Dr. Crosby" ("Dr. Crosby's Christmas"), "Pouca sorte com barbeiros" ("Poor Luck with Barbers"), and "O cosme de Riba-Douro" ("Cosme from Riba-Douro")—this last title being the story of a Portuguese immigrant who loses his life as an enlisted man in the American army during World War II. However, his most fully realized work of Portuguese-American literature is his *Um homen sorri à morte com meia cara* (A Man Smiles at Death with Half a Face) (1958), a chilling, if finally uplifting, account of his near-fatal illness and internment as a ward patient in Bellevue Hospital in the 1940s.

Onésimo Teotónio Almeida, José Francisco Costa, José Brites, Urbino de San-Payo, and Joseph M. Faria are all immigrants to the United States. Writers of short fiction, the first four write in Portuguese, the fifth in English. In *(Sapa)teia americana* (The American Snare), published in 1983, Almeida offers twenty narratives centering on Portuguese-American experiences in southeastern New England. His stories deal with the ideals and realities native to both the transplanted and the rootless, as they struggle with the English language, suffer the incurable *saudades* (a feeling of loneliness and nostalgia for things lost or left behind) of the self-exile, and scramble for that siren-like creature, money. Almeida is also the author of *Ah! Mònim dum corisco!* (Money! You Scoundrel). Published in 1978, this play is composed of interconnected incidents focusing on the difficulties of the Portuguese immigrant with school, work, authority, and language. A story like "O imperfeito do conjuntivo" ("Future Imperfect") from *(Sapa)teia americana* delves deeply and nonjudgmentally into a young woman's agonies in deciding to have an abortion. The final story of the collection, "O(s) Adriano(s)" ("Adrian, All the Adrians"), employs a multiple perspective to tell a classic case of a child's manipulation, accommodation, and acculturation in a country that is both his and not his—the fate of the Portuguese-American child, whether immigrant or firstborn—as he unfolds to the narrator both himself and his world.

The Azorean American stories in José Francisco Costa's *Mar e tudo* (1998) evoke a strong, wistful, and (at times) pained sense of a "past" place (the island of São Miguel) that is now the "lost" place of dream and hope. These are balanced by a clutch of stories, like "School Bus" and "Segundo Shift," that realize not only the pain of emigration (leaving) but that of immigration (arriving and staying) as well. The poignant story of those familiars left behind when someone emigrates is especially well told in "Fio do tempo" ("The Thread of Time").

The author of several volumes of poetry writing, José Brites also has written some highly autobiographical fiction. Some of his best fiction appears in *Imigramantes* (1984). The title, a coinage, combines a form of the word *grammar* (suffer or undergo) with the word *immigrants.* Most of these stories look to experiences in Portugal and elsewhere, but a typical story of the immigrant's experience in the United States is "Frankamente Francisco" ("Frankly Francisco"), a story of the repressed anger and frustration of an immigrant on what turns out to be his last day working for an American boss of Portuguese descent. Brites also published a novella, *Do ribatejo ao Além-Tejo* (From the Ribatejo to beyond the Tejo) (1998), and the novel *De casa para o inferno* (From Home to the Inferno) (1999).

Since emigrating over thirty years ago, Urbino de San-Payo has lived in California. Among his publications is *A América segundo S. Lucas* (1988), an epistolary novella. In these imagined letters to his wife back in Portugal, an immigrant employed in domestic service writes back with his complaints and observations. Employing the colloquialisms of daily speech and the so-called *portinglesismos* (a mixture of new words and new pronunciations) of his fellow immigrants, San-Payo provides a rich picture of Luso-American life in north Los Angeles.

Caetano Valadão Serpa's work dramatizes the sociology of immigration and the psychology of those who emigrate. In *Guiomar* (1991), he tells the story of a large family from the island of Flores largely through the consciousness of the mother, and in *Gente sem nome* (Anonymous People) (1994), he employs the device of the lightly fictionalized sketch to create, among immigrants in Massachusetts, a taxonomy of sociological types, such as the son of a fisherman and the children of divorce.

Born on the island of Pico, Manuel Ferreira Duarte has spent most of his life in California. In his work, *A banda nova e outras histórias* (The New Band and Other Stories) (1991), an entire community of immigrants is revealed in the incidents and conversations surrounding the recruitment of musicians to form a "new" band to rival the existing "old" one.

Joseph M. Faria was born on the island of Saint Michael but was brought to the United States at the age of nine months. His book of short stories, *From a Distance* (1998), organized on the model of Ernest Hemingway's *In Our Times,* with sketches intercalated so as to separate the stories, gets its impetus from the author's attempts to discover something of the life he would have lived had he never left his island. "White Elephants," with its title borrowing the central image of one of Hemingway's best-known stories, is something of a quasi-fantasy about sex with his married cousin, in which the earth does not move but they talk about it.

The corpus of fiction written by Portuguese immigrants or the descendants of those immigrants is worthy of note. Its themes are the familiar themes of immigrant and ethnic literature—hardship endured in an attempt to make a new life in a strange land, the battle to keep acculturation at bay, and the ultimate discovery of distant roots. Collectively, Luso-U.S. fiction has a voice that can be described as one of unobtrusive pride, the celebration of surviving traditions and customs, and, of course, a memorialization of loss and recovery. Moreover, although the numbers are modest, today more and generally better-written fiction is being published by Luso-Americans than ever before.

George Monteiro

References

Almeida, Onésimo T. "Two Decades of Luso-American Literature: An Overview." Pp. 231–253 in *Global Impact of the Portuguese Languages,* edited by Asela Rodriguez de Laguna. New Brunswick, NJ: Transaction, 2001.

Baden, Nancy T. "Portuguese-American Literature: Does It Exist?" *MELUS* no. 6 (Summer 1979): 15–31.

Monteiro, George. "'The Poor, Shiftless, Lazy Azoreans': American Literary Attitudes toward the Portuguese." Pp. 166–197 in *Proceedings of the Fourth National Portuguese Conference: The International Year of the Child.* Providence, RI: Multilingual Multicultural Resource and Training Center, 1979.

Pap, Leo. "Portuguese-American Literature." Pp. 183–196 in *Ethnic Perspectives in American Literature: A Source Book,* edited by Robert J. Di Pietro and Edward Ifkovic. New York: Modern Language Association of America, 1983.

Rogers, Francis M. "The Contribution by Americans of Portuguese Descent in the U.S. Literary Scene." Pp. 409–432 in *Ethnic Literature since 1776: The Many Voices of America, Proceedings of the Comparative Literature Symposium Texas Tech University,* Vol. IX, Part II. Lubbock: Texas Tech University Press, 1978.

See also: Art and Artists—Brazil; Culture; Fiction—Spanish America; Literary Relations—Portugal and the Americas; Literary Relations—Spain and the Americas; Music and Dance I–V; Poetry—Brazil; Poetry—Modern Spanish America; Popular Festivals.

FICTION—SPANISH AMERICA

Spanish American fiction has enjoyed a vigorous relationship with Spain. Early in the colonial period, Spain banned the publication of fiction in its American colonies; more than 400 years later, Spain provided Spanish American novelists with important publishing opportunities.

A royal decree issued in 1531 prohibited the publication of fiction in the colonies. Novels, it was feared, would corrupt the morality of women, youth, and indigenous peoples. This decree influenced the shape of Spanish American fiction from its inception. In order to sidestep the colonial censor, fiction had to be disguised as a different genre, such as history or autobiography. This often involved narrative acrobatics of the type that, in a later era, would become the hallmark of Spanish American novels. The kernel of the Spanish American novel's preoccupation with history can be traced to works such as *El carnero* (1638) by Juan Rodríguez Freile (1566–1640) of New Granada (Colombia and Venezuela), whose first eight chapters offer a conventionally reverent narrative of the Spanish conquest. The later chapters spin off into lurid fictional tales of the doings of prostitutes, witches, and murderers. The blending of history, fiction, and the fantastic presages central motifs of later Spanish American fiction. In *Infortunios de Alonso Ramírez* (1690) by Carlos de Sigüenza y Góngora (1645–1700) of Mexico City, a young man lives an adventurous seafaring life that enables him to tour Spain's possessions from the Caribbean to the Philippines to New Spain (Mexico). Sigüenza y Góngora succeeded in publishing this patently invented narrative by claiming that Alonso was a real boy whose life he had been commanded to record.

Spain's colonial policy rendered literary subterfuges such as these a necessary part of early Spanish American fictional narrative. The Spanish publishing industry, by contrast, filled the demand for literature. In the sixteenth and seventeenth centuries, much of the literature ordered from Spanish publishers by the readers of New Spain was in Latin; though the ban on local fiction persisted, Spanish literature, including fiction, entered the colonies unhindered. Yet in the eighteenth century, as the independence movements gathered force, Spain's influence among literary Spanish Americans was eclipsed by France, seen as the point of origin of the Enlightenment and a source of progressive and reformist ideas. In this regard, the Paris sojourn (1825–1830) of the Argentine poet, pamphleteer, and pioneering short story writer Esteban Echeverría (1805–1851), which introduced romanticism to Spanish America before its presence had begun to be felt in Spain, proved to be a harbinger of subsequent trends. Echeverría's short story "El matadero" (1840) played an important role in identifying all that was backward in Spanish America as emanating from Spain and all that was progressive and optimistic as coming from France. In "El matadero," the Argentine dictator Juan Manuel Rosas (1793–1877) and his followers are portrayed as uncouth thugs nostalgic for the era of Spanish colonialism. By contrast, the opponent of the dictatorship who is tortured to death at the story's conclusion is described by adjectives that link him to the ideals of the Enlightenment.

This binary view of the European cultural legacy meant that during the nineteenth century the quest for new forms of fictional narrative often bypassed Spain in favor of France. Young Spanish American prose writers read widely in French literature, usually ignored the literature of Spain, and, as the century progressed, longed to live in Paris. It is for this reason that the development of Spanish American fiction during the nineteenth century is frequently characterized as a series of delayed reactions to French literary "schools." One by one, major French movements such as romanticism, realism, and naturalism trooped through nineteenth-century Spanish American fiction. The influences were absorbed at different rates and in different ways in different parts of Spanish America, so that an inventory of the major novels of Spanish American romanticism would include such disparate works as *Amalia* (1851) by Argentina's José Mármol (1815–1871), *María* (1867) by Colombia's Jorge Isaacs (1837–1895), and *Cecilia Valdés* (1892) by Cuba's Cirilo Villaverde (1812–1894). The debt to France appeared in the context of the propagation of the view that Spanish American culture was being forged in the vortex of a struggle between "civilization and barbarism." The influential Argentine thinker Domingo Faustino Sarmiento proposed this duality in his work *Facundo: Civilización y barbarie* (1845), which analyzes the origins of the Rosas dictatorship. Conceiving culture in this dualistic way encouraged the idealization of France and the disparagement of Spain and its legacy.

In addition to learning from French models, many realists profited from a connection to Spain through the fascination with local customs, known as *costumbrismo.* Influenced by peninsular *costumbrista* writers such as Mesonero Romanos (1803–1882), Mariano José de Larra (1809–1837), and Estébanez Calderón (1799–1867), Spanish American writers from about 1850 onward wrote novels and sketches detailing the habits, vernacular speech, and local peccadillos of their native regions. A salient example appears in the novel *La gran aldea* (1884) by the Argentine writer Lucio Vicente López (1848–1894). Purportedly a study of the "customs" of Buenos Aires, *La gran aldea* laments the dilution of regional distinctness generated by the advent of modernity, evident in such events as the supplanting of the family-owned store by the modern business. The rise of costumbrismo appeared as a solution to the mismatch that plagued the effort to graft French literary models onto Spanish American reality. Much French realism, for example, several of the major novels of Honoré de Balzac (1799–1850), was urban, and until the late nineteenth century urban life did not play a major role in most Spanish American nations. The Chilean novelist Alberto Blest Gana (1829–1904) exemplified the dilemma of the Balzac-influenced realist at work in the more hierarchical Spanish American society. Blest Gana, who wrote of his debt to Balzac, experienced difficulty in telling tales of protagonists attempting to rise in society in a nation in which social mobility was an alien concept. His novels, *Martín Rivas* (1862) and *El ideal de un calavera* (1863), struggle with the tension between his influences and his native material. The Colombian Tomás Carrasquilla (1858–1940) wrote novels of the isolated provincial landowning class, such as *Frutos de mi tierra* (1896) and *La marquesa de Yolombó* (1926) that combined the influences of Spanish costumbrismo and French realism. Carrasquilla transcribes the particularities of rural life in often exhausting detail, yet refuses to idealize local traditions that confine his characters, particularly the women. The Peruvian novelist Clorinda Matto de Turner (1852–1909) pushed realism in the direction of confronting specifically Spanish American problems in *Aves sin nido* (1889), the first novel to focus on indigenous peoples in Spanish America. The naturalism of Émile Zola (1840–1902) also made its way to Spanish America, an influence particularly evident in the mining stories of Chile's Baldomero Lillo (1867–1923) collected in *Sub terra* (1904), in the violent and grotesque stories of the Uruguayan writer Horacio Quiroga (1878–1937), such as *Cuentos de amor, de locura y de muerte* (1917), and in the best-known novelist of the Mexican Revolution, Mariano Azuela (1873–1952), whose *Los de abajo* (1916) depicts characters acting out destinies predetermined by their environment.

In the late nineteenth century, prosperity among the new urban managerial classes lent renewed energy to Spanish America's intoxication with Paris. Many well-off Spanish Americans lived in Paris for part of the year. The Paris-based Guatemalan writer Enrique Gómez Carrillo (1873–1927) lifted praise of the French metropolis to new heights of extravagance in prose that was eagerly consumed by his Spanish American readership. The Spanish American expatriate community that thrived in Paris between the 1890s and the 1930s served as a salon where writers from different countries engaged in artistic debate. Spain's ignominious defeat in the Spanish-American War (1898), and the loss of the Philippines, Cuba, and Puerto Rico to the United States, meant that when the reaction against French influences did occur in fiction, it took the form of a deeper immersion in the particularities of Spanish American reality rather than a reclaiming of the peninsular heritage. In contrast to poetry, where a rapprochement with Spain took place, novelists turned inward; those based in Paris identified with French decadent writers such as Remy de Gourmont (1858–1915) or with André Breton (1896–1966) and the surrealists, who were in revolt against the French bourgeoisie. Novelists such as the Guatemalan Miguel Ángel Asturias (1899–1974), the Cuban Alejo Carpentier (1904–1980), and the Venezuelans Arturo Uslar Pietri (1906–2001) and Teresa de la Parra (1889–1936), all resident in Paris during the 1920s and 1930s, drew on the literary preoccupations of the French avant-garde to bring to life the cultures of nations where regional, indigenous, and African-derived elements formed an important part of the national culture. Novels such as Asturias's *El señor presidente* (1946) and *Hombres de maíz* (1948), Carpentier's *Ecue-yambo-o!* (1933) and *El reino de este mundo* (1949), Uslar Pietri's *Las lanzas coloradas* (1931), and de la Parra's *Memorias de Mamá Blanca* (1929) complemented novels written by authors resident in Spanish America, such as *La vorágine* (1924) by the Colombian José Eustasio Rivera (1889– 1928), *Don segundo sombra* (1926) by the Argentine Ricardo Güiraldes (1886– 1927), and *Doña Bárbara* (1929) and *Canaima* (1935) by the Venezuelan Rómulo Gallegos (1884–1969). Though their use of technical innovation varies widely, Spanish American landscape, local customs, and ethnic specificity acquire a talismanic force in all of these books. The background influence of Paris remained strong (Güiraldes chose to die there); Spain played a marginal role. Asturias and Carpentier each published an overlooked first book in Madrid, de la Parra studied and later died in Spain, and Gallegos went into exile in Spain from 1931 to 1935. Yet it was not until the 1960s that Spain regained a central role in debates surrounding Spanish American fiction.

During the Spanish Civil War (1936–1939) and the early years of Francisco Franco's dictatorship, Mexico City and Buenos Aires were the centers of Hispanic book production. In the 1960s, supported by measures taken by the Spanish government to ameliorate its international image, book production in Spain boomed at a time when all Spanish American nations except Cuba were experiencing a decline in publishing activity. This enabled Spanish publishers, led by Carlos Barral (1928–1989), to relaunch in Europe the publishing careers of writers such as Miguel Ángel Asturias and Alejo Carpentier, the Uruguayan Juan Carlos Onetti (1909–1994), and the Argentines Jorge Luis Borges (1899–1986), Julio Cortázar

(1914–1984), and Ernesto Sábato (1911–). Peninsular editions of these writers' works coincided with the publication in Spain of ambitious novels by young Spanish American writers such as the Peruvian Mario Vargas Llosa (1936–), whose *La ciudad y los perros* (1962) became one of the first Hispanic novels to benefit from modern promotional techniques. Success in Spain served as a springboard to translation and international publication. During the 1960s, Vargas Llosa, Cortázar, the Colombian Gabriel García Márquez (1927–) (who was published by Editorial Sudamericana in Buenos Aires), the Mexican Carlos Fuentes (1928–), and the Chilean José Donoso (1924–1996) became representatives of a movement known as the Boom, which combined daring literary technique with political engagement and aggressive commercial promotion. Many of these writers were represented by Barcelona's Carmen Balcells (1930–), the Hispanic world's most successful literary agent; for a short period in the late 1960s, nearly all of them lived in Barcelona. Their international success formed part of the rejuvenation of cultural exchange between Iberia and Spanish America that strengthened after the democratization of Spain and Portugal. In the 1990s, the Alfaguara Publishing Group, based in Madrid, took over as the prime conduit by which Spanish American writers reached the world. The collapse of the publishing industry (and, after the economic crisis of 2001, the market for books) in Argentina and the widespread pirating of books in the Andean countries have meant that, as younger Spanish American writers such as Rodrigo Rey Rosa (1958–) of Guatemala and Jaime Bayly (1965–) of Peru have stated, many contemporary Spanish American novelists receive their only secure royalty statements from Spain. This situation is certain to encourage greater literary cross-pollination between Spain and Spanish America in the future.

Stephen Henighan

References

Donoso, José. *The Boom in Spanish American Literature.* Translated by Gregory Kolovakos. New York: Columbia University Press, 1977.

Fleming, Leonor, ed. "Introducción." Pp. 11–88 in *El matadero/La cautiva,* by Esteban Echeverría. Madrid: Cátedra, 1995.

Franco, Jean. *Spanish American Literature since Independence.* London: Ernest Benn Limited/New York: Barnes and Noble, 1973.

Hart, Stephen M. *A Companion to Spanish-American Literature.* London: Tamesis, 1999.

Martin, Gerald. *Journeys through the Labyrinth: Latin American Fiction in the Twentieth Century.* London: Verso, 1989.

Santana, Mario. *Foreigners in the Homeland: The Spanish American New Novel in Spain, 1962–1974.* Lewisburg. PA: Bucknell University Press, 2000.

See also: Art and Artists—Colonial Spanish America; Censorship—Brazil; Censorship—Spanish America; Cinema; Enlightenment—Spanish America; Fiction—Portugal and the United States; Fin de Siècle; Independence I–VI; Languages; Literary Relations—Portugal and the Americas; Literary Relations—Spain and the Americas; Music and Dance I–V; Poetry—Modern Spanish America; Spanish-American War; Spanish Civil War and Latin America.

FIN DE SIÈCLE

The term *fin de siècle* means literally, "end of century." In cultural history, fin de siècle refers to the end of the nineteenth century and a corresponding sense of decline or decadence in Western civilization. During this period new ideas about subjectivity, art, popular culture, sexuality, technology, and urban life combined to challenge the prevailing middle-class faith in science, progress, and material prosperity. The result was often resignation in the face of unresolved moral and social dilemmas, especially among the intellectual and artistic elite. Perceived by some at the time as a form of social illness, in truth the fin de siècle outlook represented a temporary triumph of philosophical idealism and bohemian culture over mainstream society, as literature and popular entertainments began to engage the irrational, marginal, and unconventional aspects of daily life.

Like most nineteenth-century European cultural trends, this new set of attitudes originated in Paris. Although fin de siècle pessimism was influential in Latin America and the Iberian Peninsula, it also prompted these peripheral societies to reconsider their cultural relationship to France, as well as to each other. In this, the rise of U.S. imperialism in the Americas was a decisive factor not normally associated with the French experience.

In Western Europe, the fin de siècle lasted approximately from 1885 to 1905. The phrase first appeared as the title of a French play written by F. de Jouvenot and H. Micard in 1888. Already by 1892 this new cultural trend received an extensive and excoriating analysis by Max Nordau in his book *Degeneration,* which paradoxically remains one of the classics of fin de siècle literature. Nordau interpreted the "mood" of the period as one of childish, undisciplined contempt for traditional mores and customs in favor of artifice, imitation, and spectacle. The degeneration of culture was in fact a central idea of the turn-of-the-century period, though proponents of this attitude often paired it with a complementary call for spiritual (and usually racial) regeneration. As the balance tipped toward the latter idea in the early twentieth century, the decadent pose of the fin de siècle gave way to a violent combination of nationalism and aesthetic modernism that would dominate European culture between the world wars.

The Iberian American fin de siècle followed a slightly different trajectory, beginning with the fall of the Brazilian monarchy in 1889 and ending with the Spanish American centennial celebrations of 1910. In this period, the final vestiges of Spanish and Portuguese colonialism in the Americas were abolished, only to be replaced by the increased presence of the United States in the hemisphere's affairs. With the exception of Portugal, whose experience of the fin de siècle most closely followed that of France, the Iberian and Iberian American nations all interpreted the Parisian model through their own particular colonial or imperial legacies. Although these countries participated in a broader Western fin de siècle culture, local events prompted original understandings of ideas such as decadence and degeneration. Most importantly, intellectuals in both Spain and Spanish America saw the end of the century as a low point for Hispanic culture, and their subsequent calls for spiritual regeneration included a vision of reestablishing a transatlantic cultural community to counter the encroachment of "Anglo-Saxon" values in their societies. Though occasionally included in such Pan Iberian projects, Brazil and Portugal did not attempt a rapprochement on the same scale during this period.

Despite achieving independence from Portugal in 1822, Brazil preserved the two main pillars of colonial rule—slavery and monarchy—until the end of the nineteenth century, when both collapsed within one year of each other. Not surprisingly, concerns about race towered over Brazilian culture in the fin de siècle, as society adjusted to the emancipation of black slaves. One idea popular among turn-of-the-century statesmen and intellectuals was that the population would eventually "whiten" through intermarriage, social hygiene programs, and European immigration. Less pessimistic than its European and Spanish American counterparts, the Brazilian intelligentsia was nevertheless troubled by the sheer size of their country and the ethnic diversity of its inhabitants. In the 1890s, a messianic revolt in the peasant community of Canudos prompted new anxieties among the urban elite about the nation's vast interior. The episode also resulted in Brazil's finest turn-of-the-century literary work, Euclides da Cunha's *Rebellion in the Backlands* (1902).

For the Hispanic world, the defining event of the fin de siècle was the Spanish-American War of 1898. In this conflict, Spain lost its final American possessions, including Cuba and Puerto Rico, leaving Spaniards in a state of intense self-scrutiny about their nation's future. To many it appeared that the end of the nineteenth century was also the definitive end of the Spanish Empire, perhaps even of Spanish culture. A new group of intellectuals known as the "Generation of 1898," which included Miguel de Unamuno, Ramón María del Valle-Inclán, and others, combined literary modernism with an anguished analysis of Spain's decline to produce a unique variant of fin de siècle thought. Like their contemporaries elsewhere in Europe, these writers viewed modern life as excessively materialistic, with little room for the cultivation of spiritual or aesthetic ideals. Yet their calls for the rejuvenation of Spain were also tempered by a profound pessimism about their own society, which they considered backward in relation to the United States and much of Europe.

Spanish Americans at the end of the nineteenth century also began to express concern about the growing imperial power of the United States. Having already acquired much of the American Southwest in the Mexican-American War of 1846–1848 and de facto control over the Caribbean in 1898, the United States provoked further controversy in 1903 by supporting the secession of Panama from Colombia, a move that favored eventual U.S. control of the Panama Canal. Unlike the British, who exercised the greatest outside influence over the region in the nineteenth century, the United States sought not only to control trade relations in the hemisphere but also to promote the acceptance of their own values and institutions. Racial superiority was often invoked as a justification for U.S. tutelage. As for the Spanish American response, diplomatic attempts to prevent U.S. hegemony proved largely ceremonial, though the Southern Cone republics of Argentina, Uruguay, and Chile managed to maintain greater autonomy than those of Central America and the Caribbean.

It was in the realm of fin de siècle high culture that Spanish Americans were best able to prevent the advance of the United States by reaffirming their ties with European civilization. Governments throughout the region rebuilt their capital cities after the model of Paris; notable examples include turn-of-the-century Mexico City and Buenos Aires. Spanish American elites adorned their homes with furniture and other luxury items from Paris and London. When possible, they also spent extended periods in these cities. Elite women often found European residence to be a welcome escape from the confining social relations of their own societies; when unable to travel, they enjoyed the latest French fashions at home. By the end of the nineteenth century, Spanish American students frequently studied in French and German universities. Artists traveled to Paris, Rome, and Madrid to work with European masters, often supported by public funds. Poets, essayists, and novelists continued to look to French literature and social thought for their principal sources of inspiration. To the degree that fin de siècle decadence influenced the above areas of European intellectual and artistic activity, a similar spirit was imported into Spanish American elite culture.

The best example of such influence can be seen in the turn-of-the-century literary phenomenon known as *modernismo.* Beginning with the Nicaraguan poet Rubén Darío, Spanish American authors sought to effect a revolution in literature modeled in part on French symbolism, which called for a highly subjective style, the full use of the musical and metaphorical qualities of language, and a focus on themes of decay, dissolution, addiction, and corruption. Symbolism had been a forerunner of French fin-de-siècle culture and became an important vehicle of its transmission into Latin America. Nevertheless, modernismo came to be regarded as the first truly Latin American literary movement of international stature, and for the first time Spanish intellectuals admitted their debt to a poetic style originating in the former colonies. In terms of content, a key feature separating modernismo from French symbolism was the allegorical representation of the United States as an aggressor in the Americas. Other proponents of this movement included the Argentine Leopoldo Lugones and the Uruguayan Julio Herrera y Reissig. Brazilian and Portuguese authors like João Cruz e Sousa and Eugénio de Castro were also influenced by symbolism and performed a similar role in spreading French fin-de-siècle attitudes to their respective countries.

Yet the most significant and unique development of the Iberian American fin de siècle must be considered the restoration of intellectual and cultural ties between Spain and Spanish America. For most of the nineteenth century, Spanish Americans had treated their Hispanic heritage as an obstacle to modernization. Not only had the wars of independence in the 1810s and 1820s promoted resentment toward the mother country, but the inability of the new republics to match the material development of Europe and the United States was often attributed to the damaging effects of Spanish colonial rule. Unlike their counterparts in the United States, and to a lesser degree in Brazil, the nineteenth-century Spanish American elite had little interest in preserving cultural contact with their former imperial master. Instead, they turned to Britain and especially France for their intellectual and cultural models. Some countries, particularly Argentina and Uruguay, promoted mass immigration from other regions of Europe as a counterweight to their Hispanic cultural (and racial) inheritance. For their part, the Spanish continued to look upon the former colonies as an intellectual and cultural backwater.

This pattern reversed sharply during the turn-of-the-century period. In 1885, the Iberian American Union (Unión Ibero-Americana) began to promote trade relations and closer cultural interaction between Spain and Spanish America. Through its Pan Iberian congresses and publications, this organization facilitated greater consideration of the common traditions connecting the territories once held by the Spanish and Portuguese Empires. In Spanish America, new groups of hispanophiles attempted to counteract the persistent French influence on the region's arts, literature, and architecture. Spanish painting became popular among the Spanish American elite during the first decade of the twentieth century, winning major awards at the exhibitions held in conjunction with the centennial celebrations of 1910. Also in this period, transatlantic debates erupted over the uniqueness of Spanish American culture, particularly over the linguistic differences that had evolved in various regions of the Spanish-speaking world. Increasingly, intellectuals on both sides of the Atlantic spoke of a shared Iberian racial heritage that distinguished their societies from the materialism and individualism of the United States.

The war of 1898 deepened the sense of collective demise that characterized the fin de siècle in the Hispanic world. Common European anxieties about modern technology, popular culture, changing gender roles, and other novelties of urban life could not be distinguished from a pervasive sense of racial decline. The triumph of the United States over Spain suggested to both Spaniards and Spanish Americans that their way of life was increasingly under threat. In response, intellectuals attempted to defend Hispanic culture as an antidote to the values of material development and personal interest that they identified with the United States. In *Ariel* (1900), Uruguayan author José Enrique Rodó promoted the idea that the Americas were the site of two clashing civilizations, calling upon his fellow Spanish Americans to maintain their fidelity to the higher ideals and spiritual refinements of their Hispanic cultural inheritance. Embraced by Spanish and Spanish American readers alike, Rodó's text spawned a resurgence of idealist thought in the fin-de-siècle Hispanic intellectual community. Along with Cuban poet and independence hero José Martí's essay "Our America" (1891), it also helped renew a sense of common identity among the diverse republics of Latin America. Like the fin de siècle itself, however, these calls for Iberian and Iberian American unity eventually fell prey to the rise of an aggressive nationalism that characterized much of Western culture in the twentieth century.

Brian Bockelman

References

Baker, Edward. "*Fin de Siècle* Culture." Pp. 155–179 in *Spanish History since 1808,* edited by José Alvarez Junco and Adrian Shubert. London: Arnold, 2000.

Fey, Ingrid E. "Frou-Frous or Feminists? Turn-of-the-Century Paris and the Latin American Woman." Pp. 81–94 in *Strange Pilgrimages: Exile, Travel, and National Identity in Latin America, 1800–1990s,* edited by Ingrid E. Fey and Karen Racine. Wilmington, DE: Scholarly Resources, 2000.

Needell, Jeffrey D. *A Tropical Belle Epoque: Elite Culture and Society in Turn-of-the-Century Rio de Janeiro.* New York: Cambridge University Press, 1987.

Nordau, Max. *Degeneration.* Lincoln: University of Nebraska Press, 1993.

Pike, Fredrick B. *Hispanismo, 1898–1936: Spanish Conservatives and Liberals and Their Relations with Spanish America.* Notre Dame, IN: University of Notre Dame Press, 1971.

Rodó, José Enrique. *Ariel.* Austin: University of Texas Press, 1988.
Sayers, Raymond S. "The Impact of Symbolism in Portugal and Brazil." Pp. 125–141 in *Waiting for Pegasus: Studies in the Presence of Symbolism and Decadence in Hispanic Letters,* edited by Roland Gass and William R. Risley. Macomb: Western Illinois University Press, 1979.

See also: Architecture—Brazil; Architecture—Modern Spanish America; Art and Artists—Brazil; Art and Artists—Modern Spanish America; Columbian Exposition of Chicago; Fiction—Spanish America; Independence I–VI; Literary Relations—Portugal and the Americas; Literary Relations—Spain and the Americas; Migration—From Iberia to the New World; Migration—To Brazil; Monroe Doctrine; Nationalism; Panama Canal; Poetry—Brazil; Poetry—Modern Spanish America; Slavery I—Brazil; Spanish-American War; Universal Expositions in Spain; World War I; World War II.

FLEET SYSTEM

The fleet or convoy system provided the reliable oceanic communications that helped maintain the political and economic unity of Spain's Atlantic empire. After six decades of experimentation, the fleet system acquired the form that lasted about a century before falling into irregularity. An early eighteenth-century attempt to revive it failed after repeated efforts.

Columbus's voyages revealed the clockwise circulation of winds and currents in the Atlantic north of the Doldrums and thus set the routes that shipping followed into and out of the Caribbean. From the Canary Islands ships rode the northeast trade winds southwest and west to ca. 15 degrees North latitude to enter the Caribbean. Although ships from the islands of Puerto Rico and Hispaniola could sail back to Spain without having to sail first to Cuba, ships that went farther west in the Caribbean had to rendezvous at Havana. From there they followed the Gulf Stream through the Bahama Channel (Columbus never followed this part of the route) and then worked north and northeast to ca. 40 degrees North latitude (which he had done) to catch the westerly winds back to the Azores and then the Iberian Peninsula. This latitude sailing until land was encountered was necessary because until the late eighteenth century there was no method for determining longitude (except during unusual celestial events, and then only on land). There were no reliable clocks that could keep the time at a fixed place in Europe, which allowed the measurement of longitude by computing the difference with local time. Columbus and his immediate successors also recognized the importance of sailing to and from the Caribbean before the hurricane season began, a pattern of spring–early summer travel that also avoided most of the Atlantic's winter storms. It also imposed a one-year duration on most voyages, with winters spent at some Caribbean or Gulf of Mexico port.

Columbus's voyages also initiated the government regulation of commerce with the new discoveries. At first this was minimal; in fact, the Crown encouraged competitors to challenge Columbus's privileges. Then, in 1503, the Crown created the Casa de Contratación, or Board of Trade, at the great inland port of Seville. This institution combined a general oversight of commerce with both original and appellate jurisdiction over criminal cases arising at sea and management of the Crown's remittances from the Americas.

Ship owners, merchants, and masters soon abandoned group sailings like Columbus's first two voyages in a scramble to gain what profits they could by sailing single ships to the Caribbean; some of these ships were little more than open boats as small as 20-*tonelada* (ton) capacity. However, war with France threatened many of these small, essentially unarmed ships. French privateers often lay in wait as vulnerable Spanish ships returned to the waters off the Azores, the Portuguese capes, and the Straits of Gibraltar. In response, the Spanish Crown imposed size (an 80-tonelada minimum, later raised) and armament rules (1522) and then in 1526 declared that Spanish ships should sail in groups of at least ten. Wartime patrol squadrons off the Azores and capes of Portugal proved to be expensive, and often ineffective, supplements to such rules, primarily because ships returning across the Atlantic frequently sailed alone or were alone because they had become separated from the group with which they had left the Caribbean. Such single ships were easy prey as they made landfalls in the islands and along the shores of the Iberian Peninsula. Using patrol squadrons to convoy merchantmen ordered to assemble at the Azores (or taking a group of them to the Canaries) provided only marginal improvements to security. And many ship masters continued to go it alone, whatever the Crown ordered. The Atlantic was vast, determining accurate latitudes was not always possible, and the Azores were known haunts of French privateers best avoided if supplies of water and food allowed a direct run for Spain.

Because the Crown wanted its revenues from the Americas returned safely and cheaply to Spain, the war of 1536–1538 produced the first royal treasure fleet (of ships armed to be warships) to make the round trip to Caribbean ports (1537–1538) and a requirement that all silver and gold shipped to Spain be carried on its warships. The costs were to be apportioned among the shippers, including the Crown. Although the Crown used this fleet as a means of gathering and then confiscating (against compensation) all the precious metals shipped that year, the experience and the continued unsatisfactory nature of convoying and/or patrolling between the Iberian Peninsula and the Azores and the Canary Islands led to a decree on August 9, 1543. The decree approved a merchant proposal for a formal system of convoys to and from the Americas during wartime, paid for by an *avería* or insurance fee (often thought of as a tax because the Casa de Contratación initially collected). Two escorted groups were ordered, one to sail from Seville in March primarily for New Spain (Mexico), and the other in September primarily for the Isthmus of Panama, wintering at Cartagena (in modern Colombia). Merchantmen were required to join the escorts at Havana for the return leg to Spain.

A variant of this basic pattern from 1543 was finally made the rule in 1562–1563. The new fleet system was the result of the lobbying from Seville's *Consulado* (merchant guild created in 1543), whose members advocated the convoy system. It also reflected the presence in the Caribbean of commerce raiders (corsairs), many of whom received official licenses from Spain's European enemies, whatever the state of war or peace in Europe. Group sailings not only provided protection, but they ensured that all cargos reached the major markets at Veracruz and Nombre de

Dios (Panama, for transshipment to Peru) at the same time, which gave all merchants who shipped their goods to those markets equal opportunity to sell them. For the Crown, the convoy system meant that its revenues would return yearly, with security, and at a lower cost than if it had to send armed ships for just its own remittances from the New World.

Under the new rules, the convoys sailed in May and August from Seville, and each convoy was escorted from its winter port to Havana. Should the fleets fail to make the required rendezvous at Havana the following May or early June, each could return alone with the two escorting warships *(Capitana* and *Almiranta)* supplementing the general armament required (rules usually ignored) for each merchantman. Every effort was made to keep the ships together during the crossing so that they passed as a group through the dangerous Azores–Capes southern Spain area.

Once established, this pattern of annual convoys lasted until the 1650s. However, as early as the 1570s there were interruptions in service to Panama, which required the Crown to send its own galleons there to pick up its revenues—hence the historic name for the Tierra Firme or Panama fleet: the *Galeones.*

Estimates of the total westbound tonnage used in the trade show a peak in 1622, with declines thereafter until the system ceased its annual function in the 1650s. Eastbound tonnages, which also topped out in the 1600–1610 period, did not drop off significantly until after 1630. They were always lower because old ships were sent west to be broken up for their iron and fittings once they had delivered the bulky cargos of wine, olive oil, flour, and iron that were important parts of the trade with the colonies.

Over time, larger ships were employed both for reasons of defensibility and for the economies they offered because of their crew size. Increasing size and the silting up of the mouth of the Guadalquivir River, which was the route from the Atlantic to Seville, forced the Crown formally to shift the Iberian end of the fleet system to Cádiz in 1679, although it began to serve on occasion as a departure and (more commonly) terminus point in the 1580s. The Casa de Contratación remained in Seville, as did the Consulado, until both were moved to Cádiz in 1717.

By the 1610s, the development of import-substituting production in some of the colonies (for example, wine in Peru and cheap, coarse textiles in New Spain), the drain of silver to China for silks and other goods brought to New Spain by the Manila Galleon rather than to Seville for European cloths and manufacturers, smuggling by Spain's European rivals, and credit and other problems in the Seville-Cadiz markets had undercut the fleet system's profits to such a degree that tonnages declined dramatically. Then, after 1650, annual fleet sailings stopped, before ceasing altogether in the late seventeenth century.

Almost from the beginning, merchants and other shippers found ways to pay less than they should have toward the common expenses of the convoys. Goods were undervalued, not declared, or declared to be other than what they were. Substantial amounts of silver were smuggled back to Spain, paying no taxes or avería. This fraud continued after the Consulado took over the collection of the avería and the running of the convoys during the 1590s and changed the tax to a flat rate per bundle, barrel, or bale. Needless to say, the avería on merchandise that was declared rose sharply in a cycle that caused more fraud the higher the premium's percentage went.

Connected with the fleets during their heyday were the great fairs at Nombre de Dios, relocated in 1590 to Puerto Belo, and at Veracruz-Jalapa. Here merchants who ran the wholesale and retail trades of the Spanish colonies came to exchange silver, hides, dyes, and other products for wine, olive oil, and European manufacturers, especially cloth and metals.

The tendency of Spanish merchants to dump goods into the American market and to demand high prices soon caused troubles that continued for the rest of the empire's existence. The saturation of the South American market interrupted trade or made it less profitable. The organization of consulados at Mexico City (1592) and Lima (1613) led to concerted action by their members to break the pricing power of the convoy merchants. A refusal to buy during the fairs until the approach of the fleet's mandatory departure date usually forced the convoy merchants to agree to sell at reduced prices.

When the Crown attempted to revive the fleet system in 1720–1778, this use of a form of monopoly power to combat another monopoly, and the other factors already noted as the causes of the decline of the first fleet system, caused that attempt to fail. In addition, from 1720 to 1740 and the outbreak of the War of Jenkins' Ear, the British South Seas Company was allowed to send a 500-ton "annual ship" to each of the major Spanish American ports. Those ships' cargoes often arrived before the fleet, supplying pressing needs at lower prices than those demanded by the convoy merchants. Under the new rules, only four convoys sailed for Panama; New Spain received a dozen, each resisted by the Consulado of Mexico City. Increasingly, ships with special licenses (to carry mercury, for example) carried Spanish trade to the fleet ports. Individually licensed ships and order-books became the norm for Chile, Peru, and Ecuador in the 1740s. And except for New Spain and Venezuela, where the privilege was finally granted in 1789, after 1778 more and more parts of the empire were granted the right to trade freely with nine peninsular ports and any and all colonial ones. When that system ("free trade") was extended to New Spain and Venezuela, it marked the definitive end to the fleet system.

In sum, while the fleet system lasted, it provided the Crown with annual, inexpensive shipment of its revenues and provided the merchants of Seville (and later Cádiz) with a level playing field in the American markets as well as less expensive, secure remission of profits. Often decried as a monopoly system, and certainly having many characteristics of one, the fleet system was also an attempt to deal with a serious naval problem and to maintain order and a degree of predictability in Spain's imperial economy. The economic costs of these benefits soon outweighed the benefits for colonial consumers and sometimes even for the merchants who most directly benefited from it. That it lasted a century in its first form and had a limited life in its revived form is a testament to its value to the Crown and certain merchants and to the strength of Spain's institutions and their inertia.

Paul E. Hoffman

References

Céspedes del Castillo, Guillermo. "La avería en el comercio de Indias." *Anuario de Estudios Americanos* 2 (1945): 517–698.

Chaunu, Pierre. *Sevilla y América, siglos XVI y XVII.* Translated by Rafael Sánchez Mantero. Seville: University of Seville, 1983. (A Spanish summary of *Séville et l'Atlantique.)*

Chaunu, Pierre, and Huguette Chaunu. *Séville et l'Atlantique, 1504–1650.* 8 vols. of 10. Paris: Librairie Armand Colin, 1955–1959.

Haring, Clarence. *Trade and Navigation between Spain and the Indies in the Times of the Hapsburgs.* Cambridge, MA: Harvard University Press, 1918.

Hoffman, Paul E. *The Spanish Crown and the Defense of the Caribbean, 1535–1585.* Baton Rouge: Louisiana State University Press, 1980.

Walker, Geoffrey J. *Spanish Politics and Imperial Trade, 1700–1789.* Bloomington: Indiana University Press, 1979.

See also: Asiento; Atlantic Economy; Banks and Banking; Bourbon Reforms; Caracas Company; Casa de Contratación; Columbian Exchange—-Agriculture; Columbian Exchange—Livestock; Contraband; Credit—Colonial Latin America; Defense—Colonial Spanish America; Monopolies; Navigation; Pirates and Piracy; Ships and Shipbuilding; Wine.

FLORIDA (LA FLORIDA)

Florida-Iberian relations began and ended with the Spanish outpost at Saint Augustine. Although the Spaniards maintained a presence in many parts of northern Florida, Saint Augustine dominated Florida's social, political, and cultural landscape. Built as a defensive outpost, Florida made only limited contributions to the Spanish Empire. Plagued with a poor economy, small population, and weak mandate, Florida played only a minor role in Spain's imperial past.

While searching for the legendary Fountain of Youth in 1513, Juan Ponce de Leon landed on and named Florida. Although his initial contact did not reveal mythical fountains or hills of gold, Ponce believed that the land held potential and so he returned to build a colony in 1521. Shortly after the Spaniards arrived, the Calusa Indians attacked the colonists, fatally wounded Ponce, and drove the remaining Spaniards from Florida.

Following its initial failure, Spain maintained some interest in the area but did not seriously pursue colonization of Florida. In 1562, 150 French Huguenots landed near present-day Jacksonville. Led by Jean Ribault, the colony was founded as a refuge for displaced French Protestants. France's outpost, called Fort Caroline, presented a direct challenge to Spain's ownership of Florida. Determined to maintain its claim, Spain dispatched Don Pedro Menéndez de Aviles to establish a colony and remove the French. On September 8, 1565, Menéndez and a party of nearly 600 founded Saint Augustine. Almost immediately, the Spaniards moved to expel the French Protestants. Within three months of their arrival, the Spaniards had massacred the French interlopers. The removal of the French gave Spain military control of Florida, and to complete its cultural conquest, Spain sent Jesuit missionaries to the regional Indian communities.

Between 1566 and 1572, missionaries built ten missions from the Chesapeake to points south of Saint Augustine. The Jesuits had ambitious plans for Florida's Indian populations, but perpetual conflict strained the colony's already scant resources, and in 1572 the Jesuits were recalled. Despite their failure, the missionaries helped Spain expand its presence beyond Saint Augustine. Franciscans replaced the Jesuits in 1595. By 1655, Franciscan activities peaked in Florida as seventy missionaries made more than 20,000 converts. This success again helped expand

Spain's regional presence, but it was not enough to enlarge Florida's boundaries.

When the British settled Jamestown in 1607, Spain had reason for concern as England's presence challenged Florida's survival. But Florida did not add another city until 1698 when Pensacola was founded, largely in response to France's expansion into Louisiana and not because of population or economic growth in the region. This began a pattern that was repeated in Florida throughout the seventeenth and eighteenth centuries. Spain hoped to expand its Florida settlements but could only watch as other European powers grew and settled territory Spain had considered to be part of Florida. Often, Florida's lack of material wealth impeded its growth.

An absence of mines, extensive infrastructure, and other economic difficulties discouraged potential settlers. To most outsiders, Florida was a wasteland of swamps, mosquitoes, and dangerous Indians. Paradoxically, British forces frequently attacked Saint Augustine in hopes of taking the outpost. Spain occupied, but could not populate, and its failure to expand Florida led Britain to consider the peninsula a logical extension of its colonial holdings. But despite its lack of growth, Spanish officials deemed it important enough to defend.

Beginning in 1672, Saint Augustine built a large stone fort called Castillo de San Marcos. The *castillo* ensured that Spanish ships of the Main could be protected from pirates who preyed on the Spanish fleet as it followed the Gulf Stream back to Spain. The fort also posed a considerable challenge to would-be attackers, but this alone could not guarantee Florida's protection.

Throughout the seventeenth century, British settlements continually moved southward, and French traders and settlers, ignoring Spanish land claims, moved across West Florida. When England founded Georgia in 1732, Spain's loss of Florida appeared inevitable. Spain considered Georgia a British colony within Florida's territorial limits, as outlined in the 1670 Treaty of Madrid, but could not convince the English to vacate the land. Arguments over ownership and other disputes ultimately brought the nations to war in 1740. Known as the War of Jenkins' Ear, the conflict threatened Florida's destruction, but despite England's best efforts, Florida successfully defended itself. Still, debate over territorial limits continued in Europe, and border warfare remained a constant for the duration of Spain's tenure in Florida. Ultimately, Spain lost Florida through the events of the Seven Years' War and not direct attack from a British colony.

In the 1763 Treaty of Paris, Spain's North American holdings drastically changed. From the French, Spain received lands west of the Mississippi, but England gained East Florida and completed its control of the Atlantic coast. Florida offered little for the British as its few towns were abandoned and, according to some observers, lay in a state of perpetual neglect. Still, Saint Augustine's fort provided military support for Britain's coastal communities, and its fertile inland had the potential for agricultural wealth.

When the American Revolution began, Spanish authorities in Louisiana saw an opportunity to regain their former territory; and despite some successful battles in West Florida, Spain regained Florida through diplomacy, not conquest. In the 1783 Treaty of Paris, Britain lost all the land it had received from its victories in the Seven Years' War, and as a result, Florida reverted to Spanish ownership.

Moat and walls of Castillo de San Marcos, Saint Augustine, Florida. (David Sailors/Corbis)

During Florida's second Spanish period (1784–1819), Spain maintained Britain's east-west division of the peninsula and attempted to turn Florida into a viable colony, but most Spaniards avoided the distant outpost. Spain's benign neglect of Florida allowed many British plantations to remain intact. Spain administered Florida's government and attempted to control its economy, but this brief second period of Spanish control did not increase the colony's value. Spain's efforts to rebuild Florida came to an abrupt end in 1819, when Spain signed the Adams-Onís Treaty, which transferred ownership of Florida to the United States.

Shane Runyon

References

Bolton, Herbert E., and Mary Ross. *The Debatable Land: A Sketch of Anglo-Spanish Contest for the Georgia Country.* Berkeley and Los Angeles: University of California Press, 1925.

Hoffman, Paul E. *A New Andalucia and a Way to the Orient: The American Southeast during the Sixteenth Century.* Baton Rouge: Louisiana State University Press, 1990.

Landers, Jane. *Black Society in Spanish Florida.* Urbana: University of Illinois Press, 1999.

TePaske, John Jay. *The Governorship of Spanish Florida, 1700–1763.* Durham, NC: Duke University Press, 1964.

Weber, David J. *The Spanish Frontier in North America.* New Haven, CT: Yale University Press, 1994.

See also: American Revolution; Borderlands; Bourbon Reforms; California; Colonists and Settlers VI—Southeastern North America; Conquest VI—Southeastern North America; Conquistadors; Defense—Colonial Spanish America; Jesuits—Iberia and America; Madrid, Treaty of; Native Americans VIII—Southeastern North America; Paris, Treaty of; Pirates and Piracy; Religious Orders; Seven Years' War.

FONTAINEBLEAU, TREATY OF

This was the treaty between France and Spain, during negotiations for the Treaty of Paris (1763), in which France relinquished the Louisiana Territory to Spain in recompense for losses to Britain in the Seven Years' War. Through three "Family Compacts," the Spanish monarchy had bound itself to its Bourbon cousins in France, most recently in the 1761 Third Compact, which required Spain to enter the Seven Years' War against Britain by May 1762. The Spanish fared badly, failing in their invasion of Portugal, and losing Havana and Manila to the British Royal Navy. The British were willing to negotiate with their conquests and proposed exchanging Havana and Manila for Puerto Rico, Honduras, and West Florida, while the French agreed to give up the left bank of the Mississippi to Lake Pontchartrain, making the Mississippi the boundary line between British Canada and French Louisiana. The British were far more interested in Atlantic-facing West Florida than in all of Louisiana, which the French offered in an attempt to help the Spanish keep Saint Augustine.

Appalled that this arrangement put the British in almost complete control of the Gulf of Mexico, with easy access to Mexico, the Spanish, through Don Jerome Grimaldi, Marquis of Grimaldi, threatened to hold up the treaty process and accused France of contravening the compact by disposing of part of Louisiana without their consent. On November 3, 1762, the morning before the preliminary peace was to be signed, Louis XV of France wrote to Charles III of Spain, offering to cede Louisiana to Spain. This gesture was meant to make up for Spain's war losses, guarantee them some control over the Gulf, and unload Louisiana, which had become an expensive and unprofitable drain on France. Csar Gabriel de Choiseul, representing Louis XV, came to an agreement with Grimaldi in his private quarters at Fontainebleau Palace that morning, and Charles III unenthusiastically accepted the offer on November 13, 1763.

In gaining 900,000 square miles of territory, the Spanish also hoped to use the port of New Orleans to crack down on British smuggling in the Gulf of Mexico and lessen the blow of losing West Florida (and the fortress of Saint Augustine) to Britain in order to keep Cuba and the Philippines. Choiseul attempted to sweeten the deal somewhat by suggesting to the Spanish the vast, untapped wealth of the territory, which the French had so far been unable to find or exploit. For France, the gesture kept Spain in the Family Compact until the French Revolution, and served to rid France of an expensive drain on its treasury. The British, however, considered themselves the major beneficiaries of the negotiations, receiving Mobile Bay and Pensacola, free navigation of the Mississippi and West Florida, as well as the areas granted in the larger Treaty of Paris of 1763.

Margaret Sankey

References

Brecher, Frank. *Losing a Continent: France's North American Policy, 1756–1763.* Westport, CT: Greenwood, 1998.

Folmer, Henry. *Franco-Spanish Rivalry in North America, 1524–1763.* Glendale, CA: Arthur H. Clark, 1953.

Hargreaves-Mawdsley, W. N. *Eighteenth-Century Spain.* Totowa, NJ: Rowman and Littlefield, 1979.

Shepherd, William R. "The Cession of Louisiana to Spain." *Political Science Quarterly* 19 (September 1904): 439–458.

See also: Borderlands; Bourbon Reforms; Contraband; Cuba; Florida; Honduras; Louisiana Purchase; Paris, Treaty of; Seven Years' War.

FOOD

The exchange of foods between the Iberian Peninsula and the Americas has had profound dietary, cultural, and demographic consequences. Both hemispheres gained new sources of sustenance as the highly productive American staples, maize and potatoes, increased European agricultural productivity, while domesticated animals from the Old World offered both valuable protein and traction in the New World. Yet incorporating these new foods into existing culinary systems proved highly contentious. European disdain for all things American slowed acceptance of many beneficial elements of the indigenous culture. Native Americans likewise shared a strong culinary conservatism, particularly when Iberian conquistadors sought to use food as a tool of evangelical, economic, and ecological control. Nevertheless, food habits blended over time to create the unique, mestizo syntheses that comprise Latin American cuisines today.

Before the arrival of Columbus, three major dietary regimes prevailed throughout the diverse ecologies of the Americas. The inhabitants of tropical lowlands in the Caribbean Basin and Brazil, including Taíno, Carib, and Tupi-Guaraní peoples, depended most heavily on the tuber manioc (yucca). Cooks first grated the root, soaked it to remove poisonous juices, and then heated it over an earthenware griddle in the form of a flatbread called cassava. The natives supplemented this staple with diversified horticultural and foraging strategies: raising sweet potatoes and maize; collecting such tropical fruits and nuts as pineapples, guavas, mameys, and cashews; and hunting and fishing. This bountiful diet notwithstanding, the lowlanders possessed neither domesticated animals nor alcoholic beverages.

Mesoamerican civilizations also depended on a basically vegetarian diet of maize, beans, squash, and chili peppers. Other foodstuffs included tomatoes, avocados, herbs, and the nutritious alcoholic beverage *pulque,* fermented from the sap of the *agave* (century plant). Native Americans also ate domesticated turkeys and small dogs as well as diverse game, seafood, insects, and even lake algae. The preparation of corn tortillas was extremely labor intensive. Mesoamerican women simmered the kernels in a mineral solution, which loosened the indigestible husk and released niacin, a vitamin necessary to avoid the disease pellagra. Next they hand-ground the wet dough, called *nixtamal,* on a basalt stone, before patting the smooth dough into thin, round tortillas and cooking them on an earthenware griddle. For festive occasions, the corn dough was formed into tamales (dumplings steamed in cornhusks) or shaped as idols and eaten in communion with the corn gods. Chili pepper stews were another standard feature of Aztec and Maya banquets.

In the Andes Mountains of South America, the dietary staples were tubers, most prominently the potato, but also sweet potatoes and other root crops. Corn was grown, along with an Andean grain, quinoa, but they were less central to the diet and prepared with the less labor-intensive methods of boiling or popping. Women also used corn as the basis for a fermented alcoholic beverage called *chicha.* Unlike the Caribbean and Mesoamerica, Andean civilizations had domesticated llamas, which served as pack animals and also provided a ready source of meat. Also providing meat were guinea pigs, which were raised in every household and boiled or roasted. Highland farmers freeze-dried potatoes, called *chuño,* by leaving them overnight in the cold dry air, and also preserved llama meat *(charqui)*. These preserved foods were traded for smoked fish produced by inhabitants of the Pacific coast.

Meanwhile, Iberian diets were founded on the Mediterranean staples of wheat bread, olive oil, and grape wine. These foods were firmly established by the Roman era and later became incorporated into Catholic rituals; thus, wheat was the only grain that could be used for the Holy Eucharist. Germanic invaders in the late years of the Roman Empire emphasized pastoral traditions of cattle and sheep herding, while the Muslim occupation from 711 to 1492 enriched Iberian cuisines with the use of elaborate stews perfumed with pepper, cinnamon, clove, and mace from the Oriental spice trade. The period of Islamic rule brought about a *convivencia* in which Muslims, Jews, and Christians lived together in relative peace and shared many cultural traditions.

Old World contributions to the Americas were not limited to the Iberian Peninsula but also extended to a broad area of imperial influences. The Spanish Empire, for example, included large parts of southern Italy, and manufactured pastas became an important item on American tables by the eighteenth century. African slaves made even greater contributions to the foods of the New World, particularly in the Caribbean and Brazilian lowlands, where sugar plantations dominated the landscape. African foods, including okra, bananas, palm oil, malaguetta peppers, and various greens, became as common on the tables of plantation masters as they were in the slave quarters.

The encounter between these diverse culinary traditions caused great contention at first, particularly over the staple foodstuffs. Iberians and Native Americans alike found the taste of novel grains to be highly disagreeable. In the tropical lowlands, wheat simply would not grow, and Europeans had to depend on imported supplies. Over time, settlers acquired a taste for indigenous root crops; Brazilians, for example, eat numerous manioc cakes and pastries called *beijú*. Planters in New Spain had better luck with wheat, and Catholic missionaries in particular sought to propagate the European grain in order to replace maize gods with the Holy Eucharist. Nevertheless, indigenous farmers found the foreign grain to be unproductive, expensive to grow, and prone to disease, although some entrepreneurial natives cultivated it for sale to urban Hispanic markets. As a result, wheat bread and corn tortillas became status markers within the racial hierarchy. Maize and potatoes were carried back to the Iberian Peninsula, but they were considered animal feed at best. The problem was their lack of gluten to make raised bread. During eighteenth-century famines, however, peasants abandoned their reluctance about maize porridge, and potatoes became an essential ingredient in the Spanish omelet. Because Native American women, with their knowledge of nixtamal, did not travel to the Iberian metropolis, the lower classes that depended on maize as their staple grain were subject to the dietary-deficiency disease pellagra.

Europeans also introduced new livestock to the New World, often causing profound environmental change. In the early days of exploration, sailors dropped breeding pairs of pigs on Caribbean islands so that shipwrecked sailors would have a familiar source of meat. Livestock also rode at the vanguard of Iberian invasion, not just the conquistadors' warhorses but cattle and sheep as well. Without natural competitors, they reproduced at exponential rates, overrunning the interior. The natives of Mexico had no prior experience with livestock, and they had difficulty preventing herds of European livestock from devouring their fields. The uncontrolled grazing of herbivores soon exceeded the carrying capacity of the land, denuding once-green hills, exposing the soil to erosion, and rendering the land unfit for farming or herding. Herds of cattle and sheep reverted to a feral condition and eventually spread as far as the present-day southwestern United States. Livestock also took over much of the pampas grasslands of Argentina and southern Brazil. By contrast, Andean Indians, with their pastoral traditions, quickly became skilled herders of cattle and sheep, thus limiting the ecological damage in the region.

Both Native Americans and Iberian settlers gave critical attention to food supplies and the politics of provisioning. Andean *kurakas* (nobles) were responsible for ensuring fair distribution of food, and the Inca Empire maintained enormous granaries to support military campaigns and state feasts as well as to meet the needs of the general population. The Aztec Empire demanded tribute from throughout Mesoamerica to feed the island capital of Tenochtitlan, but they assigned less concern to the well-being of subjects. Meanwhile, the Catholic Church sought to enforce a "moral" economy to ensure fair prices for staple foods, and medieval provisioning institutions were transferred to town councils in the New World. The *alhóndiga* (municipal granary) established a reserve against hoarding in times of shortage, and a semiprivate meat monopoly called the *abasto de carne* contracted out the slaughter of livestock for sale at fixed prices.

The spread of Iberian foods provided a measure of uniformity within Latin American cuisines. A predilection for pastries and sweets, a legacy of the Moorish occupation of the peninsula, became common throughout the region. Sugar production allowed convents and households to candy virtually every available fruit and vegetable, including sweet potatoes, pineapples, quince, and coconut. Iberian stews known as *pucheros* and *cocidos* likewise appear throughout Latin America, although local ingredients hint at the diversity of pre-Columbian influences.

Indeed, the irregular nature of conquest and climate produced widely different regional cuisines. The persistence of native population was one factor shaping culinary development. Regions such as the highlands of southern Mexico and Peru preserved a far more indigenous culture than the Caribbean lowlands, where mortality from disease was highest. Moreover, the provinces of Chile and California, with climates similar to the Mediterranean, became important centers of production for Iberian staples, wheat, olives, wine, and livestock. Although the relative weight of Iberian and Native American culture varied, new mestizo cultural blends emerged as the eventual basis for national cuisines. One example of this is the renowned Mexican *mole poblano,* turkey served in a deep brown sauce combining indigenous chili pepper stews *(molli)* with the medieval Hispano-Arabic tradition of fragrant spicy dishes.

Jewish culinary influences also spread to the Americas, notwithstanding the ending of the medieval convivencia, or peaceful coexistence among Jews, Christians, and Moors, and the expulsion of the Jews from Spain in 1492 and from Portugal in 1497. Those who converted to Christianity, known as *conversos* or New Christians, were theoretically ineligible to migrate to the New World, but large numbers did so anyway. The conquistador Luis de Carvajal, a prominent converso, founded the colony of Nuevo León in northern New Spain, and the regional specialties of *cabrito* (roasted kid goat) and unleavened *pan de semita* served at Passover reflect Jewish dietary habits. Among the Portuguese nobility, Jews were quite common, and in Brazil, they acquired a stereotype as exploitative grocers, a label often applied to peninsular Spaniards in other colonies.

Iberian influence within the Americas began to decline in the nineteenth century, as the colonies gained independence while Spain and Portugal suffered instability at home. The economic and cultural ascendancy of northern European powers appeared on the dinner tables of elite Latin Americans in the form of French haute cuisine and English roast beef. Although banquet menus were invariably written in French, the actual dishes often bore scant resemblance to foods served in Parisian restaurants. Chileans were perhaps the most devoted to continental dining and even produced fine wines using imported vine cuttings from the noble growths of Bordeaux and Burgundy. Independence also brought an end to colonial restrictions on immigration. Germans and Italians became especially prominent in Argentina, Brazil, and Chile, where they contributed to local food production and culinary tastes. Breweries opened in the late nineteenth century in cities such as Buenos Aires, São Paulo, and Monterrey, and beer gradually began to replace such indigenous beverages as pulque and chicha. Meanwhile, the end of the slave trade brought coolie labor and Chinese cuisine to Peru and Cuba. Lebanese immigrants further enriched regional cuisines in the early twentieth century. Industrial processed foods from the United States such as Coca-Cola and McDonald's hamburgers later gained wide popularity.

Despite a relative decline following Latin American independence, Iberian culinary relations with their former colonies continue. Nationalist revivals of the early twentieth century led to a rejection of French haute cuisine and renewed appreciation for many traditional mestizo dishes such as Mexican mole poblano, Chilean *pastel de choclo* (a rustic clay-pot dish of chicken, maize, and olives), and Brazilian *feijoada* (a stew of indigenous black beans and manioc, African dende oil, and Portuguese chorizo). By the end of the century, fashionable nouvelle cuisines began to show cross-cultural influences, as Spanish-inspired "foams" (originally created by the renowned Catalan chef Ferran Adria) appeared in upscale Latin American restaurants. Thus, the historical bonds between Iberia and the Americas continued to reassert themselves in new and tasty ways.

Jeffrey Pilcher

References

Bauer, Arnold J. *Goods, Power, History: Latin America's Material Culture.* Cambridge: Cambridge University Press, 2001.

Coe, Sophie. *America's First Cuisines.* Austin: University of Texas Press, 1994.

Crosby, Alfred W., Jr. *The Columbian Exchange: Biological and Cultural Consequences of 1492.* Westport, CT: Greenwood, 1972.

Mintz, Sydney W. *Tasting Food, Tasting Freedom: Excursions in Eating, Culture, and the Past.* Boston: Beacon, 1996.

Super, John C. *Food, Conquest, and Colonization in Sixteenth Century Spanish America.* Albuquerque: University of New Mexico Press, 1988.

Warman, Arturo. *Corn and Capitalism: How a Botanical Bastard Grew to Global Dominance.* Translated by Nancy L. Westrate. Chapel Hill: University of North Carolina Press, 2003.

See also: Alcohol; Bananas; Cacao; Catholic Church in Brazil; Catholic Church in Spanish America; Columbian Exchange—Agriculture; Columbian Exchange—Disease; Columbian Exchange—Livestock; Culture; Independence I–VI; Islam; Jews—Colonial Latin Amerca; Kuraca; Maize; Music and Dance I–V; Native Americans I–VIII; Popular Festivals; Potato; Slavery I–IV; Sugar; Wheat; Women—Brazil; Women—Colonial Spanish America.

FOOTBALL

Modern football (soccer) originated in England, but given the skill with which they play and the success they have achieved, one might be forgiven for believing that South Americans invented the sport.

Football came to South America as it had spread across Europe. British sailors, workers, and later the British managers of banks, railways, and textile factories promoted football amongst the social clubs of the major cities. The British community in Buenos Aires, numbering 40,000 by 1890, was no different. British schools fostered the growth of football. After ten years, the football league comprised three divisions. In Brazil, the game took off largely thanks to the initiative of the Brazilian-born son of a British consul, Charles Miller, who returned from England with official balls, a rulebook, and the desire to propagate the game. São Paulo and Rio both had leagues by 1906.

Football in South America was played first by foreign and then by local elites. German, Italian, and Portuguese clubs soon followed the British. Later, sons of the local elite joined these ranks, having learned the game while traveling or studying abroad. However, within a decade football was transformed from elite pastime to a game predominantly enjoyed by the working class. British-run factories encouraged workers to play and attend games. In Rosario, Argentina, the Central Argentine Railway Company had two teams: Rosario Athletic represented the managers, and Rosario Central the workers. Peñarol of Uruguay began as the Central Uruguay Railway Cricket Club. When the company withdrew its patronage, its new name reflected the area of Montevideo where they played, the railway yards.

International competition followed the emergence of national leagues, and almost as quickly South Americans began to dominate. Uruguay won both the 1924 and 1928 Olympic football tournaments. For the 1928 Olympic Final in Amsterdam, in which Uruguay defeated Argentina, European demand for tickets outstripped supply 4 to 1. Crowds thronged Montevideo and Buenos Aires to hear minute-by-minute telegraph reports read over the radio. Uruguay hosted the first World Cup competition in 1930. The final saw Uruguay again play Argentina, with the hosts coming from behind to win 4–2. Uruguay did not compete in 1934 or 1938. Argentina's team for the 1934 finals in Italy was depleted by the loss of two stars, Luis Monti and Raimondo Orsi. Lured to Italy as professionals, they now represented the hosts through their parents' nationality. Italy won the tournament.

The 1930s saw professional as well as nonelite, and therefore nonwhite, players become more prominent. In part, professionalism was an attempt to stop the flow of players abroad. But when Argentine clubs decided to complete the 1948 championship without members of the striking players' union, many players left for Colombia. Club Atlético Millonarios de Bogotá signed eight Argentines. Led by the legendary Alfredo di Stéfano, Millonarios won the league championship four times from 1949 to 1953. Di Stéfano was one of the greatest players of all time. He joined Real Madrid in 1953 and led the Spanish giants to five straight European Cups, scoring in each final. He also led them to the inaugural World Club Championship in 1960. Di Stéfano had the unusual distinction of representing three nations: Argentina, Colombia, and Spain.

In Brazil, Vasco da Gama led the way. Prior to their promotion to Rio de Janeiro's First Division in 1923 no championship-winning team had fielded either professionals or players who were black or mulatto. The reaction of the leading Rio teams was to form a rival league. Until 1929 they required players to fill out cards stating their name, nationality, date of birth, and workplace. The effect was to exclude those with little education, such as poor whites, blacks, and mulattoes. Professionalism ultimately brought integration, though nonwhites often felt treated as heroes if they won and scapegoats if they lost. The 1938 World Cup made Brazil's black center-forward Leonidas a hero. His face adorned ads, and he went on to become a television commentator. By contrast, many blamed Brazil's defeat in the 1950 World Cup final on three black players.

The popularity of football often made it subject to political influence. In 1941, Getulio Vargas brought football under the purview, and influence, of the Brazilian government through the National Sport Council. In Argentina, President Juan Perón's finance minister, Ramón Cereijo, was a fervent supporter of the Racing Club and secured a sixty-five-year loan for the club to build a new stadium, which was dutifully named after the president. The most flagrant use of football for propaganda purposes occurred under military dictatorships. General Emilio Garrastazu Médici, president of Brazil from 1969 to 1973, exploited Brazil's victory in the 1970 World Cup, using the team's song at all official government occasions and plastering posters across Brazil with pictures of superstar player Pelé alongside the slogan "No one will hold Brazil back now." In 1978 the military government in Argentina basked in the patriotic outpouring that followed a World Cup victory on home soil. National pride and the prompting of their military rulers led many Argentines to ignore the human rights abuses carried out in their name by the government. *Somos derechos y humanos* (We are right and we are human) was their response to international and local rights protestors.

Football bears an indelible stamp of Latin American influence, particularly Brazilian and Argentine influence. The 1970 World Cup in Mexico, where Brazil triumphed for a third time, was a global feast broadcast to a hungry world audience. The style of Brazil's victory set the standard for the way people believed football should be played: attack-minded, skillful, and to the rhythm of the *samba.* Brazil's final goal in the final against Italy

Pelé shoots during Brazil's World Cup match against Czechoslovakia in Mexico, 1970. (Allsport Hulton/Archive)

saw the ball move through almost the entire team before a defender, Carlos Alberto, fired it into the net from long range. In the 1980s, an Argentine emerged whose skill rivaled that of Pelé. Diego Armando Maradona also guided his country to a World Cup victory in Mexico in 1986, but it was a victory that showed both sides of a tormented soul. Against England, Maradona recorded one goal (illegally) with his hand, before his sublime individual skill enabled him to take on half the opposing side as he dribbled from the halfway line before sliding the ball into the net.

Alistair Hattingh

References

Fédération Internationale de Football Association (FIFA). "History of the FIFA World Cup." http://www.fifa.com/en/history/history/0,1283,5,00.html (accessed February 10, 2005).

Lever, Janet. *Soccer Madness: Brazil's Passion for the World's Most Popular Sport.* Prospect Heights, IL: Waveland, 1983.

Mason, Tony. *Passion of the People? Football in South America.* London: Verso, 1995.

See also: Argentina; Banks and Banking; Brazil; Colombia; Culture; Democracy; Human Rights; Malvinas/Falkland Islands; Migration—From Iberia to the New World; Music and Dance I—Brazil; Pirates and Piracy; Popular Festivals; Race; Sports; Uruguay.

FRANCISCAN MILLENNIAL KINGDOM

The first Franciscan missionaries to the New World, and especially those who first served in Mexico, were heavily influenced by millenarian ideas popular in the late fifteenth and early sixteenth centuries. Many of these friars believed that the discovery of the New World was a sign that the coming of Christ was imminent. This notion came from two important trends in the Franciscan order.

The teachings of Joachim of Fiore were the most important source for millenarian ideas for the Franciscan friars. Fiore wrote that the history of the world fell into three periods, each associated with one person of the Trinity. The time before the arrival of Christ corresponded to the time of God the Father. The age from the time of Christ until the mid-thirteenth century was the time of God the Son. From the mid-thirteenth century on was the epoch of God the Holy Spirit. The early missionaries adopted Fiore's periodization but with different dates. They interpreted the discovery of the New World as inaugurating the third period, in which the Holy Spirit would descend to the earth in preparation for the second coming of Christ and his thousand-year reign, the millennium.

Within the Franciscan order, three groups emerged, each claiming to represent the true wishes of Saint Francis for the order. The Conventuals felt that in order to remain aloof from the temptations of the world, they should live cloistered in their convents. The Spirituals were the most radical group, espousing an extremely strict interpretation of the Rule, so much so that in the fourteenth century they were declared heretical. The Observants also sought to closely follow the Franciscan Rule, avoiding all possessions and living in simplest apostolic poverty. It was the Observants who emerged as the victorious faction in the late fifteenth and early sixteenth centuries. Although the followers of Fiore had initially been Spirituals, they eventually came to dominate the Observants.

In Spain the Observants ultimately dominated and played an important role in the reform of the order. At the same time that the Observants were developing reformed groups in Spain, the first missionaries went to the New World. The great majority of these friars came from the ranks of the reform-minded Observants.

In the New World, the Franciscan belief that the second coming of Christ was at hand colored their actions. Rather than engage in a long and protracted evangelization of the natives before offering the sacrament of baptism, the Franciscans were known for their mass baptisms. The thought was that once the last native had been baptized the second coming would be at hand. The friars also believed that the best way to convert the natives was to attract them to the faith. Consequently, even though initially they could not communicate as a result of language differences, the friars sought to convert the natives through their own lives as an example of Christian love.

The millenarianism of the Franciscans also colored their long-term expectations. When the second coming did not occur, when the natives did not embrace the faith as completely as the friars had hoped, and things seemed to be no different, many friars lost heart and became discouraged. It was hard to maintain the apostolic fervor in the face of what seemed to be defeat. By the middle of the sixteenth century, the Franciscans had moved away from their earlier ideas and had become engaged in a long-term process of evangelization.

John F. Schwaller

References

Phelan, John Leddy. *The Millennial Kingdom of the Franciscans in the New World.* 2nd ed. Berkeley and Los Angeles: University of California Press, 1970.

Rubial, Antonio. *La hermana pobreza.* Mexico City: Universidad Nacional Autónoma de Mexico, 1996.

See also: Catholic Church in Spanish America; Clergy—Secular, in Colonial Spanish America; Diabolism in the New World; Jesuits—Iberia and America; Protestant Reformation; Religious Orders; Syncretism; Virgin of Guadalupe.

FREE TRADE AREAS OF THE AMERICAS (FTAA)

The Free Trade Areas of the Americas is a regional trade agreement initiated in 1994 to create the largest free trade zone in the world among the countries of the Western Hemisphere, except Cuba. The general objective of the agreement focuses on trade liberalization, thus removing restrictions on the free movement of goods and services in the Americas by reducing tariffs and other trade barriers.

The FTAA grew out of the First Summit of the Americas, held in Miami, Florida, in December of 1994. At the summit, President Bill Clinton signed a declaration with thirty-three other leaders from the hemisphere establishing the parameters and aims of the negotiations for a project that included the FTAA, as well as negotiations dealing with the preservation of democracy, the eradication of poverty and discrimination throughout the hemisphere, and the promotion and advancement of education in the Americas. It was envisioned that this proposed free trade area would supply these thirty-four democratic countries with fair and equitable trade rules through an agreement that would be comprehensive and balanced.

During the official Second Summit of the Americas, held in Santiago, Chile, formal negotiations to establish the FTAA commenced. The countries involved in the negotiations agreed that it would be a hemisphere-wide, separate agreement negotiated by the parties that would not disrupt any current regional agreement. Moreover, the follow-up section of the Plan of Action produced at the summit committed the heads of state to continue to meet periodically to deepen cooperation and understanding among the countries of the Americas.

During the Third Summit of the Americas, held in April 2001 in Quebec City, Canada, the heads of state addressed common hemispheric issues and challenges that were identified as a result of this three-year process. These included improved access to education, alleviation of poverty, strengthening of human rights, democracy, and economic integration. The consideration of these themes and the resulting Declaration of Quebec City were designed to help determine the region's priorities and goals for the upcoming years. The most recent summit, held in Monterrey, Mexico, in January 2004, continued the themes of the Third Summit: democracy, social development, and economic growth.

The heads of state agreed that negotiations were to be completed no later than January of 2005 and that entry into force should take place no later than December of 2005. Eight ministerial conferences have advanced the process of negotiations of the current FTAA draft. Negotiations cover the following key areas: market access, investment, services, government procurement, dispute settlement, agriculture, intellectual property rights, subsidies, antidumping and countervailing duties, and competition policy.

The efforts to bind the economies of the Western Hemisphere into a single trade agreement have presented some obstacles that must be overcome before an extensive free trade zone can be properly realized. Vastly differing levels of economic development and of labor and environmental laws are concerns that will have to be addressed as these thirty-four countries attempt to integrate an extensive free trade region.

Giovanna Gismondi

References

Free Trade Area of the Americas. "Summits of the Americas," http://www.alca-ftaa.org (accessed June 5, 2004).

Patterson, P. J. "The Free Trade Area of the Americas and Smaller Economies." *Fordham International Law Journal* 27 (February 2004): 899–914.

See also: Caribbean Community and Common Market; Democracy; General Agreement on Tariffs and Trade; Human Rights; North American Free Trade Agreement; Oil; Organization of American States; Panama Canal; United Fruit Company.

FRENCH GUIANA

King Francis I of France, in defiance of the Treaty of Tordesillas, which gave rights of discovery and conquest in the New World exclusively to the Spanish and the Portuguese, funded in the 1520s and the 1530s a series of explorations designed to weaken Iberian dominion in the Americas. Although many of the early French expeditions focused on North America, by the mid-sixteenth century the French were challenging Portugal's hold on the southern colony of Brazil. In fact, in 1555 the French founded the important coastal city of Rio de Janeiro and managed to hold on to this soon-to-be-valued possession for twelve years before finally being ousted by the Portuguese in 1567.

Nonetheless, the French were determined to maintain a colonial presence in South America, and finally in the 1660s, under the military leadership of Joseph Antoine Le Febvre de la Barre, they gained possession of the island of Cayenne and the adjoining mainland territory, which came to be called *la France equinoxiale,* and later, French Guiana. As early as 1604, French citizens had settled in Cayenne and along the coastline, but as elsewhere in the Americas, skirmishes between the dominant European powers prevented any steady colonial enterprise in the region until Le Febvre's triumph over the Dutch in the mid-1660s.

Situated in the northeastern corner of the South American continent, French Guiana covers more than 90,000 kilometers of land, most of which penetrates deep into the equatorial rainforest. Over the colony's history, this discouraged widespread inhabitation of the area. Indeed, early French colonizers complained bitterly about the insalubrities of the region, as well as its stifling heat, preponderance of tropical diseases, and apparent lack of natural resources. Nevertheless, administrators like Jean Baptist Colbert (Louis XIV's minister of finance) considered French Guiana to be a coveted possession, perhaps even the entrance to the mythical lost City of Gold *(see* El Dorado). As a consequence, Colbert invested heavily in its colonization and development.

Imperial objectives, however, differed sharply from the reality of life in French Guiana throughout the seventeenth, eighteenth, and nineteenth centuries. In 1675, for example, only sixteen sugar mills were operating along the narrow coastline, and two years later (according to a census carried out by a visiting naval commander), there were only 319 white settlers, 1,374 black slaves, 48 Indian slaves, and 15 mulattoes in the entire colony.

By 1722, the sugar industry had virtually collapsed in French Guiana; only two plantations remained in the colony. The intrepid French planters who managed to survive and who were determined to stay turned progressively to alternate crops like rocou (a red dye made from the uruca plant) and coffee. Of course, most profits European plantation owners earned in French Guiana throughout these centuries came from the blood, sweat, and tears of slaves, who labored in relatively small numbers (in the early 1700s there were only 3,000 African slaves throughout the entire colony) until abolition in the mid-nineteenth century.

As a result of the Treaty of Paris, signed in 1763 by France and England, France lost Canada but maintained most of its Caribbean and circum-Caribbean possessions, including French Guiana. In its effort to rebuild the nation's colonial empire in the Americas and to finally realize France's lofty goals for Cayenne, Paris sent over 10,000 colonists from France, other parts of Europe, and Acadia (Canada) to the region to stimulate agricultural production and urban commerce. Plagued by the colonists' general lack of skill in tropical agriculture and their susceptibility to tropical diseases—an overwhelming majority died of typhoid or yellow fever—the colonization effort failed miserably, and throughout the remainder of the eighteenth century, and indeed until the 1850s, French Guiana remained an enigma to metropolitan policymakers.

In the 1850s, the French initiated two major programs for French Guiana that shaped the colony's historical development in the twentieth century. First, government recruiters lured upwards of 8,000 immigrants, mainly from India and China, to French Guiana between 1850 and 1914. This migration added rich demographic complexity to the old colony and, at least partially, solved some of the labor shortage problems that had terminally hampered its growth. Second, in 1851 the French government created the hellish "Devil's Island" Penitentiary on a small rocky island just off French Guiana's coast, and for nearly a century (it closed in 1946) it housed approximately 80,000 of France's most hardened criminals.

Home currently to approximately 190,000 people of mixed racial ancestry (blacks and mulattoes constitute the ethnic majority at 66 percent), French Guiana today is South America's only nonindependent territory. The former colony did gain new political status in 1946 when France officially converted it to an overseas *département,* granting French Guiana some representation in French government. The overseas province's principal exports are bauxite, timber, and gold, but over 25 percent of the gross domestic product is linked to the European Space Agency's launching pad located in Kourou.

Caleb P.S. Finegan

References

Burton, Richard D. E., and Fred Reno, eds. *French and West Indian: Martinique, Guadeloupe, and French Guiana Today.* Charlottesville: University of Virginia Press, 1995.

Miles, Alexander. *Devil's Island: Colony of the Damned.* Berkeley and Los Angeles, CA: Ten Speed, 1988.

Redfield, Peter. *Space in theTropics: From Convicts to Rockets in French Guiana.* Berkeley and Los Angeles: University of California Press, 2000.

Wroth, Lawrence C. *Acts of French Royal Administration Concerning Canada, Guiana, the West Indies and Louisiana.* New York: New York Public Library, 1930.

See also: Atlantic Economy; Brazil; Coffee; Conquest VI—Southeastern North America; Dyes and Dyewood; El Dorado; Engenho; Mulatto; Paris, Treaty of; Pirates and Piracy; Slavery I–IV; Sugar; Tordesillas, Treaty of.

GAUCHO

The *gaucho,* a seminomadic horseman who inhabited the plains of southern South America during the eighteenth and nineteenth centuries, is often compared to the North American cowboy. While the origin of the term remains uncertain, Spanish scientific travelers of the late eighteenth century first noted its use as a name for cattle rustlers in the territory comprising present-day Argentina, Uruguay, and southern Brazil. Gauchos were then considered the most outcast members of frontier society, lower-class men who took advantage of the scarcity of European settlement in the region and imperial competition between Spain and Portugal to engage in contraband trade.

Living for long periods on the open plains and consuming a rough diet of beef and yerba maté (a Paraguayan tea), small confraternities of gauchos pursued an independent existence during the colonial era. In truth, most of these horsemen maintained ties to more settled agricultural and ranching communities. The gaucho's equestrian skills and tolerance of solitude made him well suited to tend cattle herds on large, unfenced ranches that produced hides, salted meat, and other pastoral products. He also participated intermittently in colonial agriculture; estate records show seasonal movement of gauchos into farmwork. Informal marriages to women involved in farming provided another link to colonial society, as did children born from these unions.

From the late seventeenth century on, gauchos served as militiamen in the border wars that characterized the conflict between Spain and Portugal for control of the Río de la Plata region. In an attempt to profit from the contraband silver trade flowing from the mines of Potosí in Upper Peru, the Portuguese established Colônia do Sacramento on the eastern shore of the Paraná River in 1680. The Spaniards, who already held Buenos Aires, countered by founding the city of Montevideo in 1724. Definitive control of the area passed into Spanish hands in 1777, but the wars of independence that erupted in 1810 saw the continued presence of gaucho combatants in a new territorial struggle between Argentina and Brazil. A major result of this conflict was the founding of Uruguay as a separate nation in 1828. Further inland, gauchos took part in the civil wars that delayed the consolidation of the Argentine nation.

By 1900, the rise of commercial agriculture and the modernization of ranching had gradually transformed the gaucho into a rural peon. As he disappeared from the plains, however, the free-roaming gaucho became a heroic figure in the literature and popular culture of Argentina, Uruguay, and Rio Grande do Sul, Brazil's southernmost state (whose inhabitants are now called gaúchos). José Hernández's epic poem *Martín Fierro* (1872) identified the gaucho as the soul of Argentine civilization, a subject that sparked a transatlantic debate with turn-of-the-century Spanish intellectuals like Miguel de Unamuno. Brazilian poet José de Alencar likewise celebrated the horseman as a national hero in his *O Gaúcho* (1870). In the twentieth century, gaucho revivals became a mainstay of South American urban culture, and since the 1960s student groups have embraced gaucho customs such as the communal drinking of maté.

Brian Bockelman

References

Guy, Donna J., and Thomas E. Sheridan, eds. *Contested Ground: Comparative Frontiers on the Northern and Southern Edges of the Spanish Empire.* Tucson: University of Arizona Press, 1998.

Oliven, Ruben. *Tradition Matters: Modern Gaúcho Identity in Brazil.* New York: Columbia University Press, 1996.

Slatta, Richard W. *Gauchos and the Vanishing Frontier.* Lincoln: University of Nebraska Press, 1983.

See Also: Argentina; Armies—Colonial Spanish America; Borderlands; Brazil; Contraband; Defense—Colonial Spanish America; Estancia; Fiction—Spanish America; Hacienda; Horses; Independence I—Argentina; Independence II—Brazil; Marriage; Poetry—Brazil; Poetry—Modern Spanish America; Potosí; Silver; Uruguay.

GAY RIGHTS AND MOVEMENTS

The gay rights movement in the Iberian Peninsula and in the Americas has been tremendously influenced by the gay rights movement that originated in the United States. Both movements seek recognition, among the public as well as in the legal code, that gay people have the same rights as heterosexuals. During the 1950s and 1960s, gay bars in urban areas in the United States and Canada gradually became more common, and a gay community started to rise. Thus, a sense of gay identity began to grow. The sexual revolution of the 1960s was a key element in developing a common gay identity. Gay people eventually realized that they needed to fight for their rights and stop being treated as second-class citizens. It was not until the late 1960s that they began to organize and acquire some political and social power.

In the Iberian Peninsula and in Latin America, because of the political situation these countries were experiencing at the time (dictatorships in Spain, Argentina, Chile, and Central America; autocratic governments in Mexico, Colombia, and Peru), openly gay movements did not develop. But despite the censorship and restrictions that existed in these countries, some underground groups were able to gather and discuss the need for equal rights, and they all felt closely related to the gay rights movement that was taking place in the United States. Since the 1960s, the United States has become the model to follow, and gradually the gay rights movements in the United States gave rise to a flowering of gay movements around the world. The development of the gay rights movements in the Iberian Peninsula and in the Americas can be understood in the following manner: the United States and Canada are the pioneers, the two countries that over the past four decades have been able to secure numerous victories for gay rights; consequently, they have led the gay movements in the Americas. Then follows Spain, which has become the bridge between the Iberian Peninsula and Latin America, particularly over the last decade. There are two main reasons why Spain is becoming a bridge between these two regions: (1) pressure from other European nations, and (2) a reaction to the repression that the Spanish society suffered during Francisco Franco's dictatorship. One could place the pioneer countries of Latin America, such as Brazil, Argentina, and Mexico, in a third group. These countries have had an important role in the gay rights movements in Latin America; and despite the fact that they have followed the lead of the United States and Spain, all three countries have offered models that are considered more appropriate to Latin American realities than the conditions in the United States, Canada, or Western Europe.

The 1969 Stonewall riots are considered to be the keystone point for the modern gay rights movements in the Western Hemisphere. The participants of the Stonewall riots were fighting for equal political and social rights and recognition. The ideals that the Stonewall riot participants expressed were soon echoed in other nations, particularly in Canada and Western Europe. Thus, one can argue that Stonewall was the pioneer movement that set in motion the contemporary gay rights movements in the Western world. After Stonewall, some countries immediately followed such movements and started fighting for equal gay rights, while others took longer because of their political situation.

The Stonewall riots, consisting of various violent conflicts between gays and lesbians on one hand, and the police on the other, took place in Greenwich Village in New York City on June 27, 1969, outside the Stonewall Inn. The event marked the first time a group of gay people fought together for the same cause. Police raids were a given in gay bars and clubs prior to Stonewall, but after the riots, the movement gathered solidarity in its desire for equal rights and its message to the world that gays could fight together. The Stonewall riots gave rise to the creation of the Gay Liberation Front (GLF) in New York City. The GLF produced a document called "A Gay Manifesto" that provided the goals for the newly created gay liberation movement. This document proved very influential in other gay movements around the world.

The gay rights movement created a gay pride campaign promoting three principal ideas: (1) people should be proud of what they are, (2) sexual diversity is a gift, and (3) sexual orientation is inherent and cannot be intentionally altered. The gay rights movement has used the gay pride campaign as a way to reach people. They hold gay pride parades in different cities in the United States during which gay people celebrate their identity and show the world that they are part of the mainstream culture and that they cannot be defined using hetero-normative parameters. Symbols of gay pride include the rainbow flag, pink and black triangles, and other human rights campaign symbols. The well-known gay activist L. Craig Schoonmaker claims that he coined the term *gay pride* in a description of the 1969 Stonewall riots.

The first organized gay rights demonstration in the United States took place on October 14, 1979, in Washington, D.C. Approximately 100,000 people participated in the march. Since that time, the gay rights movements have achieved many victories, such as the case of *Oncale v. Sundowner Offshore Services.* On March 4, 1998, the Supreme Court ruled that on-the-job sexual harassment extends to situations in which both parties are of the same sex. Another example of the accomplishments of the gay rights movements in the United States is the revocation of sodomy laws in most states. In 2003 all the state laws against sodomy were ruled unconstitutional as a consequence of *Lawrence v. Texas* (2003).

The gay rights movement in the United States goes hand in hand with the international human rights organizations. One of the most influential groups in the gay rights movement is the Human Rights Campaign. Other gay rights organizations in the United States are the National Gay and Lesbian Task force (NGLTF), the Gay and Lesbian Alliance Against Defamation (GLAAD), and Parents and Friends of Lesbians and Gays (PFLAG). In addition, there are local gay community centers throughout the country. These play an important role in the gay rights movement because typically they organize the gay pride events that function as an outreach to people in the local community.

At present, a large number of companies and local governments have policies against discrimination on the basis of sexual orientation. Despite tremendous efforts, the gay rights movement has not achieved recognition of same-sex marriage or civil unions at the federal level. However, at the state level such unions have been recognized in Vermont, Hawaii, and Massachusetts. In 1969 a gay and lesbian movement in Ontario, Canada, began to press the federal government to give the gay community equal rights and protection on the basis of sexual orientation. In 1986, the Coalition for Gay Rights in Ontario achieved official recognition. Nine years later, in 1995, the Supreme Court of Canada ruled that the Canadian Charter of Rights and Freedoms could not discriminate on the grounds of sexual orientation. A year later the federal government amended the Canadian Human Rights Act to ban discrimination based on sexual orientation. By the end of the twentieth century, gay and lesbian federal employees had obtained equal partnership benefits. In the year 2000, the Act to Modernize Benefits and Obligations provided for common-law relationships, both opposite and same-sex. This new law gave gay and lesbian couples the same rights and responsibilities that heterosexual married couples possessed. In the Canadian provinces of Quebec and Nova Scotia, civil union is offered as an alternative to marriage. At the federal level, Canada recognizes common-law marriages between same-sex partners. In 2004, a court ruling of the Ontario and Quebec Supreme Courts required that the federal government grant full marriage rights to same-sex couples within two years. Canada's government proposed that marriage be defined as the "lawful union of two persons," which would legalize same-sex marriage throughout the country.

The United States and Canada are countries with many similarities, and both saw the rise of gay rights movements in their respective territories at almost the

Argentine lesbians celebrate inside the Buenos Aires City Hall after legislators voted to grant them legal status, December 12, 2002. Legislators granted legal status to gay and lesbian couples, allowing benefits such as pensions and hospital visits in a move hailed as a first in Latin America. (Reuters/Corbis)

same time. On one hand, the United States has been the model to follow in terms of gay rights movements, and many of the political ideas that these movements used around the world evolved from this model. On the other hand, Canada has accomplished more in terms of equality of rights for same-sex partners. Some scholars argue that this is because of the strong and well-organized groups that oppose the gay rights movements in the United States, such as the Christian Right and other social conservative organizations.

The pioneer country in the modern gay rights movements, the United States, has fallen behind in the realm of gay marriage and civil unions. Countries such as Canada and Spain are ahead of the United States on the issue. At the same time, such movements would probably not have been possible in Canada and Spain without the U.S. model.

During Francisco Franco's dictatorship, most human rights movements in Spain were suppressed. It was only after Franco's death in 1975 that the Spanish gay movement began to grow and become public. However, during the Franco dictatorship several underground movements were created. One of these groups was the Catalonian gay movement named Movimiento Español de Liberación

Homosexual (MELH), formed in 1971. Nine years later, the Liberation Front of Cataluña was recognized as a legal movement. Spain's political movement in the 1980s and 1990s helped the creation of gay rights movements in Spain's urban centers. However, the persecution of homosexuals continued even during the transition to democracy. This situation promoted the mobilization of well-established gay groups such as MELH to fight for their rights. The democratic euphoria that Spain experienced at the end of the 1980s helped this cause.

Another element that aided them was the international support they received from other European gay rights groups. The need to develop a common gay identity gave birth to movements such as the Front d'Alliberament Gai de Catalunya (FAGC—Catalonian Gay Liberation Front). This association sought to organize movements that would include more members of society and that, according to its founders, would be more democratic than the MELH, which was considered too elitist. According to experts on this topic, the FAGC provided more solutions to the problems that the gay population was experiencing at the time. The FAGC aided several gay groups that evolved around Spain at the end of the 1970s and early 1980s; it organized the first nationwide gay rights movement, known as the Coordinadora de Frentes de Liberación Homosexual del Estado Español (COFLHEE). This movement started in the 1970s and reached its peak in 1980.

Unfortunately, in the mid-1980s, owing to the outbreak of the AIDS pandemic, the Vatican exerted so much influence in Spain against gay movements that many of the previous years' achievements were at risk. As a result, the different organizations realized the need to make the gay rights movement a political and legal issue, and they continued their crusade against conservative groups. Gay centers began to emerge in different parts of Spain in order to create a sense of community. In 1990, Spain's federal government met with members of the gay rights movement and declared that democracy meant equality, including sexual orientation. In 1994, the government granted certain housing rights to nonmarried couples, either heterosexual or homosexual. That same year, the government of Valencia granted gay couples the right to adoption. In 1995, the legal system protected gay people against hate crimes; the first large gay pride marches started in Madrid that same year. A few years later, gay rights organizations started to press for same-sex equal rights, but they were not successful.

In February of 1997, close to 5,000 gay people demonstrated against the newly elected conservative government. However, the new government did not come out in favor of gay policies. In response, gay rights groups continued to expand around Spain. Each region developed its own groups, following Spain's autonomous model; but at the same time organizations in Madrid established links with some left-wing political parties. During his political campaign José Luis Rodríguez Zapatero announced that gay couples in Spain would be guaranteed the same rights as heterosexual couples. A year after coming into power he did what he promised, and at present gay couples in Spain can marry and enjoy the same rights as their heterosexual counterparts. Some consider this achievement one of the most significant successes in the history of gay rights movements in the world, particularly because Spain has traditionally been a Catholic and conservative country.

That Spain is the model for many Spanish-speaking countries is extremely important for the gay rights movements in Latin America and for Spain's neighbor Portugal. Latin American gay rights movements have followed the European and the North American models. In Latin America the most significant changes in favor of the gay population have occurred in the last decade. Brazil is ahead in terms of gay rights, followed by Argentina. Gay pride parades have been instrumental in gay rights movements; the first countries that organized gay pride marches were Argentina, Mexico, and Brazil. Human rights nongovernmental organizations (NGOs) throughout Latin America have played pivotal roles in the region's gay rights movements. In addition, NGOs have played a tremendous role in monitoring human rights abuses against sexual minorities and in educating the population.

From 1991 to 2004, the number of gay organizations in Brazil increased from thirteen to almost one hundred. On December 4, 1998, the Brazilian constitution was amended to include (1) protection from discrimination on the grounds of sexual orientation; (2) registered partnerships; (3) the end of the ban on lesbians and gays in the military; and (4) protection for transgendered people. This was one of the greater achievements for gay rights movements in Latin America. In 2003, the Brazilian state of Santa Catarina passed legislation that fines businesses that discriminate against gays, lesbians, bisexuals, or the transgendered. Similar antidiscrimination laws also were created in other regions, such as São Paulo, the country's largest state, Rio de Janeiro, and Minas Gerais. In May of 2004, the state of Porto Alegre passed a law that recognized civil unions of same-sex couples. Civil union couples have the rights to adoption, to inheritance, and to insurance benefits and pensions. Presently, Brazilian gay activists are seeking an amendment to the constitution that would give them equal rights in all areas of life.

In Argentina, a gay rights organization, Comunidad Homosexual Argentina (CHA), was created one year after the military dictatorship ended in 1984. After several years of struggle, in 1992, the CHA gained official recognition. That year, in July 1992, Argentina celebrated its first Gay Pride week. For many years, gay people in Argentina as well as other Latin American countries have experienced widespread discrimination and harassment. In the last couple of years, Argentina's gay rights movement has made tremendous strides. On July 18, 2003, the first civil union of a homosexual couple in Latin America took place in Buenos Aires, Argentina. The ceremony was a victory for gay rights in Latin America. However, the law does not recognize the union as marriage, nor does it extend to gay couples many of the benefits of marriage, such as health and pension benefits. Unlike the Brazilian decree, the Argentine measure does not grant gay couples legal status for their unions, and it does not allow them to adopt children or receive inheritances. Gay activists described the legislation as the most far-reaching in Spanish America.

Even though Mexican gay rights movements have not achieved the recognition of civil unions among same-sex partners, Mexican gay activists have been among the leaders in the Latin American gay rights movements. In 1979, Mexican gay activists organized the first gay parade in Latin America; it is now one of the largest in the world. The gay rights movements have long held public demonstrations seeking equal rights. Several Mexican groups, such as the Closet of Sor Juana and Diversas, have been extremely important in pursuing antidiscriminatory legislation and in including sexual minorities in human rights agendas at local and international levels. In 2002, the Mexican constitution banned any form of discrimination involving sexual orientation. The government is working with several gay organizations to define a legal framework for implementing this principle in specific laws. Unfortunately, these achievements have not been able to abolish the attitudes that many Mexicans harbor against gay people.

The gay rights movements in Latin America have been active participants in many different international forums. For example, last year Mexican gay activists participated in regional and local meetings to discuss the content and nature of the Brazilian Resolution. They have been working closely with other Latin American and Caribbean (LAC) regions. Many gay rights groups in Latin America are members of the International Lesbian and Gay Association (ILGA), the first international gay rights organization to gain consultative status with the United Nations. ILGA activists are seeking to introduce sexual orientation into the UN human rights frameworks.

Jose Guillermo de los Reyes-Heredia

References

Adam, Barry. *The Rise of a Gay and Lesbian Movement.* 2nd ed. Boston: 1987; reprint New York: Twayne, 1995.

Adam, Barry., Jan W. Duyvendak, and Andre Krouwel. "Gay and Lesbian Movements beyond Borders? National Imprints of a World Wide Movement." Pp. 344–371 in *The Global Emergence of Gay and Lesbian Politics. National Imprints of a World Wide Movement,* edited by Barry Adam, Jan W. Duyvendak, and Andre Krouwel. Philadelphia: Temple University Press, 1998.

Altman, Dennis. *Homosexuality: Oppression and Liberation.* 2nd ed. New York: New York University Press, 1993.

Blasius, Mark. *Gay and Lesbian Politics.* Philadelphia: Temple University Press, 1994.

Dudley, Clendinen, and Adam Nagourney. *Out for Good: The Struggle to Build a Gay Rights Movement in America.* New York: Simon and Schuster, 1999.

Fluvià, Armand de. "El movimiento homosexual en el estado español." Pp. 149–167 in *El Homosexual ante la Sociedad Enferma,* edited by José Ramón Enríquez. .Barcelona: Tusquets, 1978.

Pérez Cánovas, Nicolás. *Homosexualidad: Homosexuales y uniones homosexuales en el derecho español.* Granada: Editorial Comares, 1996.

Ringer, Thom. "Gay Marriage in Canada." *The Oxonian Review* 3, no. 3. (2004): 1–3.

Sanders, Douglas. "Getting Lesbian and Gay Issues on the International Human Rights Agenda." *Human Rights Quarterly* 18 (1996): 67–106.

See also: Argentina; Art and Artists—Modern Spanish America; Brazil; Catholic Church in Spanish America; Cinema; Culture; Human Rights; Mexico; Opus Dei; Papacy; Popular Festivals.

GENERAL AGREEMENT ON TARIFFS AND TRADE (GATT)

GATT represents the historical nucleus for contemporary world trade. In July 1944, the United Nations Monetary and Financial Conference was held in Bretton Woods, New Hampshire. The attending nations signed accords that would eventually establish the World Bank, the International Monetary Fund, and the GATT, signed in 1948 by twenty-three contracting nations. Nearly thirty-two bilateral trade agreements already existed with the United States by 1945, including treaties with nations in the Caribbean and Central and South America, with the 1942 Mexico agreement serving as the U.S. model for the initial draft of the GATT.

After financial and trade blunders, including the 1930 Smoot-Hawley Tariff Act and the Great Depression, as well as the two catastrophic world wars, signatories designed GATT to provide future stability in trade. Initially conceived as a stopgap or precursor to an International Trade Organization (ITO), the failure of that organization to receive approval by the U.S. Congress allowed GATT, by default, to serve as the major treaty governing trade for nearly five decades. It has been renegotiated periodically by a growing number of signatories. Because of GATT's status as a treaty rather than an organization, it lacks the necessary backbone of ordered institutional communication and internal juridical structure for enforcement.

Developing countries felt particularly weak in light of consensus-based decision making, and Latin American nations took the leadership position in voicing complaints about GATT's structure. In late 1961, Uruguay filed a complaint against all developed-country signatories of GATT that was remarkable in its wide scope and in the serious deliberation that ensued. Developing nations initially found an open environment to discuss their concerns outside of GATT in the United Nations Conference on Trade and Development (UNCTAD). Since its inauguration in 1964, UNCTAD has served as a mouthpiece for developing nations' interests and solidarity on issues of trade. By the 1970s, owing partly to pressure from this group, GATT negotiations became more mindful of their agenda.

As late as the mid-1960s, GATT tariff negotiations were on a product-by-product basis, which became complicated as the European Community emerged as a regional trade group, necessitating negotiations with its members on each product before presenting a united front at the negotiating table. The Kennedy Round, longer than any previous GATT negotiation, took over four years to reach an agreement and eliminated product-by-product decision making. From this round of negotiations forward, the European Community, especially with the 1973 addition of Britain, Denmark, and Ireland, became the world's largest trading entity. Nongovernmental interests of the 1970s, including the Organization of Petroleum Exporting Countries (OPEC), and nontariff trade barriers questioned GATT's ability to regulate trade. The Uruguay Round of negotiations began in 1986 in hopes of reaching effective rules for intellectual property rights; trade in service, agriculture, and textile sectors; and nontariff barriers, including subsidies. This round lasted more than eight years and created the World Trade Organization (WTO), which finally ended GATT's status as an all-encompassing and ever-renegotiated treaty. The WTO's charter insists that the new organization respect the signatories and framework of GATT.

Lisa Singleton

References

Hudec, Robert E. *Developing Countries in the GATT Legal System.* Thames Essay No. 50. London: Trade Policy Research Centre, 1987.

Jackson, John H. *The World Trading System: Law and Policy of International Economic Relations.* 2nd ed. Cambridge, MA: MIT Press, 1997.

See also: Caribbean Community and Common Market; Free Trade Areas of the Americas; North American Free Trade Agreement; World War I; World War II.

GOLD

Gold was considered the most precious of all metals until processes to refine pure platinum were developed at the turn of the eighteenth and nineteenth centuries. Gold ranked alongside evangelization and the search for spices as one of the major reasons for the conquest and colonization of the Americas.

The fascination of gold for the people of the Middle Ages was not merely due to the desire for wealth; it was also a result of theological and philosophical ideas relating to nature's constant struggle for perfection. Alchemists searched for the philosopher's stone, the catalyst that would perfect base metals by turning them into gold, owing to the belief that the same catalyst might restore humankind's perfection and undo the damage caused by the fall. Because of its immutability, gold was considered to be the perfect metal. In 1590, the Jesuit chronicler José de Acosta wrote that gold had always been esteemed as the most noble of all metals because it was the most durable and incorruptible.

The majority of fortune hunters who traveled to the newly discovered Caribbean, however, were not concerned with ideological explanations regarding the perfection of gold. Those who had journeyed on the premise of fabulous wealth were soon disappointed, for what gold existed seemed to be alluvial and became quickly exhausted.

The discovery and conquest of Mexico in 1519 gave new impetus to the search for gold. The conquistador and chronicler Bernal Díaz del Castillo described how the conquistadors broke up the Aztec emperor Moctezuma's treasury, while holding him captive in Tenochtitlan, saying that it was marvelous to behold so much gold. Díaz quite candidly admitted that all men coveted gold and that the more they had, the more they wanted. Much of the gold looted from Moctezuma's treasury was lost forever in the lake of Texcoco during the Spaniards' disastrous retreat from the Aztec capital, Tenochtitlan.

The craving for gold increased the desire to search for new territories to conquer. The enormous ransom that the Inca Atahualpa paid to Pizarro's men in 1533—a room filled with gold and another with silver—and the fabulous riches of Cuzco plundered by the conquistadors encouraged an endless influx of fortune-seekers from Spain. The Spaniards who captured Atahualpa became rich beyond their wildest dreams. The newly arrived who had missed this golden bonanza often tortured Andean leaders so that they would reveal the location of the gold that the Spaniards believed had been hidden.

Once the indigenous gilt-work had been plundered, the attention of entrepreneurs and the Crown (who received the fifth part of all wealth generated) turned to the systematic extraction and refining of gold. The process consisted of crushing the ore and mixing it with mercury until the gold dissolved. The slurry was then separated from the gold-mercury mixture and the mercury was evaporated. Finally, the gold was melted to burn off any remaining impurities and then cast into ingots for storage and shipment.

Andrew Redden

References

Bray, Warwick, and Julie Jones. *El Dorado: The Gold of Ancient Colombia.* New York: New York Graphic Society, 1974.

Díaz, Bernal. *The Conquest of New Spain.* London: Penguin Classics, 1963.

Fernández Armesto, Felipe. *Columbus.* Oxford: Oxford University Press, 1991.

Hemming, John. *The Conquest of the Incas.* London: Macmillan, 1993.

See also: Colombia; Colonists and Settlers I—Andes; Conquest I—Andes; Conquest V—Mexico; Conquistadors; Emeralds; Mining—Gold; Mining—Mercury; Mining—Silver; Potosí; Silver.

GRAN COLOMBIA

Under the leadership of independence hero Simón Bolívar, colonists in the Spanish Empire in northern South America created the country of Gran Colombia, consisting of modern-day Colombia, Ecuador, Panama, and Venezuela. Following Bolívar's decisive victory against the Spanish at the battle of Boyacá in August 1819, the colonists declared the creation of the new country. However, a variety of factors led to the breakup of Gran Colombia by 1830.

In the aftermath of the battle of Boyacá, the Congress of Angostura in Venezuela announced the creation of Gran Colombia in December 1819. The formation of the new country was formally approved in 1821 at Cúcuta, Colombia, with the adoption of a constitution. The capital was established at Bogotá and Bolívar was elected president, with Francisco de Paula de Santander chosen as vice-president. The new constitution provided for a highly centralized government. However, it was never very effective because the newly formed country did not possess the resources to govern. The creation of Gran Colombia was well received abroad. The United States recognized the new country in 1822, followed by Great Britain in 1825.

After the formation of Gran Colombia, Bolívar left to liberate Peru, leaving Vice-President Santander to run the country. Santander launched a liberal reform program that included the expansion of education, the abolition of slavery and Indian tribute, and some anticlerical measures.

The economy of Gran Colombia was dominated by Venezuelan coffee and Colombian gold. Venezuela's colonial cacao production never fully recovered from the independence wars. The opening of foreign trade hurt the textile industry in Ecuador, for now it could not compete with cheaper imports. The government raised a loan in Great Britain in 1824, but Gran Colombia soon defaulted on the loan.

A number of factors made the Gran Colombian union difficult to maintain. Its creation challenged 300 years of regional development and local government, making it difficult for many to submit to the authority of a distant central government. Long distances and mountainous terrain made communication difficult and economic ties virtually impossible. In Venezuela especially, many complaints were voiced about the government in Bogotá. In reality, the problem was that the Venezuelans simply did not like being subordinate. Ecuador had more legitimate complaints, inasmuch as it had no real

José Antonio Páez ousted South American liberator Simón Bolívar from Venezuela and established both an independent nation and a line of rule by caudillos, *or strongmen, in the mid-nineteenth century. (Library of Congress)*

representation in the central government, in addition to being hurt economically by tariff policies.

In 1826, conflict erupted when José Antonio Páez and his followers revolted in Venezuela. Bolívar was forced to return to his homeland to deal with the uprising, taking more direct control of government affairs. Bolívar's actions led to a period of conservative dictatorship, as he ruled by decree and abolished Congress. Although he temporarily ended the revolt, he could not completely end dissent in Venezuela. In 1829, Páez rebelled again, and Venezuela left the Gran Colombian union. The following year, Ecuador followed suit.

As Gran Colombia crumbled around him, Bolívar resigned in ill health and planned to go into exile. However, in 1830 he died in the Colombian coastal city of Santa Marta.

Ronald Young

References

Bushnell, David. *The Making of Modern Colombia: A Nation in Spite of Itself.* Berkeley and Los Angeles: University of California Press, 1993.

———. *Simón Bolívar: Liberation and Disappointment.* New York: Pearson Longman, 2003.

Bushnell, David, and Neil Macaulay. *The Emergence of Latin America in the Nineteenth Century.* 2nd ed. New York: Oxford University Press, 1994.

Lombardi, John. *Venezuela: The Search for Order, the Dream of Progress.* New York: Oxford University Press, 1982.

See also: Cacao; Coffee; Colombia; Ecuador; Enlightenment—Spanish America; Gold; Independence IV—Colombia, Ecuador, and Venezuela; Liberalism; Panama; Venezuela.

GRITO DE DOLORES

In 1810, Miguel Hidalgo y Costilla's *Grito de Dolores* (Cry from Dolores) began the armed struggle for independence in New Spain, as Mexico was known during the colonial era. Hidalgo, a parish priest turned insurrectionist leader, is considered the father of Mexican independence, which is celebrated as a national holiday every year on September 16, the anniversary of his call for rebellion.

In the latter part of the eighteenth century, a series of laws (now known as the Bourbon reforms) were passed in the hope of more effectively administering Spain's overseas empire. The reforms intensified the conflict between Creoles (*criollos*), American-born Spaniards, and *peninsulares,* European-born Spaniards who considered themselves superior and anxiously guarded their power and status. Creoles were unnerved as directly appointed officials became more responsive to the Spanish viceroy, the Crown's colonial representative, than to their local concerns. As the Crown asserted more control, Creoles advocated for local and regional autonomy. In 1804, the Crown initiated the *Consolidación de Bienes Reales,* whereby the Catholic Church's charitable funds raised in the American colonies were sent to Spain for European adventures rather than being spent locally on parishioners' needs. The Church, a major creditor, also called in loans and mortgages, causing financial hardship in the colonies.

Napoleon Bonaparte invaded the Iberian Peninsula, forced King Ferdinand VII to abdicate in 1808, and placed Joseph Bonaparte on the throne (Ferdinand would return as monarch in 1814). With the legitimate monarch replaced, Creole-dominated city councils throughout the Spanish American colonies proposed to govern themselves in the name of the monarch until Ferdinand's reinstatement. When the viceroy of New Spain did not sufficiently snuff out such potentially dangerous autonomist sentiments, he and a group of Creole leaders were imprisoned by the Spanish authorities in Mexico City.

An autonomist movement in the prosperous north-central Bajío region emerged under cover of the city of Querétaro's sympathetic magistrate and his wife. The Creole intellectual priest Miguel Hidalgo had moved into the area in 1803. Hidalgo was never on good terms with the ecclesiastical authorities. Besides holding unorthodox religious views, he gambled, read prohibited books, and fathered three children by two different women. But an enlightened sense of social justice encouraged Hidalgo's support of economic projects that improved his parishioners' lives, and thus earned him admiration and appreciation in the village of Dolores.

After Hidalgo and his fellow conspirators' plot for a mass insurrection in December to keep the peninsulares from ruling New Spain in the name of the French usurpers was discovered in September 1810, Hidalgo hastily issued his Grito de Dolores. With the cry "Death to bad government! Death to the Spaniards!" he urged his oppressed parishioners to recover the land stolen from their forefathers by the Spanish conquerors. Hidalgo was able to unite members of the Queen's Regiment, Indians, liberated prisoners, and workers on large estates angry about land tenure issues and labor conditions. His enraged mob, which included many women and children, imprisoned the Spanish authorities and local peninsulares and looted stores and estates. Hidalgo led his revolt under the banner of the Virgin of Guadalupe, the dark-skinned virgin who was believed to have appeared to a newly converted Indian in 1531 and thus represented nativist Catholicism in New Spain. The insurgents added numbers to their ranks as they captured towns. Hidalgo and his associate Ignacio Allende led 50,000 insurgents in their first military victory, taking control of Guanajuato in New Spain's most important silver-producing region.

Viceroy Francisco Venegas, who arrived in New Spain a few days prior to the issuing of the Grito de Dolores, took charge of suppressing the insurgency. Hidalgo's followers eventually assembled outside Mexico City and demanded Venegas's surrender. After three days, Hidalgo decided not to attack, owing to supply shortages, lack of support from surrounding communities, and fear of royalist troops. He retreated to Guadalajara where he solidified mass support by killing peninsulares and abolishing both slavery and the community chests that had demanded residents' contributions. He also declared communal lands inalienable. Hidalgo and Allende's army of 100,000 was decisively defeated by General Félix Calleja at Puente de Calderón on January 17, 1811. The insurrectionist leaders were captured, tried for treason, and executed. Hidalgo was defrocked the day prior to his execution. His defeat marked the end of the first stage in the war of independence in New Spain, which lasted until Mexico became an independent nation in 1821.

David M. Carletta

References

Archer, Christon I. "Bite of the Hydra: The Rebellion of Cura Miguel Hidalgo, 1810–1811." Pp. 69–93 in *Patterns of Contention in Mexican History*, edited by Jaime E. Rodríguez O. Wilmington, DE: Scholarly Resources, 1992.

Flores Caballero, Romeo. *Counter-revolution: The Role of the Spaniards in the Independence of Mexico, 1804–1838.* Translated by Jaime E. Rodríguez O. Lincoln: University of Nebraska Press, 1974.

Hamill, Hugh M., Jr. *The Hidalgo Revolt: Prelude to Mexican Independence.* Gainesville: University of Florida Press, 1966.

Tutino, John. "The Revolution in Mexican Independence: Insurgency and the Renegotiation of Property, Production, and Patriarchy in the Bajío, 1800–1855." *Hispanic American Historical Review* 78, no. 3 (August 1998): 367–418.

See also: Armies—Colonial Spanish America; Bourbon Reforms; Creoles; Independence V—Mexico; Napoleonic Invasion and Spanish America; Nationalism; Virgin of Guadalupe.

GUATEMALA

Guatemala is a country where both pre-Columbian and Spanish customs and traditions thrive. According to the 2002 Census, Guatemala has a total population of 12.2 million and is located south of Mexico, extending over 108,000 square kilometers. It boasts the biggest and strongest economy of the five Central American republics. It also has the largest Indian population in Central America, representing 52 percent of the population, as well as the largest variety of languages in the Isthmus.

Pedro de Alvarado, Hernando Cortés's lieutenant, arrived in Central America in 1523 with a force of 400 Spaniards and hundreds of Tlaxcaltecan Indians from Mexico. Alvarado's conquest was facilitated by a number of important factors. Three years before his arrival, a deadly smallpox epidemic had devastated the region. But perhaps more importantly, the Spaniards and their Indian allies were aided by the political circumstances they encountered. The early sixteenth century witnessed the rise of a powerful and expansionist Maya state, the Quiché. Over the course of their expansion in the Guatemalan highlands, the Quiché acquired numerous enemies, most notably the Cakchiquels. Taking advantage of the arrival of these newcomers, the Cakchiquels allied with the Spaniards to defeat the Quiché. However, the alliance did not last, and Alvarado soon turned against the Cakchiquels themselves, sparking a violent revolt in 1526. The Cakchiquels were defeated, and within years other Maya ethnic groups, the Tzutujil, the Chortí, the Mam, and the Pokomam, among others, fell to the European colonizers. However, the situation in Guatemala's Petén region was vastly different; in fact, it was not until 1697 that the last Maya kingdom, the Itzás, surrendered to the Spanish.

The colonizers' first step was to organize the Indian labor force. In the absence of gold and silver mines, the main source of wealth in the region was the Indian population. Initially, the exploitation of the region's dense Indian population was organized through the *encomienda* system, a grant of authority over a group of Indians. Recipients of encomienda grants, the *encomenderos,* received labor services and tribute, in return for which they were required to provide protection and religious instruction to their Indians. Some high-ranking Indians also received encomienda grants as rewards for their assistance in the conquest. Nevertheless, the system often was highly abusive, and several unsuccessful attempts were made in the sixteenth century to abolish it.

Guatemala gained independence from Spain in 1821, in part because of the eighteenth-century Bourbon reforms, which radically altered the old colonial system. The Spanish Bourbons, especially under King Charles III, promoted dramatic changes to Spain's overseas administration; commerce was pushed ahead, and many people in the colonies discovered that they could acquire wealth without the intervention of Spanish merchants. Furthermore, ideas of "liberty, equality, and fraternity" came to Central America following the French and the American Revolutions. In Central America, men from France and England fought shoulder to shoulder with the Central Americans for independence, and also in the aftermath from 1826 to 1829, during the so-called Federation Wars. The years 1821 to 1824 witnessed the establishment of the Central America Federation, a political union that integrated Guatemala, El Salvador, Honduras, Nicaragua, and Costa Rica. It was modeled after the United States, with a federal government as well as state governments in each state. However, it did not work well in Central America, and so the federation was dissolved in 1847.

Both during the colonial period and after independence, agricultural products were Guatemala's main exports. During the colonial period, the most important export was indigo; following independence it was cochineal. Both products, used to dye textiles, were in high demand in the English textile industry. After 1847, Guatemala's cochineal exports rose dramatically to supply the rising demand from England. However, the invention of artificial dyes from Germany signaled the end for Guatemala's main export product. Attention now turned elsewhere. Costa Rica had begun to grow coffee early in the nineteenth century, and once it had proved to be a successful product, Guatemalans began to cultivate coffee in the 1860s.

The coffee industry brought new demands from the landowning elite, and Guatemala's Conservative government was unable to respond. The coffee elite took office in 1871, with Justo Rufino Barrios as president and Miguel García Granados as vice president. The new Liberal administration initiated a process of modernization in communication, and a railway network was constructed. Guatemala's roads and ports were also improved. The Liberals ruled the country from 1871 until 1944, and dominated two of the longest individual presidential periods in Guatemalan history. Manuel Estrada Cabrera ruled Guatemala from 1898 until early 1920, when he was removed from office by a popular armed uprising. Jorge Ubico ruled

Guatemala from 1931 to 1944. Both presidents served the interests of Guatemala's coffee elite; their policies favored the coffee industry and benefited big international business, especially the United States' banana plantations, power companies, and railways.

In 1944, a popular uprising brought new ideas; World War II was ending, and the United States, England, and France were leading the Western Hemisphere with the ideas of democracy, liberty, and freedom of speech. Such ideas contrasted sharply with the Guatemalan reality. New ideas about democracy captured the imagination of teachers, university students, young military men, and large numbers of peasants. The revolutionary movement consumed almost the whole year of 1944; but on October 20 of that year Jorge Ubico's regime was finally ousted by an armed insurrection.

The so-called October Revolution of 1944 lasted from 1944 to 1954 and covered two presidential periods. The first revolutionary president was Juan José Arévalo Bermejo. He initiated several revolutionary changes in Guatemalan politics, and his policies favored Guatemalan workers. The second revolutionary government, led by Lieutenant Colonel Jacobo Arbenz Guzmán, was even more radical. Arbenz initiated a revolutionary agrarian reform program and confronted directly the interests of the United Fruit Company. The United States responded to the threat and provided financial support to an army of Guatemalan mercenaries who finally exiled Arbenz in 1954. Many of the revolutionary changes were reversed under the counter-revolutionary movement called the *Movimiento de Liberación Nacional;* however, the American intervention and the fall of Arbenz initiated the longest period of political unrest in Guatemalan history.

Early in the 1960s many young military officers initiated an armed movement against the Guatemalan government. The guerrilla movement took shape in the middle 1960s and was finally defeated at the end of the decade. The 1970s began with the military rule of Colonel Carlos Manuel Arana Osorio, who was followed in 1974 by General Kell Eugenio Laugerud Garcia (whose election was fraudulent). In 1978, General Romeo Lucas Garcia took office; he was forced out four years later in 1982. During that time, the guerrilla movement reorganized its forces and initiated a strong offensive. The guerrilla movement consisted of an alliance among the Army of the Poor, the Revolutionary Organization of the People in Arms, the Rebel Armed Forces, and the Guatemalan Party of the Workers (Communist). The civil war reached its peak between the years 1978 and 1982; more than 250,000 Guatemalans, most of them Maya civilians, lost their lives in the conflict. The legacy of the conflict has left deep and lasting scars.

Finally, in 1986, Guatemala began a period of relatively stable political democracy; the country elected a succession of civil presidents: Vinicio Cerezo Arevalo (1986–1991), Jorge Serrano Elias (1992–1993), Ramiro de Leon Carpio (1993–1996), Alvaro Arzu (1996–2000), Alfonso Portillo (2000–2004), and Oscar Berger who began his presidency in 2004.

In the early 1970s, Guatemala initiated a process of economic modernization and attempted to move away from a reliance on coffee. Many Guatemalans started growing vegetables such as broccoli; they also grew flowers for the export market, sugarcane, fruits (such as strawberries), and hundreds of other agricultural products. Today many Maya peasants are devoted to growing agricultural products for export. At the same time, entrepreneurs from Korea, Japan, and Taiwan arrived to invest in Guatemala's burgeoning textile industry. Such investment introduced modern industry and led to increased migration into Guatemala's capital city. At present, Guatemala City and its immediate surroundings support more than 2.5 million inhabitants. Yet in spite of its growing industrial base, both Spanish and Maya traditions continue to coexist with modernity.

Oscar Guillermo Peláez Almengor

References

Carmack, Robert M., Janine Gasco, and Gary H. Gossen. *The Legacy of Mesoamerica: History and Culture of a Native American Civilization.* Upper Saddle River, NJ: Prentice Hall, 1996.

Farriss, Nancy M. *Maya Society under Colonial Rule: The Collective Enterprise of Survival.* Princeton, NJ: Princeton Unversity Press, 1984.

Grandin, Greg. *The Blood of Guatemala: A History of Race and Nation.* Durham, NC: Duke University Press, 2000.

Jones, Grant D. *The Conquest of the Last Maya Kingdom.* Stanford, CA: Stanford University Press, 1998.

See also: Bourbon Reforms; Catholic Church in Spanish America; Coffee; Cold War—Spain and the Americas; Communism; Conquest IV—Central America; Democracy; Dyes and Dyewood; Guerrillas; Human Rights; Independence III—Central America; Laws—Colonial Latin America; Native Americans IV—Mesoamerica; New Laws of 1542; Requerimiento; United Fruit Company.

GUERRILLAS

In modern Latin America, guerrillas—small groups of armed men and women—have posed a unique political challenge to the modern state. Although earlier examples date back to the colonial period, guerrillas are primarily a twentieth-century phenomenon. Most Latin American guerrillas originated as splinter groups from established political parties in the context of political systems that did not meet increasing demands for reform. An interesting fact to emerge in studies of guerrillas is the middle- and upper-middle-class origin of most of the leaders. During the cold war, following the 1959 Cuban Revolution, groups subscribing to various forms of Marxist ideology became widespread throughout the continent and sought to fuel popular uprisings. Government responses were mainly repressive. In some cases, guerrillas sought to negotiate and enter the political system. The United States became involved in guerrilla conflicts by training Latin American militaries in counterinsurgency tactics and supporting regimes fighting against insurgencies. Although most guerrilla movements were eventually defeated, some continue to operate in the post–cold war context, most notably in Colombia, Peru, and Mexico.

As a military tactic, guerrilla warfare goes back to the premodern age. Guerrillas operate in small bands that can rely on the element of surprise to resist larger military forces. They are most effective in areas where geography helps to provide cover, such as mountains. The word *guerrilla,* meaning "little war," originated during the Napoleonic invasion of Spain (1808–1813) when Spanish *guerrilleros* formed small bands to resist Napoleon's armies. Spanish guerrillas, in conjunction with the conventional forces of the British army, inflicted much damage on the invading French army, through ambushes and interruption of supply columns.

In Latin America, the 1780 rebellion of Túpac Amaru in the Cuzco region constitutes an important precedent to modern guerrillas. Túpac Amaru used military tactics to achieve political ends. His rebellion against heavy taxation and abuses by colonial authorities soon became a widespread challenge to the Spanish colonial state. During many of the military encounters, rebels, often armed only with slings, took advantage of the Andes' rugged terrain to gain military advantage over the better organized and armed viceregal armies. Despite his defeat and eventual execution, Túpac Amaru remained a symbol of rebellion against an oppressive state. His name would be taken by two twentieth-century guerrilla movements, the Tupamaros in Uruguay (1960s–1980s) and the Movimiento Revolucionario Túpac Amaru in Peru (1980s–1990s).

During the nineteenth century, guerrillas operated primarily in the context of wars that also involved conventional armies. During the wars of independence (1810–1825), guerrillas played a role in the fighting against royalist armies. In Mexico, leaders Guadalupe Victoria and Vicente Guerrero kept alive the rebellion against the colonial state in the Sierra Madre del Sur until they eventually joined General Iturbide in declaring Mexican independence in 1821. During Peru's wars of independence, Indian guerrillas known as *montoneras* fought against the Spanish armies in the Andes. Later in the century, guerrillas helped in the resistance against foreign invaders; and during the French invasion of Mexico and the rule of Emperor Maximilian (1864–1867), liberals led by Benito Juárez used guerrilla tactics to combat the French. In Peru, during the Chilean invasion (1881–1883) that followed the War of the Pacific, armies of peasants used guerrilla tactics against the Chilean armies in the Andes.

The Mexican Revolution included guerrilla warfare at various stages. At the outset, small bands heeded Francisco Madero's call to rise up against the dictatorship of Porfirio Díaz. In the north, Pancho Villa began as a guerrilla leader. In the south, Emiliano Zapata used guerrilla tactics throughout the Revolution. Zapata's bands engaged in the classic tactics of guerrilla warfare, and when circumstances allowed them to engage advantageously in conventional encounters, they also merged to form larger armies.

During the 1920s, Augusto Sandino emerged in Nicaragua as Latin America's most successful guerrilla leader. In 1927, the United States brokered an agreement among warring political factions that led to elections in 1928 and to the creation of the Nicaraguan National Guard. Sandino refused to lay down arms and staged an insurgency against the U.S. Marines and the National Guard. During the next five and a half years, Sandino and his guerrilla forces were able to harass U.S. forces sufficiently to force a U.S. withdrawal in 1932. Sandino was eventually assassinated in 1934, but he became a symbol of nationalism and anti-Americanism. In neighboring El Salvador, the Communist leader Farabundo Martí led an uprising in 1932 that elicited a harsh government response against the peasantry, leading to a massacre known as La Matanza. Marti's legacy lived on with the emergence in the 1980s of the Frente Farabundo Martí de Liberación Nacional, a group that came close to toppling the Salvadoran government but subsequently engaged in negotiations and abandoned armed struggle.

The first successful guerrilla challenge to the modern state was the Cuban Revolution, led by Fidel Castro. Castro had originally sought to enter the political system as a congressman for the Ortodoxo Party; however, his plan was disrupted when Fulgencio Batista staged a coup and established a dictatorship in 1952. During the following years, Castro and his followers organized an armed movement. After a three-year insurgency in Cuba's Sierra Maestra Mountains, the *barbudos* (bearded ones) toppled the Batista regime in 1959. By this point, Batista had gradually lost legitimacy both nationally and internationally. Castro and his rebels gained strength and finally walked into Havana without a fight on January 1, 1959. Castro soon adopted Marxism and established Latin America's first and longest-lasting socialist experiment.

Augustín de Iturbide, a Spanish military officer who supported Mexican rebels in their drive for independence in 1820. (Library of Congress)

The Cuban Revolution became a source of both ideological inspiration and direct material support for guerrillas throughout Latin America. The most famous of Cuba's guerrilla fighters became associated with the export of revolution: Che Guevara, originally an Argentine medical student, who now holds star status in popular culture throughout the Americas. In 1960, Guevara published his practical guide to revolution: *Guerra de guerrillas* (Guerrilla Warfare), a work that popularized the idea of the *foco,* a small group of committed revolutionaries who could start the revolution, based on Lenin's idea of the *cadre.* Guevara's work emphasized the importance of individual agency in creating the conditions for revolution, in contrast to established Communist parties throughout Latin America that awaited the appropriate historical conditions and whose main struggles had been taken to organizing labor movements. Guevara's ideas were further disseminated throughout the world by the French philosopher and journalist Regis Debray. Guevara himself engaged in the project of exporting revolution and was killed in the process in 1967 while fighting in Bolivia. Soon after the Cuban Revolution, guerrilla movements emerged throughout the continent, sometimes receiving direct support from Cuba.

The oldest ongoing guerrilla war is in Colombia. Guerrillas can be traced back to the 1948 *Bogotazo,* an outburst of political violence that erupted in Bogotá following the assassination of populist leader Jorge Gaitán. In the subsequent decades of violence, guerrilla warfare became one of many tactics of confrontation among different political factions. After the 1960s, a number of groups emerged, including the FARC (Fuerzas Armadas

Revolucionarias de Colombia), which split off from the Colombian Communist Party and which continues to operate, thereby making it the longest ongoing guerrilla movement in Latin America. Another less successful guerrilla group, the ELN (Ejercito de Liberación Nacional), nonetheless had an ideological impact because of the participation of a priest, Camilo Torres, whose death in 1969 brought him a degree of fame throughout Latin America. The M-19, a group that eventually abandoned its weapons to join Colombia's political system, became famous for its armed attack against the Colombian Supreme Court on November 7, 1985, an attack that ended with the deaths of a number of judges after the army stormed the building.

Nicaragua, where the Sandinistas took over power in 1979, offers an excellent example of a closed political system, with ineffective political parties and the move toward dynastic rule under the Somoza family. Under such conditions, opposition to the regime widened among different social classes, including sectors of the elite, and allowed the Frente Sandinista de Liberación Nacional, a guerrilla group founded in neighboring Honduras in 1961, to come to power in 1979. The Sandinistas, under the leadership of Daniel Ortega, remained in power until 1990 and worked to create a socialist regime. The United States secretly funded another group of guerrillas, the Contras, who sought to undermine the Sandinista regime.

While Peru experienced a number of unsuccessful uprisings during the 1960s, the most powerful guerrilla movement emerged in the country during the 1980s: Sendero Luminoso (Shining Path). Sendero is unusual in the context of other guerrilla movements in that it began its armed struggle in 1980, precisely when Peru was making its transition to democracy after twelve years of military rule. A Maoist group born in the impoverished rural region of Ayacucho and founded by a philosopher, Abimael Guzmán (known by the *nom de guerre* Presidente Gonzalo), Sendero eventually gained global notoriety for its extreme violence and fanatical ideology. The group recruited heavily among impoverished peasants and initially gained much popular support. Yet its extreme violence, often directed against the very people it sought to represent, began to undermine its support. Through armed attacks and bombings, the group inflicted considerable damage as it implemented the Maoist tactic of moving "from the countryside to the city." The Peruvian government in turn responded with the army. Thousands of civilians were killed in the crossfire; in 2003, a Truth Commission found that 69,000 people had lost their lives in the conflict. By the early 1990s, Sendero had established its presence in the capital city of Lima and seemed close to overthrowing the government. Only careful intelligence work and the capture of Guzmán in 1991 finally dismantled Sendero's organization, although the group remains active, albeit in a weakened form.

A guerrilla group that could be placed at the opposite extreme from Sendero Luminoso because of its primarily nonviolent tactics and willingness to dialogue with the government is Mexico's Ejercito Zapatista de Liberación Nacional, which began its armed insurgency in the Chiapas region of Mexico in 1992. The EZLN is also unusual in that it did not seek to overthrow the

Mexican state but rather to push an agenda of reform focused specifically on the region of Chiapas. The EZLN has made use of the Internet to gain worldwide support for its cause.

Whereas the aforementioned movements were primarily rural-based, a new form of urban guerrilla also emerged in Latin America after the Cuban Revolution. Based primarily in the Southern Cone countries (Brazil, Argentina, Uruguay, and Chile), urban guerrillas pursued similar goals of destabilizing the state. These urban guerrillas believed that the lack of legitimacy of the military regimes they were fighting would eventually lead to popular uprisings to give the guerrillas victory. The most important theorist behind this movement was the Brazilian Carlos Marighella, who had a brief tenure as head of the Action for National Liberation (ALN), which began to operate in 1968; Marighella was shot the following year. Among the most prominent urban guerrilla movements were the Ejercito Revolucionario del Pueblo (ERP) and the Montoneros (a splinter group from the party of Juan Perón) in Argentina, and the Tupamaros in Uruguay.

The urban guerrillas of the Southern Cone were all eventually defeated by the military regimes of the region in campaigns that made famous the term *desaparecido* (disappeared), which referred to the tactic of arresting suspected militants without due process and getting rid of their bodies. During Argentina's "Dirty War" (1976–1982), over 5,000 people disappeared and thousands more were tortured and killed. Truth Commissions established in many countries since the 1980s have found that governments widely practiced such tactics throughout the region.

While guerrillas have been weakened in the post–cold war world, they continue to operate in certain countries, such as Colombia, Mexico, and Peru.

Iñigo García-Bryce

References

Castro, Daniel. *Revolution and Revolutionaries: Guerrilla Movements in Latin America.* Wilmington, DE: Scholarly Resources, 1999.

Gillespie, Richard. *Soldiers of Perón: Argentina's Montoneros.* Oxford: Clarendon, 1982.

Guevara, Ernesto "Che." *Guerrilla Warfare;* edited by Brian Loveman and Thomas M. Davies Jr. Wilmington, DE: Scholarly Resources, 1997.

Palmer, David Scott, ed. *The Shining Path of Peru.* 2nd ed. New York: St. Martin's, 1994.

Stern, Steve J., ed. *Resistance, Rebellion, and Consciousness in the Andean Peasant World, 18th to 20th Centuries.* Madison: University of Wisconsin Press, 1987.

Wickham-Crowley, Timothy P. *Guerrillas and Revolution in Latin America: A Comparative Study of Insurgents and Regimes since 1956.* Princeton, NJ: Princeton University Press, 1992.

See also: Argentina; Bandits and Banditry; Cold War—Portugal and the United States; Cold War—Spain and the Americas; Communism; Cuban Revolution; Human Rights; Independence I–VI; Liberalism; Mexico; Napoleonic Invasion and Spanish America; Populism; Rebellions—Colonial Latin America; Terrorism; Túpac Amaru Revolt.

GUYANA

Guyana is located in northern South America, bordering the North Atlantic Ocean, between Suriname and Venezuela. Most of the land area, where few people live, consists of inland highlands, rainforest, and savanna in the northeast coast of South America, due south of Newfoundland, west of Suriname (formerly Dutch

Guiana) and French Guiana, north of the northern marshes of Brazil, and east of Venezuela. It is the third smallest country in South America after Suriname and Uruguay, roughly the size of Great Britain (or Idaho). *Guyana* is the Amerindian word for "Lands of Many Waters." There is only one east-west road in the country.

The population, as measured in the 1991 Census, is 723,673, with current estimates ranging between 700,000 and 800,000, resulting from high birth rates of 3 percent per annum minus 1.3 percent emigration rates of Guyanese moving principally to the United States and Canada. Guyana's capital, Georgetown, has about 250,000 people. The only other sizable towns are Linden at 29,000 and New Amsterdam at 18,000. The ethnic groups are distinct: about half are ethnic East Indian, 32 to 36 percent African, 8 to 12 percent mixed, 4 percent Amerindian, 1 percent white, and 1 percent Chinese.

Approximately 57 percent of Guyana's population is Christian, 33 percent Hindu, 9 percent Muslim, and 1 percent other. The languages are English, Guyanese-Creole, and the Amerindian languages of Carib and Arawak. Literacy is quite high at about 96.5 percent.

Before the arrival of Europeans, the region of contemporary Guyana was inhabited by both Carib and Arawak tribes who named it Guiana, which means "land of waters." The indigenous Warrau tribe controlled the territory. The Carib Indians had driven the Arawaks north and westward into the Antilles. Sighted by Columbus during his third voyage, the area was virtually ignored by later Spanish explorers and conquistadors. The Dutch settled in Guyana in the late sixteenth century, and larger European settlements began in 1615, when the Dutch West Indian Company erected a fort and depot on the lower Essequibo River. Most of the native Carib and Arawak peoples were killed by disease or conflict over the land or forced into the interior. By the Treaty of Breda (1667), the Dutch gained all the English colonies of Guiana. The Dutch, realizing the agricultural potential of the swampy coast, drained the land with a network of dikes and canals. In the 1700s, the three Dutch colonies in present-day Guyana grew and prospered, with plantation economies based on sugarcane and slave labor. The Dutch traded with the remaining Indian inhabitants of the interior and established riverside plantations, worked by African slaves. Sugar quickly became the dominant crop.

The abolition of slavery in 1834 brought thousands of indentured laborers, primarily from India but also from Portugal and China, to Guyana to replace the slaves who labored on the sugar plantations. This led to the ethnocultural division between Afro-Guyanese, who became the majority urban population, and the Indo-Guyanese, who remained predominantly rural. Although, for the most part, the diverse ethnic groups have coexisted peacefully, the ethnocultural division has persisted and has led to occasionally turbulent politics. In 1962–1964, racial disturbances between East Indians and Afro-Guyanese erupted. However, the basically conservative and cooperative nature of Guyanese society prevented widespread violent racial tension.

With a small population and abundant natural and mineral resources, Guyana ought to be experiencing economic and social improvement. However, widespread corruption, mismanagement, extravagance, weak democratic institutions, poor economic and fiscal policies, and a huge debt burden have limited national prosperity and growth. At least half of the population lives in poverty, and children are affected more severely than any other group. One-third of the population is under eighteen years of age and, although the government provides free education through secondary school, public education and health care have deteriorated. Child labor is common, preventing high rates of school attendance.

Guyana achieved its independence from the United Kingdom in 1966 and became a republic on February 23, 1970.

Henry F. Carey

References

Gibson, Kean. *The Cycle of Racial Oppression in Guyana.* Lanham, MD: University Press of America, 2003.

Llewellyn John. "Guyana." In *Law and Judicial Systems of Nations,* edited by Charles S. Rhyne. Washington, DC: World Peace Through Law Center, 1978.

Newman, Peter. *British Guiana: Problems of Cohesion in an Immigrant Society.* London: Oxford University Press, 1964.

Rose, Euclid A. *Superpower Intervention in Guyana, Jamaica, and Greneda, 1970–1985.* Lanham, MD: Lexington Books, 2002.

See also: Abolition and Emancipation; Caribbean Community and Common Market; Childhood in Colonial Latin America; Education—Colonial Spanish America; Independence I–VI; Pirates and Piracy; Race; Slavery I–IV; Sugar.

Habsburgs

The Habsburgs were the Central European royal dynasty that also ruled Spain from 1517 to 1700. The first Spanish Habsburg was Charles I, son of Juana, the youngest daughter of Ferdinand of Aragon and Isabel of Castile; and Philip the Fair, heir of the Habsburg Holy Roman Emperor Maximilian I. Ferdinand and Isabel's other children died, leaving Juana to inherit the Spanish throne; but her descent into madness meant that power passed in 1517 to Charles, who had been raised by the Habsburgs in the Low Countries. As king of both Aragon and Castile he was Charles I; elected Holy Roman Emperor in 1519, he became Charles V.

Charles I inherited his Spanish grandparents' Caribbean possessions and soon gained Mexico and the Andes through the conquests by Hernando Cortés and Francisco Pizarro. He created the Council of the Indies in 1524 to oversee the new possessions and sent out viceroys and high courts *(audiencias)* to Mexico and Peru to strengthen royal authority in the colonies. Although the New World territories generated modest revenues, particularly with the discovery of mines in Mexico and the fabulous Andean silver lodes at Potosí, the great American treasures did not begin to reach Spain until the reign of his son, Philip II. Meanwhile, Charles struggled to protect his empire, which stretched from Germany to the Americas, from the Protestants, French, and Turks. He thus embarked on a policy that was designed to protect Habsburg interests but that eventually inflicted decades of costly wars and defeat on Spain and its empire.

In 1556 Charles abdicated and turned Spain, the Americas, and the Netherlands over to his son Philip but named his brother Ferdinand ruler of the Habsburgs' Central European territories. Philip's brief marriage (1554–1558) to Mary Tudor represented Charles's attempt to ally Spain and England against France, but after her death the two allies drifted apart. Philip II continued his father's costly imperial policies, spending Castilian revenues and massive amounts of American silver on imperial ventures. The French Wars of Religion temporarily weakened Spain's chief European rival, and the Spanish-led victory over the Turks at Lepanto in 1571 gave the Habsburgs a respite from Ottoman pressure in the Balkans and the Mediterranean. However, Philip II was unsuccessful in quelling Dutch nationalist and Protestant sentiment. English support for the Dutch eventually provoked Philip in 1588 to launch against England the great, but as it turned out not "invincible," armada. Meanwhile, Philip consolidated the Crown's hold over its American colonies, which rewarded Spain with much higher revenues than during his father's reign. However, they were insufficient to pay for the Habsburgs' imperial ambitions, and Philip declared bankruptcy three times.

Philip II's successors (Philip III, r. 1598–1621; Philip IV, r. 1621–1665; and Charles II, r. 1665–1700) reigned over the exhaustion of Spain and the extinction of the Spanish Habsburg dynasty. In a desperate attempt to maintain Spain's European hegemony, Philip IV and his chief minister, Gaspar de Guzmán, the count-duke of Olivares, attempted to consolidate the Crown's hold over its empire by imposing uniform taxes, laws, and military obligations on the disparate realms. The result was domestic turmoil and rebellion, and Spain's Golden Age ended with its crushing defeat by the French in the Thirty Years' War (1618–1648). The final Spanish Habsburg, Charles II, suffered from physical and intellectual deficiencies. His years on the throne were marked by stagnation and drift, although the remnants of the empire were able to rest from the failed ambitions of the earlier Habsburgs. When Charles died without a direct heir, the throne passed to Philip of Anjou, the Bourbon French prince, who was grandson of both Louis XIV of France and Philip IV of Spain.

Kendall W. Brown

References

Elliott, J. H. *Imperial Spain, 1469–1716.* New York: Viking Penguin, 1990.

Kamen, Henry. *Spain, 1469–1714: A Society of Conflict.* 2nd ed. New York: Longman, 1991.

Lynch, John. *Spain under the Habsburgs.* 2nd ed. 2 vols. New York: New York University Press, 1981.

See also: Administration—Colonial Spanish America; Audiencias; Bourbon Reforms; Council of the Indies; Monarchs of Spain; Potosí; Thirty Years' War; War of the Spanish Succession.

HACIENDA

Haciendas were self-contained estates with vast tracts of land cultivated and used for livestock production for internal consumption and external sale by a labor force bound to the land by economic, social, and cultural ties. Labor relations were characterized by the absence of fixed wages and the presence of legal coercion. Hacienda workers, known as *peones, gañanes, conciertos, inquilinos, acasillados,* and *yanaconas* among other terms, resided on hacienda land and labored in exchange for the right to a portion of their produce and to make payments toward debts owed to the hacienda owner, or *hacendado.* These social relations of production have led researchers to compare the hacienda with the European feudal estate. Although haciendas were social and economic institutions, hacendados also exercised political and military power. Many hacendados received land that became the foundation of their estates as a reward for military service. Some became *gamonales* or *caudillos,* men who used military power and a system of clientalism to dominate regional politics.

The hacienda's origins were in the decline of the colonial *encomienda* and the failure of alternative means of gaining access to labor. In Mexico, haciendas were established during the seventeenth-century depression when an expansion of silver mining enhanced demand for agricultural products and corresponded with a decline in the indigenous population, which was devastated by European disease. Spaniards took control over vast tracts of land, made available through the forced resettlement of indigenous peoples. They used control over land to attract indigenous laborers. Hacendados retained workers in a labor-scarce market by providing them with advances in the form of cash, store credit, seeds, and use of animals, offering them the right to settle on hacienda land and to cultivate it in exchange for a portion of the harvest, and threatening violent retribution if they left. In Central America during the same period of economic depression, Spaniards left cities to create self-sufficient ranches that did not rely on the labor of indigenous people. Thus, haciendas did not form unless there was an external market for agricultural products. Similarly, while haciendas had their origins in the Andean region in the seventeenth century, they expanded dramatically in the late nineteenth century in response to the rise of an export economy driven by European demand for llama and alpaca wool.

Although the hacienda is identified with coercive and often violent means to control labor, it also provided indigenous people with a space to reconstruct their communities. The religious *cofradía,* or brotherhood, founded to worship a community's patron saint, became the center of hacienda social, political, and economic relations. Indigenous people used cofradías to establish terms of negotiation with hacendados and to structure internal labor demand and control over resources. Hacendados acted as patriarchal figures who contracted clergy to perform fiesta masses crucial to indigenous community identity and social relations. Hacendado couples often became godparents to workers' children and were thus bound to them through a moral economy reinforced by religious rituals mediated by Catholic clergy.

In the twentieth century, Latin American governments introduced agrarian reform programs to break up haciendas whose control over land, labor, and political power appeared as obstacles to modernization.

Susan R. Fitzpatrick Behrens

References

Bauer, Arnold J. "Rural Workers in Spanish America: Problems of Peonage and Oppression." *Hispanic American Historical Review* 59, no. 1 (1979): 34–63.
Mörner, Magnus. "The Spanish American Hacienda: A Survey of Recent Research and Debate." *Hispanic American Historical Review* 53, no. 2 (May 1973): 183–216.
Thurner, Mark. "Peasant Politics and Andean Haciendas in the Transition to Capitalism: An Ethnographic History." *Latin American Research Review* 28, no. 3 (1993): 41–82.
Van Young, Eric. "Mexican Rural History since Chevalier: The Historiography of the Colonial Hacienda." *Latin American Research Review* 18 (Fall 1983): 5–61.

See also: Atlantic Economy; Caudillos; Coffee; Colonists and Settlers I–VI; Confraternities; Encomienda; Estancia; Mita; Trade—Spain/Spanish America; Yanancona.

HAITIAN REVOLUTION

The Haitian Revolution (1791–1804) was the most successful slave revolt in recorded history, emancipating close to half a million people and creating the first independent state in Latin America. From the 1600s to 1804, Haiti was known as Saint Domingue, France's largest and most profitable plantation possession. In August 1791, thousands of sugar estate slaves rose up against their masters in a colony already divided by the French Revolution (1789–1799). In 1792, as rebels fought colonists, revolutionaries in France established a republic. Colonial opposition to the French Revolution, as well as invasions by Spain and Britain, forced Saint Domingue's Revolutionary officials to ally with the former slaves. By the end of 1793, they had declared the end of slavery in Saint Domingue, and in 1794 the Revolution in France extended abolition to all French territories.

After 1794, black and mixed-race soldiers, most notably Toussaint L'Ouverture, rose to high rank in Saint Domingue. In 1797, L'Ouverture became the top French military official in the colony, and in 1801 he took the title Governor for Life. The following year, Napoleon Bonaparte sent an army to reestablish colonial control. When the French deported L'Ouverture and tried to disarm Saint Domingue's ex-slaves, a second rebellion broke out. Black and mulatto soldiers left Bonaparte's army to join the rebels and defeated the French in late 1803. On January 1, 1804, the black general Jean-Jacques Dessalines proclaimed Saint Domingue an independent nation, to be known by its Taíno name, Haiti. Referring to his men as "the indigenous army," Dessalines proclaimed, "I have avenged America!"

Dessalines did not completely expel the French, who remained in control of the former Spanish colony Santo Domingo until 1809. In 1821, when former Spanish colonists tried to establish an independent "Spanish Haiti," Haitian troops invaded the eastern part of the island. Their occupation lasted until 1844, creating lasting bitterness in what became the Dominican Republic.

The Haitian Revolution sent tremors throughout the New World wherever slavery existed. In 1805, free colored militiamen in Rio de Janeiro were found wearing buttons depicting Dessalines. Authorities in Cuba found men of color with pictures of Dessalines, expecting a Haitian invasion. Rebels in other areas took advantage of troop shortages caused by the French Revolution to stage their own uprisings. In the British West Indies, for example, 1795 saw the Julien Fédon rebellion in Grenada, a revolt of St. Vincent's Caribs, and a Jamaican Maroon War. In the Spanish Caribbean, Haiti played a role in slave conspiracies in Santo Domingo (1810 and 1818) and in Cuba (1812). On the mainland, from the 1790s through the early 1800s, contact with Haitians or news of Haitian events produced conspiracies and revolts in Louisiana (1811) and in New Granada at Coro (1795), Maracaibo (1799), and Cartagena (1799, 1809).

Despite these threats to colonial order, after 1795 Spain's empire absorbed hundreds of rebel slave soldiers and their families from Saint Domingue. As many as 14,000 black men fighting against slavery in Saint Domingue had joined the Spanish army in early 1793, when Spain declared war against Revolutionary France. As they invaded Saint Domingue from Santo Domingo, Spanish authorities had given military commissions to the leaders of the rebel slaves. The most famous of these soldiers were Jean-François, George Biassou, and Toussaint L'Ouverture, and their victories helped Spain occupy most of Saint Domingue's north province in 1794.

French Revolutionary officials countered this threat by offering emancipation to any rebel who would fight to defend the colony. In April 1794, Toussaint L'Ouverture and his men accepted the offer. Though other black officers remained loyal to Madrid, in October 1795 the Treaty of Bâle forced Spain to withdraw from Saint Domingue and Santo Domingo. Spanish authorities evacuated 707 black officers and their families from the island, sending them to various areas that needed soldiers and settlers. George Biassou and about twenty-five persons went to Saint Augustine in Florida, where he commanded the free black militia until his death in 1805. Larger groups were sent to Trinidad, to Guatemala, to Trujillo on the Honduran coast, to Campeche in the Yucatán, and to Punta Gorda in Panama. Most became farmers and militiamen, and a few bought their own slaves. Some intermarried with refugees from British or North American slavery, including French-speaking black Carib rebels deported from Saint-Vincent to Honduras. The highest-ranking refugee, General Jean-François, was sent to Cádiz in Spain with about 140 persons, including his extended family. Plans were to send him back to the New World, but Jean-François died in Spain in 1805.

Although the image of the Haitian Revolution threatened Latin American slavery, its effects actually helped sustain this labor system. After 1791, Saint-Domingue's sugar and coffee planters fled to neighboring islands, founding hundreds of new plantations in Cuba and Puerto Rico. The emancipation of French slaves created shortages of both sugar and coffee in the late 1790s, leading to a resurgence of the slave trade. Cuba's expanding sugar industry brought nearly half a million enslaved Africans to the island in the nineteenth century.

Moreover, Haiti's international isolation and internal violence led many Latin American leaders to shun it, in both colonial and national periods. The independence fighter Francisco Miranda recruited men in Haiti in 1806, and the Haitian president Alexandre Pétion provided supplies to Simón Bolívar in 1816 for his struggle against Spain. But Bolívar excluded Haiti from the first meeting of independent American nations in Panama in 1826, in part because the United States would not recognize Haiti's independence. In Cuba, those skeptical about independence from Spain cited Haitian "barbarism" as proof that a large ex-slave population was an obstacle to progress and prosperity. As late as 1912, some Cubans used the specter of "becoming another Haiti" to justify the bloody repression of black and mulatto soldiers who demanded voting rights.

John D. Garrigus

References

Dubois, Laurent. *Avengers of the New World: The Story of the Haitian Revolution.* Cambridge, MA: Harvard University Press, 2004.

Gaspar, David Barry, and David P. Geggus, eds. *A Turbulent Time: The French Revolution and the Greater Caribbean.* Bloomington: Indiana University Press, 1997.

Geggus, David P., ed. *The Impact of the Haitian Revolution in the Atlantic World.* Columbia: University of South Carolina Press, 2001.

———. *Haitian Revolutionary Studies.* Bloomington: Indiana University Press, 2002.

Helg, Aline. *Our Rightful Share: The Afro-Cuban Struggle for Equality, 1886–1912.* Chapel Hill: University of North Carolina Press, 1994.

Sheller, Mimi. "The 'Haytian Fear': Racial Projects and Competing Reactions to the First Black Republic." Pp. 285–303 in *The Global Color Line: Racial and Ethnic Inequality and Struggle from a Global Perspective,* edited by Pinar Batur-Vanderlippe and Joe Feagin. Greenwich, CT: JAI, 1999.

See also: Abolition and Emancipation; Armies—Colonial Spanish America; Bourbon Reforms; Coffee; Colombia; Cuba; Defense—Colonial Spanish America; Florida; Honduras; Independence I–VI; Panama; Puerto Rico; Race; Rebellions—Colonial Latin America; Slave Rebellions—Brazil; Slave Rebellions—Caribbean; Slave Rebellions—Spanish America; Slavery I–IV; Slave Trade; Sugar.

HENEQUEN

Henequen is the common Spanish name for *Agave fourcroydes,* a rough cordage plant indigenous to the northwestern tip of the Yucatán Peninsula. Increasing demand for henequen from the U.S. market contributed to a late nineteenth-century export boom in the region and the development of a monocrop plantation economy.

Bartolomé de las Casas's *History of the Indies* makes reference to "nequen," and early colonial reports suggest that the Maya used the plant (which they called *ki)* to make ropes, at least since the early sixteenth century. In the late eighteenth and early nineteenth centuries, Yucatecan producers of henequen fiber exported it to European and American naval yards.

In 1878, the American inventor and agricultural machinery tycoon Cyrus McCormick invented a mechanical binding machine that required twine. McCormick's invention led to an unprecedented demand for henequen. Soon Yucatán became one of the main providers of cordage to the U.S. agricultural market, and consequently Yucatán's relationship with European purchasers dwindled. While henequen production in the Yucatán increased almost tenfold between 1875 and 1900, 97 percent of it was exported, mainly to the United States. Census figures report that approximately 10,000 tons per year were produced in 1875. By 1900, that figure stood close to 90,000 tons.

The henequen plant was harvested by peasants and day-laborers hired by plantations. Plantation work was especially labor intensive since it was harvested year round. Workers harvested the henequen leaves (called *pencas* in Spanish) with a machete and loaded them onto a manual wheel barrow or a wheeled platform pulled along by a donkey. Economic growth arising from the increased demand for henequen fostered technological innovation. The first rasping machine, patented in 1875 (the "Solis," machine after the name of its inventor), mechanized the hard task of extracting the pulp and fiber from the henequen leaf. Subsequent improvements to the wooden machine added metal combs to scratch and rasp at the flesh of the plant to string out the pulp and the fiber, which then was hung out to dry out in the sun, along wooden racks especially built for this purpose.

Yucatán's railroad network also spread quickly in order to transport the fiber from the plantations to the port of Sisal, on the northern coast of Yucatán. Within the plantations, narrow-gauge rails in turn transported the henequen leaves speedily from the field to the machine room, where

A worker at a henequen plantation separates fibers with a machine, Yucatán Peninsula, Mexico. (Macduff Everton/Corbis)

the fiber was processed. The adoption of steam power late in the nineteenth century (with machines imported from Great Britain) significantly increased productivity on the plantations.

Most scholars of the period agree that there was not enough labor to satisfy the demands of the henequen economy, which led to exploitation and repressive control measures, including fostering indebtedness among the workers to tie them into a type of indentured servitude, termed *debt peonage*. The Mexican Revolution (1910–1917) redrew the relationship among workers, landowners, and the state. In Yucatán, revolutionary intentions to reform land distribution were thwarted by a powerful allegiance of landowners and major employers in the region, without whom the economy of Yucatán would have crumbled. Yucatán's commitments to export trade were not affected, and it was not until President Lazaro Cardenas's government (1934–1940) that land reform in Yucatán effectively redistributed land among peasants. However, by then plastic ropes were replacing henequen in all industries, and the importance of henequen on the international market all but disappeared.

Juliette Levy

References

Casares, Raúl E., and G. Cantón, eds. *Yucatán en el tiempo: Enciclopedia alfabética.* Yucatán: Inversiones Cares SA de CV, 1998.

Fallaw, Ben. *Cárdenas Compromised: The Failure of Reform in Post Revolutionary Yucatán.* Durham, NC: Duke University Press, 2001.

Wells, Allen, and Gilbert M. Joseph. *Summer of Discontent, Seasons of Upheaval: Elite Politics and Rural Insurgency in Yucatán.* Stanford, CA: Stanford University Press. 1996.

See also: Caste War of Yucatán; Columbian Exchange—Agriculture; Hacienda; Mexican Revolution; Mexico; Native Americans IV—Mesoamerica; World War I; World War II.

HIDALGO

The great majority of early Spanish immigrants to the New World were men, but few of these were men of high social status in their Iberian homeland. Most immigrants were skilled tradesmen of the lower middle class. They were not peasants; but they were not of the nobility, not even the lower nobility.

In the New World, as in the Old, by recognized service to the Crown, a man could advance himself to a position of acknowledged merit and distinction. He could become recognized as ranking above a commoner, and he could even establish and pass on to his progeny an admirable lineage. Such a person could become an *hijo de algo,* literally, a "son of something," the something in question being status. The elided title came to be "hidalgo," which represented the relatively exalted rank to which men of ambition aspired.

Above hidalgos on the scale of aristocracy ranked viscounts, grandees, counts, lords, marquises, barons, and dukes. Still, to achieve the status of hidalgo *(fidalgo* or *filho de algo* in Portuguese) was considered crucial, whether in Iberia or in the New World. It marked the essential divide between aristocrat and commoner, an absolute distinction.

Significant advantages accrued to an hidalgo, beyond the right to be addressed as "Don." Even if he continued to practice a trade, an hidalgo was not subject to the taxes that the Crown normally imposed on commoners. The property of an hidalgo could not be seized to settle a civil suit, nor could he be imprisoned for debt. Except in cases of treason, an hidalgo could not be tortured. If convicted of a capital crime, an hidalgo had the right to insist on decapitation as opposed to hanging, a gruesome and humiliating death unworthy of a nobleman.

The title and the practice of granting hidalgo status for meritorious service to the Crown began when the Christian kings of the northern peninsula first set out on the *Reconquista,* the campaign to drive the Moors from the Iberian Peninsula, a quest that lasted more than 700 years. Consequently, the more northern the province of one's birth, the more likely one was to be considered an hidalgo. By contrast, the farther south one lived, the less likely one was to have achieved or inherited the status. Indeed, to be acknowledged as an hidalgo, one had to prove one's *limpieza de sangre* (purity of blood) by demonstrating that one's ancestors had been Catholic at least as far back as both sets of great-grandparents.

By 1492, when the southernmost Moorish stronghold of Granada was finally overcome and Jews were also compelled to convert to Christianity, it became all the more imperative for men from central and southern Iberia, especially those whose purity of blood (religious heritage) might otherwise be questioned, to validate their loyalty, merit, and service by somehow achieving the status of hidalgo. At the same time, bastard sons of Christian aristocrats or legitimate sons whose inheritances would be minimal also sought a way to establish themselves socially and financially. An obvious place to do this was the New World, where vast territories and infidel peoples were considered ripe for conquest in the name of Crown and Church. The New World quest for "God, gold, and glory" was synonymous with the passion to prove oneself worthy of the coveted title hidalgo.

John Gordon Farrell

References

Lockhart, James. *The Men of Cajamarca: A Social and Biographical Study of the First Conquerors of Peru.* Austin: University of Texas Press, 1972.

Lockhart, James, and Enrique Otte. *Letters and People of the Spanish Indies, Sixteenth Century.* Cambridge: Cambridge University Press, 1976.

Lockhart, James, and Stuart B. Schwartz. *Early Latin America: A History of Colonial Spanish America and Brazil.* Cambridge: Cambridge University Press, 1983.

Lynch, John. *The Hispanic World in Crisis and Change, 1598–1700.* Oxford: Blackwell, 1992.

Poole, Stafford. *Juan de Ovando: Governing the Spanish Empire in the Reign of Philip II.* Norman: University of Oklahoma Press, 2004.

See also: Artisans; Catholic Church in Brazil; Catholic Church in Spanish America; Colonists and Settlers I–VI; Conquest I–VII; Conquistadors; Jews—Colonial Latin America; Migration—From Iberia to the New World; Monarchs of Spain; Moors; Native Americans I–VIII; Poverty; Race.

HISPANIOLA

The term *Hispaniola* is a poor translation from Peter Martyr's *Decades of the New World.* Throughout the sixteenth century the island was known as La Española or Isla Española. Isla Española was the original name that Christopher Columbus gave to the Antille, which the native Arawak Indians called Haiti or Quisqueya.

Columbus attempted to organize a colony based on the model established at Saint George of Mina, the great Portuguese trade establishment on the western African coast. In 1493, Columbus founded a village that he called Isabela, in honor of the Spanish queen. Three years later his brother Bartholomew founded Santo Domingo del Puerto (later known as Santo Domingo), which became the island's capital. Spanish settlers on Española had tried to exploit the gold mines of Cibao, but it was only with the discovery of the so-called new mines in the south that the economic potential of the island attracted the attention of the Crown. The Columbus period ended in October 1500, when the new governor, Francisco de Bobadilla, sent Columbus and his brothers back to Spain. The desire to establish an autonomous, almost feudal, state in Isla Española stirred constant clashes between Columbus and the other Spanish colonists. Bobadilla continued to develop the system of granting Indians to Spanish settlers in *encomiendas* or *repartimientos.*

In 1502, however, the new governor, Frey Nicolás de Ovando, began to restructure island life. Ovando moved the island's capital from the eastern to the western shore of the Ozama River, which facilitated comunication with the mining district and where there was enough ground to develop a real city. A mint was constructed beside the mines of Arbol Gordo. And in 1504 the Catholic Kings ordered the establishment of twin institutions that would monopolize trade and navigation between Spain and the New World, the Casa de Contratación (Board of Trade) of Seville and that of Santo Domingo. Ovando recommended the establishment of such institutions in order to regulate the Spanish explorations and to put an end to smuggling. The Casa de Contratación of Seville was responsible for registering the crews and settlers who sailed to the Americas. Ovando also started the construction of noble buildings (made of stone) in the capital city, paying some of them from his own pocket. He was relatively severe with the settlers; he worried about their moral life and he favored marriages. He had brought with him from Spain 1,200 settlers, seventy of whom were married women. In 1509, Bartolomé de las Casas suggested that there were 12,000 Spaniards living on the island. Ovando also improved agriculture and cattle-raising, and took a personal interest in the development of sugar plantations. The encomienda system was consolidated during his mandate, and he tried to develop a mestizo society by authorizing mixed marriages between Spaniards and

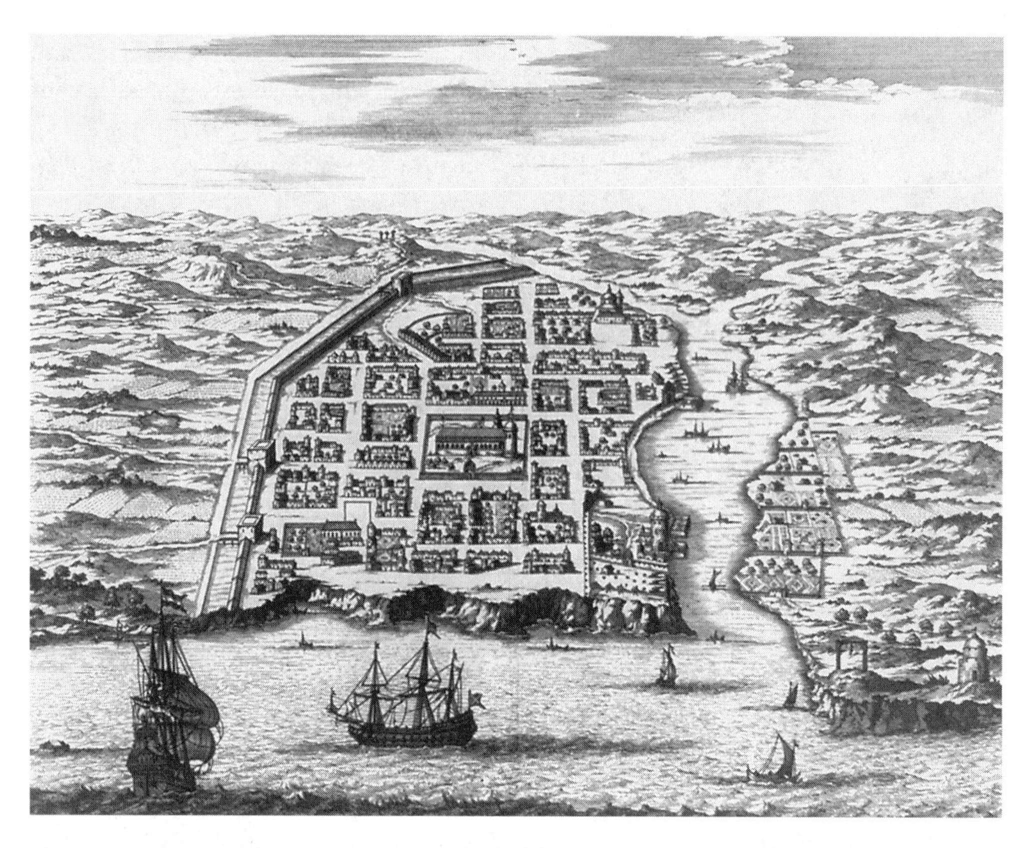

Engraving from 1671 of Santo Domingo on the island of Hispaniola. Christopher Columbus claimed the island for Spain in 1492, but after 50 years of exploiting its resources and bringing disease to its inhabitants, Spain found Santo Domingo to be an unprofitable colony. From Arnold Montanus's De Nieuwe en Onbekende Weereld, *1671. (Library of Congress)*

Indians. Law and order inspired his work. (It is important to recognize that his self-discipline was influenced by his experience as knight of the Military Order of Alcántara.) He also tried to attract Indian elites to Spanish customs and convert them into good Christians.

Before his return to Spain, Frey Nicolás de Ovando provided the resources to build the first hospital of the New World, named Saint Nicholas. His major accomplishments were to organize the expeditions that explored and conquered Cuba and Puerto Rico, as well as the foundation of twelve towns in Hispaniola. Santo Domingo was one of the first three bishoprics in the New World. The first archbishop of Santo Domingo was Garcia de Padilla. A second see for the island was simultaneously established in the city of Concepción, with Pedro Suárez de Deza serving as its first bishop. The oldest bull organizing the American bishoprics dates from 1504, and it was promulgated by Julius II; however, the Spanish Crown did not acknowledge the bull until 1511.

A magnificent cathedral was constructed in Santa Domingo over the course of the early sixteenth century. Bishop Alessandro Geraldini began the stone construction, following the traditions established in Europe in late Gothic and Renaissance style. Masons came from Extremadura or had worked on other projects in the Atlantic, probably in the Canary Islands: the apse of the cathedral was decorated in Portuguese "Manuelino" style. It is in the *Capilla Mayor,* the crypt under the main altar, that some members of the Columbus family were buried: Diego Colon (Colombus's eldest son), as well as the first admiral's brothers, Bartholomew and Diego.

In the early sixteenth century, when Spain was dominant in the New World, France, Great Britain, and Dutch privateers often disrupted Spanish shipping, stealing gold and silver and other precious items, and giving the largest share back to the supporting governments. One of the central places for these privateers to hide was just off Hispaniola's north coast, on the island of La Tortue. By the seventeenth century, privateers gave way to unsanctioned criminals, who became known as pirates, and La Tortue became the center for French pirates.

Some pirates began to cross the 16 kilometers to Haiti to hunt for food. Since they cooked over open fires, they came to be called *boukanier* (open fire men), which was translated to "buccaneers" in English. They gradually built a French settlement in Spanish territory. By the 1670s, Hispaniola's economic problems induced the Spanish to cede control of the western part of the island to the French. Disputes arose over French infringement on Spanish land; these disputes were finally settled in 1697 when the Treaty of Rystwik granted the western portion of Hispaniola to France, which named the colony San Domingue. The border was finalized in 1777. This French colony corresponds roughly to the same boundaries as modern Haiti. Sugar production dominated the economy of the island and slaves played a central role in its history.

The African slaves revolted many times, but the revolt of 1791 grew into a revolution that finally succeeded in late 1803. Spain ceded what it called Santo Domingo to France in the 1795 Treaty of Peace of Basilea, and the entire island was administratively unified in 1801. On January 1, 1804, the country of Haiti became the only republic ever formed by slaves after a victorious revolution. The Spanish had backed the insurgency, hoping to reclaim Saint Domingue. After rebel leader Jean-Jacques Dessalines declared independence for Haiti, he made himself emperor and threatened to kill the remaining French whites. An economic blockade by the European powers only served to strengthen Dessalines's position. However, he was assassinated after he tried to force the black population to return to work on the plantations.

It was not until 1818, under Jean-Pierre Boyer, that Haiti was united. Boyer also managed to conquer the remaining eastern two-thirds of Hispaniola in 1821. The newly acquired territory remained under Haitian control until 1844, when it declared independence as the Dominican Republic.

The opening of the Panama Canal in 1914 made the Windward Passage, which separates Haiti from Cuba, a strategically important shipping lane. When the Haitian president was overthrown the following year, the United States spotted the opportunity to take complete control of the passage and invaded, ostensibly to restore stability. U.S. troops seized Haiti's gold deposits, revamped the constitution, and disbanded the army, replacing it with a U.S.

police force. U.S. troops also implemented important public works, building hospitals, clinics, and roads, but the occupation faced violent resistance. The Americans departed in 1934, leaving the country in economic ruin; thereafter a series of weak governments ruled, with occasional military intervention, until 1957. The United States also invaded the Dominican Republic in 1916 but remained there only eight years.

Henry F. Carey and István Szászdi

References

Bellegarde-Smith, Patrick. *Haiti: The Breached Citadel.* Boulder, CO: Westview, 1990.

Lamb, Ursula. *Frey Nicolás de Ovando, Gobernador de las Indias (1501–1509).* Madrid: Consejo Superior de Investigaciones Científicas, 1956.

Lockhart, James, and Stuart B. Schwarz. *Early Latin America: A History of Colonial Spanish America and Brazil.* Cambridge: Cambridge University Press, 1983.

Mira Caballos, Esteban. *Las Antillas Mayores 1492–1550 ensayos y documentos.* Madrid: Vervuert-Iberoamericana, 2000.

Moya Pons, Frank. *Después de Colón: Trabajo, sociedad y política en la economía del oro.* Madrid: Alianza Editorial, 1987.

Szászdi León Borja, István. "Omizianos, final de una política penal indiana: El gobierno del comendador de lares." Pp. 587–608 in *Homenaje a Ismael Sánchez Bella,* edited by Joaquín Salcedo Izu. Pamplona: University of Navarre, 1992.

———. *Los viajes de rescate de Ojeda y las rutas comerciales indias. El valor económico del señorío del mar de los reyes católicos.* Santo Domingo: Ediciones Fundación García Arévalo, 2001.

See also: Architecture—Colonial Spanish America; Atlantic Economy; Casa de Contratación; Catholic Church in Spanish America; Clergy—Secular, in Colonial Spanish America; Conquest III—Caribbean; Conquistadors; Contraband; Encomienda; Hospitals; Laws—Colonial Latin America; Laws of Burgos; Mining—Gold; Monarchs of Spain; Monopolies; Navigation; New Laws of 1542; Religious Orders; Repartimiento; Universities; Viceroyalties.

HONDURAS

A former Spanish colony, Honduras has an area of 112,090 square kilometers and is bordered by Guatemala and El Salvador to the west and Nicaragua to the southeast. In 1502, during his fourth and final voyage to the Americas, Christopher Columbus went ashore at what is now the site of Trujillo, Honduras, and there participated in the first Catholic mass on the American mainland. Roughly twenty years passed before a more durable Spanish presence was established.

By the 1520s, the conquest expeditions radiating outward from both Panama and Mexico reached Honduras. This was a turbulent period as various *conquistadors,* including Hernando Cortés, fought over their competing claims to the northwestern coast and its hinterland. The Spanish Crown appointed the first royal governor for the province in 1525, but another decade passed before Francisco de Montejo's governorship brought a measure of stability to the region.

Preconquest Honduras straddled the dividing line between Mesoamerican "high culture" and the Chibchan culture disseminated from northern South America. Thus, one finds the Classic-period Maya city of Copán in western Honduras, as well as the less complex tribal groups of the eastern lowlands, such as the Paya and Sumu. Even before Honduras was conquered by the Spanish, the indigenous people of Honduras's north coast had been vulnerable to slave raids from Spaniards of the Caribbean islands. By the mid-sixteenth century, as a result of the shipment of thousands of Indian slaves to Panama and the Caribbean islands, internecine warfare among the conquerors, and overwork in Spanish mining operations, the indigenous population of Honduras had declined by at least 90 percent.

Most of the indigenous inhabitants of western and central Honduras, the area most heavily settled by Spaniards, were members of various chiefdoms known collectively as the Lenca. The Lenca and other Honduran indigenous groups were not complex, stratified, populous societies like those the Spaniards encountered in Peru and Mexico. Honduras offered a smaller labor supply and less moneymaking potential than those colonial centers and was therefore less attractive to Spanish colonists. Nevertheless, Spaniards did settle in Honduras and endeavored to extract such wealth as they could from the native population.

Honduras was one of the only regions of Central America that appeared to be well stocked with the precious metals that the early Spanish settlers coveted. This early mining enterprise utilized Indian slaves who were compelled to pan for gold in Honduran rivers. During the second half of the sixteenth century silver deposits were discovered in the region around Tegucigalpa, and the lure of this mineral wealth transformed Honduras. Spanish colonists were drawn to the south-central region of the province, along with a limited number of African slaves. Ultimately, however, Honduran mining never constituted a significant export for Central America; the biggest obstacle the industry faced was a shortage of labor. By the beginning of the seventeenth century, the indigenous population was severely depleted, yet the mines were not sufficiently profitable to fund the importation of large numbers of African slaves. The mines did not produce fabulous wealth for the Crown, but they did reshape local economies as agricultural and livestock production were adapted and expanded to meet the demands of the mining sectors.

Religion was, on one level, a tool for expanding and solidifying Spanish control in the colonies. In the areas of greatest Spanish settlement, it was expected that the institution of *encomienda* would provide the mechanism for converting the natives to Catholicism. However, the dispersed settlement pattern of the declining indigenous population and the shortage of parish priests combined to complicate this task. The main missionary orders active in Honduras were the Mercedarians, who were prominent in the west, and the Franciscans, who undertook several generally fruitless missions among tribal peoples of the east (such as the Jicaques and Payas) during the seventeenth and eighteenth centuries.

Lack of control over eastern Honduras posed a problem for the Spanish Crown. Whereas this territory offered scant incentive for Spanish colonization, the unoccupied northeastern coast of Honduras was attractive enough to British traders and planters who formed substantial settlements there. The threat posed by the British presence in Spanish colonial territory reached a peak in the eighteenth century. Not only did the British "Shoremen" extract the fruits of the coast and funnel contraband goods into the colony, but they also formed a close alliance with the Zambos-Miskitos who inhabited the shore and periodically harassed Spanish frontier settlements. The Spanish Crown began preparations to expel the British in the mid-eighteenth century, with the construction of Fort Omoa on the northern coast. During the War for American Independence (1779–1783), Spain seized the opportunity to attack British coastal settlements, and in agreements signed after the war the British pledged to evacuate the coast.

The Spanish Crown attempted to assert control over the northern coast by populating the region with Spanish immigrants. More than 1,200 residents of Asturias, Galicia, and the Canary Islands were recruited as colonists and sent to the coast in 1787; nearly one-fourth died en route, and the survivors faced miserable conditions onshore. Spain's belated effort to control the Atlantic coast of Honduras was a failure, with the result that at the time of independence approximately one-third of the provincial territory of Honduras lay outside of Spain's control. Even today, eastern Honduras is only sparsely populated, by people of African and indigenous descent who have only a tenuous connection with the predominantly Hispanic people and government based in western Honduras.

After Central America declared independence from Spain in 1821, Honduras was a member of the United Provinces of Central America from 1823 to 1838. Honduras did not partake in the nineteenth-century coffee boom as fully as its neighbors, owing in part to the particularly difficult topography of its coffee-growing regions. On the other hand, the north coast of Honduras proved to be ideally situated for banana cultivation. Heavily influenced by the involvement of British and U.S. capital, the banana export enclave of northern Honduras powerfully shaped the development of the Honduran economy and society as a whole.

Doug Tompson

References

Chamberlain, Robert S. *The Conquest and Colonization of Honduras, 1502–1550.* Washington, DC: Carnegie Institution of Washington, 1953.

MacLeod, Murdo J. *Spanish Central America: A Socioeconomic History, 1520–1720.* Berkeley and Los Angeles: University of California Press, 1973.

Newson, Linda. *The Cost of Conquest: Indian Decline in Honduras under Spanish Rule.* Boulder, CO: Westview, 1986.

Wortman, Miles L. *Government and Society in Central America, 1680–1840.* New York: Columbia University Press, 1982.

See also: American Revolution; Bananas; Colonists and Settlers IV—Mexico and Central America; Conquest IV—Central America; Conquistadors; Defense—Colonial Spanish America; Encomienda; Independence III—Central America; Mining—Gold; Mining—Silver; Native Americans IV—Mesoamerica; Religious Orders; United Fruit Company.

HORSES

Perhaps the most important European import to the Americas in the late fifteenth and early sixteenth centuries was the horse. Horses played key roles in the conquests of native peoples by such well-known conquistadors as Hernando Cortés and Francisco Pizarro. The horse became the essential unit of war, transportation, work, trade, and even currency in the early Iberian settlements of Latin America. While sharing early settlement with cattle, sheep, mules, pigs, chickens, and other livestock, it was the horse that became the most widespread and that had the greatest immediate impact on native peoples. Without the horse, it is hard to imagine the rapid success of the Iberian occupation, especially in Mexico and Peru.

Over the broad expanse of time, horses were no strangers to the Americas, since North America was the geographical origin of the rodent-sized Eohippus, from which several horse species developed over roughly 60 million years. Yet the most recent, *Equus,* disappeared from the Americas some 8,000 to 10,000 years ago after the closing of the Bering land bridge. It is unclear why *Equus* died out in the Americas, but earlier ancestors had migrated westward across the land bridge to establish a foothold in Asia and to subsequently proliferate throughout the "Old World." Ironically, while humans aided in the spread of the horse to all other parts of the globe over thousands of years, the peoples of the Americas had no knowledge of them until Christopher Columbus's second voyage in 1493, an act that initiated the pivotal "Columbian Exchange."

In 1493, Columbus embarked from Spain with a reported fifteen stallions and ten mares, along with other livestock. The clear intent was to establish a breeding stock to guarantee the Spanish Crown's possession of its newly claimed territories. This was a risky venture, considering that the arduous two- to three-month journey routinely exacted up to one-third mortality, while there was a long-standing deficit of horses in Spain itself. The Spanish horse was admired throughout Europe, especially for its value in war, yet by the end of the fifteenth century, cost and popular preference had caused mules to proliferate in Iberia at the expense of the horse population. The Spanish Crown then legislated possession and breeding of horses to supply the many wars of the period and to provide mounts for the landed hidalgo class, a condition that simultaneously imposed restrictions on the export of stallions and stimulated the shipment of mares to the Americas. Herds soon flourished on the islands of the Caribbean and later in Central America, and by the mid-sixteenth century breeding ranches existed in virtually all areas occupied by Spaniards. Ideal ecological conditions permitted horses to expand throughout the Americas, often well ahead of European settlers, and by the end of the seventeenth century domesticated and wild horses proliferated in the tens of thousands from Canada to the Pampas of Argentina.

The horse was instrumental in the conquest and settlement of the Americas. Though initially few in number, their speed, mobility, and shock effect contributed to several Spanish successes over indigenous armies. Horses supplied the various expeditions and conquests over the course of the sixteenth century and soon were employed in cattle ranching and in agriculture. Until mules were bred in the Ibero-American colonies, horses served as the prime source for transporting people and goods and as draft animals in mining zones and sugar plantations. The expansion of horse-raising was so rapid that by the mid-1500s no new imports were necessary into Hispaniola, and at the end of the sixteenth century New Spain (Mexico) had become the principal livestock economy in Spanish America, with as many as 150,000 equines, including mules.

The Spanish and Portuguese view of the social position of horse owners, however, meant that poor Iberians and sedentary native peoples were restricted in their access to the animals. In parts of the Spanish Empire, aboriginals had to gain special permission to own or even ride a horse, since this was reserved for the upper-class European resident of the colonies. However, such regulation could not be applied to nomadic peoples, who quickly recognized the efficacy of the horse in transportation, hunting, and warfare, and were able to steal, trade, and domesticate wild horses (*cimarrones, mesteños,* or mustangs) with little interference. The horse brought with it some profound changes and led to the expansion of some groups at the expense of neighbors, as well as Spaniards and Portuguese. In some cases it helped transform seminomadic peoples into powerful warrior-hunter-trader societies, particularly on the plains of North America and Argentina, and in Paraguay and Chile.

The breed of horses imported into the Americas was southern Iberian, largely from Andalusia. Originally from North Africa, the esteemed "Berber" stock were not the large thoroughbreds common today. Most measured thirteen or fourteen hands high (under 5 feet), weighed between 700 and 1,000 pounds, and were swift and agile animals, ideal for warfare. As they adapted and flourished in the Americas, these horses took on characteristics determined by local conditions and eventually became a separate breed, generically known as "Creole" (*criollo*). Criollos were resilient and highly adaptive, ensuring their use in cattle and sheep ranching in various environments. They became the vehicles and status instruments for the European settlement of Ibero-America, were key participants in the independence wars of the early nineteenth century, and were essential in the social and economic hierarchy until the early twentieth century. As the demands of the Industrial Revolution spread to Latin America, the criollo's value diminished in favor of larger workhorses, and eventually the railroad, tractor, and truck.

Although the modern age has led to a decline of the breed, the criollo is still found in the more rudimentary ranching complexes of the region, and many breeders raise the animals for their historic or aesthetic value. Today, the horses that dominate in most ranching, shows, and racing tend to be crossbred animals originally from Europe, the United States, or Arabia, a process that began in the late nineteenth century. Although the horse has less impact today than in the region's past, the predominantly agricultural economies of Latin America still require reliable and resilient workhorses, guaranteeing that after five centuries the horse has returned to the Americas to stay.

Robert W. Wilcox

References

Cabrera, Angel. *Caballos de América.* Buenos Aires: Editorial Sudamerica, 1945.

Denhardt, Robert M. *The Horse of the Americas.* Rev. ed. Norman: University of Oklahoma Press, 1975.

Guilmartin, John F., Jr. "The Cutting Edge: An Analysis of the Spanish Invasion and Overthrow of the Inca Empire, 1532–1539." Pp. 40–69 (esp. pp. 53–55) in *Transatlantic Encounters: Europeans and Andeans in the Sixteenth Century,* edited by Kenneth J. Andrien and Rolena Adorno. Berkeley and Los Angeles: University of California Press, 1991.

Johnson, John J. "The Introduction of the Horse into the Western Hemisphere." *Hispanic American Historical Review* 23, no. 4 (November 1943): 587–610.

Restall, Matthew. *Seven Myths of the Spanish Conquest.* New York: Oxford Univesity Press, 2003.

Worcester, Don. *The Spanish Mustang: From the Plains of Andalusia to the Prairies of Texas.* El Paso: Texas Western, 1986.

See also: Bullfighting; Cimarrones; Columbian Exchange—Agriculture; Colonists and Settlers I–VI; Columbian Exchange—Disease; Columbian Exchange—Livestock; Conquest I–VII; Independence I–VI; Migration—From Iberia to the New World; Native Americans I–VIII; Sports.

HOSPITALS

From the beginnings of Spanish colonialism in the Americas, hospitals controlled by the Catholic Church dominated formal medical care. Along with state-licensed physicians, these two groups focused more on caring for the infirm than on curing the illness. In the case of the Church, the spiritual well-being of patients was an important component of the healing process, and the job of caregivers in this context was not only to use prayer and penance as healing tools, but also to prepare patients for life after death. By the late eighteenth century, secular hospitals began to challenge the dominance of the Church in the realm of healing and healthcare. This shift continued into the nineteenth and twentieth centuries as hospitals slowly made the transition to more modern institutions of medical care.

Caring for the sick in colonial Latin America initially was understood as a missionary activity of religious orders, in particular the Franciscans, Augustinians, and Benedictines. In the first 100 years of colonial rule, roughly 120 hospitals were built in Spanish America to provide medical care for the king's subjects. Although most of these administered primarily to Spaniards, some hospitals, like the Hospital Real de Naturales (or Royal Indian Hospital), founded in 1553 in Mexico City and in 1555 in Cuzco (Peru), cared solely for Indians. The introduction of European diseases, like smallpox, decimated indigenous populations in the first decades of Spanish rule, propelling the issues of disease and care of the sick to the forefront of colonial policy and prioritizing the construction of hospitals.

Since caring for the infirm was historically part and parcel of Christian charity, the state deferred responsibility in this arena to the Church. Consequently, religious orders played an important role in healthcare, through its divine mission to care for the sick, and its presence was generally felt in the institutional setting of the hospital. Hospital care focused less on preventative medicine than on the physical and spiritual comfort of the patient. Responsibilities included keeping the hospital environment clean; bathing, feeding, and clothing patients; examining their excrements; administering medicines; tending to their spiritual needs; and, in the case of death, preparing the body for burial.

The hospital setting, however, reflected the larger racial and class divisions that existed within the colonial healthcare system. First, major hospitals generally were built near city centers, away from poorer, and predominantly mixed-raced populations of outlying *barrios.* The colonial location of hospitals made access to medical care for the urban poor particularly difficult. At the same time, only certain urban groups tended to utilize hospital care. Elites, because of their material resources and philosophical connections to European medicine, were often treated at home. Indians, on the other hand, avoided hospitals whenever possible. For example, in Mexico City, they resisted using the Hospital Real de los Naturales because they believed that it was a place where people went to die. Indians favored the more informal medical sector, based on the care of native healers, or *curanderos,* who utilized non-European forms of healing. The working poor, of mixed race and Spanish background, were most likely the largest group of hospital "consumers" during the colonial era.

Funding for hospitals came from a variety of sources, including private donations, rents from hospital-owned properties, profits from hospital-run lotteries and theaters, as well as support from local city councils in the form of tax revenues. By the end of the colonial period, however, the overall decline of the economy meant that less money was allocated to hospitals for the purposes of healthcare and maintenance. The sources of funding that hospitals relied on were precarious and never adequately covered even minimal expenses. This problem was exacerbated with independence and the ensuing political, economic, and social chaos of the first half of the nineteenth century.

Shifts away from the Church's dominance in healthcare began in the eighteenth century. An excellent example is the first secular hospital established in Mexico City, the Hospital de San Andrés. As the last major hospital built during the colonial period in the viceregal capital, it was modeled after European hospitals at the time. Its charter emphasized the idea that public service and preventative medicine superseded the doctrine of charity and focus on the spiritual well-being of the patient. Founded initially as a military hospital, it was seen as an attempt to move medicine and healthcare into a more modern era, less dependent on the perceived superstitions of the Church. Other changes during the nineteenth century included an increase in the construction of military hospitals, which reflected the growing importance of the armed forces within the independence movements as well as emerging nation-states. Secularization of the hospital continued uninterrupted into the twentieth century, as scientific and technological knowledge increased and as more modern ideas regarding healthcare permeated the hospital setting.

Sharon Bailey Glasco

References

Guerra, Francisco. *El hospital en Hispanoamerica y Filipinas, 1492–1898.* Madrid: Ministerio de Sanidad y Consumo, 1994.

Howard, David. *The Royal Indian Hospital of Mexico City.* Special Studies no. 20, Center for Latin American Studies. Tempe: Arizona State University, 1980.

Muriel, Josefina. *Hospitales de la Nueva España.* Serie Historia Novohispana 12. 2 vols. 2nd ed. Mexico City: Instituto de Investigaciones Históricos, Universidad Nacional Autónoma de México, 1990.

See also: Catholic Church in Brazil; Catholic Church in Spanish America; Cities; Columbian Exchange—Disease; Enlightenment—Spanish America; Independence I–VI; Medicine; Mestizaje; Poverty; Race; Religious Orders; Science and Scientists—Brazil/Portugal; Science and Scientists—Colonial Spanish America.

HUMAN RIGHTS

Classic human rights of the individual, defined as the inalienable rights given to each human being at birth and deriving from natural law, represent one of the fundamentals of Western civilization and have often served as a common point of reference in North America, Europe, and Latin America.

Despite the claim that they are universal and indivisible, human rights are commonly categorized into three generations: The first refers to the classic rights of the individual and combines civil (right to life, right to physical integrity, etc.) and political rights (right to vote and eligibility). The second category consists of economic, social, and cultural rights, which include rights to work, education, and an appropriate standard of living. The third category includes the rights to environment, solidarity, and development. While the first category has its roots in the thought of the European Enlightenment, the second category has its intellectual origins in nineteenth-century socialism. As regards the Ibero-American context, in the sixteenth century, after the famous "debate" between Bartolomé de las Casas and Juan Ginés de Sepúlveda, Spanish law officially recognized the indigenous population in their American colonies as human beings. This has also been subsumed under the development of the human rights idea, although African slaves were not beneficiaries of this improvement.

In Europe, the idea of human rights is closely associated with the ideals of the French Revolution; the United States and Latin Americans in turn integrated the idea of these rights into their struggles for independence. Furthermore, notions of human rights that developed in the French and the America Revolutions mutually influenced ideas both in the Americas and the Iberian Peninsula. The general understanding of human rights as principally those of the individual against the state is a common view held throughout the Americas and Europe. Social democratic and socialist positions in Western Europe have further introduced the second category into their human rights concept—an idea that is widely rejected in the United States but less so in Canada. In contrast, given the widespread socioeconomic inequality in Latin America, the collective dimension of human rights has often been emphasized.

Obviously, there have always been important differences between constitutional claims and actual respect for human rights. However, the discrepancy in Latin America has been so pronounced that the idea of human rights is often reduced to an empty promise. This has been the case throughout modern Latin American history and most apparently during the dictatorships that dominated Latin American politics from the 1960s to 1980s.

On the other hand, by pointing to continued racial discrimination, social discrepancies, and the death penalty, the portrayal of the United States as the standard-bearer for democracy and human rights has been challenged. Scholars have also disapproved of human rights concerns in U.S. foreign policy as a double standard. For instance, until the late 1980s the U.S. administration supported center-right governments of El Salvador, whose security forces committed large-scale human rights violations. At the same time that they overlooked abuses committed in El Salvador, the authorities in Washington fiercely accused the leftist Sandinistas in Nicaragua of the most egregious human rights violations.

While Europe's system of human rights has become highly sophisticated, the inter-American human rights system also has been considerably refined since 1991, in part because of the challenges of the widespread human rights abuses in the 1970s and 1980s. The Inter-American Commission (seated in Washington) and the Inter-American Court of Human Rights (San José, Costa Rica) of the Organization of American States (OAS) are the main intergovernmental human rights bodies in the Western Hemisphere. Although the response of the OAS concerning military dictatorships and human rights abuses in the 1970s and 1980s was not exemplary, since the early 1990s the organization has moved to advance human rights and the rule of law.

The human rights question became a crucial item on the transatlantic agenda in the course of the East-West conflict, particularly with regard to the Central American civil wars of the 1980s. The United States considered authoritarian and dictatorial governments to be preferable to communism, as the lesser of two evils, while many Latin American and European governments strove to fight the roots of violence and upheaval by supporting human rights. At the same time, the highlighting of the human rights issue in Latin America also led to an influential network of local and international human rights nongovernmental organizations (NGOs) in North and Latin America and Europe that have made remarkable contributions to the protection of international human rights.

Another important transatlantic issue concerns the accountability for human rights abuses committed under South American dictatorships: several European countries, in the interest of the principle of universal justice, want former junta members to be extradited in order to prosecute them for abuses committed against their citizens. In this regard, a symbolic case is the detention of former Chilean dictator Augusto Pinochet Ugarte in London in 1998 in compliance with an international warrant issued by Spain's chief prosecutor, Baltasar Garzón. In this context, the supposed coresponsibility of U.S. foreign policy for human rights violations in Latin America in the past fifty years has the potential to lead to further conflict.

Following the conclusion of the East-West confrontation, a common call has been sounded to respect human rights (and representative democracy, which is considered the natural complement of human rights), at least at the official level. Accordingly, North American and European development aid programs, as well as free trade agreements with Latin American countries, usually include human rights and democracy clauses.

In the aftermath of the terrorist attacks on September 11, 2001, in the United States, the position of human rights in the fight against international terrorism has also resulted in transatlantic disputes. Although Portugal and Spain generally supported U.S. antiterrorism efforts, several other European and Latin American countries opposed the new priorities set by Washington as part of its struggle against international terrorism by stressing their human rights concerns. After the terrorist attacks in Madrid on March 11, 2004, Spain and other European countries are expected to take a tougher stance on the issue. However, the implications for human rights are not yet clear.

Although some progress has been made in the beginning of the twenty-first century, many human rights problems remain in North and Latin America and Europe—such as the lack of significant accomplishment of indigenous rights, migrant rights, women's rights, children's rights, rights of the disabled, and protection of refugees and human rights defenders, as well as the ongoing fight against racism and xenophobia.

Klaas Dykmann

References

Cleary, Edward L. *The Struggle for Human Rights in Latin America.* Westport, CT: Praeger, 1997.

Donnelly, Jack. *Universal Human Rights in Theory and Practice.* 2nd ed. Ithaca, NY: Cornell University Press, 2003.

Harris, David J., and Stephen Livingstone, eds. *The Inter-American System of Human Rights.* Oxford: Clarendon, 1998.

Mower, A. Glenn, Jr. *Regional Human Rights: A Comparative Study of the West European and Inter-American Systems.* Westport, CT: Greenwood, 1991.

See also: Caribbean Community and Common Market; Communism; Democracy; Guerrillas; Liberation Theology; Pinochet Case; Populism; Terrorism.

HUMAN SACRIFICE

Human sacrifice was practiced by indigenous peoples throughout the Americas in the centuries leading up to the Spanish conquest and to a lesser extent into the sixteenth century. It was believed necessary in the Mesoamerican and Andean cultures primarily in order to stave off the destruction of the cosmos. In Mesoamerica, its importance was such that the need for sacrificial victims became an integral part of Aztec imperial expansion, in terms of both providing an ever-present incentive for war and terrifying their conquered territories and possible new opponents into submission.

To the newly arrived Europeans, however, human sacrifice in the Americas proved to be one of the most easily misunderstood and horrifying aspects of indigenous life. The Dominican friar Bartolomé de las Casas interpreted the practice in naturalistic terms, suggesting that human sacrifice was an entirely natural attempt by people deprived of the light of revelation to offer their most precious gift in worshiping the deity they believed created and sustained the universe. However, the sheer scale of human sacrifice in the Americas and its persistence even after a number of years of exposure to Christianity were to many Spaniards clear evidence of the diabolical nature of American religion. In 1562, for example, New Spain was rocked by the discovery of idolatrous practices in-

A wall of Aztec ritual skulls at the Templo Mayor archeaological site in downtown Mexico City. The site was the ceremonial center of the Aztec city of Tenochtitlan. (Keith Dannemiller/Corbis)

volving human sacrifice in Yucatán. Worse still, these sacrifices had sometimes taken place in churches, and the rites had apparently consisted of the crucifixion of victims in what was understood to be a demonic parody of Christianity.

Human sacrifice had an entirely different meaning for indigenous peoples. Viewed in terms of the reciprocal relationship between a society and its gods, it could be seen as the payment of an involuntary debt to deities that could devour in death those whom they sustained in life. In Mexica (Aztec) mythology, for instance, the creation of the Fifth Sun was linked to the auto-sacrifice of the god Nanauatzin, who first leapt into the fire kindled as the gods met after the destruction of the Fourth Age, and then rose from the flames as the new sun. A powerful myth then emerged: as the sun sets, he must battle through the underworld in order to rise again; should he fail to do so, the cosmos would fail and demon spirits would overrun the world and devour its inhabitants. Human sacrifice in part repaid that supreme life-giving act by the sun god, and also strengthened and sustained him as he fought his way through the underworld. Warriors killed in battle or on the sacrificial stone would assist him in the battle and would accompany him by day across the sky. Should humans fail to meet their sacrificial debt, the web of reciprocal relationships between them and their gods would break, ultimately causing the destruction of the cosmos.

Andrew Redden

References

Clendinnen, Inga. *Aztecs: An Interpretation.* Cambridge: Cambridge University Press, 1991.

Conrad, Geoffrey W., and Arthur A. Demarest. *Religion and Empire: The Dynamics of Aztec and Inca Expansionism.* Cambridge: Cambridge University Press, 1984.

Farriss, Nancy. *Maya Society under Colonial Rule: The Collective Enterprise of Survival.* Princeton, NJ: Princeton University Press, 1984.

Townsend, Richard F. *The Aztecs.* London: Thames and Hudson, 2000.

See also: Cannibalism; Catholic Church in Brazil; Catholic Church in Spanish America; Chroniclers; Clergy—Secular, In Colonial Spanish America; Conquest V—Mexico; Diabolism in the New World; Idolatry, Extirpation of; Inquisition—Luso-America; Inquisition—Spanish America; Jesuits—Iberia and America; Native Americans I–VIII; Religious Orders; Syncretism.

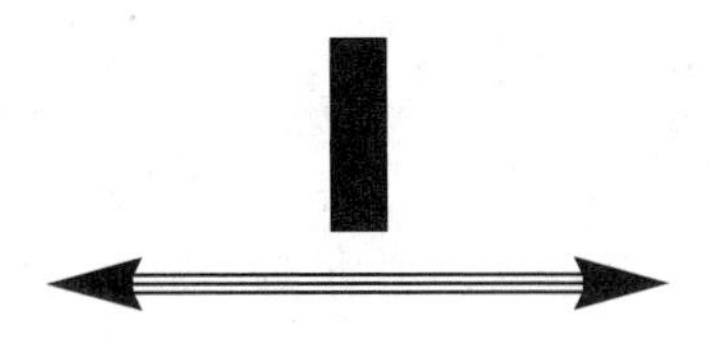

Idolatry, Extirpation of

From a European perspective, genuine adherence to Christianity by native peoples entailed the complete abandonment of indigenous religions. Throughout the sixteenth and seventeenth centuries, a vehement debate raged within the colonial Church regarding the merits of two alternative strategies: persuasion by means of word and example, and coercion through judicial process and corporal punishment. In central Mexico and the Yucatán, violent means, advocated by Franciscan bishops Juan de Zumárraga and Diego de Landa, dominated early in the evangelization (1520s–1570s) but then slowly receded; in Peru, by contrast, there was little systematic, concerted use of violent repression until the early seventeenth century, which witnessed a new missionary strategy—systematically organized ecclesiastical campaigns to extirpate, or root out, idolatry (literally "the worship of idols" but used more broadly to refer to native religions).

The idolatry investigations were sparked by a denunciation made in 1609 by the priest Francisco de Ávila to the archbishop of Lima that the inhabitants of his parish in Huarochirí were secretly worshiping their former gods, Pariacaca and Chaupiñamca, chief mountains of the district, under the guise of Christian celebrations for the feast of the Assumption of the Virgin Mary. In December 1609, before a large crowd gathered in the main square in Lima, Ávila put to the flame a large collection of confiscated native gods and ancestral mummies, and whipped and sent into exile Andean religious teacher Hernando Paucar. The event marked the beginning of a series of visitations in regions of the Central Andean Highlands within striking distance of Lima, conducted by priests of Indian parishes who presided over judicial trials for the offense of idolatry. There were two principal periods of activity: the first period between 1609 and 1622, and the second, more ambitious, one between 1649 and 1670. The timing owes most to the personal commitment of the incumbent archbishop of Lima, Bartolomé Lobo Guerrero (1608–1622) and the archbishop Pedro de Villagómez (1641–1671), respectively. The procedure for the idolatry investigations, modeled on that of the Inquisition (though without the death penalty), was set down in a manual, *The Extirpation of Idolatry in Peru (La extirpación de la idolatría del Perú)* (1621), written by the Jesuit provincial Pablo José de Arriaga.

Spanish conquerors destroying Aztec idols in Mexico. (North Wind/North Wind Picture Archives)

The effectiveness of the idolatry investigations was undermined by the lack of permanent institutional support and financial resources, by the readiness of native peoples to resort to counterlitigation, and by the contradiction at the heart of a strategy that tried to make good Christians by force. The combination of instruction in doctrine with physical punishment made rejection of the Christian message more likely. Official unwillingness to fund the costs of extirpation obliged the inspectors to enforce financial contributions from the communities subject to investigation, which only increased native cynicism and disillusionment. Indigenous communities proved extremely litigious, either bringing counteraccusations against inspectors for malpractice or extortion, which slowed down the judicial process, or exploiting the accusation of idolatry in order to remove unpopular native lords from office. As the seventeenth century wore on, prosecutions were increasingly taken out of the hands of local inspectors and revoked to Lima, where the authorities became ever more skeptical that the trials were serving their purpose. It became clear that the inspections were counterproductive because they made Andeans more distrustful and dismissive of Christian religion.

The documentation generated by the idolatry trials reveals the state of Andean religion between a century and a century and a half after the beginnings of evangelization. Although no trace remained of the imperial religion of the Incas of Cuzco, local religious life—expressed in terms of place and descent, focused on sacred beings like rocks, stones, mountains, canals, and springs, peculiar to particular communities, kin groups, families or individuals—had not only survived but also been reinvigorated. In many places, despite the material destructiveness of the inspections, the old religion had become a vehicle to resist Christianity. Persecution of native religious leaders removed many, but simply drove others into greater clandestinity. Images that had been burned or smashed to pieces were replaced by substitutes, often rationalized as "children" of the destroyed gods, or reverence was offered at the spot where their ashes had been buried and where their spirits continued to watch over the community.

To this extent, native religious rites were renewed in defiance of Christian influence, but more commonly, they blended and interpenetrated with Catholic elements to produce a mixture. Saints were adopted as protectors and intermediaries, and village celebrations merged the observance of the official church calendar and the Andean religious and agricultural cycle. Communal rituals honored both the Christian saint and the native deity at the same time. In this context, acceptance of the Christian saint was genuine, not a duplicitous cover for a purely native ceremony, as the idolatry inspectors feared. The native religious system was sufficiently adaptive to absorb the alien supernatural deities into its own structure and to make an accommodation on native terms.

Concerted campaigns of extirpation were the exception rather than the rule. Isolated idolatry investigations sponsored by individual local priests, independently of their ecclesiastical superiors, in Central Mexico, the Yucatán, and New Granada, as well as the Andes, both began before and continued long after the officially sponsored campaigns. In early and mid-seventeenth-century central Mexico, priests such as Hernando Ruiz de Alarcón, Jacinto de la Serna, and Pedro Ponce raised the cry of alarm that ancient rituals were still practiced, but their contemporaries did not take them very seriously. Here, a combination of skepticism among the political and religious authorities regarding the effectiveness of idolatry inspections and growing indifference to religious blending worked against concerted campaigns. Despite a brief recrudescence of activity in the 1720s, the same was true in the Andes in the eighteenth century. The comfortable coexistence of both religious systems in native minds no longer provoked a violent response.

Nicholas Griffiths

References

Arriaga, Pablo José de. *The Extirpation of Idolatry in Peru* [1621]. Translated by L. Clark Keating. Lexington: University of Kentucky Press, 1968.

Griffiths, Nicholas. *The Cross and the Serpent: Religious Repression and Resurgence in Colonial Peru.* Norman: University of Oklahoma Press, 1996.

Mills, Kenneth. *Idolatry and Its Enemies: Colonial Andean Religion and Extirpation, 1640–1750.* Princeton, NJ: Princeton University Press, 1997.

See also: Cannibalism; Catholic Church in Spanish America; Chroniclers; Clergy—Secular, in Colonial Spanish America; Diabolism in the New World; Human Sacrifice; Jesuits—Iberia and America; Native Americans I–VIII; Peru; Religious Orders; Saints and Saintliness; Syncretism; Virgin of Guadalupe; Witchcraft.

INDEPENDENCE I—ARGENTINA

Argentine independence was born of the Creole landholders' and merchants' wishes to break the power of the Spanish commercial and political elite and establish free trade. However, once liberated from Spain, the new elites in Buenos Aires found it impossible to maintain the territorial integrity of the former Viceroyalty of the Río de la Plata, and regional differences prevented the creation of a unified nation until the second half of the nineteenth century.

The Río de la Plata region progressed from colonial backwater in the seventeenth century to a region of central importance to Spain in the eighteenth. The cause of this rapid growth was the exchange of silver and hides for slaves and manufactured goods in the port of Buenos Aires. Buenos Aires's rapid development was not foreseen by the Spanish, who sought to channel all trade through Lima, the capital of the Viceroyalty of Peru. The economic heart of the viceroyalty was the mining center of Potosí, located in Upper Peru (modern-day Bolivia). Potosí was a magnet for goods and services from the surrounding regions; the mining center attracted Indian labor, food, hides, and pack animals to support the local population and facilitate the extraction and transport of silver. Silver was taken to Lima, then by sea to Spain, via Panama and the Caribbean. However, a certain amount of the wealth flowed to the providers of goods and services; thus, silver flowed into the cities to the northwest of Buenos Aires. Contrary to Spanish wishes, silver also began to flow out through the port of Buenos Aires, in illegal exchange for products brought by Portuguese and British merchant vessels. Foreign merchants were drawn to Buenos Aires not only by silver but also by the availability of hides and salted beef. European wars and economic expansion created demand for leather, whereas slave plantations in Brazil and the Caribbean were the chief market for salted beef. The beneficiaries of this demand were cattle ranchers (*estancieros*), many of whom were Creoles, the American-born descendants of Spanish immigrants.

In the eighteenth century, Spain recognized the growing importance of Buenos Aires. Under a series of changes known as the Bourbon reforms, Spain's new rulers, the Bourbon family, sought to reinvigorate the economy of Spain and its empire. Spain kept a monopoly on trade, keeping other Europeans out of the colonies but allowing freer trade between colonies and the mother country. *Comercio libre* was not strictly "free trade," but it encouraged commercial expansion. New officials, the intendants, arrived to oversee new territorial subdivisions and to foster economic development. Creole militias sought to better protect ocean trade and the territories themselves. In 1778, Buenos Aires became the capital of the new Viceroyalty of the Río de la Plata (including modern-day Argentina, Bolivia, Paraguay, and Uruguay). The city experienced rapid growth: shipping doubled from the 1770s to the 1790s, the export of hides grew from about 150,000 to some 330,000 per annum; the population doubled between the 1760s and 1810, and real estate values tripled.

Instead of revitalizing the empire, the Bourbon reforms led to a weakening of the ties that bound the colonies to Spain. Comercio libre was intended to encourage trade with Spain, enriching the mother country and subsidizing colonial government with the tariffs collected on trade. However, Spain could not supply the products most desired by Buenos Aires's inhabitants, namely, slaves and manufactured goods; thus, foreign merchants continued to trade in the port, even though they had to pay higher duties. The government of the viceroyalty relied on the collection of these customs to fund its bureaucracy and to pay the militia that protected the city. Continued European and Atlantic war meant that Spain also licensed foreigners to trade legally with Buenos Aires. Although these circumstances suited the cattle-ranching estancieros and the Creole merchants who had gained the right to import slaves and export hides, they did not benefit the Spanish merchants who had come out in large numbers following 1778 and who expected to make profits from monopolizing the importation and sale of Spanish products in Buenos Aires. The rivalry between Spaniards and Creoles was evident in business and in politics. One of the directives of the Bourbon reforms had been to ensure that Spaniards rather than Creoles occupied all positions of authority in colonial government. Creoles were limited to positions in the *cabildo,* the municipal government responsible for matters such as policing, sanitation, and weights and measures. However, when Creoles tried to make suggestions regarding economic policy, men like Manuel Belgrano, secretary of the merchant guild, found their opinions ignored by the Spanish colonial authorities.

In 1806–1807, successive British invasions of Buenos Aires stirred the patriotism of the Creoles. Unable to trade with Europe owing to Napoleon's Continental System, a British force had seized the port with hopes of finding an outlet for their manufactures in South America. The Spanish viceroy and his forces fled inland, leaving the city at the mercy of the invaders. After two months, however, the city rebelled, capturing the British commander. The hastily formed local militia held out against a second British invasion, forcing the invaders to flee the Río de la Plata. Commanding the militia comprised of Creoles, blacks, and Spaniards was a Frenchman in the employ of the Spanish navy, Santiago Liniers, who now became viceroy.

Almost before the territory could adapt to these new circumstances, the Spanish world was thrown into confusion by Napoleon's invasion of Iberia. Napoleon forced the abdication of Charles IV and imprisoned his heir, Ferdinand. Spain rose up under the leadership of a central council, or junta, which backed Ferdinand's claim to the throne. In Buenos Aires, a Spanish faction suggested that Liniers's French heritage made him suspect. They demanded an open town meeting, a *cabildo abierto,* in order to select a junta with which to replace the viceroy. Denied, the Spaniards planned a coup. They were thwarted in their actions by the Creole troops, commanded by Cornelio Saavedra, who came to the viceroy's rescue not out of support for his administration but motivated by their resentment of Spanish high-handedness. A new viceroy did replace Liniers in 1809, when the last outpost of loyalism in Spain, the junta in Seville, dispatched Balthasar de Cisneros to the Río de la Plata.

A new viceroy from Spain did not mean the restoration of Spanish authority in Buenos Aires. Cisneros found himself in a difficult position. In order to defend Buenos Aires from future British or French attacks, Liniers had opened the port to British goods. He used the customs revenues to equip and pay an expanding militia, which now included roughly two-thirds of the city's male population. The move had also strengthened the hand of Creole merchants such as Belgrano. Cisneros initially revoked Liniers's measures, but was soon faced with declining revenues and the troubling prospect of a militia that had not been paid. In the cabildo, a healthy debate emerged. Spanish merchants argued that British goods hurt Spanish industry. Their arguments were countered by Creole ranchers, represented by Mariano Moreno, who followed Adam Smith in arguing that specialization was the best approach to securing economic progress. Moreno argued that the region would be best served by pursuing ranching, not manufacturing. His presentation also had a strong patriotic slant, suggesting that free trade would lower consumer prices and open overseas markets to farmers. Cisneros allowed British imports but made illegal the export of silver by foreigners. He also attempted to reduce the size and influence of the Creole militia. These moves stirred leading Creoles toward revolt.

As Spanish and Creole factions began to divide in Buenos Aires, events in Spain again impelled their actions. In May 1810, news arrived that the Seville junta had fallen to the French. The Spanish colonies had essentially been cast adrift from the motherland. Cisneros called a cabildo abierto for May 22, hoping to see himself elected head of a new junta. Little more than 200 of the 450 members of the city's elite who were entitled to participate actually attended the meeting. The majority, including Spaniards loyal to Cisneros, were kept away by the rain, Creole militants, and the militia's presence. The assembly was composed of officials, clergy, lawyers and other professionals, merchants, military officials, and others. Although there was not a clear division along Spanish and Creole lines, a majority among those who supported the viceroy were Spanish. Juan José Castelli announced to the stunned Spanish contingent that the absence of a legitimate government in Spain meant that sovereignty reverted to the people of Buenos Aires. Colonists had the right to rule themselves. A further intervention by Creole loyalists on the night of May 24, when they went to cabildo members' houses to intimidate them, led to the removal of the viceroy from the ruling council.

On May 25, 1810, the new junta took office. It included Saavedra as president and Belgrano, Castelli, and Moreno among its members. The colonial order had ended, and self-government had arrived in Buenos Aires. Over the next ten years Creoles would fight successfully to maintain their independence from Spain but were unable to hold the territorial integrity of the former viceroyalty. Ultimately, Paraguay, Uruguay, and Upper Peru would reject the authority of Buenos Aires. The other interior provinces, too, would have strong reservations over accepting rule from Buenos Aires. Regional conflicts would plague Argentina long after the wars of independence ended in 1820.

The decade-long battle for Argentine independence divides into three general periods. First, in 1810–1811, came the loss of Upper Peru, Paraguay, and Uruguay. Initially successful, Castelli's forces in Upper Peru were later ejected by Spanish troops. The provinces of the northwest, which depended on commercial links with Potosí, suffered at the loss of Upper Peru. Paraguay rejected attempts by Buenos Aires to bring it into the orbit of the port city, preferring independence under the leadership of José Gáspar de Francia and Creole elites. Uruguay's Spanish governor was preparing an attack on Buenos Aires in 1811 when a rural rebellion led by José Artigas overwhelmed Montevideo. The battle for control of the eastern bank of the Río de la Plata continued for fifteen years, but this intervention both severed it from Buenos Aires's control and saved Argentina's first government.

The second phase of the independence wars saw not only ongoing battles for territorial control, but also battles within the leadership of the revolution. A reaction against free trade was developing in the interior provinces among textile manufacturers threatened by cheap British imports, and from those economically affected by the loss of Upper Peru. A triumvirate also replaced Saavedra's unwieldy rule by committee. The secretary of the triumvirate, Bernardino Rivadavia, was a liberal reformer whose ideas the provinces took as attempts to undermine the interests of the interior. Furthermore, attempts by Rivadavia's supporters to establish a constitutional monarchy threatened the provinces' desire to maintain autonomy. Internal divisions between these revolutionary factions and continued Spanish attacks destabilized government. A decision was made to reduce the members of the executive branch from three to one: from triumvirate to a single "supreme director." This made the decision-making process more efficient and direct.

In the midst of military and political conflict, on July 9, 1816, representatives of the provinces meeting in Tucumán declared the independence of the United Provinces of the Río de la Plata. The formal declaration of independence spurred the revolution into its third and final phase. A reorganization of the military under General José de San Martín added further stability. In 1817, San Martín led an army across the Andes to take the revolution to the heart of Spanish South America, Peru. Only if Spain was driven out of all parts of the continent could Argentina's independence—or that of any new nation—be secure. By 1820, the serious battles to secure Argentina's liberation were won, though many remained before unity was ensured. The chaos and dislocation brought by independence produced a series of conflicts—between centralism and federalism, representative and authoritarian government, and liberalism and protectionism. These conflicts would remain in play in Argentina for at least another century.

Alistair Hattingh

References

Bethell, Leslie, ed. *The Cambridge History of Latin America.* Vol. 3, *From Independence to c. 1870.* Cambridge: Cambridge University Press, 1985.

Halperín Donghi, Tulio. *The Aftermath of Revolution in Latin America.* Translated by Josephine de Bunsen. New York: Harper and Row, 1973.

———. *Politics, Economics and Society in Argentina in the Revolutionary Period.* Translated by Richard Southern. Cambridge: Cambridge University Press, 1975.

Lynch, John. *The Spanish American Revolutions 1808–1826.* 2nd ed. New York: W. W. Norton, 1986.

Kinsbruner, Jay. *Independence in Spanish America: Civil Wars, Revolutions, and Underdevelopment.* Albuquerque: University of New Mexico Press, 1994.

Rock, David. *Argentina 1516–1987: From Spanish Colonization to Alfonsín.* Berkeley and Los Angeles: University of California Press, 1987.

See also: Argentina; Atlantic Economy; Bolivia; Bourbon Reforms; Brazil; Cabildo; Colonists and Settlers V—Southern Cone; Contraband; Creoles; Defense—Colonial Spanish America; Estancia; Independence II–VI; Intendants/Intendancy System; Liberalism; Monopolies; Napoleonic Invasion and Spanish America; Paraguay; Potosí; Silver; Slavery I–IV; Slave Trade; Uruguay; Viceroyalties.

INDEPENDENCE II—BRAZIL

Between 1808 and 1825 a number of important changes in Brazil led to its political emancipation from Portugal. In the context of the age of revolutions, Brazilian independence represented a conservative alternative to the republican challenges that characterized Spanish-American independence, as well as the American and French revolutions.

By the end of the eighteenth century, the colonial system of the mercantile era had begun to fall apart. The system was based on the colonial pact, which provided that metropolitan traders had the privilege of intermediating the commerce of the colonies. In other words, virtually all the wealth produced in the American territory was absorbed by Europeans. Furthermore, the colonies were not permitted to export merchandise directly to other countries. Only merchandise from the respective metropolis or that coming through it was officially permitted.

In the second half of the eighteenth century, external and internal forces began to challenge Portugal's colonial system and the colonial pact. In Brazil, the echoes of the French Revolution and the successful independence of the United States influenced several anticolonialist outbursts in Brazil, in particular the uprisings in Minas Gerais (1788–1789), Rio de Janeiro (1792), and Bahia (1798). Though unique in their motivations and results, all three movements were characterized by their anticolonial nature.

In the international arena, England was undergoing its Industrial Revolution. Innovations such as the invention of the steam engine and the wage contract dramatically altered the social division of labor on a global scale. In the political sphere, Napoleon's military campaigns threatened both Spanish and Portuguese monarchies, and had international consequences. Major resistance to French imperial ambitions came from England. However, Portugal was uncomfortably positioned between both powerful enemies. Pressured by the threat of Napoleon's invasion in 1807, the Portuguese Crown finally decided to align itself with the English.

In response to the invasion of Napoleonic troops, and under British protection, the future king of Portugal, Dom João (King John VI), transferred the Portuguese royal family to Brazil. The king arrived in Brazil in January 1808, but his arrival may be considered the beginning of Brazil's political emancipation. The transfer of the Portuguese royal family across the Atlantic meant that the town of Rio de Janeiro suddenly became the headquarters of the vast Portuguese Empire. And Brazilian ports were open to friendly nations through two trade contracts (1808–1810), both of which heavily favored the British.

The opening of the ports freed Brazil's merchants from the imposed isolation of the eighteenth century. Portuguese merchants no longer enjoyed exclusive access to Brazilian goods. Brazil was opened to international commerce. However, some protections and privileges were maintained. The Royal Charter of January 24, 1808, established that the import tax on all foreign merchandise would amount to 24 percent of their value. However, to protect Portuguese interests, the prince regent John decreed a special lower tax rate of 16 percent for ships arriving from Portugal.

Not surprisingly, the British resented the arrangement and moved to pressure Dom João to sign two treaties. Through the "Friendship and Alliance" and "Commerce and Shipping" treaties Portugal lost its monopoly. Taxes on British merchandise were lowered to 15 percent. Thus, the colonial pact was abolished.

No other region in Brazil felt the impact of the arrival of the Portuguese royal family as profoundly as Rio de Janeiro. Capital of the vice-kingdom since 1763, Rio became the provisional capital of the Portuguese-Brazilian Empire. Rio's population almost doubled between 1808 and 1821, the year the royal family returned to Portugal. Already the chief export center of the south-central region of Brazil from the time of the gold rush in the eighteenth century, Rio de Janeiro had to face duly increased administrative, political, and commercial functions.

Rio's new administrative functions were already felt from the moment Dom João's royal family arrived in the harbor. Dozens of houses were divested by the Crown so that a multitude of new courtiers and bureaucrats could be housed, and at the same time, the colonial administrative bureaucracy was installed in Rio de Janeiro.

Important transformations in the customs of Rio de Janeiro residents occurred as a result of the daily contact with the foreigners, who arrived by the thousands. Rio's cultural life saw many changes with the arrival of the court, including the founding of the Royal Library and the Royal Press (1811) and the publication of Brazil's first newspapers. In the same year, the São João Royal Theater, with 1,200 seats and twelve boxes, was inaugurated. Elaborate new festivities were organized. For example, the one and only crowning of a European king outside of Europe occurred when Dom João was crowned Dom João VI on February 6, 1818.

With regard to Brazil's political emancipation, a certain intimacy between the Crown and the elites of the center-south regions became fundamental. In return for their support, Dom João VI was prodigious in granting nobility titles and property to wealthy Brazilians, especially to merchants involved in the slave trade, and in issuing credit. The relationship between the court and Rio de Janeiro's upper class occurred through the strict observance of social etiquette, as prescribed by the logic of Portuguese court society. Prince Regent Dom João played a decisive role as the manager of the encounter between the Portuguese court and the Brazilian elite. This marked the conservative nature of Brazilian emancipation.

If Brazilians were delighted with the monarch's presence, the Portuguese people, especially the upper classes, grew increasingly dissatisfied with his absence. As long as the king delayed his return to Lisbon, resident elites in Portugal started to express their discontent, especially after Napoleon's fall and the supremacy of the Holy Alliance in 1814. Complaints became increasingly vocal.

The transformation of Brazil into the United Kingdom of Portugal and Algarves in 1815 was proof that the loss of the colony was unavoidable. On both sides of the Atlantic, pamphlets circulated in favor of reestablishing the colonial pact. However, other pamphlets published in Brazil proclaimed that the pact was a disaster and that only free trade guaranteed Brazil's emancipation from the metropolis.

Instigated by the liberal revolution in Spain, a revolutionary movement broke out in the Portuguese town of Porto on August 20, 1820. A parliament *(Cortes)* was summoned, and its members called for the

A descendant of Portuguese royalty, Pedro I (also known as Dom Pedro) was the founder of the Brazilian empire and the first emperor of Brazil. (Ridpath, John Clark, Ridpath's History of the World, *1901)*

immediate return of the king and for the drafting of a constitution. The movement's echo resounded loudly in Brazil. In Portugal, groups with opposing interests united in their support of the constitutional revolt. However, the contradictions became apparent immediately and the revolution that at first defended the ideals of liberalism soon revealed its aim to reestablish Portuguese control over Brazil. Together with a new constitution and the return of the king, the revolutionaries in Lisbon desired to reestablish the *status quo ante,* when their commercial profits and privileges were assured by colonial rule.

Immediately following the Porto Revolution, Brazil's inhabitants, particularly those in Rio de Janeiro, manifested their sympathy to the idea of constitutional rule. Dom João initially resisted the demands from Porto but was ultimately coaxed into accepting the constitution. Enormous crowds gathered in the streets, and noisy demonstrations followed in Rio; during one demonstration a military division opened fire against the people in the Largo do Rocio, killing three and leaving dozens wounded. The situation became uncontrollable, and on April 25, 1821, the king was forced to return to Portugal. His son Dom Pedro remained in Brazil as prince regent.

Following the king's return to Portugal, Brazilians elected their own representatives to the Cortes in Lisbon. However, the Brazilian delegation was small and internally divided, and it soon became evident that they could do nothing to preserve Brazilian freedoms. Struggles in the Cortes echoed negatively in Brazil. The idea of independence gained broad support, reinforced by the great number of political pamphlets that incited the population and encouraged the prince regent to resist.

Dom Pedro's political position as regent was unclear, however, even though he initiated a liberal government. Portuguese society and Dom João emptied the public treasury for the king's return to Portugal. In spite of financial difficulties, Dom Pedro abolished taxes, directed the divestment of goods, and granted personal freedoms. Dom Pedro was extremely sympathetic toward the central articles of the constitution: popular sovereignty, a one-house parliament, inviolability of the king, individual and property guarantees, freedom of the press, and petition rights.

In the underground machinations that developed, the Freemason lodges that had been closed in 1818 were reopened. Important liberal leaders, Prince Dom Pedro included, participated in secret societies like the Freemasons. It is a common assumption in the historiography that secret societies, the Freemasons among them, played a central role in the Brazilian independence movement. Although one can argue that several prominent actors in the independence drama indeed were Masons, more research is needed to establish the precise role of the Masons in Brazilian independence.

As early as 1822, royal decrees from Lisbon ordered the immediate withdrawal of the prince regent and the extinction of the higher courts of Rio de Janeiro. Under a liberal flag, all politically distinct groups united against Brazil's return to colonial status. Perhaps Dom Pedro was influenced by the many demonstrations from Rio de Janeiro, São Paulo, and Minas Gerais that pleaded for him to remain in Brazil. On January 9, 1822, he decided to stay. However, the succession of events went beyond his personal will. Perhaps Dom Pedro, in accordance with most of Brazil's representatives at the Portuguese Cortes, never wished for such a separation. Yet despite the separation, Brazil's territorial integrity was safeguarded. Portuguese American independence is thus strikingly different from the independence movements in Spanish America, where regions fragmented into numerous independent countries and adopted republican regimes.

Dom Pedro adopted several measures that anticipated the road to independence and called for elections to the Council of State. Articulated by Jose Bonifácio de Andrada e Silva, in order to strengthen the "Paulista's" influence over Dom Pedro, the idea of convoking a Constituent Assembly was for the first time conceived as an option. Having the political authority in its hands, the assembly used repression and violence to contain acts of insubordination. The greatest victories of the liberals, headed by Bonifácio de Andrada, included the awarding of the title of perpetual defender of Brazil to Dom Pedro, the summoning of a Constituent Assembly, and the acclamation of the prince on October 12, 1822.

Still, the Proclamation of Independence, though formally declared on September 7, 1822, did not finalize the process of Brazilian political emancipation. Soon the Portuguese party would rise with greater force and show its conservative positions. The members of the Portuguese Party supported absolutism and chose Emperor Dom Pedro I as an instrument of their claims and aspirations. However, dissonant voices were heard from within Brazil. No other region offered more resistance to colonialism than the northeast, especially Pernambuco. This tradition arose in the eighteenth century under the influence of French ideas. A priest, Father Manuel Arruda Câmara, founded the Areópago de Itambé in 1800, a secret society with separatist ideas. The Olinda Seminary, built in the same year, was another important source of liberal ideas.

The Areópago's heritage and liberal principles were never silenced. The arrival of the royal family overtaxed the northeastern provinces, making Pernambuco's elites deeply resentful. This resulted in two major movements against the central government in Rio de Janeiro, one in 1817 and the other in 1824. In the first, a provisional republican government was formed, with five members and assisted by a Council of State. A new organic law was established that guaranteed individual rights based on the Universal Declaration of Human Rights, liberty of opinion, religion, and press.

The revolt had serious repercussions for various provinces of northeastern Brazil. Rio de Janeiro answered back by means of a counterrevolution. Recife was blockaded and the leaders were arrested. Repression was violent and hundreds of executions followed. Many convicted persons were placed on parole after the coronation of Dom João VI in February 1818. The few survivors were finally released two years later during the 1820 Porto Revolution. The revolutionary movement of Brazil's northeastern region is considered the most spontaneous and popular Brazilian uprising in its history. As in Pernambuco, many other important and bloody uprisings, such as Cabanagem in the state of Pará, the farroupilhas in Rio Grande do Sul, the Sabinada of Bahia, the Balaiada in Maranhão, and the Praieira Revolution, occurred. From a broader perspective, one may say that Brazilian independence was not complete until mid-century, when regional rebellions ceased.

Furthermore, internal struggles within the Brazilian Party reflected antagonistic interests of different social layers that joined forces together in favor of independence. For each group, emancipation carried a different meaning. The entire free but poor population, as well as black slaves, was excluded from leading roles in the independence process.

Despite its initial resistance, Portugal finally recognized Brazil's political autonomy in 1825. British diplomatic tutelage was decisive in the negotiations. After Portugal, the United States was the first country to recognize Brazilian independence. According to the treaties signed, in return for its freedom Brazil agreed to pay Portugal a compensation of £2 million. Commercial treaties guaranteed England high profits from Brazil and its commitment to the abolition of slavery, which Brazil's elites successfully postponed until the late 1880s.

In 1825, Brazil became an autonomous state; its principal duty was to build a nation, a task that would be fulfilled during the course of the nineteenth century.

Jurandir Malerba

References

Bethell, Leslie. "The Independence of Brazil." In *Brazil: Empire and Republic,* edited by Leslie Bethell. Cambridge: Cambridge University Press, 1999.

Costa, Emília Viotti da. *Brazilian Empire: Myths and Histories.* Chicago: University of Chicago Press, 2000.

Malerba, Jurandir. *A corte no exílio: Civillização e poder no Brasil às vésperas da independência.* São Paulo: Compenhia das letr 2000.

Manchester, Alan. *British Preeminence in Brazil: Its Rise and Fall.* Durham, NC: Duke University Press, 1933.

Mota, Carlos Guilherme. *1822: Dimensões.* São Paulo: Ática, 1972.

Schultz, Kirsten. *Tropical Versailles: Empire, Monarchy, and the Portuguese Royal Court in Rio de Janeiro, 1808–1821.* New York: Routledge, 2001.

See also: Architecure—Brazil; Art and Artists—Brazil; Atlantic Economy; Brazil; Enlightenment—Brazil; Human Rights; Independence I, III–VI; Migration To Brazil; Monarchs of Portugal; Monopolies; Music and Dance I—Brazil; Napoleonic Invasion and Luso-America; Napoleonic Invasion and Spanish America; Poetry—Brazil; Science and Scientists—Brazil/Portugal; Slavery I—Brazil; Sugar; Travel Literature—Brazil; Women—Brazil.

INDEPENDENCE III—CENTRAL AMERICA

Central America declared independence from Spain on September 15, 1821. Unrest related to the Bourbon reforms of the mid-eighteenth century began to percolate during the crisis that followed Napoleon Bonaparte's usurpation of the Spanish throne (1808–1814) but remained under control until Mexican independence in 1821 forced the issue upon the isthmus. The process involved separate votes from each municipality in the region, and the results varied widely, with some seeking independence from Spain and others rejecting joining Mexico. Nonetheless, broad enough support initially ensured Central America's annexation to Agustín de Iturbide's plan for a Mexican empire. However, this unwieldy and ill-managed endeavor lasted only until July 1, 1823, when an assembly representing Guatemala, Honduras, El Salvador, Nicaragua, and Costa Rica declared independence for the isthmus under the banner of the United Provinces of Central America.

Central America was poorly positioned to take advantage of Spain's imperial expansion in the early colonial period. It produced little of great export value and faced stiff competition from merchants and producers in New Spain, the region's center of colonial power. Although Central Americans capitalized on legal intercolonial trade during the sixteenth century, by the seventeenth century Spain tightened its grip on the commercial economy and enforced the mercantilist principle of trade only between colonies and the mother country. Not surprisingly, these restrictions encouraged contraband trade, and Spain's European rivals were happy to oblige. Nonetheless, by the late seventeenth century, restrictive credit, commercial weakness, and high taxes had plunged Central America into economic depression that limited much of the isthmus to semisubsistence production. This decline coincided with growing British depredations and settlements from Belize to the Caribbean coasts of Honduras, Nicaragua, and Costa Rica.

In 1700, Phillip V rose to the throne of Spain, ending the Habsburg dynasty and placing Spain under the control of the French Bourbons. Although changes came slowly at first, the new Bourbon kings of Spain began a series of policy changes designed to tighten fiscal control, promote economic development, and provide military protection in the Americas. These policies produced contradictory results; in fact, in their efforts to monitor their colonial possessions more closely and to exploit their economic potential, the Bourbon kings both strengthened and emboldened the colonies. Starting in 1717, when the Crown began to reorganize its mercantilist trading system, commercial activity began to expand, revealing the opportunities of greater competition and access. However, the most radical changes occurred after Charles III ascended to the throne. In 1774, intercolonial trade in the Americas was permitted, expanding the Central American export economies. The Bourbons never fully renounced the mercantilist system, but their policies, including the 1778 Free Trade Act, moved in that direction, teasing colonists with visions of what local economic independence would produce. As Spain and Britain warred in the late 1790s, American commerce suffered. As a result, in 1797, Spain allowed neutral countries to trade with the colonies, further opening up the Central American economies. This trade was officially closed in 1799, an act that provoked ire in Central America as the economy faced a downturn at the start of the nineteenth century.

After nearly a century of economic stagnation, the Bourbon reforms sparked an explosion of trade and economic growth, which in turn motivated new Spanish migration to Central America. By the early eighteenth century a new Spanish elite had emerged, one composed mostly of recently arrived Spaniards and centered in Guatemala. Over much of the eighteenth century, the Guatemalan merchant elite came to control most regional trade and economic production, be it Salvadoran indigo, Honduran mining, Nicaraguan cattle, or Costa Rican cacao, through their near-monopoly on credit and legal trade routes. Consequently, the reforms simultaneously illuminated the potential of provincial political and economic opportunities while restricting their expansion.

Fundamental to the Bourbon reforms were institutional changes that expanded state revenue and administrative efficiency. Fiscal reform met mixed responses, with praise for a more effective and competent bureaucracy and grumbles over increased taxation. Although export taxes were reduced, the enforcement of sales tax collection placed new demands on producers throughout Central America. Key to these changes was the 1786 implementation of the intendancy system in Central America, which distributed administrative, fiscal, and military control of Central America to *intendentes* in Chiapas, El Salvador, Honduras, and Nicaragua. The Bourbon reforms sought to decentralize American political authority while expanding Spanish imperial control. Beyond the intendancies, municipalities throughout Central America gained a measure of local autonomy that often conflicted with the supposed prerogatives of imperial authorities, especially those in the kingdom's capital of Guatemala City.

The late eighteenth century also witnessed the influence of French Enlightenment thought and the emergence of progressive politicians and intellectuals who campaigned for economic and political liberalism. The weekly newspaper *Gazeta de Guatemala* provided a forum for discussions about free trade, representative government, and popular sovereignty. Out of these debates began to crystallize the split between Conservatives, who supported traditional monarchical authority, corporatism, and limited political participation, and Liberals, who advocated republicanism, anticlericalism, political equality, and free trade.

Crisis erupted in 1808 when Napoleon Bonaparte invaded Spain and deposed Ferdinand VII. Napoleon placed his brother Joseph on the throne, an action that sent the Spanish into rebellion. Resisting the French required organization and political legitimacy, both of which the rebels hoped to conjure up by convening Spain's first modern parliament (or *Cortes*) in Cádiz. The new assembly worked to restore the deposed Ferdinand and hold the empire together. Although some regions of the Americas responded with cries for independence, the Kingdom of Guatemala rebuked Napoleon's invasion and supported Ferdinand VII through the rebel assembly in Cádiz. The news of the Hidalgo revolt in Mexico did incite brief revolts in El Salvador, Honduras, and Nicaragua, but these rebellions were suppressed under the stern rule of Captain General José de Bustamante y Guerra. Fears of further uprisings remained, but the isthmus remained comparatively quiet until after 1821.

Over the eighteenth century, the non-Indian *casta* (mixed-race) population, often referred to as *ladinos,* grew in size and importance. This shift was recognized in the debates of the Cortes of Cádiz over whether castas should be represented in the assembly. Although "ladino" is often defined as "mestizo" in current usage, at the time of independence it also included mulattoes and blacks, groups that in many cities outnumbered mestizos. Census figures from the late 1780s in Nicaragua, for example, report that mulattoes outnumbered mestizos 3 to 1, numbers that were likely matched in Honduras and El Salvador. Given its tenuous authority, the Cortes had to provide colonial representation if it was to maintain imperial legitimacy in the face of Spanish disarray. Nonetheless, peninsular Spaniards were unwilling to allow representatives of the 16 million people of the colonies to outvote those speaking for Spain's 11 million people and, initially, limited political personhood to Europeans and Creoles (colonial-born whites), meaning that Spain held a 3-to-1 majority in the Cortes.

Peninsular control of the Cortes did not create a conservative assembly. In fact, liberals dominated the Cortes, and in 1812, after two years of debates and maneuvering, the Cortes produced a new Spanish constitution that enshrined the values of Enlightenment liberalism and provided for a political system that limited monarchical power, organized political authority through provinces and municipalities, and strengthened Spanish control over the colonies. Municipal institutions had grown in importance thanks to the Bourbon reforms; the Spanish constitution of 1812 furthered this trend and the scale of municipal power by privileging any town with a thousand residents to claim a city council with the same political authority as any of the principal capitals that had ruled the provinces until then. The constitutional debates in Cádiz also engaged the question of casta political participation. In the end, Indians and mestizos gained the right to compete with Spaniards for election to these city councils, but mulattoes remained disqualified from such privileges until after independence. Although revolts were limited in Central America, the news of independence struggles in other parts of the Americas and the liberal character of the 1812 constitution emboldened the Creoles and politicized the isthmus in profoundly new ways.

Ferdinand VII returned to the Spanish throne in 1814 following Napoleon's defeat. The king rejected the 1812 constitution's limits on his power and its liberal character and swiftly tossed out the charter. Creoles and politically active ladinos, having tasted political opportunity offered by the constitution, were deeply disappointed. In 1820, the Riego revolt in Spain forced the restoration of the 1812 constitution, clearing the way for open political dissent in Central America while weakening Spain's ability to send military reinforcements to the colonies. Despite this turn of events, it was Mexico's declaration of independence and independence leader Agustín de Iturbide's effort to incorporate Central America into a new Mexican empire that ultimately forced the issue of independence on the isthmus. On September 15, 1821, Central Americans declared their acceptance of what had already become a fact. However, the nature of independence was more widely contested, with different municipalities choosing different tacks. Some favored independence from Spain but adhesion to Mexico, while others rejected both. Still others added Guatemala to the list of authorities to renounce. Nonetheless, the allure of Iturbide's constitutional monarchy over the more radical and untried option of republicanism favored the annexation of Central America to Mexico.

Almost immediately it became clear that the costs of maintaining Agustín de Iturbide's Mexican empire had proved greater than its benefits. Despite the initial Central American enthusiasm for the empire, Iturbide was forced to send troops under Vicente Filísola to enforce the project, especially against the defiance of El Salvador and Nicaragua. Moreover, provincial juntas continued to compete with Guatemala rather than work with it. Throughout the colonial period, provincial officials had bemoaned the difficulties of communication and travel between their capitals and Guatemala City, a situation that was exacerbated during the rainy season. The effort to link these increasingly localist provinces to a distant Mexico City only worsened the complaints.

The long-term tendency toward greater atomization of regional authority meant that even the former colonial provinces could not be relied upon for unity. Instead, dozens of municipalities clamored to speak for local and regional needs. By early 1823, the Mexican empire was collapsing, and when Vicente Filísola convoked an *Asamblea Nacional Constituyente* (National Constitutional Assembly) on March 29, 1823, Central Americans heeded the call. Representatives were elected from Guatemala, Honduras, El Salvador, Nicaragua, and Costa Rica and joined together to declare their complete independence and the formation of a federation. Mexico held on to Chiapas, to which it had long had greater economic ties. The notion of a *patria grande* remained attractive, but its implementation engendered decades of conflict. The structure of the federation favored Guatemala, something that even rival national factions often agreed was unfair. One solution was to move the federal capital from Guatemala City to other provincial locations, but this alternative failed to resolve the basic conflict. Moreover, the federation did nothing to dispel the legitimacy of municipal authority and its challenge to larger state formation projects in each of the former provinces. Over the ensuing decades, these conflicts came increasingly to be fought out in struggles over national unification rather than fragmentation.

Justin Wolfe

References

Karnes, Thomas L. *The Failure of Union: Central America, 1824–1975.* Rev. ed. Tempe: Center for Latin American Studies, Arizona State University, 1976.

Lanning, John Tate. *The Eighteenth-Century Enlightenment in the University of San Carlos de Guatemala.* Ithaca, NY: Cornell University Press, 1956.

Pinto Soria, Julio César. *Centroamérica: De la colonia al estado nacional, 1800–1840.* Guatemala: Editorial Universitaria de Guatemala, 1986.

Rodríguez, Mario. *The Cádiz Experiment in Central America, 1808–1826.* Berkeley and Los Angeles: University of California Press, 1978.

Troy, Floyd. *The Anglo-Spanish Struggle for Mosquitia.* Albuquerque: University of New Mexico Press, 1967.

Wortman, Miles. *Government and Society in Central America, 1680–1840.* New York: Columbia University Press, 1982.

See also: Atlantic Economy; Belize; Bourbon Reforms; Constitution of Cádiz; Contraband; Cortes of Cádiz; Costa Rica; Creoles; Defense—Colonial Spanish America; El Salvador; Enlightenment—Spanish America; Grito de Dolores; Guatemala; Honduras; Independence I–II, IV–VI; Intendants/Intendancy System; Mestizaje; Mexico; Monopolies; Napoleonic Invasion and Spanish America; Nicaragua; Panama; Race.

INDEPENDENCE IV—COLOMBIA, ECUADOR, AND VENEZUELA

When France attacked Spain in 1808, it forced King Ferdinand VII from the throne, placed Napoleon's brother on the throne instead, and thereby threw the Spanish world into disarray. Spanish legal tradition held that, in the absence of the king, sovereignty reverted to the people and they were entitled to determine their own fate. The inhabitants of Spain's American colonies faced four choices: declare loyalty to the French, who now occupied the throne in Madrid; declare loyalty to the struggling Spanish governments (alternately the Junta Central, the Council of Regency, and the Cortes); declare autonomy, meaning temporary independence until King Ferdinand VII returned to the throne; and declare full independence and secede from the empire with no intention ever to return. The groups that sought independence came to be called Republicans or patriots, whereas those that remained subordinate to the Spanish government were called Royalists.

Americans declared autonomy or independence for several reasons. Many areas declared autonomy to ensure that they would not come under French rule. Already resentful of the preponderance of Spaniards in administrative posts, Americans desired greater opportunity in the state bureaucracy and more self-governance. The influence of Enlightenment thought and the examples of revolution in the United States and France also imbued some Americans with a desire for liberal political-economic structures (such as elected officials, representative government, civil liberties, and a free market economy) that they considered impossible under the absolutist Spanish system.

When war erupted, however, Americans fought as much among themselves as they did against the Spanish. The fighting concerned not only independence from Spain but also struggles for autonomy, racial conflict, civil war, competition between centralists and federalists, and cities resisting the hegemony of other cities. Under the colonial system, New Granada (today called Colombia), Ecuador (*note:* the region now called Ecuador was at the time known as Quito. This entry uses the anachronism "Ecuador" to distinguish the larger region from the city of Quito), and Venezuela had all belonged to the same viceroyalty centered at Bogotá. However, because each of these colonies possessed its own juridical and administrative apparatus, the colonies had been largely autonomous, and Bogotá's authority over them had been nominal. Furthermore, individual cities within each region often enjoyed considerable autonomy owing to the colonial administrative structure as well as the constraints of a vast and rugged geography. When the cities began to fight each other, the conflicts were often indistinguishable from the Royalist-Republican fight as a city might declare itself Royalist simply because it could hope for greater self-rule as a subject of Madrid than as a subject of Bogotá, Caracas, or Quito. The reasons for and character of the fighting changed dramatically over time, and it was not until the last years of the war that these three regions joined together in a unified movement.

Quito, the principal city of Ecuador, was the first Spanish American city to declare autonomy. On August 9, 1809, the city's government declared that it would govern itself in the name of Ferdinand VII until he returned. However, Guayaquil, Ecuador's main coastal city, and Lima, Peru, viewed this as an act of rebellion, and so troops from both cities attacked and occupied Quito. Although the soldiers from Guayaquil departed, the occupying Peruvian soldiers behaved like conquerors, oppressing the residents and arresting those complicit in the autonomy movement. The Peruvian troops left in August 1810, when their general realized that their looting was only making the situation worse. Finding themselves free again, Quito's leaders convened a junta that declared they would recognize the authority only of the Regency in Spain and therefore would be independent from Bogotá and Lima. Quito then took the offensive, attacking surrounding cities to regain its authority over most of Ecuador.

In Caracas, Venezuela, the organs of government split as the *audiencia* (high court) and captain general wanted to declare loyalty to the Spanish government, while the *ayuntamiento* (municipal council) wanted to form a local junta with governing powers. The captain general, fearing this was an independence movement, arrested the projunta faction. A new captain general arrived and mollified the growing tensions, but the arrests had weakened the formation of a strong moderate faction that could have headed off the pro-independence radicals. By the end of 1810, as the French won more victories and the Spanish government retreated to Cádiz, Caracas's elites created a junta and declared autonomy. While some Venezuelan cities supported the move, several others (Coro, Maracaibo, and Guayana) declared loyalty to the Regency. When the Caracas junta refused to dissolve, the Regency sent ships and blockaded Venezuelan ports. This event, coupled with the news that Peruvian troops had looted Quito, horrified many of the Caracas elite and increased the power of the proindependence radicals.

Similarly, Bogotá also saw a split between the autonomists and Royalists. In November 1809, the Royalists suppressed the autonomists for fear that they intended full rebellion, thus stifling the moderates who could have controlled the radicals. Nonetheless, in July 1810, Bogotá formed the Junta Suprema de Nueva Granada and invited the other provinces to send representatives for a congress. The Bogotá junta at first took a moderate autonomist course, swore loyalty to the Regency, and, as competition between factions grew more violent, imprisoned many of the radicals and expelled the colonial officials from the country. Meanwhile, throughout 1810 other cities formed their own juntas and declared autonomy not only from Spain but also from Bogotá. This began what has been called the Patria Boba (Foolish Fatherland, 1810–1816), as cities, towns, and provinces all broke away from each other, splintering New Granada into smaller and smaller states. Warfare broke out as cities fought against each other and against their own hinterlands.

Events in Spain took dramatic turns that profoundly affected American events.

Although the French occupied virtually all the peninsula, in 1812 the Spanish Cortes at Cádiz produced a progressive, liberal constitution that gave some Americans a restored willingness to remain loyal. Two years later, the Spanish expelled the French invaders and put Ferdinand VII on the throne. This freed Spanish resources to be sent to the Americas to suppress the independence movements. However, Ferdinand VII also intensified Americans' desire for independence when he threw out the 1812 constitution, repressed the liberals, and attempted to restore absolutist rule.

In Venezuela the independence movement began before the king's return. In July of 1811 an elected congress declared independence, and in December it produced a constitution. However, Venezuela's First Republic enjoyed uneven support; within a year a Royalist army had landed on the coast and defeated the Republicans. In 1813, the Republicans returned to the fight, though their leadership was even less unified than before. Whereas race had been a factor in the previous year's fighting, it became even more important now. Although both sides offered freedom to slaves who joined their cause, the slaves, along with free blacks, *pardos* (people of mixed race), and poor whites, joined the Royalists in greater numbers. The poor and the nonwhites tended to trust the Spanish more than the Creoles to protect their rights, and also saw an opportunity for revenge against the Creole elite that had enslaved and oppressed them. Supporting the Royalists, Tomás Boves raised an irregular cavalry composed of poor southern plainsmen who deeply resented the wealthier Venezuelans and fought largely for the opportunity to rape and pillage. One of the Republican generals, Simón Bolívar, issued a declaration of "War to the Death," asserting that Republicans would kill all Spaniards unless they actively supported the independence movement. Both sides terrorized the civilian population. In June of 1814 Boves defeated the Republican army, again sending their leadership into hiding; however, Boves fell in a skirmish that December. In April 1815 another Spanish army arrived and restored order to the land whose population had been devastated by civil, racial, and regionalist warfare.

In New Granada, the junta of Bogotá declared itself the capital of a new, autonomous state called Cundinimarca (1811). The new president, Antonio Nariño, attempted to form a highly centralized state, but congress produced a federalist constitution and ratified the Act of Federation of the United Provinces of New Granada. Cundinimarca rejected this act so that by the end of 1811 the stage was set for fighting among three main divisions: Cundinimarca, the United Provinces (composing most of the rest of Republican New Granada), and the Royalists. The situation became further complicated as centralists (associated mostly with Cundinimarca) struggled with federalists (associated largely with the United Provinces), and as Cartagena and Cundinimarca separately declared independence (1811 and 1813, respectively). In 1813–1814, Cundinimarca and the United Provinces joined forces against the Royalists, but the Royalists prevailed and sent Nariño to prison. This period also saw Venezuelans assisting the New Granadans; Bolívar fought for the United Provinces when he was not fighting in Venezuela. After their defeat in 1814, more Venezuelans came and helped the United Provinces to defeat Cundinimarca,

Simón Bolívar leads in signing the Declaration of Independence for Venezuela from Spanish rule, July 5, 1811. (Bettmann/Corbis)

thereby temporarily uniting the New Granadan Republicans. Bolívar then received the title of the captain general of New Granada and led the fight against the Royalists. New Granadans again fought each other, however, as Bolívar turned against Cartagena. The Royalists exploited this disunity, and thus defeated the republicans in 1815. Bogotá fell to the Royalists in May 1816 and the Patria Boba came to an end.

Ecuador also experienced violence but less than its northern neighbors. In December 1811, Quito severed ties to the Regency and again declared itself autonomous. But Royalist forces fought back, and by the end of 1812 they had defeated the autonomist movement. Still, Spain's 1812 constitution granted so much liberty that Ecuador existed peacefully within the Spanish system. When the king returned in 1814 and revoked the constitution, most autonomy leaders were already in prison, exiled, or dead, so Ecuador saw little protest.

As the king revived absolutist structures, the Royalists punished Republicans in Venezuela and New Granada with prison sentences, confiscation of property, and execution. These acts galvanized a weakened Republican cause. In 1816, the president of Haiti, Alexandre Pétion, gave Bolívar the supplies and finances that elevated him to the leadership of the Venezuelan Republicans and enabled him to launch another campaign that year. Although other generals challenged Bolívar's supremacy, by 1819 he had become the uncontested leader of the independence movements in both Venezuela and New Granada. In August 1819 Bolívar led his troops from Venezuela across the Andes where he defeated the Royalists at Boyacá, took Bogotá, and gained control of almost all of New Granada. In December of that year the Republican congress in Angostura (eastern Venezuela) declared the Republic of Gran Colombia, which included Venezuela, New Granada, and Ecuador.

Although the Republicans had only a tenuous hold after these victories, Spain could not send reinforcements because in 1820 liberals revolted throughout the country, demanding that the king restore the 1812 constitution. Bolívar's forces now had time to solidify their strength. In May 1821, a Republican congress met in Cúcuta (eastern New Granada) and shortly produced a constitution for Gran Colombia. Though liberal in many respects, with a bicameral elected legislature, the government would be highly centralized with a powerful president. Both congresses—the one that declared Gran Colombia's existence and the one that wrote the constitution—had poor representation from Gran Colombians. No Ecuadorians were present at either congress, and Venezuelan delegates came only from those areas that were under Republican control. This poor representation came to haunt the state of Gran Colombia, and regional differences eventually tore it apart in 1830.

Also in 1821, the Republicans took the offensive in Venezuela. By June they had defeated the Royalists at the battle of Carabobo, and Bolívar rode triumphantly into Caracas. By the end of 1821, Cartagena and Panama had joined the republic, and Bolívar became Gran Colombia's first president. His forces could now turn south to Ecuador.

In 1820, the city of Guayaquil, which previously had been Royalist, declared independence in response to Spain's absolutist policies. Royalists and Republicans fought throughout Ecuador, and they soon reached a stalemate, with Royalists controlling the highlands and Quito. The president of independent Ecuador, José Olmedo, spent two years trying to enlist support from Bolívar without promising to join Gran Colombia, expressing a vain hope to gain help without being subjugated. In 1822, Bolívar's general, Antonio Sucre, entered Ecuador and defeated the Royalists in two key battles. Gran Colombia then annexed Ecuador, over the strenuous protests of the leaders of Ecuador's independence movement who viewed this more as conquest than liberation.

The following year, 1823, the Republicans defeated the last Royalist holdouts in Venezuela's coastal cities, and Gran Colombia became independent from the Spanish Empire.

Reuben Zahler

References

Andrien, Kenneth J. *The Kingdom of Quito, 1690–1830: The State and Regional Development.* New York: Cambridge University Press, 1995.

Lynch, John. *Bolívar and the Age of Revolution.* London: University of London Institute of Latin American Studies, 1983.

———. *The Spanish American Revolutions 1808–1826.* New York: W.W. Norton, 1986.

McKinley, P. Michael. *Pre-Revolutionary Caracas: Politics, Economy, and Society 1777–1811.* Cambridge: Cambridge University Press, 1985.

Rodríguez, O., and E. Jaime. *The Independence of Spanish America.* Cambridge: Cambridge University Press, 1998.

Uribe-Uran, Victor. *Honorable Lives: Lawyers, Family, and Politics in Colombia, 1780–1850.* Pittsburgh: University of Pittsburgh Press, 2000.
———, ed. *State and Society in Spanish America during the Age of Revolution.* Wilmington, DE: SR, 2001.

See also: American Revolution; Audiencias; Bourbon Reforms; Colombia; Constitution of Cádiz; Cortes of Cádiz; Creoles; Ecuador; Enlightenment—Spanish America; Gran Colombia; Independence I–III, V–VI; Napoleonic Invasion and Spanish America; Race; Venezuela.

INDEPENDENCE V—MEXICO

In 1810, approximately half of the population of Spanish America (between 6 and 7 million people) resided in New Spain (Mexico). This statistic as well as the fact that the province produced so much wealth explains why, despite its own struggle against the French (1808–1814), Spain contributed expeditionary troops to prevent Mexican independence. Prior to the French invasion of Spain in 1808 that provoked Spanish Americans to consider their options, many Mexicans (*Novohispanos)* opposed the administrative and fiscal reforms introduced by the Bourbon monarchs. Centralization of the regime served to eliminate some traditional powers of the Creoles (*criollos)* and oppressed the Indian and mixed-race population with higher taxes and other demands. The catalyst for change occurred in 1808 with the shocking news that Napoleon had invaded Spain, removed King Charles IV and his son Ferdinand VII, and installed his brother Joseph on the Spanish throne.

Shortly thereafter, representatives of several Spanish juntas arrived in Mexico to ask for recognition as the legitimate interim Spanish government and to insist that funds normally sent to Madrid be remitted to them. Like so many Bourbon administrators in the Americas, Viceroy José de Iturrigaray of New Spain failed to handle the political ramifications of this imperial crisis. During the summer of 1808, Iturrigaray appeared to concur with the *ayuntamiento* (city government) of Mexico City and many Creole leaders who called for an interim junta to govern New Spain. With much of New Spain's army already serving in cantonments at Jalapa, Córdoba, and Orizaba to protect against a possible French or British invasion, the powerful but small *gachupín* (peninsular Spanish) minority perceived political changes that might lead to independence. On the night of September 15–16, 1808, merchant militiamen of Mexico City commanded by a wealthy gachupín merchant and *hacendado,* Gabriel Yermo, invaded the viceregal palace, overthrew Viceroy Iturrigaray, and established an interim government. For decades, Mexicans blamed the gachupines for staging the first *golpe de estado* (coup d'état) and for unleashing chronic disorder.

Over the next two years conspiracies and invasion threats kept New Spain in a state of agitation. Some Creoles proposed the mobilization of large Indian forces to defend the country against invasion. Others wished to resist the haughty and acquisitive gachupines who had seized control. In 1809, the regime suppressed a conspiracy in the Intendancy of Valladolid. The following year, there was a much broader conspiracy in the Bajío region to the north and west of Mexico City that embraced the cities of Querétaro, Celaya, Guanajuato, Valladolid, San Miguel, and many smaller towns. In addition to chronic competition for the possession of land, poor harvests reduced maize production and drove up food prices. Authorities in Guanajuato and other towns strove to fill their granaries and threatened force if necessary, thus exacerbating instability and disseminating new rumors among the rural agrarian populace.

The upheaval that produced over a decade of revolutionary and civil warfare began at the town of Dolores under the local *cura* (curate), Father Miguel Hidalgo y Costilla (1753–1811), a controversial leader who remains a legendary hero of the Mexican republic. Accompanied by a handful of supporters, on the night of September 16, 1810, Hidalgo launched an insurrection that almost instantaneously galvanized the regional population to the cause of rebellion. Adopting the cry of "Long live the Virgin of Guadalupe, Death to bad government, Death to the gachupines," rural people, some Creoles, and parts of the regional provincial militia regiments declared rebellion. What began as a small, poorly armed force exploded into a great movement that surged into local towns and quickly occupied the great mining city of Guanajuato. Moreover, Hidalgo dispatched revolutionary emissaries to spread the revolutionary message well beyond the Bajío region where they ignited many new centers of rebellion. For a short while, the uprising gave the impression that Hidalgo had released an inexorable force that might sweep away the existing regime. Well beyond the regions affected, the gachupines and some Creoles fled from their home provinces to seek refuge in Mexico City.

Father Miguel Hidalgo y Costilla was the author of the Grito de Dolores (Cry from Dolores), *the passionate speech of Dolores that ignited the independence struggle in Mexico on September 16, 1810. (Library of Congress)*

At first, the regime appeared to be shocked and incapable of making a meaningful response. The new viceroy, Francisco Xavier de Venegas (1810–1813), one of the few Spanish army commanders with battlefield successes against the French invaders in Spain, sought the assistance of an experienced regular army officer, Félix Calleja del Rey. Calleja had been active in New Spain since 1789, and in 1810 he was commander of the Tenth Militia Brigade, based at San Luis Potosí. Mobilizing two provincial militia dragoon regiments and recruiting new units of mounted lancers and some poorly armed infantry, Calleja organized a force of about 5,000 soldiers called the Army of the Center. Gradually, the Royalist forces illustrated that organized troops armed with flintlock muskets and able to fire volleys could cut down the ill-equipped and disorganized rebel masses. At first, Hidalgo appeared to be intent upon occupying Mexico City until a small dug-in force from the capital halted the attacks of a rebel multitude of some 80,000 people near Toluca at the battle of Monte de las Cruces. After that, Calleja's reinforced Army of the Center crushed the insurgents at the one-sided battles of Aculco, Guanajuato, and Calderón near Guadalajara.

During the insurgent occupations of Guanajuato, Valladolid (Morelia), and Guadalajara, brutal treatment and in a few cases the clandestine executions of groups of male gachupines reminded many Creoles that they could be the next victims of the revolution. However, after the battle of Calderón (January 17, 1811), Hidalgo, Ignacio de Allende who replaced him, and other leaders fled northward where in March 1811, the Royalists captured them by surprise, committed them to trials, and executed them. Notwithstanding his failures, Hidalgo, who was the last to die before a firing squad on July 30, 1811, emerged in death as one of the great heroes of the independence epoch. The revolution fragmented into many new uprisings and insurgencies, including that of Father José María Morelos.

Much more capable in terms of military organization, planning, logistics, and strategy, Morelos operated in the regions to the south of Mexico City. He built upon strong popular support from the disaffected racially mixed populations of the tropical lowlands as well as the interior. His grand strategy of 1812 was to surround, isolate, and force the surrender of Royalist power in Mexico City. Calleja, still occupied in the Bajío region, had to move his Army of the Center southward to confront the new peril. In addition, Royalist forces struggled to protect Puebla and to keep open the interdicted roads from the capital to the strategic port of Veracruz. However, while French armies still occupied parts of the metropolis, the first Spanish expeditionary infantry battalions arrived at Veracruz. Morelos fortified the town of Cuautla Amilpas south of Mexico City, believing that his forces could draw the Royalists into a protracted siege that they could not win. Although both sides suffered incredible hardships, after seventy-two days starvation forced the insurgents to break out and to flee. Morelos moved southward to occupy Oaxaca and then besieged and occupied Acapulco; in the process he moved his campaign away from the major populated centers of New Spain. In response to Royalist firepower, from 1812 to 1821 many insurgent chiefs adopted defensive warfare, employing effective guerrilla tactics and forcing the Royalists to undertake sieges. The defense of rugged mountain fortifications and isolated islands in lakes produced many Royalist victories owing to their superior firepower and logistics; however, over time the effort caused exhaustion, low morale, and desertion.

After 1812, in many respects the conflict became a civil war, with the insurgents occupying the less populated rural zones and the Royalists holding the major cities and towns. Calleja and his commanders introduced a classic form of counterinsurgency: they fortified the Royalist towns and cities with parapets and established hard targets that would compel attackers to use artillery and siege equipment. The Royalists militarized the populace, introducing taxes to support the war, raising urban and rural militia forces for urban defense, and patrolling surrounding rural districts. The Royalists sometimes concentrated village and hamlet inhabitants into fortified towns protected by armed garrisons, palisades, and ditches. The idea, though often unsuccessful, was to clear the countryside so that anyone encountered there could be treated as an enemy. Although these methods succeeded in some provinces, the insurgents managed to turn the region around Lake Chapala in Nueva Galicia into a zone of near-constant bloody combat. With a strong insurgent fortress on the island of Mezcala in Lake Chapala, the Royalists had to confront enemy canoe flotillas with cannon launches and galley warfare. Years of skirmishes around the littoral of the lake left some districts totally devastated. The struggle in the Bajío region continued with the insurgents blockading the cities and controlling rural areas. Often, Royalist commanders failed to cooperate so that provincial or military district boundaries provided rebel guerrilla bands opportunities to escape pursuit. During these years, Royalist commanders such as José de la Cruz (Nueva Galicia), Agustín de Iturbide (Guanajuato), and Ciriaco de Llano (Puebla) became powerful figures who sometimes enriched themselves and governed as despots of their provincial commands.

On the political side, many Mexicans welcomed the Spanish constitution of 1812, which established representative government and authorized elections to the town and city councils, the province, and the Spanish *Cortes* (parliament). Although elections were held, in 1814 Ferdinand VII returned from exile to abrogate the constitution and restore absolutism. The insurgents under Morelos also held elections, but they did not occupy major populated centers. In 1813, the Congress of Chilpancingo declared the independence of Mexico from Spain, and the next year the insurgents adopted the Constitution of Apatzingán, establishing a republic. However, renewed Royalist military pressures prevented the actual creation of a new government. In November 1815, Royalist forces captured Morelos and sent him to Mexico City for a show trial, condemnation, and on December 22, execution by firing squad at Ecatepec just outside the capital.

Although some Royalists hoped that victory was near, the economy was in ruins, communications and commerce were interrupted, and soldiers went unpaid. The proliferation of guerrilla and bandit bands *(gavillas)* compelled commanders to divide and subdivide their regiments and battalions for garrison duties, patrols, and service in armed convoys needed to move commerce. After 1817, Spain no longer dispatched fresh expeditionary units to bolster morale. Gradually, the Royalist army lost its capacity to field operational armies or to engage in difficult counterinsurgency campaigns. Viceroy Juan Ruiz de Apodaca (1816–1821) introduced a generous amnesty program to attract insurgents, often incorporating former rebels directly into the Royalist military. Beset by financial crises, loss of discipline, disease, and increasing levels of desertion, after 1816 the Royalist army lost much of its fighting capacity. In the meantime, some veteran rebel leaders, such as Vicente Guerrero, Guadalupe Victoria, and other guerrilla and bandit chiefs, blockaded roads, raided from isolated fortresses, and interdicted vital commercial routes. In 1819, Royalists lost control of the strategic road from the interior to Veracruz. Without major battles or outstanding insurgent chiefs to command broad national support, the Royalist army illustrated every sign of debilitation and exhaustion.

After more than ten years of war, the independence of Mexico came as something of a distinct anticlimax. In 1820, the restoration of the Spanish constitution once again generated elections in New Spain, and many argued that the constitution invalidated the counterinsurgency system with its heavy local taxation. Some city governments disbanded urban and district militias and stacked their arms. At the same time, Viceroy Apodaca named Brigadier Agustín de Iturbide to attack the implacable insurgent bands, including that of Vicente Guerrero in the rugged territory of today's Guerrero State. Rather than chase these bands according to his instructions, Iturbide met with Vicente Guerrero and other rebel chiefs. They issued the Plan de Iguala, signed on February 24, 1821. The plan contained three major guarantees, proclaiming religion (the Catholic faith), independence (proposing Ferdinand VII or a member of his family to rule), and union (referring to the unification of the populace of New Spain). Few could disagree with these broad goals, and both Royalist and insurgent leaders joined the movement. Forming the Army of the Three Guarantees and beginning what was little more than a victory march about the country, the Royalist side crumbled and remnants of the military and the bureaucracy retreated to Mexico City. When Juan O'Donojú arrived in July 1821 as captain general and superior political chief of the new constitutional Spanish government, he met with Iturbide and signed the Treaty of Córdoba, which recognized the independence of New Spain. Iturbide entered Mexico City on September 27, 1821, the day of his thirty-eighth birthday. When news arrived that the Spanish government rejected the Treaty of Córdoba, Iturbide's followers pressed for his candidacy to lead the new nation. On May 1, 1822, soldiers of Iturbide's regiment proclaimed him emperor and forced the congress to agree. His authoritarian reign lasted ten months; his resignation in March 1823 opened the way to the proclamation of the fully independent Mexican republic and to the Constitution of 1824.

Christon I. Archer

References

Anna, Timothy E. *The Fall of the Royal Government in Mexico City.* Lincoln: University of Nebraska Press, 1978.

Archer, Christon I., ed. "Fighting for Small Worlds: Wars of the People during the Independence Era in New Spain." *Cuadernos de Historia Latinoamericana* 6 (1998): 63–92.

———. *The Birth of Modern Mexico, 1780–1824.* Wilmington, DE: Scholarly Resources, 2003.

———. "The Indian Insurgents of Mezcala Island on the Lake Chapala Front, 1812–1816." Pp. 84–128, 158–165 in *The Pax Colonial and Native Resistance in New Spain,* edited by Susan Schroeder. Lincoln: University of Nebraska Press, 1998.

Guedea, Virginia. *La insurgencia en el Departamento del Norte: Los Llanos de Apan y la Sierra de Puebla, 1810–1816.* Instituto de Investigaciones Históricas. Mexico City: Universidad Nacional Autónoma de México (UNAM), 1996.

Hamill, Hugh M. *The Hidalgo Revolt: Prelude to Mexican Independence.* Gainesville: University of Florida Press, 1966.

Hamnett, Brian R. *Roots of Insurgency: Mexican Regions, 1750–1824.* Cambridge: Cambridge University Press, 1986.

Robertson, William S. *Iturbide of Mexico.* Durham, NC: Duke University Press, 1952.

Rodriguez O., Jaime E., ed. *The Independence of Mexico and the Creation of the New Nation.* Los Angeles: UCLA Latin American Center, 1989.

———. *The Independence of Spanish America.* Cambridge: Cambridge University Press, 1998.

Van Young, Eric. *The Other Rebellion: Popular Violence, Ideology, and the Mexican Struggle for Independence.* Stanford, CA: Stanford University Press, 2001.

See also: Armies—Colonial Spanish America; Bandits and Banditry; Bourbon Reforms;

Constitution of Cádiz; Cortes of Cádiz; Creoles; Defense—Colonial Spanish America; Enlightenment—Spanish America; Grito de Dolores; Guerrillas; Independence I–IV, VI; Intendants/Intendancy System; Mexico; Monarchs of Spain; Napoleonic Invasion and Spanish America; Rebellions—Colonial Latin America; Transportation—Colonial; Viceroyalties.

INDEPENDENCE VI—PERU

Peru moved fitfully toward independence, struggling to overcome internal Royalist sentiment but aided by external forces determined to liberate the South American colonies from Spanish control. Napoleon's invasion of Spain and overthrow of the monarchy in 1808 created a constitutional crisis in the Spanish Empire. Forcing Charles IV and his son Ferdinand VII to abdicate, Bonaparte placed his brother Joseph on the throne. The empire refused to accept Joseph as its legitimate ruler, however, and patriotic Spaniards established a central committee (junta) to organize resistance to the French and attempt to rule the overseas colonies, including Peru.

On the surface, Peru seemed a likely hotbed of anticolonial sentiment. Creoles (American-born Spaniards) had long resented the preference given to peninsular Spaniards in appointments to political and ecclesiastical office, and as the Bourbon monarchy heightened that discrimination in the late eighteenth century, the Creoles' bitterness grew. They also disliked many of the changes that resulted from new Bourbon policies intended to strengthen the Crown's control over the empire and increase the amount of revenue collected from the colonies. Lima lost its sense of privilege with the creation in 1776 of the new Viceroyalty of the Río de la Plata. With its capital at Buenos Aires, the new viceroyalty stripped away from Lima regions that became Argentina, Uruguay, Paraguay, and Bolivia. The eighteenth century also witnessed serious rebellions in the Andes, some of which aimed to drive the Spaniards from Peru. Most were indigenous uprisings, sometimes with Creole complicity, but they gave Peru an air of political instability that worried Madrid. Liberalism had also made modest inroads into Peru, leaving some to ponder the significance of the revolutions in British America, France, and Haiti.

When news arrived of the political crisis in Spain, Peru might have joined with the regions of Spanish America, such as Buenos Aires, that rejected the junta's attempt to rule. Yet Peruvian Royalists maintained firm control over the colony. A number of factors contributed to the Peruvians' reaction. The Great Andean Rebellion of the early 1780s, an indigenous uprising that spread over the southern Peruvian and the Bolivian highlands, left tens of thousands dead and made the Creole white elite fearful of arming the indigenous lower classes to overthrow Spanish rule. Better, the Creoles reasoned, to live in colonial status than to run the risk of inciting the lower classes to violence against the Crown and then having the uprising consume both Spaniards and Creoles. Peru also lacked the nationalist sentiment that had developed in regions such as Mexico. There was little sense of shared nationhood between the largely indigenous highlands and the coastal towns and cities, which contained a much higher proportion of Creole and mestizo residents.

The latter despised the Indians and considered them culturally inferior. The Royalist cause in Peru also benefited from the presence of an able, energetic viceroy, José Fernando de Abascal, who governed from 1806 to 1816.

Thus, as rebellion engulfed Spanish America, Peru remained relatively stable. In March 1809, when word arrived of the crisis in Spain, Lima soon recognized the Junta Central's authority to rule the empire until the king was able to return. Meanwhile Viceroy Abascal acted quickly to organize Peruvian defenses against threats from external rebel forces. He replaced unpopular royal officials and took other pragmatic measures to curb Creole complaints, and he dealt forcefully with conspirators who talked about setting up a Peruvian junta. That minor plot in mid-1809 was apparently the most serious internal threat to royal authority before 1814. In Spain, the junta convened a *Cortes* (representative assembly) to write a constitution. Invited to send delegates, Peru sent representatives to participate in the Cortes. While drafting what turned out to be an exceptionally liberal document, the Cortes issued decrees that complicated Abascal's rule in Peru, such as the edict of March 13, 1811, that abolished indigenous tribute. This weakened the state's fiscal control over the majority of the population, deprived the government of much-needed revenue, and eventually undermined its ability to fight against independence. Abascal protested, but he could not avoid implementing the decree or the constitution of 1812. Rather than pressing for independence, Peruvian liberals such as José Baquíjano y Carillo contented themselves with demands for free trade and relaxation of other economic restrictions.

The chief menace to the viceregal government prior to 1814 came from outside Peru. Argentine forces invaded Upper Peru, and Abascal sent an army there under General José Manuel de Goyeneche in 1809 to crush the rebels. Tumult in Quito required another force. Abascal provided funds to support the Royalist cause in Montevideo against Buenos Aires insurgents and in 1813 sent troops to Chile. His actions appeared successful but strained the Peruvian treasury.

In 1814, conditions in Peru shifted. The French were driven from Spain, and Ferdinand VII returned to claim the throne. A reactionary, Ferdinand VII abolished the constitution of 1812 and dashed the liberals' hopes for transforming the empire. In Cuzco discontent produced conspiracy and a serious uprising. Liberal Creoles there insisted on implementation of the promised constitutional reforms and increasingly resented Lima's domination of their region. Frustrated by the intransigence of the city's *audiencia* (high court), which was controlled by conservative Royalists, the liberals plotted to seize power. They needed military force and consequently opened negotiations with Mateo Pumacahua, an indigenous *kuraca* (chieftain) who had remained loyal to the Crown during the Great Andean Rebellion of 1780–1781 and whose army played a crucial role in defeating the rebels. By 1814, Pumacahua was old and frustrated. He believed the government had failed to deliver on its promises to improve indigenous conditions and felt that he had not been properly rewarded for his services. The Cuzco conspirators persuaded him and his army to join their insurgency. They sent out three forces in an attempt to take control of southern Peru: one to Puno and La Paz, another to Huamanga and Huancavelica, and the third to Arequipa. They massacred the Europeans at La Paz and killed the intendant of Arequipa but failed to consolidate their gains. By mid-1815, Royalist forces had crushed the Cuzco revolt and captured and executed Pumacahua and many of the Creole leaders.

Nonetheless, the Royalist successes proved transitory. In 1816, Abascal retired and was replaced as viceroy by Joaquín de la Pezuela, who had been commanding the Royalist forces in Upper Peru. Pezuela inherited a government bereft of funds and a colony whose commerce and mining the wars had disrupted. Royalist Creoles were rethinking their allegiances. Furthermore, the new viceroy concentrated troops and resources in Upper Peru, failing to anticipate invasion by sea from Chile until it was too late. It came in the person of José de San Martín, the resourceful and astute Argentine general who not only saw Peru as the linchpin of Royalist power in South America, but also believed that Peru could only be liberated via the Pacific rather than overland through the mountains of what would become Bolivia. From Argentina San Martín took his army over the Andes into Chile, helped secure its independence, and then began preparing for an invasion of Peru. He obtained naval forces under the command of the British mercenary commander Thomas Cochrane, who destroyed Spanish naval power in the Pacific and wreaked havoc on Peruvian commerce by blockading the coast.

In September 1820 San Martín invaded Peru, landing his forces at Pisco, south of Lima. Rather than seeking a decisive battle with Pezuela's formidable forces, San Martín waited, anticipating that the Peruvian population would rise in favor of independence. On December 29, 1820, the intendant of Trujillo, the Marquis of Torre Tagle, and that city's *cabildo* (town council) pronounced in favor of independence, and most of northern Peru followed. As pressure on Lima mounted, so did criticism among Royalists of Pezuela's conduct of the defense, and on January 29, 1821, they removed the viceroy and put General José de la Serna in his place. Attempts by San Martín to negotiate a peaceful transition to independence failed, even when he proposed converting Peru into a constitutional monarchy headed by a prince from the Spanish royal family. In July 1821, La Serna withdrew from Lima to the interior, although royal forces continued to hold the fortifications at the port of Callao. Occupying Lima, San Martín declared Peru independent on July 28, 1821. The capital's Creoles went along, less out of ardor for independence than out of fear of mob rule should San Martín not hold the city's lower classes in check.

Following the declaration of independence, San Martín, as Peru's civil and military protector, issued decrees to carry out a social transformation of the nation. He emancipated all children born of slaves after July 28, 1821, abolished Indian tribute and the *mita* (forced indigenous labor), expelled all Spaniards, and confiscated half their property. San Martín sought to turn Peru's Indians into full citizens. His decrees failed because the Peruvian Creoles showed little enthusiasm for their enforcement and because the Royalists continued to control important regions in the interior of the country. An election produced Peru's first parliament, which convened on September 20, 1822. San Martín failed to press the military campaign against the enemy forces, did not attack the Royalists when

The Spanish army meets defeat at the hands of troops led by Bolivian general Antonio José de Sucre on December 9, 1824. (North Wind Picture Archive)

they finally evacuated Callao, and caused rising indignation for his persecution of Spaniards in Lima.

Meanwhile, Simón Bolívar's Colombian forces moved through Ecuador to occupy the port of Guayaquil. With both Bolívar and San Martín determined to drive the Spanish forces from Peru, the issue of their cooperation became crucial. The two liberators met at Guayaquil in late July 1822 and disagreed regarding the future government for Peru: Bolívar insisted on republicanism, whereas San Martín argued that monarchy was more suited to Peru's traditions and experience. In the face of Bolívar's determination and upon discovery of infighting and turmoil among his supporters in Lima, San Martín ceded the stage. Independence had not proved as popular among Peruvians as he had hoped, and Lima did not provide the resources needed for defeating the Spanish forces in the interior. San Martín left South America for Europe, and Spanish, Peruvian, Chilean, Colombian, and Argentine soldiers fought to decide Peru's fate.

Disunity among the allies and Peruvian political factionalism threatened to defeat the movement for independence. Congress appointed José de la Riva-Agüero Peru's first president, but when it disagreed with his actions, it named José Bernardo Torre Tagle to replace him. With his power base in northern Peru, Riva-Agüero refused to step aside for Torre Tagle, who drew most of his support from Lima. With the resulting chaos, Royalist forces temporarily occupied Lima and regained control of almost all of Peru in mid-1823. The crisis forced Bolívar himself to go to Peru. He arrived in Lima on September 1, 1823. The Peruvian parliament gave Bolívar command of all the armies fighting for the nation's liberation. Many Peruvians distrusted Bolívar and feared that he came as a conqueror with Napoleonic ambitions. Unlike San Martín, he had no illusions that out of patriotic and nationalist zeal Peruvians would rise to the banner of independence. Bolívar consequently concentrated on building an army to carry the fight into the mountain stronghold of the Royalists. In early 1824, the Spanish cause received a devastating blow when General Pedro Antonio Olañeta, commander of the Royalist army of Upper Peru, rebelled against Viceroy La Serna and installed himself as the political and military ruler of the region. This threatened La Serna's rear and deprived him of reinforcements and supplies. On July 6, 1824, La Serna suffered defeat near Jauja at the battle of Junín. Antonio José de Sucre, Bolívar's deputy, completed the destruction of Royalist power in the highlands, routing La Serna at Ayacucho on December 8, 1824, and defeating Olañeta the following April in Bolivia. Despite the victory at Ayacucho, which made Peru's independence inevitable, a few Royalist forces held out at Callao through 1825 before their surrender on January 23, 1826, marked the end of the conflict.

Nearly two decades of turmoil and warfare had devastated Peru. The mines that had produced its colonial wealth were destroyed or abandoned. Its commerce lay moribund. Despite the liberators' decrees, the status of the indigenous population remained unsettled, and there was no consensus regarding political organization. To create a new nation proved as daunting as liberating the colony.

Kendall W. Brown

References

Anna, Timothy E. *The Fall of the Royal Government in Peru.* Lincoln: University of Nebraska Press, 1979.

Humphreys, R. A. *Liberation in South America, 1806–1827: The Career of James Paroissien.* London: University of London Press, 1952.

Lynch, John. *The Spanish American Revolutions, 1808–1826.* 2nd ed. New York: W. W. Norton, 1986.

Masur, Gerhard. *Simón Bolívar.* Albuquerque: University of New Mexico Press, 1948.

Miller, John. *Memoirs of General Miller, in the Service of the Republic of Peru* [1829]. 2nd ed. 2 vols. New York: AMS, 1973.

Mitre, Bartolomé. *The Emancipation of South America: A Condensed Translation of the History of San Martín.* Translated by William Pilling. Buenos Aires: Stockcero, 2003.

Rojas, Ricardo. *San Martín, Knight of the Andes.* Translated by Herschel Brickell and Carlos Videla. New York: Cooper Square, 1967.

See also: Bourbon Reforms; Cabildo; Creoles; Enlightenment—Spanish America; Independence I–V; Intendants/Intendancy System; Monarchs of Spain; Napoleonic Invasion and Spanish America; Nationalism; Peru; Rebellions—Colonial Latin America; Túpac Amaru Revolt; Viceroyalties.

INQUISITION—LUSO-AMERICA

The Portuguese Inquisition was a predominantly ecclesiastical tribunal established in 1536 with the papal bull *Cum ad nil magis* to police the behavior and beliefs of the subjects of the Portuguese Crown. The expulsion of the Jews from Spain in 1492 stimulated a flood of Jewish refugees into Portugal, which increased tensions and ethnic hatreds there. Pressured by Spain to expel the Jews as part of a royal marriage agreement, the king, Dom Manuel (1495–1521), finally issued an expulsion order in 1496 for all Jews who would not convert to Christianity. Rather than allow the Jews to leave, Dom Manuel engaged in forced baptisms (creating the so-called New Christians) and restricted Jewish migration from Portugal. He also resisted all attempts to create an Inquisition. Consequently, the institution was not established until the reign of Dom João (1521–1557) (King John III). Despite the 1536 bull, the Inquisition did not begin to take its final form until 1547 with a new papal bull.

The Portuguese Inquisition organized itself roughly on the model of the Spanish Inquisition established in 1478. The Inquisition established tribunals at Évora (1536), Lisbon (1539), Coimbra (1541), Lamego (1541), Porto (1541), and Tomar

(1541). The last three survived only until 1546 or 1547. The tribunal in Portuguese India was created in Goa in 1560.

The regulations or bylaws (called *Regimentos*) that governed inquisitional activity were first systematized in 1552 and modified again in 1570, 1613, 1640, and 1774. Each new Regimento increased the centralization and bureaucratization of the Inquisition and modified its practices to suit the political, social, and ideological climate of the empire.

The inquisitor general oversaw all inquisitional activity in the Portuguese Empire. He sat as president of the *Conselho Geral* (general council), which included at least three deputies, a secretary, and a solicitor. The general council served as a centralizing agent and as a forum for the resolution of disputes between the different tribunals. The deputies of the general council were superior in authority to the inquisitors of the tribunals. They handled all difficult cases, oversaw inquisitional inspections and the compilation of lists of prohibited books, acted as the final court of appeals on all matters of inquisitional procedure and organization, and oversaw the appointment of inquisitional officials.

The inquisitors of the various tribunals sat as judges. They were collectively responsible for the litigation of all cases brought before the tribunal. This included gathering information, questioning witnesses and accused heretics, and passing judgment. The tribunals benefited from an army of lesser officials, including *promotores* (prosecutors), *notários* (notaries), *meirinhos* (bailiffs), *alcaides dos carceres* (jailers or wardens), *procuradores dos presos* (attorneys of the criminals), *comissários* (commissioners), and *familiares* (lay officials).

Brazil never received a tribunal of its own, and, together with the other Atlantic territories of Portugal, it remained under the authority of the Lisbon Tribunal until the abolition of the Inquisition in 1821. After the creation of the bishopric of Bahia in 1551, bishops held inquisitorial authority in the colony. But in the sixteenth century, the bishops did very little in this regard. It was not until after Spain assumed the Portuguese throne in 1580 that the Inquisition made its presence felt in Brazil. This long delay helped Brazil become a refuge for New Christians fleeing persecution in Portugal.

The Inquisition sent several *visitas* (visitations or investigations) to Brazil in an attempt to rein in the heterodoxy of the colonists. Father Heitor Furtado de Mendonça oversaw the first visitation to Brazil (Bahia, 1591–1593, and Pernambuco, 1593–1595). Father Marcos Teixeira visited Bahia in 1618–1620, and Father Giraldo de Abranches visited Grão-Pará from 1763 to 1769. These visitations prosecuted crypto-Jews and every other unorthodox behavior including sodomy, bigamy, blasphemy, and witchcraft. But these visitations were brief and infrequent, and the Inquisition had to establish a more effective way of policing the morals of the inhabitants of Portuguese America.

The result was a system based on the utilization of noninquisitional institutions and personnel. The Inquisition relied heavily on high-ranking ecclesiastical authorities such as bishops, rectors of Jesuit colleges, priors of convents, and vicars.

After 1690, the Inquisition moved to replace this system with a network of resident inquisitional officials. Comissários formed the backbone of inquisitional power in Brazil and oversaw all inquisitional activity. They were assisted by a network of lay officials called familiares.

The period of most intense inquisitional activity in the Portuguese Empire occurred between 1584 and 1674. Between 1606 and 1674, the Inquisition investigated 22,481 cases and sent 863 individuals, either in person or in effigy, to the civil authorities for execution. The next 100 years saw a marked decrease in this type of inquisitional activity. Between 1675 and 1767, only 12,142 cases came before inquisitional tribunals, and 446 faced the flames either in person or effigy.

Of the 28,266 individuals who appeared in the *autos-da-fé* (public acts of reconciliation) during the tenure of the Inquisition, 1,817 were burned, 1,175 in person (4.2 percent) and 642 in effigy (2.2 percent). Most of the executions occurred in the sixteenth and seventeenth centuries, and several years often passed between executions (for example, in Évora only twelve after 1691 and none between 1706 and 1755, in Coimbra none after 1718, and in Lisbon none after 1765). Of the 44,817 individuals prosecuted by the Inquisition between 1536 and 1821, 28,266 were punished (63 percent), and 1,175 (2.6 percent) of them actually perished in the flames.

The list of the autos-da-fé from Lisbon shows that 556 individuals from Brazil were punished, most frequently for the "crimes" of Judaism and bigamy. Brazil experienced two relatively intense periods of activity against New Christians. Between 1709 and 1728, most of those punished in the autos-da-fé were New Christians from Rio de Janeiro. Between 1731 and 1741, a large group of related individuals from Paraíba was also punished. Men represented the majority of those punished in Lisbon (372 or 66.9 percent), while women represented 33.1 percent (184).

Anita Novinsky has identified 1,819 men and women accused, or suspected by the Inquisition, of Judaizing in Brazil in the eighteenth century alone. She has also identified 1,076 prisoners, both men and women, sent from Brazil to Lisbon. Inquisitional activity occurred all over Brazil but was concentrated in the regions with dense populations. Rio de Janeiro produced 306 (55 percent) of those from Brazil punished in autos-da-fé. Pernambuco and Bahia followed with 64 (11.5 percent) each.

This evidence suggests that during the eighteenth century, inquisitional activity in Brazil provided a significant portion of the total inquisitional activity in the empire. Between 1709 and 1737, Brazilians frequently represented more than 50 percent of those punished in the Lisbon autos-da-fé. Between 1600 and 1787, fully 13.85 percent of those punished in the autos-da-fé came from Brazil. During the eighteenth century alone, 21.25 percent came from Brazil. The high percentage rate of individuals from Brazil being punished at the autos-da-fé suggests the increasing importance of Brazil as a locus for inquisitorial activity and the successful efforts of the Inquisition to detain and punish those it identified as offenders.

The eighteenth century witnessed an extended period of reform and decline for the Portuguese Inquisition. After 1690, the number of sentences handed down by inquisitional tribunals declined sharply. At the same time, appointments of familiares and comissários rose dramatically until the 1770s in Portugal and the 1790s in Brazil. This disparity in sentences and appointments suggests that the Inquisition had shifted its focus from repression to social promotion. Growing numbers of lay officials sought appointments to the Inquisition to gain access to inquisitional privilege and, more importantly, to acquire solid, publicly recognized credentials as defenders of the faith and persons of pure blood. Inquisitional appointment supported claims to honor and social prestige and could be used to gain access to prestigious brotherhoods and to public office.

The Inquisition also underwent considerable reform in the eighteenth century. Sebastião José de Carvalho e Melo, later the Marquis of Pombal, the chief minister of the kingdom under Dom José I, energetically reformed the Inquisition. In 1768, he stripped the power of censure from the Inquisition and invested it in a new institution called the Real Mesa Censória. He eliminated the legal distinction between New and Old Christians and rescinded the pure blood laws in 1773. In 1774, he issued new regulations for the Inquisition that constrained the use of secret testimony and single witnesses, the confiscation of property, and the use of torture. The new regulations also eliminated the pure blood requirement for those seeking inquisitional office.

Despite, and perhaps because of, these reforms, the Inquisition continued to decline. By the late eighteenth and early nineteenth centuries, inquisitional officials everywhere began refusing to serve the Inquisition. The Inquisition's values had become painfully out of sync with the popular ideals of the Enlightenment that began to take hold in Portugal and Brazil in the last quarter of the eighteenth century. These external pressures, combined with the internal rot, brought the institution to a close by the vote of the liberal Cortes in Lisbon in March 1821.

James E. Wadsworth

References

Bethencourt, Francisco. *História das inquisições: Portugal, Espanha, e Itália.* Lisbon: Temas e Debates, 1996.

Herculano, Alexandre. *Historia da origem e estabelecimento da inquisição em Portugal.* Vols. 1–3. Lisbon: Ed. Livraria Bertrand, 1975.

Novinsky, Anita. *Rol dos culpados: Fontes para a história do Brasil, século XVIII.* Rio de Janeiro: Expressão e Cultura, 1992.

———. *Inquisição: Prisioneiros do Brasil, séculos XVI–XIX.* Rio de Janeiro: Expressao e Cultura, 2002.

Siqueira, Sonia A. *A inquisição portuguesa e a sociedade colonial.* São Paulo: Editora Ática, 1978.

Vainfas, Ronaldo. *Trópico dos pecados: Moral, sexualidade e inquisição no Brasil colonial.* Rio de Janeiro: Nova Fronteira, 1997.

Wadsworth, James. "Agents of Orthodoxy: Inquisitional Power and Prestige in Colonial Pernambuco, Brazil." Ph.D. dissertation, University of Arizona, 2002.

See also: Bigamy, Transatlantic; Catholic Church in Brazil; Clergy—Secular, in Colonial Spanish America; Comissários; Confraternities; Converso; Diabolism in the New World; Enlightenment—Brazil; Familiares; Idolatry, Extirpation of; Independence II—Brazil; Inquisition—Spanish America; Jesuits—Brazil; Jews—Colonial Latin America; Liberalism; Monarchs of Portugal; Napoleonic Invasion and Luso-America; Religious Orders; Saints and Saintliness; Visita; Witchcraft; Women—Brazil.

INQUISITION—SPANISH AMERICA

Founded in 1478, the Spanish Inquisition was transferred into the New World in the sixteenth century to eliminate from non-Indian society all heresy, heterodoxy, and offenses against God. The Inquisition set up tribunals in Mexico City, Lima, and Cartagena de Indias (in today's Colombia), which soon became not only a privileged royal instrument to enforce religious orthodoxy by punishing crimes ranging from blasphemy to Judaizing, but also a primary cause of colonial misrule and even a source of institutional chaos. Contrary to popular belief, the Spanish American Inquisition enjoyed the support of both members of the elite and the popular masses until the late eighteenth century, when the tribunals entered an era of social, economic, and political decline culminating in the tribunals' suppression in 1820 and 1821.

In the early years of Spanish colonization, the investigation of heresy was a duty of the bishops and, in their absence, of the friars. In 1517, the bishop of Puerto Rico, Alfonso Manso, became the first inquisitor of the New World. Because of the scarcity of bishops, the pope also granted inquisitorial powers to missionaries in a 1522 bull known as *Omnímoda.* Although jurisdiction reverted to the bishops upon their appointment in the colonies, the friars maintained inquisitorial authority in regions without ministers of that rank. The bishop's inquisitorial powers were officially ended in January 1569, when King Philip II decreed the establishment of the Tribunal of the Inquisition, appointing Pedro Moya de Contreras and Licenciate Serván de Cerezuela as inquisitors of Mexico and Peru, respectively. The Spanish king's decision stemmed from the need to put an end to the constant abuses of power by the poorly trained episcopal ministers and the need to stop the distribution of Protestant printed matter in his possessions across the Atlantic. A circular forbade the bishops from punishing religious crimes and ordered them to transfer all pending cases to the tribunals, but the religious ministers refused to give up their jurisdiction, thus forcing the Supreme Council of the Inquisition to repeat such injunctions in 1585 and 1586. The newly appointed inquisitors were entrusted with the impossible task of supervising a territory twenty to thirty times bigger than that assigned to their counterparts on the Spanish Peninsula. At a time in which the largest tribunals in Spain, such as Valladolid, encompassed a territory of 90,000 km^2, the Mexican tribunal had jurisdiction over an area of nearly 2 million km^2, including Mexico, Guatemala, Nicaragua, northern Panama, the Caribbean islands, and the Philippines. For its part, the Peruvian Inquisition was in charge of a territory of close to 3 million km^2 comprising southern Panama, Colombia, Venezuela, Ecuador, Peru, Bolivia, Argentina, Uruguay, and Paraguay. The creation of a third tribunal in Cartagena de Indias in 1610, with a territorial jurisdiction of 2.5 million km^2 encompassing Colombia, Panama, Venezuela, Puerto Rico, and Cuba, offered some relief to both tribunals but was clearly not enough. Starting in 1620, repeated petitions were written to create another tribunal in Buenos Aires to control the entrance of Portuguese Judaizers, but the Crown refused to incur such an expense and did nothing.

From their inception, the colonial tribunals shared some characteristics that set them apart from their peninsular counterparts. While in Spain the establishment of the Inquisition in 1478 responded to the fear of converted Jews who allegedly observed Jewish rites while practicing formal Christianity, King Philip II created the American tribunals with the main purpose of prosecuting Protestant foreigners and censoring heretical books to control the spread of Reformist ideas in the New World. This notwithstanding, the tribunals also carried out fierce campaigns against crypto-Jews, especially during the seventeenth century when such prosecutions reached extraordinary proportions. Another important characteristic of the Spanish American tribunals was that, in contrast to their counterparts in Spain, they did not have jurisdiction over the vast majority of the population. Indeed, the Inquisition regularly tried Spaniards, Africans, and mixed-bloods, but it had no authority over the Indians; jurisdiction over the natives had been reverted to the bishops and their ecclesiastical judges or *provisores* in 1569. This injunction was generally respected, but inquisitors occasionally received denunciations against Indians and even ordered investigations about their transgressions, thus giving way to conflicts of competence with the *provisorato.* The Spanish American tribunals were also more autonomous than those in Spain. At a time in which the Supreme Council of the Inquisition (the Suprema) increased its control over peninsular tribunals, colonial inquisitors could appoint minor officers, create commissions, pronounce sentence, and even prohibit books without waiting for the authorization of the Supreme Tribunal (the Suprema) in Madrid. Colonial tribunals were required, however, to send reports of their current affairs and the state of pending cases, a practice that allowed the Suprema to supervise the tribunals' activities and ponder the fairness of the sentences imposed. Additional mechanisms, such as sending an inspector with extensive faculties and deposing especially abusive inquisitors, allowed the Suprema to exert some degree of control over the tribunals.

The Spanish American Inquisitions also offered their ministers unique opportunities of social ascension. Serving in the Inquisition became a means of reaching the episcopate (normally after an average of four years of service) or getting promoted to a more prestigious position in another colonial district (Cartagena and Lima being the lowest and highest in the hierarchy, respectively). This is clearly exemplified by the impressive case of Pedro Moya de Contreras, first inquisitor of Mexico, who became archbishop of New Spain after three years of service in the tribunal and was later appointed viceroy and president of the Council of the Indies. Similarly, Inquisitor Bonilla, who arrived in Mexico as prosecutor in 1571, became inquisitor in 1573 and archbishop of Mexico in 1592; and Bartolomé Lobo Guerrero, inquisitor in Mexico, was given the see of Bogotá in 1596. Finally, at a time in which peninsular Spaniards occupied most of the high posts in the colonies, the Inquisition also opened its doors to Creoles (American-born Spaniards) and even Indians, thus constituting a precious venue of social climbing for members of both groups. Indeed, Creoles were not only appointed as prosecutors and secretaries but also as inquisitors. By the seventeenth century, Indians were also serving as *familiares* in Mexico and there were petitions to grant similar privileges to Indians in Peru.

The organization of the Spanish American Inquisition essentially mirrored that of the Spanish districts. Like their counterparts in Spain, the colonial tribunals consisted of salaried and unsalaried officials who, in addition to the specific qualifications of their positions, had to demonstrate their purity of blood, that is, the absence of Jewish or Muslim ancestors. The salaried personnel were normally composed of two inquisitors (occasionally three), one prosecutor, one notary, one secretary, one treasurer, one constable, one jailor with assistants, an advocate of prisoners, and minor officers such as a barber, a physician, a surgeon, and a porter. These officers served in the Inquisition's headquarters in Mexico, Lima, and Cartagena de Indias, and along with their families, enjoyed special privileges such as being exempt from taxation, and judicial immunity *(fuero)* in both civil and criminal matters. Although the vast majority of the officials were unsalaried, they also benefited from the social and economic advantages of serving in the Inquisition, which explains why these posts were keenly sought. Those serving as nonsalaried personnel were the theologian consulters, the censors or *calificadores* who pondered the gravity of the crime committed, the commissioners or representatives of the Inquisition in all major towns (normally chosen among the clergy), their notaries and constables, and finally, the numerous familiares recruited among the nobility and other individuals of high social standing who acted as lay police for the Inquisition, arresting suspects and enforcing the Inquisition's mandates.

Colonial inquisitors relied especially on the inspecting and policing work of commissioners and familiares, for in contrast to their peninsular counterparts, they were not required to travel their districts receiving denunciations and taking testimony, and it was only through these officials that the Inquisition learned of crimes committed in ports, mining towns, and rural areas. Years of experience had shown the Crown, however, that these functionaries tended to abuse their authority and, from the very first years, the king tried to limit their power. The instructions given to the inquisitors of Lima and Mexico in 1569 and 1570 asked them to be especially careful when appointing commissioners, a mandate rarely obeyed, and clearly specified the jurisdictional boundaries of these functionaries. Commissioners could conduct investigations and take testimony, but they had no authority to perform arrests unless it was clear that the case concerned the Inquisition, there was enough evidence against the culprit, and it was highly possible that the offender would escape. Unfortunately, these conditions were not always met, especially in distant regions, where the abusive behavior of these officers was a source of constant complaint. As in Spain, however, it was the familiares who constituted the most troublesome group. Usually selected from laymen of the highest social echelons, the familiares formed a precious network that allowed the Holy Office to both police the land and secure the support of influential groups of colonial society. The familiares were the largest number of officers working for the tribunals, and like the commissioners, they were appointed to serve in the episcopal sees and the capitals of the viceroyalties, but also in "Spanish towns." Knowing that these officers tended to abuse their immunities, the Spanish Crown placed strict limitations on the number of positions available and restricted their privileges. Thus, the familiares enjoyed immunity in criminal matters like other members of the Holy Office, but they were subject to the vice-regency for civil matters. In practice, however, the tribunals never hesitated to protect them, and their infamous actions constituted a source of endless disputes over matters of jurisdiction with secular authorities.

As in Spain, the colonial Inquisition went through periods of economic dependence, growth, and decay, which responded to the vicissitudes of royal policy, the changing cycles of inquisitorial repression, and a perennial lack of funds. During the first decades, the Spanish Crown paid for the salaries of the inquisitors, prosecutors, and secretaries. Colonial tribunals were expected to cover all other expenses (including the salaries of other minor officers) from fines and confiscations; nevertheless, the tribunals found it difficult to make ends meet. By the 1620s, however, inquisitors had found new sources of income, and the deficit started to disappear. Among these alternative sources were the "donations," which the tribunals obtained by collecting other people's debts and charging a commission of 33 to 50 percent. The Inquisition also profited from the popularity of gambling in the colonies by fining those who breached their promise, attested by a notarial deed known as *escritura de compromiso,* not to gamble again. Other sources included lending money at high interest (*censos*), exploiting Indian laborers through the system of *repartimiento,* and selling appointments as minor officers to the Inquisition; finally, the tribunals also accumulated property and money as beneficiary in the wills of pious Christians. In 1628, Philip IV obtained from the Vatican the extension of the system of suppressed prebends (*canonjías supresas*) to the New World, which allotted to the tribunals an annual stipend from the revenues of every cathedral and church in the colonies. A few years later, the tribunals received a major financial boost when they initiated proceedings against wealthy Portuguese merchants of Jewish origin on charges of Judaizing, or secretly practicing their religion. In Peru, the most lucrative confiscations took place from 1634 to 1639, while in New Granada the Judaizers were tried from 1636 to 1638. Finally, in Mexico the first arrests were made in the 1580s, but the greatest repression was carried out between 1640 and 1649. The benefits for the tribunals were sizable, as clearly shown in the case of the Peruvian Inquisition, which received more than 1 million pesos between 1635 and 1646. In spite of the economic bonanza, the tribunals consistently underreported and even refused to give account of their earnings to the Supreme Council in order to continue receiving the generous royal subvention (which, in the case of Peru, the most expensive tribunal, amounted to 10,000 pesos per annum).

Because of the tribunal's autonomy and its fierce determination to maintain and even expand its jurisdiction and privileges over both temporal and spiritual spheres, the Spanish American Inquisition frequently became involved in quarrels with both ecclesiastic and royal authorities. The bitter jurisdictional disputes, the settlement of which were known as *competencias,* were often compounded by the inquisitors' penchant to excommunicate opponents and even to prosecute anyone who attempted to curb their pretensions as an "impeder" of the Holy Office. Conflicts with ecclesiastic authorities centered on two main issues: the deprivation of the bishops' jurisdiction over religious transgressions and the exemption of abusive ecclesiastics serving in the tribunal from prosecution in episcopal courts. The collection of the suppressed prebends was also a matter of dispute, for bishops often tried to use those resources to solve the Church's needs or simply refused to hand them over. Although the inquisitors' relationships with government officials were not always abrasive, there were also many sources of contention. Three in particular are noteworthy: the tribunals' dubious jurisdiction over crimes not necessarily involving heresy (such as bigamy, which was also punished by civil courts), the disputes over the collection of fines and confiscated goods from individuals punished by the Holy Office, and the fueros enjoyed by its representatives. Inquisitors were sensitive to matters of etiquette, and the breach of protocol by both ecclesiastic and secular authorities in masses, meetings, and rituals of public punishment often triggered heated disagreements that easily escalated into serious confrontations. In an effort to restore peace, Philip III asked for the advice of members of both the Council of the Indies and the Suprema, who after much deliberation elaborated the famous *Concordia* of 1610, which put significant limits on the Inquisition's excesses. The document set new standards of behavior by forbidding inquisitors from excommunicating a viceroy in jurisdictional disputes, or protecting commissioners or familiares in frauds or abuses of authority. To avoid the expensive and tiring process of sending jurisdictional complaints to Madrid, the Spanish Crown also ordered the creation of councils *(juntas de competencias)* in the colonies involving the parties in contention. But news of irreconcilable disputes continued pouring into the Suprema, and in 1633 the king felt forced to issue a new Concordia containing new prohibitions for the Holy Office's representatives and precise rules of etiquette to be observed by the inquisitors, the bishops, and the colonial authorities in public ceremonies. This decree was followed by another one of 1640, which regulated the etiquette to be followed in the juntas. Since the meetings were to take place at the Holy Office's headquarters, the royal decree tacitly reasserted the social precedence of the Inquisition over its enemies.

The repressive activity of the colonial tribunals followed the procedures and forms of punishment also in force in Spain. Every three years, on a Sunday during Lent or on a feast day, inquisitors were expected to promulgate the Edict of Faith in an impressive ceremony to be held in cities that were the seat of a tribunal. The lengthy document contained a detailed description of Jewish and Muslim practices and asked the faithful to denounce within six days, under penalty of excommunication, anyone who practiced such rites or customs or was a follower of Mohammedanism, Protestantism, or Mystic Illuminism, or who committed crimes such as blasphemy, witchcraft, bigamy, perjury, solicitation of women in confession, divination, astrology, or possessed heretical books. In the smaller towns, the commissioners were to read copies of this proclamation to the faithful, while confessors were instructed to refuse absolution to penitents who did not denounce offenses to the Christian faith. Although highly irregular because of conflicts of etiquette and sheer negligence, the publication of the Edict of Faith in the colonies was frequently followed by an abundant harvest of denunciations and self-denunciations.

After receiving a denunciation, the Inquisition undertook a detailed investigation of the charges involved. A number of theologians determined whether the case warranted prosecution, and if the evidence gathered was judged sufficient, an order of arrest was issued. Since punishment of some crimes included confiscation of property, inquisitors ordered the seizure of all possessions at the moment of arrest. In accordance with the traditional procedure, neither the names of the denouncer nor the charges were disclosed to the defendant.

Thus, when asked if they knew the reason for the trial, the culprits sometimes confessed to crimes unknown to the inquisitors. Prisoners were allowed to have a lawyer, but this minor officer of the court could do no more than advise the culprits to confess and ask for mercy. Contrary to popular belief, torture was used only in a small number of cases to obtain confessions. After spending months (sometimes years) in prison, the culprits were sentenced. Although arbitrariness was common, inquisitors tended to take into consideration the importance of the crime committed, the culprit's social standing, and the prisoner's willingness to repent. They thus condemned the offenders to abjure of their crimes *de levi* (for minor offenses) or *de vehementi* (for those more egregious) and to punishment that ranged from spiritual penances (such as reciting a number of Paternosters) to scourging, public disgrace by being paraded naked to the waist with insignia of their offenses, forced labor in presidios and textile workshops, work as an oarsman in the king's galleys, or exile from certain cities. The ultimate punishment was death at the stake, a sentence carried out by state authorities on behalf of the Holy Office and normally reserved for unrepentant or relapsing heretics.

Many of these sentences were announced in an auto-da-fé, an elaborate ceremony of punishment held either in private or in public during which the culprits were paraded wearing penitential garments (*sambenitos*), cone-shaped hats (*corozas*), and gags. Both secular and religious authorities attended the autos held in public, which soon became a popular way of edifying the faithful and promoting the tribunals' achievements. The largest autos of the colonial period took place in 1639 and 1649. The first one was staged in Peru and featured sixty Judaizers among the seventy victims, of which eleven were burned. Four of them repented at the last moment and were thus strangled before the flames were lit. Ten years later, Mexico celebrated an auto-da-fé in which all of the 109 penitents but one were Judaizers. This notwithstanding, punishment for heresy represented a small percentage of the total offenses. The vast majority of the Inquisition's repressive activity involved crimes such as blasphemy, heretical propositions, superstition, and bigamy, which deserved a milder punishment.

The Spanish American Inquisition also tried to prevent the dissemination of unorthodox ideas by taking measures against the entry of heretical literature into the colonies. This was another area in which the Spanish American tribunals enjoyed more autonomy than their peninsular counterparts. While in Spain, only the Suprema could issue edicts prohibiting books; in the colonies, the tribunals inspected and banned books without awaiting approval from Madrid. Colonial inquisitors were expected to read the Suprema's edicts in public, but they also issued some of their own, listing the books to be banned, which not surprisingly featured Protestant literature as a major source of concern along with works deemed superstitious or against Catholic religion and moral norms. The edicts of prohibited books also included books in Arabic and Hebrew, vernacular or heretical translations of the Bible, and devotional works in the vernacular; and like the Edicts of Faith, instructed the people to denounce those who read, owned, or sold such works. But the Inquisition did not only rely on denunciations to control the circulation of prohibited books. Following a royal injunction of 1558, the tribunals carried out minute inspections of all ships arriving in American ports to prevent the importation of heretical books. Since ships were to be inspected before they could unload their merchandise, this practice created constant friction with secular authorities, who generally regarded it as a time-consuming hindrance to trade. The Holy Office also undertook highly irregular inspections of bookshops, as well as private and institutional libraries, practices normally restricted to big towns where there was an inquisitorial presence, and reviewed inventories of books owned by the dead before relatives could take possession of them. In all these errands, the tribunals found precious guidance in the systematic catalogues of prohibited and expurgated books (that is, books with censored passages but not banned as a whole) issued by Madrid in the form of an index, which by the seventeenth century consisted of several volumes. The tribunals also issued special permits to read prohibited books to individuals and institutions such as convents and schools that could demonstrate the need to do so because of their functions or métier. In spite of all these control mechanisms, the tribunals' attempt to monitor the circulation of books in the colonies seems to have been plagued by inefficiency, foot-dragging, and plain incompetence.

By the eighteenth century, the Spanish American Inquisition entered an era of gradual decadence prompted by the combined effect of important economic and political changes. Economically, the tribunals faced a declining income, as evidenced by the Holy Office's difficulties in collecting debts in times of agricultural crises, the smaller income from fines and confiscations resulting from the decrease in the tribunals' repressive activity, and the sharp decline of revenues from loans stemming from a significant decrease in interest rates. The economic descent of the Holy Office is dramatically exemplified by the case of the tribunal of New Granada, which in 1739 was in such a state of poverty that the inquisitors felt forced to sell most of the houses they possessed. To further compound their dire situation, their palace was bombarded two years later during a French attack on the colony, and they were not able to rebuild it until 1766. As expected, the financial crisis negatively affected the personnel's salaries and made it difficult to fill the vacancies on account of the low pay and the sharp decrease in prestige, economic benefits, and social prerogatives normally attached to those positions. Indeed, with the advent of the Bourbon dynasty and its absolutist inclinations, a new royal drive was launched to restrict the Inquisition's political privileges, and even to reduce its jurisdiction. In 1760, a royal decree abolished the fuero of the familiares in its entirety and limited that of salaried officials to cases in which they acted as defendants in criminal and civil matters. The Spanish Crown further undermined the Inquisition's authority a few years later by declaring that the Inquisition would have no jurisdiction over the crime of bigamy. Paradoxically, the Holy Tribunal later became an important tool of absolutism in the colonies, by concentrating its energies of the last decades on the prosecution of liberals, Freemasons, and even insurgents.

The final suppression of the Spanish Inquisition in America came as the result of a rapid succession of political events. In 1808, after occupying Madrid, Napoleon issued a decree abolishing the Holy Office.

After the expulsion of the French, representatives of the patriotic forces gathered in the Cortes at Cádiz declared the suppression of the Inquisition on February 22, 1813. The edict was published in Mexico in June and later in Peru. In Cartagena, a popular rebellion had already suppressed the tribunal since November 1811, but the inquisitors refused to abandon the colony and remained in Santa Marta. The abolition was short-lived. Yielding to pressures from conservative forces, Ferdinand VII restored the tribunal on July 21, 1814, but six years later, on May 9, 1820, the king confirmed its suppression. That same year, Mexico and Peru declared the abolition of their tribunals, while that of Cartagena de Indias ceased to exist by 1821.

Javier Villa-Flores

References

Alberro, Solange. *Inquisición y sociedad en México, 1570–1700.* Mexico City: Fondo de Cultura Económica, 1988.

Alvarez Alonso, Fermina. *La inquisición en Cartagena de Indias durante el siglo XVII.* Madrid: Fundacion Universitaria Española, 1999.

Castañeda, Paulino, and Pilar Hernández Aparicio. *La inquisición de Lima.* Vols. I and II. Madrid: Deimos, 1995 and 1998.

Greenleaf, Richard E. *The Mexican Inquisition in the Sixteenth Century.* Albuquerque: University of New Mexico Press, 1969.

Lea, Henry Charles. *The Inquisition in the Spanish Dependencies.* London: Macmillan, 1908.

Lewin, Boleslao. *La inquisición en Hispanoamérica: Judíos, protestantes y patriotas.* Buenos Aires: Paidos, 1967.

Liebmann, Seymour B. *The Jews in New Spain: Faith, Flame and the Inquisition.* Coral Gables, FL: University of Miami Press, 1970.

Maqueda Abreu, Consuelo. *Estado, iglesia e inquisición en Indias: Un permanente conflicto.* Madrid: Centro de Estudios Políticos y Constitucionales, 2000.

Millar Carvacho, René. *La inquisición de Lima,* Vol. 3. Madrid: Deimos, 1998.

Perez Villanueva, Joaquin, and Bartolomé Escandell Bonet, eds. *Historia de la inquisición en España y América.* 3 vols. Madrid: Biblioteca de Autores Cristianos/ Centro de Estudios Inquisitoriales, 1993.

See also: Bigamy, Transatlantic; Bourbon Reforms; Cannibalism; Catholic Church in Spanish America; Censorship—Spanish America; Clergy—Secular, in Colonial Spanish America; Cortes of Cádiz; Council of the Indies; Creoles; Diabolism in the New World; Familiares; Idolatry, Extirpation of; Independence I–VI; Inquisition—Luso-America; Islam; Jews—Colonial Latin America; Laws—Colonial Latin America; Missions; Moors; Napoleonic Invasion and Spanish America; Native Americans I–VIII; Papacy; Protestant Reformation; Religious Orders; Repartimiento; Syncretism; Witchcraft.

INTENDANTS/INTENDANCY SYSTEM

The intendants or intendancy system was the centerpiece of the Bourbon dynastic reforms, which were meant to invigorate and modernize the military, commercial, and administrative structures of the Spanish Empire. Borrowing from their French relatives, the Bourbons introduced the intendancy system to Spain in 1718, but the process was slow and was not completed until 1749. It was only at the end of the Seven Years' War (1756–1763) that Spain introduced the system in the New World, but there, too, innovation was gradual.

In 1763, England's return of Havana to the Spanish after a ten-month occupation and Spain's acquisition of Louisiana made Cuba and Louisiana logical choices for the introduction of the new system of rule. From there, the system spread throughout the empire. In 1769, intendants were appointed for California and Sonora, and one was designated for Caracas in 1776. Quito received one in 1782, while Río de la Plata received eight, with Puno being added in 1784 as a ninth intendancy, although later it was placed under Peru. In 1784, Peru received six intendants, and the Philippines and Puerto Rico received one each. In 1785, Guatemala, Nueva Vizcaya, and Puebla, and in 1786, Valladolid, received one each. Also in 1786 the one for the Philippines was divided up into five, and those in Mexico were reconstituted with new ones there that totaled twelve. In 1787, Chile acquired two. In 1812, the single intendancy of Cuba was divided into three units, and in 1814, Puerto Rico's was divided into two. Implementation in volatile Colombia was delayed until the Spanish *Reconquista* (1815–1816) under General Pablo Morillo. Independence brought an end to the intendancies, and in the Caribbean, Spain abolished the system in 1854.

The chief proponent of the system and the person under whom it reached its full flowering was the Spanish statesman and reformer José de Gálvez. As minister of the Indies (1776–1787), Gálvez wanted a new provincial administrator, the intendant, who would govern the intendancy without interference and who could bypass the viceroy or captain general and deal directly with Madrid. Gálvez saw the host of local officials throughout the Spanish Empire—governors, *corregidores,* and *alcaldes mayores*—as backward, slow, corrupt, and responsible for Spain's stagnation.

The intendant's generous salary of 5,000 to 8,000 pesos, his military experience, and his superior training and education were supposed to bring about a more progressive and efficient administration that would generate more revenue and allow Spain greater control and flexibility over its far-flung empire. Revenues increased considerably in the late colonial period, but as the workhorses for Gálvez's reform program, the intendants created much heated opposition, especially among Creoles. By placing the powers and functions of many local officials in the hands of a single bureaucrat who ruled over a large region, the intendancy system promoted regionalism and supplied the structural basis for nineteenth-century federalism throughout Spanish America. The geographical boundaries of the intendancies in Mexico, for example, paralleled those of many of its present-day states—Guanajuato, Puebla, and Veracruz, for example—or the modern nation-states of Central America—Honduras, Costa Rica, Nicaragua, and El Salvador.

Maurice P. Brungardt

References

Fisher, John R. *Government and Society in Colonial Peru: The Intendant System, 1784–1814.* London: University of London Press, 1970.

Fisher, Lillian Estelle. *The Intendant System in Spanish America.* Berkeley and Los Angeles: University of California Press, 1929.

Lynch, John. *Spanish Colonial Administration: The Intendant System in the Viceroyalty of the Río de la Plata.* London: Athlone, 1958.

See also: Administration—Colonial Spanish America; Bourbon Reforms; Corregidor/Corregimiento; Costa Rica; Creoles; Cuba; El Salvador; Honduras; Independence I–VI; Mexico; Nicaragua; Seven Years' War; Viceroyalties; War of the Spanish Succession.

ISLAM

Islam has affected the New World since the Americas were discovered. The year 1492 was not only the year that Columbus reached the Indies; it was also the year the

Spanish *Reconquista* ended, with the fall of Iberia's last Muslim kingdom, Granada. Castile's Queen Isabella wished to continue the war against Islam in Africa, and the Spanish court hoped to establish a Holy League against the Turks. Also in 1492, Spanish Jews were told to choose between conversion to Christianity and permanent exile. It was in this context that the discovery of America occurred.

It was thought that the Great Khan of China was a friend of Christiandom and that sending an embassy to him would facilitate a world alliance against Turkish power. The Turks were considered the power of Muslim expansion, a reflection of evil on earth. In 1492, King Ferdinand and Queen Isabella sent a messenger to Jerusalem to give news to the Latin Christians of their victory in Granada; this provoked an exchange of ambassadors between them and the king of Georgia, Constantine II, who sought their friendship and alliance against the Turkish power. The fate of the Moorish Kingdom of Granada seemed at first not to affect the relations between Spain and other friendly Muslim states in the Mediterranean such as Egypt, but the sultan feared the Ottoman Turks more than he did his Christian allies, the Catholic Monarchs. During the entire sixteenth century, Spain was occupied in the struggle between Christianity and Islam and the conquest and colonization of the New World.

If Islam had a notorious influence on Spanish Christian culture, it also became the stimulus of a warrior society. Muslim Spain had evolved over almost eight centuries, from 711 until 1492. From its days of superiority over the northern Christian kingdoms, from the eighth to the tenth centuries, the Spanish Muslim states became tributaries of the Christians until the end of the fifteenth century. Nevertheless, Muslims influenced the peninsula's Christians in both war and peacemaking, as well as protocol. Christian-Muslim relations also informed the conquistadors in the Americas, who always kept the Moors as a reference when treating the Indians. The Royal Fifth, the *requerimiento,* and the practice of hostage taking are some elements inherited from Muslim traditions.

From 1501 onward, Muslims, Jews, heretics, and their children were forbidden to travel to the New World. The same prohibition was extended to Muslim black slaves. It is worth noting that a number of white Muslim slaves appeared in colonial Spanish America, but their presence was exceptional.

From 1580 and especially after 1600, the Atlantic crossing became dangerous because of Muslim pirates from the Barbary Coast. Seizures were recorded from Spanish vessels sailing to the Canary Islands, Azores, Madeira, Brazil, Santo Domingo, Virginia, and Newfoundland; and these are just a few examples. Attacks occurred along the coasts of Portugal, Galicia, the Gulf of Biscay, Brittany, Normandy, and in the English Channel. The danger of suffering captivity by Moors and Turks in the Atlantic was real.

But this is not the real link between Islam and the New World, for the Turkish sultan and his closest ministers seemed to maintain a special curiosity and interest in the Indies. For example, in the nineteenth century a copy of Admiral Piri Reis's map was discovered at the Topkapi Palace in Istanbul. The map shows the American Atlantic coastline from Central America to South America; it was finished at Gallipoli in April 1513 under the direction of the Turkish admiral Piri Reis, who had received the details from a slave, most probably a pilot, who had traveled three times with Christopher Columbus to the New World. Later, the slave had been taken captive with an original chart made by Columbus himself. The slave also provided his Turkish master with accurate information of the Antilles and its inhabitants, naming and drawing the most important islands. It is reasonable to believe that Piri Reis may have had a plan to attack Hispaniola, the Spanish base in the West Indies. In 1517, he was responsible for leading Turkish ships to Cairo in order to invade Egypt. And in 1547 he was in charge of the naval expedition sent by the sultan to conquer the Portuguese fortress of Aden; for his success he was promoted to admiral of the Indian Sea. However, in 1553 Reis was defeated by the Portuguese in waters close to the island of Ormuz.

The esteemed French scholar Ferdinand Braudel has explained that maize was first cultivated in significant amounts in Europe in the Balkans; this occurred in the sixteenth century when Turkish authorities introduced the new crop to feed their vassals. For that reason, American corn was known in Central Europe in the sixteenth century as Turkish corn. The same occurred with chili—paprika—which the Turks introduced to Hungary as early as 1526 and was called *vöros Törökbörs,* or red Turkish pepper. Long before Europeans learned the benefits of these American goods, the Turkish sultan had ordered their introduction as foodstuffs and had incorporated them into their agriculture. The same thing happened with tobacco. In fact, many goods, plants, and animals that originated in the Indies were mistakenly thought to come from the Turkish Empire; for example, the turkey birds originated from North and Central America.

Interest in the New World developed early in Turkish territories, perhaps because of the Sephardic Jews and Morisco exiles. Extracts from Bartolomé de las Casas's works were read in sixteenth-century Turkey, providing even more information about the Americas to the Ottoman powers. However, Turkish authors also addressed the topic. Completed in about 1580, the *Tarih Hind-i garbi* is the Islamic world's most important source for the discovery and conquest of America. Some of its historical sources have been traced in the works of Francisco López de Gómara, Gonzalo Fernandez de Oviedo, Pietro Martire d'Anghiera (Peter Martyr), and Agustín de Zárate.

Finally, it has been suggested that the Spanish sailor who first saw land on the horizon on October 12, 1492, was cheated from the reward that Columbus had promised to the first man to spot land; feeling bitter, the sailor returned to Spain in 1493 and departed for Morocco, where he converted to Islam.

István Szászdi

References

Farah, Cesar E., ed. *An Arab's Journey to Colonial Spanish America: The Travels of Elias al Musili in the Seventeenth Century.* Syracuse, NY: Syracuse University Press, 2003.

Goodrich, Thomas. *The Ottoman Turks and the New World.* Wiesbaden: Otto Harrassowitz, 1990.

Ladero Quesada, Miguel Ángel. "Isabel and the Moors." Pp. 171–193 in *Isabel la Católica, Queen of Castile: Critical Essay,* edited by David A. Boruchoff. New York: Palgrave Macmillan, 2003.

Szászdi León-Borja, István. "El derecho marítimo en las Yndias: La navegación regulada." Unpublished Ll.D. dissertation, University of Valladolid, 1994.

———. "Después de la inter caetera, ruptura y cambio en la política indiana de Alejandro VI." Pp. 1577–1629 in *Memoria del X Congreso del Instituto Internacional de Historia del Derecho Indiano,* II. Mexico City: Escuela Libre de Derecho–Universidad Autónoma de México, 1995.

See also: Chroniclers; Columbian Exchange—Agriculture; Conquest I–VII; Conquistadors; Food; Jews—Colonial Latin America; Maize; Migration—From Iberia to the New World; Moors; Pirates and Piracy; Requerimiento; Slavery I–IV; Tobacco; Tordesillas, Treaty of.

JESUITS—BRAZIL

The Jesuits were the main conduits of religious and cultural transformation among native populations in early-modern Brazil. For more than two centuries, from the arrival of the first fathers in 1549 until their expulsion from all Portuguese territories in 1759–1760, the Jesuits played a central role in the spiritual and expansionist endeavors undertaken by the Portuguese Crown. The Society of Jesus's activities in Brazil included not only missionary work among the Amerindians, but also the education of the entire population and the ownership and administration of vast multipurpose estates and sugar plantations as well as urban properties. Following the reestablishment of the order in 1814, the first Jesuits returned to Brazil in 1841, this time with a much more restricted participation in social, political, cultural, and economic terms. In this second phase, the Jesuits' activities were related mainly to running educational facilities.

By the time the Society of Jesus was founded (1540), the king of Portugal, King John III (whose reign extended from 1521 to 1557), had just initiated efforts to establish more effective royal control and to create better conditions for the defense and economic exploitation of Brazil. Given that the system of proprietary captaincies in force since the 1530s was partly flawed, the king dispatched a royal governor and staff who were to erect the city of Salvador, in All Saints Bay, centrally located on the coast. Having learned about the king's plans, the founder of the order in Portugal, Simão Rodrigues (1510–1579), sought authorization to lead a group there. Authorization was granted, and in 1549 four priests and two brothers arrived in Bahia, accompanied by the governor Tomé de Souza. The mission's superior was Manuel da Nóbrega (1517–1570), a resolute priest who endured various hardships; Nóbrega traveled tirelessly, deploying his fellow fathers among the recently formed settlements. During the sixteenth century, other members of the Society were sent to Brazil; among them was José de Anchieta (1534–1597), who earned the reputation of "Apostle of Brazil." In 1600, their number was 169. Just before the expulsion, there were more than 600 Jesuits in Brazil, including those who worked in the state of Maranhão, which at the time was a separate province. Nóbrega and the superiors who followed him sought to establish missions in different parts of the colony, from the furthest reaches in the Amazonian rainforest to the Colônia do Sacramento in the far south.

Jesuit letters and other writings, which cover different stages of the contact with Brazil's indigenous populations, are the best sources of information about the ways of life and beliefs of the Indians. The correspondence often indicates the Jesuits' tenacity and ability to face obstacles of various kinds. A difficulty they had to deal with in Brazil, as suggested in many passages of their correspondence, was isolation from each other and from Europe. But this was only one among many obstacles; other problems related to accommodation, food supply, infectious diseases that devastated local indigenous populations, and conflicts with Portuguese colonists and members of the secular clergy. Many authors who have studied the European colonial enterprise of the early modern period recognize and have illustrated the Society of Jesus's adequacy regarding its structure, principles, and education of its members, to put into practice the evangelization project in the Americas. The order was organized in a military fashion, with its members trained to do battle against Protestantism and paganism. The uniformity of doctrinal matters, and a sophisticated education in logic, language, and rhetoric, were common features of the Society of Jesus.

Another relevant common feature was the order's flexibility toward Amerindian beliefs and practices. Soon after the Society of Jesus was founded, Ignatius Loyola oriented his disciples to adopt an attitude of selective tolerance with respect to cultures with which Europeans were not familiar. By accepting certain customs of the different peoples, the Jesuits often were able to gain their sympathy and thus advance their missionary work. In Brazil, as in the various other parts of the world in which they worked, Jesuits made significant adaptations to Catholic practices, translated Christian faith in terms that were more familiar to local populations, and sought to link the latter's beliefs and ethical values to Christian principles.

Initially, Brazil's Indians appeared receptive to evangelization, but soon it became clear how difficult it was to make them abandon customs such as ritual cannibalism, warfare, polygamy, and their reliance upon local shamans. As Indian behaviour continued to frustrate the missionaries' initial expectations, the Jesuits started to adopt a stricter posture, resorting to coercive methods to reach their goals. Following the policy of pacification undertaken by the governor-general Mem de Sá (1557–1572), Brazil's Jesuits began to gather and instruct the natives in villages under their guardianship (*aldeamentos*), where they endeavored to foster the Indians' acculturation and assimilation, thus creating an indigenous peasantry. In doing so, they offered an alternative to the enslavement and slaughter of the Indians, practices followed by many of Brazil's early colonists.

The different ways in which historians have interpreted the Jesuits' participation in the early history of Brazil generated a polarization between a tendency to emphasize the order's role in humanizing the colonizing process and the Jesuits' importance in promoting a Portuguese system of domination. More recently, the prevailing interpretation is that power directly related to the central government and to economic exploitation, on the one hand, and the imposition of cultural change, on the other, are two components of the same general process. With their control of Indian communities placed near white settlements, Jesuits served the interest of the Crown in promoting the organization and development of the colony. Missionary action was not simply an attempt to convert the Indians to the Christian faith or to protect them from enslavement and from the colonists' greed. Evangelization was an enterprise intended to transform the Amerindians in a radical way, requiring that they renounce their culture and become like Europeans. Moreover, the fathers were not against the "just" enslavement of Indians, that is, the bondage of communities regarded as hostile; in fact, the Jesuits sometimes owned Indian chattels.

The frequent conflicts between Jesuits and colonists in Brazil over the problem of the colonists' enslavement of the Indians are documented in much of the Jesuit correspondence of the second half of the sixteenth century. These conflicts are best expressed, however, in the writings of António Vieira (1608–1697), a former court preacher and diplomat born in Portugal but educated in the Jesuit college in Bahia. Vieira was the superior of the mission of Pará and Maranhão in the Amazon from 1655 to 1661. In his sermons, Vieira vehemently condemned Indian slavery and their forced removal from the interior forests. His constant pleas to Dom João IV (King John IV) (1640–1656) to prohibit expeditions against tribes and the inhumane treatment they received from the colonists resulted in a law passed in 1655 that gave the Jesuits control in the recruitment of indigenous labor and made an unprecedented conversion of hostile tribes possible. Such accomplishments disquieted the colonists and the members of other religious orders, a process that led to the expulsion of the Jesuits from the residences of São Luís and Belém in 1661.

Besides their central involvement with the cathequization of Indians, and later also the conversion of newly introduced African slaves, the Jesuits sought to erect colleges in Brazil's urban centers. During the sixteenth century, the colleges of Bahia (1553), São Vicente (1553), Piratininga (1554), Rio de Janeiro (1567), and Olinda (1568) were founded. Instructional houses were also created in Ilhéus, Porto Seguro, and Espírito Santo. In these institutes, whites and mestizos were taught Portuguese, Latin, and the disciplines of the arts curriculum, and, of course, they also received religious instruction. The Society of Jesus's facilities in the cities included preparatory schools, colleges, churches, and probationary houses in which the friars lived.

The Society also became a major property owner in Brazil. Jesuit properties in Brazil were obtained through donations by the Crown and private owners, exchanges, and purchase, both direct and through the intervention of third parties. The Society also owned large livestock and multipurpose estates, as well as sugar plantations. Sugar production furnished a significant part of the colleges' income in Bahia, Pernambuco, Rio de Janeiro, Espírito Santo, and Maranhão. From the end of the seventeenth century until the expulsion, stockraising had a growing importance among the Jesuits' economic interests. The order's income also derived from trading ventures and their role as landlords, through which they received the payment of rents from rural and urban tenants.

Because of the success achieved in developing their holdings, the Jesuits became important agents in the colonial economy, acquiring a visibility that made them the target of increasing criticism. In Brazil, as in other parts of the Portuguese Empire, they were constantly accused of having forsaken their spiritual mission and of becoming preoccupied only with economic gain. This ultimately led to their expulsion from all imperial dominions and the confiscation of the order's patrimony. This process has to be examined in relation to the rise of Sebastião José de Carvalho e Mello, the Marquis of Pombal, who was secretary of state for war and foreign affairs in Portugal from 1750 to 1777, and a stepbrother of the governor of Greater-Pará and Maranhão, Francisco Xavier de Mendonça Furtado (1751–1759). Mendonça Furtado's letters to Pombal recounted the accusations leveled against the Jesuits by their fiercest opponents. The fathers were accused of deliberately failing to convert or civilize Indians, of being committed to the acquisition of wealth, of exerting a despotic rule in the missions, and of keeping the natives in miserable conditions. Pombal, suspecting that the Jesuits were sabotaging his administration, blamed the Jesuits for almost everything that went wrong. Following the publication of Luís António Vernei's *Verdadeiro methodo de estudar* (1746), the idea that the courses offered by the Jesuits in their colleges and universities were outdated became current among Portuguese scholars. Economic motivations were central to Pombal's persecution of the Jesuits. Furthermore, many of Brazil's colonists wanted to explore the "spices of the sertão" using Indian labor, without the missionaries' mediation. The Crown was interested in the settlers' prosperity, believing that their financial success would increase the Crown's tax base. In June 1755, Pombal persuaded King José I (1750–1777) to declare the freedom of the Indians of Pará and Maranhão, who acquired a status equal to ordinary citizens. Mission villages were transformed into towns, and Indians descended from the forests were to receive land grants. Another edict prohibited missionaries from having temporal authority, ending Jesuit control of Indian affairs. In April 1758, a papal bull forbade the fathers to engage in commerce, hear confessions, and preach. An attempt to assassinate the king in the same year led to the suspicion that the Society of Jesus was involved. Finally, in September 1759, the Jesuits were expelled from Portugal and its colonies.

Lígia Bellini

References

Alden, Dauril. "Economic Aspects of the Expulsion of the Jesuits from Brazil: A Preliminary Report." Pp. 25–71 in *Conflict and Continuity in Brazilian Society,* edited by Henry E. Keith and S. F. Edwards. Columbia: University of South Carolina Press, 1969.

———. *The Making of an Enterprise: The Society of Jesus in Portugal, Its Empire, and Beyond, 1540–1750.* Stanford, CA: Stanford University Press, 1996.

Hemming, John. *Red Gold: The Conquest of the Brazilian Indians.* London: Macmillan, 1978.

Kiemen, Mathias C. *The Indian Policy of Portugal in the Amazon Region, 1614–1693.* Washington, DC: Catholic University Press, 1954.

Leite, Serafim. *História da Companhia de Jesus no Brasil.* 10 vols. Lisbon: Portugália; Rio de Janeiro: Civilização Brasileira, 1938–1950.

Leite, Serafim, ed. *Monumenta brasiliae.* 5 vols. Rome: Archivum Romanum Societatis Iesu, 1956–1968.

Loyola, Ignatius. *Monumenta Ignatiana . . . Sancti Ignatii de Loyola Societatis Jesu fundatoris, epistolae et instructiones.* 12 vols. Madrid, 1903–1911.

See also: Bourbon Reforms; Brazil; Clergy—Secular, in Colonial Spanish America; Education—Brazil; Education—

Colonial Spanish America; Enlightenment—Brazil; Jesuits—Expulsion; Jesuits—Iberia and America; Jesuits—Paraguay; Madrid, Treaty of; Monarchs of Portugal; Papacy; Paraguay; Religious Orders.

JESUITS—EXPULSION

The Society of Jesus was expelled from Portugal, France, Spain, and their dominions between 1759 and 1767. The expulsions were followed by papal suppression of the Jesuit Order from 1773 to 1814. While directly triggered by political circumstances in Europe, European reaction against the order was spurred by Jesuit activity in the Americas. Jesuit organization, ideology, successes, and competing propaganda about their transatlantic missions led European monarchs to consider the Society of Jesus a threat to royal authority. In mid-eighteenth-century Europe, an attempted regicide, a much-publicized bankruptcy, and a series of riots, respectively, provided Dom João I (King John I) of Portugal, King Louis XV of France, and King Charles III of Spain with justification to act against the order. The ensuing removal of several thousand Jesuits from their posts in Iberia, France, and the Americas was meticulously organized, and had immediate consequences for the hundreds of Jesuit colleges and missions of the Old and New Worlds. The missions were slowly restaffed and reorganized, often by missionaries from other religious orders.

Until the mid-eighteenth century, Jesuits enjoyed the support of many European monarchs as well as popes. Jesuits were favored as educators and confessors of the Bourbon kings of France and Spain, and the Braganza royal house of Portugal. However, royal patronage did not translate into unconditional support in the colonies. For example, in seventeenth-century Brazil, Jesuits challenged local slaveholders in the northeastern part of the country over the enslavement of the Indian population. In an attempt to ban the practice, Jesuits approached their provincial superiors and finally Pope Urban VIII, who not only condemned Indian slavery, but in 1639 issued a papal edict that threatened all slaveholders with excommunication. In response, the colonists of São Paulo forcibly removed the Jesuits from the area.

Across the Atlantic, however, royal and papal backing successfully bolstered Jesuits in key positions, especially as educators. By the eighteenth century, Jesuits staffed the majority of Europe's schools and universities. It was also at that time that they came to be labeled as ultramontanists, leading to a change in attitude toward the Society. Ultramontanists supported papal theocracy and believed that the pope had authority over kings. The gallicanists in France and the regalists in Spain challenged that view and pressured leaders of the Catholic Church to answer to national rulers rather than to the pope. The Jesuits were seen as particular servants of the papacy because of their fourth vow of obedience to the pope and their Rome-based centralization. Jesuit recruitment of non-Iberian and non-French foreigners to staff their overseas missions was seen as another indication that the Jesuits, by virtue of their international membership, were subverting the authority of individual monarchs and serving a new transnational papal empire. Finally, some Jesuits advanced theologically controversial doctrines, including probabilism (the belief that if one is in a difficult moral situation, one can act on a "probable opinion" derived from theological authorities), populism (the idea that people have the right to depose a tyrant), and, in 1701, the position taken by several prominent Jesuit missionaries that certain Chinese rites that were similar to Catholic rituals should be tolerated and used to promote conversion to Christianity.

Jesuits were noteworthy not only as educators and theologians, but also as active participants in transatlantic commerce. When the Portuguese minister, the Marquis of Pombal, founded the Commercial Company of Great-Parà, giving himself exclusive rights over navigation in northern Brazil, Jesuits vigorously protested the new monopoly for blocking their means of supporting their missions. Jesuits also garnered opposition to their financial administration from within the Catholic Church. In seventeenth-century Mexico, Bishop Juan de Palafox y Mendoza rebuked the Jesuits for their insistence upon the privilege of exemption from paying the tithe, the annual 10 percent tax on agricultural production paid to the Church. But the economic conflicts surrounding the Jesuits were most evident in Paraguay. Since 1576, the Jesuits had attempted to create financially self-sustaining reductions among the Guaraní Indians, opposing colonists' demands for Guaraní labor and tribute. The reductions garnered income from selling homegrown tea and paid lowered royal tributes in exchange for the Indians' service as a permanent border militia. A group of Paraguayan colonists, irritated by the reductions' prosperity, accused the Jesuits of using Indian labor to work hidden gold mines within their reductions. Even after the Council of the Indies investigated and refuted the accusation in 1743, the widespread rumor that the Jesuits profited financially from their frontier missions did not subside.

The political repercussions of the 1750 Treaty of Limits again cast the Paraguay reductions and the Jesuits into the European spotlight. The treaty settled New World border disputes between Spain and Portugal by ordering the Guaraní Indians to leave their towns in Spanish territory so that the land could be ceded to Portugal in exchange for Brazil's colony of Sacramento. Together with local Guaraní chiefs, Jesuit missionaries appealed to both kings and protested the treaty before finally being commanded by Jesuit superiors to obey the treaty. The Indians of the Paraguay reductions resisted two joint Spanish-Portuguese military expeditions before the treaty was finally annulled. Portugal's Marquis of Pombal publicly blamed the Jesuits for the failure of the Treaty of Limits. His voice was amplified and embellished in the anti-Jesuit press of the eighteenth century.

The explosive growth of news publications in countries like France contributed to the spread of propaganda by both Jesuits and their adversaries, who in France included the Enlightenment intellectual Voltaire and the Jansenists, followers of Bishop Cornelius Jansen (1585–1638). The leading eighteenth-century Jansenist newspaper, the *Nouvelles Ecclésiastiques,* issued up to 6,000 copies a month, largely devoted to criticism of the Society of Jesus. The Jesuits countered with regular newspaper *suppléments* to refute this and other popular Jansenist journals. These media brought events in the Americas to the center of debates over Jesuit power in Europe.

In 1759, Portuguese Dom João I (King John I) officially expelled all Jesuits from his dominions, though Jesuit missionaries had begun to be removed from service in Brazil as early as 1751 in response to the Guaraní Wars. In 1755, the Marquis of Pombal declared the Indians of Brazil free of Jesuit authority. For years the Marquis of Pombal had been competing for the king's ear with the king's Jesuit confessor, José Moreira. Portugal's Royal Treasury had been emptied to finance the military campaigns in Paraguay and in reconstructing Lisbon, which had suffered great damage in the earthquake of 1755. On September 3, 1758, an attempt was made on the life of the king by an unknown instigator. The Marquis of Pombal accused several of his personal enemies from Portugal's wealthiest noble families, along with the Jesuits whom he denounced for having agreed to the ambush. The nobles and, later, one prominent Jesuit, Gabriel de Malagrida, were publicly executed. In spite of the protests and the attempted negotiations of Pope Clement XIII, the Jesuits of Portugal were imprisoned and their properties sequestered. Following this repudiation, the representative of the papacy was also exiled from Lisbon in 1760, thus severing diplomatic relations between Portugal and the papal court of Rome.

The Spanish king's wariness of the Jesuit Order grew as he watched the Portuguese expulsion and the decisions of his Bourbon ally, the king of France. In France, although the Jesuits had been targets of defamation campaigns by Voltaireans and the Jansenists, their position had seemed more secure. However, the Jesuit Antoine Lavallette had engaged in unsuccessful commercial speculation in Martinique without the permission of his superiors and was forced to declare bankruptcy. He appealed his case to the French parliament in 1761, when the parliament, made up largely of Jansenist sympathizers, turned the civil case into a criminal case against the entire Society of Jesus. Parliament decreed that the Jesuits were harming the rights of both the Catholic Church and society. King Louis XV was sympathetic to the Jesuits at first and annulled parliament's decree but requested internal reform of the Society of Jesus in France. In 1762, when Pope Clement XIII and the Father General of the Society of Jesus both opposed the king's suggested reforms, the king signed a decree disbanding the Jesuit Order in France. By 1765, nearly 4,000 French Jesuits were living in exile.

In Spain, the Hat and Cloak Riots in Madrid in March 1766 directly precipitated the Jesuit expulsion. These riots were part of fifty subsistence riots across Spain that spring. The residents of Madrid demanded removal of the unpopular Italian-born minister of finance, Leopoldo de Gregorio, the Marquis of Squillace. Squillace's reforms had increased taxation, organized a monopoly of staple foods which raised food prices, and attempted to reduce street crime in Madrid by forbidding the wearing of traditional broad-brimmed hats and long capes. The king entrusted Pedro Rodríguez de Campomanes (1723–1802), a finance minister, with investigating the cause of the riots. In his final report, Campomanes blamed the Jesuits for the riots. He wrote that Jesuits did not see themselves as vassals of the king, but continually defied Spanish royal authority: they accumulated riches by protesting payment of the tithe, incited rebellion and ruled as despots over their missions in Paraguay, adopted non-Christian customs, and espoused tyrannicide and probabilism. He also referred to France and Portugal's earlier expulsions as solutions. In 1767, other Spanish ministers and the king's Franciscan confessor advised that Jesuits be banished from the realm and their property confiscated. They were replaced with secular priests under direct control of Spanish bishops.

Pope Clement XIII died in February 1769 and was replaced by Clement XIV, who was more sympathetic to the Bourbon monarchs of France and Spain. In his July 1773 papal brief *Dominus ac Redemptor,* Clement XIV suppressed the Jesuit Order in all of Christendom. From Spanish dominions alone, the popes had been obliged to harbor 5,000 Jesuits, among them many Creoles from the Americas. Many ex-Jesuits remained in Rome while others took refuge in Prussia and Russia, where the papal bull never took effect because the ruling monarchs there did not legally approve it. In 1814, Pope Pius VII reinstated the Jesuit Order.

In the Americas, the expulsion legislation took many months because of the remoteness of many Jesuit missions. The strongest resistance was in the Mexican mining region of San Luis de Potosí, where Indian riots were brutally put down by troops led by New Spain's visitor-general, José de Galvez. More typically, the banishment of the Jesuits was quiet, and the Jesuits themselves helped to calm the mission Indians. At the Chiquitos and Moxos missions in Upper Peru, many of the Indians fled the reductions in response to rumors of Jesuit removal. The governor of Buenos Aires, Francisco de Paula Bucareli, was in charge of the expulsion at the Paraguay reductions. He invited the thirty chiefs of the Guaraní villages to come to the colonial capital to try to gain their sympathy and to hold them as potential military hostages. After the Jesuit removal, Bucareli stayed in the reductions for ten days with his troops to remind the Indians of the authority of the king.

The most far-reaching consequences of the Jesuit expulsion were in the areas of finance, education, and overseas missions. Economically, Portugal, France, and Spain did not profit from Jesuit coffers as much as they had expected, in part because of the exaggerated reports of Jesuit wealth, but also because of the costs of transporting exiled Jesuits. However, in South America impounded Jesuit properties provided a new land base for colonial elites. The banishment of Jesuit intellectuals from universities on both sides of the Atlantic Ocean allowed university reform to be controlled by national monarchies. In some missions in the Americas, soldiers replaced Jesuits as administrative heads. On the border of Brazil, these soldier-administrators were often abusive, leading to depopulation and deserters. In California, however, Franciscans expanded and improved on the Jesuit network of missions.

Karin Vélez

References

Alden, Dauril. *The Making of an Enterprise: The Society of Jesus in Portugal, Its Empire, and Beyond, 1540–1750.* Stanford, CA: Stanford University Press, 1996.

Cottret, Monique. *Jansénismes et Lumières: Pour un autre XVIIIe siècle.* Paris: Editions Albin Michel, 1998.

Mörner, Magnus, ed. *The Expulsion of the Jesuits from Latin America.* New York: Knopf, 1965.

Tietz, Manfried, ed. *Los jesuitas españoles expulsos: Su imagen y su contribución al saber sobre el mundo hispánico en la Europa del siglo XVIII.* Madrid: Iberoamericana, 2001.

Van Kley, Dale. *The Jansenists and the Expulsion of the Jesuits from France, 1757–1765.* New Haven, CT: Yale University Press, 1993.

See also: Bourbon Reforms; Brazil; Catholic Church in Brazil; Clergy—Secular, Colonial Spanish America; Education—Brazil; Education—Colonial Spanish America; Enlightenment—Brazil; Enlightenment—Spanish America; Jesuits—Brazil; Jesuits—Iberia and America; Jesuits—Paraguay; Madrid, Treaty of; Monarchs of Portugal; Monarchs of Spain; Papacy; Paraguay; Religious Orders.

JESUITS—IBERIA AND AMERICA

By the mid-eighteenth century, members of the Society of Jesus made up one-sixth of the total Iberian missionary presence in the Americas and thus constituted the second largest group of missionary personnel in the New World after the Franciscan Order. The Society of Jesus was a relatively young religious organization compared to the orders of missionaries who had arrived earlier in the Americas—the Franciscans, Mercedarians, Dominicans, and Augustinians. In 1549, less than a decade after the founding of their Society, six Portuguese Jesuits led by Manoel da Nobrega (1517–1570) arrived in Brazil. The first Jesuit missionaries sent to the Americas by Spain's Council of the Indies arrived in Florida in 1566. The Jesuits gradually expanded their American evangelization in the seventeenth and early eighteenth centuries. Like the Franciscans, the Jesuits were active in most American territories, but the Jesuits administered their missions centrally from Rome and often managed them exclusively, especially in the case of well-known missions on the frontiers of Spanish colonial control such as northwestern Mexico and Paraguay. Jesuit missions in Latin America were also frequently staffed by foreign, or non-Iberian, Jesuits. Building on the tradition of their schools in Europe and the East Indies, Jesuits in colonial Latin America showed particular interest in the education of indigenous peoples, African slaves, and already evangelized populations. Finally, Latin American Jesuits sent regular correspondence to the Rome-based headquarters of the Society of Jesus, where their letters were edited, translated, published, and distributed throughout the world. The transoceanic communication networks of the Society of Jesus brought the Jesuit missions of the Americas far-ranging publicity that was further amplified by their expulsion from all Iberian dominions in 1767.

Jesuit missions were administered centrally, with a small number of provinces answering directly to provincial superiors and ultimately to the Father General of the Society of Jesus, resident in the papal capital of Rome. In Latin America the Jesuit provinces included Brazil (1550s), Peru (1568), New Spain (1572), the Philippines (1605), Paraguay (1606), the Vice-Province of Chile (1624), Quito (1696), and New Granada (1696). Jesuits in the Americas largely supported their work by acquiring rural estates through donations, bequests, and purchases, cultivating the lands to be as self-sustaining as possible. This was the case in Cuba, where in the early 1700s Jesuits managed sugar plantations run by slave labor to support their new college in Havana. Jesuits also procured mission assignments on frontiers such as California and Paraguay, where their locations on disputed borders led the Iberian Crowns to rely on their mission populations in a military capacity. These factors—having supranational, Rome-based administration, owning independent sources of income, and being crucial to border defense—occasionally allowed Jesuits to negotiate successfully with the Crowns, Church, and local governments for more control over the management of their missions. However, at times Jesuit successes brought conflict with other religious orders such as the Capuchins, who sought intervention from the Spanish Crown in 1744 to keep Jesuits from infringing on their established mission towns on the Meta River (Colombia). It also rankled authorities such as the bishop of Puebla, Juan de Palafox y Mendoza (1639–1649), who argued that the Jesuits had acquired excessive privileges in New Spain (Mexico).

The Society of Jesus on the Iberian Peninsula had insufficient personnel to cover its expanding mission circuits and therefore, as did other religious orders, it recruited foreigners. Most of the non-Iberian Jesuits working in the Spanish and Portuguese territories came from Italy, Germany, and Bohemia. Attitudes toward foreign recruitment fluctuated over time. The Spanish Crown at first permitted foreign Jesuits to go to Spanish territories, then restricted foreign participation in the early 1600s, only to allow it to burgeon again in the early eighteenth century. Portuguese kings also wavered, sharply curtailing the number of foreign Jesuits allowed to travel to Brazil in the 1650s but loosening travel restrictions in later decades. Within the Society of Jesus itself, there were conflicting attitudes toward the nature of participation and inclusion. Debates over the ordination of mestizos (persons of mixed European and indigenous American descent) occurred in the last third of the sixteenth century in Spanish America, ending with the decision not to extend the privilege. Controversy also swirled around the participation of American-born Jesuits, or Creoles, in mission work in the Americas. Restrictions were placed on the number of Creole novices that Ibero-American provincials could accept. The attempt to limit Creole membership in the Society of Jesus was not always successful. One Jesuit provincial in Brazil, Simão de Vasconcelos (1569–1671), disregarded these restrictions and actively recruited Creoles. Nonetheless, Jesuits in Latin America were predominantly European-born and educated.

In the cities and towns of the early Americas, Jesuits were most active in the field of education. Jesuit colleges did not charge tuition and primarily claimed the sons of Spaniards and the secular clergy as students. The Jesuit College of Máximo and San Gregorio in Quito, Ecuador, was one prestigious place of study, with its library of European scientific and classical titles eventually housing 14,000 volumes. In New Spain alone, Jesuits established twenty-two colleges in the most important urban centers. Jesuits also focused their urban missions on Indian outreach, preaching in the prominent indigenous tongues and founding schools such as the College of San Gregorio in Mexico City (1582) to educate the sons of the indigenous elite. Some of their colleges became centers for translation projects: the Jesuit College in Cartagena de Indias, Colombia, hired twenty-one translators of African dialects to compose liturgies in the native languages of the slaves. Many Jesuits working in Latin America became key intellectual figures. Of note to historians and anthropologists are José de Acosta (1540–1600), who wrote on the Indians of Peru; Andrés Pérez de Ribas (1576–1655), who reported on missions in New Spain (Mexico); and Alonso de Sandoval (1576–

1651), who described customs of African slaves in Cartagena de Indias (Colombia). Seventeenth-century cartographers of the Amazon River Basin included Raimundo de Santa Cruz, Enrique Richter, and Samuel Fritz. Noteworthy Baroque playwrights were Matías de Bocanegra (Mexico) and Pedro López de Lara (Peru). Among the best known Latin American Jesuit authors were Creoles exiled to Europe after 1767 whose descriptions of the Americas are credited with inspiring Creole nationalism. Francisco Xavier Clavijero (Mexico), Juan Bautista Aguirre (Ecuador), Rafael de Landívar (Guatemala), and Juan Pablo Vizcardo (Peru) were among these ranks.

Jesuits had contradictory stances on how to convert the Indians in the vast hinterlands of the Americas. One debate among Jesuit missionaries was whether to employ force of arms. Some Jesuits, like Paraguay martyrs Roque González, Alonso Rodríguez, and Juan del Castillo, killed by Guaraní Indians in 1628, insisted on proselytizing without weapons. Others noted the practical necessity of combining missionaries with troops of soldiers when establishing missions in dangerous frontier regions. Whether or not Jesuits initiated their missions in conjunction with Iberian soldiers varied by region and could change with local circumstances. In the case of the frontier between Spanish Paraguay and Portuguese Brazil, Jesuits acquired permission for the converted Indians in their missions to bear arms against the Brazilian slave raiders who attacked their towns almost annually between 1614 and 1638, capturing more than 300,000 Indians.

Other sharp differences of opinions concerned Jesuit participation in ecclesiastical initiatives such as the campaigns to extirpate Indian religious error, initiated sporadically in the seventeenth- and early-eighteenth-century Archdiocese of Lima, Peru. Early Jesuit proponents of the extirpation, such as Pablo José de Arriaga (1564–1621), supported the participation of Jesuit preachers and confessors as part of the inspection teams that spread through the Andean parishes. But other Jesuits, whose opinions won out by the 1650s, argued that the Jesuits' positions on the right hand of secular priests, where they might serve commissions as idolatry judges, threatened the trust that many Andean Christians had built for Jesuits as their confessors and nonparish advocates.

The use of indigenous languages in conversion was also controversial. Blas Valera (1544–1597), a mestizo Jesuit from Peru, was admonished by his superiors for advocating the usefulness of Inca religious concepts and the Quechua language for converting native Andeans. At the same time, some Jesuits were renowned and admired for their linguistic abilities, such as the Italian Jesuit Francisco Rugi, who worked in the province of Quito in the seventeenth century. Rugi was said to have known sixteen languages and translated the catechism into all of them. Amid opinions from other religious and political officials who favored the spread of Spanish or Portuguese among the Indians, and who increasingly suspected exclusionary Jesuit motives, the norm for Jesuit missionaries in Latin America became working in the local language. Along the Amazon River in the Maynas missions alone, Jesuits learned and employed thirty-nine indigenous languages to catechize various Indian groups between 1638 and 1768.

Jesuits were keen to extend the boundaries of Catholicism in Latin America and therefore frequently accepted missionary

A Spanish Jesuit missionary and explorer, Eusebio Francisco Kino founded a mission system and converted thousands of Indians to Catholicism. (Library of Congress)

posts on the edges of Iberian dominions. Eusebio Francisco Kino (1645–1711) walked more than 6,000 leagues in his thirty years as a missionary in northern Mexico, pushing the Spanish frontier northward. In remote areas of South America, temporary missions were often conducted by pairs of Jesuits traveling from *residencias* (secure houses) and colleges in urban centers and evangelization bases such as Julí, Potosí, or Santa Cruz de la Sierra. These bases functioned as training centers where missionaries could learn indigenous languages and techniques before setting out in the field. Early forays from these sites created the foundation for later reductions.

Jesuit reductions (Spanish *reducciónes* and Portuguese *aldeias*) were offshoots of sixteenth-century Iberian schemes to bring Catholic order and organized labor recruitment to indigenous life. Indian towns and villages were segregated from colonial settlements with the double intent of indoctrinating Indian inhabitants in European ways and at the same time protecting them from Iberian and African corruption. By the 1570s, reductions became a central part of political policy, epitomized by the reorganization of Andean peoples pursued by the Viceroy of Peru Francisco de Toledo (1569–1581). The most famous Jesuit reductions in Paraguay were built on such models of political resettlement. They were significant not for their originality as a system, but for the prolonged success of the Jesuits there in sheltering the towns from external administration.

Jesuit attitudes toward African slaves in Latin America sometimes conflicted. Jesuits were prominent slaveholders in Cuba in the early 1700s. Yet in the cities of Lima, Veracruz, Santiago de Chile, Hispaniola, and Havana, "black missions" were organized in the early 1600s. Jesuit evangelical outreach to African slaves was most noteworthy in the Jesuit "Mission of Guinea" (1608–1683), which was run out of Lima (Peru) and Cartagena de Indias (Colombia). The Jesuit colleges of San Pablo de Lima and Cartagena de Indias taught and promoted the Angolan language, publishing catechism manuals and grammars and training groups of priests and lay brothers for the black ministry. Cartagena de Indias was also home to Saint Pedro Claver (1580–1654), a Spanish Jesuit who was said to have paid daily visits to recently arrived slave ships and to have baptized 300,000 slaves.

Jesuits serving in Latin America were strongly connected to Europe via frequent correspondence and annual reports to the headquarters of the Society in Rome. In order to recruit new Jesuits and promote public relations, the Society of Jesus published edited excerpts from these letters and distributed them widely. Two of these Jesuit compilations, *Lettres édifiantes et curieuses* in France and *Der neue Weltbott* in Germany, were top sellers in the 1700s. Occasionally, this information network led to transfers of ideas between Jesuits working under the auspices of the Iberian Crowns and Jesuits serving elsewhere. In the 1640s, for instance, the Jesuits of New France tried to imitate the reductions of the Jesuits in Paraguay and created the short-lived mission town of Sillery among the Montagnais and Algonquin of Canada. Over the seventeenth and eighteenth centuries in Europe, Jesuits circulated more published reports about their overseas missionary work than any other religious organization. This created widespread recognition of Jesuit activity in the Americas and the world; it also contributed to exaggerated popular perceptions of Jesuit influence.

In the seventeenth and eighteenth centuries, the most trumpeted Jesuit missions in Latin America were far flung, administered from Peru, New Spain, Paraguay, Chile, and Quito. Southeast of Cuzco, on the shore of Lake Titicaca, Julí (1576) was the most important early mission center in the Andes region. In the flat highlands on the frontier of Brazil, Jesuits established two more major mission centers, Moxos and Chiquitos. The Moxos missions were established with the help of soldiers who fought alongside the Moxos Indians against their enemies, the Caracurae Indians. In 1734, this Jesuit area consisted of twenty-one reductions inhabited by 35,000 Indians, sustained by agriculture and raising livestock. At their height, around forty Jesuits ministered to the Moxos reductions, with a central headquarters at their oldest reduction of Loreto (1682), from whence they also organized missions among the Baúres and Movimas Indians. South of Moxos, the Chiquitos missions (1691) were managed by Jesuits from the College of Tarija as a Spanish barrier to Portuguese incursions. Early reductions there, like the town of San Javier, had to be defended by local Spaniards and moved several times to avoid attacks from Brazilian slavers.

In northern New Spain (Mexico), Jesuit missions among the Laguneros Indians were acclaimed successes, with the Laguneros taking to Catholicism so quickly that by the seventeenth century the missions had been turned over to the secular clergy. Further north and west, the Jesuits were assigned the task of missionizing the peninsula of Baja California, where they resettled populations into seven mission towns centered around the fortified mission of Loreto, continuing their northward explorations and hiring ships to regularly bring them supplies from New Spain. The Spanish militia was integrated into these frontier missions alongside the Indians. The missions served as defense, agricultural suppliers, and central communications posts for the region. Also stepping off from New Spain were Jesuit missions to the Philippines, where they arrived in Manila in 1581. Jesuits were especially active there in Mindanao, acting as intermediaries between the *mahometanos* (Muslim inhabitants) and Manila. In Manila, they founded two colleges and compiled tagalog vocabularies and histories of the islands.

On the border between Paraguay and Brazil, Jesuits had their largest network of reductions, ranging west of Asunción among the Guaycuru Indians, along the Paraná and Uruguay rivers with the Guaraní and Itatine Indians, and northward near Paranapamena, inhabited by the Guayrá Indians. In the early 1700s, there were twenty-six reductions with over 100,000 Indians. Each of the agriculturally self-sustaining reductions was run by one to three Jesuits, who acted as spiritual authorities, and thirty to forty Indian leaders, who decided on secular matters. Jesuits who had been soldiers also gave military training to the Indians, who were constantly under attack by slave raiders from Brazil. By 1631, nine of the eleven reductions of Guayrá had been destroyed in these raids. Jesuit Antonio Ruiz de Montoya (1585–1652) sparked controversy by transplanting the remaining two reductions of San Ignacio and Loreto, loading 12,000 Indians onto 700 rafts and moving them closer to Spanish territory and protection. Continued attacks led him to travel to Madrid for assistance, where in 1640 he procured permission for the Indians to use firearms to defend themselves from the slavers. In 1750, negotiations between the Portuguese and Spanish Crowns led to the Treaty of Limits, which was disastrous for the Paraguay reductions, resulting in the Guaraní Wars.

In Chile, Jesuits initiated missions among the Araucanians. After their uprising in 1598, Jesuit Luis de Valdívia (1561–1642) attempted to approach these Indians and offer peaceful conversion rather than war. Valdivia thus became a key negotiator between Araucanian leaders and Spanish officials. His brief experiment in unarmed outreach ended when three Jesuits were killed by Araucanians in Elicura in 1612 and when the Bishop Pérez de Espinosa, threatened by Valdívia's growing authority, requested his removal.

The Jesuit province of Quito (Ecuador) financed the extensive Jesuit missions of Maynas in the Amazon Basin. The flourishing capital of these missions, Santiago de la Laguna, included a church, school, language seminary, and artisan workshops, and was a crossroads for Indians of different language groups. By 1768, the Jesuits had attempted eighty-eight reductions along the many tributaries of the Amazon, including the Marañón, Ucayali, and Napo rivers. Entire reduction populations were sometimes lost here due to internal warfare, dispersal, epidemics, and slave raids.

Karin Vélez

References

Alden, Dauril. *The Making of an Elite Enterprise: The Jesuits in the Portuguese Assistancy, 16th to 18th Centuries.* Minneapolis: University of Minnesota, Associates of the James Ford Bell Library, 1992.

Bailey, Gauvin Alexander. *Art on the Jesuit Missions in Asia and Latin America, 1542–1773.* Toronto: University of Toronto Press, 2000.

Borges, Pedro, ed. *Historia de la Iglesia en Hispanoamérica y Filipinas (Siglos XV-XIX). Volumen I: Aspectos Generales; Volumen II: Aspectos regionales.* Madrid: Biblioteca de Autores Cristianos, 1992.

Crosby, Harry W. *Antigua California: Mission and Colony on the Peninsular Frontier, 1697–1768.* Albuquerque: University of New Mexico Press, 1994.

Ganson, Barbara. *The Guaraní under Spanish Rule in the Río de la Plata.* Stanford, CA: Stanford University Press, 2003.

García Rodríguez, Mercedes. *Misticismo y Capitales: La Compañía de Jésus en la economía habanera del siglo XVIII.* Havana: Editorial de Ciencias Sociales, 2000.

O'Malley, John, Gauvin Alexander Bailey, Steven J. Harris, and T. Frank Kennedy, eds. *The Jesuits: Cultures, Sciences, and the Arts, 1540–1773.* Toronto: University of Toronto Press, 1999.
Pérez de Ribas, Andrés, *History of the Triumphs of Our Holy Faith among the Most Barbarous and Fierce Peoples of the New World* [1645]. Edited by Daniel Reff. Tucson: University of Arizona Press, 1999.
Ruiz de Montoya, Antonio, *The Spiritual Conquest* [1639]. Translated by C. J. McNaspy. St. Louis, MO: Institute of Jesuit Sources, 1993.

See also: Borderlands; California; Catholic Church in Brazil; Catholic Church in Spanish America; Congregaciones; Credit—Colonial Latin America; Creoles; Defense—Colonial Brazil; Defense—Colonial Spanish America; Education—Brazil; Education—Colonial Spanish America; Enlightenment—Brazil; Enlightenment—Spanish America; Idolatry, Extirpation of; Jesuits—Brazil; Jesuits—Expulsion; Jesuits—Paraguay; Languages; Mestizaje; Monarchs of Portugal; Monarchs of Spain; Native Americans I–VIII; Paraguay; Religious Orders.

JESUITS—PARAGUAY

Beginning in 1607, the Jesuits established missions in the Río de la Plata region. They eventually operated thirty missions in modern Paraguay. Rosseau wrote about the "Jesuit Republic" in Argentina and Brazil, as well as in northern Paraguay and Bolivia.

The Jesuits assumed a variety of roles in the fabric of colonial society in Spanish America. In urban centers, the Jesuits operated *colegios* to educate the children of the elite, and they maintained farms and ranches as well as urban properties that produced income to support the colegios and other Jesuit activities. On the frontiers, the Jesuits staffed missions designed to incorporate native peoples into colonial society and to convert natives to Catholicism. In the Province of Paraguay, the role of the Jesuits in establishing missions, also known as *reducciones,* was more important than any other activity.

In 1604, the Jesuits received royal authorization to establish the Province of Paraguay, and three years later in 1607 the king granted the Jesuits permission to establish missions. The Franciscans had established missions in Paraguay beginning in the late sixteenth century, but the Jesuit missions were different. Unlike the Franciscans, the Jesuits sought converts among native groups not bound in *encomiendas;* they also established their presence on the frontier of Spanish authority in South America. The Spanish in Paraguay already had to cope with twenty-two native uprisings and hoped that Jesuit missionaries would be able to stabilize their position in the region. In 1609, the Jesuits established their first mission, named San Ignacio Guazu, in what today is southeastern Paraguay. Within two decades, the Jesuits were pushing their mission program into Tape (modern Brazil), Guayra (Brazil), and Itatin (northern Paraguay and Brazil). However, slave raids by settlers from São Paulo called *bandeirantes* forced the Jesuits to retreat in the 1630s to districts located west of the Uruguay River. As a consequence of the slave raids, the Jesuits organized a mission militia that defeated the Paulistas at the battle of Mborore in 1641. The Jesuits maintained the mission militia, and local government officials mobilized Guarani troops on numerous occasions to battle the Portuguese and rebel colonists in Paraguay.

The Jesuits stabilized the missions after 1641 and, beginning in the 1680s, following the establishment of Colonia do Sacramento by the Portuguese, they ventured back into western Rio Grande do Sul in Brazil. By the 1720s, the Jesuits operated thirty missions in southeastern Paraguay and in parts of Brazil and Argentina. It was this group of missions that earned the epithet "Jesuit Republic" and the fancy of Rosseau in the Hollywood film *Candide.* In 1732, 141,000 natives lived on the thirty missions. The missions were in many ways self-governing indigenous communities, organized on the model of the *pueblos reales* of the Andean region and Mesoamerica. The Jesuits retained the social and political structure of the Guarani intact within the missions. Although the Jesuits introduced Iberian municipal government with a *cabildo* or town council, the caciques or traditional political leaders continued to exercise control within the mission communities. The missionaries assigned each cacique (native ruler) a block of housing for the natives subject to their *cacicasgo* (chieftaincy), and in records such as censuses and registers of baptisms and burials, the missionaries identified the neophytes as also belonging to the cacicasgos. This practice continued in Paraguay into the early 1840s. The Jesuits shared power with local caciques and cabildos.

The Jesuits and the Guarani neophytes participated extensively in the regional economy, producing food crops, cattle hides, cotton, and yerba maté. The missions controlled extensive *estancias* (farmland) in the Banda Oriental, several of which measured in the thousands of square hectares and included such improvements as chapels, storehouses, and bunk rooms for the Guarani *vaqueros* (cowboys). There was a division of labor within the missions, divided between labor on communal projects under the supervision of the missionaries and labor controlled by the caciques for the benefit of the communal group and the individual family. This meant that the Jesuits controlled surpluses, but so, too, did the Guaranís, and they actively participated in regional trade under the orders of the Jesuits as well as on their own.

The Jesuits directed the construction of extensive building complexes that included the sacred precinct of the church, which dominated the main square of the mission community. Missions also included the residence and office of the missionaries, shops for the manufacture of cloth and other craft goods, housing for the neophytes, and the *coti guacu,* a dormitory for single women and widows. Census records show a distinct gender imbalance in the missions and large numbers of widows as compared to only small numbers of widowers. Men went away on service with the militia or on building projects for the Crown, but there was also outmigration.

The peak of building construction in the missions dated from about 1720 to about the 1760s. The early missions had buildings of wattle and daub, compressed earth, or adobe bricks. During the last phase of construction at many of the missions, stone structures replaced the older churches and cloisters, although not all buildings, particularly neophyte housing, was rebuilt with stone. Jesuit officials insisted on the use of tile roofs to prevent fires, and documents suggest that there was a common plan for the development of mission communities.

In the decades that followed the arrival of the Spaniards in Paraguay, devastating epidemics spread through the native populations. Although the limited documentation speaks of high mortality rates, the sources do not comment on the recovery of the Guaraní populations. Epidemics were horrific episodes that caught the attention of Spanish chroniclers, officials, and priests, but the slow recovery of the population was not as dramatic and therefore did not receive the same attention in the written record. In the late seventeenth and first half of the eighteenth centuries, the Guaraní mission populations grew at slow to moderate rates, punctuated by major mortality crises that occurred approximately every generation. However, unlike other frontier native populations brought to live on missions, the Guaraní populations rebounded or recovered following epidemics. For example, thousands of Guaraní died during the 1730s, and the population of the missions dropped from 141,000 to 73,900 in just eight years, but then recovered and grew.

The Guaraní missions were not the only missions the Jesuits managed in the province of Paraguay. In the late 1740s, the Jesuits established San Estanislao and San Joaquin in Itatin in northern Paraguay, and Belén in 1760. Further to the north, in what is now southeastern Bolivia, south and east of Santa Cruz de la Sierra, the Jesuits established ten missions in the Chiquitania between 1691 and 1760. San Francisco Xavier was the first. The Chiquitos missions were different from the Guarani missions in a number of ways. First, the Jesuits continued to organize expeditions to congregate large numbers of non-Christians (called gentiles) to the mission communities. The Jesuits in Paraguay settled small numbers of non-Christians from time to time, but the mission populations were more stable. The mission populations were also smaller. In 1732, the average Guarani mission had a population of 4,708, compared to an average population of 2,379 in the Chiquitos missions in 1766. The Jesuits stationed in the Chiquitos missions participated in the regional economy but on a much smaller scale. The missions exported wax and cloth. Between 1750 and 1768 (there are gaps in the record), the Chiquitos missions exported cloth with a value of 21,554.50 pesos and wax worth 29,545.75 pesos. The pattern of sales of wax suggests that prices increased during the periods of international war, such as the Seven Years' War (1755–1763), stimulating the export of wax from the missions.

Although the Jesuits developed the Chiquitos mission communities along similar lines to the Guarani missions, there were differences in building materials. The Jesuits used stone to build just one mission, San Jose, and the others were constructed of plastered wattle and daub or plastered wood. The churches and other structures were colorfully decorated inside and out, and the churches had overhanging roofs supported by large wooden beams that provided some shade. In recent years, efforts have been made to restore the surviving Chiquitos mission churches.

In 1767–1768, the Spanish Crown ordered the expulsion of the Jesuits from its territories and placed the ex-missions under the control of civil administrators. Although there was continued outmigration following the Jesuit expulsion, for decades the ex-missions continued to exist as viable communities. The seven missions located east of the Uruguay River fell to a Portuguese colonial militia force in 1801 and in the 1820s were attacked and partially depopulated during regional civil wars. The ex-missions located between the Paraná and Uruguay rivers, in modern Misiones, Argentina, were damaged during civil wars and Brazilian invasions between 1810 and 1820. The ex-missions, located in what is now southeastern Paraguay, continued to function as autonomous communities, until Carlos López ordered them secularized in 1848, with the state taking livestock and other assets. Over time, the surrounding forest reclaimed many of the buildings of the former missions.

Robert H. Jackson

References

Carbonell de Masy, Rafael. *Estrategias de desarrollo rural en los pueblos Guaranies (1609–1767).* Barcelona, 1992.

Cardiff, Guillermo Furlong. *Misiones y sus pueblos de Guaranies.* Buenos Aires, 1962.

Ganson, Barbara. *The Guarani under Spanish Rule in the Río de la Plata.* Stanford, CA: Stanford University Press, 2003.

Hernandez, Pablo. *Organizacion social de las Doctrinas Guaranies de la Compania de Jesus.* 2 vols. Barcelona, 1913.

Maeder, Ernesto. *Misiones del Paraguay: Conflictos y disolucion de la sociedad guarani (1768–1850).* Madrid, 1992.

Radding, Cynthia. "From the Counting House to the Field and Loom: Ecologies, Cultures, and Economies in the Missions of Sonora (Mexico) and Chiquitania (Bolivia)." *The Hispanic American Historical Review* 81, no. 1 (2001): 45–87.

———. "Comunidades en conflicto: Espacios politicos en las fronteras misionales del noroeste de Mexico y el oriente de Bolivia." *Descatos* 10 (2002): 48–76.

See also: Bandeirantes; Borderlands; Brazil; Cabildo; Caciques; California; Catholic Church in Brazil; Catholic Church in Spanish America; Clergy—Secular, in Colonial Spanish America; Jesuits—Brazil; Jesuits—Expulsion; Jesuits—Iberia and America; Native Americans I–VIII; Paraguay; Religious Orders; Seven Years' War.

JEWS—COLONIAL LATIN AMERICA

Both the Jewish presence and absence in colonial Latin America were the direct results of events in the Iberian Peninsula. The Acts of Expulsion, passed in Spain in 1492 and in Portugal in 1497, turned Jews living in Spain and Portugal into either New Christians (by forced conversion) or immigrants to other European countries with more liberal religious policies. Both *conversos* (those who had accepted the new faith and became "true" Christians, as well as those who secretly kept their Jewish beliefs—crypto Jews) and migrants crossed the Atlantic and settled in Spanish and Portuguese America, and in Dutch colonies, respectively.

Many historians have documented the presence of Jewish conversos among the Spanish conquistadors and government officials at the beginning of the imperial project, even suggesting that "former" Jewish individuals helped finance Columbus's explorations. Luis de Carvajal y de la Cueva, for example, held positions of power in the Cape Verde Islands, was Spanish fleet admiral, and eventually became governor of the New Kingdoms of Leon (Monterrey). He and several members of his family were later arrested by the Inquisition, accused of being Judaizers, and killed by the Inquisition.

The office of the Inquisition, created in 1483 in Spain, was a powerful arm of the Spanish Crown in helping establish and later defend the religious integrity of the newly "reconquered" state. Once Spain had extended its dominions to Central and South America, the Inquisition was also set up in the colonies in order to extirpate heretical practices (including the practice of non-Catholic religions) among the non-Indian population of these new territories. The persecution of New Christian "Judaizers" in the colonies, however, did not reach full force until the arrival of large numbers of Portuguese New Christians after 1580. This date marked the temporary fusion of Spain and Portugal, opening up the possibility of Portuguese individuals to settle in the Spanish imperial domains. Several scholars have argued that the Inquisition's persecution of the Portuguese New Christians was fueled by fears that went beyond religious issues. These individuals were viewed as economic as well as social threats. Economically speaking, Portuguese New Christians belonged to important commercial networks that heightened the envy (and therefore the religious zeal) of Old Christians who also made commerce their source of income. New Christians were also suspected of having close connections with Indians and blacks owing to their involvement in commercial activities, and of being disloyal to the Spanish Crown. They were accused of practicing magical rituals (like the Indians), engaging in activities associated with the black/slave population, and conspiring against Spanish domination. The Inquisition served to defend not only the Catholic religion from extraneous belief, but also to make sure that the social fiber of the colonial world and the economic predominance of Old Christians were not challenged by the presence of "foreign" forces.

Although the Office of the Inquisition never existed in Brazil, inquisitors visited Brazil periodically after the Spanish and Portuguese Crowns were united. The persecution of "infidels" did take place, however, and the accused were returned to Portugal for trial.

The Dutch captured several Brazilian ports (Bahia, from 1624 to 1625; Olinda, and Recife), and former New Christians were allowed to practice their religion under their new colonial masters. Synagogues were built, contacts with the Jewish community in Amsterdam were established, and new congregations flourished. It is estimated that half of the European civilians living in Dutch Brazil were Jewish. In 1654, however, Dutch occupation ended after a nine-year war, and all Jews were given permission by the new Portuguese authorities to leave Brazil. Almost all Jews chose to leave; many moved back to Amsterdam, while others remained in the Americas: on Caribbean islands (like Curaçao and Barbados) and in the Dutch colony of New Amsterdam (later to become New York). A group of twenty-three Jews, after leaving Recife, founded the famous Shearith Israel, the Spanish Portuguese synagogue in New York City.

The Dutch accepted the settlement of Jewish people in the aftermath of the Acts of Expulsion. These Jews were then able not only to practice their religion, but also to participate in the development of the market economy that characterized European economic activity at the time. Jews became important actors in commercial ventures that involved seeking new markets, and they extended commercial networks by making use of family ties. In 1651, the Dutch West India Company gave twelve families permission to settle in Curaçao, an island off the coast of Venezuela, taken from the Spanish in 1634. Here, although not able to develop sugar production (as the company had hoped), the Jewish population, which had reached 1,500 by 1745, was able to thrive economically by taking advantage of the familial networks (which extended to the Mediterranean) and the geographical location of the island.

From Curaçao, Jews moved to other islands in the Caribbean, where they participated in the local economy and founded several congregations. The Jewish communities on some of these islands, however, were short-lived, because natural disasters and changes in the economy forced these groups to seek other areas in which to settle.

Spanish and Portuguese Jews also arrived in the Americas and settled on French and English colonies such as Jamaica, Haiti, and Saint Thomas. In British North America, for example, there were communities in Newport, Savannah, Charleston, Philadelphia, and Richmond.

The Jews who settled in Latin America during the colonial period were searching for a place in which they could both practice their religion and participate in economic activities without restrictions. Banned from doing this in the Iberian Peninsula, they either became crypto-Jews and moved to Spanish colonies, or moved to Amsterdam, from which some crossed the Ocean to the Dutch colonies in the area. True converts, though believers in Christianity, were nevertheless often suspected of being Judaizers who threatened religious, economic, national, and social priorities. This association continued to exist until the end of the Spanish and Portuguese domination of their colonies.

Adriana Brodsky

References

Angel, Marc D. *La America: The Sephardic Experience in the United States.* Philadelphia: Jewish Publication Society of America, 1982.

Hordes, Stanley M. "Inquisition and the Crypto-Jewish Community in Colonial New Spain and New México." Pp. 207–215 in *Cultural Encounters: The Impact of the Inquisition in Spain and the New World,* edited by Elizabeth Perry and Anne J. Cruz. Berkeley and Los Angeles: University of California Press, 1991.

Israel, Jonathan. "The Sephardim in the Netherlands." Pp. 189–212 in *Spain and the Jews: The Sephardi Experience 1492 and After,* edited by Elie Kedourie. London: Thames and Hudson, 1992.

Metz, Allan. "'Those of the Hebrew Nation . . .' The Sephardic Experience in Colonial Latin America." Pp. 209–233 in *Sephardim in the Americas: Studies in Culture and History,* edited by Martin A. Cohen and Abraham J. Peck. Tuscaloosa, AL: American Jewish Archives, 1993.

Silverblatt, Irene. "New Christians and New World Fears in Seventeenth-Century Peru." *Comparative Studies in Society and History* 42, no. 3 (2000): 524–546.

Stern, Malcolm H. "Portuguese Sephardim in the Americas." Pp. 141–178 in *Sephardim in the Americas: Studies in Culture and History,* edited by Martin A. Cohen and Abraham J. Peck. Tuscaloosa, AL: American Jewish Archives, 1993.

See also: Atlantic Economy; Catholic Church in Brazil; Catholic Church in Spanish America; Converso; Idolatry, Extirpation of; Inquisition—Luso-America; Inquisition—Spanish America; Islam; Jews—Modern Latin America; Migration—From Iberia to the New World; Monarchs of Portugal; Monarchs of Spain; Moors; Sugar; Witchcraft.

JEWS—MODERN LATIN AMERICA

As soon as the former Spanish colonists began the revolutionary movements that ended colonial domination, Jews already settled in the Caribbean (mostly under Dutch control) took the opportunity to settle in the continent. The island of Curaçao, whose Jewish community was made up of descendants of Spanish-Portuguese Jews who had lived on the island since the middle of the seventeenth century, was the center from which Jews moved into the newly created republics. Some Jews were accepted in Gran Colombia after Bolívar granted freedom of religion in 1829. Other Jews, seeking refuge from natural disasters and the outbreak of plagues in Curaçao, moved to the port cities of Venezuela, in particular Coro, where they remained, though in small numbers, until the end of the eighteenth century. Curaçaoan Jews participated in trade transactions with ports in Colombia, Venezuela, Mexico, Cuba, and Puerto Rico. It was some of these Jewish merchants who, after deciding to settle in these ports in order to facilitate commercial ventures, organized and helped the growth of several Jewish communities on the Latin American continent. Just as Amsterdam had aided the development of the Curaçaoan communities in the past, Curaçao helped the small handful of Jews who tried their luck on the mainland.

Other descendants of Spanish and Portuguese Jews, who had left for North Africa after the Acts of Expulsion, took advantage of the newly granted religious freedom and chose to migrate to several different countries in Latin America. Moroccan Jews traveled to Brazil and peddled their goods in the Amazon, where they built synagogues (as early as 1824) and bought land to organize their cemeteries. Some of these Jews had already migrated from Morocco to the Azores, and from there they moved to the former Portuguese colony in Latin America. From Brazil, these Jews later migrated to other Latin American countries, especially Venezuela and Argentina, where Spanish, a language they knew, was spoken. Soon thereafter, these countries began receiving small numbers of recent migrants from Morocco. The Alliance Israelite Universelle, the French organization that had set up schools in Morocco beginning in the 1860s to train and educate the local Jewish population, advocated the teaching of Spanish because so many Jews were migrating to Spanish-speaking countries. Young Moroccan men (and their wives) trained in Paris at the Alliance Israelite were later sent to Argentina, Venezuela, and Peru to teach the Jewish communities who were beginning to arrive on those Latin American countries from Europe. The Jewish Colonization Association, which had bought land in various Latin American countries to establish agricultural colonies, used these teachers in the colonies' schools, as their knowledge of Spanish made them especially welcomed by the local Latin American authorities who had devised educational plans that required, among other things, the teaching *of* Spanish and *in* Spanish.

Other Sephardic groups later followed the Moroccans to Latin America. Jews living in the Ottoman Empire suffered many economic setbacks during the late nineteenth century. Trade routes changed, and towns in Turkey, Aleppo, and Damascus, which had until then enjoyed some prosperity, experienced a marked decline. Also, during the first years of the twentieth century, political as well as religious issues changed the circumstances that Jews had enjoyed in this region. The 1908 revolution of the Young Turks, which forced Jews (as well as Christians) into compulsory military service, and the nationalist decisions taken by the newly established Balkan states furthered the migratory movement of Jewish communities. Argentina received most of the Ottoman emigrants, who, once in Argentina, founded their own self-aid societies (which, whenever possible, respected towns of origin as the guiding principle), built their own communities, and bought land to set up their own cemeteries. As with the Moroccan Jews who had arrived earlier, the former Ottoman Jews found peddling to be a lucrative activity that would perhaps provide the necessary income to own a store and later open branches in other parts of the republic. Ottoman Jews also settled in the United States, Canada, Brazil, Mexico, Cuba, Venezuela, Peru, Chile, and Uruguay.

After the creation of the state of Israel, the situation of Sephardic Jews in the Arab world became more dangerous. Most fled to Israel, but many migrated to Latin America. For example, Egyptian Jews settled in Brazil, and the remaining Moroccan Jews moved to Buenos Aires. Sephardim, then, were the first and last Jews to arrive in Latin America.

Sephardic Jews chose to create their own institutions and remain separate from the Ashkenazim, which made up the majority of Jews now living in Latin American countries. Citing cultural as well as religious differences, these two groups were, at first, intent on keeping their distance. Important cities like Buenos Aires, for example, had five Sephardic cemeteries as well as an Ashkenazic one. The first generation of Argentine Sephardic Jews usually only married other Sephardic Jews from their own congregations. Social, cultural, and religious organizations gathered those who had arrived from the same region, town, or country. It took one more generation to break those cultural barriers.

Heirs to a rich culture, Sephardic Jews in Latin America have come together in a federation of Sephardic Jews: Federacion Sefaradi Latinoamericana (FESELA). Aware of their minority status within the countries in which they live, and because Ashkenazic culture has become dominant, Sephardic Jews have become active in promoting cultural events and educational projects in an effort to maintain their cultural legacy alive.

Adriana Brodsky

References

Angel, Marc D. *La America: The Sephardic Experience in the United States.* Philadelphia: Jewish Publication Society of America, 1982.

Dias, Fátima S. "The Jewish Community in the Azores from 1820 to the Present." Pp. 19–34 in *From Iberia to Diaspora: Studies in Sephardic History and Culture,* edited by Yedida K. Stillman and Norman A. Stillman. Leiden: Brill, 1999.

Igel, Regina. "Haquitía as Spoken in the Brazilian Amazon." Pp. 446–450 in *From Iberia to Diaspora: Studies in Sephardic History and Culture,* edited by Yedida K. Stillman and Norman A. Stillman. Leiden: Brill, 1999.

Lesser, Jeffrey. "(Re)creating Ethnicity: Middle Eastern Immigration to Brazil." *The Americas* 53, no. 1 (1996): 45–65.

Miller, Susan Gilson. "Kippur on the Amazon: Jewish Emigration from Northern Morocco in the Late Nineteenth Century." Pp. 190–209 in *Sephardi Middle Eastern Jewries: History and Culture in the Modern Era,* edited by Harvey E. Goldberg. Bloomington: Indiana University Press, 1996.

Mirelman, Victor. "Sephardic Immigration to Argentina Prior to the Nazi Period." Pp. 33–44 in *The Jewish Presence in Latin America,* edited by Judith Laikin Elkin and Gilbert W. Merk. Boston: Allen and Unwin, 1987.

———. "Sephardim in Latin America after Independence." Pp. 235–265 in *Sephardim in the Americas: Studies in Culture and History,* edited by Martin A. Cohen and Abraham J. Peck. Tuscaloosa, AL: American Jewish Archives, 1993.

See also: Amazon; Atlantic Economy; Catholic Church in Brazil; Catholic Church in Spanish America; Gran Colombia; Independence I–VI; Inquisition—Luso-America; Inquisition—Spanish America; Islam; Jews—Colonial Latin America; Migration—From Iberia to the New World; Moors; World War II.

JUREMA

Jurema is a drink extracted from a plant of the same name commonly found in northeastern Brazil that contains hallucinogenic properties and is used extensively in indigenous religious rituals and Afro-Brazilian cults. Jurema was used by at least two large indigenous groups in northeastern Brazil, the Jê and the Kararí.

There are several types of jurema. The two most common are *Jurema Preta* (*Mimosa Hostilis*) and *Jurema Branca* (*Mimosa Verrucosa*). In processing the plant, the bark is stripped from the roots and pounded to remove the dirt and outer bark. It is then soaked in water and pressed repeatedly until a thick reddish liquid remains. The bark may also be boiled. The active ingredient in jurema is dimethyltryptamine (DMT). The precise recipe for the early jurema mixture is not known, although more recent practices suggest that it may have included honey and the roots of other plants.

The *mestres de jurema* (masters of jurema) possessed the secret to mixing the drink and became the leaders of the various jurema ceremonies or cults. These masters developed rituals that included the use of tobacco, the maraca, dancing, and the drinking of the jurema.

In the eighteenth century, participants drank the jurema and then danced until they collapsed and experienced powerful hallucinations interpreted as religious experiences. Some local priests in Paraíba denounced the practitioners to the Inquisition in the eighteenth century. There is some indication that the Indians used the cult as a way of resisting conversion and the power of colonial authorities.

The indigenous cult surrounding the use of jurema experienced a resurgence in the mid-eighteenth century in northeastern Brazil after the expulsion of the Jesuits. The practice apparently continued throughout the nineteenth century but fell into decline and was thought to have been lost by the twentieth century. It continued, nonetheless, and has resurfaced among detribalized Indians seeking recognition from the Brazilian government. These groups tout the use of jurema as a distinctive characteristic of Brazilian Indians.

Jurema consumption has also become an important part of several Afro-Brazilian religious traditions in which the drug is used to help induce trances. There are several spirit deities who bear the name *jurema.* The most common is the Caboclo Jurema.

Jurema has been used in Candomblé rituals since at least as early as 1905. The modern drink used in Candomblé is a mixture of the jurema extract, honey, herbs, and alcohol. Some Candomblé practitioners may also mix it with the blood of sacrificial animals. Originally, the pot used to serve the jurema was made from a stump with feathers around the edge indicating its indigenous origins.

James E. Wadsworth

References

Mota, Clarice Novaes da. *Jurema's Children in the Forest of Spirits: Healing and Ritual among Two Brazilian Indigenous Groups.* London: Intermediate Technology Publications, 1997.

Sangirardi, Junior. *O índio e as plantas alucinógenas: Tribos das 3 Américas e civlizações pré-colombianas.* Rio de Janeiro: Editorial Alhambra, 1983.

Schultes, Richard Evans, and Albert Hofmann. *Plants of the Gods: Their Sacred, Healing, Hallucinogenic Powers.* Rochester, VT: Healing Arts Press, 1992.

Wafer, Jim, *The Taste of Blood: Spirit Possession in Brazilian Candomblé.* Philadelphia: University of Pennsylvania Press, 1991.

See also: Alcohol; Drugs; Inquisition—Luso-America; Jesuits—Brazil; Jesuits—Expulsion; Music and Dance I—Brazil; Native Americans II—Brazil; Slavery I—Brazil; Syncretism; Tobacco.

Knights of Columbus

The Knights of Columbus is the largest organization of Roman Catholic laity in the world. Membership in the fraternal order is open to all adult Catholic males. The order is internationally active, with headquarters located in New Haven, Connecticut. The four principles of the order are charity, unity, fraternity, and patriotism. Established in 1882, the order had over 1.5 million members at the end of the twentieth century.

The Knights of Columbus was established by a Catholic priest, Michael J. McGivney, and a group of Irish American laymen at St. Mary's Church in New Haven. The Roman Catholic Church condemned secret societies; however, they flourished in the United States in the late 1800s and early 1900s, when such membership greatly advanced networking opportunities for social and business success. McGivney witnessed the popularity of fraternalism among Protestants and sought to create for Catholic men the same sort of sanctuary from the severely competitive and divisive character of industrial life. The order's principal function was to provide insurance to women and children in the event of a knight's death, but the addition of the noninsurance or associate membership greatly increased membership.

The Knights astutely chose Christopher Columbus as their patron: Columbus symbolized the legitimate presence of Catholics in the United States. Protestants evoked the *Mayflower* as part of their American identity. The Knights showed pride in their American Catholic heritage by celebrating Columbus Day, honoring the earlier arrival of the *Santa Maria,* which brought Catholic Christianity to the New World. The rise of nativist Protestant, anti-Catholic immigration activism created the need to publicly display the affinity of Catholicism and patriotism. In addition to its antidefamation agenda, the Knights promoted Catholic unity and worked against Catholic ethnic particularity. The leaders were all second-generation Irish Americans, but the order established the German-American Teutonia Council and Italian-American Ausonia Council in Boston in the 1890s. The Knights were a Catholic demonstration of the patriarchy, manliness, and muscular Christianity that was endorsed by fraternal organizations of the era. The 1892 celebrations of the quadricentennial of

Columbus's landfall in the Western Hemisphere and the national patriotic fervor during the 1898 Spanish-American War animated the order's character.

In nineteenth-century Mexico, anticlerical freemasons had been highly influential in politics. Many Mexican Catholic leaders welcomed the Knights of Columbus (Caballeros de Colón in Spanish) as a countervailing organization. The order was established in Mexico in 1905 by an American expatriate hacienda owner and was welcomed by Porfirio Díaz, the opportunistic dictator who was also grand master of the Masons. The first members in Mexico were mostly Americans, and the order was viewed with suspicion as an imported American organization. In 1911, Díaz went into exile. In the aftermath of the Mexican Revolution, which produced the anticlerical Constitution of 1917, thirty-four of the fifty-eight Knights' lodges were forced to close. President Plutarco Calles stalwartly enforced the anticlerical provisions of the constitution, leading to the Cristero Rebellion (1926–1929), in which over 90,000 Mexicans lost their lives. The U.S. Knights raised $1 million to bring the conflict to the world's attention and encouraged Mexican Catholics to resist, though their efforts to influence American foreign policy against the revolutionary Mexican government were unsuccessful. After the government's nonimplementation of key constitutional provisions, church-state conflict in Mexico came to an end in the 1940s.

In the United States, the Knights created religious and recreational centers for the spiritual needs of Catholic servicemen and the social needs of all American soldiers, regardless of their religious affiliation, stationed along the Mexican border in 1916. As a result of the success of this program, the order offered the same service to the U.S. government when it entered World War I the following year.

After World War I, U.S. Knights set up employment bureaus for veterans, established evening academic and vocational schools, and sponsored college scholarships. A historical commission was created in the 1920s to promote the contributions of non-Anglo-Saxon U.S. immigrant groups. During the Great Depression, the order revived its anti-Socialist and anti-Communist activities, linking them to the anti-Fascist cause. In the 1960s, the Knights reformed their admissions policy to become racially integrated. Today, the order sponsors numerous charitable activities.

David M. Carletta

References

Kauffman, Christopher J. *Faith and Fraternalism: The History of the Knights of Columbus, 1882–1982.* New York: Harper and Row, 1982.

———. *Patriotism and Fraternalism in the Knights of Columbus: A History of the Fourth Degree.* New York: Crossroads, 2001.

Redinger, Matthew. "'To Arouse and Inform': The Knights of Columbus and United States-Mexican Relations, 1924–1937." *Catholic Historical Review* 88, no. 3 (July 2002): 489–518.

Rich, Paul, and Guillermo de los Reyes. "The Mexican Revolution and the Caballeros de Colón." *Catholic Southwest* 10 (1999): 60–74.

See also: Mexican Revolution; Nationalism; Opus Dei; Papacy; Spanish-American War; World War I; World War II.

KURACAS

Kuracas were the agents of Indian societies who best embodied the inextricability of Iberian-Indian relations in the colonial Andes. Crucial to the existence of their groups, kuracas played a major role in the relations established between Spaniards and natives. By the late eighteenth century, in response to pressures imposed by the colonial administration over their people, some kuracas led massive Indian uprisings that ravished the Andes and challenged Iberian control of the area.

Hereditary local rulers, kuracas, a *Quechua* term for "native chiefs," have usually been in charge of their ethnic units' well-being since the earliest stages of social organization in the Andes. At the time of the expansion of the Inca Empire, they constituted the bond between the Incas' authority and local ethnic groups. Kuracas were traditionally responsible for organizing and mobilizing labor using customary bonds of mutual obligation, a practice known to anthropologists as "uneven reciprocity." Once incorporated into the Inca Empire, ethnic groups were asked to pay their taxes in labor, which was used to complete crucial state-sponsored projects, such as roads, storehouses, and bridges. Incan administration, therefore, confirmed and heavily relied on the power of local kuracas. From the commoners' perspective, loyalty to their native chiefs guaranteed them access to a major network of trade that constituted the main incentive to join the Inca Empire. As for religion, Andean tradition dictated that corpses of influential kuracas should be mummified and worshiped by their communities in order to guarantee good harvests.

Spaniards recognized the influence of kuracas over their communities and, soon after the conquest, allotted their earliest *encomiendas* according to the chiefs' names and places of residence. Since early colonial times, Iberians made sure that kuraca positions remained in the hands of few families. Usually, lineages that could prove an ancestral position of authority among their fellow Indians were confirmed in those positions. In exchange for the official imperial recognition, kuracas served as middlemen between Spaniards and Indian communities, a role key to the functioning of the colonial economy. In so doing, native chiefs facilitated a delicate equilibrium between the Spaniards' demands and the resources that Indian groups could and were willing to offer.

The eighteenth-century Bourbon reforms brought deep changes to the Andes. As taxes were increased and their collection was reinforced, Indians began to complain. Above all, the practice of *repartimiento,* the forced selling of unwanted European goods to Indian communities, became the main target of the natives' protests. In 1780, José Gabriel Condorcanqui, a wealthy kuraca from the central Andes, started a massive Indian uprising. Under the name of Túpac Amaru, one of the last Inca kings, Condorcanqui organized a huge army that threatened the future of Spanish presence in the Andes. Although Túpac Amaru was eventually captured and executed, the rebellion took over 100,000 lives and constituted the most expensive military operation since the conquest. Most importantly, it spread among Creoles in the Andes the dread of race warfare and strengthened their loyalty to Spain, delaying the area's independence.

Maria Marsilli

References

Spalding, Karen. *Huarochirí: An Andean Society under Inca and Spanish Rule.* Stanford, CA: Stanford University Press, 1984.

Stern, Steve J., ed. *Resistance, Rebellion, and Consciousness in the Andean Peasant World.* Madison: University of Wisconsin Press, 1987.

See also: Colonists and Settlers I—Andes; Conquest I—Andes; Encomienda; Mita; Native Americans V—Central and Southern Andes; Peru; Repartimiento; Túpac Amaru Revolt.

L

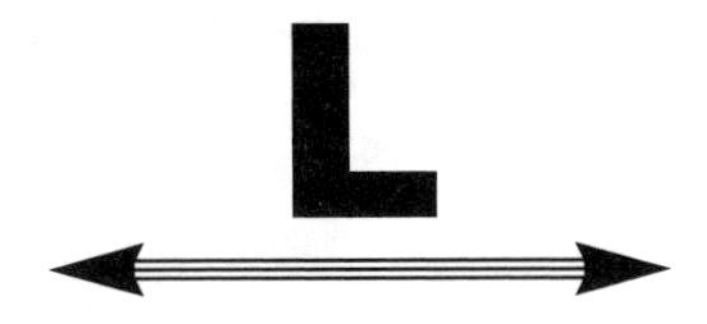

Labor Relations—Portugal/Brazil

Portugal exported its own labor systems and created new ones on the Atlantic islands and on American soil, but over time the transplanted labor systems changed and adapted to local conditions. The most important form of labor brought by the Portuguese was slavery. However, slavery in Portuguese America differed from slavery in Portugal in important ways. From its use in marginal economic activities in Portugal, slavery became the dominant labor system in one of the most important slave societies and economies in world history: colonial and early independent Brazil. Nonetheless, the main characteristics of Portuguese (and in general Iberian) slavery were to be found in nonplantation Brazil and, in particular, in towns and cities. Furthermore, other coercive forms of Portuguese labor (servitude) tainted labor relationships of free workers in Brazil. In general, Portugal's legacy in this field is linked with the establishment of nonfree forms of work in the Atlantic world, both through the slave trade and the direct use of labor.

By the end of the fifteenth century, Portugal had a relatively small population, with roughly between 1 and 1.4 million inhabitants, unevenly distributed throughout the country. In the demographic context of the Iberian Peninsula, Portugal had far fewer inhabitants than Castile and Aragon; like its Spanish counterpart, the Portuguese population was recovering from the ravages of the fourteenth-century Black Death.

Portugal's population included Jewish and Arab minorities; however, their numbers and importance were far less than in other parts of the Iberian Peninsula. Some Jews were bankers and professionals under the protection of Portugal's king, but most were artisans and craftsmen, such as tailors, goldsmiths, blacksmiths, and cobblers. Still fewer Portuguese Jews were peasants and sailors. The expulsion of the Jews from Spain in 1492 benefited Portugal because many Spanish Jews crossed into the region, where they remained until the middle of the seventeenth century when conditions worsened for Jews everywhere in the Spanish and Portuguese worlds. The Moors were visible in Portugal in the most southern part of the country, where a relatively large population of Christianized Moors (Moriscos) toiled the fields and worked as artisans in towns and cities.

Portuguese society was highly stratified, which became an essential part of the Portuguese legacy in Brazil. Issues of honor shaped social and labor relations in important ways. The majority of the population was comprised of commoners, engaged in agricultural or pastoral activities. As in Spain, Portuguese peasants shared their crops with the landowner in return for a more or less stable tenure; still, many landowners attempted to legally and effectively tie the laborers to the soil. Permanent labor shortages in the Lisbon and Oporto hinterlands allowed peasants some bargaining power, and therefore day laborers *(jornaleiros)* were able to demand higher wages and better working conditions. However, this was not enough to modify significantly the general tendency of the Portuguese labor market. Rigid property rules, small holdings, and large families combined to make it difficult for the rural youth to remain in their towns of birth. Peasants tended to migrate from the countryside to cities such as Lisbon and Oporto, hoping to find economic opportunities. Instead, they increased the ranks of the urban poor; in response, many joined Portuguese sailing crews and left for Goa or Brazil. Sixteenth- and seventeenth-century plagues and famine in Portugal influenced decisions to emigrate as well.

Portugal had only a few large cities other than Lisbon and Oporto, and neither of those became important industrial centers; rather, Portuguese cities were commercial entrepôts. This pattern certainly influenced the Portuguese colonial experience in colonial Brazil. The vast majority of the urban settlers were domestic servants, dependent workers of artisan shops, and street vendors and peddlers comprising the *povo,* or people, who bore the greatest share of the tax burden. Portuguese guilds, unlike their Spanish counterparts, were less rigid and dominated by the merchant elites; this flexibility in industrial matters was transplanted to Brazilian cities.

High levels of potential labor migration constituted one of the greatest problems for the Portuguese economy. The demographic impact of Portuguese emigration on adult manpower was considerable; for example, during the sixteenth century, roughly 2,400 able-bodied and unmarried young men left Portugal annually. In the fertile northern provinces of Minho and Douro and in the Atlantic islands of Madeira and the Azores, emigration created labor shortages that seriously threatened local agriculture. After approximately 1570, Brazil began to attract more migrants than India and the East because of health considerations and better economic opportunities. Furthermore, an increasing number of Portuguese women crossed the Atlantic to settle in Brazil.

Portuguese emigrants were more fortune-seekers than settlers. However humble their social origins might have been, most were unwilling to perform manual work if they could avoid it. Yet conditions in the colonies often were different from what many expected, and, therefore, most were obliged to work in trades, crafts, and on the land. Craftsmen and artisans worked as stonemasons, carpenters, coopers, tailors, cobblers, or goldsmiths. Others served as overseers or foremen on sugar plantations, or as stockmen on cattle ranches. Few newcomers arrived in Brazil with enough economic resources and appropriate social networks to become the *sehnores de engenho,* or sugar mill and plantation owners. As in other colonial experiences around the world, the Portuguese in Brazil attempted to exploit the colonized. However, since Brazilian Indians resisted labor demands, colonizers turned to forced labor to meet the labor needs of Brazil's expanding agriculture. In so doing, the Portuguese simply extended to Brazil a practice they had established earlier on the Atlantic islands.

The first two centuries of modern slavery were closely linked with the Portuguese slave trade. After the Treaty of Alcaçovas in 1479 with Spain, Portuguese slavers obtained slaves from their African outposts to supply both the Old and New World. The uninhabited Atlantic islands of Madeira, the Azores, and Cape Verde, and the islands of São Tome, Principe, Ascension, Saint Helena, and many others in the Gulf of Guinea were a kind of commercial and production laboratory of the early Portuguese colonial experience. In particular, Madeira and later São Tome, the Azores, and Cape Verde became major sugar producers. The Azores also produced wheat, while several islands played important intermediary roles in the passage of slaves from the African mainland to their subsequent distribution in Europe and the Americas. In their search for workers, Portuguese colonizers used different free and coerced labor, including free workers, Iberian migrants, and Berber or black African slaves; all were put to work (under various terms) on the islands. However, the preference for slave labor on the Atlantic islands later influenced the labor patterns the Portuguese would use in plantation Brazil.

Indeed, the Portuguese institutionalized the slave trade before the end of the fifteenth century. At first, hundreds of African slaves were sold in European markets; however, Brazil, the Caribbean, and continental America soon became the major markets for millions of African slaves. The changes in numbers reflected the changes in the nature of slavery itself. Slavery had long been known in Iberia, but slaves never constituted more than a small percentage of society. By 1492, although more than 35,000 black slaves had been introduced in Portugal, most of them were intended to be reexported to other European markets and to the Americas. By 1550, there were 9,500 African slaves in Lisbon—comprising nearly 10 percent of the total population—and 32,370 slaves and 2,580 freedmen in Portugal as a whole. Black slaves increasingly replaced slaves from other racial origins as the Portuguese became less involved in the wars against the Turks in the Mediterranean and in general against Muslims.

Like contemporary slavery in other European countries, slavery in Portugal was marginal both to the economy and to the society. Most slaves worked as domestic servants of the elites, or as unskilled laborers. Slavery was mostly an urban phenomenon. In a way, slaveholding was a source of social prestige as well as a source of labor. Portuguese slavery, like its Spanish counterpart, rested heavily on the Roman, Visigothic, and Muslim law and practice. That is, slavery was a temporary situation in which freedom was always the ultimate goal. In the meantime, however, slaves were salable servants, heavily dependent on their masters, though never deprived of their religious and economic rights. There were several formal ways of manumission, from the master's grant to the self-purchase of freedom for good service; and bondsmen had the right to change masters if they had received cruel treatment or sexual abuse. In general, royal courts could intervene in slave-master relationships. Slave marriage was protected by the Church. Portuguese slavery inherited the Roman *peculium,* the practice by which slaves could have their own property and reap the fruits of their work.

All of these characteristics were in force in Brazil. However, conditions were undoubtedly better in the cities. On sugar plantations (*engenhos*) the protective regulations were disregarded, and it is not surprising that colonial Brazil was widely known as a hell for slaves. In effect, Portuguese conquerors and settlers relied largely on Indian slave labor provided by slaving expeditions (*bandeiras*), despite the royal prohibition of the enslavement of Indians in 1570, first for harvesting brazilwood and then for sugar plantations; however, by the early seventeenth century, the sugar plantations of Pernambuco and Bahia were worked almost exclusively by African slaves.

Francisco F. Quiroz

References

Anderson, James M. *The History of Portugal.* Westport, CT: Greenwood Press, 2000.
Birmingham, David. *A Concise History of Portugal.* Cambridge: Cambridge University Press, 2003.
Blackburn, Robin. *The Making of New World Slavery: From the Baroque to the Modern, 1492–1800.* London: Verso, 1997.
Boxer, Charles R., *The Portuguese Seaborne Empire, 1415–1825.* Exeter: Carcanet, 1991.
Lane, Ann J., ed. *The Debate over Slavery: Stanley M. Elkins and His Critics.* Urbana: University of Illinois Press, 1971.
Levine, Robert M. *The History of Brazil.* Westport, CT: Greenwood Press, 1999.
Meade, Teresa A. *A Brief History of Brazil.* New York: Facts on File, 2003.
Russell-Wood, A.J.R. *A World on the Move: The Portuguese in Africa, Asia, and America 1415–1808.* New York: St. Martin's Press, 1992.
Schwartz, Stuart B. *Slaves, Peasants, and Rebels: Reconsidering Brazilian Slavery.* Chicago: University of Illinois Press, 1992.
Skidmore, Thomas E. *Brazil: Five Centuries of Change.* New York: Oxford University Press, 1999.

See also: Bandeirantes; Brazil; Cimarrones; Colonists and Settlers II—Brazil; Conquest II—Brazil; Donatary Captaincies; Engenho; Jews—Colonial Latin America; Labor Relations—Spain/Spanish America; Laws—Colonial Latin America; Migration—From Iberia to the New World; Moors; Palenque; Slave Rebellions—Brazil; Slavery I–IV; Slave Trade; Sugar; Women—Brazil.

LABOR RELATIONS—SPAIN/SPANISH AMERICA

Spanish American labor systems are similar and, at the same time, differ from those that existed in Spain during the Age of Discovery. Spanish American possessions had unique and varied pre-Columbian influences, and peninsular labor systems adjusted differently to local social, demographic, and economic conditions.

By the mid-fifteenth century, the Spanish population was expanding as it continued to recover from the ravages of the fourteenth-century Black Death. Castile, the largest kingdom in the peninsula, also supported the largest population (about 4.5 million). Its predominance increased even more after Castile subjugated Granada in 1492 and occupied Navarre in 1512. Aragon had more than 1 million inhabitants, while the still Muslim Granada had half a million people. Navarre was the smallest independent realm, with roughly 250,000 inhabitants.

At the time, Spain's population included Jewish and Arab minorities. Spanish Jews numbered 100,000 and lived mostly in Castile. Contrary to common beliefs, most of them were not rich. Aside from a small portion of wealthy and influential people, the majority of Spanish Jews were workers. There was a large population of Christianized Moors (moriscos) as well, most of whom were peasants living in Valencia and Granada; some of them were even slaves. Arab artisans were especially important in pottery and building industries. Forcibly converted to Christianity, Jews and Moriscos were still subject to persecutions and banned from traveling to the American colonies; nonetheless, many found ways to avoid this restriction. In fact, Jewish influence in trade and finances and Muslim contributions in crafts in colonial Latin America are topics that just recently have received scholarly attention.

The majority of Spain's population was comprised of commoners engaged in agricultural or pastoral activities. Although many were tied to the land (*siervos*) and others actually owned small lands (*labradores*), most worked a noble's land, sharing the crop with him in return for a more or less stable tenure (*aparcería*). While personal serfdom was abolished, the rural population was still subject to seigniorial charges and rents (tithes, sharecropping, payments for the use of seigniorial monopolies such as mills, forests, pasture lands, and the like). Legal servitude of the Catalan *payeses* remained in force until Ferdinand's *Sentencia arbitral* of Guadalupe abolished it in 1486. Only a small part of the rural population worked as wage-earning day laborers for the wealthiest owners and tenants.

Slaves were marginal to the Spanish economy, even in Andalusia, Extremadura, the southeastern coastal regions, and the Balearic and Canary Islands, where slavery was most prevalent. By 1565, for instance, the 14,500 African slaves in the Bishopric of Seville constituted only 3.5 percent of the total population; in the city of Seville, African slaves comprised just 7 percent of the population. Most slaves in peninsular Spain worked as domestic servants or as assistants to master artisans.

Spanish American slavery differed from slavery in the Iberian peninsula in several important respects; however, the Iberian experience helps explain the way it evolved. Roman, Visigothic, and Muslim law and practice influenced the way in which slavery developed in Castile. Slavery was then a multiracial phenomenon, very different from the racial slavery that certain parts of the New World witnessed later. Moreover, white Christians could and did become slaves of the Muslims if they happened to fall captive. White female Muslim concubines accompanied the conquerors and first settlers to the New World, where they and their descendants were subsequently freed. The practice of enslaving Muslims as enemies of the faith was extended to the Americas. After several discussions on the issue, the Spanish Crown allowed the enslavement of Indians who refused to acknowledge the Crown's authority and to convert to Christianity. As a result, thousands of Indians were enslaved in Central America, northern Mexico, Chile, and Argentina.

In reality, Castilian slavery was a temporary situation, a kind of transition to full inclusion into society. Indeed, Spanish law and practice considered slaves to be human beings, salable human beings of course, but never deprived of all rights. This is clear from the thirteenth-century code that was in force at least well into the eighteenth century in both Spain and Spanish America. Known as the *Siete partidas* of Alfonso the Wise, the code reflects a society comprised of serfs and lords in which slaves were more salable servants than chattel merchandise. To be sure, captured enemies of the faith could be enslaved as could the offsprings of female slaves; they therefore could be sold, rented, donated, and so on. Masters had wide powers over their slaves. At the same time, slaves had certain religious and economic rights as well as obligations. There were several formal ways of manumission, ranging from the master's grant to the self-purchase of freedom for good service; bondsmen also had the right to change masters if subjected to cruel treatment or sexual abuse. In general, royal courts could intervene in slave-master relationships. Slave marriage was protected by the Church. And lastly, Spanish slavery inherited the Roman *peculium* or the practice by which slaves could possess their own property and enjoy the fruits of their labor.

All of these characteristics appeared in Spanish America. As in other aspects of cultural legacies, however, there could be large gaps between the legal status of slaves and the reality of their conditions. Moreover, local legislation in Spanish America was repressive in nature, restricting slave mobility and punishing slaves for carrying arms, running away, or fraternizing with Indians. In plantation Spanish America, slavery acquired the common severe features that characterized racial plantation slavery elsewhere, especially in Cuba.

In another important pattern introduced by Spaniards to the New World, the majority of the peninsular population lived in towns and cities rather than scattered in the countryside. Several Spanish urban centers were large in contemporary European terms. In the late fifteenth century Seville, Granada, and Toledo were really large cities with nearly 50,000 inhabitants.

The vast majority of these urban settlers were domestic servants, artisans, and street vendors and peddlers. They comprised the lower levels of the social ladder. Castilian guilds and confraternities ranked by prestige, with silversmiths the most honored and cobblers the least, lacked the economic and political power of their Catalan counterparts, but they did influence the lives and work of urban dwellers. Yet, by the sixteenth century, the guild system in Spain was experiencing important transformations. Guilds began to resemble less and less the medieval closed corporation they used to be; instead, they turned into more dynamic corporations dominated by large producers and merchants who organized (or at least intended to organize) production for large markets.

Social and labor conditions at home influenced Spanish migration to America. To begin with, Spanish migration differed roughly from that of other European countries. Unlike northern Europeans, the Spanish conquered the most densely populated and politically developed territories of the Americas, and the nature of their colonies was heavily influenced by preconquest Native American institutions. In general, the Spaniards never found acute labor shortages in the economic activities they encouraged. And although native populations decreased in numbers in some areas during the first century after conquest, growth after 1650 provided a potential labor force able to cover the internal demand for workers.

It is impossible to know the total number of Spanish emigrants and returnees. Scholars' educated guesses reveal that nearly 225,000 Spaniards and other Europeans officially entered Spanish America by 1600. Unfortunately, there are no studies for the seventeenth century, a period of population decline in Spain; similarly, it is unclear how many arrived during the remainder of the colonial period. In any case, Spanish migrants were mainly free persons in search of fortune or at least a better way of living in America. If they hoped to return with wealth and honor, only a few fulfilled their expectations. This is clear from the fact that many Spaniards migrated alone to the New World, leaving their spouses, mothers, and sisters behind.

Unlike the British emigration, the Spanish rested heavily on family and social ties. Relatives (real and spiritual) helped pay the costs of the trans-Atlantic passage. Despite the negative attitude from local elites, the newly arrived had unique opportunities in the Americas, other than becoming dependent workers. To be sure, these peasants, petty traders, and craftsmen did not reject menial work absolutely, but they expected to establish themselves independently as farmers, merchants, and industrialists.

Francisco F. Quiroz

References

Blackburn, Robin. *The Making of New World Slavery: From the Baroque to the Modern, 1492–1800.* London: Verso, 1997.

Burns, Robert I. *Las Siete Partidas.* 5 vols. Philadelphia: University of Pennsylvania Press, 2001.

Freedman, Paul. *The Origins of Peasant Servitude in Medieval Catalonia.* Cambridge: Cambridge University Press, 1991.

Ruiz, Teofilo F. *Spanish Society, 1400–1600.* London: Longman, 2001.

Stella, Alessandro. *Histoires d'esclaves dans la Péninsule Ibérique.* Paris, Éditions de l'École des Hautes Études en Sciences Sociales, 2000.

See also: Artisans; Cimarrones; Columbian Exchange—Agriculture; Columbian Exchange—Livestock; Family—Colonial Spanish America; Food; Islam; Jews—Colonial Latin America; Labor Relations—Portugal/Brazil; Laws—Colonial Latin America; Marriage; Migration—From Iberia to the New World; Moors; Native Americans I–VIII; Palenque; Race; Slavery I–IV; Women—Colonial Spanish America.

LADINO

The term *ladino* is of uncertain origin in Spain, but it generally referred to foreigners, often slaves, who had become Spanish speakers and professed the Christian faith. Over time its meaning shifted, so that by the late nineteenth century it meant "non-Indian," and it increasingly became synonymous with "mestizo." In early colonial Spanish America, the term *ladino* applied almost exclusively to African slaves and native peoples of the Americas as in the usage "*negros ladinos*" or "*indios ladinos*" to mean the same as it did in Spain. Ladino tended to be used as an adjective to describe populations that were otherwise considered foreign to the Spanish. By the eighteenth century, the comparative decline in native populations that could not communicate in Spanish and the attendant growth in mixed-race populations transformed the use of "ladino" so that it became synonymous with mixed-race *castas,* especially mestizos and mulattoes. Although the word lost favor in many parts of Latin America after independence, it remained a key term in Central America, where it is still used today. Throughout the nineteenth century, ladino was still used to mean mixed-race, but it also came to have an increasingly cultural meaning, defining people who lived a Europeanized lifestyle. In this way "ladino" began to revert to its original meaning, defining a set of cultural values. But unlike the precolonial and early colonial eras, it shifted from being an aspect of identity to being a defining characteristic. Indians could become ladinos by leaving their communities and casting off traditional clothing, language, and other signs of community affiliation. In so doing, however, they ceased to be Indian. In the twentieth century, ladino has often been used interchangeably with mestizo, and is used to mean biological mixture as much or more than a cultural mode of being. This contemporary usage tends to erase the mulattoes included in the term's meaning in the late colonial period.

Justin Wolfe

References

Gould, Jeffrey L. *To Die in This Way: Nicaraguan Indians and the Myth of Mestizaje, 1880–1965.* Durham, NC: Duke University Press, 1998.

Taracena, Arturo. "Contribución al estudio del vocabulo 'ladino' en Guatemala (S. XVI-XIX)." Pp. 89–104 in *Historia y antroplogía de Guatemala: Ensayos en honor de J. Daniel Contreras R.,* edited by Jorge Luján Muñoz. Guatemala: Faculty of the Humanities, University of San Carlos of Guatemala, 1982.

See also: Catholic Church in Spanish America; Clothing in Colonial Spanish America; Languages; Mestizaje; Mulatto; Native Americans I–VIII; Race; Syncretism.

LANGUAGES

Spanish is a Romance language that derived from Vulgar Latin, the spoken variant of Latin, the official language of the Roman Empire. Other national Romance languages include Portuguese, French, Italian, and Romanian; others such as Catalan, Galician, Occitan, Rheto-Romance, and Sardinian are regional languages. Vulgar Latin was spoken by the Roman legionaries and merchants who arrived in the Iberian Peninsula at the end of the third century BC.

The Spaniards arrived in the Americas in 1492 already possessing Castilian as a common language that had been made official not long before. The same year, Antonio de Nebrija's *Gramática* was published to set standards for the users of the Spanish language, that is, Castilian vernacular enriched with other peninsular dialects.

Once in America, the diversity of aboriginal languages presented major communication difficulties for the Spaniards. The interpreters who accompanied the explorers were fluent in Arabic and Hebrew, languages that because of their commercial relevance between the Middle and the Far East were believed to be potentially useful. These languages proved to be useless in the Americas; therefore, the other recourse was to train interpreters. To this end, they captured natives, took them to the court, and taught them Spanish.

In 1514 the *requerimiento*—a judicial formula requiring the natives to recognize the Holy Trinity and the rights of the king of Spain—was enforced, but it was written in Spanish, a language foreign to the natives. Refusal to accept this requerimiento brought on a "just war" of countless injustices and acts of violence. Concerned for the well-being of the natives, many priests, especially those from the Franciscan, Dominican, Augustinian, and Jesuit orders, learned the languages of the conquered. Thus, missionaries published numerous vocabularies, grammars, and religious works in two, three, and even four languages simultaneously. The difficulty posed by the vast number of indigenous languages encouraged the missionaries to use *linguae francae.* Thus, the universities in Mexico and Lima provided instruction in Nahuatl for Mexico and Central America, Quechua for the former Inca Empire, and Guaraní for the areas covering present-day Uruguay, Paraguay, and Argentina. The teaching of indigenous languages was also instituted at the University of Salamanca in the sixteenth century, a practice that continued until 1770, when King Charles III banned their use.

Contact situations with Native American languages contributed to the enrichment of the Spanish language. In America, Spanish settlers came into contact with new flora, fauna, people, cultures, and meteorological phenomena, along with the corresponding lexicon. Words of Caribbean origin were spread throughout Spanish America by subsequent explorers, replacing local words. Terms like *ají* (pepper), *hamaca* (hammock), *huracán* (hurricane), *canoa* (canoe), and *maíz* (corn) became common throughout Central and South America as well as in Spain. In addition, the prestige associated with having visited the Americas led many explorers and merchants to deliberately use Americanisms on their return to Spain, and writers such as Cervantes, Lope de Vega, and Quevedo diffused those words to a broader public.

Although the population of the Antilles became almost extinct soon after the arrival of the Spanish explorers, they left a lexical legacy such as *guacamayo* (macaw), and *tabaco* (tobacco). Africans imported as slaves left words like *banano* (banana), *mucamo* (servant), *conga,* and *samba.*

In Mexico, the Aztecs possessed a phonetic hieroglyphic writing system to represent Nahuatl. In Mesoamerica, Maya-Quiché was the main language, with approximately thirty dialects and a complex hieroglyphic writing system. The contributions of Nahuatl and Maya-Quiché to Spanish are mainly nouns such as *aguacate* (avocado), *tuna* (prickly pear), and *chocolate.*

Quechua, the official language of the Inca Empire, was spoken in southern Colombia, Ecuador, Peru, and northwest Argentina. Aymara was spoken in Bolivia and parts of Peru. Terms that entered the Spanish system from those languages include *papa* (potato), *palta* (avocado), *guagua* (infant), and *choclo* (corn).

The Araucan people occupied the continent's Southern Cone, and their language became the *lingua franca* there. The Tupi-Guaraní language family extended from the Andes to the Atlantic Ocean and from Guyana to the Río de la Plata. Guaraní was principally spoken in present-day Paraguay, where, with Spanish, it is still an official language. In their roles as wives, domestic servants, and nursemaids to Spanish settlers and their children, indigenous women provided another channel for the diffusion of Native American terms into Spanish. During most of the colonial period, men outnumbered women among European settlers, especially in areas that required prolonged military action. Ethnically mixed unions ensued in which an indigenous woman with an incomplete command of Spanish became the primary caregiver and linguistic role model for Spanish and mestizo children. This did not happen in the Antilles, Argentina, Uruguay, Chile, and Central America where the natives were driven away, leaving few linguistic remains. In the Amazonian Basin, linguistic assimilation of the indigenous population is still in process.

Although lexical items generally entered Spanish more easily than phonetic or syntactic ones, indigenous phonetic and syntactic elements did affect Spanish in areas of long-term sociolinguistic contact. The borrowing of phonetic traits from native languages is perceived in the Spanish varieties in contact with Quechua and Guaraní. For example, Andean Spanish tends toward raising the mid-front and back vowels, and Paraguayan Spanish exhibits glottal stops between words.

Despite the Amerindian substratum differences as well as the diversity of peninsular dialects prevalent in Spain in the early colonial period, American Spanish was relatively homogeneous, as early documents reveal.

Seville was the staging area where speakers from diverse regions of Spain came into contact for the first time. This created ideal conditions for language leveling. Castilians and Andalusians provided the main foundations of American Spanish; in fact, the similarities between sixteenth- and seventeenth-century Andalusian and Castilian included nearly all aspects of the language. As a result, although speakers of other dialects had to shed their regional accents, few Andalusians or Castilians had to alter their speech patterns in order to communicate with each other. This shows that dialect leveling was in progress early and was hastened by emigration.

Peninsular and American Spanish underwent parallel developments, with some exceptions. For example, in 1492 the Spanish language contained three pairs of sibilants, voiced and voiceless as illustrated here (the parallel brackets represent the pronunciation, and the round brackets represent the spelling):

	Voiceless	*Voiced*
1	/s/ (ss) as in English *face*	/z/ (s) as in English *phase*
2	/t^s/ (c) as in pizza	/d^z/ (z) a voiced realization
3	/§/ (x) as in English *show*	/ʒ/ (g, j) as in French *jour*

/s/ and /z/ were apico-alveolar, similar to the pronunciation of contemporary Castilian /s/. The merger of the alveolar fricatives and affricates (groups 1 and 2), which were the precursors of *seseo,* began in Andalusia by the end of the fifteenth century. In America and in western Andalusia, all the sibilants merged to form /s/. In the rest of Spain, /t^s/ and /d^z/ became the interdental fricative /θ/ as in English *think.* This innovation did not take root in Latin American Spanish.

At the end of the fifteenth century, *vos* and *tú* were the formal and familiar pronouns, with *vos* also used frequently as a plural. *Vos* later disappeared from the dialects of Spain but was retained in much of Spanish America, particularly in Venezuela, Argentina, and Uruguay.

Major parallel developments include the pronunciation of the aspirated [h] of word-initial /f/ in words like *farina* (flour), modern Spanish *harina,* which has disappeared from modern Latin American Spanish and Castilian. In 1492, /b/ and /v/ were separate phonemes in Spain, but later both phonemes merged into one: /b/. The formal pronouns *usted* and *ustedes,* which developed from *vuestra merced* and *vuestras mercedes,* appeared in the seventeenth century.

Generally, Latin American Spanish remained sensitive to linguistic developments in Spain up to the end of the seventeenth century, and many regions continued to absorb the linguistic innovations of the peninsula. In terms of culture, in the sixteenth and seventeenth centuries, Spain was heavily influenced by two main currents, the Italian Renaissance and Erasmian Humanism, which also spread to America. However, after the abdication of Charles V (1556), Phillip II, a champion of Catholic orthodoxy, inaugurated an era of absolutism and intolerance. The works of Erasmus were burned, Spaniards were forbidden to study or to teach abroad, and intellectual leadership was left to other countries. Despite the repression imposed by Spain's sixteenth- and seventeenth-century rulers, there was an explosion of literary masterpieces by authors like Lope de Vega, Cervantes, and Góngora. In contrast, fields such as politics, economics, and philosophy did not achieve comparable linguistic eminence.

Although Spanish lacked a rich lexical database in these areas at this particular time, intellectuals have entertained the ideals of language purity and standardization since the 1492 publication of Nebrija's *Gramática.* This is exemplified by Correas's *Arte grande de la lengua española castellana* (1626), a grammar book for Spanish speakers. Later, the Royal Academy of the Spanish Language was founded in 1713 to guard and preserve the language.

Despite the Academy's vigilance, French influence increased during the eighteenth and nineteenth centuries; Purists saw this trend as a threat. The Venezuelan philologist Rafael María Barlat attempted to combat the trend by publishing a *Diccionario de galicismos* (1855). However, the free trade policies of the time encouraged an uninhibited exchange of ideas, and some Americans, considering linguistic purism to be a limitation on the intellect, even suggested building an "American language" free from the Academy's approval.

In his *Gramática de la lengua castellana,* Nebrija argued that Spanish must be written the way it is pronounced and pronounced the way it is written. His goal was to standardize Spanish spelling in such a way as to establish a balance between phonology and orthography, while respecting the classical origins of words and avoiding revolutionary change. Nebrija published his *Ortografía* in 1517; numerous others came out in the sixteenth and seventeenth centuries, a time when Spanish experienced its major phonetic revolution. The desire to remove superfluous letters such as silent *h* and to use a single grapheme for each sound is seen in Correas's *Ortografía* (1630).

In 1823, while Spanish America was in the midst of its Wars of Independence, Andrés Bello and Juan García del Río announced the need for new orthographic reforms. Contending that there must be a one-to-one correspondence between pronunciation and spelling, they ultimately introduced three changes: *j* for aspirated *g; i* for *y;* and *z* for *c* before *e* and *i.*

In 1843, Domingo Faustino Sarmiento also proposed orthographic changes, which he presented to the University of Chile's Faculty of Humanities; however, Sarmiento's suggestions were rejected because his radical innovations would alienate Chileans not only from the literature of the past, but also from future writers in Spain and America who would continue to use the system prescribed by the Royal Academy.

At the turn of the century, a group of Chilean scientists also attempted to purify

Domingo Sarmiento, an influential essayist, educator, and polemicist, served as president of Argentina from 1868 to 1874. (Library of Congress)

the spelling system by launching their *ortografía rrazional,* an aseptic version of what the Royal Academy prescribed. By 1900, the ortografía rrazional was being used by several scientists and nonscientists in Chile.

A countercurrent existed at the same time, which instead of standardization, espoused individual rights. This current became so strong that in 1911 Chile's Council of Public Education advised Spanish-language examining committees to accept whatever orthographic system their individual institutions had adopted. In view of the orthographic anarchy that resulted, upon assuming the presidency in 1927 Carlos Ibáñez decreed adherence to the prescribed orthographic system of Spain's Royal Academy. Thus, the ortografía rrazional and every other system fell into disuse.

During the nineteenth and twentieth centuries, use of Spanish had increased throughout the Americas. Factors such as the vast European migration to Spanish America, the role of the Church in the establishment of academic institutions for Spanish-speaking communities, upward social mobility owing to new industry and technology, and the migration of people from rural to urban centers, all contributed to a widespread use of Spanish.

Wars and social movements also played a part in diffusing Spanish. For example, in 1913, the Mexican revolutionary Pancho Villa assembled an army of 4,000 soldiers in less than two months and within a year was in charge of 300,000 people of different indigenous backgrounds. Of necessity, the lingua franca was Spanish.

The future of Spanish as a unified language or as a multitude of varieties was a topic of great discussion in the twentieth century. Many scholars envisioned a fragmented Spanish comparable with the fragmentation of Latin into the various Romance languages. However, from the perspective of the twenty-first century, this outcome seems unlikely owing to two main factors. First, the pressures to diverge, which divided the Romance languages, are not likely to recur in the future. From the Roman period to the twelfth century, communication between the various Romance-speaking regions was weak. As a result, local changes remained local, leading to increasing diversification of speech. From the twelfth century, different forms of Romance were associated with different medieval states and could be promoted as national languages in those states. At present there is no evidence pointing to the adoption of separate spelling and grammatical codes in different countries. Nor is there evidence to promote any local variety as a national language distinct from those used in other parts of Spanish America or Spain.

Second, pressures toward convergence are greater than before. Collaboration between the academies, which have a presence in practically all Spanish-speaking countries, including the United States, ensures linguistic uniformity, especially in official publications and the media. Similarly, migration, tourism, and high-tech communication afford speakers of different varieties of Spanish unprecedented personal contact, which promotes similarity of linguistic usage. Although regional variation is noteworthy, especially in the lexis, Spanish speakers are able to communicate easily.

Today Spanish is an international language; it occupies third place in terms of number of speakers, after English and Chinese. A crucial factor in spreading and maintaining language presence is that, with the exception of Spain, Equatorial Guinea, and the Philippines (spoken as a second language), most of the main Spanish-speaking nations border other Spanish-speaking nations.

In the legal, political, and economic domains, Spanish is recognized as the official language in twenty-one countries and is one of the official languages in international organizations such as the United Nations and the European Union. However, in terms of economic power, its rank varies because many of the Spanish American nations are still relatively poor and underdeveloped; the most significant economies are those of Spain as well as Chile, Mexico, and some of the Southern Common Market (Mercosur) countries. The economic power of Spanish speakers significantly increases when one includes Spanish speakers in the United States.

In science and technology, however, there is a trend for Spanish speakers from Spain and Spanish America to publish and communicate mainly in English in order to reach a wider audience. It is also in these domains that a vast number of Anglicisms have entered the Spanish language. In education and culture, Spanish is the language of instruction where it is also an official language. It is also widely taught as a foreign language in the United States, Japan, Australia, and Europe. Spanish literary distribution outside Spain and Spanish America has increased notably, as has the translation of popular English literary titles, television programs, and movies (especially from the United States) into Spanish. However, an often inadequate translation of these has introduced a myriad of Anglicisms in Spanish. Tourism, Spanish American pop culture, and emerging Hispanic artists in the United States, as well as the vast number of Hispanics living in the United States, have helped raise awareness of Spanish, thus encouraging nonnatives to learn it as a second language.

According to the U.S. Bureau of Census 2000, the number of "Latinos" in the United States is estimated at approximately 35 million. However, Spanish is not the mother tongue of all of them, and intergenerational transmission of Spanish has been weak. The Spanish spoken in the United States is heavily influenced by English and is the subject of much controversy with language purists. To some, this new form of speaking is *Spanglish,* that is, half Spanish and half English, but to others it is simply a natural evolution of any other Spanish-speaking community outside Spain and Spanish America over time. The Spanish variety spoken by Hispanics in the United States is stigmatized as rural or inadequate, demonstrating its speakers' undereducated origins or their linguistic incompetence in learning either Spanish or English. On the other hand, others seek to validate the appropriateness of U.S. Spanish as a genuine form of language living and developing in U.S. Spanish-speaking communities.

Rosario Gómez

References

Canfield, Lincoln. *Spanish Pronunciation in the Americas.* Chicago: University of Chicago Press, 1981.

Glickman, Robert J. *Fin del Siglo: Retrato de Hispanoamérica en la época modernista.* Toronto: Canadian Academy of the Arts, 1999.

Instituto Cervantes. *El español en el mundo; anuario 2000.* Centro Virtual Cervantes. http://cvc.cervantes.es/obref/anuario.

Lipski, John, M. *Spanish American Spanish.* London: Longman, 1994.

Lodares, Juan Ramón. *Gente de Cervantes: Historia humana del idioma español.* Buenos Aires: Taurus Pensamiento, 2001.

Makenzie, Ian. *A Linguistic Introduction to Spanish.* Munich: Lincom Europa, 2001.

Mar-Molinero, Claire. *The Politics of Language in the Spanish-Speaking World: From Colonization to Globalization.* London: Routledge, 2000.

———. "Spanish as a World Language." *Spanish in Context* 1, no.1 (2004): 3–18.

Penny, Ralph. *A History of the Spanish Language.* 2nd ed. Cambridge: Cambridge University Press, 2002.

Pountain, Christopher. *A History of the Spanish Language through Texts.* London: Routledge, 2001.

See also: Conquest I–VII; Conquistadors; Culture; Education—Brazil; Education—Colonial Spanish America; Independence I–VI; Ladino; Mestizaje; Mexican Revolution; Migration—From Iberia to the New World; Moors; Native Americans I–VIII; Requerimiento; Slavery I–IV; Syncretism; Travel and Tourism; Universities; Women—Brazil; Women—Colonial Spanish America; Women—Modern Spanish America.

LAWS—COLONIAL LATIN AMERICA

A complex set of laws, customs, and doctrines, commonly referred to as *derecho indiano,* governed Hispanic America and the Philippines from the late fifteenth century until the promulgation of the Latin American codes in the second half of the nineteenth century. These laws were also applied to some regions of North America that today form part of the United States.

Shortly after Columbus returned from his first voyage to the New World, the Catholic monarchs requested that Pope Alexander VI issue a papal concession of the new lands, as according to medieval custom, the pope had universal secular control over territories inhabited by pagans. Furthermore, Isabel and Ferdinand were anxious to limit Portuguese claims to the western zone of the Atlantic. The pope acceded, and on May 3, 1493, Alexander VI promulgated the first *Inter Caetera* Bull that granted the Catholic kings jurisdiction over all islands and *tierra firme* to the west not governed by Christian rulers. On the same day, Alexander VI issued the *Eximiae devotionis* Bull, which gave the Spanish monarchs the same privileges that had been granted to the Portuguese in Guinea and East Indies in the papal bulls of 1452, 1454, 1481, and 1484.

On May 4, 1493, Alexander VI issued a second *Inter Caetera* Bull that more explicitly granted (in perpetuity) to the Catholic kings and their successors control over lands situated west of an imaginary line, located one hundred leagues from the Azores Islands and Green Cape. In return, the Spanish monarchs were to provide for the Christianization of the inhabitants of those territories. However, the bulls were not considered enough to justify Spanish sovereignty over the Indies. Consequently, on June 7, 1494, following careful negotiations between Castile and Portugal, the Treaty of Tordesillas was signed. Under the terms of the treaty, the line previously set by Alexander VI was modified, and a new line was drawn from pole to pole 370 leagues to the west of the Green Cape Islands. The agreement effectively divided the world between Spain and Portugal; the Portuguese considered that their interests in Africa would be protected, and the Spanish Crown considered that the treaty would protect their new discoveries in the Caribbean.

Because the lands Columbus had discovered were granted to the Crown of Castile, the Indies were considered Spanish territory, and therefore its native inhabitants should have been considered legal Spanish vassals, with all the rights accorded to Spaniards. However, colonial realities required a transformation in Spanish law; as a result, a new juridical system arose, known as the *derecho indiano.* This system consisted first of the laws that were especially prescribed for the Indies, whether they originated in Spain or in the Americas, by authorities who were conferred the right to legislate. The derecho indiano referred basically to laws associated with public matters and legal issues that had arisen since the New World was discovered. For example, jurists discussed the legal status of the Indians, the legitimacy of the conquest, and the economic, legal, and political organization in Spain's new colonies. Indian customs were to be respected, provided that they did not challenge colonial rule or offend the Catholic faith.

The historical development of the derecho indiano occurred in four phases. In phase one (1492–1511), we find the first traces of the derecho indiano in the Capitulaciones de Santa Fe, signed by the Catholic Kings and Columbus on April 17, 1492. Very few laws were issued at the beginning of Spanish colonial rule, and therefore Castilian law took precedent in all cases. The second phase (1511–1566) was critical. It was during this phase that jurists debated the nature of Spanish rule and the right of the Crown to exploit the new lands and its inhabitants. In 1511, the Dominican friar Antonio de Montesinos denounced the abuses of the colonizers. His words raised great commotion and opened a debate that deeply touched theologians and jurists in Spain. In 1512 a junta was gathered, and it issued the Laws of Burgos, which declared the natives to be free human beings who deserved humane treatment, although they could be ruled by Spaniards once they converted to Christianity. Juan López de Palacios Rubios, one of the most notable jurists of the court, drafted the *requerimiento,* or requirement, a document that had to be read to the native peoples before engaging them in war. The curious document explained that Jesus had named the pope as God's representative on earth and had granted the Indies to the Spanish kings, and therefore they had to accept his power. If they did not do so, the document warned, they would be responsible for what followed.

Still, many Spaniards continued to challenge Spain's legal right to colonize the New World and exploit the native populations. As a consequence of the tireless campaign of the famous Dominican bishop Bartolomé de las Casas, Charles V called a meeting of jurists to resolve the controversy. As a result, the New Laws were promulgated on November 20, 1542. Through these laws, the administrative organization of the colonies was structured, freedom was granted to the Indians, and their rights were recognized. Furthermore, the New Laws called for the abolishment of the *encomienda* system. The laws caused great commotion in Spain's colonies; in Peru the Spanish population rebelled and Peru's first viceroy, Blasco Nuñez Vela, was executed. Charles V was obliged to repeal the laws, and the encomienda system continued, in some areas until the end of the colonial period. During this important second phase, a large corpus of laws was issued from the Council of the Indies. It is also important to note that many new laws were created in America itself, laws that later became the origin of a Creole Indian law.

In the third phase (1566–1680), the derecho indiano grew and increasingly distanced itself from Castilian law. Finally, the fourth phase (eighteenth and nineteenth centuries) began with the accession of the Bourbon dynasty in Spain and continued through the independence movements of the nineteenth century. The Bourbon monarchs initiated important changes in Indian political organization.

Over time, the burgeoning corpus of new laws forced the Spanish monarchs to consider the possibility of gathering them together to faciliate consultation and application. This project was carried out in America and in Spain over the course of more than a century, beginning in 1560. It was then that King Philip II ordered the viceroy of Peru to gather all the laws issued for that province. At the same time, the Council of the Indies began an analogous project, headed by Juan de Ovando. Many jurists worked to gather the laws in the so-called *cedularios* and *sumarios,* in which laws were placed thematically and chronologically, with the indication of the date of their original publication. This monumental task was carried out successively by various jurists. But it was the *Licenciado* Fernando Jiménez Paniagua who finalized it, building on the work of his predecessors. The result was the *Compilation of the Laws of Indies,* which was promulgated in 1680 by King Charles III. The work is divided into nine books, which deal mainly with religious matters, the Council of the Indies, audiencias, courts, legislation, viceroys, general captaincies, discoveries, mines, magistrates, lawsuits, crime and punishment, and taxes. After release of the *Compilation of the Laws of Indies,* many jurists wrote comments on it, such as that of Juan del Corral Calvo de la Torre in 1737. As the kings continued to promulgate new laws, it was soon necessary to update the *Compilation of the Laws of Indies,* which was decided by a royal decree dated May 9, 1776. The *fiscal* (public prosecutor) of the Council of Indies Juan Crisóstomo de Ansotegui was appointed, but he only managed to complete the first book, and finally the Crown abandoned its intention to update the *Compilation of the Laws of Indies.*

The principles and techniques that inspired the derecho indiano did not differ much from those of the Castilian laws. This was understandable because the laws and the doctrine came from jurists whose ideas had been formed under a common school: Humanism. The only differences were based on the peculiar conditions of the Indies, which made adjustment to local conditions necessary. Still, when there was no specific local custom or tradition, Castilian law had to be applied, which explains the importance of Castilian laws in the Indies, especially in criminal, civil, and procedural matters where Indian regulations were few.

In the case of Portuguese colonial law, local norms prevailed until the middle of the eighteenth century, in part because of the great autonomy granted to the conquerors. This law was formed by customs, *capitulaciones* and *cartas de donación,* and norms disclosed by the municipal chambers, but the influence of the Amerindian and African customs was negligible. Unlike the derecho indiano, which was compiled in the *Compilation of the Laws of Indies,* Brazilian colonial law was not.

The significance of the derecho indiano lies in the fact that although independence movements replaced Spanish rule all over Latin America, the norms, methods, customs, and doctrine applied during the colonial period did not disappear; in fact, they survived well into the late nineteenth century.

Viviana Kluger

References

Benton, Lauren. *Law and Colonial Cultures: Legal Regimes in World History, 1400–1900.* Cambridge: Cambridge University Press, November 2001.

Cruz Barney, Óscar. *Historia del Derecho en México.* Mexico: Oxford University Press, 1999.

Cutter, Charles. *The Legal Culture of Northern New Spain, 1700–1810.* Albuquerque: University of New Mexico Press, 1996.

Herzog, Tamar. *Upholding Justice: State, Law and the Penal System in Quito.* Ann Arbor: University of Michigan Press. (forthcoming).

Mirow, Matthew. *Latin American Law: A History of Private Law and Institutions in Spanish America.* Austin: University of Texas Press, 2004.

Tau Anzoátegui, Víctor. *Casuismo y Sistema: Indagación histórica sobre el espíritu del Derecho Indiano.* Buenos Aires: Instituto de Investigaciones de Historia del Derecho Indiano, 1992.

———. *Nuevos horizontes en el estudio histórico del Derecho indiano.* Buenos Aires: Instituto de Investigaciones de Historia del Derecho Indiano, 1997.

See also: Administration—Colonial Spanish America; Capitulations of Santa Fe; Catholic Church in Spanish America; Conquest and the Debate over Justice; Corregidor/Corregimiento; Council of Castile; Council of the Indies; Defensor de Indios; Encomienda; Laws of Burgos; Native Americans I–VIII; New Laws of 1542; Papacy; Religious Orders; Requerimiento; Tordesillas, Treaty of.

LAWS OF BURGOS

The Laws of Burgos were decrees issued by King Ferdinand of Spain in 1512–1513 to regulate relations between Spaniards and the indigenous inhabitants of Hispaniola. The king was reacting to reports, especially by Dominican friars such as Antonio de Montesinos, regarding abuse of the islanders by the Spanish.

The Crown convened a group representing widely varying views on the Indians to discuss the issues. Montesinos himself voiced the humanitarian side of the dispute, whereas Alonso del Espinal represented the colonists, many of whom held *encomiendas*—the right to receive tribute in kind and labor from the indigenous population. Montesinos argued that unbridled tribute extraction was inhumanely depopulating the Caribbean. The *encomenderos* (those who held encomiendas) contended that their livelihoods and Spain's economic interests in the islands depended on indigenous labor. Other participants maintained that the islanders were what Aristotle had called "slaves by nature," too primitive to live freely as Spanish subjects: prone to laziness they needed tutelage and had to be forced to work.

The Laws of Burgos approved by Ferdinand on December 27, 1512, were a compromise, the product of more than twenty meetings held by the committee. On one hand, the laws recognized the importance of indigenous labor and approved the encomiendas as a means of mobilizing it. Spaniards could require a third of the islanders to mine for gold. On the other hand, the decrees required Spaniards to construct housing for the workers, provide religious instruction, and furnish them with adequate food and clothing. Encomenderos and clergy were to educate the children of chieftains in the hope of Hispanicizing the islands' inhabitants. Indeed, the Crown envisioned a time when tutelage and coercion would no longer be required. Encomenderos could not force pregnant women to mine for gold, and they were restricted in the physical punishment they could use to coerce workers. Each community was to provide two inspectors to ensure that the laws were enforced.

In early 1513, the Dominican provincial arrived from Hispaniola and insisted on several changes to the laws. These included provisions that the islanders be required to wear clothes; that children be permitted to learn trades and crafts, if they so desired; and that to prevent idleness the Indians be forced to work three-fourths of the year for the Spanish. The amendments became known as the Clarification of the Laws of Burgos and were promulgated on July 28, 1513.

The Laws of Burgos represented the first formal attempt by the Spanish Crown to regulate indigenous/Spanish relations in the New World. They reflected the tension between the Crown's humanitarian concern for its new subjects in the Caribbean and its ambitions to turn the colonies into economically profitable ventures for itself and the settlers who migrated there.

Kendall Brown

References

Hanke, Lewis. *The Spanish Struggle for Justice in the Conquest of America.* Boston: Little, Brown, 1965.

The Laws of Burgos of 1512–1513: Royal Ordinances for the Good Government and Treatment of the Indians. Translated and edited by Lesley Byrd Simpson. San Francisco: J. Howell, 1960.

See also: Administration—Colonial Spanish America; Catholic Church in Spanish America; Colonists and Settlers III—Caribbean; Conquest and the Debate over Justice; Conquest III—Caribbean; Encomienda; Laws—Colonial Latin America; Native Americans I–VIII; New Laws of 1542; Religious Orders; Requerimiento.

LIBERALISM

Liberalism was one of the two main nineteenth-century political thoughts and movements in Latin America. It reached a dominant position in the latter half of the century, a time some have called the "liberal reform period," following earlier periods of conservative dominance. The transition was facilitated as the continent became more economically internationalized. Liberalism underscored accountable government, the private sector, and the rule of law. It focused on economic modernization, initially through agriculture, export promotion, the minimization of religious influence, and the protection of individual rights.

In practice, the other political movement, conservatism, which opposed the antilocal, antidomestic, anticommercial, elite, pro-urban bias of liberalism, actually adopted many of the same liberal practices, even though it theoretically emphasized order, tradition, and religious inspiration. By the same token, there were repressive, liberal dictatorships, a seeming oxymoron since liberalism was supposed to protect individual rights.

Liberalism dominated the nineteen postcolonial states of Latin America in the nineteenth century. Adherents believed in the rule of law for all and the separation of government powers. The combination was to prevent the undue concentration of authority in and over the government while stimulating economic development. Different country conditions and elite compromises to obtain power or achieve political stability rendered liberal practices different from the theories they espoused. As merchants were favored under liberalism, some states like Peru established illiberal, economic protectionism. Some states soon failed in their liberal projects; Haiti, the first independent Latin American state and the first one in the world with universal equality, established an autocratic monarchy that soon disintegrated into civil war, autocracy, and political instability. Postcolonial Paraguay was illiberal in every respect except in its diminution of Church power.

Liberalism was an imported idea, though not primarily from Spain; furthermore, liberalism transmuted into different forms throughout the Americas. As the leading philosophy of the postcolonial regimes, its proponents were as much inspired by the liberal ideals of the U.S. and French revolutions and against Spanish corporatist ideals. Despite the similar colonial institutions and liberal tenets, different choices and timing characterized the adaptations. Argentina began liberalism at the earliest stages of independence and undertook some of the most radical reversals after the end of liberalism in the twentieth century. Paraguay delayed its liberal project until after it was conquered. Anticlericalism was much stronger in Paraguay than in Argentina.

Liberals in Latin America behaved differently depending on the relative strengths of the bourgeoisie, peasantry, and landed aristocracy. Unlike Europe, which was under rapid industrialization, Latin America rarely produced a strong enough business class to negotiate democratization reforms over time under conditions of relatively equal bargaining power. In depicting liberalism in Central America, James Mahoney concluded that Guatemala and El Salvador represented "radical liberalism" (attacked communal landholding, encouraged capitalism, and ended protectionism), somewhat similar to the Fascist forms in Europe that imposed labor-repressing policies in the countryside. By contrast, Costa Rica's "reformist liberalism" (more moderate changes with protection for medium-sized farms) resulted from commercialized, small coffee farms displacing large landowners from repressive policies, while labor was sufficiently strong to negotiate political rights as well. Honduras's and Nicaragua's "aborted liberalism" (the postcolonial state and large landowners survived intact) resulted from the lack of political development, reflecting the incomplete economic transformation of either the commercial or agricultural sectors. The strong role of the military in Guatemala and El Salvador resulted from the prior radical liberal project, whereas the democracy that has prevailed in Costa Rica benefited from the moderate liberal reforms that were undertaken.

In assessing liberalism, recent scholarly efforts have underscored the liberal bias of the historians themselves. In these recent critical appraisals, contemporary historians have reached less benign assessments. Some scholars maintain that the Western roots of liberalism made the approach dominant, yet inappropriate for Latin America. Caudillos, or strongmen, were the dominant elites in Latin America, as opposed to the bourgeoisie in Western Europe, which negotiated with the aristocracy for shared power. Without a local industrial class, Latin American merchants lacked the bargaining power of their European counterparts. Instead, some Latin American caudillos often represented most liberal interests without the typical liberal social base and interests. Liberal movements with more diverse, broad leadership and support, which were more industrialized, were more likely to realize liberal regimes.

The most well-known liberal reformers, such as Benito Juárez of Mexico, José María Samper of Colombia, and Domingo F. Sarmiento of Argentina, sought to promote freedom by opposing the interests of the Church, landed oligarchy, and the army. The last two provided memoirs advocating liberal ideas and praising their overthrow of the Rosas dictatorship to promote liberal reforms. The most authentic liberal regimes, which enjoyed such a heterogeneous base, included federalist Venezuela and Chile through the middle of the nineteenth century, Peru under Ramón Castilla, and Colombia under Francisco de Paula Santander.

Clearly, the postcolonial state was formed by liberal principles while continuing many illiberal colonial practices. The illiberal elites came to power during independence wars, often with the military remaining empowered; this meant that the postcolonial state was quite illiberal from the beginning and arguably never attempted a liberal project. This is in stark contrast to the United States, where George Washington went into retirement and the new state demobilized its military. Latin America, like Europe, did not enjoy the stopping power of water and had to maintain much larger standing armies, which were also powerful politically. Subsequently, frequent civil wars, involving national and elite rivalries, rendered many states less liberal.

Furthermore, liberalism has been seen as an elite-driven and self-serving ideology that failed to educate enough citizens to exploit the espoused advantages of capitalism. Instead of free trade, some sectors were protected whereas others subsidized foreign business partners, both practices violating liberal principles. Still, there were many examples where the economy was opened by reducing tariffs, such as the foreign investment in railroads, the telegraph, and electricity in Argentina. Ultimately, this led to a backlash, with patriotic appeals leading to protectionism in the twentieth century and alliances by the nationalist capital and labor forces, as prior liberal reformers like Sarmiento and Mitre became vilified.

Continuing social exclusion by whites or white-dominant mestizos prevented large-scale participation in economic and political life among the majority of the population, which were often of indigenous or mixed race. In Guatemala, the Indian majority was excluded from political participation by the conservative and then by the first liberal government of Rufino Barrios from 1870 to 1885. Alternatively, genocide was perpetrated in the Southern Cone. Instead of supporting Iberian colonialism, the poor masses were forced to obey the postcolonial elites empowered during colonialism.

Henry F. Carey

References

Clergern, Wayne M. *Origins of Liberal Dictatorship in Central America: Guatemala, 1965–1973.* Niwot: University Press of Colorado, 1994.

Gudmundson, Lowell, and Héctor Lindo-Fuentes. *Central America, 1821–1871.* Tuscaloosa: University of Alabama Press, 1995.

Halperín Donghí, Tulio. *Historia Contemporánea de América.* Madrid: Alianza Editorial, 1975.

Mahoney, James. *The Legacies of Liberalism: Path Dependence and Political Regimes in Central America.* Baltimore, MD: Johns Hopkins University Press, 2001.

Peloso, Vincent C., and Barbara A. Tenenbaum, eds. *Liberals, Politics and Power: State Formation in Nineteenth-Century Latin America.* Athens: University of Georgia Press, 1996.

Rippy, J. Fred. *Latin America in the Industrial Age.* New York: G. P. Putnam's Sons, 1944.

See also: American Revolution; Argentina; Caudillos; Coffee; Colombia; Communism; Costa Rica; Fin de Siècle; Guatemala; Guerrillas; Independence I–VI; Mestizaje; Nationalism; Peru; Populism; Race; Terrorism.

LIBERATION THEOLOGY

Liberation Theology is generally associated with the Latin American Roman Catholic Church and describes a process of modernization and change in Church emphasis and priorities beginning in the 1960s. Liberation theologians identified with the poor, the rural, and the suffering in Latin America and the world. They connected politics with economics in order to more fully understand theology and God's divine plan for humanity. The term *Liberation Theology* was used for the first time at a July 1968 conference of Peruvian Roman Catholic priests meeting at Chimbote, a coastal Peruvian city 240 miles north of Lima. There, Father Gustavo Gutiérrez delivered a talk titled *Hacía una teología de la liberación.* That conference formed the base of his 1971 major work *Teología de la liberación: Perspectivas,* which was published in Lima and is still considered the foundational text of Liberation Theology.

The theories of Liberation Theology developed as modernization, urbanization, and nationalism forced Latin Americans to confront growing poverty and unresolved social tensions in the region at the conclusion of World War II. Two events, one in the Americas, the other in Europe, were critical to the emergence of a Latin American Theology of Liberation. First, the 1959 Cuban Revolution proved that violent political and social revolutions could succeed in Latin America. This revolution underscored historical fractures in Cuba, societal indifference to the plight of the poor, and structures of authority that prevented modernization, fair distribution of resources, or democracy. The Church came under attack during and after the revolution for supporting and legitimizing this historically imbalanced society. Next, from 1962 to 1965, the Roman Catholic Church leadership met in Rome to "renovate" the Church in light of modern challenges. The meeting, popularly referred to as Vatican II, resulted in significant changes for the Church. For example, cardinals and bishops authorized more equal distribution of power to the laity of the Church, they agreed that the Catholic mass would be recited in the vernacular rather than Latin, and they began working more forcefully in the "here and now" rather than speculating excessively on the afterlife.

The reforms enacted at Vatican II fell short of the expectations of Latin American

Church leaders. Since European cardinals and bishops controlled the major committees and authored the primary texts at Vatican II, many Latin American cardinals and bishops felt that the challenges of Latin American society had not been integrated by the Church hierarchy at the Second Vatican Council. Such challenges were reinforced when Father Camilo Torres Restrepo of Colombia was killed in February 1966 while fighting against the Colombian army. He had joined the Marxist Army of National Liberation (ELN) some four months earlier.

The Catholic hierarchy in Latin America responded to the unique needs of their region with their own meeting of bishops, a meeting designed to implement social change within the framework of the Church hierarchy. At Medellín, Colombia, about one-third of all Latin American bishops met from August 26 to September 6, 1968; clearly, the bishops derived inspiration from Vatican II, but Latin Americans in the late 1960s faced severe and deepening poverty, growing violence, and revolutionary struggle. The structure and parameters of Liberation Theology emerged at this meeting.

Priests and bishops at Medellín spoke of sociology, history, and economics; they were not afraid to apply Marxist social analysis as a "tool" to help identify societal problems. Consciousness raising, the CBC (Christian Base Community), and a new interpretation of sin as "structural" were some of the innovative ideas and reforms that emerged from Medellín. Priests were encouraged to leave the comfort of urban parishes and move to the countryside; they were challenged to meet and work directly with the poor. Priests, nuns, and laity worked together to raise the people's consciousness in the hope that Latin America's poor would become agents of their own liberation from material poverty and deprivation. The CBC, or small, local groups working to solve specific social or economic problems, became the structure through which Liberation Theology spread. Rather than wait for indifferent governments and politicians to build roads and dig wells, communities took action on their own, with support from the local parish. Liberation Theology encouraged people to reflect on specific passages from the Old Testament, such as the story of Exodus, where Jews organized and fought their way out of slavery in Egypt. For Liberation Theologians, the definition of sin expanded beyond the traditional boundaries of the Ten Commandments. After Medellín, sin became associated with social and economic structures that kept the vast majority of citizens in Latin America poor while a small percentage enjoyed unprecedented material prosperity. Landholding patterns at the second half of the twentieth century, such as the Colombian case where about 2 percent of the population controlled 75 to 80 percent of all arable land, were characterized by Liberation Theologians, simply, as sinful.

The year 1979 was critical for Liberation Theology as two proponents of the movement helped lead the Sandinista Revolution in Nicaragua. Father Miguel D'Escoto was named foreign minister of Nicaragua, and Father Ernesto Cardenál became minister of culture. Pope John Paul II, elected to the papacy a year earlier, was skeptical of Marxist analysis, disapproved of priests' involvement in politics, and believed that Scripture and tradition were the only appropriate sources of theology. In January 1979, at the Third General Conference of the Latin American Episcopate (at Puebla, Mexico), John Paul II warned that "the concept of Christ as a politician, a revolutionary, a subversive from Nazareth does not fit with the Church's catechesis" (Puebla Documents, p. 10, author's translation from Spanish).

The Puebla Meeting encoded the concept of the Latin American Church's "preferential option for the poor" based on Jesus' tireless work with the poor during his public ministry. But it is clear that Liberation Theology has been on the defensive since the early 1980s. One of the most public and serious challenges to Liberation Theology came in 1985 when the Brazilian theologian and theoretician Leonardo Boff was "silenced" for ten months by Cardinal Joseph Ratzinger, at that time the Vatican's prefect of the Congregation for the Doctrine of the Faith. Ratzinger was elected Pope in April 2005 and took the name Benedict XVI. Pope John Paul II (1978–2005), through his consistent appointment of moderate to conservative men as bishops, archbishops, and cardinals, significantly diminished Liberation Theology discourse and action in Latin America and the world.

Michael LaRosa

References

Berryman, Phillip. *Liberation Theology: The Essential Facts about the Revolutionary Movement in Latin America and Beyond.* Philadelphia: Temple University Press, 1987.

Boff, Clodovis, and Leonardo Boff. *Introducing Liberation Theology.* New York: Orbis, 1987.

Gutiérrez, Gustavo. *A Theology of Liberation.* New York: Orbis, 1973.

United States Catholic Conference. *Medellín Conclusions.* New York: Second General Conference of Latin American Bishops, 1973.

See also: Catholic Church in Brazil; Catholic Church in Spanish America; Colombia; Communism; Cuban Revolution; Guerrillas; Nationalism; Nicaragua; Opus Dei; Papacy; Populism; Religious Orders; World War II.

LITERARY RELATIONS—PORTUGAL AND THE AMERICAS

Understanding literary relations between Brazil and Portugal requires an awareness of the fundamental realities of literary activity in both the metropolis (Portugal) and its colony (Brazil). During the colonial period, Portugal did not deviate from the European norm, which tended to ignore or denigrate American artistic and intellectual expression.

For some 300 years after Pedro Álvarez Cabral's discovery of Brazil, Brazil was a colony of Portugal, subject to all the imposed and generally accepted assumptions of relative cultural inferiority attendant to metropolis/colony relations. For another eighty-one years, from 1808 to 1889, the Empire of Brazil was increasingly independent of Portuguese cultural hegemony, turning instead to English and French models. From the first proclamation of the Brazilian Republic in 1889 to the present day, Portuguese/Brazilian literary relations have been characterized by the fact that the impact of Portuguese models on Brazilian literature has increasingly been an issue of greater significance to the Portuguese than to the Brazilians.

This can be attributed to at least two important factors. First, the Portuguese—as do their Spanish, French, and English counterparts—remain jealous and protective of their mother tongue, not only in its transitory spoken form but especially in its written manifestation. The Instituto de Lexicologia e Lexicografia da Lingua Portuguesa, a division of the Academia das Ciencias de Portugal, continuously strives to combat deviation from the linguistic norms established in the academic centers and political capital of the motherland. Second, Brazil, with 184 million people as compared to Portugal's 10.5 million, is a much larger and more dynamic society than Portugal. This naturally leads to a greater tendency for spoken language in Brazil to deviate from existing standards. Moreover, Brazilian society, despite herculean efforts at public education, continues to suffer a high rate of illiteracy—13.6 percent in 2004 compared to a rate of 6.7 percent in Portugal. This widespread inability among many of its citizens to comprehend written texts has led Brazilian popular culture to favor film, television, radio, and music over literature.

Yet, it was not always so. Certainly, during the three centuries of colonial rule, educated Brazilians looked to Lisbon and especially to the Portuguese national university at Coimbra to set the norms of literary discourse. The fact that during all this time neither a university nor a printing press was permitted to exist in Brazil meant that almost any Brazilian literary endeavor would necessarily be subject to Iberian standards and be judged primarily in terms of a metropolitan critique. Even as the French Enlightenment began to make its presence felt in the Iberian Peninsula, and Brazilian scions came to matriculate not only at Coimbra, but also at such French academic centers as Montpellier, Brazilians with literary ambitions had to meet the expectations of the educated populace of Lisbon, based on an almost six-centuries-old tradition of Portuguese literature.

The earliest texts in Portuguese were courtly poems of the thirteenth century, based on French models from Provence. These troubadour poems, mainly amorous and satirical, were followed in the fourteenth century by more popular lyrical ballads in narrative form, with themes common to the time: chivalry, heroic battles, religious legends, and grand adventures, many oriented to the sea. Early prose works included chronicles, genealogies, and lives of the saints. Pastoral poetry and drama developed in the sixteenth century. The Renaissance in Portugal saw a flourishing of poetry, history, criticism, and theology that lent the aura of a Golden Age to the late sixteenth century.

Much of the best writing of this era took the form of travel accounts and chronicles of the extraordinary Portuguese achievements in seafaring discovery, primarily in the Far East, but also in the New World. Chief among these is the crown jewel of Portuguese literature, the epic poem *Os Lusiadas,* by Luis Vaz de Camoes (1524–1580), who also wrote exceptional lyric and love poetry.

Portuguese works of the seventeenth century are generally considered inferior to those of the preceding century, owing mainly to an increase in royal absolutism and the influence of the Inquisition, as well as the sixty-year period during which the Portuguese and Spanish Crowns were combined and Portuguese writers of ambition chose to abandon their native tongue for Spanish. Nonetheless, during this time, ecclesiastical sermons, such as those of the Jesuit António Vieira (1608–1697), reached new heights of imaginative power and eloquence.

The founding text of Brazilian literature is the 1500 report by Cabral's lieutenant, Pero Vaz de Caminha (1450–1500), telling Portuguese king Manuel I of the discovery of the land that would come to be known as Brazil. Caminha's letter, effusive in its praise of the lush land, its wealth of natural resources, abundance of water, exotic flora and fauna, fertility, and generally attractive climate, served as the model for many of the early descriptive writings to emanate from the colony.

A priest, José de Anchieta (1534–1597), wrote poetry even as he sought to convert the indigenous peoples and founded the city of São Paulo. During the mid-seventeenth century, the aforementioned António Vieira is sometimes considered the first Brazilian nationalist. His brilliantly persuasive sermons defended the indigenous peoples while excoriating the Dutch invaders of Brazil. By the late seventeenth century, the satirical poet Gregório de Matos Guerra was ably criticizing Brazilian colonial society.

Not until the eighteenth century did self-identified Brazilians begin to contribute to the annals of Portuguese literature. After almost three centuries of colonial rule, echoes of the French Enlightenment, however distant and muted, were heard in Brazil, particularly in the wealthy province of Minas Gerais. Leading Brazilians had long been sending their sons to Portugal to study at Coimbra; many of these young men went on to attend "cultural finishing school" at French universities. By the mid- to late eighteenth century, many such sons of privilege had returned with ideas that undermined the existing social and political order. Leading works of the time include the epic poem *O Uraguai* (1769), by José Basílio da Gama, and *Marília de Dirceu* (1792), a pastoral love poem by Tomás Antonio Gonzaga.

Despite the absence of a printing press in the colony, French ideas challenging the divine right of kings made their way to Brazil. Small but influential coteries of free thinkers who gathered in private "academies" decried and sometimes actively conspired against the authority of the Portuguese monarchy, notably during the *Inconfidencia Mineira* or so-called Tiradentes Conspiracy of 1789. The conspiracy, centered in the wealthy colonial mining region of Minas Gerais, sought to replace Portuguese colonial rule with an independent, republican government. These incipient urges toward Brazilian nationalism were prodded by the Pombaline reforms of the late eighteenth century. These new administrative regulations imposed by Portuguese prime minister the Marquis de Pombal to promote more effective government and more efficient taxation in the colonies eroded the financial and political power of native-born Brazilian elites.

Although the Napoleonic invasion of the Iberian Peninsula in 1807 proved the impetus for much of Spanish America's independence from Spain, it initially had the opposite effect on Portugal. Thanks to timely transportation by their British allies, the entire Portuguese royal family and court escaped to Brazil. Safely ensconced in Rio de Janeiro, Dom Joao VI (King John VI) took pains to develop the intellectual, cultural, and scientific life of his Brazilian colony, which, given the reality of his own royal presence, he declared a kingdom coequal with Portugal.

Braganza family patronage provided Brazilians with their first printing press, national library, university, and many other intellectually and artistically stimulating resources. In 1822, defying the will of the Portuguese legislature, Dom João's son, Dom Pedro I, proclaimed his intention to remain in his New World dominion, thus achieving for Brazil a relatively smooth and bloodless independence from Portugal.

Writers in Brazil, encouraged both by nationalistic impulses and European literary trends, began to express themselves according to the currently popular tenets of romanticism. However, conflicting notions as to what was truly "Brazilian" complicated their efforts.

Linguistically, Brazilian romanticists insisted on employing *tupinismos,* words and phrases of indigenous origin, thus foreign to the Iberian Portuguese language. Simultaneously, a larger question arose: Was it their proper role to describe Brazilian experience in terms of typical national characters, such as Indians, backwoodsmen of the *sertão,* pioneering *bandeirantes,* African slaves, cattlemen, and planters, none of which were to be found in Portugal? Or did this produce an excessively self-conscious, inherently quaint, and thus limited national literature?

Outstanding works of this period include the poetry of Antonio Gonçalves Dias, noted for his romantic adulation of indigenous peoples and cultures, and that of the abolitionist poet Antonio de Castro Alves. Among the earliest novels written by a Brazilian were *O Guarani* (1857) and *Iracema* (1865), both by José de Alencar.

With the end of the six-year War of the Triple Alliance (Paraguayan War), in which Brazil joined with Argentina and Uruguay to oppose a militarily resourceful and surprisingly determined Paraguay, Brazilian literature began to evolve toward a more realistic portrayal of the national experience. Brazil came to be presented not in terms of exoticism, but frankly and directly, as a patriarchal society, in a tropical climate, based on an agricultural economy, founded on African slavery, and racially commingled, both willingly and rapaciously. Exemplars of such realism were *Memórias de um sargento de milicias* (1854–1855) by Manual Antonio de Almeida, *Inocencia* (1872) by Alfredo d'Escragnolle Taunay, and *O Mulato* (1881) by Aluísio de Azevedo. This trend toward realism in Brazilian letters, however, continued to reflect European trends of the time, when the works of Emile Zola set the standard.

In Brazil, the bridge between the old romanticism and the new, realistic literature was Joaquím María Machado de Assis (1839–1908), who ranks in the highest echelon of Brazilian writers. Machado added an element of psychological reflection to his novels, chief among them *Memórias póstumas de Brás Cubas* (1891) and *Dom Casmurro* (1900), which paved the way for a stark new realism of which he himself sometimes disapproved. Even (or especially) when such realism emanated from Portugal, Machado found it not to his taste. For example, he carried on a polemic against the works of the Portuguese realist Eça de Queiróz (1845–1900), a leading light of the Portuguese literary generation known as the Group of Ten.

Machado took issue with Eça de Queiróz's novels *O Primo Basílio,* with its theme of incestuous and cynical adultery, and *O Crimen do Padre Amaro,* recounting the illicit love affair of a young priest. Though they disagreed as to what constituted proper themes and their appropriate portrayal, both men sought to get a better understanding of the relationship between Portuguese and Brazilian literatures, and the work of Eça de Queiróz was widely lauded in Brazil.

The principal work of turn-of-the-century literature was Euclides da Cunha's *Os Sertoes* (1902). Based on actual events, the work described a rebellion in the backlands of northeastern Brazil, where indigenous, African, and Portuguese races mixed to forge a resilient and resourceful opposition to the existing political and social power structure. The surprising effectiveness and determined resistance of the Canudos religious fanatics led da Cunha to question profoundly the essence of the Brazilian national character.

The effort to define a specifically Brazilian literature characterized Brazilian modernists of the early twentieth century. In the 1920s, the urge to assimilate the best of European culture, while rejecting whatever seemed antithetical to Brazilian culture and identity, reached its apogee in the movement known as anthropophagism, which played upon the historical reality of ritual cannibalism practiced by the indigenous Tupi peoples, the original inhabitants of the Brazilian national territory. Innovative and antirationalist, the movement had much in common with European cubism, futurism, surrealism, and dadaism; but it was self-consciously Brazilian. Its defining manifestos and manifestations, notably those emanating from the São Paulo–based Week of Modern Art in 1922, included eclectic works by Menotti del Pichia, Mário de Andrade, and Oswald de Andrade. With the advent of anthropophagism, Brazilian literature definitively proclaimed its independence from that of Portugal.

John Gordon Farrell

References

Coutinho, Afranio. *An Introduction to Literature in Brazil.* Translated from the Portuguese by Gregory Rabassa. New York: Columbia University Press, 1969.

Dictionary of Brazilian Literature. Edited by Irwin Stern. New York: Greenwood, 1988.

Franco, Jean. *The Modern Culture of Latin America: Society and the Artist.* London: Pall Mall, 1967.

Haberly, David T. *Three Sad Races: Racial Identity and National Consciousness in Brazilian Literature.* Cambridge: Cambridge University Press, 1983.

Marchant, Alexander. "Aspects of the Enlightenment in Brazil." Pp. 95–118 in *Latin America and the Enlightenment,* edited by Arthur P. Whitaker. Ithaca, NY: Cornell University Press, 1961.

Rector, Monica, and Fred M. Clark, eds. *Portuguese Writers: Dictionary of Literary Biography,* Vol. 287. Farmington Hills, MI: Gale Group/Thomson Learning, 2004.

See also: Art and Artists—Brazil; Bandeirantes; Brazil; Cannibalism; Cinema; Colonists and Settlers II—Brazil; Conquest II—Brazil; Education—Brazil; Enlightenment—Brazil; Independence II—Brazil; Inquisition—Luso-America; Jesuits—Brazil; Languages; Monarchs of Portugal; Music and Dance I—Brazil; Napoleonic Invasion and Luso-America; Paraguayan War; Poetry—Brazil; Science and Scientists—Brazil/Portugal; Travel Literature—Brazil; Universities.

LITERARY RELATIONS—SPAIN AND THE AMERICAS

Literary relations between Spain and the Americas have enjoyed two periods of particularly vibrant exchange: (1) the colonial era, when Spain imposed strict censorship on Spanish American writing and yet also provided the colonies with their sense of literary taste, a source of books and publishers, and in some cases an outlet for Spanish American writers seeking broader horizons; and (2) the period since the 1960s, when Spanish publishers have been crucial to the international expansion of the market for Spanish American fiction, and when some Spanish American writers have chosen to live in Spain. Creative exchange between writers from Spain and Spanish America also occurred intermittently during the early twentieth century.

Relations between the literatures of Spain and Spanish America began with the conquistadors. Bernal Díaz del Castillo (1495–1584), a soldier in the army of Hernando Cortés (1485–1547) during the conquest of Mexico in 1519–1521, wrote his *Historia verdadera de la conquista de Nueva España* (1632), the most vivid, complete, and credible account of the Spanish conquest of the New World, in response to the publication in Zaragoza of Francisco López de Gómara's *Historia General de las Indias* (1552). Díaz del Castillo was stirred to correct the account of the conquest provided by López de Gómara, which he considered fanciful and riddled with errors. Such beginnings suggest the close relationship and persistent tensions that characterized literary relations between Spain and Spanish America. Spain served as both a provocation and a source of literary and publishing opportunities. Draconian colonial censorship, including a ban on the publication of novels, did not prevent colonial Spanish American writers from enjoying literary success in Iberia. One of the earliest examples was Garcilaso de la Vega (1539–1616), known as "el Inca" to distinguish him from the Spanish poet of the same name (to whom he was related). Born of a liaison between a conquistador and an Inca woman, Garcilaso left his native Peru to seek his fortune in Spain, where he lived for the rest of his life. His *Comentarios reales de los Incas* (1609) and *Conquista del Perú* (1613) idealized Inca society for Spanish readers and preserved much information about preconquest Peruvian culture, although many of his more fanciful assertions about the Incas cannot be trusted. Garcilaso's ability to elicit sympathy is evident in the fact that in 1782, in the aftermath of the rebellion against Spanish rule led by the neo-Inca Túpac Amaru II (1740?–1781), the *Comentarios reales* was banned in Spain's American colonies.

The colonial writer who made the most lasting impression on Spanish literature was Juan Ruiz de Alarcón y Mendoza (1581?–1639), whose plays constitute an indispensable part of the canon of Spanish Golden Age drama. Born in the mining town of Taxco, in New Spain (Mexico), and educated at the universities in Mexico City and Salamanca, Alarcón settled in Madrid in his mid-thirties. In spite of his success, he was the object of relentless ridicule directed at him by other Golden Age dramatists, in part because he was born a hunchback but possibly also because of his origins as an "Indiano" (a Spaniard born in the colonies). Alarcón's discomfort with life in Madrid is evident in his persistent, unsuccessful efforts in his later years to obtain a government post that would enable him to return to New Spain. Alarcón's career casts some doubt on the degree to which colonials were accepted into Madrid society, but there is no denying the centrality of his plays, such as *La verdad sospechosa* (1619), to the achievement of Golden Age drama. Many colonial writers who did not travel to Spain, such as the poet Sor Juana Inés de la Cruz (1651–1695), were also widely published there.

During the late eighteenth century, Spanish America's literary relations with

Spain fell victim to rising hostility to colonial rule and the growing influence of French writing, which gained its first significant foothold in the Americas with the translation from French of pamphlets propounding the principles of the Enlightenment. In the bitter aftermath of the wars of independence, French literary models prevailed, particularly in prose. During much of the nineteenth century, literary exchange with Spain was limited and often tainted with mutual disdain, although Spanish *costumbrismo* exercised an important influence on Spanish American realism, accentuating its regional qualities. Channels of communication reopened toward the end of the nineteenth century. The subdued lyricism of the Spanish romantic poet Gustavo Adolfo Bécquer (1836–1870) influenced the Nicaraguan poet Rubén Darío (1867–1916). Darío, who is credited with founding the poetic movement known as *modernismo,* was a crucial figure in healing the long-standing transatlantic literary rift. His first book, *Azul* (1888), rejected the materialism of the new Spanish American middle class for a poetry of resuscitated classical forms and allusions to European culture, particularly Greek mythology. Extended stays in Chile, Argentina, Spain, and France made Darío a figure in tune with the literary movements of most of the cultures central to Hispanic literary production. Darío's second visit to Spain in 1898 prompted the propagation of *modernista* theories that would shape the careers of major Spanish poets such as Antonio Machado (1875–1939) and Juan Ramón Jiménez (1881–1959). As the first literary movement originating in the Americas to have substantial repercussions in Spain, modernismo represents the beginning of a more equitable two-way literary exchange between Spain and its former colonies. After the disaster of the Spanish-American War of 1898, Darío turned *modernismo* away from its immersion in distant times and places, sketching in *Cantos de vida y esperanza* (1905) a form of Pan Americanism that trusted in the peninsular heritage of the Spanish language and the Catholic religion as a bulwark against the threat of the United States' cultural domination.

This renewed emphasis on Spanish America's inheritance from peninsular culture helped to elicit Spanish American solidarity with Republican Spain during the Spanish Civil War (1936–1939). At the second Conference of Anti-Fascist Intellectuals, held in Madrid and Valencia in 1937, Spanish American writers expressed their support for the Republic. Among those present were the Chilean poets Pablo Neruda (1904–1973), who was stripped of a diplomatic post because of his pro-Republic politics, and Vicente Huidobro (1893–1948), the Mexican poet Octavio Paz (1914–1998), the Cuban poet Nicolás Guillén (1902–1989), the Cuban novelist Alejo Carpentier (1904–1980), and the Peruvian poet César Vallejo (1892–1938). After the victory of the Falangist forces in 1939, many Spanish intellectuals went into exile in Mexico, where they nourished the faculty of the Universidad Nacional Autónoma de México (UNAM), influencing the education of younger Mexican intellectuals such as Carlos Fuentes (1928–). In 1949, the exiles founded El Ateneo Español de México. Transatlantic exchange grew during the 1960s when the increased heft of the Barcelona-based Spanish publishing industry, taking over the publication of Spanish American writers from companies in Buenos Aires and Mexico City, projected the fiction of writers such as

Fuentes, the Argentines Jorge Luis Borges (1899–1986) and Julio Cortázar (1914–1984), the Peruvian Mario Vargas Llosa (1936–), the Colombian Gabriel García Márquez (1927–), and the Chilean José Donoso (1924–1996) into the international publishing arena, in a phenomenon that became known as "el Boom." The Boom novel's quest for national self-definition through the innovative narration of history stimulated a heightened awareness of distinct cultural identities within Spain, provoking a series of "mini-Booms" in the Canary Islands, Catalonia, and Andalusia. The dissemination of Spanish American concepts of identity in peninsular writing is evident in the friendship between Fuentes and the Spanish novelist Juan Goytisolo (1931–). Goytisolo's rewriting of Spanish history to stress the "impure" Arabic elements enriches and is informed by Fuentes's depiction of Mexican cultural and racial syncretism.

During the 1980s, when dictatorship swept Spanish America, it was Spain's turn to be adopted as a refuge by Spanish American writers. The Uruguayans Juan Carlos Onetti (1909–1994), Mario Benedetti (1920–), Eduardo Galeano (1940–) and Cristina Peri Rossi (1941–) were among the many writers, notably from the Southern Cone countries, who lived in exile in Spain. The literary impact of their presence is evident in cases such as Onetti's friendship with and mentoring of the peninsular novelist Antonio Muñoz Molina (1956–). The elaborately patterned prose of Muñoz Molina's novel *El jinete polaco* (1992) reflects his discovery, through Onetti, of the U.S. novelist William Faulkner (1897–1962), a major literary influence in Spanish America but little absorbed in Spain prior to Muñoz Molina's novel. In spite of greater openness and more equitable exchange between Spain and Spanish America, tensions still arise. In 1994, furious criticism greeted Vargas Llosa's decision to take out dual Peruvian-Spanish citizenship, suggesting that for many Spanish Americans, unflagging commitment to the nation remains a sine qua non for the writer. In a different vein, Alfaguara, the Madrid conglomerate that publishes much contemporary Spanish American fiction, is regarded with both approval and opprobrium. By dividing its publishing empire into regional units and failing to distribute many writers outside their own regions, some contend, Alfaguara reproduces the Spanish colonial system of viceroys who reported to Madrid but were permitted minimal communication with their compatriots in other areas of Spanish America.

Stephen Henighan

References

Díaz del Castillo, Bernal. *The Discovery and Conquest of Mexico, 1517–1521.* Cambridge, MA: Da Capo, 1996.

Gonzalez, Mike, and David Treece. *The Gathering of Voices: The Twentieth Century Poetry of Latin America.* London: Verso, 1992.

Goytisolo, Juan. *Saracen Chronicles.* Translated by Peter Bush. London: Quartet, 1992.

Henriquez Ureña, Pedro. *A Concise History of Latin American Culture.* Translated by Gilbert Chase. New York: Praeger, 1966.

Santana, Mario. *Foreigners in the Homeland: The Spanish American New Novel in Spain, 1962–1974.* Lewisburg, PA: Bucknell University Press, 2000.

See also: Art and Artists—Colonial Spanish America; Art and Artists—Modern Spanish America; Censorship—Brazil; Censorship—Spanish America; Cinema; Culture; Enlightenment—Spanish America; Fiction—Spanish America; Independence I—VI; Literary Relations—Portugal and the Americas; Music and Dance I–V; Spanish-American War; Spanish Civil War and Latin America; Syncretism; Universities; Viceroyalties.

LOUISIANA PURCHASE

In a brief ceremony on December 30, 1803, the United States flag was hoisted over the government buildings in New Orleans, Louisiana. The occasion marked the United States' acquisition from France of the Louisiana Territory, an area approximately 838,000 acres, for which the United States paid just 3 cents per acre. To the Spanish government, the United States was the recipient of stolen property.

Originally, Spain claimed the territory as part of its colonial conquests, but owing to a lack of settled Indian groups or natural wealth, Spain never gave much attention to Louisiana. Sovereignty over the territory became more complicated in 1682, when French explorers claimed the region for France, hoping to fulfill the dream of linking French Canada with French colonies in the Caribbean. However, lack of money and a greater interest in European affairs meant that the French never pursued the territory's development. Although Spain had never abandoned its claim to the territory, in 1761, France offered the territory to Spain in return for a declaration of war against Britain in the Seven Years' War. The 1763 Treaty of Paris recognized Spain's control of Louisiana, but at the same time the treaty granted Britain control of West Florida (the territory between New Orleans and Pensacola). The 1783 Treaty of Paris that ended the American Revolution sanctified Spain's ownership of Louisiana and also the return of West Florida. Because the 1783 Paris treaty established the boundary of the newly independent United States at the eastern bank of the Mississippi River, Spain immediately closed the river and the port at New Orleans to U.S. commerce, a decision that was reversed with the 1795 Treaty of San Lorenzo (also known as Pinckney's Treaty).

As the nineteenth century ended, the Spanish government recognized its inability to impede westward expansion of the United States, a view shared by France's Napoleon I. At the same time, the French leadership envisioned the establishment of a French empire in the Caribbean, with Louisiana as its granary and future safety valve for a growing population. Thus, the governments in Paris and Madrid shared similar interests and so concluded a secret pact at San Ildefonso on October 1, 1800. In return for Louisiana, France was to grant the Italian state of Tuscany to the son-in-law of Spanish king Charles IV, with a promise to return Louisiana to Spain if he failed to deliver Tuscany. With Napoleon slow to deliver on his promise, Charles IV received more assurances, including Napoleon's pledge never to transfer Louisiana to a third party. In the meantime, Napoleon prepared for his empire in the Western Hemisphere by sending troops to occupy the Caribbean Island of Santo Domingo and begin preparations for the occupation of New Orleans and its environs.

In October 1802, France closed the Mississippi River and port of New Orleans to the United States. The closure prompted demands for war against Spain across the American West. An alarmed President Thomas Jefferson dispatched James Monroe to assist Minister Robert Livingston in Paris, where they were authorized to offer up to $10 million for the purchase of New Orleans and West Florida. But fate offered more. Napoleon's troops in Santo Domingo fell victim to a successful slave revolt and to an outbreak of yellow fever, prompting Napoleon to abandon plans for a Western Hemispheric empire and instead focus on European expansion. To finance his continental plans, Napoleon offered Louisiana to the United States for $15 million. Livingston and Monroe accepted the offer, and the U.S. Senate ratified the treaty on October 10, 1803.

Understandably, the government in Madrid was outraged at the loss of a territory that was not France's to negotiate. And because Napoleon failed, perhaps purposely, to identify Louisiana's western and northern boundaries, Spain encountered continued diplomatic difficulties with the United States until signing the Transcontinental Treaty in 1819 (also known as the Adams-Onis Treaty).

Thomas M. Leonard

References

DeConde, Alexander. *This Affair of Louisiana.* New York: Charles Scribner's Sons, 1976.

Kaplan, Lawrence S. *Thomas Jefferson: Westward Course of Empire.* Wilmington, DE: Scholarly Resources, 1999.

See also: American Revolution; Bourbon Reforms; Colonists and Settlers VI—Southeastern North America; Defense—Colonial Spanish America; Monroe Doctrine; Napoleonic Invasion and Spanish America; Paris, Treaty of; Seven Years' War; War of the Spanish Succession.

Madrid, Treaty of (1670)

The Treaty of Madrid was negotiated between Spain and England in 1670, recognizing England's possessions in the Caribbean, including Jamaica. Earlier, in 1655, having failed to take Santo Domingo, the English instead conquered Jamaica, which they established as a naval base from which to disrupt trade on the Spanish Main and encourage logging in Belize. In 1664, Thomas Modyford, Jamaica's new governor, in response to a lack of funding from London, began to defend the island using dubious privateers, who raided Campeche, Mexico, and the Isla de Providencia in Nicaragua. The Spanish were furious, and the queen mother Maria Ana, acting for Charles II of Spain, issued the *cédula* (a royal warrant) of April 20, 1669, granting reprisal commissions and declaring a limited war on the English below the Tropic of Cancer.

Not wanting an outright war, which would please France and the Dutch, Charles II of England began negotiating with Madrid for a cessation of hostilities, while giving Governor Modyford ambiguous instructions about his letters of marque, which were licenses issued by the English crown authorizing attacks on Spanish ships as legal reprisals for previous depredations by the Spanish. As a result, captains of both England and Spain carried out continued raiding while the negotiations proceeded, the most spectacular of which were the governor of Saint Augustine Manuel de Condoya's raid on Charleston, Henry Morgan's sack of Panama and Portobello, and a Scottish-led attack on the Spanish mission at Guala.

Sir William Godolphin and the Conde de Peñaranda arrived at an acceptable treaty, which was signed on July 8, 1670, in Madrid and published in the Caribbean by July 1671. In Spain's first recognition of any other nation's New World possessions, England's ownership of Jamaica and Virginia and any other place held on the date of signing was specifically confirmed, although this ownership was nebulously defined. In addition, the treaty revoked all letters of reprisal issued by Spain and required reciprocal aid to ships in distress, with permission to repair in each other's ports.

The treaty was deeply hated in Spain, where it was seen as an admission of weakness. However, it was a great boon to the English, who used it to position the Royal African Company in the Caribbean slave trade as a partner of Portugal. Almost immediately, the Spanish protested that the English failed to punish Modyford or Morgan, that there was no repayment of damages done to Portobello and Panama, and that the English were constantly encroaching on Spanish land. Logging camps in the Yucatán, a Scottish settlement at Stewart's Town near Port Royal, and the terms of the Charter to the Proprietors of Carolina, which gave them claims near the 29th parallel, all violated the terms of the treaty.

Margaret Sankey

References

Barbour, Violet. "Privateers and Pirates of the West Indies." *American Historical Review* 16 (April 1911): 529–556.

Davenport, Frances Gardiner. *European Treaties Bearing on the History of the United States and Its Dependencies,* Vol. 2. Gloucester, MA: Peter Smith, 1967.

Howat, G. M. D. *Stuart and Cromwellian Foreign Policy.* New York: St. Martin's, 1974.

Peterson, Mendrel. *Funnel of Gold.* Boston: Little, Brown, 1975.

Wright, J. Leitch. *Anglo-Spanish Rivalry in North America.* Athens: University of Georgia Press, 1971.

See also: Fleet System; Madrid, Treaty of; Monarchs of Spain; Panama; Pirates and Piracy; Slave Trade; Slavery II—Caribbean.

MADRID, TREATY OF (1750)

In 1750, Spain and Portugal signed the Treaty of Madrid, which called for an exchange of territory in South America. Sometimes referred to as the "Boundaries Treaty," it was the most important agreement between the two countries over issues of overseas possessions since the Treaty of Tordesillas (1494). The agreement was a result of a dispute over colonial boundaries that had led to a conflict over the settlement of Colônia do Sacramento on the Río de la Plata during the first half of the eighteenth century.

Under the terms of the treaty, Portugal ceded Colônia and other lands along the Río de la Plata to the Spanish. The Portuguese also guaranteed Spain free navigation of the river. In exchange, the Spanish surrendered territory between the Uruguay and Ibicui rivers, where seven Jesuit missions were located. In addition, Portugal also received lands in northern Brazil in the Amazon region.

The treaty was the result of many years of conflict. In 1680, the Portuguese founded the settlement of Colônia do Sacramento on the east bank of the Río de la Plata. Colônia soon became the center of contraband trade with Buenos Aires, an increasingly important port city in Spanish South America. Located just fifteen miles across the estuary from Buenos Aires, Colônia was vulnerable to Spanish attacks. The Spanish attacked the Portuguese settlement on numerous occasions, notably in 1735 when the governor of Buenos Aires led an attack.

By the mid-1700s, both countries sought an agreement. For Spain, the presence of Colônia meant the loss of silver revenue through contraband trade. Furthermore, conflict with Portugal also meant potential conflict with Great Britain, a Portuguese ally. Portugal in turn sought settlement for all of Brazil's frontier disputes. By surrendering Colônia, Portugal hoped to make gains elsewhere. After three years of negotiations, the two countries agreed to the treaty on January 3, 1750.

Significant opposition to the treaty came from powerful interests in both Spain and Portugal. The success of the agreement was also complicated by the presence of the Jesuits' missions. The Jesuits were required to withdraw from these missions under the treaty. Not surprisingly, the Jesuits opposed the treaty, and between 1754 and 1756 there was open resistance among the missionaries and the Guaraní Indians. Such opposition was one of the factors that eventually led to the expulsion of the Jesuits from Portugal and its territories by 1760.

Because of this opposition and because Spain and Portugal never fully carried out the terms of the agreement, the two countries abrogated the treaty in 1761 with the signing of the Treaty of El Prado. Soon Spain and Portugal renewed their conflict over the disputed territories. Spanish troops once again took Colônia as well as coastal Rio Grande in Brazil.

Ronald Young Jr.

References

Alden, Dauril. *Royal Government in Colonial Brazil.* Berkeley and Los Angeles: University of California Press, 1968.

Burkholder, Mark, and Lyman Johnson. *Colonial Latin America,* 5th ed. Oxford: Oxford University Press, 2004.

Mauro, Frederic. "Portugal and Brazil: Political and Economic Status of Empire, 1580–1750." Pp. 441–468 in *The Cambridge History of Latin America,* Vol. 1, edited by Leslie Bethell. Cambridge: Cambridge University Press, 1984.

See also: Brazil; Jesuits—Brazil; Jesuits—Expulsion; Jesuits—Iberia and America; Jesuits—Paraguay; Madrid, Treaty of; Missions; Native Americans II—Brazil; Paraguay; Tordesillas, Treaty of; Uruguay.

MAIZE

Indigenous to America, *zea mays* is the most important cereal in Africa and Latin America and the second most important cereal on earth. Descending from wild grasses by paths that still cause debate, maize (or corn) emerged as long as 10,000 years ago in Mesoamerica. Several thousand years later maize had spread north to what is now the United States and Canada, and south to Peru. Spanish and Portuguese merchants and migrants brought it to Europe and Africa, and from there it spread, carried by Arab traders and others, to the rest of the world.

In Mesoamerica, maize has had magical and sacred properties both before and after the Spanish invasion. People considered it a divine gift and the substance from which the deities molded human beings. Its cultivation in preinvasion Mesoamerica was of such importance that it stimulated massive technological innovation. Irrigation systems, floating gardens (*chinampas*), and hydraulic projects, including raised fields and long-distance aqueducts, led to dense populations and the rise of cities.

Alkali processing *(nixtamal)* in Mesoamerica involves soaking grain with ground limestone or other alkali so that the hull can be removed by washing, and the kernel is then ground to flour for making tortillas. Almost as popular are recipes in which the dough is wrapped in leaves, with meat, chilis, and other ingredients, and then served as *tamales.* In North Africa maize is eaten as couscous. Soups and stews (*pozole* in Mesoamerica; *kenkey, ogi,* and other local names in Africa) are also common. In the United States, maize is widely used to feed cattle but is also popular in the cuisine as grits, scrapple, cornbread, and corn on the cob. Popcorn and breakfast cereals of maize such as cornflakes have spread worldwide. Alcoholic drinks made from this cereal range from the *chicha* beers of Andean America to the bourbon whiskeys of the United States and Canada. In these two countries, high-fructose corn syrup has now surpassed natural sugar as a nondiet sweetener in processed foods.

Maize, a nutritious plant, also has some notable deficiencies. It is low in calcium, niacin (part of the vitamin B complex), and, above all, in its "white maize" form, in vitamin A. Some diets heavy in maize, such as those of poor people in Mesoamerica, compensate by introducing alkalis during food preparation and by combining maize with beans, squashes, and chilis. Among the poor in some parts of the world, heavily maize diets have caused pellagra, a niacin and amino acid deficiency, and kwashiorkor, a protein deficiency. Some of these problems have been attacked by encouraging the consumption of supplementary dietary foods and by developing new varieties of maize with higher vitamin and protein contents.

In recent years the uses of maize have increased rapidly. Though still used primarily as food and alcohol, with its adaptability, yields, and caloric content all better than those of wheat or rice, it has also been harnessed for industrial uses. Fuel and textile manufacturers and the paper industry have all found uses for the plant. Disposable diapers, road "salt," and biodegradable "plastics" such as tableware can all be made from "corn." Maize is perhaps the ultimate miracle cereal, not least because of its remarkable spread from its Mesoamerican homeland and because of the variety of its uses.

Murdo J. MacLeod

References

Mangelsdorf, Paul C. *Corn: Its Origins, Evolution and Improvement.* Cambridge, MA: Harvard University Press, 1974.

Warman, Arturo. *Corn and Capitalism: How a Botanical Bastard Grew to Global Dominance.* Translated by Nancy L. Westrate. Chapel Hill: University of North Carolina Press, 2003.

See also: Alcohol; Atlantic Economy; Bananas; Cacao; Coca; Coffee; Columbian Exchange—Agriculture; Cotton; Food; Henequen; Milpa; Native Americans I–VIII; Potato; Sugar; Tobacco; Trade—Spain/Spanish America; Wheat.

MALVINAS/FALKLAND ISLANDS

Known by the British as the Falkland Islands and by the Argentines as Las Islas Malvinas, these islands in the South Atlantic have been the focus of a bitter battle over sovereignty between the two nations for almost 200 years. Britain claims the islands based on settlement and, at present, as a means to protect the self-determination of the islanders, the vast majority of whom are of British descent. Argentines believe that they inherited Spanish sovereignty over the islands following their nation's independence from Spain in the early nineteenth century. In 1982, Britain and Argentina fought a war over the islands.

The Falklands/Malvinas consist of two main islands and several hundred smaller islands that altogether make up an area roughly the size of Northern Ireland. The islands lie some 300 miles off the coast of South America in the Atlantic Ocean, and during the seventeenth and eighteenth centuries hosted French, British, and Spanish settlements. Argentina claimed sovereignty on Spain's expulsion from the Americas after 1810. In 1833, Britain established a naval command post on the islands, expelling the Spanish-speaking inhabitants and preventing further migration from the mainland. In the 1850s, the Falkland Island Company took over the running of the islands, and wool became the principal export. In 1965, the United Nations acknowledged that the islands fell under their 1960 resolution to end colonialism, and so urged Britain to begin negotiations with Argentina to transfer sovereignty. Negotiations lasted from 1966 until the outbreak of war in 1982. The British appeared willing to concede sovereignty to Argentina but were limited by the islanders' reluctance to accept the transfer.

As negotiations over the islands continued, the political situation in Argentina worsened dramatically. The military had carried out a coup in 1966, after eleven years of trying to manufacture a political solution that excluded former president Juan Perón and his followers. Various military governments between 1966 and 1973 failed to create economic growth or provide political stability. At the same time, a series of guerrilla groups emerged across Argentina, staging bank robberies, kidnappings, and attacks on military installations. The military as well as clandestine right-wing groups began to strike back at leftist targets. In 1973, the military recognized their political and economic failures and allowed Perón to return as president. Perón was now seventy-eight years old. During his less than one year in office (he died in July 1974), the political situation continued to unravel. Toward the end of his regime, and during the twenty months that his widow and vice president Isabelita ruled, the conflict between the guerrillas and the military reached a crisis. A group believed to have links to the federal police, the Argentine Anticommunist Alliance, began abducting and killing leftist opponents.

On March 24, 1976, the military staged another coup and initiated what they called the Process of National Reorganization. The military set out to destroy the guerrillas and any potential sympathizers. From 1976 to 1983, somewhere between 10,000 and 30,000 people "disappeared" at the hands of the military, police, or clandestine right-wing organizations. Union leaders, medical students, doctors, psychiatrists—people from all walks of life—were taken and held in police stations, military installations, or schools. There, they were tortured and some were executed, their bodies disposed of in unmarked graves. At first, the population had welcomed the military's intervention, given the chaos of the Perón's government. Soon, those who opposed the government were cowed into submission. However, as in the period 1966–1973, the military were unable to manufacture political stability or economic growth.

In December 1981, a new military commander took over at the head of the dictatorship, General Leopoldo Galtieri. Galtieri sought to gain popular support for the military's mission. Along with navy commander Admiral Jorge Anaya, Galtieri planned an invasion of the Falkland Islands, intended for one of Argentina's patriotic holidays in May or July. As pressure mounted on the regime, they moved the invasion forward to April 1, 1982. A small British force was quickly overcome by the Argentine invaders, and reinforcements were sent to support the newly named governor of the Islas Malvinas, General Mario Menéndez. The invasion sparked mass protests of support for the regime in

Buenos Aires, precisely what the government had wanted. The military government had calculated that Britain would not defend the islands and that the United States would support the Argentine claim. The latter assumption was based on the close relations that had been established between Buenos Aires and Washington with regard to U.S. actions against leftist activities in Central America. Galtieri was proved wrong on both counts.

Under Margaret Thatcher, herself looking for popular support in the midst of a campaign to remake British society, Britain mobilized a naval task force and elite army troops. The United States condemned Argentina's illegal use of force in taking the islands, as did most of the European Community. All of Latin America, excluding Pinochet's Chile, backed Argentina. In the battle for the islands, over 200 Britons and more than 700 Argentines perished. In the sinking of the Argentine cruiser *General Belgrano,* which occurred outside the exclusion zone established by the British, 400 crewmen died. Argentina's Exocet missile attack on the British destroyer *Sheffield* resulted in twenty deaths. On land, the British troops overwhelmed a force of Argentine conscripts. The Argentine military, rather than reinforcing the islands with regular troops, had sent raw conscripts. Elite Argentine troops were left guarding the border with Chile, with whom the military government had stoked a confrontation over claims to the Beagle Channel, yet another attempt to garner popular support for the regime.

The Argentine military's failure in the Falklands/Malvinas brought down the government. When the army surrendered, it uncovered the misinformation they had been broadcasting to the country regarding the mission's success and undermined the authority of the military government's claim to legitimacy. Galtieri resigned from office, and in 1983 popular elections swept Raúl Alfonsín into office as Argentina's new president.

Alistair V. Hattingh

References

Burns, Jimmy. *The Land that Lost Its Heroes.* London: Bloomsbury, 1986.

Hastings, Max, and Simon Jenkins. *The Battle for the Falklands.* New York: W. W. Norton, 1983.

Rock, David. *Argentina 1516–1987: From Spanish Colonization to Alfonsín.* Berkeley and Los Angeles: University of California Press, 1987.

See also: Argentina; Brazil; Chile; Cold War—Spain and the Americas; Communism; Democracy; Football; Guerrillas; Independence I—Argentina; Pinochet Case; Populism; World War I; World War II.

MANIFEST DESTINY

Manifest Destiny is the theory that the United States of America was divinely ordained to expand its domain across the North American continent and overseas. Many proponents of this theory also believed that Anglo-Saxons were superior peoples fated to spread their social, political, economic, and religious culture. Although some of the ideas behind Manifest Destiny can be traced back to early British North American settlement, the term was coined in 1845 by the Irish American intellectual John L. O'Sullivan. Born during the War of 1812 in Gibraltar, where his father was U.S. consul to the Barbary States, O'Sullivan grew up in Europe while his father pursued shipping in the Mediterranean and the Americas. O'Sullivan's mother returned with her children to the

United States after her husband's death on the high seas. Upon graduating from Columbia College in 1834, O'Sullivan began practicing law in New York City. Three years later, he cofounded the *United States Magazine and Democratic Review.* In 1841, O'Sullivan was elected to the New York Legislature, where he served one term.

From 1841 to 1846, O'Sullivan was sole editor of the review, which published monthly many great American literary figures such as Nathaniel Hawthorne, Henry Wadsworth Longfellow, and Edgar Allan Poe. The review's first subscriber was Democratic president Andrew Jackson (1829–1837), who tried to purchase Texas from Mexico and hoped that the United States would someday take over Spanish North America. O'Sullivan used his magazine to help win the New York vote for James K. Polk, the Democratic presidential candidate in 1844. President Polk (1845–1849) won on a platform of expansion regarding Texas and Oregon. As the plan for the U.S. annexation of the Republic of Texas (1836–1845) was underway, O'Sullivan printed an editorial in the July–August 1845 issue of the review denouncing opposition to "the fulfillment of our manifest destiny to overspread the continent allotted by Providence for the free development of our multiplying millions." O'Sullivan's term rationalized the fervor of land-hungry northern Europeans migrating to the United States and heading west. He predicted that Canada would sever its colonial ties with England and be annexed by the United States.

In 1845, O'Sullivan was also the editor of another New York Democratic organ, the *Morning News,* from which comes the second appearance of his term, in an editorial on December 27, 1845. The U.S. Congress was debating President Polk's request to terminate the 1818 agreement with Great Britain by which the two nations occupied the Oregon country. O'Sullivan argued that the U.S. claim to Oregon was "by the right of our manifest destiny to overspread and to possess the whole of the continent which Providence has given us for the development of the great experiment of liberty and federative self-government entrusted to us." The following week, Representative Robert C. Winthrop of Massachusetts became the first to use the phrase in Congress after he quoted O'Sullivan's editorial in a speech opposing Polk's expansionist policy in Oregon.

Manifest Destiny became a catchphrase in the Oregon controversy and the Mexican War (1846–1848), but in 1846 the *Morning News* folded and O'Sullivan sold the review. That same year, O'Sullivan became a regent of the University of New York. He continued for many years to write editorials for the review, arguing that uncivilized Native Americans and corrupt Mexicans would assimilate and be lost in the more highly developed races overrunning the continent. In 1848, he convinced President Polk to attempt to purchase Cuba from the Spaniards. He then supported several unsuccessful filibustering attempts against Cuba. President Franklin Pierce (1853–1857) appointed him U.S. minister to Portugal. O'Sullivan died poor and forgotten in 1895. Three years earlier, the Republicans had written Manifest Destiny into their party platform. Soon after O'Sullivan's death, the phrase was again popular with U.S. citizens looking to Hawaii and the remnants of Spain's empire in Cuba, Puerto Rico, Guam, and the Philippines as places in need of a civilizing mission.

David M. Carletta

References

Haynes, Sam W., and Christopher Morris, eds. *Manifest Destiny and Empire: American Antebellum Expansionism.* College Station: Texas A & M University Press, 1997.

Pratt, Julius W. "The Origin of 'Manifest Destiny.'" *American Historical Review* 32, no. 4 (July 1927): 795–798.

———. "John L. O'Sullivan and Manifest Destiny." *New York History* 14, no. 3 (July 1933): 213–234.

Widmer, Edward L. *Young America: The Flowering of Democracy in New York City.* New York: Oxford University Press, 1999.

See also: Cuba; Democracy; Mexico; Monroe Doctrine; Nationalism; Spanish-American War; USS Maine.

MAPS

Maps have played an important role in defining and organizing space in Latin America since the earliest encounters between Europeans and indigenous populations in the late fifteenth century. Both groups had distinct ways of representing the world around them, which reflected their cultural differences and conflicting views of the world. Yet, as both the Spanish and Portuguese solidified their power in the New World, European mapmaking quickly displaced indigenous forms of spatial representation. The form and function of maps also changed. Scientific gains during the eighteenth and nineteenth centuries made maps much more accurate. By the late nineteenth century, maps also became a tool in understanding and analyzing urban problems, such as disease, crime, and poverty. Moving into the twentieth century, maps continued to represent these dynamics, while at the same time focusing on contemporary issues of place and space.

While Spanish conquistadors were encountering the New World, their fellow countrymen back in Spain were creating images of their countries, their provinces, and their cities, making the surrounding world visible through maps. Not only Iberian but European cartography in general exploded during the sixteenth century, as the European Renaissance brought developments in mathematics and graphic arts that improved mapmaking and urban cartography considerably. The European experience in the Americas was now accessible to a much wider audience, through engravings and woodcuts. With European world maps reaching new levels of geometrical precision, Spaniards and Portuguese were given a vehicle for envisioning the New World. As the century progressed, the outlines of their possessions in the New World were defined, classified, and introduced to the broader world.

The clash between the Spanish and Native American populations during conquest and colonization has been well investigated through a number of political, economic, social, and cultural arenas. This is also true using the lens of cartography. The difference between the European and indigenous worlds of the Americas was seen most starkly in the early maps of the region, in particular the mapping of the Mexica capital of Tenochtitlan. Early European visions of the city mixed two popular systems of projection into one seamless image of the city. The first, Euclidean, emphasized the geometric dimensions of the city by focusing on a grid pattern to depict space. The second, Albertian, offered a more panoramic view of the city by surrounding Tenochtitlan with Lake Texcoco and other cities along the lakeshore. Both of these styles of representation grew out of the European understanding of space as a series of connected points, reducible by geometric means. In a larger sense, these map styles fit within a European high culture that embraced an emerging scientific rationalism, with man at the center.

In comparison, Mexica (Inca) depictions of its capital city focused on the social rather than geometric dimensions of the city. In one such map from the Codex Mendoza, Tenochtitlan was divided into four triangles intersected by four of the city's numerous canals, each triangle representing the four major neighborhoods of the capital. Embedded in these triangles were not landmarks, such as buildings, streets, or public spaces, but rather the ten original founders of the empire, each within their corresponding neighborhood. At the same time, the massive lake surrounding the island city was reduced to a narrow border strip. Clearly, the Mexica image, unlike its European counterpart, was not based in scientific rationality. Rather, it was a humanistic, or social, projection of the physical space of the city; the organizing principles themselves were the social, rather than physical, layout of the city. Residents of Tenochtitlan recognized the space around them as defined and structured by social relationships. This use of social organization to structure both the understanding and the representation of space was as common in Ancient Mexico as the use of geometry to define space was in Europe.

Very quickly, however, as the Spanish and Portuguese increased their control and influence in the New World, the European understanding of space began to dominate the formal construction of maps. As more and more of the New World became known to the conquerors, maps increasingly came to depict this space but in European physical and cultural terms. By the eighteenth century, increasingly powerful and centralized governments had the resources necessary to impress themselves physically on the design of maps, as well as in the representation of towns, cities, and broader geographical areas. In general, maps and plans of the eighteenth century were more accurate, owing to the increasing improvements in surveying methods brought about by the Scientific Revolution and the Enlightenment focus on scientific methods. In the representation of cities, for example, the rectangular grid plan that had dominated urban planning throughout the colonial period continued to be the preferred pattern. The Bourbon Reforms, in particular, with their focus on structure, efficiency, and order, also emphasized the use of maps to illustrate change. New Spain's coastlines were explored and mapped in an effort to define the geographical outlines of the Spanish Empire. Foreigners like Alexander von Humboldt played a prominent role in mapping the geography of New Spain and in the process encouraged colonists to do the same. This, coupled with a greater focus on science and mathematics in the educational system, meant that a new generation of cartographers would emerge, with the skills to produce more accurate and technically sophisticated maps. New political boundaries, changing economic activities, shifting trends in urbanization, and efforts to improve public services and delivery of resources were all represented in maps. The symmetry, detail, and organization of these maps illustrated the larger mission of these reforms, in a visual manner.

The spatial changes that came about as a consequence of independence became a particular focus of cartographers in the early nineteenth century. For example, new

A Spanish map of Tenochtitlan, now known as Mexico City, designed by Hernando Cortés. The Aztec city was surrounded by water, a natural barrier, but Cortés managed to conquer it in 1521. (Corbis)

maps illustrated the larger mission of these reforms, in a visual manner.

The spatial changes that came about as a consequence of independence became a particular focus of cartographers in the early nineteenth century. For example, new political boundaries now had to be defined for purposes of national identity, unity, and security. The political struggles of the early century were often reflected in shifting borders and conflict over national territory. These struggles gave way to new concerns by the late nineteenth century. Another major shift in mapping and spatial representation took place, as thematic mapping for social means became an important tool for Latin American governments. This shift was encouraged in part by increasing militancy among the working classes, and also as a response to increasing urbanization and the physical and social consequences of urban growth. By creating visual texts that highlighted the issues of poverty, crime, and unemployment, for example, mapping helped put a tangible face on social problems that many questioned even existed, while at the same time providing municipal agencies with important information in developing their responses to urban problems. These new "social" maps also aided local leaders in maintaining elements of order and control over what they viewed as an increasingly unruly urban population by focusing attention on certain areas of cities that were deemed especially problematic.

Another theme of the late nineteenth century was mapping the distribution and spread of disease, especially cholera and yellow fever. This was pushed forward in Latin America by the Great Cholera Epidemic of 1832 in Western Europe, where maps had been used extensively in organizing responses to disease outbreaks. As another consequence of urbanization and material growth, city governments in Latin America struggled in dealing with epidemics, which, given the physical realities of overcrowding, poverty, and poor public services, meant that disease could and did wreak havoc in the urban setting. As with other issues, such as crime and unemployment, mapping disease outbreaks gave public health officials valuable data in developing their responses.

For Latin America, the process of modernization in the twentieth century has naturally propelled the demand for, and creation of, more modern maps. Demographic growth, rapid urbanization, dis-

with technical developments, have meant that cartographers in Latin America have been able to meet that challenge in providing valuable visual texts, much like their predecessors had during the colonial period and the nineteenth century.

Sharon Bailey Glasco

References

Elliot, James. *The City in Maps: Urban Mapping to 1900.* London: British Library, 1997

Levenson, Jay, ed. *Art in the Age of Exploration: Circa 1492.* New Haven, CT: Yale University Press, 1991.

Mignolo, Walter. *The Darker Side of the Renaissance: Literacy, Territoriality, and Colonization.* Ann Arbor: University of Michigan Press, 2003.

Mundy, Barbara E. *The Mapping of New Spain: Indigenous Cartography and the Maps of the Relaciones Geográficas.* Chicago: University of Chicago Press, 1996.

Woodward, David. "Maps and the Rationalization of Geographic Space." Pp. 83–87 in *Art in the Age of Exploration: Circa 1492,* edited by Jay Levenson. New Haven, CT: Yale University Press, 1991.

See also: Bourbon Reforms; Cities; Columbian Exchange—Disease; Conquest I–VII; Conquistadors; Culture; Education—Brazil; Education—Colonial Spanish America; Enlightenment—Brazil; Enlightenment—Spanish America; Environment; Independence I–VI; Languages; Nationalism; Native Americans I–VIII; Poverty; Science and Scientists—Brazil/Portugal; Science and Scientists—Colonial Spanish America; Science and Scientists—Modern Latin America; Travel and Tourism.

MARRIAGE

Catholic marriage was one of the most fundamental social institutions that the Iberians brought to the New World. At least in theory, the Catholic marriage stipulated the proper relations between men and women, between their respective families, and between parents and children. Furthermore, it determined to some extent the social standing of husband and wife; it served as one of the most important ways of property transmission between families, and it was one of the most effective means of forming networks and political alliances. Yet the Catholic marriage underwent significant changes between 1500 and 1800, and modern readers are often surprised when confronted with the fluidity of definitions of what constituted a legitimate marriage in the early modern Western world. The ideal that marriage was a sacred union between unmarried or widowed persons of the opposite sex, publicly instituted in front of witnesses, licensed, authorized, and registered by a parish priest, with the approval of the couple's parents was only codified by the Council of Trent in the Tametsi Decree of 1563. New World marriage practices between 1500 and 1800 were shaped by medieval marriage ideals brought from Spain and Portugal, further modified by specific demographic conditions in the postconquest societies of the New World, general cultural and legal developments in the Catholic world, and the varying results of cross-cultural encounters between European, American, and African kinship systems.

Before the Council of Trent, religious and secular perspectives on marriages differed in several important regards in Europe. Secular courts and aristocratic circles generally emphasized the material aspects of the marriage contract and insisted on parental control and required public ceremonies, either in church or in front of a notary, to regard marriages as legitimate and legally binding. The Church defended a vision in which marriage was primarily a mystical and sacred union instituted in every instance by God, where only the verbal promise of the spouses and the physical union of their bodies were necessary for the marriage to be legitimate. The Tametsi Decree was a compromise between the two views. It required the couple to have banns published on three consecutive Sundays, receive the priest's blessing in front of two witnesses, and register the marriage in the parish church. Although paternal consent was not made mandatory for marriages to be legitimate, the Council adverted that it "detested" unions made against the wishes of the parents. After 1563, the Catholic Church sought to instill this new practice in the New World, but the older ideal that marriage was valid simply if a promise had been made lingered on in the popular conception for a surprisingly long time in the New World.

The first generations of Iberians who came to the Americas were overwhelmingly male. This gender imbalance, combined with the small number of priests in the sixteenth-century New World, the popular Iberian acceptance of consensual unions as legitimate marriages, the power imbalance between conquerors and conquered, the Iberians' willingness to take native spouses, and the practice of many indigenous societies of offering women to create political and military alliances—all contributed to a profusion of marriages as well as other types of unions between Iberian men and Indian women during the first decades of Iberian rule. The conquistadors of the early sixteenth century were constantly on the move, and many took wives in several locations, although secular as well as canon law recognized only the first marriage to be legitimate until the death of one of the spouses. The offspring of unions between Spanish males and Indian females were labeled mestizos, a term that soon came to be regarded popularly as a synonym for illegitimacy.

Gradually, the standardizing effects of the tridentine regulations became apparent, and over time Iberians of high social standing increasingly preferred to wed Iberian women. However, the number of Iberian women who migrated to the Americas remained low throughout the colonial period, ensuring a high social price being placed on them in the marriage market. Indeed, social status among Iberian elites came to rest in large part on the concept of "purity of blood." Simultaneously, it became a concern to protect the material wealth amassed during the conquest, which also contributed to the new significance of contracting marriages with those perceived to be social equals. Material concerns and paternal control for the marriages of the elites were further cemented by the extensive use of the dowry, at least until the early eighteenth century when this custom seems to have withered. The dowry was given to a daughter when she married, and although the husband administered it, the dowry was legally the woman's property for life. The size of dowries corresponded to the social and economic standing of the woman's parents. Husbands were also expected to provide wives with an *arras,* a gift of money or valuables that legally belonged to the wife. Although the Church continued to emphasize that the free selection of partners was a condition for legitimate marriages, there is much evidence to suggest that parents or other family members often arranged marriages among colonial elites. In both Brazil and Spanish America, women tended to be considerably younger than men at the time of their first marriage, averaging around twenty-two years for females and thirty for males. Marriages between cousins or couples who were related to the fourth degree were also common among elites; however, these unions required formal dispensation from the bishop.

Among the less wealthy Hispanic or Hispanized population, material concerns were usually less prominent in both the choice of spouses and in obeying the rigid exigencies of posttridentine marriage legislation. Hispanic nonelites generally had their marriages registered later, if at all, than their social superiors. Various factors may explain this phenomenon. Fees demanded by parish priests for banns and ceremonies could be excessive. Distances to the nearest church could be considerable, especially in rural areas. The old and popular notion that mutual verbal promises were sufficient for a marriage to be valid also seems to have been long-lived, which meant that many couples probably felt that they were legitimately married even though their union was not formally registered or licensed by the Church. To colonial elites, including representatives of the Church and the Iberian monarchies, the marriage practices of the popular classes were frequently dismissed as disorderly, and the view that equated *mestizaje* with illegitimacy was further cemented.

Of all social groups in colonial Latin America, slaves were the least likely to marry. Generally, slaves on plantations in rural areas and those who had recently arrived from Africa were barred from entering the marriage market. Urban slaves born in the Americas had a much greater chance of establishing a legal family, especially if they held an occupation that provided the opportunity to accrue some material wealth. Neither Spanish America nor Brazil imposed legal impediments against slaves' marriages. On the contrary, colonial legislation emphasized the duty of slave owners to ensure that slaves lived in accordance with religious and social norms. Nevertheless, in practice slave owners were reluctant to let slaves marry, especially if the couple belonged to different owners. Married slaves were often seen as less loyal to the owner than unmarried slaves. The low marriage propensity among slaves, particularly those born in Africa, may also be interpreted as a sign of resistance against the imposition of an alien and dominant culture, but in revolts or disputes between masters and slaves where marriage was an issue, slaves generally fought for the right to marry and maintain legal families, not against this institution.

Colonial authorities placed great importance on converting the native population to Christianity. One of the most important tasks assigned to the regular clergy was to transmit the principles of the Catholic marriage and family living to the natives. The degree to which the friars succeeded in making the Indians adopt Catholic marriage depended largely on the success of the particular missions themselves. Some of the peripheral areas of Spanish America and Brazil were never fully controlled during the colonial period, and there the Church and the religious orders made little headway in introducing Christian concepts of sexuality and family life. In more central areas, however, and particularly in the highland areas of Spanish America, most of the Indians who were firmly under European domination seem to have appropriated the European marriage institution a generation or two after the conquest. Indeed, during the mid- and late colonial period, the Indians living in pueblos showed the largest number of marriages registered by the Church, and they were also the group that married at the earliest age and among whom illegitimacy rates were the lowest. This may be seen as a sign of the close religious and social vigilance exercised by the Church and the religious orders in the Indian pueblos, but the figures may also be a function of more general economic and demographic factors. Village-dwelling Indians, in general, found partners from their own pueblos.

During the last decades of colonial rule, from the mid-eighteenth century onward, Spanish and Portuguese governments sought to reform marriage practices through a series of legislative reforms. Inspired by the ideas of the Catholic Enlightenment and guided by the absolutist pretensions of the Bourbons in Spain and the Marquis de Pombal in Portugal, several decrees and new laws were issued to enhance parental control over the choice of partners for their offspring. Modeled on laws and legal codes previously introduced in some of the Italian states and in Protestant areas in northern Europe, the new marriage legislation required couples under a certain age (the exact age was modified several times) to obtain parental consent (or from guardians when parents were dead or absent) before marrying. In the event of parental disapproval, cases were to be heard by civil instead of religious authorities. These new laws, especially the 1776 *Pragmática sanción* on "unequal marriages" and the 1778 royal decree which made the 1776 law valid in Spanish America, have been interpreted as bans on interracial marriages. But the laws themselves did not explicitly forbid marriages between couples of different racial groups; racial disparity was just one of several reasons cited by unhappy parents or other relatives when they opposed a marriage. The new laws certainly reduced the difference between Catholic and Protestant regions with respect to marriage legislation and strengthened the material and economic aspects of marriage as a contract in relation to the compromise reached at the Council of Trent. However it is still an open question whether the new legislation had much bearing on marriage practices in Latin America. The late-eighteenth-century marriage legislation was generally adopted and continued by the new republics after independence, until the introduction of civil marriages in the mid-nineteenth century.

Steinar Andreas Saether

References

Arrom, Silvia Marina. *The Women of Mexico City, 1790–1857.* Stanford, CA: Stanford University Press, 1985.

Gutiérrez, Ramón. *When Jesus Came the Corn Mothers Went Away: Marriage, Sexuality and Power in New Mexico, 1500–1846.* Stanford, CA: Stanford University Press, 1991.

Lavrín, Asunción, ed. *Sexuality and Marriage in Colonial Spanish America.* Lincoln: University of Nebraska Press, 1989.

Martinez-Alier, Verena. *Marriage, Class and Colour in Nineteenth-Century Cuba.* Cambridge: Cambridge University Press, 1974.

Nazzari, Muriel. *Disappearance of the Dowry: Women, Families, and Social Change in São Paulo, Brazil (1600–1900).* Stanford, CA: Stanford University Press, 1991.

Rípodas Ardanaz, Daisy. *El Matrimonio en Indias. Realidad social y regulación jurídica.* Buenos Aires: FECIC, 1977.

Seed, Patricia. *To Love, Honor, and Obey in Colonial Mexico: Conflicts over Marriage Choice, 1574–1821.* Stanford, CA: Stanford University Press, 1988.

Socolow, Susan Migden. *The Women of Colonial Latin America.* Cambridge: Cambridge University Press, 2000.

Twinam, Ann. *Public Lives, Private Secrets: Gender, Honor, Sexuality, and Illegitimacy in Colonial Spanish America.* Stanford, CA: Stanford University Press, 1999.

See also: Bigamy, Transatlantic; Bourbon Reforms; Catholic Church in Brazil; Catholic Church in Spanish America; Childhood in Colonial Latin America; Clergy—Secular in Colonial Spanish America; Council of Trent; Enlightenment—Brazil; Enlightenment—Spanish America; Family—Colonial Brazil; Family—Colonial Spanish America; Laws—Colonial Latin America; Mestizaje; Migration—From Iberia to the New World; Native Americans I–III; Race; Religious Orders; República de Indios; Slavery I–IV; Women—Colonial Spanish America.

MEDICINE

In the first century of contact between Europeans and the indigenous peoples of the Americas, native populations declined by as much as 90 percent, owing mainly to their lack of immunity to Old World diseases. Despite the far-reaching implications of this tragic fact, the history of medicine in colonial Latin America has received comparatively little attention from English-language scholars. However, its importance for understanding colonial society has attracted growing interest of late so that a general outline of the topic is possible, if still preliminary.

Colonial medicine existed on two different levels: a colonial, "official" level that employed the theories and practices of Western medicine and a "popular" level that used a mixture of local indigenous, African, and European customs drawn from both medical and religious traditions. The practitioners of official medicine were few in number, lived almost exclusively in the viceregal capitals or audiencia (high court) seats, and treated a European clientele. Popular practitioners treated the majority of the plebeian populations, both urban and rural, despite the fact that their services were technically illegal according to the colonial medical establishment. Yet notwithstanding the separation of the two medical traditions, there is some evidence that they did interact with and influence one another.

Much information is available concerning the official practice of colonial medicine. Medical practitioners arrived with the first Spanish fleets and included among their ranks doctors, surgeons, and apothecaries. Of these professions, doctors enjoyed the highest social prestige because they were required to have university degrees, which they could obtain in the medical schools of American universities as early as 1578. Doctors typically did not perform surgeries. The colonial surgeon, who performed amputations, bloodletting, and pulling teeth, enjoyed much lower status than doctors; surgeons had no formal educational requirement. Finally, apothecaries occupied an ambivalent position in the medical hierarchy. Although they were required to be literate and know Latin, they, too, performed manual tasks of preparing and dispensing medicines, and they could obtain a license to practice after a three-year apprenticeship.

In spite of these differences, colonial medical practitioners had many things in common. First, they all had to be of Spanish descent and had to prove it by presenting certificates of *limpieza de sangre* (purity of blood) in order to obtain a medical license. Second, they all practiced according to European medical theory that derived from the teachings of ancient

Greek and Roman doctors. The Greek Hippocrates, perhaps the most influential of these doctors, proposed the theory that the body was made up of four different fluids called *humors* and that disease occurred when there was an imbalance among them. It was the practitioner's responsibility to restore humoral balance, which was done most commonly by extracting the humor in excess through a variety of methods such as inducing vomiting, sweating, diarrhea, or by drawing blood or applying poultices. Practitioners also had access to over 1,500 different kinds of medicines made from herbs, animal parts, and minerals as well, most of which came from the ancient "recipes" of Galen, though some recipes did incorporate New World plants using indigenous knowledge as well.

All official practitioners had to obtain a medical license in order to practice legally. They received this license from the Protomedicato, a medical board consisting of three Protomédicos (high-ranking physicians) and three examiners who regulated the practice of medicine in both Spain and the colonies. Though a product of medieval Castilian legislation, the Protomedicato was formally organized during the reign of Philip II (1556–1598) and brought to the Americas in the seventeenth century, with Protomedicatos established in the viceregal capitals of Lima and Mexico City. There the Protomédicos oversaw the legal and ethical practice of medicine in the colonies, at least in theory. Protomédicos were expected to carry out regular inspections of medical establishments, and the Protomedicato acted as a judicial court for cases of fraud and medical malpractice.

Despite the Protomedicato's wide powers, it does not appear to have been particularly effective at controlling the illegal practice of medicine. Not only were the medical boards located only in the capital cities and thus far removed from the rural populations that dominated colonial America, but there were also few licensed practitioners in relation to the population as a whole. Thus, the majority of people had to turn to popular practitioners, termed *curanderos,* for medical treatment. An impressive network of hospitals, many specifically designed to cure the "poor-sick" who could not otherwise afford Western treatment, was simply not enough, and the Protomedicato was in no position to be able to control practices outside the reach of its effective jurisdiction.

A level of popular medicine, therefore, continued to thrive throughout the colonial period despite its illegal status, thus preserving many of the indigenous and African medicoreligious traditions from which it derived. Unfortunately, research in this area of medicine is in a preliminary stage, though traces of indigenous practice and syncretism with Western medical practice are visible in a number of sources. Officials from the Audiencia of Guadalajara, for example, entreated the Protomedicato in 1799 to allow the legalization of *curanderismo* in places where no licensed practitioner was available. This practice, which they termed the "Doctrine of Tolerance," was summarily rejected by the Protomédicos. Furthermore, modern anthropologists have marked the similarity between Aztec and Hippocratic medicine, both of which recognized the cause of disease as an imbalance of four main bodily fluids. In addition, both the Spanish and Portuguese

Crowns sought information on New World medicinal plants, whose healing properties were no doubt described by indigenous informants. In 1571, for example, Philip II ordered the Protomédico Francisco Hernández to study and catalogue all medicinal plants in the New World, and Spaniards such as Gregorio López and Juan de Esteyneffer described both indigenous and European practices in their medical books. Indigenous plants were incorporated into the European pharmacopoeia as well, with quinine as the most famous example; American pharmacies drew a significant amount of their stock from local resources. In this way, the two levels of colonial medicine at times combined to form an original form of medical theory and practice.

Paula DeVos

References

Cook, Noble David. *Born to Die: Disease and New World Conquest, 1492–1650.* Cambridge: Cambridge University Press, 1998.

Hernández Saénz, Luz María. *Learning to Heal: The Medical Profession in Colonial Mexico, 1767–1831.* New York: Peter Lang, 1997.

Lanning, John Tate. *The Royal Protomedicato: The Regulation of the Medical Professions in the Spanish Empire.* Edited by John Jay TePaske. Durham, NC: Duke University Press, 1985.

Varey, Simon, Rafael Chabran, and Dora Weiner, eds. *Searching for the Secrets of Nature: The Life and Works of Dr. Francisco Hernández.* Stanford, CA: Stanford University Press, 2001.

See also: Audiencias; Bourbon Reforms; Columbian Exchange—Disease; Enlightenment—Spanish America; Hospitals; Inquisition—Spanish America; Jesuits—Expulsion; Poverty; Science and Scientists—Brazil/Portugal; Science and Scientists—Colonial Spanish America; Syncretism; Universities; Viceroyalties.

MESTIZAJE

Mestizaje, which refers to the Spanish American concept of racial mixing, was based on another concept known as *limpieza de sangre,* or purity of blood. The concept of mestizaje formed the basis for Spanish colonial society in the Americas and for the *sistema de castas* or the caste system.

Mestizaje, the process of biological mixing between peoples of different ethnic backgrounds, formed the basis for the colonial society in Spanish America. The sistema de castas was the way that the Spanish differentiated between themselves and peoples of color, including peoples of mixed European, indigenous, and African ancestry. The Spanish created a series of generally denigrating terms to identify peoples whom they categorized as being of mixed ancestry. The caste terms included *mestizo, mulatto, lobo,* and *coyote,* among others. The root of the term *mulatto,* for example, is *mula,* which is a mule or a hybrid animal. Hence, the clear connotation was that a person categorized as being a mulatto was a hybrid animal. Other caste terms such as lobo and coyote carried similar connotations of being animal-like and thus less than human. Spanish census-takers and priests recorded and assigned caste terms to individuals in censuses and sacramental registers. Being categorized as a *casta* brought certain legal liabilities, such as exclusion from certain professions, and a social stigmatism and certain assumptions about collective behavior.

The Spanish American caste system and the assumptions regarding the process of mestizaje have their roots in medieval Iberia. Iberia was a multiethnic and multireligious society during the Middle Ages encompassing the Romanized population in the peninsula, Germanic peoples, Arabs, and peoples from North Africa. Northern Iberia had more in common in social and cultural terms with northern Europe, whereas large parts of central and southern Iberia formed a part of the larger Mediterranean Basin culture. During the long process of the Christian reconquest of the Muslim-controlled areas of Iberia (711–1492), the Christian kingdoms became increasingly exclusivistic; that is, all non-Christians and recent forced converts did not enjoy equal status with Christian families that traced their roots to the northern part of the peninsula. By the sixteenth century, the idea of limpieza de sangre had become an established legal principle. In order for individuals to serve in the Spanish government or hold a high position in the Catholic Church, they had to document their Old Christian roots with no "taint" of Muslim, African, or Jewish ancestry. This legal concept formed the basis for the Spanish American caste system.

The second basis for the caste system was the corporate organization of Spanish society. Corporate society stressed identities based on membership in a group, with common rights and obligations to the Crown. In a corporate society there was little possibility of social mobility. A peasant was born a peasant, died a peasant, and passed on his status to his children. The liberal concept of equality before the law, meaning that all were judged by a single law code, did not apply. Rather, each group had distinct laws that applied to them, and there was inherent inequality between groups. *Castas* faced limitations in the choice of profession and were also subject to sumptuary laws that the Spanish used to create visible barriers between themselves and inferior peoples of color. For example, peoples of African ancestry could not wear clothes made of silk.

The Spanish used the process of what they defined as mestizaje to identify and stigmatize people as being a part of the corporate group of mixed ancestry. Priests who recorded the baptisms of newly born children assigned a caste status to individuals they believed to be of mixed ancestry. The different terms used reflected what the Spanish believed to be different gradations of mixing.

Spaniards attributed certain patterns of behavior to people of mixed ancestry and in turn used these assumptions about behavior to justify the discriminatory laws applied to castas. People of mixed ancestry were believed to be naturally violent and child-like, and laws prohibited them from carrying certain types of weapons or from serving in the military where they would learn martial skills. The Spanish also believed that people of mixed ancestry were naturally inclined to vice and inherited the worst elements of European, indigenous, and African society and culture. Although some newly independent Spanish American countries abolished the use of caste terms in the nineteenth century, the stigmatism of mixed-ancestry birth persisted among Spanish-American elites well after independence.

The Spanish viewed the distinctions between peoples of mixed ancestry placed into different categories as being rigid, but in reality there was considerable fluidity in the caste system and the distinctions were artificial. Limited social mobility was possible, and individuals could change their status, often by moving to a community where they were not known. Moreover, the adage that money whitens applied, in limited instances, to the caste system. In terms of social relations, culture, and daily interactions between people, the rigidity that the caste system implied did not always match reality.

Robert H. Jackson

References

Chance, John. *Race and Class in Colonial Oaxaca.* Stanford, CA: Stanford University Press, 1978.

Cope, Douglas. *Limits of Racial Domination: Plebeian Society in Colonial Mexico City, 1660–1720.* Madison: University of Wisconsin Press, 1994.

Jackson, Robert H. *Race, Caste, and Status: Indians in Colonial Spanish America.* Albuquerque: University of New Mexico Press, 1999.

Mörner, Magnus. *Race Mixture in the History of Latin America.* Boston: Little, Brown, 1967.

See also: Creoles; Ladino; Laws—Colonial Latin America; Marriage; Mulatto; Native Americans I–VIII; Race.

METHUEN TREATY

In 1703, Great Britain and Portugal signed the Methuen Treaty in Lisbon. John Methuen of Great Britain and the marques de Alegrete of Portugal negotiated the treaty. The agreement reinforced existing trading relations between the two countries. It gave preferential tariffs to British wheat, textile, and manufactured exports to Portugal. In exchange, the British granted some preferential treatment to Portuguese wine and olive oil. For example, the Portuguese would pay about two-thirds the rates that the British charged for French wine imports

Anglo-Portuguese relations date to the fourteenth century. Initially, Portugal had the upper hand in the relationship because it dominated the seas. Then, between 1580 and 1640, Portugal was ruled by Spain, which of course greatly weakened Portuguese power. Since the end of the Iberian union in 1640, Portugal had looked to Great Britain for military and diplomatic aid against Spain. In return, Portugal granted commercial privileges to Great Britain. Starting in 1642, Portugal opened domestic and imperial ports to British ships. Portugal also pledged to purchase British ships for Portuguese fleets and to limit tariffs on imports from Great Britain. Such developments largely excluded Portuguese merchants from trade with Great Britain. At the same time, Great Britain discriminated against Portuguese products in favor of goods from its own colonies, as was the case with sugar.

After 1670, Portugal attempted to introduce protectionist legislation. However, internal and external interests led to the signing of the Methuen Treaty. The 1703 agreement, which cemented the Anglo-Portuguese alliance in the War of the Spanish Succession (1701–1714), only served to reaffirm British superiority in the relationship between the two countries

Overall, the treaty had negative effects on Portugal. The arrangement discouraged industrial development in Portugal and strengthened dependence on British industry. It had become easier to buy British goods with Brazilian gold and diamonds rather than to produce the same goods in Portugal. Increasingly, British merchants and ships were reexporting Brazilian goods from Lisbon to British ports. After 1750, the Marquis de Pombal sought to reverse this trend. Furthermore, after the mid-1700s, the supply of Brazilian gold and diamonds declined, forcing Portugal to adjust by attempting to produce goods that once had been imported.

The treaty paved the way for the enormous expansion of the port wine trade in the eighteenth and nineteenth centuries. Port was introduced in Britain as early as the fourteenth century, and sales grew in the sixteenth century when British ships began to call on Portugal to trade for New World products. Then, when Great Britain awarded favorable terms to Portuguese wines in order to cut into French wine profits, the demand for port wine in Great Britain grew dramatically. The first thirty years of the eighteenth century saw an unprecedented expansion of wine making in the Douro Valley in Portugal. A number of British businessmen bought controlling interests in the port trade and operated foreign trading stations in the city of Oporto. To this day, most of the names on port wine labels are in English and almost all the factories in Portugal are run by Englishmen.

Ronald Young Jr.

References

Bakewell, Peter. *A History of Latin America,* 2nd ed. Oxford: Basil Blackwell, 2004.

Baumgartner, T., and T. R. Burns. "The Structuring of International Economic Relations." *International Studies Quarterly* 19, no. 2 (1975): 126–159.

Smith, Joseph. *A History of Brazil, 1500–2000: Politics, Economy, Society, Diplomacy.* London: Longman, 2002.

See also: Atlantic Economy; Bourbon Reforms; Brazil; Enlightenment—Brazil; Independence II—Brazil; Madrid, Treaty of; Monopolies; War of the Spanish Succession.

MEXICAN REVOLUTION

Diplomatic relations between Mexico and Spain reached an apogee of stability during the centenary celebrations of Mexican independence in 1910 and then unraveled with the outbreak of revolution that shook Mexico from 1910 to 1920.

Prior to the revolution, Spanish-Mexican ties had been improving under Mexican president Porfirio Díaz, who had ruled since 1876 and who encouraged immigration and foreign investment. Although only 100,000 immigrants came to Mexico by 1910, half of them were Spaniards, mainly merchants and large landowners with close ties to the Mexican elite. Mexico also received extensive foreign capital, mostly from the United States.

Díaz was wary of the United States, however. In an effort to limit U.S. influence, he invited Europeans to invest in Mexico. Spain was less important for its capital than France, Germany, and Great Britain, but it enjoyed a special relationship with Díaz, based in part on the influence of Spanish nationals in Mexico's economy and on a common desire to curb U.S. ambitions in Latin America. After losing Cuba and Puerto Rico to the United States in 1898, Spain tried to regain some influence in the region through *hispanismo,* a policy that emphasized its cultural and historical affinities with its former American colonies.

Spanish ambassador Bernardo Cólogan organized Spain's participation in the centenary, including the return of independence hero José Morelos's uniform to Mexico. Of the thirty-one nations attending the celebrations, Spain received the warmest welcome. Díaz later sent Mexican novelist Federico Gamboa to thank King Alfonso XIII and proposed elevating Mexico's legation in Madrid to an embassy. Alfonso accepted, but the outbreak of revolution in Mexico vastly complicated relations.

The Mexican Revolution began on November 20, 1910, after fraudulent elections returned Díaz to office. Díaz had rigged votes and jailed his opponent, a *hacendado* (estate owner) from Coahuila named Francisco Madero. Following his release, Madero fled to Texas where he issued the Plan of San Luis Potosí, a document that called for armed rebellion to win democracy and liberal political reforms. The revolution gained support from more radical quarters, as in Morelos where peasants led by Emiliano Zapata demanded land reform.

At first, Cólogan thought that Díaz would prevail, but as the regime collapsed, he worried that the U.S. government might intervene or that antiforeign outbursts might threaten Spanish lives and property. In March, tensions mounted as U.S. troops mobilized on the Texas border and as U.S. and British warships plied Mexican waters. Cólogan advised Madrid against sending its navy, believing this would antagonize Mexico and harm Spanish interests. He also warned that relying on U.S. consuls to protect Spanish nationals would imply support for the Monroe Doctrine and undermine Spanish policy in Latin America.

Cólogan instead sought guarantees from Díaz and Madero and urged Spanish citizens to act prudently. At this point, there were few serious attacks against foreign nationals. In May, the worst incident occurred in Torreón, where revolutionaries massacred 3,000 Chinese nationals. Assaults on Spaniards involved looting and some deaths and injuries. In April, Mexican rebels shot ten Spanish hacienda employees in Atencingo, Puebla. In May, rebels sacked a factory in Metepec, Puebla.

The first phase of the revolution ended in May 1911 with the Treaty of Juárez, which ousted Díaz but left Mexico's state and army intact under a caretaker government headed by Francisco León de la Barra. In November 1911, Madero won the presidential elections but failed to stabilize Mexico. Conservative opponents rejected his reforms, while Madero's moderation alienated many revolutionaries. Zapata renewed armed struggle when Madero hedged on land reform. The crisis deepened when ex-Maderista general Pascual Orozco allied with conservatives and rebelled in the north.

Mexico also endured conflict with U.S. ambassador Henry Lane Wilson, who harbored animosity toward Madero. On the other hand, Cólogan supported Madero. Since Spain's diplomatic position was weak, it opted to protect its interests by maintaining friendly relations with the Mexican government.

Cólogan's task was complicated by conservative Spanish hacendados and merchants, led by Iñigo Noriega, who opposed agrarian and political reform. But peasant hostility simmered in regions where Spaniards owned estates or operated *tiendas de raya,* the company stores that many Mexicans saw as hated symbols of debt peonage. This made Spaniards targets for the insurgents.

Anti-Spanish sentiments flared in the summer of 1911 when Mexican newspapers reported that Noriega was bankrolling the presidential campaign of Bernardo Reyes, a porfirian (supporter of ex-president Porfirio Díaz) general and politician. This coincided with General Victoriano Huerta's campaign to pacify the Zapatistas, who responded with attacks against Spanish textile factories in Puebla.

In December 1911, Noriega was the target of street protests when leading Maderistas accused him of seizing peasant lands at Xochimilco. As verbal attacks against Spaniards mounted, the Spanish community rallied to Noriega. Cólogan demanded protection for Noriega and insisted that the government prosecute those who threatened him. In the absence of a physical attempt on Noriega, the Mexican government declined.

Relations between Spain and Mexico remained cordial to this point, but Spanish involvement in Mexican politics was still an issue. Asserting the principle of noninterference, the government expelled a handful of Spaniards in 1911–1912. Cólogan protested in some cases, but he accepted Mexico's right to do so.

In view of Ambassador Wilson's campaign to oust Madero, Madrid was sensitive to Mexico's insistence on noninterference. Like Wilson, Madrid wanted a government that would maintain the privileges foreigners enjoyed under Díaz. However, Madrid also feared U.S. intentions and found itself compelled to support Madero. Madrid's view changed as internal disorders mounted and as Wilson's efforts gained ground.

On February 9, 1913, Generals Bernardo Reyes and Félix Díaz launched a revolt in Mexico City that ended with Madero's resignation and his subsequent execution. Known as the Ten Tragic Days, the mutiny brought General Huerta to the presidency in an attempt to restore the old order. Ambassador Wilson may have had a hand in the plot, but his role has never been proven. It is clear that Wilson threatened military intervention if Madero refused to leave office. Madero resisted at first, but Wilson received support from the Spanish, German, and British diplomats. Cólogan personally presented their joint resignation demand to Madero and tried to suborn officers loyal to the president. Madrid had decided that Madero could not restore peace to Mexico, and that only his departure could forestall U.S. intervention.

Spain quickly recognized Huerta, but it badly misunderstood the situation. In the United States, President-elect Woodrow Wilson disavowed his ambassador's actions and refused to recognize Huerta on constitutional grounds. In April 1914, he sent U.S. marines to occupy Veracruz and drive out Huerta. Meanwhile, Mexican revolutionaries returned to battle under Zapata in the south and Venustiano Carranza in the north. Rather than restore order, Huerta's usurpation sparked the worst fighting in the Revolution and led to the greatest loss of Spanish lives and property in Mexico since the War of Independence.

Spanish diplomacy became much more difficult. Many Spanish nationals supported Huerta with financial aid and military volunteers. And with the withdrawal of the U.S. ambassador, the Spanish embassy acquired eminence in Mexico City, where it denounced U.S. intervention. But it lost influence in zones where revolutionaries dominated. As a result, Spain was obliged to rely on the United States to protect Spanish nationals in northern Mexico.

Huerta's regime crumbled as the revolutionaries gained momentum. Meanwhile, Carranza maneuvered for recognition. He offered reparations to foreigners for losses of life and property, and he ordered his generals to respect foreign interests in their zones. However, some revolutionary leaders were bitter toward Spain for its role in Huerta's coup. Early in 1914, Pancho Villa expelled Spaniards from Chihuahua and seized their properties. Later, Villa, too, angled for recognition, and he allowed Spaniards to return but would not restore lands outside the Valley of Mexico.

Huerta fled Mexico for Barcelona in July 1914, and Spain withdrew Cólogan, replacing him in September with José Caro. Meanwhile, Carranza sent Juan Sánchez Azcona to seek recognition in Madrid. Talks broke down when the revolutionaries met in Aguascalientes in October to form a government but split into hostile factions. Zapata and Villa were allied in the more radical Conventionist camp and occupied Mexico City. Carranza's Constitutionalists held Veracruz.

Spain was left with very little diplomatic influence as civil war developed in Mexico between contending revolutionary regimes. Forced to improvise, Spain recalled Caro and adopted the U.S. approach, sending confidential agents to Villa (Emilio Zapico) and Carranza (Rafael Casares), while Emilio Moreno operated in Mexico City.

At first, Spanish agents expected Villa and Zapata to win. Their forces seemed stronger, and Villa enjoyed good relations with Washington. But in the spring of 1915, Constitutionalist general Alvaro Obregón dealt a series of crushing blows to Villa, precipitating his decline as a political contender. Moreover, Carranza's distaste for land reform and radicalism was more appealing to Madrid and to Spanish citizens in Mexico.

In October 1915, the U.S. government extended de facto recognition to Carranza. Spain followed suit in November and sent Juan Francisco Cárdenas to negotiate with Mexico. By August 1916, Alejandro Padilla arrived as Spain's minister plenipotentiary. The normalization of relations developed in the context of Carranza's desire to preserve Mexican sovereignty by cultivating Europe as a counterweight to the United States. Carranza also hoped—fruitlessly, as it turned out—to secure arms and private bank loans from Spain.

The Spanish government hoped to restore its influence, to protect the lives and properties of Spanish citizens, and to secure reparations for damages incurred since 1911.

At the same time, hispanophobia had been relatively limited throughout the period 1910–1919. During these years, the violence of the revolution claimed the lives of 1,477 foreign victims. Of these, 550 were from the United States, 471 were Chinese, and 209 were Spanish. Of the remaining victims, there were 111 Arabs, 38 British citizens, 16 Italians, 14 French, 10 Japanese, and 58 from other countries. Spanish nationals clearly suffered serious economic losses, but in terms of lives lost, they were far from the most affected in either absolute or relative terms.

Still, Spain had an image problem that its minister plenipotentiary, Alejandro Padilla, worked hard to improve by developing excellent relations with the Mexican government. While he complained about publications that encouraged rancor toward Spain, he also encouraged more prudence among Spanish residents who continued to embrace antirevolutionary views. Padilla's efforts had an effect, although

Spain's influence on Mexican policies was limited.

The Mexican government began returning property to Spanish landowners, but this action did not end Spanish difficulties. Fighting continued in Morelos until the government assassinated Zapata in 1919. Villa did not surrender until 1920. Attacks, expropriations, and expulsions against Spaniards continued in some regions, although they declined in intensity.

In 1917, Padilla and Madrid were alarmed by nationalist, agrarian reform as well as anticlerical provisions that appeared in Mexico's new constitution. The Constitution of 1917 mandated restitution of land illegally seized from peasants, expropriation of uncultivated land, and property redistribution; it also prohibited foreigners from owning land or waters, or possessing subsoil property rights. Finally, the constitution secularized education and marriage, banned public religious worship, and imposed strict controls on the Catholic clergy.

Madrid tried to forge a European consensus against the Constitution of 1917 and even threatened to withdraw recognition as Portugal had done. Although this effort failed, Spain did win minor concessions. The Mexican government agreed to allow a small number of exiled Spanish priests to return and agreed further to tolerate public observances of Catholic worship by the Spanish colony.

Despite these problems and other conflicts, Madrid and most Spanish residents were able to reconcile themselves with Carranza and the Revolution, so that by 1920 Spain and Mexico had achieved a high degree of cooperation.

Chris Frazer

References

Flores Torres, Oscar. *Revolución Mexicana y diplomacia española: Contrarrevolución y oligarquía hispana en México, 1909–1920.* Mexico City: Instituto Nacional de Estudios Históricos de la Revolución Mexicana, 1995.

Katz, Friedrich. *The Secret War in Mexico: Europe, the United States and the Mexican Revolution.* Chicago: University of Chicago Press, 1981.

MacGregor, Josefina. *México y España: del porfiriato a la revolución.* Mexico City: Instituto Nacional de Estudios Históricos de la Revolución Mexicana, 1992.

———. *Revolución y diplomacia: México y España 1913–1917.* Mexico City: Instituto Nacional de Estudios Históricos de la Revolución Mexicana, 2002.

See also: Bandits and Banditry; Caste War of Yucatán; Chaco War; Communism; Cuban Revolution; Mexico; Nationalism; Oil; Populism; World War I; World War II.

MEXICO

Mexican-Iberian relations have been shaped by 300 years of colonial rule. Not surprisingly, relations deteriorated after Mexican independence in 1821 and were characterized by anti-Spanish sentiments in Mexico and a desire for imperial restoration in Spain. Relations did not improve until the late nineteenth century. But the Mexican Revolution ended a short period of close cooperation. Ties were broken briefly in 1914–1915 and continued strained until 1931. Mexico supported the Republic during the Spanish Civil War of 1936–1939, but relations formally ended in 1940 with the victory of Spanish Fascism. Ties were not restored until 1977 but have since been very warm. Mexican ties with Portugal were virtually nonexistent

Hernando Cortés and Aztec ruler Montezuma meet in November 1519 on Cortés's expedition to conquer Mexico. (Library of Congress)

during the colonial period and have been negligible since independence.

The conquest of Mexico began in 1519 when Hernando Cortés and his men arrived on Mexico's Gulf coast. Two years later, in 1521, Cortés and his Indian allies defeated the Aztecs (Mexica) and established Mexico City on the rubble of the Mexica island capital of Tenochtitlan. The Spanish imposed Catholicism, tribute, and the *encomienda* system, a form of labor service, on the conquered peoples. However, overwork and disease reduced Mexico's indigenous population from more than 12 million in 1519 to less than 1 million by 1630. The Habsburg monarchy abolished the encomienda system and created a separate legal system to govern indigenous subjects. Mexico's indigenous population stabilized and accepted Spanish rule, although there were still revolts against colonial domination.

King Carlos I sent the first viceroy in 1535 to enforce royal control over New Spain, or Mexico. With the discovery of silver in the mid-sixteenth century, New Spain became the Crown's most important colony and developed a society dominated by mine-owners, merchants, and *hacendados* (large landowners), linked to royal and ecclesiastic officials. Peninsular and Creole (American-born) Spaniards sat atop a mercantile system that exploited mestizos (children of Spanish and indigenous parents), African slaves, and indigenous people.

Silver was a major source of revenue for the Crown, but by 1650 New Spain's increased productivity in agriculture and basic goods combined with the exhaustion of its mines to reduce its trade with Spain. Trade remained stagnant until 1750. In the eighteenth century, the Bourbon monarchy, facing bankruptcy, introduced reforms to make its colonies more profitable. Mexican mining revived and the increased revenues from silver and other sources flowed to Spain. However, the reforms also increased tensions between Creoles and peninsulars.

Spain's imperial crisis and Napoleon's invasion in 1808 led to Creole demands for autonomy. Viceroy José Iturrigaray allowed a provisional junta, but peninsulars arrested Creole leaders and replaced the viceroy. On September 16, 1810, Creole priest Miguel Hidalgo urged his indigenous and mestizo parishioners in Dolores to rebel. The poorly armed and undisciplined army sacked Guanajuato, massacring both Creoles and peninsulars. The violent nature of the plebeian uprising united most Creoles with peninsulars against the independence movement.

The royal army executed Hidalgo in 1811, but the revolt continued as a guerrilla war until 1820, when a liberal rebellion in Spain abolished seigneurial rights, introduced a limited franchise, and ended military and religious privileges. However, the new government unintentionally hastened Mexican independence when it rejected colonial autonomy. Mexican Royalists refused to be governed by anticlerical liberals in Spain.

The Creole Royalist Agustín Iturbide made a deal with insurgent leader Vicente Guerrero to proclaim independence based on the Plan of Iguala, which invited Fernando VII to be monarch of Mexico. It preserved military and religious privileges (*fueros*), declared equality between *peninsulares* and Creoles, and established an interim regime of liberals and conservatives to govern until a Mexican congress was elected. However, Fernando VII and the Spanish Cortes rejected the plan.

Following independence, Mexican liberals and conservatives fell into a power struggle that culminated in civil war from 1858 to 1867. In Spain, the loss of its colonies—except Cuba and Puerto Rico—eliminated a major source of taxes and precious metals and drastically reduced its access to export markets. This hastened Spain's decline as a European power and sparked conflict between liberals and conservatives. Tensions between Spain and Mexico did not fade until the late nineteenth century.

In 1827, Mexico expelled Spanish residents. In 1829, Spain tried to retake Mexico with 3,000 troops. They were defeated by General Antonio López de Santa Ana. The conflict only deepened Mexican antipathy toward Spain. However, sober-minded leaders in Spain and Mexico salvaged commercial relations between the two countries.

In 1830, Spain reciprocated a Mexican decision to allow Spanish merchant vessels to enter its ports, but Spanish-Mexican trade remained marginal. Even fifty years later, Spain purchased only 6 percent of Mexican exports, and Spanish goods only accounted for about 3 percent of Mexico's imports.

Improved trade relations—and the death of Fernando VII in 1833—led to renewed diplomatic relations in 1836 when

Mexico and Spain signed a peace and commerce treaty. The first Spanish minister, Angel Calderón de la Barca, arrived in 1839. In 1843, his wife, Francis, published her acclaimed account, *Life in Mexico.* Mexico signed its first treaty with Portugal in 1843; however, relations were relatively insignificant.

Relations between Spain and Mexico were cordial but troubled. They disagreed over the payment of Mexico's colonial debt to Spain, the status of Spanish residents in Mexico, compensation for damages during the endependence war, and Spanish demands for commercial privileges. Mexican liberals were wary of Spain's imperial ambitions, whereas Madrid viewed Mexico as central to restoring its Latin American domains and preserving its hold over Cuba and Puerto Rico. Madrid supported a Bourbon revivalist movement in Mexico, but the campaign collapsed when the U.S. army invaded Mexico and acquired half its territory in 1848. Alarmed by U.S. expansionism, Madrid began promoting pan-Hispanic solidarity.

Nearing financial insolvency and faced with more U.S. territorial claims in 1853, Mexico turned to Europe for loans and protection. Mexico borrowed heavily from Britain and settled debt payment terms with Spain but failed to negotiate defensive alliances with either nation. Moreover, ongoing strife between liberals and conservatives polarized Mexican politics, leading to the War of the Reform in 1858–1861. This conflict coincided with an upsurge in Spanish imperial ambitions under Queen Isabella II and an interventionist policy under the Liberal Union government headed by General Leopoldo O'Donnell.

When Benito Juárez's liberals defeated the conservatives in 1861, they suspended Mexico's debt payments to Britain and Spain, and repudiated the French debt acquired by their conservative foes. In response, a Franco-British-Spanish coalition formed to collect on the claims. The Treaty of London stipulated preservation of Mexican independence, but Spain and France had imperial designs that dovetailed with the interests of Mexican conservatives who were seeking a European monarch and military support. France's Napoleon III saw an opportunity to conquer Mexico, while O'Donnell and Queen Isabella were angling toward a return to eminence in Latin America and Europe.

Allied troops embarked from Cuba and landed at Veracruz in 1861, but Britain withdrew when it discovered Napoleon's aims. Then Isabella opposed Napoleon's choice of Archduke Maximilian of Austria as the Mexican emperor. Isabella ordered General Juan Prim, who sympathized with Juárez anyway, to leave Mexico in April 1862. The War of the French Intervention ended with a Mexican victory in 1867. When Juárez executed Maximilian, Spain and Portugal severed relations with Mexico. Juárez then cut ties with nations that had recognized Maximilian and repudiated the 1853 debt treaty with Spain.

It was not until 1871 that Spain renewed relations with Mexico. Portugal followed in 1884 with the opening of a Mexican consulate in Lisbon. Spanish rapprochement resulted from a liberal revolt in 1868 that replaced Isabella II with King Amadeo. General Prim and other Spanish leaders abandoned policies based on imperial restoration. The new Spanish minister to Mexico, Feliciano Herreros, concentrated on winning Mexican neutrality toward an anticolonial insurgency in Cuba (1868–1878). Spain hoped to neutralize U.S. influence and reduce Latin American support for the rebels. Mexico's positive response reflected a desire to end its isolation from Europe.

While Mexican president Sebastián Lerdo de Tejada granted citizenship to exiled Cuban rebels exiles, he also preferred a Cuba dominated by Spain rather than by the United States. This remained the Mexican policy until 1898 and the outbreak of the Spanish-American War, when it opposed U.S. intervention in Cuba and Puerto Rico.

Between 1876 and 1910, Mexican-Spanish relations were excellent. Both nations enjoyed relative political stability and economic growth, driven by an export boom and foreign investment in railroads, agriculture, and mines. Growth benefited the elites, but foreign investment earnings were usually repatriated so that development was uneven. Social disparities widened in Spain and Mexico.

In Mexico, the regime of Porfirio Díaz (1876–1880, 1884–1911) wooed Europeans in order to counter U.S. influence. Meanwhile in Spain, *hispanismo* shaped foreign policy, which emphasized Spain's cultural and historical affinity with Latin America, and promoted pan-Hispanic solidarity in order to expand Spain's influence in the Americas and to strengthen its hold on Cuba and Puerto Rico. When Spain lost these colonies in 1898, it relied even more heavily on hispanismo as a foreign policy instrument.

Hispanismo first became predominant under the liberal regime of Mateo Sagasta, which formed the Unión Iberoamericana in 1885. Some Latin American nations preferred the pan-Americanism sponsored by the United States, but Mexico participated in the Union and formed its most important national committee in 1886, headed by Manuel Romero Rubio. Mexico sent delegations to Madrid for the fourth centennial of Columbus (1892) and the Ibero-American Social and Economic Congress (1900).

Positive relations between Mexico and Spain led to the settlement of Mexico's debt with Spain in 1894, cultural treaties in 1892 and 1903, and an agreement on scientific, literary, and artistic property in 1895. Leading Mexican novelists like Emilio Rabasa and Federico Gamboa embraced hispanophilia, whereas writers like Manuel Payno, Ignacio Manuel Altamirano, and Vicente Riva Palacio were all appointed to diplomatic posts in Spain and published major works there. After 1888, Mexico permitted the entry of conservative Spanish religious orders like the Company of Santa Teresa de Jesús and the Sisters of Mary, who set up schools for males and females.

Mexico and Spain produced and sold similar items on the world market, so that commercial exchanges were limited. Mexico tried to diversify by enticing European immigrants with capital. However, most immigrants preferred the United States, Argentina, Chile, or Brazil. By 1910, there were only about 100,000 foreigners in Mexico, but nearly half were Spaniards. Of these about 80 percent were merchants or landowners who enjoyed privileges and close ties with the Mexican elites.

Ties between Spain and Mexico also led to the circulation of radical ideas and the migration of artisans and workers. Mexican socialist Sotero Prieto acquired his political views in Madrid, as did the Greek-Mexican anarchist Plotino Rodhakanaty. Meanwhile, Spanish revolutionaries arrived in Mexico; among them was the anarchist printer Antonio Pellicer y Paraire, who helped form workers' associations, cooperatives, and unions. Founded in 1878, the Mexican labor federation, the Gran Círculo de Obreros (Grand Circle of Workers), was modeled after the Conferación Nacional del Trabajo (National Confederation of Labor, or CNT) in Spain.

Diplomatic relations between Mexico and Spain reached their height during the centenary celebrations of Mexican independence in 1910. The Mexican government viewed the independence celebrations as a showcase for the country's stability and strength. For Spain, the government and King Alfonso XIII saw the celebrations as a chance to consolidate relations with a key Latin America nation and further pan-Hispanic solidarity. Both countries organized events to build momentum for the celebrations. This included a visit by Spanish jurist and historian Rafael Altamira for academic conferences and public lectures to promote the establishment of a university in Mexico and to strengthen cultural and intellectual ties.

The Casino Español de México, representing Spaniards in Mexico, sponsored the return of independence hero José María Morelos's uniform to Mexico. However, in deference to Mexican sensitivity, Spain canceled plans to send a statue dedicated to conquistador Hernando Cortés. More than thirty countries attended the celebrations, including a warmly received Spanish delegation led by General Camilo García de Polavieja, whose mother was Mexican. Afterward, Mexican President Díaz proposed to open a Mexican embassy in Madrid. However, talks were interrupted in 1910 with the outbreak of the Mexican Revolution, which toppled Díaz in May 1911.

Spain's position was weak during the revolution, since it was no longer a major power in the Americas or in Europe. Its main concern was with respect to the U.S. position and the internal stability of Mexico, to ensure the protection of Spanish lives and property and maintain friendly relations with the Mexican government. Relations with the revolutionary government of Francisco Madero were friendly until February 1913. In the wake of a conservative military revolt, the Spanish minister Bernardo Cólogan collaborated with U.S. ambassador Henry Lane Wilson to compel Madero's resignation.

Mexican general Victoriano Huerta seized power and executed Madero, despite efforts by Cólogan and others to save his life. Madrid recognized Huerta and enjoyed a brief eminence in Mexico City, but Huerta's government fell in July 1914, defeated by revolutionary forces led by Venustiano Carranza and Emiliano Zapata. Triggered by Cólogan's role in forcing out Madero, anti-Spanish sentiments surged, and Spaniards suffered serious losses of lives and property. Their lands were expropriated in Chihuahua and Morelos, and more than 200 Spaniards were killed during the revolution.

Complicating matters, Spain lacked stable relations with Mexico until it recognized the Carranza government in November 1915. Relations improved with the arrival of Spanish ambassador Alejandro Padilla in 1916, although they stumbled over nationalist and anticlerical provisions in Mexico's Constitution of 1917. Portugal cut its ties with Mexico on this issue and did not permanently restore them until 1929.

Spain replaced Padilla with Antonio de Zayas, the duke of Amalfi, who identified with antirevolutionary Spaniards, especially the hacendados who still controlled 95 percent of foreign-owned agricultural land in Mexico. Amalfi disliked Mexicans and their government, and felt Madrid was ignorant of the realities in Mexico. Madrid withdrew Amalfi in February 1920.

Mexican-Spanish relations were cordial but strained. Spain objected to Mexican president Alvaro Obregón's land reforms in 1921 and threatened to refuse the credentials of Mexican diplomat Alessio Robles. In response, Obregón limited land redistribution and issued bonds worth 50 million pesos, amortized to twenty years and bearing interest of 5 percent, to cover indemnifications for expropriations. By 1923, Spanish hacendados had lost 96,691 hectares, valued at nearly 40 million pesos.

Meanwhile, Mexico began to deemphasize its Spanish heritage in favor of its indigenous roots. To the mid-1930s, the dominant figure in Mexican politics was Plutarco Elías Calles, president during 1924–1928. Calles was anti-Spanish, but his views were muted by conflicts with the United States and by his need for good relations with Latin American countries who had friendlier ties with Spain.

In 1931, the Second Republic in Spain replaced the monarchy and the totalitarian regime of Miguel Primo de Rivera. Spain's new constitution drew from a variety of models, including the Mexican Constitution of 1917. Mexico was the only Western state that supported the republic during the Spanish Civil War. General Francisco Franco's rebels were backed by Fascist Italy and Nazi Germany. Mexico's left-nationalist president, Lázaro Cárdenas (1934–1940), shipped weapons, fuel, food, and clothing to the republic and represented it in those nations where Spain's diplomats defected to Franco.

Mexico received refugees and severed relations with Spain when Franco defeated the Republicans. In 1945, the Mexican government hosted José Giral's government-in-exile and campaigned to isolate Franco diplomatically. Mexico successfully sponsored a United Nations resolution to have member nations withdraw their ambassadors from Madrid until Spain returned to democracy. The campaign lost steam by the 1950s, but Mexico did not renew relations with Spain until after Franco died in 1975.

Diplomatic ties were reestablished in 1977, but they cooled when the Spanish government of Leopoldo Calvo Sotelo criticized Mexican support for the Sandinistas in Nicaragua and socialist Cuba. In the early 1980s, relations warmed when Felipe González's socialists came to power in Madrid and strengthened Spain's influence in Latin America. Thus, Mexico and Spain cooperated in supporting the Contadora initiative to bring peace to Central America and in opposing U.S. policies in the region.

Economic ties also improved. In 1990, Mexico and Spain signed an agreement that called for Mexico to receive $4 billion in investments between 1990 and 1994. It also canceled half of Mexico's debt to Spain. Spain became Mexico's second-ranking trading partner and a major customer for PEMEX, Mexico's state-owned oil company, purchasing 100 to 150 million barrels of oil a day. Meanwhile, PEMEX became an investor in the Spanish oil company Repsol. This made Spain the largest European destination for Mexican exports. In recent years, Mexico's balance of trade with Spain hovered at $1 billion.

The 1990s have witnessed something of a rejuvenation of hispanismo in Mexican-Iberian relations. In 1991, Spain and Portugal attended the first annual Ibero-American summit, hosted by Mexico in Guadalajara. The following year, Spain hosted the summit in Madrid.

Chris Frazer

References

Carr, Raymond. *Spain, 1808–1975.* Oxford: Clarendon Press, 1982.

Flores Torres, Oscar. *Revolución Mexicana y diplomacia española: Contrarrevolución y oligarquía hispana en México, 1909–1920.* Mexico City: Instituto Nacional de Estudios Históricos de la Revolución Mexicana, 1995.

Katz, Friedrich. *The Secret War in Mexico: Europe, the United States and the Mexican Revolution.* Chicago: University of Chicago Press, 1981.

Lynch, John. *Bourbon Spain, 1700–1808.* Oxford: Blackwell, 1989.

———. *The Hispanic World in Crisis and Change.* Oxford: Blackwell, 1992.

MacLachlan, Colin M., and William H. Beezley. *El Gran Pueblo: A History of Greater Mexico.* Upper Saddle River, NJ: Prentice Hall, 2004.

MacLachlan, Colin M., and Jaime E. Rodríguez. *The Forging of the Cosmic Race.* Berkeley and Los Angeles: University of California Press, 1990.

Mares, Jose Fuentes. *Historia de un conflicto: Mexico-España.* Madrid: CVS Ediciones, 1975.

Roett, Riordan, ed. *Mexico's External Relations in the 1990s.* Boulder, CO: Lynne Rienner, 1991.

See also: Altepetl; Armies—Colonial Spanish America; Colonists and Settlers IV—Mexico and Central America; Conquest V—Mexico; Conquistadors; Hacienda; Independence V—Mexico; Liberalism; Mestizaje; Mexican Revolution; Music and Dance V—Mexico; Napoleonic Invasion and Spanish America; Native Americans IV, VI; North American Free Trade Agreement; Oil; Organization of American States.

MIGRATION—FROM IBERIA TO THE NEW WORLD

Since the end of the fifteenth century, transatlantic migration has been one of the most important processes in the complex relations between Iberia and the Americas. Undoubtedly, transatlantic migration entails the most important and massive geographical movement of population in human history. With the "discovery" of the New World, its vast spaces, and the news of its rich natural resources and wealth, the inhabitants of Spain found themselves confronted with a fantastic promised land, a land where it would be possible to obtain easy riches. For this reason, permanent European settlements were established from the earliest transoceanic voyages. Subsequently, early explorations and wars of conquest mobilized an appreciable number of young men who went to the New World in search of adventure, wealth, fame, and social distinction. If possible, these individuals sought to gain enormous riches and return home.

Far from a free, spontaneous undertaking, migration from Iberia to the New World remained under royal vigilance throughout the colonial period. In the beginning, the Catholic monarchs Ferdinand and Isabella saw the Indies as an ideal destination for prisoners condemned to banishment or forced labor. However, they soon discarded the idea. In the following years, as indicated to the governor of Hispaniola, Nicolás de Ovando, royal policies encouraged and facilitated the emigration of poor, Catholic families to work in the Indies, preferably in agriculture. Charles V even decreed the return of single settlers to Spain in order to take their spouses and children to the Indies. Through this measure, the Crown attempted to resolve the conflict posed by an important number of adventurers and vagabonds who wandered about the New World in search of fortune. On the other hand, the emigration of single women was encouraged because their scarcity in the Indies posed serious problems like prostitution and a high degree of illegitimate unions and births, mainly between Spaniards and natives.

From its foundation in 1503, the Board of Trade (Casa de Contratación) became the royal institution charged with controlling emigration. This it did by issuing permissions or licenses for embarkation. In this way, officials attempted to avoid spontaneous migrations and, at the same time, obtain the archetype of the suitable emigrant preferred by the state. The principal objective was to create an ideal Christian society without the defects of the old continent in America. According to this principle, from 1501 the Laws of the Indies impeded the passage to the New World of Jews and Moors expelled from Spain, new Christians (*moriscos* and *judeoconversos*), any person processed by the Inquisition, heretics, gypsies, and delinquents. The list of prohibited persons also included foreigners, since the Crown considered the Indies an exclusive monopoly of Spain. Nevertheless, from 1526 through 1531, Charles V permitted the subjects of other nations he ruled to travel to America. Later, these foreigners would be excluded, although extraordinary licenses were frequently conceded, as in the case of those accorded to foreign men who had resided in Spain for ten years and were married to Spanish women.

In reality, this system of control never worked perfectly and continually presented grave deficiencies. The government lacked efficient means of information and vigilance, a situation complicated by the habitual corruption of its functionaries. For these reasons, persons excluded by law frequently reached the Americas. Clandestine emigration hardly would have been so common without the connivance of the officials of the Board of Trade, ship captains, and sailors. One of the usual strategies, in addition to the falsification of documents and witnesses required for the concession of licenses, was embarkation as a sailor or soldier in order to desert upon reaching one's destiny. Others registered themselves as servants of relevant personages, who sometimes profited from the sale of licenses. If caught, illegal migrants typically were issued a fine, and authorities usually legalized cases of clandestine emigration found in the Indies.

In sixteenth-century Spain, demographic expansion increased the pressure on the region's already scarce vital resources. Moreover, the human demands of the conquest, exploration, and settlement of America led the Crown to encourage emigration; royal policies and decrees promoted the departure of families of farmers by conceding them free passage, land, laborers, and tax exemptions. On the other hand, the seventeenth century witnessed a period of demographic crisis, which brought the imposition of tighter restrictions on emigration to the New World. However, the restrictions did not endure. With the demographic resurgence of the eighteenth century, Spain's Bourbon monarchs, dedicated to the economic recovery and geographical expansion of the Indies, once again promoted emigration.

The qualitative and quantitative analysis of Spanish emigration to the Indies during the colonial period presents a series of problems that prevent determining precise numbers. Rulers during this prestatistical age had no consciousness or means of assessing the utility and repercussions of the quantification of social phenomena. Thus, the most important surviving archival source and basis for most studies remains the licenses of embarkation. Nevertheless, these documents register only part of the official emigration record. In spite of these obstacles, the patient efforts of specialists have provided an approximate idea of the nature of the population movement.

The sixteenth and seventeenth centuries generally presented homogeneous tendencies. Most early emigrants came from Andalusia, which accounted for almost 40 percent of the emigrants (although this percentage declined slightly during the seventeenth century). The region of Extremadura accounted for 18 percent of the total, a percentage nearly equaled by those of New Castile, Old Castile, and Leon. Therefore, emigrants from the Kingdom of Castile accounted for nearly 90 percent of the total. The remaining 10 percent of emigrants came from the Basque Country, Galicia, Navarre, the Crown of Aragon, and the Canary Islands, in descending order. The majority of emigrants came from cities, especially Seville. This is not surprising because at the time Seville was the site of the Board of Trade and served as the obligatory point of departure for all boats destined for the New World. After Seville came Badajoz, Toledo, Cáceres, and Valladolid, together representing more than 50 percent of the total. Foreigners accounted for less than 1 percent of the official number of emigrants; they were usually Portuguese or Italians, followed by Flemish, Greeks, and French.

With respect to the emigrants' gender, men manifestly outnumbered women. Although women did not exceed 5 percent of total emigrants during the conquest period, by the middle of the sixteenth century, female emigration had risen to 28 percent. Among these women, 40 percent were married, accompanying their husbands or going to meet them, and 54 percent were single, some of them in search of convenient marriages to newly rich Americans. The socioprofessional structure of the migrants, on the other hand, was diverse and is inextricably connected to urban developments in the Indies. For example, in the early stages of colonization, the warring hidalgos of the conquest predominated, followed by evangelizing clerics, mariners, and adventurers of undefined occupation. Subsequently, the number of functionaries, soldiers, and ecclesiastics increased, as did the numbers of servants, merchants, artisans, and professionals (doctors, professions, scribes). The poor could rarely afford to travel to the Indies. The price of the voyage could reach more than one-half of an artisan's annual salary.

Another important aspect of colonial migration was the emigrants' destinations. In the beginning, the Antilles was the most common destination; however, with the conclusion of the conquest in the mid-sixteenth century, the American mainland, in particular Mexico and Peru, emerged as the declared destinations of choice. Peru attracted 49 percent of emigrants and Mexico 35 percent until the mid-seventeenth century. Subsequently, Mexico emerged as the preferred destination. In general, colonization had a remarkably urban character; for this reason, the districts of the Audiencias of Mexico, Lima, and Charcas, which contained the largest cities (Mexico, Lima, Potosi), attracted the most emigrants. Destinations such as La Florida, Guatemala, Honduras, Nicaragua, Costa Rica, Panama, Chile, Río de la Plata, and New Granada lagged far behind, each drawing fewer than 2 percent of all emigrants.

In the eighteenth century, the internal configuration and regional provenance of emigration underwent important changes. Furthermore, the number of bureaucrats, officials, and military engineers increased. The number of servants also continued to rise, as did the number of merchants. Passengers' origins also diversified. Andalusia now accounted for 24 percent of the emigrants, followed by Castile with 15 percent. At the same time, emigration from northern Spain increased significantly, with Basques making up 11 percent of all emigrants, Galicians (6 percent), Cantabrians (6 percent), and Austurians (4 percent). The rise of emigrants from Catalonia (5 percent) and the Canary Islands also is noteworthy, as is the dramatic decline of emigrants from Extremadura (to 1 percent), roughly the same total as Aragon and the Balearics. These figures reveal the effects of Bourbon policies aimed at giving Spain's peripheral regions a greater role in the Indies. The index of foreigners rose to 20 percent, consisting mainly of Italians, Portuguese, French, Irish, and English. Similarly, the proportion of women fell to 14 percent; 50 percent of the women were married, whereas 82 percent of the men were single. Regarding their destinations and in response to state policy, previously marginal areas grew in importance, namely, the Río de la Plata, New Granada, the Antilles, and Florida, and particularly the cities of Cartagena de Indies, Buenos Aires, and Havana.

The most difficult problem is determining the actual number of emigrants. The absence of reliable sources and necessary data makes specialists' figures approximate and provisional. Current estimates place the number of sixteenth-century emigrants at roughly 250,000, a figure that would fall to 100,000 in the seventeenth century. The eighteenth century saw another 100,000 emigrants, with an additional 25,000 during the first third of the nineteenth century. According to these calculations, the entire colonial period produced some 500,000 emigrants, or an average of 3,000 individuals per year.

Following the successful independence movements in most of Spanish America, Spain's laws from 1836 through 1853 attempted to prohibit Spanish migration to the Americas, with the exception of Cuba and Puerto Rico, which remained part of Spain's colonial empire. Nevertheless, in the second half of the nineteenth century, Spaniards comprised 28 percent of the 11 million Europeans who migrated to Hispanic America. The majority moved from overpopulated areas with scarce agricultural development, such as Asturias, Galicia, and the Canary Islands. The destination of preference was now the regions of important agricultural expansion: Argentina, Brazil, Uruguay, and Cuba. Although the Great Depression of the 1930s occasioned the return of many migrants, the Spanish Civil War of 1936 provoked an exodus of exiled Republicans, many of whom found a generous and sympathetic refuge in countries such as Mexico and Argentina, where they made important intellectual and professional contributions. Yet the story does not end there. Today the tendency has inverted, and it is Spain that receives thousands of Hispano-Americans who search for prosperity in the Old World.

Carlos Alberto González Sánchez

References

Boyd-Bowman, Peter. *Patterns of Spanish Emigration to the New World (1493–1580).* Buffalo: State University of New York at Buffalo, 1973.

Martínez Shaw, Carlos. *La emigración española a América (1492–1824).* Gijón, Spain: Fundación Archivo de Indianos, 1994.

Mörner, Magnus. *Adventurers and Proletarians: The Story of Migrants in Latin America.* Pittsburgh, PA: University of Pittsburgh Press, 1985.

Sánchez Albornoz, Nicolás. *The Population of Latin America: A History.* Berkeley and Los Angeles: University of California Press, 1974.

See also: Atlantic Economy; Casa de Contratación; Cities; Colonists and Settlers I–VI; Conquest I–VII; Conquistadors; Contraband; Converso; Exiles: Iberians in the Americas; Explorers; Migration—To Brazil; Monarchs of Spain; Pirates and Piracy; Spanish Civil War and Latin America; Women—Brazil; Women—Colonial Spanish America.

MIGRATION—TO BRAZIL

Throughout its history, Brazil received significant numbers of both Spanish and Portuguese immigrants. However, it was not until the end of the nineteenth century that a significant number of Spaniards arrived in Brazil. The Portuguese comprised the most important immigrant group in Brazil. During the colonial period, the bulk of Brazil's free white population came from Portugal. They occupied virtually all of the administrative positions in the colony, and Portuguese colonists owned the greatest number of large landholdings. In general, these individuals remained in Brazil only temporarily, and in most cases they were males who did not take their families with them. Yet, among the immigrants in the colonial period were others who arrived because they had been issued land grants. Most of those individuals established themselves permanently in the country.

The exact number of Portuguese who settled in Brazil during the colonial period is uncertain; colonial records do not permit reliable population estimates. What is known is that Portuguese settlers and their descendants made up most of Brazil's white population during the sixteenth, seventeenth, and eighteenth centuries.

Following Brazil's independence, the flow of Portuguese immigrants did not stop. Even greater numbers of settlers began to arrive in the region during the nineteenth century. In fact, the people who arrived in the colonial period were only a fraction of those who arrived in the late nineteenth and early twentieth centuries.

Therefore, it is important to note that, even though Portuguese immigrants were nationals of the (or former) mother country, the majority of them arrived not as colonizers but as individuals who were seeking better economic and social conditions in the Americas. Initially, these immigrants did not comprise an elite group, since many of them were poor people who had moved to Brazil for economic reasons.

In the first half of the nineteenth century, the Portuguese continued to constitute the largest group of free immigrants to Brazil. In the second half of the nineteenth and in the early twentieth centuries, the flow of Portuguese immigrants increased significantly. Although the majority of these individuals continued to be young males, the number of women increased dramatically, and families began to migrate together, particularly after the late nineteenth century. By this time, Brazil also began to receive significant numbers of Spanish immigrants.

The push factors that motivated Spanish and Portuguese individuals to leave their countries had to do with demographic growth and with the lack of opportunities in the rural and urban job markets in Iberia. The pull factors that attracted immigrants to Brazil were mostly related to economic opportunities; following independence, Brazil experienced significant economic growth, largely as a result of its export economy. The two Latin American countries that received the largest numbers of European immigrants, Argentina and Brazil, were also the two countries that experienced the most significant economic growth. Therefore, the flow of immigrants was directly related to the booming economy.

There were two major groups of migrants: those who financed their own immigration and those who were sponsored to immigrate. Usually, migrants who were sponsored to move to Brazil were hired by plantation owners. Portuguese and Spanish immigrants, among others, were sponsored specifically to work on coffee plantations. These immigrants began to replace the slave labor lost when Brazil abolished its slave trade in 1850. Immigrants were also brought to Brazil in order to supply the increasing demand for labor in the burgeoning coffee industry.

Immigrants who financed their own transfers to Brazil usually did not settle in the rural regions. Indeed, the majority of the Portuguese and Spanish immigrants who found their way to Brazil in the nineteenth and twentieth centuries settled in large urban centers. Because most land was controlled by large landowners, there were fewer good opportunities for advancement in Brazil's countryside. And those who could afford to settle in urban Brazil avoided the exploitative conditions of plantation life. Immigrants who were hired in the coffee plantations usually faced extremely difficult working conditions. Brazil's plantation owners were used to exploiting slave labor, and many of them believed that they could treat immigrants in a similar manner. Still, vast numbers of workers arrived to work on the coffee plantations. São Paulo, which was the coffee center of Brazil, was the state that sponsored the majority of the immigrants. In the late nineteenth century, an average of 90 percent of all immigrants arriving in São Paulo had been subsidized to come to Brazil.

Sponsored immigrants could find themselves in a never-ending cycle of debt. The immigrants, after having had their tickets paid, received money in advance in order to sustain themselves during their first months in the new country. Therefore, they arrived in Brazil already having incurred significant debt. While they were obliged to pay back the farmers all of the money that had been spent, the plantation owners also charged interest on the debts. Furthermore, the immigrants usually had to pay for the rent of a small house. They also received a small plot of land to produce food crops, half of which they had to give to the landowner. In addition, the immigrants would shop at the farmer's store, where they did not need to pay immediately for the goods. In doing so, they only increased their debt, since the farmer was always discounting large sums of money from the immigrants' share of the profits. Immigrants thus found themselves in a situation of indentured labor. They could not leave the plantation before they had paid all of their debt—an impossible challenge for most workers. Many complained that plantation owners were not fair when they counted their profits, and some disgruntled workers eventually revolted against the landowners and abandoned the farms.

Some immigrants who had been sponsored to the rural regions moved to urban centers where they constituted a significant proportion of the working and merchant classes. The cities also received immigrants who financed their own travel to Brazil. Among these urban immigrants, a large majority worked in the urban retail sector; others owned commercial establishments. Today the stereotype of a Portuguese immigrant owning, or working in, a food store is still present in Brazil. For instance, people still associate a Portuguese immigrant as the owner of a bakery or a *botequim* (a small café).

Another pull factor for European immigrants was the fact that most Brazilian governments welcomed European immigrants as a way to whiten their population. During the nineteenth century, Brazil was influenced by the European ideas of Darwinism and Positivism. These ideologies gave Brazilians a "scientific" justification for something they already believed: the superiority of Europeans over Amerindians and Africans. Among other things, Positivism defended the idea that even though Africans and Asians were superior to Europeans as an agricultural labor force, Europeans were more intelligent than the Asians, who in turn were more intelligent than the Africans.

Therefore, many politicians and intellectuals believed that in the interest of Brazil's future, it was better if the region were to be populated by whites, especially those from northern Europe. It was thought that its large African population would keep Brazil "uncivilized." Thus, Brazilian rulers wanted to stimulate European immigration to offset the large numbers of blacks in Brazil. The Brazilian elite attributed Brazil's backwardness in relation to the United States and Europe to a racial problem.

Most of the Spanish and Portuguese migrants who went to Brazil were from the poor northern region of the Iberian Peninsula. Therefore, in Spain, people from Galicia (a region just north of Portugal, and whose language is a dialect of Spanish and Portuguese) comprised the majority of the immigrants, not only in Brazil but in Latin America in general. Of all the regions in Latin America, it was only in São Paulo that people from Galicia did not predominate. In that Brazilian state, roughly 60 percent of all Spanish immigrants came from Andalusia in southern Spain. This was a consequence of an intensive immigration campaign to attract workers for São Paulo's coffee plantations.

Similarly, the northern region of Portugal also exported the largest numbers of immigrants to the region. In general, immigrants from northern provinces such as Viana, Braga, Porto, Vila Real, and Bragança chose Brazil as their main destination. The Portuguese Atlantic islands of the Azores also experienced significant immiigrant growth. Yet, most of the Azoreans tended to immigrate to the United States and, later in the twentieth century, to Canada.

Portuguese immigrants had the advantage over their European counterparts because large numbers of Portuguese had already established themselves in Brazil dating back to the colonial period. These individuals often served as important contacts for others in finding jobs and housing. Indeed, young males who arrived in Brazil had been enticed to migrate because there was already another Portuguese who offered them employment or some other kind of assistance.

This important network of friends and relatives influenced the immigrant's decision of where he should settle. Even though some immigrants chose their place of settlement for economic reasons, it was much more common for immigrants to move to places where they had friends or relatives already established.

The majority of the Portuguese and Spanish settlers who arrived in Brazil were young males, and they were overwhelmingly also single. Yet, there was a small but significant flow of women as well. In the late nineteenth and early twentieth centuries, an increasing number of women found their way to Brazil, as more families began to immigrate together. The São Paulo region received the largest number of women and children in all of Latin America. This was also a consequence of the subsidy program of that state.

In terms of occupation patterns for women, domestic service was the most common area of employment for both Spanish and Portuguese immigrant women in Brazil. However, a small minority of women ended up working as prostitutes.

After Argentina, Brazil received the largest number of European immigrants. Based on the available statistics, Argentina received an average of 6.5 million immigrants between 1856 and 1932, and Brazil received approximately 4.5 million between 1821 and 1932. However, available statistics do not provide a complete view of the number of immigrants arriving in Latin America. For instance, the statistical data do not take into consideration clandestine immigrants who arrived in Brazil without a passport and who were never officially counted as immigrants.

Another fact that makes it difficult to calculate the precise number of immigrants who entered Brazil is the lack of reliable statistics on the number of individuals who returned to Europe or who migrated to other regions in the Americas. In other words, not everyone who migrated settled permanently in their first destination.

Even though Brazil is a Portuguese-speaking country, it was the third largest recipient of Spanish immigrants in Latin America. This was a consequence of the large number of immigrants that Brazil attracted during the nineteenth and twentieth centuries. In the case of the Portuguese, until the mid-twentieth century, Brazil attracted the majority of all Portuguese who emigrated from Portugal. Indeed, from 1855 to 1960, Brazil attracted an average of 80 percent of all registered Portuguese emigrants. Between 1891 and 1911, the percentage of Portuguese emigrants whose destination was Brazil was as high as 93.

The Spanish and Portuguese comprised two significant and constant immigrant groups throughout Brazil's history. The Spanish immigrated to Brazil mostly as subsidized immigrants at the end of the nineteenth and the early twentieth centuries. The Portuguese immigrated as subsidized and independent immigrants. They also comprised the largest and most consistent migrant groups to Brazil. Their presence in the region contributed to a growing urbanization in cities like São Paulo and Rio de Janeiro. In addition, their labor force and their investments in Brazil's commercial sector, as well as in some industries, contributed to the region's economic growth.

Rosana Barbosa Nunes

References

Baily, Samuel L., and Eduardo José Míguez. *Mass Migration to Modern Latin America.* Wilmington, DE: Scholarly Resources, 2003.

Barbosa Nunes, Rosana. "Immigration to Rio de Janeiro, 1822–1850," *The Americas* 57:1 (July 2000): 37–61.

———. "Portuguese Immigrants in Brazil: An Overview." *Portuguese Studies Review* 18, no. 2 (Spring/Summer 2000): 27–44.

———. "Immigration, Xenophobia and the Whitening of the Brazilian Population." *Journal of Transatlantic Studies* 3 (Spring 2004).

Martinez, Elda Evangelina Gonzales. "O Brasil Como País de Destino para os Migrantes Espanhóis." In *Fazer a América. A Imigração em Massa para a América Latina,* edited by Boris Fausto. São Paulo: Câmara Brasileira do Livro, 1990.

Moch, Leslie Page. *Moving Europeans: Migration in Western Europe since 1650.* Indianapolis: Indiana University Press, 1992.

See also: Architecture—Brazil; Argentina; Art and Artists—Brazil; Brazil; Coffee; Colonists and Settlers II—Brazil; Conquest II—Brazil; Enlightenment—Brazil; Family—Colonial Brazil; Independence II—Brazil; Music and Dance I—Brazil; Native Americans II—Brazil; Positivism; Slavery I—Brazil; Travel Literature—Brazil.

MILPA

Derived from the Nahuatl word *tlalmilli, milpa* is a term used primarily in Mexico and Central America for a small plot of land worked by a peasant household to grow corn, beans, squash, chilis, and other vegetables. Milpa agriculture is a system of shifting cultivation in which forestland is cleared of brush and trees, the debris is burned, and seeds are planted manually at the beginning of the rainy season. Plots are worked for about two years and then abandoned to lie fallow. The system requires a favorable ratio of land to local population, enabling families to meet their subsistence requirements. Productivity varies according to climate and elevation, annual rainfall, soil quality, and use of chemical fertilizers.

Milpa agriculture was practiced before the Spanish conquest in regions where cultivation was not organized around extensive irrigation works, terracing, or other technologies that required large numbers of workers. It became common throughout Mesoamerica with the decline of the Indian population in the sixteenth century. Since the nineteenth century, population growth and land shortages, efforts to end communal land tenure and limit the political autonomy of rural municipalities, and the promotion of large-scale commercial agriculture, especially for export, have undermined local *milpa* economies. Yet the practice persists, especially in southern Mexico and western Guatemala. Studies of this form of shifting cultivation are important in many fields of study that focus on the history of rural social groups, the "agrarian question" in the politics of Latin America, or the impact of globalizing economic forces on the rural poor. The environmental impact of slash-and-burn cultivation, because of its contribution to deforestation and soil erosion, has been of special interest in recent debates about sustainability, biodiversity, and global warming.

Milpa agriculture also is associated with the preservation of local and regional ethnic cultures, and with the persistence of community-based practices that define local identity, set standards for proper conduct, recognize reciprocal rights and obligations, and structure a calendar of household and community ceremonies. The distribution of land and water rights is linked to the history of families and larger kinship groups; norms regarding the work of men and women ground local ideas of masculinity and femininity; and representations of the sacred nature of the physical landscape, in prayers and rituals, draw on indigenous and European religious traditions. The material culture of milpa agriculture, including tools and methods of demarcating land boundaries, figures prominently in local constructions of history and social memory.

Kevin Gosner

References

Nash, Manning, ed. *Social Anthropology.* Vol. 6 of *The Handbook of Middle American Indians: Social Anthropology.* Robert Wauchope, gen. ed. Austin: University of Texas Press, 1973.

Watanabe, John M. *Maya Saints and Souls in a Changing World.* Austin: University of Texas Press, 1992.

Wolf, Eric R. *Sons of the Shaking Earth.* Chicago: University of Chicago Press, 1959.

See also: Altepetl; Caciques; Cah; Columbian Exchange—Disease; Estancia; Guatemala; Hacienda; Maize; Mexico; Native Americans IV—Mesoamerica.

MINING—GOLD

Gold is a rare element usually found in and around ancient, eroded mountain ranges. Its appeal derives from its unusual luster, malleability, ductility, and corrosion resistance. In much of the Old World, gold functioned as money, rendering it still more desirable. In early-colonial Latin America, most gold was found in secondary or alluvial deposits, but in some instances shafts were sunk to pursue gold-bearing veins of quartz and other host minerals deep underground. Therefore, early gold mining was a labor-intensive, low-technology industry. In the tropics, gold mine work was rarely done voluntarily; most often, mine owners forced native peoples held in *encomienda* or slaves of African descent to dig for treasure. The pursuit of gold was perhaps the single most important stimulus for European colonization in the Americas and with it the expansion of forced labor.

Christopher Columbus, who had visited the famous Portuguese trading post of Mina on the Gold Coast of present-day Ghana, reached the Caribbean in 1492 in search of gold. Under the circumstances, discovery of even the tiniest amount of this metal justified the expense of Columbus's otherwise ill-advised voyages and served as the spark driving future explorations. First the Caribbean, then mainland Spanish America, and next Brazil experienced gold rushes in colonial times. But gold mining did not end with colonialism. Since independence in the 1820s, Brazil has continued to produce substantial gold, with Colombia, Chile, Venezuela, Peru, Mexico, Ecuador, Bolivia, and the Dominican Republic also contributing significant quantities.

Gold was discovered first on the island of Hispaniola in the 1490s, then in Cuba, though in smaller amounts, then in Panama, Venezuela, and Mexico. The Taíno and Carib peoples of the Greater and Lesser Antilles appear to have preferred a copper-gold alloy called *guañín* over pure native gold, which they considered too raw, yellow, and soft to properly represent divinity. By contrast, the Aztecs seem to have favored high-karat, cast gold ornaments, a strong inducement to conquistadors such as Hernando Cortés. Immediately after Mexico's conquest in 1521, mines were developed along rivers flowing southwestward into the Pacific.

Much richer was the Inca Empire, with its twin capitals of Cuzco and Quito. The Andes were laced throughout with gold deposits, from Venezuela to Chile. Like Europeans and many others, the Incas and other Andeans associated gold with divinity, in the Inca case the sun god, Inti. By association, as "sons of the sun," gold was the metal of the Inca rulers themselves. For the conquistador Francisco Pizarro and his followers, this translated into great hoards of gold in few hands. The Inca Atawallpa's ransom, collected between 1532 and 1533, consisted of several tons of worked gold objects.

The Spaniards immediately sought out placer, or riverine, deposits, most of them long known to indigenous peoples. They were led to rich mines in the various tributaries of the Amazon, including the Napo and Santiago River basins of modern Ecuador, the Chachapoyas district of northern Peru, and Carabaya, east of Cuzco. Placer deposits were also located in central Chile, but attempts to exploit them were mostly thwarted by the indomitable Mapuche and neighboring indigenous groups.

Although gold sources were scattered throughout Mexico, the Caribbean, and the Andes, it was in the area constituting modern Colombia that they proved most concentrated. New Granada, as the Spanish called the region, served as Spain's El Dorado until independence. By far the largest gold strikes in Spanish America occurred there, with sporadic regional booms and busts the standard pattern throughout the colony's history. Indeed, the economic history of colonial Colombia is at root the story of shifting gold mining frontiers, and with it the expansion of African slavery. Gold was only slowly displaced by coffee after independence. Colombia's Pacific coast was the last region to be exploited, although highland mines continued to produce.

For the Portuguese, the bonanza came in 1695 with the discovery of gold in the interior highlands north of Rio de Janeiro. This strike led to the world's greatest gold rush prior to 1849. Nearly half a million Portuguese migrated to Brazil by 1750, the African slave trade ballooned, and the relatively pristine natural environment of Brazil's south-central interior was permanently altered. The rush yielded at least 1 million kilograms of gold but did little to develop either the Brazilian or Portuguese economies.

Portugal in fact became highly dependent on England following the Methuen Treaty of 1703, and Brazil was blanketed with laws and taxes restricting trade, innovation, and industrialization. The colony was nevertheless elevated to a viceroyalty in 1720, and its capital was moved from Salvador to Rio de Janeiro in 1763. The first stirrings of independence arose in Minas Gerais, or "General Mines," as the core gold district was called. Mining frontiers extended far into the interior as well, with important eighteenth-century placer works in Goiás and Mato Grosso. The Amazon region was only exploited in the twentieth century, stimulated largely by spiking gold prices in the 1980s.

Together, New Granada and Brazil produced the bulk of world gold in the colonial era, and both depended almost entirely on enslaved African laborers. Independence here and elsewhere in Latin America in the 1820s led to waves of foreign investment, first British, then U.S., then a mixture of French, Dutch, German, and more recently Canadian, Australian, Japanese, and other nations' firms. Free labor displaced slavery by the late nineteenth century throughout Latin America, but gold mining techniques have continued to run the gamut from primitive prospecting to highly mechanized, deep-shaft excavation.

Native Americans had mined gold both above and underground in pre-Columbian times. Europeans simply expanded the scale of operations and introduced new tools. Placer or alluvial deposits were first exploited, usually using a combination of iron-tipped handtools and wooden gold pans (*bateas/bateias*). The banks of flowing streams and rivers were excavated and sifted first, using gravity and water. Older terraces were eventually exploited as well, a process requiring more coordinated labor and planning. The most complex placer works entailed massive forest clearing, along with construction of elaborate dams, holding tanks, and canals. Such works consumed many hands and often took decades of preparation before any gold washing took place. Though small by modern standards, pit placer mines led to significant deforestation, river sedimentation, and other environmental problems. In colonial times this was most evident in Brazil. Miners were frequently dependent on neighboring indigenous inhabitants for food supplies as well, encouraging the further expansion of swidden agriculture. All told, the majority of gold mine work in colonial and early national Latin America was of this "pit placering" type.

Male Native American workers between the ages of eighteen and fifty were forced to mine by early Spanish *encomenderos* as both slaves and quasi-serfs. Such coerced mine labor was curbed by the Spanish Crown as early as the 1510s, although it persisted in frontier regions into the eighteenth century. A solution to the resultant labor shortage was to import enslaved Africans. These workers, whose welfare Iberian monarchs cared less about, soon outnumbered indigenous gold washers in most districts. African miners, male and female, were at work in Hispaniola within decades of Columbus's arrival. In both New Granada and Brazil in their eighteenth-century heyday, tens of thousands of African and African-descended slaves toiled in the gold fields. Descendants of enslaved colonial miners continue to produce gold in Colombia, Brazil, Ecuador, Venezuela, Bolivia, and Peru.

In New Granada particularly, African and African-descended men, women, and children all participated in the complex process of gold washing. Enslaved African miners appear to have learned techniques from native miners in some areas, while others probably had experience in either gold, copper, or iron mining and metallurgy in western Africa. Blacksmiths, who supplied miners with essential tools, were almost universally African. In Brazil, few indigenous workers could be found in the mines of the eighteenth-century core districts—and almost no women of any ethnicity. Skewed sex and age ratios were a common feature of most mining districts but were especially notable in gold rush–era Brazil.

Underground gold mines were rarer than alluvial ones, but several were exploited in colonial times in Honduras, New Granada, Ecuador, Peru, and Brazil. In Mexico gold was often a by-product of silver mining, which had reached extraordinary depths by the late eighteenth century. The deepest gold mines of the modern Americas are now found in Minas Gerais, Brazil. As with silver mining, following gold underground was a more capital-intensive process than placering and one that relied heavily on imported techniques and machinery.

Initially, tunneling in hard rock was arduous and done mostly without explosives. Iron and steel tools were consumed in notable quantities. Refining required expensive crushing apparatus and complex chemical treatments. Mercury was frequently used in the cleanup, or final separation of gold particles from waste material, but not to the extent found in silver refining. Smelting, which consumed precious fuel, was also practiced. Some African slaves were used in underground mining in both Brazil and Spanish America, but more often the Spanish established indigenous draft labor systems (*mita/repartimiento*) resembling those set up for the much larger silver mines. Some of these persisted beyond independence. For all workers mine labor was highly dangerous and frequently deadly.

Mine work did not become safer with independence, but it grew in complexity. British firms introduced steam-pumps, elevators, railroads, and other mechanical apparatus throughout Latin America, but slave and otherwise coerced labor was retained in many places. A case in point is Minas Gerais, Brazil. Free labor became common only with the Liberal reforms of the later nineteenth century. In this era, U.S. mining companies introduced large dredges, pneumatic drills, and new refining processes, many of them developed in California, Alaska, Australia, and South Africa. Nations such as Brazil and Bolivia nationalized mineral assets in the twentieth century in hopes of keeping profits in country, but this trend has been largely reversed since the 1990s. As in colonial times, both high-investment and small-scale gold mining have continued to generate huge environmental problems, along with social discord.

Kris E. Lane

References

Bakewell, Peter J., ed. *Mines of Silver and Gold in the Americas.* Aldershot: Variorum, 1997.

Boxer, Charles R. *The Golden Age in Brazil, 1695–1750: Growing Pains of a Colonial Society.* Berkeley and Los Angeles: University of California Press, 1964.

Cleary, David. *Anatomy of the Amazon Gold Rush.* Iowa City: University of Iowa Press, 1990.

Higgins, Kathleen. *Licentious Liberty in a Brazilian Gold Mining Region: Slavery, Gender, and Social Control in Eighteenth-Century Sabará, Minas Gerais.* State College: Pennsylvania State University Press, 1999.

McFarlane, Anthony. *Colombia before Independence: Economy, Society, and Politics under Bourbon Rule.* Cambridge: Cambridge University Press, 1993.

Russell-Wood, A. J. R. "The Gold Cycle, c.1690–1750." Pp. 190–243 in *Colonial Brazil,* edited by Leslie Bethell. Cambridge: Cambridge University Press, 1987.

Sharp, William F. *Slavery on the Spanish Frontier: The Colombian Chocó, 1680–1810.* Norman: University of Oklahoma Press, 1976.

Twinam, Ann. *Miners, Merchants, and Farmers in Colonial Colombia.* Austin: University of Texas Press, 1982.

West, Robert C. *Colonial Placer Mining in Colombia.* Baton Rouge: University of Louisiana Press, 1952.

See also: Amazon; Brazil; Childhood in Colonial Latin America; Coffee; Colombia; Colonists and Settlers I–VI; Conquest I–VII; Donatary Captaincies; El Dorado; Encomienda; Environmentalism; Gold; Independence I–VI; Methuen Treaty; Mexico; Migration—From Iberia to the New World; Mining—Mercury; Mining—Silver; Mita; Native Americans I–VIII; Peru; Repartimiento; Silver; Slavery I–IV.

MINING—MERCURY

Because colonial Spanish American silver refiners processed most of their ores through amalgamation, mercury or quicksilver was essential to the imperial economy. In 1555, Bartolomé de Medina invented a method of refining silver ores through amalgamation (processing of gold with quicksilver had been developed earlier). The process involved mixing salt and mercury with a crushed ore slurry. The mercury combined with the silver to form an amalgam. Workers then washed away the dross, separating out the amalgam, which they heated to volatilize off the mercury, leaving the silver. This process made it possible to refine lower-grade ores; it also consumed less fuel. The new technology spread throughout Spanish America, and by 1572 it was introduced at Potosí. Amalgamation quickly became the predominant refining technique in the Spanish Andes.

The mercury used in Spanish America came from two principal sources: Almadén (Spain) and Huancavelica (Peru). On a few occasions Spain purchased mercury from Idrija (Slovenia) or from China. Punitaqui (Chile) and Cuernavaca (Mexico) also produced small amounts of quicksilver during colonial times. Although miners occasionally encountered elemental mercury, they typically extracted and refined cinnabar (mercuric sulphide).

Throughout the colonial era, Huancavelica generally supplied quicksilver to Andean mines, with Potosí monopolizing most of what was produced; Almadén's output went to Mexico. However, during the 1600s, the Crown shifted part of Almadén's mercury to the Andes. The government took responsibility for the distribution of mercury to the mines, aiming to promote bullion production and to ensure the refiners' payment of mining taxes, as there was generally a relationship (*correspondencia*) between the amount of mercury used and the quantity of silver it yielded: 100 pounds of mercury could be expected to refine approximately 100 marks of silver.

Almadén was the world's richest mercury district and had been active since Roman times. Charles V gave the Almadén concession to the Fuggers, the great German banking family, because their loans helped underwrite his election as Holy Roman emperor. However, the Fuggers had great difficulty supplying sufficient quicksilver to satisfy the colonial silver refiners' demands for mercury. Struggling to attract sufficient labor to increase mercury output, they persuaded the Crown to send convicts to work at Almadén. The workforce consequently consisted of free laborers, slaves, and convicts. Almadén's output expanded until the 1620s, when it reached 4,000 to 5,000 *quintales* (a quintal was 100 pounds) annually and then declined. In 1645 the Crown rescinded the Fugger concession and took over direct operation of the mines. By the 1690s, annual output fell to little more than 1,000 quintales. In 1698, however, the discovery of rich deposits and the opening of El Castillo mine touched off an expansive phase, and Almadén reached more than 20,000 hundredweight per year in the 1780s and 1790s. The great Mexican silver boom of the eighteenth century would have been impossible without the flood of quicksilver from Almadén.

Andeans revealed the rich Huancavelica deposits to Spaniards in 1563, and the following year mining began. In the 1570s, Viceroy Francisco de Toledo asserted the monarchy's right to the deposits and expropriated them from the claimholders. Toledo then established a contract with a guild of miners to exploit Huancavelica. Such contracts stipulated the amount of mercury to be produced annually and the price the government paid the guild for it. The contracts also provided the operators with cheap forced indigenous labor (*mita*) to supplement whatever free workers the guild could attract. Huancavelica produced as much as 8,000 quintales per year with its virgin ores, but output gradually declined over the 1600s, beset by labor scarcities and exhaustion of the best pits. In the early 1600s, the mines were so poorly ventilated and inflicted such mortality on the indigenous labor force that Viceroy Luis de Velasco stopped underground work. But his proscription did not last, given the economy and the Crown's dependence on colonial silver. The guild took four decades to dig a long adit, which intersected the lower part of the mine and ventilated it. Its final stretches were excavated by blasting. Around 1700 Huancavelica's production fell to as little as 2,000–3,000 quintales per year. It recovered briefly in the mid-1700s but during the second half of the century was unable to meet demand from the Andean silver mines. In 1779 visitador general José Antonio Areche abolished the Huancavelica guild and turned the mines over to a single operator, Nicolas Saravia. Areche's hope of increasing production and cutting the cost of mercury to the silver refiners died with Saravia in 1780. The government then took over direct management of Huancavelica. The top half of the mine collapsed in 1786, and although Huancavelica continued to produce some mercury, the Andes became ever more dependent on European quicksilver.

Work at the mercury mines was dangerous not only because of the cave-ins and silicosis that characterized early modern mining, but also because of quicksilver's high toxicity. While they toiled, miners inhaled mercury-impregnated dust and absorbed the poison through their skin. It attacked their nervous systems, causing some to tremble so violently that they could not walk or feed themselves. Their gums ulcerated and their teeth fell out. Thousands died. A colonial official called Huancavelica a "public slaughterhouse," some indigenous mothers allegedly crippled their sons to incapacitate them for work there, and many men abandoned their villages, migrating to areas not subject to the Huancavelica *mita.* Exposure to mercury fumes at the refining ovens was even more dangerous than underground mining.

Technological exchanges between Huancavelica and Almadén benefited both mining districts. The *aludel* ovens remained the standard means of refining cinnabar for more than a century. Assisted by Spanish experts from Almadén, Jerónimo de Sola y Fuente introduced systematic blasting at the Peruvian mine, and the Nordenflycht technical mission visited Huancavelica in the 1790s in a failed attempt to provide a solution to the mine's 1786 collapse and to introduce large refining ovens.

Silver mining continued to depend on amalgamation until the end of the nineteenth century. By then Huancavelica deposits were exhausted, making silver refiners dependent on Almadén, then a Rothschild monopoly. In a historical irony, given the long search for a source of mercury within Mexico, the discovery came in 1845 in Santa Clara County, California, on the eve of California's independence: the New Almadén quicksilver deposits broke the Rothschild monopoly and provided abundant and much cheaper mercury to stimulate mining throughout the Americas.

Kendall Brown

References

Brown, Kendall W. "Workers' Health and Colonial Mercury Mining at Huancavelica, Peru." *The Americas* 57, no. 4 (April 2001); 467–496.

Pike, Ruth. *Penal Servitude in Early Modern Spain.* Madison: University of Wisconsin Press, 1983.

Whitaker, Arthur P. *The Huancavelica Mercury Mine: A Contribution to the History of the Bourbon Renaissance in the Spanish Empire.* Cambridge, MA: Harvard University Press, 1941.

See also: Atlantic Economy; Bolivia; California; Colonists and Settlers I—Andes; Mining—Gold; Mining—Silver; Mita; Monopolies; Peru; Potosí; Visita.

MINING—SILVER

Unlike gold, silver usually occurs in nature in massive compounds rather than its native, "free" state. As a result, silver mining has traditionally been underground, and silver refining is a complex and expensive process. To compensate, silver tends to be far more abundant and concentrated than gold. Although there is little evidence of significant silver mining in pre-Columbian Mesoamerica, it appears to have been an ancient and widespread activity in the Andes. The Incas and their subjects were only the last of a long line of pre-Columbian silver miners and workers. Silver, as in the Western tradition, was associated with the moon and the female sex in the Andes.

Silver was not found in the Caribbean or Brazil but proved abundant throughout the rugged sierras of Mexico and western South America. Mines were developed in the 1530s at Taxco and Pachuca, near Mexico City, and then north and west at Zacatecas and Guanajuato in the mid-1540s. In Upper Peru, old Inca mines were reactivated at Porco in the 1530s, and apparently new ones developed at Potosí by 1545. In the sixteenth and early seventeenth centuries, Potosí, in present-day Bolivia, outshone all other Spanish American silver mining districts. By the 1580s, production from the several hundred mines of this so-called *Cerro Rico,* or Rich Hill, reached the tens of millions of ounces per annum. Even in decline, Potosí remained Spanish America's single most productive silver camp.

Silver mining was demanding, sometimes deadly work. Amerindian laborers were most prevalent in both Mexico and the Andes in colonial times, supplemented by enslaved Africans and free workers of varying ethnicities. Almost no Spaniards or other Europeans were directly engaged in mine labor despite being called *mineros;* the term *minero,* or miner, was reserved for owners or renters of mines.

To meet the labor demands of owners, the Spanish Crown institutionalized native corvées, called *mitas* in the Andes and *repartimientos* in Mexico. Wherever developed, such corvées rotated thousands of indigenous men between the ages of eighteen and fifty into mining and refining stints lasting up to a year. Draft labor of this kind was barely compensated and quite disruptive of subsistence agriculture and other aspects of indigenous livelihoods. These stresses, along with cyclical disease epidemics, soon led to demographic collapse and internal migration. As a result, mine owners moved to wage labor supplemented by African slavery by the early seventeenth century. Still, production generally declined, in part owing to the growing depth of the mines.

Silver mining was cyclical. There was often a brief boom following discovery and exploitation of friable, oxidized ores near the surface, followed by diminishing production. As mines deepened, ores became more compact and chemically complex, and flooding became a problem. Next came long dead periods in which highly capitalized mine owners, often dealers in silver bullion, paid workers to excavate long, horizontal tunnels by hand. Few explosives were used before the late seventeenth century. These tunnels, or adits (*socavones*), which could cost more than a full-size Baroque church to build, served to drain the mines and ease access to deep ore shoots. Some adits were large enough to allow mule teams to enter. Once the great tunnels reached paying ore, a new cycle of prosperity began, usually lasting longer than the first.

Silver refining was revolutionized in the late sixteenth century with the massive implementation of mercury amalgamation. The other known process, smelting, was somewhat inefficient in extracting silver from raw ore, particularly refractory sulphide ore; more importantly, smelting proved ravenous of fuel. Charcoal was the fuel of choice, given the scarcity of coal, but since most silver mines discovered in this era were located high in semiarid, subalpine environments, even bushes were scarce. Most timber was in fact used for underground props and refinery construction. Virtually all of it had to be imported from distant lowlands on the backs of mules.

The alternative to smelting was mercury amalgamation, and by chance Spain boasted a near-world monopoly on this liquid metal. The ancient mines of Almadén, in New Castile, were revived and staffed with convicts, and a major Peruvian source, Huancavelica, was discovered around 1564. As with Potosí, Huancavelica's labor needs were met by the mita draft. Mercury mines at Idrija, in Habsburg Slovenia, proved yet another source, though not a significant one, until late in the colonial period. Mercury amalgamation had been a known means of separating gold and silver from crushed ores since Antiquity, but only in Spanish America was a large-scale amalgamation process developed. A key innovator was Bartolomé de Medina, whose work at Mexico's Pachuca mines in the 1550s led to the open-air method later known as the *patio process.*

Silver ore, finely crushed by hydraulic mills, was heaped in outdoor patios. Mercury was slowly dripped upon the heaps until they flattened into large, round "cakes." The mixture was then periodically stirred by native workers and horses, with sunlight providing a bit of extra energy. After several weeks, blobs of amalgam were removed from the cake and washed, then fired in condensing ovens. Mercury was thus recovered, and silver blooms were left behind. These were subsequently smelted into bars and sorted by purity. By the 1570s, mints producing silver "pieces of eight" (*pesos de a ocho*) were established in Mexico City, Lima, and Potosí.

Owing in part to the spread of amalgamation, Spanish American silver production skyrocketed in the late sixteenth century. Some 11 million kilograms of silver were registered by the first decade of the seventeenth century. The mines were less consistent in the seventeenth century, but a general revival was under way by 1700. Eventually, Mexico's mines eclipsed Peru's, although Potosí remained important. Combined production in Peru and Mexico in the seventeenth century averaged at least 50 million pesos per decade. By the second quarter of the eighteenth century, mining output exceeded that of the first boom years and continued to climb. Mexico alone produced some 25 million ounces annually by 1800, Peru almost 9 million. Free wage workers were found in many districts, but the mita and African slavery were also revived.

Spanish American silver camps came in many shapes and sizes. Some were abandoned long before the end of colonial times. Other deposits, some of them substantial, were discovered relatively late in the colonial period and occasionally in areas not known for their silver potential. Other regions followed a steady, imperialist logic. Mexico's long religious and military push to the north in the seventeenth and eighteenth centuries, for example, was the result of expanding silver mining frontiers in both the western and eastern Sierra Madre Ranges. Whatever their size or productivity, silver mines served as the primary motor of colonial Spanish American political economy from the 1550s to the 1820s. In Mexico, Peru, and Bolivia, dependence on silver carried on well into the national period.

Historians debate the overall significance of Spanish America's silver mining heritage, but most agree that this industry left deep and lasting effects throughout the region. The export of raw wealth, reliance on forced labor, and chronic underdevelopment of local infrastructure and industry have all been cited as legacies of colonial silver mining. Some of these patterns have persisted to the present day. Other historians have argued that mining spurred interregional commerce, local technical innovation, and settlement of otherwise inhospitable or unattractive frontiers. For better or worse, silver was always at the heart of Spanish colonialism in the Americas.

Kris E. Lane

References

Bakewell, Peter. *Silver Mining and Society in Colonial Mexico: Zacatecas, 1546–1650.* Cambridge: Cambridge University Press, 1971.

———. *Miners of the Red Mountain: Indian Labor in Potosí, 1545–1650.* Albuquerque: University of New Mexico Press, 1984.

———. *Silver and Entrepreneurship in Seventeenth-Century Potosí: The Life and Times of Antonio López de Quiroga.* Albuquerque: University of New Mexico Press, 1988.

Brading, David A. *Miners and Merchants in Bourbon Mexico.* Cambridge: Cambridge University Press, 1971.

Brading, David A., and Harry Cross. "Colonial Silver Mining: Mexico and Peru." *Hispanic American Historical Review* 74 (1972): 545–579.

Brown, Kendall. "Workers' Health and Colonial Mercury Mining at Huancavelica, Peru." *The Americas* 57, no. 4 (April 2001): 467–496.

Couturier, Edith B. *The Silver King: The Remarkable Life of the Count of Regla in Colonial Mexico.* Albuquerque: University of New Mexico Press, 2003.

Craig, Alan, and Robert C. West. *In Quest of Mineral Wealth: Aboriginal and Colonial Mining and Metallurgy in Spanish America.* Baton Rouge: Louisiana State University Press, 1994.

Randall, Robert W. *Real del Monte: A British Mining Venture in Mexico.* Austin: University of Texas Press, 1972.

Tandeter, Enrique. *Coercion and Market: Silver Mining in Colonial Potosí, 1692–1826.* Albuquerque: University of New Mexico Press, 1993.

See also: Atlantic Economy; Colonists and Settlers I–VI; Columbian Exchange—Disease; Conquest I—VII; El Dorado; Encomienda; Environment; Gold; Independence I–VI; Methuen Treaty; Mexico; Migration—From Iberia to the New World; Mining—Gold; Mining—Mercury; Mita; Monopolies; Native Americans I–VIII; Peru; Pirates and Piracy; Repartimiento; Silver; Slavery I–IV.

MISSIONS

The mission was the quintessential Spanish frontier institution, designed to subjugate at a lower cost native groups living on the fringes of Spanish America and to implement social, cultural, and religious change among the native populations. This entailed settlement in permanent villages, changes in many social practices including marriage, a new labor regime, and adherence to a new religion. In Brazil, the equivalent became a labor camp for Portuguese settlers to recruit workers.

The Spanish and Portuguese brought with them a form of Catholicism forged in the crucible of the *reconquista,* the seven-century sporadic war to reclaim Iberia from Muslim domination. Iberian Catholicism was militant and saw as its mission the conversion of all non-Catholics. Moreover, Iberian Catholicism developed in a multiethnic and multireligious society. As the Catholic kingdoms on the peninsula emerged as the dominant political force, Iberian Catholicism became increasingly intolerant, and governments and Church leaders became concerned to maintain religious orthodoxy as large numbers of Jews and Muslims became new Christians, often by force. In the late fourteenth and fifteenth centuries, there were anti-Jewish pogroms in Catholic Iberia, particularly in Castile, and many newly converted Jews and Muslims became suspect in their beliefs. In the late fifteenth century, Isabel of Castile created the first national Inquisition, designed specifically to insure that the forced converts did not secretly practice their own beliefs and to make sure that Jewish and Muslim religious practices did not contaminate the one and true faith. Iberian Catholicism also had a strong mystical belief in Marianism; it was Iberian clerics who promoted the doctrine of the Immaculate Conception adopted at the Council of Trent that ended in 1565.

This was the faith that the Spanish and Portuguese brought to the Americas, and the government assumed that the native populations would have to become Catholics. Moreover, the papacy conceded extensive authority over the Church in the Americas to the Crown of Castile, known as the *real patronato.* The papacy theoretically was responsible for organizing missions to non-Catholics, but in the late fifteenth century the popes did not have the resources to fund missions and were distracted by convoluted Italian politics. The papacy granted the Crown of Castile the right to nominate clerics for positions in the Church, to create new ecclesiastical jurisdictions such as parishes, to collect the tithe to finance Church entities, and to keep a portion of the monies collected. The Crown was also given authority to censor papal bulls, or decrees on doctrine and other issues related to the operation of the Church. In return the Crown assumed responsibility for evangelization of the native peoples in the Americas.

In Mesoamerica and in the Andes region, the Spanish encountered native peoples living in hierarchical and stratified state systems, in which native peoples paid tribute and provided labor for the benefit of the state. The Spanish harnessed and modified the existing tribute and labor system to produce income and laborers for their own purposes. In the coastal region of Brazil the natives lived in tribal societies; the Portuguese had to use coercion to get men to provide labor and used the mission communities called *aldeias* to congregate natives into nucleated communities under the supervision of a missionary, where they could be required to work for the Crown or for settlers. On the fringes of Spanish America, native peoples were either sedentary farmers living in clan-based tribal societies who often practiced seasonal migration to exploit wild food sources, or were nomadic hunters and gatherers living in small bands exploiting food resources generally in well-defined territories. Military conquest of these peoples proved to be elusive or overly expensive. Therefore, colonial officials turned to missionaries to organize communities, based on the blueprint of the politically autonomous *pueblos reales* in Mesoamerica and the Andean region, where natives would be congregated, converted to Catholicism, and subjected to a program that attempted to transform the natives into sedentary farmers who paid tribute and provided labor. In cases where natives already lived in permanent communities, such as in the case of the pueblo peoples of New Mexico, the missionaries established the mission on the fringe of the existing community. These communities were known by different names including *doctrina, misión,* and *reducción,* and came into existence only through royal fiat, and received varying levels of financial support from the Crown.

Members of religious orders staffed and managed the missions and generally were independent of secular authority, which frequently became a source of tension between local bishops and the missionaries. Missionaries claimed exemption from the payment of tithes and episcopal mandates and in some instances received authority to confirm, which was normally a privilege of the bishops. The mission was to be a short-term measure, and when the natives were deemed ready to assume their role in the new colonial order, missions were to be turned over to episcopal authority. Royal legislation in the 1570s limited the authority of the missionaries to a decade, but many missions operated for as long as a century or more. In the late seventeenth century, the papacy organized a special bureaucracy to help manage the growing number of missions in the Americas and other areas in the world, known as the Congregation of Propaganda Fide. The bureaucrats of Propaganda Fide in turn attempted to institute measures to provide future missionaries with training to serve on the missions, such as the organization of Apostolic Colleges by the Franciscans that managed groups of missions and provided the missionary personnel to staff the missions. The Jesuits and Franciscans were the most important missionary orders in Spanish America, but Dominicans, Augustinians, and Mercedarians also staffed missions.

The Crown established missions across the northern tier of territories in northern Mexico as well as Florida. There were also missions along the frontier of Spanish South America from the Venezuelan *llanos* (plains) to southern Chile, and in the Río de la Plata region. These missions experienced different levels of success, as defined by the goals of both royal officials and the Crown. Missionaries faced difficulties in areas where they had to compete with local settlers, many of whom demanded native labor for mines, farms, and ranches. One example of this was Nueva Vizcaya in northern Mexico, where Jesuit and Franciscan missionaries administered communities that were essentially labor camps, and were accused by native peoples of being organizers of exploitation. There were frequent uprisings and flight by the natives. When missions operated in relative isolation or with limited settler pressure on native labor, land, or water rights, such as in the Jesuit missions of Paraguay, the missionaries achieved more success in creating stable native communities.

Two case studies, the Jesuit missions of Paraguay and the Franciscan missions of Texas, provide a sense of the range of experiences on frontier missions. In 1604, the Jesuits received authorization to establish the Province of Paraguay, and three years later the king gave the Black Robes permission to establish missions. The Franciscans had established missions in Paraguay beginning in the late sixteenth century, but the Jesuit missions were unique because they sought converts among native groups not bound in *encomiendas* and on the frontier of Spanish authority in South America. The Spanish in Paraguay had already had to cope with twenty-two native uprisings and hoped that the missionaries would be able to stabilize their position in the region. The Jesuits established their first mission (San Ignacio Gauzu) in 1609, in what today is southeastern Paraguay. Within two decades, the Jesuits were pushing their mission program into Tape (modern Brazil), Guayra (Brazil), and Itatin (northern Paraguay and Brazil). However, slave raids by settlers from São Paulo forced the Jesuits to retreat in the 1630s to districts located west of the Uruguay River. As a consequence of the slave raids, the Jesuits organized a mission militia that defeated the Paulistas at the battle of Mborore in 1641. The Jesuits maintained the mission militia, and local government officials mobilized Guaraní troops on numerous occasions to battle the Portuguese and rebel colonists in Paraguay.

The Jesuits stabilized the missions after 1641 and, beginning in the 1680s, following the establishment of Colonia do Sacramento by the Portuguese, ventured back into western Rio Grande do Sul in Brazil. By the 1720s, the Jesuits operated thirty missions in southeastern Paraguay and in parts of Brazil and Argentina. It was this group of missions that earned the epitaph of the "Jesuit Republic," and the fancy of Rosseau in *Candide.* In 1732, roughly 141,000 natives lived on the thirty missions. The missions were in many ways self-governing indigenous communities on the model of the *pueblos reales* of the Andean region and Mesoamerica. Within the missions, the Jesuits retained the social and political structure of the Guaranís intact. Although the Jesuits introduced Iberian municipal government with a *cabildo* or town council, the caciques or traditional political leaders continued to exercise control within the mission communities. The missionaries assigned each cacique a block of housing for the natives subject to their old jurisdictions, or *cacicasgos,* and in records such as censuses and registers of baptisms and burials the missionaries identified the neophytes as also belonging to the cacicasgos.

This practice continued in Paraguay into the early 1840s. The Jesuits shared power with the caciques and cabildos.

The Jesuits and the Guaraní neophytes participated extensively in the regional economy, producing food crops, cattle hides, cotton, and yerba maté. The missions controlled extensive estates in the Banda Oriental, several of which measured in the thousands of square hectares and included such improvements as chapels, storehouses, and bunk rooms for the Guaraní *vaqueros.* There was a division of labor within the missions, divided between labor on communal projects under the supervision of the missionaries and labor controlled by the caciques for the benefit of the communal group and the individual family. This meant that the Jesuits controlled surpluses, but so too did the Guaraní, and they actively participated in regional trade under the orders of the Jesuits as well as on their own.

The Jesuits directed the construction of extensive building complexes that included the sacred precinct of the church, the residence and office of the missionaries, shops for the manufacture of cloth and other craft goods, housing for the neophytes, and the *coti guacu,* a dormitory for single women and widows. Censuses show a gender imbalance in the missions, with large numbers of widows compared to the small numbers of widowers. Men went away on service with the militia or on building projects for the Crown, but there was also outmigration. The peak of building construction in the missions dated from about 1720 to about 1760. The early missions had buildings of wattle and daub, compressed earth, or adobe bricks. During the last phase of construction, stone structures replaced the older churches and cloisters, although not all buildings, particularly neophyte housing, were built of stone. Jesuit officials insisted on the use of tile roofs to prevent fires, and documents suggest that there was a common plan for the development of mission communities.

In the decades following the arrival of the Spaniards in Paraguay, epidemics spread through the native populations. Although the limited documentation speaks of high mortality, the sources do not comment on the recovery of the Guaraní populations. Epidemics were horrific episodes that caught the attention of Spanish chroniclers, officials, and priests, but the slow recovery of the population would not have been as dramatic. In the late seventeenth and first half of the eighteenth centuries, the Guaraní mission populations grew at slow to moderate rates, punctuated by major mortality crises that occurred approximately every generation. However, unlike other frontier native populations brought to live on missions, the Guaraní populations recovered following the epidemics.

In 1767–1768, the Spanish Crown ordered the expulsion of the Jesuits from its territories and placed the missions under the control of civil administrators. Although there was continued outmigration following the Jesuit expulsion, the ex-missions continued to exist as viable communities for decades. The seven missions located east of the Uruguay River fell to a Portuguese colonial militia force in 1801 and in the 1820s were attacked and partially depopulated during civil wars in the region. The ex-missions located between the Parana and Uruguay rivers, the region that today is the modern Argentine province of Misiones, were damaged during civil wars and Brazilian invasions between 1810 and 1820. The ex-missions located in what today is southeastern Paraguay continued to function as autonomous communities, until Carlos López ordered them secularized in 1848, with the state appropriating the livestock and other assets. The surrounding forest reclaimed many of the buildings of the former missions.

Franciscans first established missions from 1690 to 1693 among the Hasinais (Caddoes), sedentary agriculturalists who lived in a sophisticated tribal confederation in the east Texas Piney Woods. The impetus for colonization was sparked by French interest in the lower Mississippi River Valley. In the mid-1680s, La Salle established a short-lived colony on the Texas coast. Royal officials in Mexico City dispatched expeditions to locate the French colony and in 1690 sent a group of Franciscans accompanied by soldiers to east Texas. However, the Spanish abandoned the missions three years later under duress. The Spanish government authorized a new effort to colonize Texas in 1716 after Louis Juchereau de St. Denis, the French commander of the recently established outpost at Natchitoches, arrived at San Juan Bautista presidio on the Rio Grande with orders to establish trade with Mexico. St. Denis convinced Spanish officials in Mexico City that the Hasinais would accept the return of the missionaries. The Franciscans returned and eventually established six missions in the Piney Woods. Reports of a French trader on the Trinity River east of modern Houston prompted the establishment of Nuestra Senora de la Luz de Orcoquisac in 1756.

During the course of four decades, the Spanish established twenty missions in Texas. The missions were in four regions: the Piney Woods of east Texas, including Orcoquisac mission; central Texas, which included the area of modern San Antonio and a district on the San Xavier mission northeast of San Antonio; the Coastal Bend or Gulf Coast region; and missions established for the Lipan Apaches west and northwest of San Antonio. There were other missions established within the boundaries of modern Texas, but these missions were jurisdictionally never a part of Texas and were established by Franciscans dispatched from New Mexico and Nueva Vizcaya.

The Franciscans established six missions among the Hasinais but in 1731 relocated three to sites on the San Antonio River in the modern city of the same name. The Hasinais benefited from being located on the Spanish-French colonial frontier, and preferred to trade rather than accept conversion. The Franciscans failed to congregate the natives and baptized very few (only around 300 individuals) over more than fifty years. Those baptized were mostly adults, who accepted conversion on their deathbeds. In 1763, at the end of the Seven Years' War (1755–1763), Spain acquired Louisiana from France and no longer needed the expensive missions as a buffer. The government abandoned the three remaining missions in the early 1770s. As noted above, in 1756 the Franciscans established a mission among the Orcoquisac on the Trinity River. The Orcoquisac were also sedentary agriculturalists, and some had previously congregated for a short period of time on the San Xavier missions. The mission languished for fifteen years and also failed to congregate or convert the natives.

In 1722, the missionaries established Espiritu Santo mission near the site of the failed French settlement near the coast of the Gulf of Mexico. They later added the Rosario (1754) and Refugio (1793) missions. The principal native group in the Coastal Bend region was the Karankawas, members of bands of hunters and gatherers who practiced season transhumance between permanent village sites on the coast and creeks and rivers in the interior. The Franciscans failed to congregate the Karankawas, who often came and left the missions as they saw fit and apparently worked the mission as an additional source of food when needed. The Franciscans expressed frustration over their inability to control the Karankawas, and over what they perceived to be the failure of the Spanish military to provide more support.

From the 1720s to 1749, Apache Indians raided Spanish settlements in Texas, and the Spanish military garrisons tried to stop the raiding. In the early 1750s, royal officials approved a plan to establish missions for the Lipan Apaches, and in 1757 a group of Franciscans and soldiers founded San Saba mission and presidio. The Apaches visited but did not settle, and evidence suggests that they attempted to embroil the Spanish with their enemies the Comanches. In early 1758, a force of 1,500 to 2,000 Comanches and their allies, including some Hasinai, destroyed San Saba mission. In 1762, the commander of San Saba presidio relocated to the Upper Nueces River, where the missionaries established two missions. Some Apaches settled, but it appears that the band leaders left women, children, and the elderly at the missions while they went off to hunt buffalo and attack the Comanches. The Comanches located the two missions and raided the settlements, thus ending the effort to settle the Apaches on missions.

The final group of missions comprised the five missions established on the San Antonio River between 1718 and 1731, and the three San Xavier missions dating to the late 1740s. The Spanish initially authorized a mission on the San Antonio River as a way station between the Rio Grande and the new establishments in the east Texas Piney Woods. The Franciscans founded the first, San Antonio de Valero, in 1718, and added a second mission they designated San José y San Miguel de Aguayo two years later in 1720. In 1731, the Franciscans relocated three establishments from east Texas to the San Antonio River. When compared to the other Texas missions, the five San Antonio establishments attained a relatively high level of stability, and following the abandonment of the east Texas settlements the San Antonio area communities became the center of Spanish Texas. In the late 1740s, the missionaries established three missions on the San Xavier (San Gabriel) River for different bands of natives but abandoned the three missions after eight years because of drought, an epidemic, and a conflict with the commander of the military garrison ostensibly assigned to protect them. Supplies from the three missions went to the Apache mission program, and the neophytes still living at the missions relocated to the San Antonio missions.

The Franciscans congregated members of bands of hunters and gatherers collectively known as the Coahuiltecos from the scrublands between San Antonio and the Rio Grande, and into Coahuila. Whereas other native groups in Texas demonstrated ambivalence toward the Spanish mission programs, the Coahuiltecos apparently saw a benefit from moving to the missions. The prevailing interpreta-

The facade of the Mission Nuestra Señora del Espiritu Santo de Zuniga at the Goliad State Historical Park, Texas. (Danny Lehman/Corbis)

tion is that increased warfare between Apaches and Comanches left the Coahuiltecos caught in the middle, and by settling on the missions they also cemented a military alliance with the Spanish. A second less plausible interpretation is that the Coahuiltecos obtained a more reliable supply of food in the missions; this theory ignores the fact that the natives had a highly sophisticated economy based on hunting and the collection of wild plant foods. The threat of raids by hostile natives prompted the Franciscans to modify the design of the mission-building complexes to include military features such as bastions armed with cannons and to completely enclose the mission communities in walls. These adaptations afforded additional protection but also forced the native neophytes to live in close quarters within the walls, which facilitated the spread of contagious crowd diseases such as smallpox.

The Franciscans baptized thousands of natives in the five San Antonio missions. Reports on conditions in the missions recorded the total of baptisms and burials. Between 1720 and 1761, the missionaries stationed on San José baptized 1,972 natives and recorded 1,247 burials, and from 1731 to 1761 the Franciscans at La Purísima, San Juan Capistrano, and San Francisco baptized 792, 847, and 815, respectfully, and recorded 558, 645, and 513 burials. Altogether, the missionaries at the four communities baptized 4,426 and buried 2,963. These figures highlight the one element that eventually undermined the mission program, the demographic collapse of the native population. By the 1790s, the population of the five missions had declined to some 200, and in 1794 the government ordered the secularization of San Antonio mission, an action taken because of the greatly decreased population, but also because of the need to provide land to settlers forced to abandon the east Texas settlements in the early 1790s. Final secularization of the remaining four missions occurred in 1824.

The mission as an institution on the frontier of Spanish America came under attack in the late eighteenth century, as royal officials influenced by Enlightenment ideas argued that the missionaries actually prevented the natives from being integrated into colonial society. Moreover, settlers criticized the missions but were often motivated by desires to gain access to native labor, lands, and water rights. In the 1720s, for example, a coalition of settlers and royal officials in Sonora on the northern frontier of Mexico petitioned unsuccessfully to have the Jesuits removed from the missions. In the Río de la Plata region, settlers complained about competition in the yerba maté trade from the Jesuit missions. In 1767, King Carlos III ordered the expulsion of the Jesuits from Spanish territory, an action that followed the expulsion of the Black Robes from Portuguese dominions in 1759 and from French territories in 1764. The king never gave his reasons for his decision, but it is generally accepted that the Jesuits, who answered directly to the pope, unlike the other orders such as the Franciscans who had a separate national organization within each country, were seen as not being under complete royal control.

Missions continued to operate into the nineteenth century, although under increasing attack. In 1813, the liberal Cádiz Cortes decreed the secularization of all missions in the Americas, but the dissolution of the Cortes the following year prevented the implementation of the order. Mexican liberal reformers called for the closing of all missions following independence in 1821 and ordered the closing of remaining missions in 1833 during a short stint in power. The decree only affected the California missions, as most other missions on the northern Mexican frontier were in a state of decline. Paraguay's government closed the surviving ex-Jesuit missions in the Río de la Plata region in 1848 and confiscated remaining assets. This antimission ideology, tied to growing anticlericalism, viewed the missions as anachronisms that prevented the complete integration of natives into society and also retarded economic development. However, this did not spell the end of the use of missions. Several national governments, including Bolivia, reintroduced missions in the nineteenth century to help with recalcitrant natives on several frontiers. In Bolivia, Franciscans established missions among the Chiriguanos and the different native groups in the Chaco. These missions operated for decades, and the last one was not closed until the late 1940s. However, the Republican missions differed from the colonial-era establishments in a number of ways, particularly the legal status of the natives. During the colonial period, the natives were considered to be wards of the state and were legally subject to the missionaries. The closing of the colonial missions also included emancipation of the natives. Settlement on the missions was voluntary, and, as has been shown for the Chiriguano missions, many of the neophytes came and went as they chose, and many went to work on sugar plantations in northern Argentina. The missionaries of the nineteenth and twentieth centuries did not enjoy the same level of state support as they had during the colonial period.

Robert H. Jackson

References

Crosby, Harry. *Antigua California: Mission and Colony on the Peninsula Frontier.* Albuquerque: University of New Mexico Press, 1994.

Deeds, Susan. *Defiance and Deference in Mexico's Colonial North: Indians under Spanish Rule in Nueva Vizcaya.* Austin: University of Texas Press, 2003.

Ganson, Barbara. *The Guarani under Spanish Rule in the Rio de la Plata.* Stanford, CA: Stanford University Press, 2003.

Jackson, Robert H. *The Spanish Missions of Baja California.* New York: Garland, 1991.

———. *Indian Demographic Decline: The Missions of Northwestern New Spain, 1687–1840.* Albuquerque: University of New Mexico Press, 1994.

———. *From Savages to Subjects: Missions in the History of the American Southwest.* Armonk, NY: M. E. Sharp, 2000.
Jackson, Robert H., and Edward Castillo. *Indians, Franciscans, and Spanish Colonization: The Impact of the Mission System on California Indians.* Albuquerque: University of New Mexico Press, 1995.
Langer, Erick, and Robert Jackson, eds. *The New Latin American Mission History.* Lincoln: University of Nebraska Press, 1995.
Radding, Cynthia. "From the Counting House to the Field and Loom: Ecologies, Cultures, and Economies in the Missions of Sonora (Mexico) and Chiquitania (Bolivia)." *The Hispanic American Historical Review* 81, no. 1 (2001): 45–87.
Saeger, James. *The Chaco Mission Frontier: The Guaycuruan Experience.* Tucson: University of Arizona Press, 2000.

See also: Borderlands; Bourbon Reforms; Brazil; California; Catholic Church in Brazil; Catholic Church in Spanish America; Clergy—Secular, in Colonial Spanish America; Florida; Jesuits—Brazil; Jesuits—Expulsion; Jesuits—Iberia and America; Jesuits—Paraguay; Madrid, Treaty of; Native Americans I–VIII; Ordenanza del Patronazgo; Paraguay; Religious Orders.

MITA

Mita is the system of rotating, forced indigenous labor established in the colonial Andes. Before the Spanish conquest of Peru, the Incas required able-bodied adult males to provide temporary labor service (*mit'a*) to the state. Mit'a obligations centered on public projects, such as construction and maintenance of roads and bridges, as well as military service. Following the conquest, Spanish officials perpetuated the obligation, as the *mita,* but its objective was less the well-being of Andeans and more the prosperity of the colonial state and the Spanish conquerors.

Especially during the sixteenth century, before Old World diseases devastated much of the native population, mita conscripts (*mitayos*) provided seasonal labor for Spanish agriculture, worked as carriers and teamsters, and toiled in textile sweatshops. The mita was most infamous, however, for the labor it supplied to the mines, especially the fabulous silver mines at Potosí and the mercury mines of Huancavelica. Discovered in 1545, Potosí initially offered rich surface ores that could be smelted, but by the 1560s refiners had to amalgamate lower-grade ores in order to maintain a high level of silver output. Anxious to promote mining, Spanish viceroy Francisco de Toledo ordered a census of the viceroyalty and used its data to establish mitas at both Potosí and Huancavelica to ensure that mine operators had sufficient cheap labor.

The Potosí mita drew workers from a vast highland area stretching nearly to Cuzco to the north and included the provinces immediately south of Potosí. All able-bodied males between the ages of eighteen and fifty (with a few exceptions such as *kuracas,* or chieftains) were to serve every seventh year. In the 1570s, this amounted to approximately 13,000 *mitayos* per year for Potosí, where they worked in the mines and refining mills every third week and in theory rested from the obligation the other two weeks. Mitayos received a wage, generally a third to half of what free laborers earned. They were also to be paid for the time it took them to travel to the mines. Mita wages were too low to support the worker and his family, and mitayos usually had to take food and other provisions with them in order to survive their term of service at the mines.

At Huancavelica, the mita was smaller, initially numbering 3,000 and dropping to 620 in the mid-1600s. Given the poisonous conditions in the mercury mines, Spanish officials soon had to modify the mita there into two-month shifts, again drawing on a seventh of the potential conscripts at a time.

The mita mobilized workers for the colonial economy but devastated indigenous society. Many mitayos died during service, especially at Huancavelica. Others fled to avoid conscription. For the colonial government, the mita's cheap, albeit unskilled, labor subsidized the mining industry. In the eighteenth century, it would have been impossible to continue exploiting the exhausted ore bodies at either Potosí or Huancavelica if operators had paid market rates for wages. With the onset of the wars of independence, the Spanish Cortes abolished the mita in 1812, in part hoping to retain the indigenous population's loyalty to Spain.

Kendall Brown

References

Brown, Kendall W. "Workers' Health and Colonial Mercury Mining at Huancavelica, Peru." *The Americas* 57, no. 4 (April 2001): 467–496.

Cole, Jeffrey A. *The Potosí Mita, 1573–1700: Compulsory Indian Labor in the Andes.* Stanford, CA: Stanford University Press, 1985.

Tandeter, Enrique. *Coercion and Market: Silver Mining in Colonial Potosi, 1692–1826.* Albuquerque: University of New Mexico Press, 1993.

Wiedner, David L. "Forced Labor in Colonial Peru." *The Americas* 16, no. 4 (April 1960): 357–383.

See also: Administration—Colonial Spanish America; Bolivia; Columbian Exchange—Disease; Independence VI—Peru; Mining—Mercury; Mining—Silver; Native Americans V—Central and Southern Andes; Peru; Potosí; Yanaconas.

MONARCHS OF PORTUGAL

In its eight centuries of monarchy, Portugal was ruled by five dynasties, thirty-two kings, and two queens. Some of them were indistinct figures, overshadowed by favorites who governed on their behalf or, in the nineteenth century, by elected politicians. Most, however, left a deep imprint on Portugal, whether because of their personal contributions or their inability to measure up to the demands of their times.

Each dynastic period coincided with a very distinct period in Portuguese history. The Burgundian dynasty (1143–1385) oversaw the emergence of Portugal as an independent kingdom formed partly from the country of Portucale, a former province of Leon, and substantial territorial gains between the Mondego and Tagus rivers, wrestled by the founding king, the legendary Afonso Henriques (b. 1109?, *r.* 1128–1185), from Muslim powers. His successors, Sancho I (b. 1154, *r.* 1185–1211), Afonso II (b. ?, *r.* 1211–1223), and Sancho II (b. 1209, *r.* 1223–1248), were able to add to these gains, whether by their own initiative or military entrepreneurs acting in their name. The reconquest was completed early in the reign of Afonso III (b. 1210?, *r.* 1248–1279), when the Kingdom of Algarve was added to the Portuguese Crown. All the kings of the Burgundian dynasty struggled with imposing effective central control over their kingdom, faced with turbulent nobility and ambitious clergy bent on autonomy. The kingdom stabilized under Afonso III and flourished economically and culturally under Dinis I (b. 1261, *r.* 1279–1325), distinguished both as a ruler and as an artist. Neither Dinis nor his successor Afonso IV, however, managed fully to overcome the problems of governing a kingdom that was always at risk for noble rebellions. For Pedro I (b. 1320, *r.* 1357–1367) and Fernando I (b. 1345, *r.* 1367–1383), these difficulties were vastly compounded by the devastating impact of recurrent plagues. Fernando's three disastrous wars with neighboring Castile greatly weakened the country, compounding the preexisting economic, demographic, and social problems. Fernando died without a male heir in 1383, leaving the kingdom in the state of a chaotic interregnum.

Through election in the Cortes (parliament) the throne eventually went to João I (John I) (b. 1357, *r.* 1385–1433), Fernando's youngest illegitimate brother and former master of the military order of Avis. João's accession marked the beginning of the most brilliant period in Portuguese history, the "Golden Age" of Portugal, defined by the ambitious and rapid overseas expansion in the Atlantic and Indian oceans, which reached its climax in the first half of the sixteenth century. Yet the new dynasty was long haunted by the stain of illegitimacy.

João's first decades were spent in a seemingly endless series of wars with the kings of Castile, other pretenders to the throne, and noble insurgents; however, João gradually consolidated his kingship. In 1411, Castile agreed to a ten-year truce and in 1431 to a perpetual peace treaty recognizing the rights of the Avis dynasty. The conquest of the Moroccan city of Ceuta in 1415 greatly enhanced the international prestige of João I and his dynasty, further cemented by a series of dynastic marriages in the first half of the fifteenth century.

Domestically, the early years of the Avis dynasty were even more challenging. The economic crises and recurrent epidemics, coupled with the monetary debasements and growing costs of war and preferment, created a potentially explosive situation that had to be continually diffused. The wars in Morocco (Ceuta, 1415; Tangier, 1437; Alcáçer Seguer, 1458) and the expansion in the Atlantic were two of the methods employed to gain economic and social means to quell the growing dissatisfaction. While his great prestige guaranteed João I the posthumous appellation "of Good Memory," his son Duarte I (b. 1391, *r.* 1433–1438) was forced to deal with the accumulated problems with both hands tied behind his back.

Duarte's early death in 1438 left the throne to a six-year-old boy, Afonso V (b. 1432, *r.* 1438–1481). Throughout Afonso's reign, the social situation in the kingdom deteriorated. The records of the Cortes reveal disorder, violence, and instability in every aspect of public and daily life. Afonso, chivalric and idealistic, found it easier to govern by appeasing the turbulent nobility through gifts, opportunities, and preferments than by imposing order and fostering the economy. His son, João II (b. 1455, *r.* 1481–1495), joked bitterly that his father left him the king of the roads of Portugal, having given away all else. Nonetheless, Afonso V gained considerable international reputation by his conquests in Morocco (Arzila and Tangier, 1471), which earned him the appellation "the African." But he squandered his good repute in his unsuccessful bid for the Castilian throne (1475–1479).

The fortunes of the dynasty peaked only during the reigns of João II and Manuel I (b. 1469, *r.* 1495–1521). João II and Manuel took advantage of the increase in revenues and means of preferment provided by the overseas expansion to stabilize the domestic situation and extend the central power of the Crown. Both shared a vision of Portugal as a world empire. In the four decades of their reigns, Portugal's expansion reached its climax. The Portuguese claimed outposts from the coasts of Brazil and Africa to the Indian subcontinent and Indonesian archipelago. Manuel also pressed the expansion in Morocco, adding a number of coastal cities to his predecessors' conquests. Recognizing the role of the overseas enterprises in his expanding fortunes, he added to his royal titles "Lord of Conquest, Navigation, and Commerce, and Conquests in Ethiopia, Arabia, Persia, and India."

His successor, João III (b. 1502, *r.* 1521–1557), trapped between inflated expectations stemming from Portugal's increased stature on the international scene and the overwhelming demands on the resources of a small kingdom, was forced to choose to surrender most holdings in Morocco to keep those in the Indian Ocean. Between 1537 and 1554, the Portuguese royal family was decimated by a number of premature deaths. All of João's legitimate children died before him. The tragedies transformed João from a secular, Renaissance prince into a grim, deeply religious figure of the Counter-Reformation. He was the founder of the Portuguese Inquisition and a promoter of the new Jesuit order. He died in 1557, leaving his four-year-old grandson Sebastião to inherit the throne. Sebastião (b. 1554, *r.* 1557–1578) was a difficult young man who refused to marry but presided over some promising policy measures in the 1570s. However, his strong commitment to renewed conquests in Morocco resulted in his presumed death in the disastrous battle of Alcáçer Quibir in 1578. The throne passed to his great uncle, the elderly and childless Cardinal-King Henrique (b. 1512, *r.* 1578–1580) whose death precipitated a change of dynasty.

The most powerful claimant to the Portuguese throne was King Philip II of Spain (b. 1527, *r.* 1580–1598), a grandson of Manuel I. The resulting personal union of Portugal and Spain united the Iberian Peninsula for the next sixty years. Although Philip II (Filipe I of Portugal as he dutifully styled himself) and his successors, Filipe II (Philip III of Spain, b. 1578, *r.* 1598–1621) and Filipe III (Philip IV of Spain, b. 1605, *r.* 1621–1640), largely respected Portugal's administrative and political autonomy, the process of integration was almost unavoidable, especially where the elites were concerned. Portugal at first profited from the opening of Spanish commercial and financial markets, but it also became a target of Spain's numerous enemies, in particular the Dutch. The costly demands to support Spain's European wars created additional dissatisfaction.

The discontent that erupted in many parts of Habsburg Spain in 1640 brought about the restoration of Portuguese independence under the new Bragança dynasty. João IV (b. 1604, *r.* 1640–1656), the former duke of Bragança and a grandson of Catarina, the niece and closest natural heir of João III, headed the successful rebellion of the provincial Portuguese nobility, alienated from the cosmopolitan Habsburg court. The fragile independence did not, in the short run, bring Portugal either prosperity or international recognition. Spain acknowledged it only in 1668. João IV did not live to see the moment—he died in 1656, leaving the throne to his son, Afonso VI (b. 1643, *r.* 1656–1683). Afonso was handicapped both physically and mentally. He was removed from power in 1667 when discontent with his chief minister peaked and Afonso's inability to conduct marital relations became obvious. His youngest brother, Pedro, ruled in his stead, first as prince regent and, from 1683, as King Pedro II (b. 1648, *r.* 1683–1706). Pedro II, though capable and determined, was faced not only with overwhelming economic and social problems but also with a power gridlock that drove his talented minister, the count of Ericeira, to despair and suicide in 1690. It was only the discovery of the Brazilian gold deposits that changed the dismal situation.

Pedro II's successor, João V (b. 1689, *r.* 1706–1750), presided over a rich empire centered on Brazil. His long rule was marked by the flowering of the Portuguese baroque, with large investments in impressive public buildings and public residence of the aristocracy, churches, libraries, and art. The court pomp and the conspicuous consumption of the elites were not matched, however, by an increase in the standard of living of the masses or structural development of the economy. Portugal remained dependent on England for manufactured goods and markets for its agricultural products and raw materials. The Catholic Church and the Inquisition continued to hold firm power over the cultural and intellectual life in both the metropolis and the colonies.

The political, social, and cultural limitations of early modern Portugal were challenged only during the reign of João's successor, José I (b. 1714, *r.* 1750–1777). His chief minister, the Marquis de Pombal, pursued a policy of modernization and enlightened despotism, marked by a frontal attack on the most reactionary elements of Portuguese society—the high nobility and clergy. The Jesuits represented a particularly odious target for Pombal, and he succeeded in expelling them both from Brazil and continental Portugal, secularizing higher education to some degree. Through various mercantilist policies, such as chartered companies and subsidies to domestic manufacturing, he also tried to reduce Portuguese dependence on England.

Although José's death in 1777 resulted in Pombal's downfall, the ministers serving Maria I (b. 1734, *r.* 1777–1816) and her consort, King Pedro III (1717–1786), did not entirely lose sight of his objectives, despite the personal ineffectiveness of both the queen and king. Deeply religious and mentally ill, Maria I left the business of government to her officials and her son João VI, co-ruler since 1792. She demanded a restoration of Church authority, however. Her reign was severely disrupted by the Napoleonic invasion in 1807, which forced the flight of the royal court to Brazil. The French were eventually repelled by a British expeditionary force, which remained in Portugal for two decades, making England utterly unpopular and feeding the revolutionary liberal movement of the period.

Upon his return to Portugal, her son and successor João VI (b. 1767, *r.* 1816–1826) found himself facing radical constitutional demands that made the absolutist monarchy a matter of the past. For the next decade Portugal was embroiled in a series of political and military conflicts between progressive and conservative elements, a turmoil accompanied by a dynastic confrontation that pitted the conservative Miguel (b. 1802, r. 1828–1834, d. 1866) against his brother Pedro IV (b. 1798, r. 1826, d. 1834; Emperor Pedro I of Brazil, 1822–1831) acting on behalf of his daughter, Queen Maria II (b. 1919, r. 1826–1853). Queen Maria, though conservative by inclination, was forced to accept constitutional constraints and to preside, together with her husband, King Consort Fernando II (Ferdinand of Saxe-Coburg, 1816–1885), over Portugal's rocky transformation into a constitutional monarchy. The final stage of the Portuguese liberal revolution took place in 1851, two years before the queen's death in childbirth. Since the 1840s, however, active political power had been mostly in the hands of elected politicians, headed by the prime minister.

The first two kings of the Bragança-Saxe-Coburg dynasty, Pedro V (b. 1837, *r.* 1853–1861) and Luís I (b. 1838, *r.* 1861–1889), played a largely ceremonial role in the political life of the country, although both made contributions to the cultural and intellectual scene and represented Portugal abroad. In 1906, Carlos I (b. 1863, *r.* 1889–1908) broke with the tradition by appointing a prime minister of his own choosing. The prime minister, João Franco, attempted to introduce liberal reforms backed by authoritarian measures. His policies led to the assassination of Carlos I and the crown prince in 1908. Carlos was succeeded by his younger son, Manuel II (b. 1889, *r.* 1908–1910, d. 1932). Manuel was ready to rule constitutionally, but the existing republican movement was too powerful for the monarchy to survive. The young king was deposed in 1910, and, despite several strong monarchist movements, Portugal became an enduring republic.

Ivana Elbl

References

Ackerlind, Sheila R. *King Dinis of Portugal and the Alfonsine Heritage.* New York: Peter Lang, 1990.

Bebiano, Rui. D. *João V: Poder e espectáculo.* Aveiro: Livraria Estante Editora, 1987.

Benton, Russell E. *The Downfall of a King: Dom Manuel II of Portugal.* Washington, DC: University Press of America, 1977.

Birmingham, David. *A Concise History of Portugal.* 2nd ed. Cambridge: Cambridge University Press, 2003.

Mantero, Inês, ed. *A monarquia portuguesa: Reis e rainhas na história de um povo.* Lisbon: Selecções do Reader's Digest, 1999.

Marques, A. H. de Oliveira. *History of Portugal.* 2nd ed. New York: Columbia University Press, 1976.

Maxwell, Kenneth. *Pombal, Paradox of the Enlightenment.* Cambridge: Cambridge University Press, 1995.

Sanceau, Elaine. *The Reign of the Fortunate King, 1495–1521.* Hamden, CT: Archon, 1969.

Schultz, Kirsten. *Tropical Versailles: Empire, Monarchy, and the Portuguese Royal Court in Rio de Janeiro, 1808–1821.* New York: Routledge, 2001.

See also: Architecture—Brazil; Brazil; Catholic Church in Brazil; Enlightenment—Brazil; Habsburgs; Independence II—Brazil; Inquisition—Luso-America; Jesuits—Brazil; Jesuits—Iberia and America; Monarchs of Spain; Napoleonic Invasion and Luso-America.

MONARCHS OF SPAIN

Since the dynastic unification of the Crowns of Castile and Aragon in 1479, historians have identified the sovereigns of a shifting accumulation of Iberian, European, American, and Pacific territories as the Monarchs of Spain. Alongside the plurality of these Hispanic kingdoms, the unitary ideal of a Spanish monarchy has persevered over the centuries. Sixteenth- and seventeenth-century monarchs eased the incorporation of different regions into a composite Hispanic monarchy by respecting their customs, laws, tribunals, and fiscal systems. The eighteenth-century Bourbon rulers, while imposing standard laws, taxes, and administrative bureaucracies in most regions, opened up commercial relations between American and Spanish ports other than Cádiz. After the Napoleonic Wars and a brief experiment in republican government, the Spanish monarchs of the nineteenth century oversaw the loss of Spain's overseas colonial empire, nostalgically invoked in the commemorative activities of 1929 and 1992.

Historians generally cite the personal union between Ferdinand of Aragon and Isabel of Castile as a cornerstone in the foundation of the Spanish monarchy. This dynastic alliance, though far from irreversible in its day, set a crucial precedent for the aggregation of different territories. The sovereigns titled themselves monarchs of Castile, Leon, Aragon, Sicily, Toledo, Valencia, Galicia, Majorca, Seville, Sardinia, Cordoba, Corsica, Murcia, Jaen, the Algarves, Algeciras, Gibraltar, and the Canary Islands, counts of Barcelona, lords of Viscaya and Molina, dukes of Athens and Neopatria, counts of Rousillon and Cerdeña, and marquises of Oristan and Goceano. In 1492, this collection of titles grew to include the Kingdom of Granada and the "islands and land of the ocean sea" that Christopher Columbus encountered. At times Ferdinand also styled himself king of Jerusalem. Although this enumeration of distinct titles headed royal decrees, the monarchs employed the abbreviated expression "kings of Spain" on coins and international treaties. The title "the Catholic Monarchs," which Pope Alexander VI conferred upon Ferdinand and Isabel in 1493, recognized their pretensions to extend their realms alongside the Catholic faith. Isabel's demise in 1504, leaving Ferdinand as king of Aragon and regent of Castile, led Italian ambassadors and historians to continue calling him the "King of Spain" as distinct from his daughter, Juana, and her husband, Philip (d. 1506), the monarchs of Castile. As regent, Ferdinand witnessed the Spanish conquest of strategic posts on the coast of North Africa (Mazalquivir, Oran, and Bujía) and used a combination of diplomatic pressure and military force to incorporate Navarre into the Kingdom of Castile.

The Hispanic monarchy's territorial expansion by war and diplomacy, including marriage alliances, could produce unintended results. Hence the death of three heirs in fewer than three years led to the succession of Queen Juana, the second daughter of Ferdinand and Isabel, to Castile and, following the 1516 demise of Ferdinand, to Aragon. Upon that occasion, Juana's eldest son, Charles I (Charles V of the Holy Roman Empire), assumed the title of king of Castile and Aragon jointly with his mother, adding the Low Countries to the Iberian and American patrimony that he claimed. Charles accumulated even more territories in 1519 when elected king of the Romans and future Holy Roman emperor, a title that took precedence over those of his Hispanic inheritance. In addition to facing rebellions in Castile and Valencia in 1520–1521, Charles found his Italian patrimony contested by Francis I of France, confronted the threat of Turkish expansion in the Mediterranean, and combated the spread of Protestant creeds in Germany and the Netherlands. In 1556, Charles divided the burdensome "universal monarchy" that he had acquired and attempted to defend between his younger brother, Ferdinand, king of Hungary and Bohemia, successor to the Holy Roman Empire, and his son, Philip, thereafter

Philip II of Spain (1556–1598). Meanwhile, the conquests of Mexico, Peru, and the Philippines vastly extended the Hispanic monarchy. The death of the Portuguese king, moreover, enabled Philip to press his claims to that Crown, formally incorporated into the Spanish monarchy in 1581. Upon returning to Madrid, Philip II created the Council of Portugal, which, like the Councils of Aragon, the Indies, and later Flanders, would administer those territories. Other regions, such as Navarre, Sardinia, Sicily, Naples, Mexico, and Peru, had their own resident viceroys whose courts mediated between regional elites and the Spanish monarchy. Inheriting his father's role as defender of the Catholic faith, Philip II continued to combat Turkish advances in the Mediterranean and intensified the struggle against rebels in the Low Countries. An attempt to curtail English piracy and support for the Dutch uprising led to the "Invincible Armada" beaten by the elements and the English navy in 1588.

The Spanish monarch's role as a defender of the faith included his image as a patron of the arts, architecture, and learning. Philip II enshrined these values in the palace and monastery of San Lorenzo de El Escorial built outside Madrid from 1570 through 1584. His son and successor, Philip III (1598–1621), guided by his friend and favorite, the duke of Lerma, pursued a policy of peace in Europe that featured a twelve-year truce recognizing Dutch independence. On the same day that he signed the truce, the monarch decreed the expulsion of the Morisco population of Islamic origins from Spanish territory. Subsequently Philip III constructed a splendid Plaza Mayor (principal square) in Madrid, where his court had returned after five years in Valladolid. Philip IV (1621–1665) and his own favorite, the count-duke of Olivares, would sponsor another monumental project, Madrid's Buen Retiro Palace, where they enjoyed theatrical productions and assembled a collection of the finest paintings of their day. Confronting the economic and military demands of the Thirty Years' War, Olivares developed a plan for the fiscal and legislative unification of the Spanish kingdoms. These attempted reforms produced rebellions in Catalonia, which made its peace with Madrid in 1652, and Portugal, which regained its independence from Spain in 1668. The reign of the last Habsburg monarch, Charles II (1665–1700), initially guided by his mother, the regent Queen Mariana, featured competition between French and Austrian candidates to the Spanish throne.

Although Charles II designated the French candidate, Philip of Anjou, as his successor, the Archduke Charles of Austria received support from Catalonia, Aragon, Valencia, Germany, England, and Holland in the War of the Spanish Succession that followed the death of Charles II. Concluding this war in 1713, the Peace of Utrecht confirmed Philip V as monarch of Spain and the Indies, while ceding the Netherlands to Charles of Austria, and Menorca and Gibraltar to England. Although Philip V declared his intention to govern all of "the continent of Spain" by the laws and customs of Castile, in practice he only abolished the local privileges of those territories that had favored his opponent, Aragon, Valencia, and Catalonia. On the other hand, Navarre and the Basque provinces retained their own laws. The trend toward monarchical absolutism, which drew upon deep roots in Roman law, reached its height under the Bourbon monarchs of Spain and the Indies. As steps toward state centralization, Philip V created secretaries or ministers responsible for different departments (State, Justice, War, Marine, and Finance) and established a system of intendants rather than viceroys to represent the Crown in distinct provinces. To proclaim the grandeur of the new dynasty, Philip V also constructed a new palace at La Granja (Segovia) modeled on Versailles and undertook important reforms in that of Aranjuez. His successor, Ferdinand VI (1746–1759), further strengthened the state by bolstering the navy to enhance and safeguard commerce between Spain and its American colonies. Further applying his predecessor's mercantilist principles, Charles III (1759–1788), perhaps the most famous of Spain's "Enlightened absolutist" monarchs, introduced a new fiscal bureaucracy, tighter administrative controls, and standing armies in the Americas. He also created the Archive of the Indies in Seville as a depository for all documents pertaining to Spain's overseas colonial empire, which included the Louisiana territory from 1762 through 1803.

Challenging any absolutist pretensions, the French Revolution and Napoleonic Wars overtook Charles IV (1788–1808). Charles IV and his chief minister, Manuel Godoy, had established an alliance with Napoleon Bonaparte, only to find French troops marching on Madrid in the spring of 1808. Popular uprisings around these events forced Charles IV to abdicate on behalf of his son, Ferdinand VII. Napoleon would entertain both monarchs in France while naming his own brother, Joseph, king of Spain. In the "absence and captivity" of their lawful sovereign, opponents of French rule convoked the Cortes of Cádiz and drafted the 1812 constitution of Naples and Spain for "all Spaniards of both hemispheres." Notwithstanding the liberal aspirations recorded in the document, the Napoleonic invasion offered Creole elites throughout Spanish America an opportunity for self-rule, which many extended by rebelling against the Spanish Crown after Ferdinand VII (1814–1833) returned to Spain and annulled the Constitution of 1812. In rapid succession, Chile, Colombia, Venezuela, Mexico, Central America, Peru, Bolivia, and Uruguay declared their independence from Spain. Peninsular turmoil and military intervention in government affairs nevertheless kept Ferdinand VII, his wife, the regent queen María Cristina, and their daughter, Isabel II (1833–1868), from fully attending to the loss of the majority of their American colonies. A climate of discontent forced Isabel II into exile in 1868 and led to Spain's first republican government, which proved even less stable than its constitutional monarchy. Eventually, the throne was restored to Isabel's son, Alfonso XII (1875–1885) and grandson, Alfonso XIII (1885–1931).

Dependent upon influential ministers, Alfonso XII and XIII exercised increasingly little practical authority and generally presided over a system of electoral fraud and alternation in office between conservative and liberal leaders. The loss of Spain's remaining overseas colonies, Cuba, Puerto Rico, Guam, and the Philippines, in the Spanish-American War of 1898 entailed a greater blow to Spanish pride and prestige than the independence of other American territories. As a last vestige of imperial power, Morocco became increasingly important and gave the charismatic dictator,

Miguel Primo de Rivera, a pretext to seize power with the acquiescence of Alfonso XIII in 1923. Among other costly projects, Primo de Rivera promoted an Ibero-American Exposition in Seville designed to emphasize Spain's historical and cultural ties to its former colonies. Curtailed by the financial crisis of 1929, this Exposition coincided with Primo's last days in power. The dictator's fall preceded that of Alfonso XIII and the inauguration of a Second Republic (1931–1936).

After emerging as the Nationalist leader in the Spanish Civil War, a second twentieth-century dictator, Francisco Franco, made certain gestures toward monarchist sentiment without permitting a restoration of the monarchy itself until his own death in 1975. After succeeding to the throne, Juan Carlos I guided Spain's transition toward democracy, accepting the Constitution of 1978, which considers the Spanish monarch a "symbol of the unity of the Spanish nation." Three years later the monarch played a crucial role in quelling an attempted military coup. Although his predecessors never crossed the Atlantic, Juan Carlos has been an ambassador from Spain to Latin America before and after the five hundredth anniversary celebrations of "the Age of Discovery" in 1992 inspired debates about Spain's historical legacy on both sides of the Atlantic.

Bethany Aram

References

Artola, Miguel. *La Monarquía de España.* Madrid: Alianza Editorial, 1999.

Brading, D. A. *The First America: The Spanish Monarch, Creole Patriots, and the Liberal State, 1492–1867.* Cambridge: Cambridge University Press, 1991.

Carr, Raymond. *Modern Spain, 1875–1980.* Oxford: Oxford University Press, 1980.

Elliott, J. H. "A Europe of Composite Monarchies." *Past and Present* (November 1992): 42–71.

Fernández Albaladejo, Pablo. *Fragmentos de monarquía.* Madrid: Alianza, 1992.

Lynch, John. *Bourbon Spain, 1707–1808.* Oxford: Blackwell, 1989.

See also: Administration—Colonial Spanish America; Armies—Colonial Spanish America; Bourbon Reforms; Constitution of Cádiz; Cortes of Cádiz; Council of Castile; Council of the Indies; Defense—Colonial Spanish America; Habsburgs; Intendants/Intendancy System; Islam; Louisiana Purchase; Monarchs of Portugal; Moors; Napoleonic Invasion and Spanish America; Pirates and Piracy; Spanish-American War; Thirty Years' War; Utrecht, Treaty of; Viceroyalties; War of the Spanish Succession.

MONOPOLIES

Monopolies in Spanish America were grants of exclusive rights to individuals or interest groups for the production or commercialization of goods and services. Such monopoly grants were pervasive in colonial Spanish America. Under mercantilism, which was the predominant economic doctrine at the time, protectionist policies were seen as necessary tools for the expansion of the wealth and power of nations.

The foremost example of Spanish mercantilist policies was the monopoly of trade it imposed over its American possessions. In the early colonial period, control over Spanish American trade was in the hands of the Board of Trade (Casa de Contratación), which was established in Seville in 1503. The Board of Trade was in charge of licensing and supervising ships, passengers, and in general, all goods traded between the American colonies and the metropolis. Monopoly rights over trade were ceded to the wealthiest merchants of Seville and to the colonial *consulados* (merchant guilds) in New Spain and Peru. Only a few ports were allowed to participate in this commercial exchange: Seville in the peninsula and three American ports, Veracruz in New Spain, Cartagena in New Granada, and Nombre de Dios on Isthmus of Panama (replaced with Portobelo in 1598). In order to monitor compliance with monopoly regulations and to protect the treasury shipments coming from the New World, trade was organized around convoys protected by warships. In addition, the fleet system served to reduce the risks and vulnerability of ships to natural hazards. Two fleets sailed from Seville every year: the *flota* which was sent to trade with Mexico and the *galeones* which traded indirectly with the Peruvian viceroyalty through Panama. This system lasted with only minor modifications throughout the Habsburg period; however, over time it gradually failed to provide regular service.

Monopoly of trade within the Spanish American colonies was in the hands of local merchant guilds, composed for the most part of the Creole elite. These merchant guilds extracted high economic rents, mainly through the imposition of high prices but also through the forced sales of goods. Traditionally, the *repartimiento de mercancías,* as the forced sales of goods came to be known, has been viewed as a mechanism of exploitation of the Indian communities. Study of the Mexican *cochinilla* industry, however, illustrates that the Indians viewed the repartimiento de mercancías as a mechanism through which they could gain access to an otherwise elusive credit "market." Beyond the concession of monopoly rights to the colonial consulados, the Crown heavily regulated commerce within the colonies, including intercolonial trade. The best developed intercolonial trade in the Habsburg era was the Peru–New Spain–Manila connection, which basically served for the exchange of Peruvian silver for Chinese silks and porcelain. (The Crown had restricted the trade between America and Asia to the port of Acapulco.) In an effort to avoid further diverting silver from the Atlantic system, the Crown banned all trade between New Spain and Peru in 1631.

The monopolistic conditions of the trading system between Spain and its American colonies created serious economic challenges: namely, high prices and shortages, which provoked high levels of contraband. The Habsburg system, however, effectively protected a large portion of the Crown's treasure shipments. During the reign of Philip II until the 1620s, commerce showed a dramatic increase and functioned relatively well. By the time the inefficiencies inherent to such a rigid monopoly manifested themselves, vested interests in both the colonies and the metropolis had too much at stake to permit drastic reforms.

It was only until after the War of the Spanish Succession that the Bourbon monarchs sought simultaneously to strengthen control over their American possessions and to increase the gains from trade. In the last decades of Habsburg rule, contraband reached epidemic proportions. The Bourbons realized that in order to reestablish control over commerce, they had to relax the heavy regulations that were restricting legal trade. Although a few mild reforms were passed early in the eighteenth century, the core of the Bourbon plan was progressively adopted after Spain's defeat in the Seven Years' War. The most important component of the commercial reforms was the "free trade" law *(Reglamento para el comercio libre)* of 1778. The new law did not imply a drastic change in the monopolistic conditions of the trading system. Under the new system, the metropolis still enjoyed a monopoly over commerce with its American colonies. The main difference with the old system was the expansion of the number of ports allowed to participate in trade. Thirteen Spanish ports acquired rights to trade directly with America (upsetting the monopoly of Cádiz, which had replaced Seville in the early 1700s). The number of American ports also expanded dramatically to include ports in Venezuela and Río de la Plata among others. Another important goal of the new regulations was to develop the empire trading system as a market for Spanish manufactured products and a source of cheap raw materials for the peninsula, in accordance with the mercantilist prescriptions of the time. In terms of the structure of trade, the reforms did not achieve what the Bourbons had hoped. There is considerable evidence that agriculture in the peninsula was much more responsive to the new incentives than other industries and that in spite of some industrial growth, Spain continued to reexport large volumes of foreign manufactured products to its American possessions.

Overall, the reforms gave an important impulse to trade. Exports of American products increased tenfold from 1778 to 1796. Imports also experienced a fourfold increase. However, by 1797 an entirely new commercial arrangement emerged as a result of the outbreak of the Napoleonic Wars. Spain's alliance with France provoked the British blockade of its Atlantic ports and brought the commercial expansion to an end. In the final analysis, the introduction of neutral commerce undermined the very foundations of the new trading system, a change that proved to be irreversible.

Beyond the monopoly of trade, there were many other areas in which the colonial state intervened. The Crown required the acquisition of licenses to engage in many economic activities and prohibited specific groups from engaging in particular trades or industries. It also restricted production of certain goods and commodities to certain geographic areas, as was the case with the production of cochinilla in Mexico. Some of the most heavily regulated industries included the production of mercury and tobacco.

Beginning in the second half of the sixteenth century, mercury became a key ingredient in the production of silver. The process of amalgamation required mercury for the effective separation of silver from the ore. This technique was widely adopted in the mining industry for centuries and made mercury a much sought after commodity. Its commercialization was monopolized in 1572 and remained heavily regulated until the early nineteenth century. In contrast with the monopoly on trade, which restricted commerce and raised prices, the rationale for the monopolization of mercury was to subsidize the production of silver through cheap mercury and to monitor silver output. The mercury monopoly did not directly raise much revenue for the Crown. Indirectly, however, it had some positive effects on revenue because it allowed for better monitoring of silver output, which in turn permitted a better management of taxes on silver production.

Perhaps the most successful case of Bourbon intervention in the late colonial economy, judging by its contribution to

Crown revenues, was the tobacco monopoly. In the years of its maximum expansion (1780s and early 1790s), taking the region as a whole, the tobacco monopoly became the second largest source of Crown revenue, following silver.

The Crown monopolized tobacco distribution starting in 1717 in Cuba. Later, a monopoly over the industry was established in Peru in 1752, in Chile and La Plata in 1753, in New Spain in 1765, in Costa Rica in 1766, and in most other areas of Spanish America including New Granada, Paraguay, and Venezuela in the 1770s. By the late 1770s the tobacco industry was heavily regulated in nearly all of Spanish America.

Tobacco monopoly regulations were originally based on Spanish regulations of the industry in the peninsula. These regulations were progressively adapted to the needs of the Spanish American industry. In most areas, the monopoly included strict rules not only over the production of the tobacco leaf, but also over its distribution and final transformation for consumption. In Mexico and Peru, factories for the production of cigars and cigarettes were established. The tobacco factories were among the most sophisticated economic organizations in Spanish America, resembling in many respects the new factory organization that was evolving in Great Britain at the time. Nonetheless, the motive for these organizational changes was the reduction of monitoring costs and the control of contraband. In contrast to the textile factories in Britain, for example, no major technological changes or economies of scale were associated with their development.

The monopolistic practices and control over trade that were such an important part of economic life in Spanish America were not uncommon, with counterparts throughout many kingdoms of Europe and their colonies. In the view of many observers at the time, they provided the state with secure revenue in a hostile international environment and one in which the methods of modern direct taxation had not been contemplated. The view that these policies had disastrous negative economic effects that actually reduced long-run political stability was long in the making. A wave of liberal thought, originating in Scotland with David Hume and Adam Smith in the latter half of the eighteenth century, vigorously attacked mercantilist policies; however, the influence of such writers on Spanish policymakers was negligible in the years leading to independence.

Catalina Vizcarra

References

Baskes, Jeremy. *Indians, Merchants and Markets: A Reinterpretation of the Repartimiento and Spanish-Indian Economic Relations in Colonial Oaxaca, 1750–1821.* Stanford, CA: Stanford University Press, 2000.

Deans-Smith, Susan. *Bureaucrats, Planters and Workers: The Making of the Tobacco Monopoly in Bourbon Mexico.* Austin: University of Texas Press, 1992.

Dobado González, Rafael. "El monopolio estatal del mercurio en Nueva España durante el siglo XVIII." *Hispanic American Historical Review* 82, no. 4 (2002): 685–718.

Fisher, John R. *The Economic Aspects of Spanish Imperialism in America.* Liverpool: Liverpool University Press, 1997.

Klein, Herbert. *The American Finances of the Spanish Empire: Royal Income and Expenditures in Colonial Mexico, Peru and Bolivia, 1680–1809.* Albuquerque: University of New Mexico Press, 1998.

Vizcarra, Catalina. "Markets and Hierarchies in Late Colonial Spanish America: The Royal Tobacco Monopoly in the Viceroyalty of Peru, 1752–1813." Ph.D. dissertation, University of Illinois at Urbana-Champaign, 2001.

See also: Alcohol; Artisans; Atlantic Economy; Bourbon Reforms; Casa de Contratación; Contraband; Credit—Colonial Latin America; Creoles; Fleet System; Habsburgs; Independence I–VI; Mining—Mercury; Mining—Silver; Monarchs of Spain; Napoleonic Invasion and Spanish America; Pirates and Piracy; Repartimiento; Seven Years' War; Silver; Tobacco; Viceroyalties; War of the Spanish Succession.

MONROE DOCTRINE

In his annual message to Congress on December 4, 1823, U.S. president James Monroe declared that henceforth the Western Hemisphere was no longer open for European colonization, nor was it to be subjugated to European political philosophies; furthermore, Monroe proclaimed that the United States had no intention of becoming involved in European affairs. Although these pronouncements had long-term roots in U.S. history, including its colonial experience, the immediate context of Monroe's pronouncement was rooted in European events regarding Spain.

Following Napoleon's defeat in 1815, a "Holy Alliance" emerged in Europe. Steered primarily by Austrian prince Clemens Metternich, the Alliance—Austria, Prussia, and Russia—aimed to thwart liberal/republican movements across Europe. Spain fell within the Alliance's purview. In 1820, King Ferdinand VII was forced to support a constitution that led to widespread hostility and conflict in Spain. Open revolution appeared on the horizon in July 1822 when an attempted coup in Madrid failed; however, the insurgents established control over a section of northern Spain. This was followed by the detention of Ferdinand VII and the establishment of a regency. The European powers convened at Verona in October 1822 where they approved French military intervention to restore Ferdinand VII to the Spanish throne, an act that brought into question the status of Spain's New World colonies.

Although no one denied the legitimacy of Spain's colonial claims, Iberian realities in 1822 made that point irrelevant. Beginning in 1810, rebellions in the New World resulted in the loss of most of Spain's American colonies. The Holy Alliance refused to consider Ferdinand VII's request for assistance to restore the Spanish Empire. Still, Britain feared that France had commercial designs in the New World. It did not have such designs, however—a fact confirmed by the Canning-Polignac Memorandum of October 12, 1823, even though neither had yet to recognize the independence of any one of the newly founded Latin American nations. By 1823, only the United States had recognized the independence of several Latin American states.

The British also approached the United States about issuing a joint statement declaring Latin America off-limits to recolonization. But the Monroe administration refused, preferring to address the issue on its own. In December 1823, confident that the European powers would not restore the colonies to Spain and anxious to establish a U.S. political and commercial presence in the region, President Monroe issued his unilateral statement.

In Europe, Monroe's message fell on deaf ears. Both the French and British recognized Monroe's inability to enforce his proclamation. The independent action of the United States also embarrassed the British, who quickly closed its West Indian trade to the North Americans. The leaders of the "Holy Alliance" scoffed at Monroe's brazen actions, a sign that they understood little about U.S. political culture. Though disappointed that the Europeans did not come to his assistance, Ferdinand VII, like Spanish rulers before him, interpreted Monroe's statement as yet another example of U.S. expansionist interests. Largely because the United States offered no official assistance during their independence movements, Latin Americans were suspicious of U.S. intentions in 1823. A generation later, their suspicions would be proven correct. In 1846, U.S. President James J. Polk coined the phrase "Monroe Doctrine" to justify war with Mexico. Since then, the Monroe Doctrine has been used to justify U.S. intervention in Latin America.

Thomas M. Leonard

References

May, Ernest R. *The Making of the Monroe Doctrine.* Cambridge, MA: Belknap Press of Harvard University Press, 1975.

Perkins, Dexter. "Europe, Spanish America and the Monroe Doctrine." *American Historical Review* 27 (January 1922): 207–218.

See also: American Revolution; Constitution of Cádiz; Cortes of Cádiz; Independence I–VI; Louisiana Purchase; Monarchs of Spain; Napoleonic Invasion and Spanish America.

MOORS

The term *Moors,* derived from Mauritania, designated those Muslims and their descendants from the north of Africa who established themselves in Spain through different waves of Islamic invasions beginning in 711. In general, the Christian monarchs who conquered Iberian dominions from Islam during the Middle Ages respected the customs and religion of the *mudejars,* or Muslims among Christians, in exchange for obedience and heavy taxes. These mudejars, in spite of their marginal status, reached important numbers at given times and places. Toward the end of the fifteenth century, mudejars constituted a minority in Castile and Navarre. On the other hand, in the Kingdom of Granada the mudejars vastly outnumbered old Christians. Large groups of Moors also resided in Aragon and, above all, in Valencia, where nobles received and protected them in their seigniorial dominions in exchange for submission and cheap labor. In spite of appearances, there was always a fragile equilibrium in the coexistence, not *convivencia* (harmonious cohabitation), between Muslims and Christians. In addition to an ancestral hatred, those Christians who, encouraged by the Crown, settled in the Moors' territory also usurped their principal economic resources. At the same time, ecclesiastical authorities persistently worked to coerce and to assimilate the Islamic population. Together, these circumstances produced an inevitable clash of civilizations.

Such confrontations culminated in the rebellion of the Moors of the Alpujarras region of Granada in 1499, which led the Catholic Monarchs to order the general conversion of all of the mudejars of Granada to Christianity and the expulsion of those who refused baptism. The forcefully converted were known as *moriscos,* or new Christians. Although Charles V conceded the moriscos forty years grace from the Inquisition in order to achieve full integration in the Christian population, many continued practicing their religion and defending their customs against the acculturating policies of Church and Crown. Philip II, confronting the failure of his father's policy, dictated a series of laws that attempted, though without great success, to prohibit the Moors from using their language, clothing, and daily customs, carrying arms, or possessing slaves. Such measures led to a general uprising of the moriscos in 1568, provoking, in turn, a war, cruel on both sides, which lasted until 1570, with the victory of an army led by Juan de Austria. The moriscos of Granada were then resettled throughout the interior of Castile. In Valencia and Aragon, where violent incidents rarely occurred, moriscos remained beneath the tutelage of their lords. Yet the history of the Muslims and their descendants in Spain did not conclude until 1609, when Philip III, heeding rumors that accused the moriscos of betrayal and favoring Turks, French, and Berber pirates, decreed their expulsion from Spain. The ensuing exodus concluded in 1613, with a total of 300,000 moriscos exiled under very distressing conditions. The majority went to North Africa.

No doubt the Moors pertain more to the Mediterranean than to the Atlantic, a space with which they had little contact. Among other factors, from 1501 the Crown, in its desire to preserve the racial and religious purity of the colonization of the New World, prohibited Moors and their descendants from establishing themselves in the Indies. Nevertheless, their civilization influenced other Spaniards in diverse ways and, thereby, that of Spain's American colonies. Moreover, the evangelical methods and strategies for acculturation that Spanish authorities applied to the Moors provided an experiential basis for those that they developed with Native Americans. These methods, at least, entailed many similarities and proved equally destructive and intransigent with respect to the beliefs and customs of the defeated.

Carlos Alberto González Sánchez

References

Cardaillac, Louis. *Moriscos y cristianos: Un enfrentamiento polémico (1492–1640).* Mexico City: Fondo de Cultura Económica, 1979.

Domínguez Ortiz, Antonio y Vincent, Bernard. *Historia de los moriscos: Vida y tragedia de una minoría.* Madrid: Alianza, 1997.

See also: Capitulations of Santa Fe; Catholic Church in Spanish America; Colonists and Settlers I–VI; Converso; Inquisition—Spanish America; Islam; Jews—Colonial Latin America; Migration—From Iberia to the New World; Monarchs of Spain; Pirates and Piracy; Race; Religious Orders.

MULATTO

The term *mulatto,* designating people of mixed African and European descent, represents one of the several categories created to describe people born through the process of miscegenation between Iberian, Indian, and African groups. The expression originated from the derogatory Spanish word *mulo,* referring to the offspring of a horse and a mule. The number of mulattoes in a given society remains difficult to calculate and varied considerably according to location and to the extent to which plantation slavery developed.

In slave societies, mulattoes might have been slaves or free persons. If free, their status tended to remain precarious. In Spain's colonial territories, the category mulatto was but one of constituent parts of the stratified *sociedad de castas,* a hierarchical ordering of racial groups based on the proportion of a person's blood deemed Spanish. The *casta* system was created under colonial rule as an elaboration of the earlier dichotomy between Spaniards and Indians. It also involved the transference to the Americas of the hierarchical, estate-based, corporate society of the Iberian Peninsula. Although the system could contain in excess of thirty categories, practical necessity reduced this number to seven groups: Spaniards, *castizos, moriscos,* mestizos, mulattoes, Indians, and blacks. Position in the caste system informed a person's legal status, which then held implications for treatment under the law, corporate privileges, and proscriptions regarding marriage, residence, and social mobility.

In practice, it proved difficult to identify someone as mulatto in the absence of clear documentary evidence. Providing proof of someone's lineage, something rarely possible even for elites, became less likely through the generations because of interethnic mixing and social mobility. Accordingly, someone might be designated *mulatto* on the basis of prevailing notions of skin color and associations of physical attributes, or phenotype, a method lacking precise standards. Further complicating matters, people described themselves in ways that did not conform to Iberian definitions. The complexity of these categories led to the creation of a broad vocabulary, in Spanish as in Portuguese, reflecting a subdivision of the category *mulatto.* Such Spanish terms included *mulato amarillo* (yellow mulatto), *mulato blanco* (white mulatto), and *mulato negro* (black mulatto), among many others.

Toward the end of the colonial period, the sociedad de castas lost most of its practical value for Spanish administration, and the system collapsed entirely with the coming of independence. The modern period did not bring an end to stereotypes, discrimination, and issues surrounding notions of race. Historians have yet to arrive at a consensus regarding the fate of mulattoes. The term appears to have gone largely into disuse: some suggest that the category *mulatto* collapsed under general terms for people of African descent; or, alternatively, mulattoes "passed" into white society. Tracing the fate of mulattoes proves difficult partly because of an absence of the term in contemporary documents and partly because mulatto identity was complicated by issues of class and nationality. The historian Magnus Mörner has observed that terms like mulatto gradually fell from use once they ceased to reflect an ethnic reality.

Richard Conway

References

Blackburn, Robin. *The Overthrow of Colonial Slavery, 1776–1848.* New York: Verso, 1988.

Cope, R. Douglas. *The Limits of Racial Domination: Plebeian Society in Colonial Mexico City, 1660–1720.* Madison: University of Wisconsin Press, 1994.

Davis, Darién J., ed. *Slavery and Beyond: The African Impact on Latin America and the Caribbean.* Wilmington, DE: Scholarly Resources, 1995.

Mörner, Magnus. *Race Mixture in the History of Latin America.* Boston: Little, Brown, 1967.

See also: Colonists and Settlers I–VI; Ladino; Laws—Colonial Latin America; Mestizaje; Native Americans I–VIII; Race; Slave Trade; Slavery I–IV.

MUSIC AND DANCE I—BRAZIL

Since the so-called discovery, there has been continuous cultural interaction between Brazil and Portugal. This interaction has helped shape the music and dance traditions in both regions. The Iberian influence on the Brazilian spheres of music and dance is particularly visible and can be noted in the strong presence of guitars, quatrain poetic verse forms, functional harmony, couples dancing, and countless other expressive elements. However strong the metropolitan cultural presence may be in Brazil, the colony also had an impact in Portugal, and the Portuguese cultivated a fascination toward colonial culture, particularly in the arenas of music and dance.

The first accounts of Brazilian music and dance to reach Europe arrived through the illustrations and writings produced by explorers, missionaries, and travelers. Their representations fluctuated between shocking reports of savagery, cannibalism, and nudity to images of a paradise inhabited by people of a childlike innocence. The music, dances, and musical instruments of the natives were central in evincing the fascination and repulsion Europeans felt toward Amerindians. Just as they could be represented as a group of beautiful goddesses gaily dancing in a circle to the sound of a maraca, they could also appear in fearful war dances around a burning body, accompanied by rattles and flutes made from human skulls and bones.

Such images fueled the sense of urgency to embark upon the evangelization of the natives, marking the beginning of what has been the strongest cultural force sustaining the links between Portugal and Brazil over the centuries: Roman Catholicism. In their crusades to convert the Amerindians, missionary priests enacted morality plays (*autos*) in which music played a central role. The Jesuits in particular found they could achieve the acculturation of the Amerindians through musical instruction, and by the mid-1600s, the Guaranís who lived in Jesuit missions in southern Brazil were not only playing European organs, harpsichords, woodwinds, and various stringed instruments, but masterfully manufacturing them. Their ability to perform European music became a major argument in a scholastic debate as to whether or not Amerindians had souls. Cultural interchange within the missions was essentially unilateral, though some scholars have claimed that the priests also used native forms of music and dance; the most probable legacy of this practice is the *cateretê,* a southeastern line-dance marked by hand-clapping and foot-stamping.

Outside the missions, the Roman Catholic Church remained weak. Although some large plantation owners maintained priests to service their families and workers, small hinterland communities of subsistence farmers could go for years without a priest's visit. In the absence of active priests, the colonists developed lay forms of devotion, based on traditions brought from Portugal, many rooted in late medieval musical forms. As in Portugal, the saints that became the objects of popular devotion in Brazil—the Virgin Mary, the Magi, Saint John, among others—were depicted with all-too-human characteristics, and quite frequently they were fun-loving musicians and dancers. The legacy of these practices is still present throughout Brazil, and frequently their links with the metropolis can be detected.

The biblical Magi, for example, are a focus of devotion in both Brazil and Portugal, with traditions centering on visitations by mummer-like musical ensembles known as *folias de reis.* In southeastern Brazil these ensembles tend to be made up of men who employ a cumulative vocal style that resembles that of the women's polyphonic choruses still found in the Minho region of Portugal. In both Brazil and Portugal, Saint Gonçalo, who was born in Amarante around 1250, is sought out by hopeful spinsters in their search for a husband. Unlike Portugal, in Brazil, the saint is typically depicted with a *viola* (guitar-like instrument with five double courses) in hand to indicate his role as the patron of the *violeiros* (viola players). The Brazilian form of devotion to the saint centers on the Saint Gonçalo dance, a double line-dance similar to the cateretê. In the hinterlands of the Northeast, medieval modes are common in both religious and secular traditions.

In the urban centers of colonial Brazil, religious life focused on lay brotherhoods (*irmandades*). These voluntary associations built churches and maintained charitable institutions, while their main public activities centered on the celebration of patron festivals: thus, they played a critical role in promoting the musical life of the colony. The special significance of the lay brotherhoods became particularly evident in Minas Gerais during the 1700s, where the discovery of gold in the late seventeenth century generated the wealth necessary to finance grand artistic projects, both in Brazil and in Portugal.

In the mining regions, towns grew up over night, swelled by prospectors from all over the country as well as from Europe. Although mass immigration waves greatly depleted the metropolitan population, in the colony it had a strong Europeanizing impact. This is especially evident in the artistic fields sponsored by the lay brotherhoods, such as church architecture, sculpture, painting, and music. The major mining towns of Vila Rica (now Ouro Preto), Sabará, Mariana, Arraial de Tejuco (now Diamantina), São João del Rey, and São José del Rey (now Tiradentes) as well as numerous other smaller centers still preserve this legacy, heralding it as an emblem of local identity.

One factor affecting artistic production at the time was the intense competition among the lay brotherhoods in their efforts to outdo one another in the promotion of their grand festivals. Indeed, the high demand for superior craftsmanship created the conditions for the emergence of professional artists and musicians to service the brotherhoods. Between 1760 and 1800, there were nearly a thousand active musicians in the region, many of whom were free mulattoes, trained in family-based musical establishments, where they studied Latin, voice, and instruments, and learned to read and copy music and to set liturgical texts to melodic lines. For each festival, the lay brotherhoods contracted a composer to generate new music for the event and to organize the necessary musicians to perform it. Some of the most prominent composers of the period, such as José Joaquim Emérico Lobo de Mesquita (1746–1805), Marcos Coelho Netto, both father (1746–1806) and son (1763–1823), Jerônimo de Souza Lobo (d. ca. 1803), and Manoel Dias de Oliveira (ca. 1735–1813), operated in the "modern style," often involving a four-part mixed chorus with an orchestral accompaniment provided by two violins, viola (or cellos), bass, and two French horns, and occasionally oboes, flutes, and harpsichord. Clearly, colonial musicians were aware of the European musical trends, and indeed copies of the work of both baroque and classical European composers can be found in many Brazilian eighteenth- and nineteenth-century manuscript collections. In many former mining communities today, community choirs, orchestras, and bands still perform a colonial repertoire, with the most elaborate performances taking place during Holy Week.

Slaves and freed slaves in the mining communities were also linked to brotherhoods, particularly the confraternity of Our Lady of the Rosary. The black brotherhoods promoted festivals involving the coronation of black kings, which the slaves were allowed to elect from time to time since at least the early eighteenth century. After the coronation, the slaves processed through the streets dancing and singing to commemorate their new leadership. By housing their practices within a Catholic festival, Brazil's African populations and their descendants were able to carve out safe niches to preserve their cultural heritage. These coronations gave rise to the African-Brazilian ensembles currently known as *congos* and *congados* (also *congadas*) as well as a diversity of other processional music and dance groups, such as *moçambiques, candombes,* and *marujadas,* among others.

In Portugal the gold from Brazil allowed for the founding of a music school and the expansion of the royal chapel to a patriarchal chapel in 1716, which attracted numerous foreign musicians, including Domenico Scarlatti. Opera, in particular, flourished during the first half of the eighteenth century, and several opera houses were built in Lisbon as well as other major Portuguese towns. Furthermore, a notable collection of opera scores was amassed, which is still housed in the Ajuda Library.

As the gold supply dwindled, the population in the mining regions began to disperse, and the levels of artistic production declined. Many prospectors returned to Portugal, taking their gold as well as their colonial experiences with them, marking the first major wave of colonial cultural influence upon the Mother Country.

Alongside the religious sphere, colonials engaged in lively secular traditions, many of which evinced strong African influences. From the time of their arrival, African slaves used what free time they were granted to engage in singing and dancing, activities that greatly fascinated their white owners, even though they were generally considered indecent and lascivious. Numerous travelers' accounts indicate that slaves were invited to perform for white visitors, and in some cases, to the shock of their guests, the white masters joined in the dance. African dances were also widely performed by white Brazilians and mulattoes throughout the country in both rural and urban settings. Sometimes they underwent processes of domestication that toned down their more offensive movements, but generally this was insufficient for many Europeans, for whom the dances heightened metropolitan notions of the rusticity and degenerate morality of the colonials.

Nonetheless, a number of Brazilian dances made their way to Portugal. Perhaps the first of these was the *fofa.* Though references to the fofa in Brazil are rare, a mid-eighteenth-century popular pamphlet printed in Lisbon claimed that it had originated in Bahia. The emergence of the fofa in Portugal coincided with the initial phase in the decline of gold production, suggesting that, if indeed it was of Brazilian origin, it probably arrived in Portugal with the first wave of returning immigrants and the slaves they brought with them from Brazil. In Portugal, its main milieus were the African neighborhoods of Lisbon, most notably the riverside quarter of Alfama, as well as other major Portuguese towns, where slaves and other dark-skinned low-income workers resided. As the number of returning Portuguese increased toward the later part of eighteenth century, another Brazilian dance, which according to some was equally "immoral," would become popular in the metropolis: the *lundu.* Like the fofa, it too fused with African Portuguese dances in the poorest and darkest districts of Portugal, but occasionally it emerged even in respectable parlors.

Another major immigration wave took place when the Portuguese royal family, with an entourage of around 10,000 subjects, arrived in Rio de Janeiro in 1808 to flee from the Napoleonic threat. The ways in which this relocation is linked to the complex Atlantic interactions between Portugal and Brazil are especially highlighted in the story of the *modinha,* a style that has been heralded as the first "authentically Brazilian" musical form. In both Portugal and Brazil, the term *moda* was used to refer to any type of folk song, but by the late eighteenth century, its diminutive form, modinha, had become associated in Portugal with a particular type of operatic parlor love song. Although there was also a Portuguese form of the modinha, it was distinguished from the more rhythmic and syncopated Brazilian modinha.

Received accounts of the development of the Brazilian modinha typically begin with Domingos Caldas Barbosa (1738–1800), a native of Rio de Janeiro who emerged in the Portuguese parlors around 1775 with his *viola de arame* (wire-strung viola), which he used to accompany a vast repertoire of morally questionable tunes that he called modinhas and lundus. Caldas Barbosa was perhaps the strongest force in instigating the modinha craze that swept the metropolis in the late eighteenth century. However, it was the Portuguese who reintroduced the genre in Brazil a few decades later. By the time the modinha made its way back to Brazil, it had undergone considerable domestication, its shameful themes suppressed in favor of more respectful forms of amorous expression.

The presence of the court in Rio had an especially strong Europeanizing effect on the colony. Like other Portuguese monarchs before him, Dom João VI (King John VI) was a great patron of the arts and sciences, and during his stay in Brazil he graced Rio with the National Library, the Medical School, the Botanical Gardens, the School of Fine Arts, and many other institutions. Music received special attention, and Dom João VI brought musicians from Europe. This ensured the success of his musical institutions, among which was the Imperial Chapel, which sustained fifty singers, a full orchestra, and two chapel masters. He also built the Royal Theater of Saint John, modeled on the great Saint Charles Theater in Lisbon, which introduced opera to Rio's elites.

The shift instigated by the transfer of the court is epitomized in the place pianos came to acquire within Brazilian polite society. Pianos were one of the great novelties introduced by the Portuguese; they rapidly became central status symbols among Brazil's elites. Families of sufficient means scrambled to acquire one, and young ladies enhanced their marriage prospects by learning to play it. The demand was so great that by 1834, pianos were being constructed in Brazil, and local publishers were supplying the market with modinhas as well as the latest European dances, such as waltzes, polkas, schottisches, quadrilles, country dances, and others. European sheet music of both popular styles and serious music was also widely available.

When the Portuguese court returned to Lisbon after a thirteen-year stay in Brazil, the entourage consisted of 4,000 people, and several more thousand soon followed. Just as the Portuguese had repatriated the modinha, the court's return was an important catalyst in the development of Portugal's national musical style: the *fado.* In Brazil the fado was yet another dance with strong African links that had gained popularity in the colonial parlors of the early nineteenth century, once it had been sufficiently domesticated. It was as a dance that the fado was first performed in Portugal as well, and like other Brazilian dances before it, this dance found its home in neighborhoods where Africans, mulattoes, and their descendants were concentrated. By the mideighteenth century, however, in Portugal the term *fado* no longer referred to a dance, but to a style of solo singing that had developed in Lisbon among small home-based craftsmen, such as cobblers, match and cigar makers, typographers, cabinet makers, and others, who drew upon the improvisational structure of the songs that had accompanied the dance.

Meanwhile, in Brazil, the impact of the Portuguese court still lingered in the musical life of Rio, particularly in the taste for opera and orchestral music. Although the prince-regent-turned-emperor, Dom Pedro I, could not sustain the music institutions his father had established, the growth of the coffee economy in the 1840s allowed his son, Dom Pedro II, to invest rather lavishly in the arts. Nevertheless, the funds still were insufficient to match the demands of an emerging bourgeoisie in search of cultural spaces worthy of their station. Thus, Rio's elites took to founding exclusive "clubs" and "societies," some more well-endowed than others, which became the main organizations for the promotion of secular concerts of serious music from the 1830s to the late nineteenth century. Each society promoted regular soirées, with a staple diet of Italian and French arias as well as light instrumental pieces and selected movements from chamber and orchestral repertoires; often poetry readings and short theatrical productions were featured alongside the vocal and instrumental performances. After the official program, dinner or refreshments were served, and the evening typically closed with a ball. These events were more social than artistic, but the performance of European art music served to demarcate the discerning tastes of those in attendance.

The trends in popular music that reached Brazil underwent processes of localization. Rio's popular musicians, for example, took to the modinha, readapting it to the guitar. The style remained popular in Brazil well into the early twentieth century, only losing centrality with the emergence of samba. European dances that had found favor in imperial drawing rooms also spread into the streets, and by the 1870s a Brazilianized way of playing the polka had developed into an identifiable instrumental style that came to be known as the *choro.* This style, too, remained popular well into the 1930s and even spawned a revival in the late twentieth century.

The establishment of the republic in Brazil in the latter part of the nineteenth century brought the emergence of nationalist sentiments, and Brazil's elites began to take stock of their unique cultural heritage. Early assessments, however, were rather pessimistic in their representations of Brazilian culture, emerging, as they did, within debates on how best to explain the country's stunted development. Drawing on the racial and climatic theories prevailing in Europe at the time, Brazilian cultural inferiority was seen to be rooted in the country's racial makeup and its tropical climate. The solutions proposed, therefore, centered on the need to "whiten" the population.

The primary way through which the Brazilian population was to be whitened was by encouraging racial miscegenation. Paradoxically, this policy actually led to the "triethnic myth" of Brazilian culture, which claimed that only that which had emerged from the meeting and mixing of Amerindians, Africans, and Europeans within the Brazilian territory could be defined as truly Brazilian. Initially, this dictum was viewed primarily in relation to rural traditions, in line with European nineteenth-century romantic nationalist movements. By the 1930s, however, with the rise of the populist regime of Getúlio Vargas, the Brazilian musical canon shifted its focus to center on urban popular music, ultimately placing samba in the position of Brazil's national style and making carnival Brazil's national festival.

The mass immigration program implemented to combat the rise in slave prices after 1850 dovetailed with the whitening project, bringing over 1.5 million immigrants, primarily Italians, but also Portuguese, Spaniards, Germans, Poles, and Japanese into Brazil. Many worked on coffee plantations, whereas others found niches in the country's nascent industries. The immigrants formed tightly knit communities in which they cultivated their national traditions. Along with several small bands that performed for community events, the Portuguese in São Paulo also maintained a full orchestra. The musical life of the immigrant communities has been largely neglected because it challenged the Brazilian triethnic ideal. However, today the descendants of these immigrants are organizing performance groups, and their cultural heritage is being documented.

Since the 1950s, both Brazil and Portugal have undergone significant changes. Brazil has experienced a dramatic population increase, exceeding 175 million people, rapid industrial development, and a shift from a predominantly rural to an urban society. Portugal too has become predominantly urban, with only 10 percent of its population still living in a rural setting. Yet, while Brazil has been undergoing economic stagnation, the Portuguese economy has been on the rise, attracting an ever larger Brazilian community. This, coupled with dramatic growth in the Brazilian culture industry, has made it perhaps possible today to speak of the Brazilianization of Portugal. Brazilian popular music, especially MPB (Música Popular Brasileira) and the soap operas (*novelas*) produced by Rede Globo, now one of the largest television networks in the world, dominate the Portuguese media. This cultural invasion is stimulating a greater awareness of Portugueseness among a new generation of Portuguese musicians, and they are turning to the nation's heritage for inspiration.

Suzel Ana Reily

References

Appleby, David P. *The Music of Brazil.* Austin: University of Texas Press, 1983.

Araújo, Alceu Maynard. *Folclore nacional.* 3 vols. São Paulo: Melhoramentos, 1964.

Béhague, Gerard. *Music in Latin American: An Introduction.* Englewood Cliffs, NJ: Prentice-Hall, 1979.

Brito, Joaquim Pais de, ed. *Fado: Voices and Shadows.* Lisbon: Museu de Etnologia, 1994.

Castelo-Branco. Salwa El-Shawan, ed. *Portugal e o mundo: O encontro de culturas na música/Portugal and the World: The Encounter of Cultures in Music.* Lisbon: Dom Quixote, 1997.
Fryer, Peter. *Rhythms of Resistance: African Musical Heritage in Brazil.* London: Pluto Press, 2000.
Mariz, Vasco. *História da música no Brasil.* 2nd ed. Rio de Janeiro: Civilização Brasileira, 1983.
Oliveira, Ernesto Veiga de. *Instrumentos musicais populares Portugueses,* 2nd ed. Lisbon: Fundação Calouste Gulbenkian, 1982.
Perrone, Charles, and Christopher Dunn, eds. *Brazilian Popular Music and Globalization.* Gainesville: University Press of Florida, 2001.
Reily, Suzel Ana, ed. "Brazilian Musics, Brazilian Identities." Special issue of the *British Journal of Ethnomusicology* 9, no. 1 (2000).
Schreiner, Claus. *Música Brasileira: A History of Popular Music and the People of Brazil.* New York: Marion Boyars, 1993.

See also: Architecture—Brazil; Art and Artists—Brazil; Brazil; Culture; Independence II—Brazil; Jesuits—Brazil; Migration—To Brazil; Missions; Music and Dance I–V; Napoleonic Invasion and Luso-America; Poetry—Brazil; Popular Festivals; Travel Literature—Brazil.

MUSIC AND DANCE II—COLONIAL SPANISH AMERICA

Music and dance in colonial Spanish America were a hybrid of indigenous, African, and European musical traditions. Even so, musicologists usually agree that indigenous music was largely overshadowed by its European counterparts and by the impact of neo-African influences carried to the Americas through transatlantic slavery. That feature of colonial music was brought about by a variety of forces and is testimony to the ways in which music was used as a tool of religious and political domination within the colonial context. Nonetheless, the melding of these various musical traditions led to a complex music that has stubbornly resisted attempts to conclusively trace precise influences and roots. Even while the diversity of styles was usually presented within European musical idioms, both liturgical and secular, the music of Spanish America is inherently New World in its conception.

From their first contact Europeans wrote that Amerindians were skilled musicians who learned European musical forms and instruments easily and who valued music highly. Although we know relatively little about precontact indigenous music, there is no reason to suppose that it was static in nature. Even while much indigenous music was based on the pentatonic scale, particular groups in the Amazon area and southern Chile did not adhere to this melodic convention; clearly, there were structural variations in Amerindian music. Beyond this, since indigenous people interrelated on economic, social, and political levels it is likely that they influenced each other's musical styles. It is also true that there were a variety of musical characteristics among the different indigenous groups themselves.

For example, music was the means through which Nahuatl texts were memorized and knowledge of history and traditions was maintained. Song was an integral part of Nahuatl communication and was represented by a flowery volute in the codices of ancient Mexico. In his account of Inca society before the Spanish invasion, Felipe Guaman Poma de Ayala depicts many musical instruments. Music was an integral part of spirituality, intellectual activity, and technological production and thus was an obvious target of Spanish attempts to destroy those indigenous attributes. As a result, it was in the areas most remote from Spanish domination that indigenous musical traditions were able to survive the longest. This historical process was traced out by Bernardino de Sahagún when he wrote that even in the late sixteenth century the Indians still sang their songs and danced their dances to their old gods. Yet the growing economic and political power of the Catholic Church and the European colonial system allowed for the gradual eradication of indigenous musical traditions.

African musical traditions were more acceptable to Europeans since they had already experienced those practices and styles in the Iberian Peninsula. Typically associated with particular rhythms, such musical influences were also sensitive to the ethnic origins of the Africans regrouped in specific parts of the Americas. African influences were evident in the types of songs and in the rhythms associated with them. These included *guineos, negros,* and *negrillas,* which were *villancicos* or songs of praise in the vernacular, composed using African musical traditions. For example, poems written by Sor Juana Inés de la Cruz in the latter part of the seventeenth century were set to music in this style, using a type of black dialect text with refrains and repetition of African words, syncopated rhythms that corresponded to displaced accents in the text, as well as major tonalities. Much of the music associated with African influences is based on a rhythmic analysis of particular dances, such as the *cumbia* in New Granada (Colombia), the *merengue* in the Dominican Republic, and the *rumba* and *conga* in Cuba. Ironically, while Europeans permitted and even encouraged African musical performance and dance because they could provide solace for the hardships of enslavement in the New World, those same musical practices could also serve as a means of resistance to domination.

Indigenous music was characterized by wind and percussion instruments such as flutes and whistles, often made of pottery or sometimes of reeds (*quena*), especially in the Andes. The Aztec drum, the *hueyhueytl,* was a typical percussive instrument; different types of shakers and rattles were also common. Some instruments were made from animal bones, such as the drums made of llama skulls in Peru; and there are, of course, questionable references to groups of indigenous cannibals who made instruments from the bones of the people they had eaten. Whereas the typical African contributions to musical instruments are associated with drumming and percussive instruments, the Europeans generally were most influential in the stringed instruments they brought. The *vihuela* was the most popular during the colonial period, although the guitar also became common. Spaniards also brought organs and a variety of other European instruments, such as the *chirimia* and *bajón,* two wind instruments that figured largely as conversion tools used in the missions of northern New Spain.

The use of music by missionaries is a well-documented historical process in colonial Spanish America; missionaries and churchmen recognized music as a powerful tool for conversion. The first bishop of Mexico, Juan de Zumárraga, wrote that the Indians loved music and were more easily converted by music than by other means such as preaching. Thus, the complete apparatus of sacred music was transported en masse to the colonies. Liturgical music came to characterize one of the major streams of musical production in Spain's colonies, and professional musicians often were associated with the Church. At the outset, indigenous musicians trained by the missionaries, or enslaved Africans trained by their owners, were the main actors in this music production. Indigenous and African instrument makers quickly became recognized for their skills, and the Jesuit missions in Paraguay gained widespread fame for their instrument-making workshops. Some musicologists argue that because Iberians had a disdain for manual labor they viewed musical performance negatively, and thus it became the purview of traditionally marginalized groups in the colonies. Women, Indians, blacks, and racially mixed groups were the ones who were trained in music. One of the characteristics of European practices during the Renaissance and the Baroque periods was that women were not allowed to perform liturgical music. Therefore, children, falsetto singers, and every now and then the rare castrato were used to sing the high parts. Notwithstanding this practice, in Spanish America women's voices often were heard in churches, especially in the missions, and this caused some clergy to try to eradicate the practice.

The study of musical norms and practices in colonial Spanish America once again reflects the rich diversity that existed simultaneously in this vast area. Thus, at the same time that a chapel master in Guatemala was composing music incorporating obvious African instruments, a high prelate had ordered the destruction of indigenous musical instruments in Peru. The result of the mixing of a variety of influences in Spanish America meant that even though Europeans and Creoles composed in European forms and used European instruments, the results were often a hybrid of influences from Amerindians, Africans, and Europeans. The genius of the Americans was reflected in their ability to engage in musical production within European norms and still create something quite unique because of the incorporation of local elements.

Renée Soulodre-La France

References

Béhague, Gerard. *Music in Latin America: An Introduction.* Englewood Cliffs, NJ: Prentice-Hall, 1979.

Den Tandt, Catherine, and Richard A. Young. "Tradition and Transformation in Latin American Music." Pp. 236–257 in *The Cambridge Companion to Modern Latin American Culture,* edited by John King. Cambridge: Cambridge University Press, 2004.

Koegel, John. "Spanish and French Mission Music in Colonial North America." *Journal of the Royal Musical Association* 126 (2001): 1–53.

Mendoza de Arce, Daniel. *Music in Ibero-America to 1850. A Historical Survey,* Lanham, MD: Scarecrow, 2001.

Robertson, Carol E. *Musical Repercussions of 1492: Encounters in Text and Performance.* Washington, DC: Smithsonian Institution Press, 1992.

See also: Art and Artists—Colonial Spanish America; Catholic Church in Spanish America; Cimarrones; Codices; Colombia; Creoles; Cuba; Culture; Jesuits—Iberia and America; Jesuits—Paraguay; Missions; Music and Dance I, III–V; Native Americans I–VIII; Palenque; Race; Religious Orders; Slave Rebellions—Spanish America; Slavery I–IV; Slave Trade; Women—Colonial Spanish America.

MUSIC AND DANCE III—CUBA

At the time of first contact with Cuba's native inhabitants, Spanish chroniclers observed and recorded local Taíno dances. While holding hands, the dance leader would lead the entire group in dance steps forward and backward. At times, the genealogy of the caciques or chiefs would be recited along with their accomplishments.

However, nonnative Cuban music and dance had its early influences in Spanish and European Renaissance music. One of the earliest composers of non-European music was Miguel Velázquez, who sang at the Cathedral of Santiago de Cuba. Zarzuelas were in vogue as early as the mid-sixteenth century. Popular dances included the zapateo and the fandango. Over the next two centuries, Cuban musical tastes continued to follow those of Spain and Europe, and dances were those usually presented at royal court.

In the late eighteenth and early nineteenth centuries, Cuban music consisted mainly of the waltz, minuet, and mazurka. *Villancicos,* another popular form of music, were short three-part *cantatas.* Esteban de Salas, a priest, was a popular and successful composer of *villancicos.* And although African music existed (and still exists) on the island, it was not allowed into the mainstream and remained strictly within the dominion of the slave population.

By the early nineteenth century a new musical dance, the *contradanza,* appeared on the Cuban musical scene. It was most popular in the province of Santiago de Cuba where most French refugees from Saint Domingue settled. The San Pasqual Bailón, from 1803, is the earliest dance still in existence. At the same time, the *tumba francesa,* mutual aid societies from Saint Domingue, also appeared in Santiago. Their *carnaval* dances, such as the *comparsas,* enlivened Cuban carnivals. In addition, the white Spanish population enjoyed lavish productions of music and theater at the Teatro de Tacón in Havana.

In 1870, the *danzón* first appeared in Havana; it remained popular well into the twentieth century. By the late nineteenth century, African slaves had been freed and were allowed to establish societies or *cabildos* for mutual aid. Under the auspices of the Catholic Church, each society was required to have a patron saint, usually that of the church at which it was registered.

In Santiago and Havana, these cabildos celebrated carnival in their own ways. In the former, carnival was a month-long celebration that lasted from June 24 until July 26, while in Havana carnival took place on January 6. Lavish costumes and masks were worn. Representations of various gods and evil spirits were shown as part of ritualistic performances. By the mid-twentieth century, carnivals in Havana and Santiago de Cuba were world famous and included floats, called *carrozas,* singing groups, clowns, and modern music.

In effect, these cabildos merged and fused African music, dances, and culture with those of the Catholic Church and other Cuban influences. At the same time, the practice of *santería,* or saint worship, was born. African gods became synonymous with various Catholic saints. Elements of native religion were incorporated into Church ceremonies and vice versa. Cuban music and dance combined these rhythms to form such Cuban genres as the mambo, son, cha cha cha, and modern salsa.

African rhythms in Cuban music came from West African people such as the Yoruba, also known as Lucumi in Cuba,

Cubans performing the national Zapateado *dance, ca. 1890. (Historical Picture Archive/Corbis)*

and the Congo. Their songs and dances were intended to call their gods in various ceremonies. It is not surprising that the cabildos would hold their particular celebrations on the feast or saint day of their patron saint. These lavish religious ceremonies emerged as a popular form of music and spread throughout the island and extended beyond Cuba's African population.

Mambo was developed in the 1930s and became highly popular in the United States, perhaps most famous under the banner of Pérez Prado. The rumba, a mixture of stylized African rhythms which developed from African dances, also gained in popularity. The *guaguanco* is the modern form of rumba. By the 1950s, such groups as the Sonora Matancera, with Celia Cruz as the lead singer, helped to popularize Afro-Cuban music and dance far beyond Cuba's borders. Many of Celia's songs have elements of African origins.

In the period after 1959, the *mozambique* became popular. The mozambique is a cross between the conga and the mambo. Modern salsa is nothing more than a renaming of Cuban, Puerto Rican, and Dominican music for North American audiences. It is a mixture of the rumba, cha cha cha, and son, stylized to modern "Latin" music of North America. Salsa's popularity grew as a result of the large influx of Cubans to South Florida, and Puerto Ricans and Dominicans to New York.

Peter E. Carr

References

Clark, Walter A. *From Tejano to Tango: Latin American Popular Music.* New York: Routledge, 2002.

Manuel, Peter L., Kenneth Bilby, and Michael Largey. *Caribbean Currents: Caribbean Music from Rumba to Reggae.* Philadelphia: Temple University Press, 1995.

Salazar Primero, Max. *Mambo Kingdom: Latin Music in New York.* New York: Schirmer, 2002.

Steward, Sue. *Musica! The Rhythm of Latin America: Salsa, Rumba, Merengue, and More.* San Francisco: Chronicle, 1999.

See also: Catholic Church in Spanish America; Cuba; Cuban Revolution; Culture; Music and Dance I–II, IV–V; Popular Festivals; Saints and Saintliness; Slave Rebellions—Caribbean; Slavery II—Caribbean; Syncretism.

MUSIC AND DANCE IV—INDIGENOUS

Ancient cultures of the Americas used music and dance for religious and most likely for social purposes as well. Numerous archaeological studies reveal sound-producing instruments, music, and dance in pre-Encounter America. Musical artifacts and iconographic records (such as figurines, codices, and murals) offer some clues about ancient music and music performance, but much is and will remain speculation, even if supported by the writings of Spanish chroniclers and missionaries from the early years of the conquest or based on observations of contemporary Amerindian music-making. Since native performance practices had been mostly determined by rituals, which Spanish authorities successfully banned or suppressed after the subjugation of the indigenous populations, musical instruments and performance changed or disappeared altogether. Thus, the precise uses of musical artifacts are often unknown. Unearthed Mayan and Aztec multitubed duct flutes that can produce several pitches at a time, for example, imply the production of multipart musical textures that challenge European acoustical theory and aesthetics. As such, flutes are no longer in use today, both sound and performance context are obscure.

Because music, song, and dance were important elements of pre-Christian worship, missionaries quickly realized the power of music to convert the Indians. Symbolism of the conquering Catholic Church merged with pre-Encounter religious, life-cycle, and agricultural rites and led to performance practices that show unique patterns. Although Amerindians have often voluntarily appropriated one another's styles and repertories since before Columbus, native musical traditions changed drastically under Iberian economic, political, and cultural dominance. Music based on harmony and sacred texts, as well as harp, violin, and guitar, were introduced early during the colonial period and have become central to traditional native music-making. Despite the obvious cultural syncretism, Iberian and Amerindian traits often exist side by side, and some Renaissance musical practices of the conquerors have been preserved in Latin America only. The physical and cultural disappearance of Amerindians caused by subjugation, conversion, assimilation, modernization, and migration had a devastating effect on native traditions, but some continuity between pre- and post-Encounter musical traditions still exists, in particular music's close relationship to religion and the spiritual world. Many ancient dances associated with shamanistic ritual, for example, continued after the conquest by replacing the native deities with Catholic saints.

The number of studies on today's Amerindian culture is limited. Most knowledge about music and dance in the twentieth century was acquired in inhospitable, isolated areas where such groups were able to preserve their own essential character relatively unaffected by European or mestizo traditions. Each group has its own specific experiences with other cultures, its own values and intentions, and its own performance styles and repertories, all of which defy generalization. Nevertheless, there are common cultural traits in large geographical areas and among ethnic groups with similar historical developments. Many Native Americans have gender-, age- or kinship-based musical preferences. Distinction of gender is apparent in men's dominant roles in public ceremonies. Men also play a greater number of musical instruments than women. Women's musical activities are often restricted to singing in the domestic realm. Yet, lullabies and children's songs are absent from most native repertories. Social groups are sometimes identified by styles of performance or specific genres. Besides the creative mixing of native and foreign elements of musical traditions, many Amerindians have maintained a few relatively unchanged genres, which usually are closely related to ritual and religion.

Among indigenous communities shamanism is widespread. Transformation into animals, ancestors, or spirits is achieved through ritual structure, which often involves singing, music-making, and dancing. Shamans communicate with nonhumans in order to cure or inflict illnesses, produce rain, increase hunters' fortunes, and restore harmony in community life. Musical instruments used for such communication often emulate the voices of the ancestral and supernatural realms. The symbolic significance of musical instruments and their extramusical power are vital. Among Native Americans, flutes, trumpets, conch shells, and a variety of drums and rattles proliferate, as do the violin and harp, instruments originally introduced by the missionaries but long since perceived as indigenous. Musical traditions are transmitted by oral and aural means, without musical notation. Practice is part of performance, as no institutions for musical enculturation exist. Musical traditions are based on concepts of sound, time, and space, as well as on a variety of timbres, tunings, and other sonic and performance preferences that do not exist in European music theory and practice. Most native music features a single, fairly steady, rhythmic pulse, with slight melodic syncopation in the vocal part. Indigenous aesthetics stresses repetition and uses few tonal materials. Sounds and their associated movements are often defined in a single word, for they are inextricably linked. Music and dance are usually restricted to the appropriate ceremonial period and are judged for their efficacy. Although music and dance have social functions, they are not considered entertainment in a Western sense.

Interaction between Amerindians and non-Indians over the centuries has led to many syncretic forms. Variations of the fifteenth-century dramatic performance of the *baile de moros y cristianos,* the dance of the Moors and Christians, which represents the triumph of good over evil, are found in virtually all of Latin America. Most native music-making is associated with Christian religious beliefs and thus occurs on the major holidays of the Catholic calendar (Christmas, Easter, saints' days).

Today's complex sociocultural reality has challenged simplifying colonialist classifications of America's peoples into groups of indio, mestizo, and criollo. Although many mestizos celebrate their Indian heritage, the mass media and popular culture industries have reached the most isolated Amerindian communities. Public festivals in particular mirror national, ethnic, and community-based identities and the struggle over cultural representation and self-representation. In recent decades, revivals and reinventions of historical music-dance dramas with elaborate costumes and choreographies have served not only as tourist entertainment but also as self-representation of communities. This kind of "re-Indianization" and affirmation of native identity works against the ongoing process of mestizaje.

External influences increased in the last few decades of the twentieth century. Protestant missionaries are fiercely recruiting Amerindians, thus estranging them from traditional life. Radio and cassette recorders, and more recently video recorders, have made tremendous inroad into native communities. Although these new technologies encourage innovation and alter musical practice and ceremonial life, tape and video recorders also serve to preserve them for future generations.

Helena Simonett

References

Mendoza, Zoila. *Shaping Society through Dance: Mestizo Ritual Performance in the Peruvian Andes.* Chicago: University of Chicago Press, 2000.

Olsen, Dale. *Music of the Warao of Venezuela: Song People of the Rain Forest.* Gainesville: University Press of Florida, 1996.

Seeger, Anthony. *Why Suyá Sing: A Musical Anthropology of an Amazonian People.* Cambridge: Cambridge University Press, 1987.

Stevenson, Robert. *Music in Aztec and Inca Territory.* Berkeley and Los Angeles: University of California Press, 1968.

See also: Art and Artists—Colonial Spanish America; Art and Artists—Modern Spanish America; Catholic Church in Spanish America; Childhood in Colonial Latin America; Chroniclers (Cronistas); Clothing in Colonial Spanish America; Codices; Conquest I—VII; Creoles; Culture; Islam; Mestizaje; Moors; Music and Dance I–III, V; Native Americans I–VIII; Saints and Saintliness; Syncretism.

MUSIC AND DANCE V—MEXICO

Music and dance in Mexico are a combination of traits from different musical traditions. Like its racially mixed peoples, the mestizos, musical traditions have an essential mestizo character. Iberian music and dance brought to Mexico have been kept alive and have blended with native traditions. Afro-mestizo traditions are mainly found along the Gulf coast and in the Pacific coastal area. Amerindian music, dance, and ritual are still thriving throughout Mexico, but most of native musical events coincide with the Catholic liturgical calendar and feature a syncretic mixture of European and Amerindian elements.

Except for the African-derived *marimba* (xylophone), found throughout southern Mexico, all folk instruments are adopted and adapted from European instruments. The violin, the diatonic harp, and the guitar were all introduced early during the colonial period. The import of brass and wind instruments from Europe in the second half of the nineteenth century led to the formation of municipal and community bands. The diatonic button accordion was brought to Mexico's northeast region by German and Czech immigrants in the late 1800s.

The Iberian folk and popular religious repertories diffused by missionaries during the colonial period had a significant influence on music and dance in New Spain, still evident in the many folk religious plays associated with Christian holidays. As Spanish dominance deteriorated in the late eighteenth century, music and dance with a more local character began to emerge. Transformations of Spanish folk expressions into local genres and styles gained in popularity after Mexico's independence (1821). Although the Mexican upper classes continued to enjoy a musical life dominated by Italian opera and lighter musical theater derived from the Spanish zarzuela, local tunes and dances (*sones* and *jarabes*) found their way into the musical comedies featured at the cities' theaters. Upper-middle-class parlors resounded with song and romantic piano music. It was not until the last decades of the nineteenth century, however, that a definable Mexican national style emerged.

As one of Europe's most significant cultural exports of the nineteenth century, the brass band was introduced to every colony overseas. Facilitated by the mass production of brass instruments and new valve mechanisms, *bandas populares* (popular bands) became a ubiquitous feature of Mexico's musical life in the late nineteenth century and thrived in both rural and urban areas. *Bandas* performed at various outdoor celebrations such as bullfights, cockfights, horse races, parades, saint days, weddings, and funerals. Like the military bands at that time, popular bands played an eclectic repertory of marches, operatic selections, and popular dances such as the waltz, polka, and schottische. The urban *orquesta* (a small orchestra dominated by string instruments), favored by the upper and expanding middle classes for serenades and private events, played a similar repertory.

In the early twentieth century, Mexico's composers trained in the European classical tradition "discovered" the ancient Aztec legacy. They began to integrate not only reconstructed Aztec music but also mestizo folk idioms into their compositions. Far from resembling the people's artistic expressions, these nationalistic works were essentially stylized arrangements of popular material.

After the Mexican Revolution (1910–1920), existing traditional practices were modified and institutionalized for the new nationalism. Efforts were made to develop an "official" folklore that would blur regional differences so as to create a more integrated society. Cultural missionaries were sent out by the government to study and collect folk songs and dances throughout Mexico. The mariachi, a string ensemble from Jalisco originally consisting of harp, *guitarra de golpe* (guitar type), and one or two violins, was established as the national musical ensemble. The urbanized mariachi replaced the harp with the *guitarrón* (bass guitar). The developing radio, film, and recording industries of the early 1930s were influential in forming the "typical" mariachi ensemble with added trumpets. Nationalistic radio laws issued by the Mexican government privileged certain popular cultural forms in order to ensure that the medium would disseminate a uniquely Mexican culture and thereby promote a sense of national solidarity. Although mariachi and marimba fit the kind of national ideology propagated by the postrevolutionary government, many distinctive local ensemble types remained virtually unknown outside their regions of

A folk dancing group performs a Mexican hat dance to the music of a mariachi band, Mexico City. (Sergio Dorantes/Corbis)

origin. Some of these marginalized styles survived the century, though mostly in modernized versions, and were ultimately embraced by the national and international popular music industries. The accordion-driven *conjunto norteño,* for example, a small ensemble from rural northern Mexico whose repertory consisted of schottisches, redowas, polkas, *canciones* (songs) and *corridos* (folk ballads descended from the Spanish *romance*), migrated with the peasants to the cities, where it eventually spread from the working-class neighborhoods to the dance halls of the middle classes. Nowadays, *norteño* figures among Mexico's commercially most popular music styles.

Emerging in the 1930s, the *comedia ranchera* (ranch comedy), the most enduring genre of Mexican cinema, helped to establish the *canción ranchera,* a kind of romantic pseudofolk song performed by famous singing actors, such as Jorge Negrete, Pedro Infante, and José Alfredo Jiménez, with mariachi accompaniment. After World War II, the *canción romántica,* a more refined and sentimental version of the *canción ranchera,* arose and gained in popularity, in particular among middle-class urbanites. Popularized by the guitar-based trio, the bolero and the *canción-bolero* flourished for more than a decade until they gave way to new musical developments which enraptured Mexico's youth in the early 1960s: rock and roll and an international ballad type popularized by the famous crooners Frank Sinatra and Julio Iglesias. In the following decades, composers and songwriters largely drew from previously popular styles. In the 1990s Luis

Miguel, a young Mexican pop star, was instrumental in reintroducing the romantic bolero to a new, transnational generation.

In the mid-1980s emerged the *grupo* (group) ensemble with its synthesized instruments and lead vocalist as one of Mexico's commercially most successful forms of popular music. Led by the prolific singer and songwriter Marco Antonio Solís, Los Bukis dominated the romantic pop *grupero* music scene and inspired dozens of other groups. *Tecnobanda* (technoband), a *grupo*-version of the traditional acoustic *banda sinaloense* (a regional band from the state of Sinaloa), emerged in the late 1980s in Guadalajara, Jalisco, and was popularized in the 1990s by Mexican immigrant communities in the American Southwest.

Helena Simonett

References

Geijerstam, Claes af. *Popular Music in Mexico.* Albuquerque: University of New Mexico Press, 1976.

Jáuregui, Jesús. *El mariachi: Símbolo musical de México.* Mexico City: Banpaís, 1990.

Moreno Rivas, Yolanda. *Historia de la música popular mexicana.* Mexico City: Consejo Nacional para la Cultura y las Artes and Alianza Editorial Mexicana, 1989.

Simonett, Helena. *Banda: Mexican Musical Life across Borders.* Middletown, CT: Wesleyan University Press, 2001.

See also: Art and Artists—Colonial Spanish America; Art and Artists—Modern Spanish America; Bullfighting; Catholic Church in Spanish America; Fiction—Spanish America; Independence V—Mexico; Mestizaje; Mexican Revolution; Mexico; Music and Dance I–IV; Saints and Saintliness; Syncretism.